TO FOLLOW IN
THEIR FOOTSTEPS

TO FOLLOW IN THEIR FOOTSTEPS

THE CRUSADES AND FAMILY MEMORY IN THE HIGH MIDDLE AGES

NICHOLAS L. PAUL

CORNELL UNIVERSITY PRESS

Ithaca and London

This book was published with the generous assistance of a Book Subvention Award from the Medieval Academy of America.

First published 2012 by Cornell University Press
First paperback printing 2017

Printed in the United States of America

Library of Congress Cataloging-in-Publication Data

Paul, Nicholas, 1977–
    To follow in their footsteps : the Crusades and family memory in the high Middle Ages / Nicholas L. Paul.
        p. cm.
    Includes bibliographical references and index.
    ISBN 978-0-8014-5097-6 (cloth : alk. paper)
    ISBN 978-1-5017-1064-3 (pbk. : alk. paper)
    1. Crusades—Influence. 2. Upper class families—Europe—History—To 1500. 3. Nobility—Europe—History—To 1500. 4. Families of military personnel—Europe—History—To 1500. 5. Social history—Medieval, 500–1500. 6. Europe—Social conditions—To 1492. I. Title.
        D160.P38 2013
        909.07—dc23   2012018009

For my parents

❦ Contents

✎ ILLUSTRATIONS

ILLUSTRATIONS

🐌 ACKNOWLEDGMENTS

This book would not have been possible without the help and encouragement of a great number of people. In a series of classrooms I had the good fortune to find myself taught by a sequence of wonderful teachers, including Terence Gilheany, Jonathan Berkey, Gail McMurray Gibson, Robert Bartlett, and Paul Magdalino. The debt that I owe to Jonathan Riley-Smith is beyond reckoning. As a postgraduate student at Cambridge, I enjoyed the collegiality that he fostered among the group of crusade historians that gathered in his office each week. It was in that place of wisdom and friendship that I met a brilliant and inspiring historian and the love of my life, Caroline Smith. At some point my footsteps carried me along the path across Emmanuel College that connected Professor Riley-Smith's office with that of another generous mentor, Elisabeth van Houts, thus joining, for me, the world of crusaders with that of family memory.

I was no less fortunate in finding support while I completed this work in North America. Thomas Madden and his graduate students at Saint Louis University provided another outstanding setting for the exchange of ideas about the crusades. The vibrant community of medievalists at Fordham University, and in particular my colleagues Richard Gyug, Maryanne Kowaleski, Wolfgang Mueller, Nina Rowe, and Suzanne Yeager, all offered advice and assistance on numerous points. In 2009–10 I spent a wonderful year as an Andrew W. Mellon fellow at the School of Historical Studies at the Institute for Advanced Study, where I enjoyed the hospitality of Caroline Bynum, Giles Constable, and the other faculty. My work was truly transformed by this experience, due in no small part to inspiring conversations with my fellow medievalists and other members of the IAS class of '09–'10. Björn Weiler and John Gillingham kindly provided me with their copies of the editions of the *Historia Welforum* and the chronicle of Geoffrey of Vigeois. Richard Barton, Alexandra Cuffel, Marilynn Desmond, Adam Kosto, Anne Lester, Jonathan Phillips, Vincent Ryan, Michael Staunton, Suzanne Yeager, and the anonymous readers from Cornell University Press provided critical feedback on the manuscript. Peter Potter at Cornell has been a stalwart supporter of this project for many years, and his advice and comments were essential in shaping the work in its final form.

Funding for this project was provided at different stages by the Overseas Research Trust and the Lightfoot Fund at Cambridge University, by a Faculty Research Grant and a Faculty Fellowship from Fordham University, and by the Andrew W. Mellon Foundation for a Fellowship for Assistant Professors at IAS. Steve and Laurence Bouchayer kindly offered me a beautiful place to stay and transportation to Le Chalard, where the Tenant de La Tour family allowed me to view the church and the tomb monument of the Lastours family. For their assistance, I am also grateful to the archivists at the departmental archives in Limoges and Angers, at the Arxiu de la Corona d'Aragó in Barcelona, and at the Bibliothèque nationale in Paris and the Bibliothèque municipale in Angers. Fordham's outstanding interlibrary loan office was indispensable for access to materials otherwise unavailable in New York. As the work neared completion, I was delighted to find that my friends, who always gave their unflagging encouragement, also offered their technical expertise. Maps and genealogical charts were prepared by Kurt Fesenmyer and Alexis Boehmler, respectively.

The greatest debt of all I owe to my family. From the start, my parents, Douglas and Elizabeth Paul, have shown unwavering enthusiasm and support for my research. The Smith family in Coventry provided a base of operations for writing and research trips, and, just as important, a steady supply of tea and good cheer. To my amazing wife, Caroline, who read every word of the manuscript and endured marathon discussions of the project's finest details I can offer only all my thanks and my love, and perhaps a rest. When this book was in its final stages, we welcomed our daughter, Anthea Jean. We look forward to imparting to her the memories and traditions of the families we are so lucky to share.

❧ Abbreviations

Printed Texts

AS   *Acta Sanctorum.* Edited by Jean Bolland, Jean Carnedet, et al. 70 vols. Paris, 1863. Reprint, Brussels, 1965.

ASOB   *Acta Sanctorum ordinis sancti Benedicti.* Edited by Jean Mabillon. 9 vols. Venice, 1733–38.

CCA   *Chroniques des comtes d'Anjou et des seigneurs d'Amboise.* Edited by Louis Halphen and Renée Poupardin. Paris, 1913.

CCCM   *Corpus Christianorum: Continuatio Medievalis.* Vols. 121–. Turnhout, 1967–.

GCB   *Gesta comitum Barcinonensium.* Edited by Lluís Barrau Dihigo and Jaume Massó Torrents. Croniques Catalanes 2. Barcelona, 1925; reprint, 2007.

GM   Gislebert of Mons. *La Chronique de Gislebert de Mons.* Edited by Léon Vanderkindere. Brussels, 1904.

GND   *The "Gesta Normannorum ducum" of William of Jumièges, Orderic Vitalis, and Robert of Torigny.* Edited and translated by Elisabeth van Houts. 2 vols. Oxford, 1992–95.

GV   Geoffrey of Vigeois. "*Chronique* (première partie)." Edited by Pierre Botineau. Thesis, École des Chartes, 1968.

GVPA   Geoffrey of Vigeois. *Chronica Gaufredi prior Vosiensis: Pars altera.* Edited by Philippe Labbé. In *Novae Bibliothecae manuscriptorum librorum, tomus secundus rerum Aquitanicarum praesertim bituricensium uberrima collectio...opera ac studio,* 330–342. Paris, 1657.

LA   Lambert of Ardres. *Historia comitum Ghisnensium.* Edited by Johann Heller. *MGH SS* 24: 550–642.

MA   *Monasticon Anglicanum.* Edited by William Dugdale and Roger Dodsworth. 8 vols. London, 1817–30. Reprint, Farnsworth, 1970.

MGH SS	*Monumenta Germaniae historica: Scriptores in folio.* Edited by Georg Heinrich Pertz. 38 vols. Hanover, 1826–.
MGH SS rer. Germ.	*Monumenta Germaniae historica: Scriptores rerum Germanicarum.* 75 vols. Hanover, 1871–2002.
OFCC	*The Old French Crusade Cycle.* Edited by Jan A. Nelson and Emmanuel L. Mickel. 10 vols. Tuscaloosa, AL, 1977–2003.
OV	Orderic Vitalis. *Historia ecclesiastica.* Edited and translated by Marjorie Chibnall. 6 vols. Oxford, 1969–80.
PL	*Patrologia cursus completus: Series latina.* Edited by J-P. Migne. 217 vols. Paris, 1844–91.
RHC Occ.	*Recueil des historiens des croisades: Historiens occidentaux.* Edited by the Académie des Inscriptions et Belles Lettres. 5 vols. Paris, 1844–95.
RHGF	*Recueil des historiens des Gaules et de la France.* Edited by Martin Bouquet. 24 vols. Paris, 1737–94. Reprint, Farnborough, 1967.
RS	[Rolls Series] *Rerum Britannicarum medii aevi scriptores: Chronicles and Memorials of Great Britain and Ireland.* Edited by William Stubbs et al. 99 vols. London, 1858–96.
WT	William of Tyre, *Chronique.* Edited by R. B. C. Huygens with Hans Eberhard Meyer and Gerhard Rösch. *CCCM* 63. 2 vols. Turnhout, 1986.

Shelf Marks

ACA	Barcelona, Arxiu de la Corona d'Aragó
ADHV	Limoges, Archives Départmentales de la Haute-Vienne
ADML	Angers, Archives Départmentales de Maine-et-Loire
BAV	Rome, Bibliotheca Apostolica Vaticana
BNF	Paris, Bibliothèque Nationale de France

TO FOLLOW IN
THEIR FOOTSTEPS

Introduction

Although the vow by which a medieval Chris-
tian assumed the legal and spiritual status of a crusader was, at least in theory,
a contract of a highly personal nature between that individual and his God, in
practice crusading was always a family affair. Husbands and wives debated the
merits of taking the cross in the marital chamber; departing crusaders enacted
charters for the well-being of their spouses and children and hired ships with
their cousins. Crusaders traveled, fought, and died in the company of their
kin, while other relatives cared for their property and prayed for their success
and safe return. So critical were kinship networks in providing support for
crusading activities that, from a practical point of view, crusading would seem
to have been almost impossible without the support of kindred.[1]

Kinship and crusading were also connected in another important way.
From at least the middle of the twelfth century, those who issued calls to

---

1. For husbands and wives, see James Brundage, "The Crusader's Wife: A Canonistic Quandary,"
Studia Gratiana 12 (1967): 425–442 (repr. in Brundage, *The Crusades, Holy War, and Canon Law* [Lon-
don, 1991]); Christoph Maier, *Crusade Propaganda and Ideology: Model Sermons for the Preaching of the
Cross* (Cambridge, 2000), 121. For the provisions for family and estates, see Jonathan Riley-Smith, *The
First Crusaders, 1095–1131* (Cambridge, 1997), passim, but especially 93–105, 129–143, 169–189;
Jonathan Phillips, *The Second Crusade: Extending the Frontiers of Christendom* (New Haven, CT, 2007),
110–114; Caroline Smith, *Crusading in the Age of Joinville* (Aldershot, UK, 2006), 175. For prayer,
see Anne E. Lester, "A Shared Imitation: Cistercian Convents and Crusader Families in Thirteenth-
Century Champagne," *Journal of Medieval History* 35:4 (2009): 353–370.

crusade, both clerical and lay, commonly referred to the obligations of men and women of the warrior aristocracy to imitate and uphold the accomplishments of their ancestors. Papal letters issued from the time of the Second Crusade (1147–49) until the pontificate of Pope Innocent III (1198–1216) enjoined the nobility to recall the efforts of their forefathers (*strenuitas patruum*) and to follow or walk in their footsteps (*vestigia subsequere* or *inhaerere*). One historian has argued that during this period ancestral obligation represented "the most prominent motif used by those who sought to recruit for crusades to the East," replacing, in the papal letters, an earlier focus on the imitation of Christ.[2]

We cannot know the identity, let alone the complete ancestry, of the majority of participants in crusade expeditions, so it is impossible to say with certainty how central this particular idea may have been in building support for new campaigns. Studies of individual crusade expeditions and of crusading more generally, however, have noted that many of those who can be identified as having taken the cross from the time of the Second Crusade onward through the later Middle Ages could count participants in earlier expeditions among their ancestors.[3] That there existed among certain noble families a strong sense of obligation to reverence and imitate the deeds of crusading ancestors is, moreover, suggested by the numerous examples of families from both the princely and the more local aristocracy whose members joined crusade expeditions over the course of multiple generations. Connections of kinship can often be established between two or three generations of crusaders, but in some cases the commitment continued further. Noble families with patterns of participation lasting between four and six generations can be identified across the Latin West. They included the continental princely dynasties of Austria, Catalonia, Champagne, Dreux, Flanders, and Thuringia,

---

2. William Purkis, *Crusading Spirituality in the Holy Land and Iberia, c. 1095–c. 1187* (Woodbridge, UK, and Rochester, NY, 2008), 115.

3. Norman Housley, *Contesting the Crusades* (Malden, MA and Oxford, 2006), 89–90; Christopher Tyerman, *England and the Crusades, 1095–1588* (Chicago, 1988), 180–181; Jonathan Riley-Smith, "Family Traditions and Participation in the Second Crusade," in *The Second Crusade and the Cistercians,* ed. Michael Gervers (New York, 1992), 101–108; Jonathan Phillips, "The Murder of Charles the Good and the Second Crusade: Household, Nobility, and Traditions of Crusading in Medieval Flanders," *Medieval Prosopography* 19 (1998): 55–76; Phillips, *The Second Crusade,* 51–52, 99–102, 147, 150; Elisabeth Siberry, "The Crusading Counts of Nevers," *Nottingham Medieval Studies* 34 (1990): 64–70; Kathleen Thompson, "Family Tradition and the Crusading Impulse: The Rotrou Counts of the Perche," *Medieval Prosopography: History and Collective Biography* 19 (1998): 1–33; Penelope Adair, "Flemish Comital Family and the Crusades," in *The Crusades: Other Experiences, Alternate Perspectives,* ed. Khalil I. Semaan (Binghamton, NY, 2003), 101–114; Jean Longnon, "Sur les croisés de la quatrième croisade," *Journal des savants* 2:2 (1977): 119–127; James Powell, *Anatomy of a Crusade, 1213–1221* (Philadelphia, 1986); Michael Lower, *The Barons' Crusade: A Call to Arms and Its Consequences* (Philadelphia, 2005), 47–48; Smith, *Crusading,* 172–174; Purkis, *Crusading Spirituality,* 75, 90–94, 112–119.

and the seigneurial houses of St. Pol in Flanders, Lusignan in Poitou, Coucy in Picardy, and Joinville in Champagne. In England, Simon Lloyd has identified twelve baronial families that contributed crusaders for four or more generations.[4]

In these and other families, commitment to crusading was demonstrated through active participation not only across but also within generations, as some individuals took the cross on multiple occasions (some as many as four times) and often in the company of spouses, children, siblings, and cousins. Whether or not they traveled and fought, all adult members of the family could be involved in the effort. The minnesinger Hartmann von Aue would say that, in their prayers, women who stayed at home were as much crusaders as their husbands who traveled and fought far away.[5] Women did, however, accompany their husbands, and, although this was exceptional, widows or unmarried women might take the cross on their own.[6] In Austria, for instance, it was the widowed duchess Ida, leader of her own contingent on the crusade of 1101, who stood at the beginning of her dynasty's long-standing commitment.

For the European nobility, crusading represented an opportunity to combine the normally sinful acts of violence associated with their lives as members of a military aristocracy of landed lords with the redemptive act of penitential pilgrimage, a widespread and popular expression of lay piety. Like other aspects of church law and custom, the rites by which an individual assumed the status of a crusader, the legal privileges and protections that crusaders enjoyed, and the precise conception of the spiritual reward that they hoped to earn were only fully rationalized toward the year 1200.[7] From the time of the First Lateran Council (1123), however, we find those who answered papal calls to fight against the enemies of the church taking vows, marking themselves with the sign of the cross, and receiving assurances of protection for their lands and families during their absence.[8]

Even as the status of the crusader was recognized within canon law, crusading and pilgrimage remained closely intertwined. In the language used to describe crusades (*peregrinatio, iter, expeditio*) and in the behavior of those that

---

4. Simon Lloyd, *English Society and the Crusade, 1216–1307* (Oxford, 1988), 103.

5. Hartmann von Aue, "Swelch vrowe sendet lieben man" (The Wife Who Sends Her Cherished Lord), in *Kreuzzugsdichtung,* ed. Ulrich Müller (Tübingen, 1969), 57. See also Lester, "A Shared Imitation."

6. Christoph T. Maier, "The Roles of Women in the Crusade Movement: A Survey," *Journal of Medieval History* 30:1 (2004): 61–82; Natasha R. Hodgson, *Women, Crusading, and the Holy Land in Historical Narrative* (Woodbridge, UK, 2007), 117–124.

7. Christopher Tyerman, "Were There Any Crusades in the Twelfth Century?" *English Historical Review* 110:437 (1995): 553–577.

8. Purkis, *Crusading Spirituality,* 73–74.

undertook them crusading and pilgrimage are often hard to distinguish. Henry the Lion, Duke of Saxony, for instance, undertook an apparently peaceful pilgrimage to Jerusalem in 1172, during a period of enforced truce between Latins and Muslims in the Levant. On the one hand, it is not impossible that a nobleman like Henry could have wanted to make a peaceful pilgrimage to the Holy Land. But it seems difficult to imagine that the duke, who was armed, and who retraced the steps of his crusading great-grandfather Welf IV of Bavaria and publicly demonstrated great largesse toward the military orders of the Temple and the Hospital while touring sites and listening to stories associated with the First and Second Crusades, would not have fought if he had been given half the chance.[9] The chronicler Arnold of Lübeck presented Henry's pilgrimage as neither chiefly oratory nor military but rather something else, an adventure or tour de force in the Holy Land, a journey that won fame and honor just like the wars he fought against the pagan Slavs, at least one of which was a papally sanctioned crusade.[10] If high-medieval writers working in the orbit of the nobility were generally less concerned about questions of definition than are modern historians, they were also more likely to place what we consider crusades within their own historical matrices, which linked crusading with events that long predated the First Crusade. Henry and Arnold would have agreed that the first "Jerusalemite prince," whose efforts anticipated those of even Henry's earliest crusading ancestors, was the Byzantine emperor Heraclius (r. 610–641).[11]

Henry the Lion's armed pilgrimage, which was not timed to coincide with any offensive campaign in the East, is also a reminder that crusades could take a number of forms. Large-scale expeditions, precipitated by papal pronouncements and preaching campaigns, often saw local and regional groups of crusaders join together under the leadership and patronage of regional princes and (less frequently) crowned monarchs. These largest, Pan-European projects are the ones that have received the traditional numbering—First (1095–99), Second (1147–49), Third (1189–92), Fourth (1201–4), and Fifth (1213–21)—but they were not by any means the only crusades.[12] In fact, there was hardly a moment in the twelfth and thirteenth centuries when members of the European nobility were not setting out on expeditions to the

---

9. Arnold of Lübeck, *Chronica Slavorum,* ed. Johann Martin Lappenberg, *MGH SS* 21:115–125.

10. See, for example, the epitaph for Henry in Arnold of Lübeck, *Chronica Slavorum,* 201–202.

11. Arnold of Lübeck, *Chronica Slavorum,* 122. For Henry's patronage of a Holy Cross cycle (featuring Heraclius) in the church of St. Blasien in Brunswick, see Barbara Baert, *A Heritage of Holy Wood: The Legend of the True Cross in Text and Image,* trans. Lee Preedy (Leiden and Boston, 2004), 187.

12. For the numbering of crusades, see Giles Constable, "The Historiography of the Crusades," in *Crusaders and Crusading in the Twelfth Century* (Aldershot, UK, 2008), 24, and "Appendix B: The Numbering of the Crusades," 353–356, in the same volume.

Holy Land. While more powerful princes like Henry might bring a sizable retinue with them from their domains, at various times during the twelfth century we find local castle lords setting out for the East individually and in small groups.

Just as members of a single noble family might demonstrate their support for crusading in different ways, those who took vows as crusaders could choose to fulfill them in different theaters of war. There is now general agreement among most crusade historians that, as early as the first decade after the conquest of Jerusalem in 1099, the memory of what the First Crusade had accomplished was invoked to apply the idea of crusading to other fronts.[13] By the time of the Second Crusade, crusading privileges were extended to those fighting against both pagans in the Baltic and Muslims in the Iberian Peninsula, and the early years of the thirteenth century would also see crusades prosecuted against political enemies of the church who were themselves Christians. While for the majority of those who did not already live near the northern and Iberian frontiers, as indeed for the papacy, the effort to retain control over Jerusalem remained the central crusading priority, we do find some noble families whose members would take the cross in succeeding generations to fight on different fronts. The grandson and great-grandsons of the 1101 crusader Ida of Austria, for example, would go on to fight against Muslims in the East and in Spain, against those accused of supporting the Cathar heresy in the Languedoc and against pagans in the Baltic.

Given the great dangers to health, wealth, and familial security that went hand in glove with crusading, and the more general uncertainties that surrounded the exercise of dynastic lordship during this period, it is striking that so many families were able (much less willing) to demonstrate such consistent commitment to crusading projects. While in a very small number of cases, for instance that of the lords of Lusignan in Poitou, crusading led to circumstances that might materially benefit the family in the West, building bridges of power and patronage—miniature crusading empires that stretched across the Mediterranean—most crusaders did not set off with the goal of accumulating land and wealth, and for nearly all of the other families mentioned above, crusading more often resulted in death, political difficulties, and severe financial strain.[14]

---

13. Giles Constable, "Early Crusading in Eastern Germany: The Magdeburg Charter of 1107–8," in *Crusaders and Crusading*, 197–214; Purkis, *Crusading Spirituality*, 124–125.

14. For the dangers of crusading, see Smith, *Crusading*, 94–98; for a complete review of the crises that beset dynastic lordship in this period, see Thomas N. Bisson, *The Crisis of the Twelfth Century: Power, Lordship, and the Origins of the European Government* (Princeton, NJ, 2009).

The real fate of most crusaders, and the difficulties that participation caused for their families, make the patterns of continued participation over the generations all the more striking. Why did they continue to go? Among historians of the crusades, for whom questions of motivation have been a primary concern, the answer has generally been associated with what is termed "tradition." But "tradition," in the words of John D. Niles, "is no hypostatic entity, airy and transcendent. Nor can we think of it as hard and durable, like an old chair passed down from hand to hand. . . . It is a volatile process."[15] Traditions are being continuously invented, dropped, stopped, and restarted, and those that continue do so because of the "tradition bearers" that keep them running. "In the case of practices and institutions made up of human actions," wrote Edward Shils in his classic study of traditions, "it is not the particular concrete actions which are transmitted." Instead "the transmissible parts of them are the patterns or images of actions which they imply or the beliefs requiring, recommending, regulating, permitting, or prohibiting the re-enactment of those patterns."[16] To put it another way, "traditions" in the behavioral sense cannot be understood without first understanding the "traditions" in the narrative sense that lay behind them: the stories, images, and ideas about the past that conditioned the nobility's responses to calls for crusades. It is the latter sense that is the focus of this inquiry. The argument presented in this book is that the support of the medieval nobility for crusade expeditions in the twelfth and thirteenth centuries was shaped fundamentally by knowledge and attitudes that were preserved, transformed, and transmitted in the social or collective memories of the families themselves. This book is, then, about the mechanisms through which collective memory functioned, the forms and meanings of the knowledge about the past that was transmitted, and the forces that governed its interpretation and reception. Before considering how we might access the collective memories of noble families, however, it is worth going back to locate the origins of our tradition of "crusading traditions."

Our Crusading Ancestors

That the enthusiasm demonstrated by many nobles for crusading could to some degree be explained by medieval conceptions of noble lineage is, for crusade historians, a safe conclusion based on decades of prosopographical identification of crusade participants and important discoveries in the

---

15. John D. Niles, *Homo Narrans: The Poetics and Anthropology of Oral Literature* (Philadephia, 1999), 173.

16. Edward Shils, *Tradition* (Chicago, 1981), 12.

language of ancestral obligations emanating from the papal chancery. By resorting to the power of tradition as an explanation of crusader motivations, however, scholars were also reaffirming much older popular ideas about the medieval aristocratic world. The concept of "crusading traditions" corresponds closely, almost perfectly, with long-standing general conceptions of the medieval nobility: that their power was based on hereditary privilege, that they subscribed to a customary law, that they respected codes of honor and a martial culture of chivalry that celebrated both military prowess and the fulfillment of Christian duty, and most of all that they revered their ancestors.

It is well known that Europe in the nineteenth and twentieth centuries saw a romantic revival of interest in the Middle Ages, and in particular in medieval aristocratic culture. At the same moment that European governments were undertaking overseas projects of colonization and empire—projects that were proudly compared in some quarters to the efforts of medieval crusaders—we find a longing to connect with explicitly ancestral crusading traditions of the past. In England, for instance, we find the widespread (and erroneous) belief that the cross-legged pose of the knightly effigies that populated parish churches and chantries of hundreds of English villages designated a figure as a crusader. This meant not only that whole families of local gentry might be taken as crusaders, but that nearly every community had a "crusading ancestor" on hand to admire and contemplate. The occupants of nearby English manor houses with pretensions to ancient nobility were offered such handsome volumes as James Cruickshank Dansey's *English Crusaders* (1850), which named the participants in every crusading expedition, with their (often anachronistic) arms, and occasionally mentioned their living descendants. In France, King Louis-Philippe's announcement in 1843 that he would decorate his Salles des Croisades at the palace of Versailles with the arms of crusading families resulted in a brisk trade in forged medieval documents that created new crusading ancestors for the modern nobility.[17]

As European imperial involvement in North Africa and the Near East escalated, so too did the rhetoric of crusading traditions, if mainly among

---

17. For crusading in the nineteenth and early twentieth centuries, see Elizabeth Siberry, *The New Crusaders: Images of the Crusades in the Nineteenth and Early Twentieth Centuries* (Aldershot, UK, 2000); and Adam Knobler, "Holy Wars, Empires, and the Portability of the Past: The Modern Uses of Medieval Crusades," *Comparative Studies in Society and History* 48:2 (2006): 293–325. For the popular idea of the cross-legged crusader and its refutation see H. A. Tummers, *Early Secular Effigies in England: The Thirteenth Century* (Leiden, 1980), 118–120. Robert-Henri Bautier, "La collection des chartes de croisade dite 'Collection Courtois'," *Comptes-rendus des séances de l'Academie des Inscriptions et Belles Lettres* (1956): 382–386; David Abulafia, "Invented Italians in the Courtois Forgeries," in *Crusade and Settlement: Papers Read at the First Conference of the Society for the Study of the Crusades and the Latin East and Presented to R. C. Smail,* ed. Peter W. Edbury (Cardiff, 1975), 135–147; Siberry, *The New Crusaders,* 51–52, 169–170.

members of the aristocracy. During his 1898 journey to Palestine and Syria, which featured a triumphal entry into Jerusalem by knights on horseback dressed as crusaders, Kaiser Wilhelm II of Germany had an image installed in a new German hospice on the Mount of Olives depicting himself and the empress Augusta Victoria surrounded by eight German crusading kings.[18] A British officer in Palestine during the capture of Jerusalem in 1917 wrote to his family that he was thinking of his "old crusading ancestor who killed a Saracen and a lion on those very hills!"[19] Even in the 1930s, in the fading twilight of this world, the aristocratic protagonists of the novels of P. G. Wodehouse and Dorothy L. Sayers were said to be the descendants of companions of Richard I on the Third Crusade.[20]

These strong undercurrents of popular belief do nothing to vitiate what historians of the crusades have more recently proposed about the ways that the medieval nobility understood and acted on appeals to take the cross, but they do help us to understand the shape and limits of their inquiries. For although historians of the crusades have become increasingly aware of the patterns of familial involvement in crusades, and have argued for an awareness of and pride in such family traditions among the nobility, the strength and meaning of "tradition" as an almost metaphysical force in itself have been largely assumed.

Crusading Traditions

Not surprisingly, the importance of family traditions to understanding the mentalities of crusaders first occurred to historians who studied the later crusade expeditions—naturally, such traditions needed time to develop and flourish. In the late 1970s, after an intensive prosopographical inquiry into the participants in the Fourth Crusade, Jean Longnon concluded that not only were many of the crusaders on that expedition related to one another or to veterans of earlier crusades, but that "for others, in taking the cross, they were following a family tradition."[21] Although James Powell, writing about the Fifth Crusade a decade after Longnon, found that only about 20 percent

18. Jonathan Riley-Smith, "Islam and the Crusades in History and Imagination, 1 November 1898–11 September 2001," *Crusades* 2 (2003): 151–167; and Riley-Smith, *The Crusades, Christianity, and Islam* (New York, 2011), 58–59.

19. Quoted in Eitan Bar-Yosef, "British Propaganda and the Palestine Campaign, 1917–18," *Journal of Contemporary History* 36:1 (2001): 94 and, for the discourse of crusade ancestry surrounding the British campaign in Palestine more generally, see 93–96.

20. P. G. Wodehouse, letter to the *Times,* November 30, 1937 (for the Sieur de Wooster); Charles Wilfrid Scott-Giles, *The Wimsey Family: A Fragmentary History Compiled from Correspondence with Dorothy L. Sayers* (London, 1977), 16–31.

21. Longnon, "Sur les croisés," 120.

of identifiable participants had known ties of kinship to other crusaders, he nonetheless concluded that family traditions were important to the aristocracy.[22] He suggested, for instance, that the veteran preacher James of Vitry may have chosen the crusader James of Avesnes, who died at Arsuf in 1191 during the Third Crusade, for an exemplum in one of his sermons because the audience of the sermon would be aware of the Avesnes family's distinguished crusading tradition.[23] Even clearer evidence of appeals to ancestry in thirteenth-century troubadour songs and *chansons de geste* were identified by Caroline Smith, who considered family tradition, together with personal piety, to be the primary reason why John, the lord of Joinville and seneschal of Champagne (d. 1317), took the cross in 1248.[24]

John of Joinville stands as a landmark figure in discussions of family crusading traditions because of an epitaph he composed in the vernacular for his great-grandfather Geoffrey III (d. 1188) and had inscribed at Clairvaux in 1311. The epitaph gives the names of several of Joinville's male ancestors, taking special care to mention those who had fought "on this side of the sea and on the other."[25] In the epitaph John also claimed that the lion in his family's coat of arms had been granted to his grandfather Geoffrey IV by Richard I, with whom he had fought on the Third Crusade.[26] As Simon Lloyd first noted, the epitaph provides crucial evidence of a noble's self-consciousness of his place in a longer family tradition of crusading.[27] The great prestige that went with crusading ancestry in what Lloyd called "chivalric circles" brings into sharper focus the importance of certain cultural productions,[28] such as the four painting cycles commissioned by the English king Henry III for his palaces at Westminster, Winchester, and Clarendon and at the Tower of London, which depicted the battle of Antioch, where his ancestor Robert Curthose was believed to have performed heroic deeds.[29] As Christopher Tyerman observed, the prestige associated with crusading ancestry did not diminish in the later Middle Ages. Pointing to later medieval monuments, such as the genealogical rolls composed by John Rous for the Beauchamp

---

22. Powell, *Anatomy of a Crusade,* 82–83. In this finding, Powell was in agreement with the nearly contemporary work of Constance Bouchard, who demonstrated that family traditions lay behind the patterns of benefactions to monastic institutions. See Bouchard, *Sword, Miter, and Cloister: Nobility and the Church in Burgundy* (Ithaca, NY, 1987), passim, esp. 130–149.

23. Powell, *Anatomy of a Crusade,* 59–60.

24. Smith, *Crusading,* 89–91, 176.

25. *Chronicles of the Crusades,* trans. Caroline Smith (London and New York, 2008), 346–347.

26. Smith, *Crusading,* 172.

27. Lloyd, *English Society,* 101–102.

28. Lloyd, *English Society,* 102.

29. Simon Lloyd, "King Henry III, the Crusade, and the Mediterranean," in *England and Her Neighbours, 1066–1453: Essays in Honor of Pierre Chaplais,* ed. Michael Jones and Malcolm Vale (London, 1989), 102–103. Nearly all of these paintings are now lost.

family in the 1470s and 1480s or the castle built by the crusading order of the Hospital in Bodrum in southwestern Anatolia in 1401 and decorated with the coats of arms of many families with crusading ancestry, Tyerman has argued both for the longevity of these traditions and for a clear sense of pride in them.[30]

The Joinville epitaph, the references to paintings and monuments, and the later medieval genealogies are all critical evidence of the prominence of the crusades in the discourse about the family past, but they have two limitations. First, in relation to the history of the crusades to the Holy Land, they are quite late. Even the epitaph inscribed at Geoffrey III of Joinville's tomb, was, as Lloyd noted, written at a time when the Joinville tradition was already long, and too prominent to be ignored.[31] Such sources are also limited by their form. While genealogies have been heralded as the most lucid expressions of aristocratic self-perception in the central and later Middle Ages, they can, necessarily, tell only part of the story. This is because, as we will see in a moment, they cannot express the plurality of ideas that individuals might have about their kin and ancestors. Most genealogies are also not descriptive. Even Joinville's epitaph, which is more discursive than contemporary genealogies, only hints at the stories Joinville must have known, describing where and with whom his ancestors fought, how they died and where they lay, and how they had won honor for themselves and for their descendants. The epitaph itself tells us little about these matters, and nothing about how Joinville knew about his ancestors, how he felt about them, and when he talked about them. Like the sculptures of equestrian figures charging down non-Christian foes that decorate the Romanesque churches patronized by crusading families throughout Aquitaine, these sources tell us about the existence, but not the content or the operation of a family's sense of the past.[32]

Collective Consciousness and Family Memory

Both Christopher Tyerman and Jonathan Riley-Smith have argued that the systems of ideological transmission that led to the development of crusading traditions had their roots in the first half of the twelfth century. Tyerman, for instance, was convinced that for many English families, "the true

---

30. Tyerman, *England and the Crusades,* 180–181, 315.

31. Lloyd, *English Society,* 102.

32. Linda Seidel, "The Holy Warriors: The Romanesque Rider and the Fight against Islam," in *The Holy War,* ed. Thomas Patrick Murphy (Columbus, OH, 1976), 33–77; and Seidel, *Songs of Glory: The Romanesque Façades of Aquitaine* (Chicago, 1981), 55–81.

history of how the [crusading] ideal became a habit of mind and action to be passed down to succeeding generations" lay "in the experience of those who... embark[ed] for Jerusalem in the years before 1150." "In these years," he continued, "family traditions were established which later sustained the whole movement."[33] This hypothesis was greatly expanded and corroborated in Jonathan Riley-Smith's study of the earliest crusaders. Building on the earlier work of Marcus Bull on the response to the preaching of the First Crusade in the Limousin and Gascony,[34] Riley-Smith associated the act of taking the cross for the First Crusade with older family traditions of pilgrimage and support for local religious communities.[35] Riley-Smith's painstaking genealogical and prosopographical study of crusaders in the first decades of the twelfth century convinced him that during this time "the crusading movement itself was as much in the collective consciousness of certain noble and knightly families as in action and the thinking of theoreticians."[36]

It is the objective of this study to uncover what Riley-Smith called the "collective consciousness" of noble families and what Tyerman termed the "habit of mind" surrounding the early crusades. To do this it is necessary to go beyond the methods so far employed by crusade historians, who have sought mainly to identify family networks of crusaders or to find appeals to tradition in calls to take the cross. Between the actions of certain family members and the appeals that were made to them by preachers and poets lay a discourse that was fundamental to every member of the medieval nobility. This was a discourse centered on the ancestry of a particular kin-group, a continuous conversation between and about members of a family that helped to define that family's identity and to inform the behavior and decisions of its members over the course of succeeding generations.[37] This discourse is part of what medieval historians call *memoria*—the wider set of liturgical and commemorative practices that kept alive the memory of the dead—and it is termed here simply "family memory."[38]

---

33. Tyerman, *England and the Crusades*, 35.
34. Marcus Bull, *Knightly Piety and the Lay Response to the First Crusade: The Limousin and Gascony* (Oxford, 1993), 204–249.
35. Riley-Smith, *The First Crusaders*, 93–97.
36. Riley-Smith, *The First Crusaders*, 13.
37. Shils's classic study, *Tradition*, outlines the actors and props necessary to maintain traditions over time.
38. For overviews of the scholarship, see Michael Borgolte, "*Memoria*: Bilan intermédiaire d'un projét de recherché sur le Moyen Âge," and Michel Lauwers, "*Memoria*: À propos d'un objet d'histoire en Allemagne," both in *Les tendances actuelles de l'histoire du Moyen Âge*, ed. Jean-Claude Schmitt and Otto Gerhard Oexle (Paris, 2002), 53–70 and 105–126; and Joseph Morsel, "Inventing a Social Category: The Sociogenesis of the Nobility at the End of the Middle Ages," in *Ordering Medieval Society: Perspectives on Intellectual and Practical Modes of Shaping Social Relations*, ed. Bernhard Jussen and trans. Pamela Selwyn (Philadelphia, 2001), 221–222.

The collective consciousness of the family is best understood as the collective memory of the family as a social group. The concept of social memory has been applied to other groups in medieval society, such as monastic houses, the lawyers of Italian towns, or much more broadly to the Frankish kingdoms of the earlier Middle Ages, but Maurice Halbwachs, the sociologist who first proposed the study of social or collective memory, could think of no better example of a group that identified itself through reference to its own, distinct past than the family.[39] Taking inspiration from Halbwachs's ideas about social memory, which continue to be expanded and explored as they are applied across the social sciences, as well as from more recent, comparable approaches by Karl Schmid, Otto Gerhard Oexle, Elisabeth van Houts, and others, family memory will here be treated as inherently social, forged from the interactions among members of a family, between the family and their household, and between the family and other individuals and local religious communities.[40] Looking at how ideas and images associated with the crusades became part of the collective memories of noble families promises to reveal the appeal and the importance of crusading not only to those families with long and distinguished crusading traditions, but to the nobility as a whole. But what do we mean by a "family," and how can we hope to access a family's memory?

Lineage, Memory, and Identity

Beginning in about the middle of the eleventh century, writers throughout Latin Christendom began committing to writing many different kinds of works, including genealogies, epitaphs, and numerous other types of memorials that were primarily focused on the ancestry of powerful aristocratic

---

39. Amy Remensnyder, *Remembering Kings Past: Monastic Foundation Legends in Southern France* (Ithaca, NY, 1995); Chris Wickham, "Lawyer's Time: History and Memory in Tenth- and Eleventh-Century Italy," in *Studies in Medieval History Presented to R. H. C. Davis,* ed. Henry Mayr-Harting and R. I. Moore (London, 1985), 53–71; Rosamund McKitterick, *History and Memory in the Carolingian World* (Cambridge, 2004); Matthew Gabriele, *An Empire of Memory: The Legend of Charlemagne, the Franks, and Jerusalem before the First Crusade* (Oxford, 2011). See also the relevant sections of Chris Wickham and James Fentress, *Social Memory* (Oxford, 1992); Maurice Halbwachs, *Les cadres sociaux de la mémoire* (Paris, 1925), trans. Lewis Coser as *On Collective Memory* (Chicago, 1992), 54–74.

40. For the intersections between memory studies and the study of the Middle Ages and the crusades, see Nicholas Paul and Suzanne Yeager, introduction to *Remembering the Crusades: Myth, Image, and Identity* (Baltimore, 2012), 1–25. For memory as socially constructed, see Halbwachs, *On Collective Memory,* 38. Otto Gerhard Oexle, "Welfische *Memoria:* Zuglich ein Beitrag über adlige Hausüberlieferung und die Kritierien ihrer Erforschung," in *Die Welfen und ihr Braunschweiger Hof im Hohen Mittelalter,* ed. Bernd Schneidmüller (Wiesbaden, 1995), 61–63. For Van Houts's contribution, see Elisabeth M. C. van Houts, *Memory and Gender in Medieval Europe, 900–1200* (Basingstoke, UK, 1990); Van Houts, *History and Family Tradition in England and the Continent, 1000–1200* (Aldershot, UK, 1999); and the collection of essays Van Houts, *Medieval Memories: Men, Women, and the Past* (Harlow, UK, and New York, 2001).

families. Most striking, however, is the great flowering in the twelfth and early thirteenth centuries of longer narrative texts that traced the ancestry of a particular family from the origins of its claim to noble lordship until the writer's own time. Most of these texts were composed in Latin, with a few notable exceptions written in Romance. Nearly all were composed by literate clerics, although one, whose author we shall meet in the first chapter of this book, was written during the early stages of the First Crusade by a lay prince himself.[41] These longer narratives, rich with detailed information on the attitudes of noble families toward their ancestry, have served as both the inspiration and the point of departure for this study.

The modern discovery of these genealogies and florid historical narratives generated two interrelated strands of historical scholarship that culminated, in the late 1960s and early 1970s, in the publication of groundbreaking articles by the German historian Karl Schmid and the French historian Georges Duby.[42] In 1968 Schmid, who had been among a team of historians at the universities of Freiburg and Münster investigating the structure of aristocratic families in the earlier Middle Ages,[43] turned his attention to the textual and artistic depictions of the Welf dynasty from the twelfth century.[44] Drawing from a range of sources, including a genealogy and a longer dynastic narrative dedicated to the ancestry of the twelfth-century Welf dukes, Schmid noted that the narrow agnatic lineage described in these texts ignored most members of the larger kin-group (*Sippe*) of Welfs that could be identified operating in the Frankish kingdoms since the Carolingian period. According to Schmid, over the course of the eleventh century members of the Welf kindred had developed a "self-consciousness" as a lineage (*Geschlecht*). The twelfth-century narrative of the family's ancestry, the *Historia Welforum,* was a manifestation and expression of this new dynastic consciousness, containing the "lore" of the family's origins as a noble "house" (*Haus*), and associating them with both land and title.

At the same time that Schmid began his work on the expression of noble "self-consciousness" in the Welf dynastic texts of the twelfth century, the

---

41. See below, chapter 1, 21–23.

42. For the background to this scholarship, see John B. Freed, "Reflections on the Medieval German Nobility," *American Historical Review* 91:3 (1986): 553–575, esp. 560–564 (Freed does not discuss the implications of Schmid's and Duby's research for dynastic historical narratives); David Crouch, *The Birth of Nobility: Constructing Aristocracy in England and France, 900–1300* (Harlow, UK, 2005), 106–107.

43. Otto Gerhard Oexle, "Gruppen in der Gesellschaft: Das wissenschaftliche Oeuvre von Karl Schmid," *Frühmittelalterliche Studien* 28 (1994): 410–423.

44. Karl Schmid, "Welfisches Selbstverständnis," in *Adel und Kirche: Gerd Tellenbach zum 65 Geburtstag dargebracht von Freunden und Schülern,* ed. Josef Fleckenstein and Karl Schmid (Freiburg, 1968), 390–416.

French historian Georges Duby had already begun to recognize points of harmony between the work of the Münster-Freiburg historians on early medieval family structures and his own views about the dramatic transformation of western society (later called the *mutation feodale* or *mutation de l'an mil*) that he saw taking place around the year 1000.[45] Duby associated the shift in family structures identified by Schmid and his colleagues with the proliferation of hereditary lordship after the collapse of Carolingian authority in the tenth century that he had described in detail in his earlier work on the Mâconnais in Burgundy.[46] As the land and fortifications from which lordship was projected became hereditary, so paternal ancestry and agnatic lineage became the all-important elements in the identity of those who possessed them. One result of this new focus on lineage, Duby argued, was the writing of genealogical lists and, gradually emerging from them, dynastic historical narratives.

Both Schmid and Duby's arguments have been enormously influential; their model has been the subject of ongoing commentary and criticism. Duby, in particular, has been the touchstone both for subsequent studies of the dynastic narratives themselves and for more general theoretical treatments of the place of genealogy within the Old French historical and literary tradition.[47] This legacy is, however, complicated by the fact that the theories of social change and the structure of the family that underlay Schmid and Duby's reading of the dynastic texts have now been challenged.[48] Studies of the aristocracy in the earlier Middle Ages, and of high medieval England, Touraine, Champagne, and the German empire have demonstrated

---

45. Georges Duby, "Structures de parenté et noblesse, France du Nord, XI-XII siècles," in *Miscellania Medievalia in Memoriam Jan Frederik Niermeyer* (Gröningen, 1967), repr. in Duby, *Hommes et structures du Moyen Âge: Recueil d'articles* (Paris and The Hague, 1973); trans. as "The Structure of Kinship and Nobility: Northern France in the Eleventh and Twelfth Centuries," in *The Chivalrous Society*, trans. Cynthia Postan (Berkeley, 1977), 134–148; Duby, "Remarques sur la littérature généalogique en France aux xi et xii siècles," *Comptes rendus des séances de l'année 1967: Académie des Inscriptions et Belles Lettres* (Paris, 1967); trans. as "French Genealogical Literature," in *The Chivalrous Society*, 149–157. For an earlier and more thorough survey of material from the empire, see Hans Patze, "Adel und Stifterchronik," *Blätter für deutsches Landesgeschichte* 100 (1964): 8–81, and 101 (1965): 67–128. On Duby's thinking, see Crouch, *The Birth of Nobility*, 105–106.

46. Georges Duby, *La société aux XIe et XIIe siècles dans la région mâconnaise* (1953; repr., Paris, 1971).

47. See Leah Shopkow, "Dynastic History," in *Historiography in the Middle Ages*, ed. Deborah Mauskopf Deliyannis (Leiden, 2003), 217–248. As Shopkow indicates (esp. in comments at 247 n. 1), Duby was cited as an influence by R. Howard Bloch, *Etymologies and Genealogies: A Literary Anthropology of the French Middle Ages* (Chicago, 1983), 64–91; see also Gabrielle Spiegel, "Genealogy: Form and Function in Medieval Narrative," in Spiegel, *The Past as Text: The Theory and Practice of Medieval Historiography* (Baltimore, 1997), 104; and Spiegel, *Romancing the Past: The Rise of Vernacular Prose Historiography in Thirteenth-Century France* (Berkeley, 1993), 351 n. 141.

48. Richard E. Barton, "Aristocratic Culture: Kinship, Chivalry, and Court Culture," in *A Companion to the Medieval World*, ed. Carol Lansing (Malden, MA, 2009), 500–504; Dominique Barthélemy, *The Serf, the Knight, and the Historian*, trans. Graham Robert Edwards (Ithaca, NY, 2009).

that family structures were both more complex and more fluid than the original *mutationiste* thesis allowed.[49] In these regions, members of aristocratic families can be observed celebrating both paternal and maternal lineage, but also associating and acting together with wider kin-groups. The structure and self-identity of a family might be determined by a variety of factors. The nobility of Angevin England might choose to adopt the arms of their paternal or maternal ancestors, depending on which lineage was considered the most distinguished.[50] In France, even in the mid-thirteenth century, a wide network of kin, cousins, and allies might come to the aid of a noble-man in need of assistance.[51] The plurality of possible family identities is clearly expressed in the works of John of Joinville, the thirteenth-century crusader whose writings have been so important for historians' ideas about family traditions of crusading. In the epitaph that he composed for his great-grandfather, Joinville proudly wrote of a sequence of patrilineal ancestors, but in recalling his time on crusade, he revealed an awareness of a wider group of relatives. Recounting his experiences on crusade in the *Vie de Saint Louis,* for instance, he described the brothers Geoffrey II of Sarrebruck and Gobert of Apremont as his "cousins," referring apparently to a marriage between their families that had occurred a century and a half (three genera-tions) previously. Joinville went so far as to describe the Count of Jaffa, John II of Ibelin, as "a member of the Joinville lineage," although the two could at most have been second cousins; their relationship was affinal.[52]

Joinville, who wrote exclusively of his male ancestors and relatives, would make an excellent case for Duby's grand thesis of the high-medieval con-ception of the noble family as a male-dominated and patrilineal (if not pri-mogenital) lineage. More recent studies of other individuals, families, and

---

49. David Crouch, "The Historian, Lineage, and Heraldry," in *Heraldry, Pageantry, and Social Display in Medieval England,* ed. Peter Coss (Woodbridge, UK, and Rochester, NY, 2002), 17–37, esp. 34–37; Theodore Evergates, *Aristocracy in the County of Champagne* (Philadelphia, 2007), 82–100; Pauline Stafford, "The *mutation familiale:* A Suitable Case for Caution," in *The Community, the Family, and the Saint: Patterns of Power in Early Medieval Europe,* ed. J. Hill and M. Swan (Turnhout, 1998), 103–125; Stephen White, *Custom, Kinship, and Gifts to Saints: The* laudatio parentum *in Western France, c. 1050–c. 1150* (Chapel Hill, NC, and London, 1988); Amy Livingstone, *Out of Love of My Kin: Aristocratic Family Life in the Lands of the Loire, 1000–1200* (Ithaca, NY, 2010); Stuart Airlie, "The Aristocracy," in *The New Cambridge Medieval History,* vol. 2, *700–900,* ed. Rosamund McKitterick (Cambridge, 1995), 438; Jonathan Lyon, "Cooperation, Compromise, and Conflict Avoidance: Family Relationships in the House of Andechs, ca. 1100–1204" (PhD diss., University of Notre Dame, 2004); John B. Freed, *The Counts of Falkenstein: Noble Self-Consciousness in Twelfth-Century Germany,* Transac-tions of the American Philosophical Society, n.s. 74:6 (Philadelphia, 1976), 1–13.

50. Crouch, "The Historian," 28–37.

51. Dominique Barthélemy, "L'État contre le lignage: Une thème a développer dans l'histoire des pouvoirs en France aux xi, xii, et xiii siècles," *Médiévales* 5:10 (1986): 48–50.

52. Jean of Joinville, *Vie de Saint* Louis, ed. and trans. Jacques Monfrin (Paris, 1995), 76 §158 and note; trans. Caroline Smith in *Chronicles of the Crusades,* 184–185 and n. 7.

regions—including Joinville's own county of Champagne—are revealing, however, that women had a much greater role to play in aristocratic society than Duby's patrilineal model had originally allowed. From the eleventh through the thirteenth century, we find women wielding power, either through the family or directly, as lords in their own right.[53] Rather than seeing the family as arranged around a lineal sequence of male lords, Theodore Evergates has argued that "the nuclear or conjugal family...constituted the elementary form of the aristocratic family long before the twelfth century, and it passed through the millennial divide without fundamental change."[54] Around this conjugal unit, lines of affinity and kinship could be drawn in various ways and would probably include those who held offices in the household, including clergy and servants. Research on patterns of monastic patronage and, of greatest relevance to this study, on patterns of involvement in crusades, has suggested that women played an important role in preserving family traditions as well as in introducing new religious ideas into their husband's families. This was potentially because, as Elisabeth van Houts has argued, women were often the transmitters of oral traditions about the family past—strong, although often invisible links in the chain of family memory.[55]

Since nobility itself, as Oexle has observed, like reputation, glory, honor, and perhaps most importantly lordship, was fundamentally derived from the past, ancestry would constitute one of the most important ways through which the noble man and woman at the center of the family identified themselves.[56] "Lineage," then, was not a fixed social structure, but a way for the family to talk about their shared past, and thus their collective identity. Conceptions of the family were fluid, reflecting both changes in attitude over an individual's lifetime as older generations died, marriages were made and broken, and children were born, and situational—often politically motivated—choices. Seen not as passive reflections of a new social structure, but as active statements of a lineage that was deliberately constructed, dynastic histories were clearly important statements of identity.[57] More than any other, these are the sources that can reveal how members of particular noble communities thought about crusading and its place in their shared past.

---

53. Kimberly LoPrete, *Adela of Blois: Countess and Lord (c. 1067–1137)* (Dublin, 2007).

54. Evergates, *Aristocracy,* 88.

55. For noble women and family patterns of monastic patronage, see Constance Bouchard, *Sword, Miter, and Cloister: Nobility and the Church in Burgundy* (Ithaca, NY, 1986), 136–137, 141–148. For women and the diffusion of enthusiasm for crusading, see Riley-Smith, *The First Crusaders,* 98–100. Van Houts, *Memory and Gender,* passim.

56. Oexle, "Welfisches *Memoria,*" 61–65.

57. For the fluid structure of the family and the aristocratic life cycle, see Crouch, *The Birth of Nobility,* 121–123; and Evergates, *Aristocracy,* 82–100.

The use of textual sources as evidence for the mentalities of a group, most of whom had only second hand access to the written word is an exercise that can be performed only with the greatest caution. With this in mind, a key assumption of this book is that a large number of our written sources, whether in Latin or the vernacular, reflect memories that were shared by the wider community and constructed at points of social interaction. As is demonstrated in the first chapter, the nobility of the later eleventh and twelfth centuries demonstrated through their actions and, although more rarely, through their writings that they were fully aware of and engaged with monastic discourses of ancestral responsibilities and obligations. Ideas about the past could be transmitted in a variety of different contexts, but in the second chapter it is argued that moments when the itinerant nobility visited particular sites within their domains presented opportunities for formal evocations of the past and storytelling. The surviving dynastic historical narratives are not transcripts of storytelling *séances,* but the demand for these narratives among a variety of different types of literate communities suggests that the stories they contained were popular and widely used for the purposes of commemoration, moral instruction, and the enhancement of familial honor and reputation. Our textual sources also provide a wealth of evidence of the material framework around which social memory was constructed, and this framework is the subject of the third chapter.

Perhaps the most important elements in the material framework of any family's memory were the bodies of their dead relatives. As chapter 4 demonstrates, however, the very act of crusading posed a major threat to this aspect of noble commemorative culture. Dynastic narratives and a host of other sources attest to the crises that could result from the loss of control of familial remains caused by crusading. Having the names, deeds, and bodies of ancestors in an ordered set was important because it helped to structure the narrative of the family past as an episodic sequence that closely resembles the structure of medieval epic cycles. The fifth chapter explores the place of the crusades within these commemorative sequences and suggests that one particular motif, that of the closed gate, was used to foretell and explain the family's participation in the crusades, and as a metaphor for crusading more generally.

While the first part of the book establishes something of the mechanisms through which ideas and images about the crusades were preserved and transmitted within the collective memory of noble families, as well as the meaning of these memories and their place in the family past, the second part demonstrates the role that ancestry played in the attempts to persuade two figures—first Henry II of England and then Alfonso II of Aragón—to take the cross in the second half of the twelfth century. These two men offer ideal case studies, as both of their reigns are well documented and coincided with the descent into crisis of the crusading situation in Spain and the Holy Land. Both figures were, therefore, subjected to sustained appeals from within their own domains, from Rome, and from the East to take the cross. Although both ultimately held royal titles, Henry and Alfonso had complex dynastic identities because both were descended, in the male line, from old families of regional nobility. It was their noble, rather than their royal, ancestors who had participated in crusades, and thus in the increasingly heated debates about whether to take the cross, it was their noble identity that came to the forefront. What these two case studies reveal is how appeals from afar, for instance from Rome and Jerusalem, were met in a landscape thick with sites, objects, and stories reminding the two men of their crusading ancestors.

Henry and Alfonso are in many ways special cases. Their royal status, the direct appeals made to them to take the cross, and their participation so shortly before their deaths set them apart from the vast majority of crusading nobles in the twelfth century. As the first part of this book will reveal, however, these two men participated in a culture of family remembrance that can be identified as operating in generally similar ways for nobility across the Latin West. While acknowledging the varieties of local customs and social structures that must have existed across the landscape of lordship in Europe, like other studies of crusading and crusaders, this book takes a comparative approach. Both crusading and the existence of a class of hereditary nobles were Pan-European phenomena and can be studied most profitably in the wider, transregional perspective. Across different regions, we find remarkable similarities in the systems through which ideas about the past were transmitted, the potential meaning of these ideas to families and wider communities, and the shape that the narrative of the past could take. Our investigation of these aspects of family memory—its mechanics, semantics, and poetics— must begin by establishing why crusading, in particular, came to occupy such an important place within the collective memory of so many families. We will therefore first examine the special resonance of the crusading ancestor.

PART I

*Family Memory:
Form and Function*

❧ CHAPTER 1

Ancestor, Avatar, Crusader

In the year 1096, twenty-eight years after seizing control of the county of Anjou from his elder brother, Geoffrey III the Bearded, Count Fulk IV le Réchin of Anjou initiated the creation of a brief written memorandum regarding his family.[1] Dictating his work to a scribe who was probably a cleric of his household or one of the religious communities of his principality, Fulk indicated that the first part of his work would encompass "how my ancestors had acquired their *honor* [a term that denoted the lands and rights that were the basis of princely power] and how they held it until my own time."[2] Rendered in basic Latin prose, devoid of any scriptural allusions or classicizing turns and seeming utterly alien to the normally high Latinate style associated with the Loire schools of his principality, Fulk's account began with a simple genealogy of his four earliest ancestors, repeated "just as my uncle Geoffrey Martel told it to me," and proceeded with a summary of the careers of his predecessors beginning with his great-grandfather Geoffrey Greymantle.[3] When this had been completed, Fulk reached the second, more difficult

---

1. The text is edited in two parts as "Fragmentum historiae Andegavensis," in *CCA*, 232–246, and as *Gesta Andegavensium Peregrinorum*, in *RHC Occ.* 5: 345–347. For its textual history and on Fulk as the author, see Nicholas Paul, "The Chronicle of Fulk le Réchin: A Reassessment," *Haskins Society Journal* 18 (2007): 19–35.
2. "Fragmentum historiae Andegavensis," 232.
3. "Fragmentum historiae Andegavensis," 232.

stage of his composition, in which he would account first for the eight-year war he had waged against his elder brother and then for his own, troubled rule as count. "I held that *honor* for twenty-eight years until that time when I arranged to make these writings," said the count, "if you want to hear what I did in these twenty-eight years and in the eight which came before, follow what I am writing now and you will know what occurred."[4]

Looking forward to the literary patronage of Fulk's yet far-off descendants, the Plantagenet rulers of England, historians have contented themselves that what drove the count to undertake this adventure, however simple, in Latin historiography, was a preternatural interest in letters.[5] In fact the reason was more pragmatic. Evidence from another text suggests that at the time Fulk was writing, the very matters he chose to describe—the legacy of his ancestors and his own treatment of that legacy—were at the center of a heated and potentially dangerous debate.

Within ten years of the time that Fulk began his narrative, another historian, this one an accomplished writer of historical prose with a solid education in the Latin classics, wrote his own work about the counts of Anjou.[6] Therein he described with distaste how Fulk had seized power from his brother, ultimately imprisoning him, and how in the course of their eight-year conflict and the ensuing disaster that was Fulk's reign as count, the Angevin patrimony had been dramatically weakened, with the loss of major towns and castles in the Touraine, the Saintonge, and the Gâtinais. What was left of the family's lands was menaced internally by the uprisings of the greater castellans and externally by their neighbors in Normandy, Aquitaine, and Blois-Chartres.[7]

New hope had dawned as Fulk's capable, popular, eldest son, Geoffrey, came of age and began to challenge the wicked ways of his usurping father. Word of the boy's virtues, the chronicler asserted, even reached the ears of his old uncle Geoffrey, still alive after nearly thirty years of captivity. The imprisoned former count gave his blessing and sent words of encouragement to his nephew and namesake: "I am pleased that with regard to the worthiness (*probitas*) of our ancestors, you

---

4. "Tenui igitur honorem illum viginti octo annis usque ad terminum illum quo scriptum facere disposui. In quibus viginti octo annis et in aliis octo qui precesserunt, si vis audire que gessi, prosequere que scribo et cognosces que facta sunt." "Fragmentum historiae Andegavensis," 237.

5. James Westfall-Thompson, *The Literacy of the Laity in the Middle Ages* (Berkeley, 1939), 129; Leah Shopkow, *History and Community: Norman Historical Writing in the Eleventh and Twelfth Centuries* (Washington, DC, 1997), 28. For the question of Fulk's literacy, see Paul, "The Chronicle of Fulk le Réchin," 19–21.

6. The earliest surviving version of this work, the *Chronica de gestis consulum Andevagorum*, is a redaction probably written in the second or third decade of the twelfth century by Thomas, prior of the collegiate church at the comital castle of Loches. Internal evidence from this redaction, most notably a closing *envoi* to the reader written before the death of Fulk le Réchin in 1109, strongly suggests that the original text was written before this date. *CCA*, xxx.

7. *CCA*, 64–65.

do not depart from it."[8] Presumably at the encouragement of the young heir, his uncle was released from prison and allowed freedom of movement, under guard, around what was left of his former domains. According to the anonymous chronicler, these events occurred near the time when Pope Urban II held a great church council at Clermont in the Auvergne, which was in November 1095, the year before Fulk began writing.[9]

The immediate context for the creation of Fulk's narrative of his ancestry and his rule was thus a crisis, not so much of direct, military control over the county, as of reputation, tradition, and dynastic identity. The words of praise that the anonymous Angevin dynastic chronicler placed in the mouth of Fulk's brother suggested that the count's rule had been illegitimate not because he had acquired it through military force, but because he had failed to defend what his ancestors had achieved, to match in his own deeds the strength and virtue that they had demonstrated in theirs. The Latin term that the chronicler used, *probitas*, might be translated as "worthiness" "uprightness," or "honesty." This characteristic, later rendered in the vernacular as *preudommie*, was the bedrock of virtue on which the idea of nobility rested, the forerunner to the code of aristocratic conduct known as *chevalerie*.[10] David Crouch has argued that in the age before the appearance of a self-conscious code of chivalry, which was codified first around 1220, noble conduct was instead the product of the noble *habitus*—the horizon of expected behavior adopted unself-consciously by young aristocrats. Before there was a code, Crouch argues, there were models, "avatars," of nobility from whom proper behavior was adopted.[11] At the time of the First Crusade, the market for avatars was thriving. It featured martyred soldiers, saints, and hermits and the heroes of *chansons de geste*. But as the discourse at Angers around the year 1100 suggests, ancestors were models of particular importance. As avatar, the ancestor was more closely connected to the individual noble than any other

---

8. "Gaudeo te ab avorum probitate non degenerare." *CCA,* 65.

9. *CCA,* 65.

10. David Crouch, *The Birth of Nobility: Constructing Aristocracy in England and France, c. 900–c. 1300* (London and New York, 2005), 29–86, esp. 30–37. For commentary on Crouch's ideas, see Richard E. Barton, "Aristocratic Culture: Kinship, Chivalry, and Court Culture," in *A Companion to the Medieval World,* ed. Carol Lansing and Edward English (Malden, MA, 2009), 504–511. The resonance and meaning of the term *probitas* have generally been overlooked in studies of the Latin terminology of virtue. C. Stephen Jaeger, for instance, in *Origins of Courtliness: Civilizing Trends and the Formation of Courtly Ideals, 939–1210* (Philadelphia, 1985), 32, 134, saw *probitas* as among the more "common" ethical terms associated with *mores.* Where I have found it related to noble conduct in the twelfth century, however, it stands alone, or coupled with *nobilitas.* For a discussion of *probus* functioning like *preudommie,* see Barton, 508.

11. David Crouch, "Courtliness and Chivalry: Colliding Constructs," in *Soldiers, Nobles, and Gentlemen: Essays in Honor of Maurice Keen,* ed. Peter Coss and Christopher Tyerman (Woodbridge, UK, 2009), 41–44; Crouch, *The Birth of Nobility,* 46–56.

figure. Where the inheritance, defense, and enlargement of *honors* were concerned, the contrast between the present generation and the past was glaringly,
even dangerously, obvious.

Fulk's written work was a deft response to the accusations that he had become
estranged from the *probitas* of his ancestors, and that he had failed to uphold their
achievements; he framed it in precisely such a way as to refute these charges.[12]
Beginning with Geoffrey Greymantle (d. 987) "whose *probitas* we cannot even
relate" and moving next to Fulk Nerra (d. 1040) "whose *probitas* was great and
wonderful," and then to his uncle Geoffrey Martel (d. 1060) "whose *probitas* and
prudence in worldly matters were great," he told of their strength and wisdom,
of the building of castles and glorious victory in battle.[13] Fulk's interest did not
usually extend to acts of piety, but he did refer to the famous (and one might say
glorious) pilgrimages of his grandfather Fulk Nerra to Jerusalem.[14] What Fulk
produced was thus an account of virtuous deeds, what Latinate historians knew
as *gesta* and vernacular writers would refer to as *gestes*. By writing about deeds,
he was demonstrating his awareness of what had been achieved by his ancestors
and of their tradition of *probitas*.

We may safely assume that in the second, autobiographical part of his work,
Fulk intended to show how he had defended the accomplishments and upheld
the traditions of his ancestors. This is something we have to assume because the
second part of Fulk's chronicle does not survive—the sole manuscript witness to
what he wrote breaks off shortly after the point where he stated his intention to
give an account of himself.[15] Whether he even finished his work is itself unclear,
because at the very moment that he was preparing it, he became distracted by
another series of events. They began with the unprecedented arrival of a Roman
pontiff, Urban II, in Fulk's lands during the pre-Lenten season of Septuagesima
in 1096.[16] Urban, who sought to secure an alliance with the count, drew on

---

12. The centrality of *probitas* in the text was noted by Jane Martindale, "Secular Propaganda and
Aristocratic Values: The Autobiographies of Count Fulk le Réchin of Anjou and Count William of
Poitou, Duke of Aquitaine," in *Writing Medieval Biography, 750–1250: Essays in Honour of Professor Frank
Barlow*, ed. David Bates, Julia Crick, and Sarah Hamilton (Woodbridge, UK), 146.

13. *CAA*, 233–235.

14. *CAA*, 234. Fulk IV thought that his great-uncle had gone to the Holy Land twice, but it is
generally believed that he went at least three, if not four, times. See Bernard S. Bachrach, *Fulk Nerra, the
Neo-Roman Consul, 987–1040: A Political Biography of the Angevin Count* (Berkeley, 1993), 243; Bachrach,
"The Pilgrimages of Fulk Nerra, Count of the Angevins, 987–1040," in *Religion, Culture, and Society in the
Early Middle Ages: Studies in Honor of Richard E. Sullivan*, ed. Thomas F. X. Noble and John J. Contreni
(Kalamazoo, MI, 1987), 205–217.

15. BAV, Reg. Lat. 173, f. 8v. For the MS, see André Wilmart, *Codices Reginenses Latini* (Vatican City,
1937–45), 1: 407–409; and Paul, "The Chronicle of Fulk le Réchin," 31.

16. For Urban's journey through the Loire Valley, see now Jean-Hervé Foulon, *Église et réforme au
Moyen Âge: Papauté, milieu réformateurs et ecclésiologie dans les Pays de la Loire au tournant des xie-xiie siècles*
(Brussels, 2008), 181–186.

an arsenal of ritual and pomp to bolster the count's standing. On February 10, in a gesture of potentially great significance given the arguments about the count's failure to respect the traditions of his ancestors, Urban himself conducted the ceremonial translation of the body of Fulk's uncle Geoffrey to a new tomb before the high altar.[17] Then, at the official beginning of Lent on Quadragesima Sunday (March 2) in Tours, the site of the shrine of Saint Martin and therefore the most sacred location in Fulk's domains, the pope presented the count with a precious object, a golden flower, which the count decreed would always be carried before him and his successors "out of love and memory" of the event. In ritual, at least, Fulk's pious observance of his ancestors, and his place in the glorious line of counts, were assured.

The primary reason for Urban's visit to Anjou was not, however, to repair the reputation of its embattled count. The pope had come to spread the message he had first propounded four months earlier on November 27 at the closing of the Council of Clermont.[18] It was, according to Fulk, that the people "should go to Jerusalem that they might expel the gentile people who had occupied all of the lands of the Christians up to Constantinople."[19] The events that unfolded in response to this call were of such consequence that they led Fulk, who had begun to write once again in 1098, to abandon the narrative project he had planned and to transcribe the news he was receiving of other deeds, done by a faraway army that had reached northern Syria. The significance of these deeds dwarfed the accomplishments of the count's own career and captured the imagination of the medieval West, forever changing the measure of aristocratic Christian achievement.[20] The enormity of the reports that had reached Fulk's ears was such that he went back to the beginning of the year he had been describing (1096) to mention the "signs and portents" that had been seen in the land, and that he now knew to have prophesied the coming of the First Crusade.

At the very moment Fulk was writing, setting out to defend with the written word how he was fulfilling his dynastic responsibilities, the European nobility were being presented with a new, collective responsibility: the defense of eastern lands understood (using a lexicon of power familiar to them) as the patrimony of Christ, their Lord.[21] Like the domains they

17. *CCA*, 238.

18. H. E. J. Cowdrey, "Pope Urban II's Preaching of the First Crusade," *History* 55 (1970): 181, repr. in *The Crusades: Essential Readings,* ed. Thomas Madden (Oxford, 2005), 20–21; Jonathan Riley-Smith, *The First Crusaders: 1095–1131* (Cambridge, 1997), 59.

19. *CCA*, 238.

20. *Gesta Andegavensium Peregrinorum,* 345–347.

21. Christopher Tyerman, "Were There Any Crusades in the Twelfth Century?" *English Historical Review* 110:437 (1995): 554, called the First Crusade "an old way of gaining reward, by loyal service to a master (the pope or, more generally, Christ) writ large." For the related idea of crusading

inherited from their own forebears, these lands had been earned through suffering and the shedding of blood. Those who took up this responsibility and
became crusaders, who suffered and died in the Lord's service and whose efforts
restored Jerusalem and the holy places to Latin control set an example of *probitas,* of worthiness, so unlike any other that most contemporaries resorted to
Old Testament examples, to the Maccabees or Gideon, in order to appropriately
describe it.[22] In the words of a sermon intended for the Feast of the Liberation of
Jerusalem, celebrated annually on the anniversary of the city's conquest by the
crusaders (July 15), they were no longer just knights, "but on the contrary, the
flower of knighthood (*ymo militum flores*)."[23] For their relatives and descendants,
a new standard of worth had been set.

In the decades after the First Crusade, the novel spiritual, social, and military
experience of crusaders became, for many noble families, fused with the responsibilities of noble lineage. Attempts to harness these sentiments to further the
crusading cause are often associated with the encyclical authored by Pope Eugenius III in 1145, which sought assistance for the beleaguered Latin Kingdom that
the crusaders had established in 1099. His letter, *Quantum praedecessores,* invoked
the precise concerns that are manifest in the writings of Fulk le Réchin and the
anonymous Angevin chronicler, and it did so in similar language:

> It will be seen as a great token of nobility and worthiness (*nobilitatis et
> probitatis*) if those things acquired by the efforts of your fathers are vig-
> orously defended by you, their good sons. But if, God forbid, it comes
> to pass differently, then the bravery of the fathers will have proved to be
> diminished in the sons.[24]

In his study of crusading spirituality in the twelfth century, William Purkis has
pointed to numerous appeals to ancestral efforts (*strenuitas patrum*) in writings by
or concerning crusaders, which appear with increasing frequency from around
the time of the Second Crusade.[25] This message, which "struck a resounding
chord with the arms-bearers of western Europe," came to replace the earlier

---

as vengeance in the name of God and the patrimony of Christ, see Susanna Throop, *Crusading as an Act
of Vengeance, 1095–1216* (Farnham, UK, 2011), 57–61, 108–114.

22. Nicholas Morton, "The Defence of the Holy Land and the Memory of the Maccabees," *Journal
of Medieval History* 36:3 (2010): 275–293, esp. 276–281.

23. John France, "The Text of the Account of the Capture of Jerusalem in the Ripoll Manuscripts,
Bibliothèque Nationale (Latin) 5132," *English Historical Review* 103:408 (1988): 653.

24. "Maximum namque nobilitatis et probitatis indicium fore cognoscitur, si ea quae patrum strenuitas acquisivit, a vobis filiis strenue defendantur. Verum tamen si, quod absit! secus contigerit, patrum
fortitudo in filiis imminuta probatur." Eugenius III, "Epistolae et privilegia," *PL* 180, col. 1064.

25. William Purkis, *Crusading Spirituality in the Holy Land and Iberia, c. 1095–c. 1187* (Woodbridge,
UK, 2008), 90–92.

rhetorical focus on the imitation of Christ.[26] Crusaders who had once been called to walk in the footsteps of Christ were now increasingly called to follow the footsteps (*vestigia subsequere*) of their ancestors.

Indeed, while it is possible to admire the sympathy of Eugenius and Bernard for the concerns of the warrior elite, we might just as well be surprised that it took the papacy forty years to realize the potential effectiveness of such language in its communications. To the nobility themselves, the importance of ancestral participation in the crusades was immediately apparent. So much is obvious not only from patterns of recruitment for the early crusade expeditions, which, as Jonathan Riley-Smith has shown, reflect strong commitment to crusading within certain kindreds,[27] but also, as we will see below, from what was written by and about those who did and did not take the cross. This chapter will demonstrate that although the First Crusade undoubtedly had a transformative effect on the way that warrior aristocrats thought about their own status and responsibilities, as a devotional act as much as an exotic adventure, the image of the crusader fit effortlessly into discourses of ancestry, tradition, and responsibility that were already firmly in place at the time of Urban's preaching at Clermont in 1095. Those normative discourses of ancestry, which above all sought out heroic and exemplary figures from the past around which to model aristocratic conduct, were not just the preserve of monks, bishops, and popes, but also that of the nobility, and the concern to locate such figures can be observed as easily at the end of the twelfth century as at the beginning. From the time of the First Crusade, the identification and exaltation of virtuous ancestors enjoined on their descendants not only abstract ideas of good conduct, but a strong sense that it was their responsibility to uphold particular ancestral efforts and achievements. In certain circumstances crusading might even be seen as a hereditary obligation.

Ancestry and Behavior

The importance of what ancestors were believed to have done and how they were believed to have comported themselves was made manifest to nobles in a variety of contexts. The discourse of ancestry and responsibility with which historians of the nobility are the most familiar is the one associated with the nobility's hereditary sense of reputation and honor. Honor was, as Richard Barton has shown with reference to the county of Maine, a key element in the glue that bound fighting men to their lords, and thus a constituent

---

26. Purkis, *Crusading Spirituality,* 91, 115.
27. Riley-Smith, *The First Crusaders,* 93–105, 169–195.

element in the power wielded by magnates.[28] Honor was also, as Matthew Strickland has demonstrated, hereditable. The idea that flight from battle would bring lasting dishonor on one's descendants was manifested in England as early as the tenth century; by the thirteenth it was such a characteristic feature of aristocratic culture that during the battle of Mansourah in Egypt in 1250 a crusading knight barricaded in a house and surrounded on all sides sought the assurance of his colleagues that going in search of assistance would not bring dishonor on his descendants.[29]

Honor was clearly important, and in the years before the First Crusade characters and episodes from *chansons de geste,* like the debate between Oliver and Roland over the merits of tactical withdrawal at the battle of Roncesvaux in the *Chanson de Roland,* provided knights and nobles with a theater of imagined deeds and conduct in which the contours of what constituted honorable behavior could be actively negotiated.[30] But alongside this broader discourse of noble behavior was a much more specific one focused not on heroic avatars but on ancestral ones. This normative discourse of ancestry is better documented and potentially even more important than images of heroism in vernacular literature in understanding the mentalities of early crusaders.

In his groundbreaking study of aristocratic piety at the time of the First Crusade, Marcus Bull pointed to the many ties that bound the lords of eleventh-century Francia to their local Benedictine and Augustinian religious foundations.[31] Nobles seeking access to the intercessory prayers of religious communities and the power of the saints whose shrines they guarded made benefactions of land and lordship. Members of noble families also adopted the religious life, some as child oblates, but others later in their lives, creating ties of kinship between the two communities. As Bull demonstrated, the rhetoric deployed in the texts composed at these religious houses, both for the monastic communities themselves and in the context of their dealings with local knights, gave clear warning to the laity of the sin associated with their lives of violence, and of the attendant punishments that would be visited upon them in the hereafter. The clear recognition by the eleventh-century laity of the redemptive effects of monastic intercession, the widespread support of the laity for the local monasteries, and the close correspondence between the rhetoric of punishment used by monastic writers with the language of the charters of departing crusaders

---

28. Richard Barton, *Lordship in the County of Maine, c. 890–c. 1160* (Woodbridge, UK, 2004), 77–111.

29. Matthew Strickland, *War and Chivalry: The Conduct and Perception of War in England and Normandy, 1066–1217* (Cambridge, 1996), 98, 123–124. Referring to John of Joinville, *Vie de Saint Louis,* ed. and trans. Jacques Monfrin (Paris, 1995), 110–112, §224–246.

30. For the use of the *Chanson de Roland* as evidence of discourses of honor and courage, see Strickland, *War and Chivalry,* 98–121.

31. Marcus Bull, *Knightly Piety and the Lay Response to the First Crusade: The Limousin and Gascony* (Oxford, 1993), 115–203.

explains, Bull argued, the great appeal of the crusade, which offered the promise of salvation to all those who took part with a contrite heart.

If, in their dealings with the laity, professed religious engaged in a discourse of sin, punishment, and redemption they were no less involved in discussions about traditions and customs. As the primary lords of the land, nobles and monks were inevitably involved in many negotiations over rights of lordship. These rights were hereditary, and they necessarily involved the two parties in a dialogue about the past. "Actions of the living," Michel Lauwers has written of this world, "are based on tradition, on precedents, that is to say, on the memory of ancestors and the pronouncements of the old."[32]

When the balance of power in a locality changed, and in particular when the heir of a lordship came of age, local religious houses often asked the new lord to validate and reaffirm matters agreed with an institution by their parents and ancestors.[33] The form of the resulting confirmation charters would suggest that the business of the lord's ancestor was read aloud, the circumstances and characters of the previous generation coming briefly to life before the lord enacted the confirmation, placing his or her name, autograph mark, and increasingly by the mid-twelfth century also his or her seal beside those of the earlier generation. An 1180 charter of Count Philip of Flanders for the Augustinian house of Voormezele demonstrates the sense of continuity generated by these confirmations.

I likewise confirm those things which my ancestors, the outstanding counts of Flanders Robert, Baldwin, Charles, [and] my father Thierry gave to that aforesaid church, confirming those writings of theirs, which I saw and I heard and I recognized by the placement of their seals.[34]

The process of securing confirmations resulted in the compilation of dossiers of written acts bearing the names and validating marks of several generations of a family, which might then be recopied in book format as cartularies, representing small monuments to that family's good relations with a community and perhaps also with a particular saint.[35]

32. Michel Lauwers, *La mémoire des ancêtres, le souci des morts: Morts, rites, et société au Moyen Âge* (Paris, 1997), 322.

33. See, for example, *Cartulaire de Sainte-Croix d'Orleans* (814–1300), ed. Eugène Jarry and Joseph Thillier (Paris, 1906), no. 66.

34. "Illa quoque predicte ecclesie similiter confirmoque preclari comites Flandrie antecessores mei Robertus, Balduinus, Karolus, Theodericus pater meus illi in elemosinam contulerunt, scriptis suis ea confirmantes, que vidi et audivi et recognivo per eorum sigilla apposite." *Oorkonden der graven van Vlaanderen (juli 1128–setember 1191)*, ed. Adriaan Verhulst and Thérèse de Hemptinne (Brussels, 2009), 102, no. 584.

35. Damien Carraz, "Mémoire lignagère et archives monastiques: Les Bourbouton et la commanderie de Richerenches," in *Convaincre et persuader: Communication et propagande aux XIIe et XIIIe siècles*, ed. Martin Aurell (Poitiers, 2007), 465–502.

That it was the responsibility of lay lords to respect the established customs of the region (*consuetudines*) and the established precedents (*traditiones*) of their ancestors is made most evident in cases where relations broke down. To use the formulation of Henk Teunis, "when rulers exhibited 'hegemonic' conduct, the monks countered with the collective memory of what was just."[36] The charters of the nuns of Holy Mary of Charity (known as Le Ronceray) in Angers, which, like many of the documents written in northwest Francia in the eleventh century are notable for their narrative quality, reveal that ancestral behavior occupied a central place in this collective memory. The nuns complained, for instance, that Peter Rubiscallus had "in his tyranny, [gone] against the law (*jus*) of his ancestors."[37] In another charter, which described a lengthy dispute between the nuns and the family of the lords of Matheflon at the time of the First Crusade, the evil usurpations of Lord Fulk of Matheflon were compared with the generous concessions of his son Hugh. When, after a long interval, during which Fulk of Matheflon participated in the First Crusade, the lord, together with his son, daughter-in-law, daughter, and grandson, came to an agreement with the nuns of Ronceray, the normalization of relations was sealed with the lord's "humble decree" that "just as he, so far as is in his power, must defend the castle of Matheflon that had been built by the early counts and given to him by the agreement of his illustrious father, so he must do for the land of Mary against all men who do not accept the law."[38] The nuns' victory was apparently in convincing Fulk of Matheflon that his responsibility to protect the rights of the Virgin and her community at Le Ronceray was equivalent to his well-understood responsibility to defend the achievements of his ancestors, which he associated with their strong stone fortress.

Not surprisingly, given the long memories of monastic communities and their active engagement with the past, the behavior of earlier generations of a noble family could permanently influence how monks perceived living members of a dynasty. At the court of the Count of Anjou in 1047, for instance, the canons of Saint-Lézin attempted to bolster their argument against Eudes of Blaison by describing him as only the most recent generation of a family that had continually harmed their community.[39] This kind of rhetoric found its greatest exponent in

---

36. Henk Teunis, *The Appeal to the Original Status: Social Justice in Anjou in the Eleventh Century* (Hilversum, 2006), 7.

37. "Cartularium monasterii beatae Mariae caritatis andegavensis," ed. Paul Marchegay, in *Archives d'Anjou* 3 (Angers, 1854), 68–69, act no. 90.

38. "planoque predicavit sic castrum Mateflon ab antiquis comitibus constitutum suoque patri tali conditione datum ut terram S. Mariae contra homines omnes, nulla accepta consuetudine, pro posse defenderet." "Cartularium monasterii beatae Mariae caritatis andegavensis," 93–95, act no. 130.

39. For the Eudes of Blaizon case, see Teunis, *The Appeal*, 28–29; and Richard E. Barton, "Making a Clamor to the Lord: Noise, Justice, and Power in 11th and 12th century France," in *Feud, Violence, and Practice: Essays in Medieval Studies in Honor of Stephen D. White*, ed. Belle Tuten and Tracey Billado (Farnham, UK, and Burlington, VT, 2010), 224–226.

the poison pen of that indefatigable enemy of the castle lords of the Seine basin Abbot Suger of Saint-Denis. He described some lords, like Hugh of le Puiset, as having grown wealthy "by his own and his ancestors' tyranny" (*propria et antecessorum tyrannide sola opulentus*), and others, like Guy of La Roche Guyon, as "breaking with the evil traditions of his ancestors" (*antecessorum nequitiae rupta propagine*).[40] If the nuns of Ronceray sought to associate a tradition of justice with the Matheflon family's defense of their hereditary castle lordship, Suger, in one of his most colorful moments, blamed the long tradition of evil that haunted the family of the lords of La Roche Guyon on their "terrible and ignoble castle," the veritable hell mouth of Lucan's *Pharsalia*.[41] When Guy of La Roche Guyon attempted to reverse his family's tradition of evil, he was "overcome by the evil of that ill-fated place," and beheaded by his brother-in-law.[42]

The normative discourse of ancestry with which monks like Suger attempted to reform the behavior of the lay nobility would only have been effective if the laity were eager to see themselves as virtuously following the honorable and pious traditions of their ancestors. Charters of the later eleventh century reveal not only that nobles actively participated in this discourse of ancestral traditions, but they in fact describe lay lords making extravagant gestures of deference to these traditions. As Stephen White has argued was true of most pious benefactions by lay clients of religious communities, these gestures were often made at critical moments in the lives of nobles: as they lay dying, at the funeral obsequies of their loved ones, in recognition of the succession of a new lord, or, as happened in the case of our next example, when they departed on crusade.[43]

At virtually the same moment that Count Fulk le Réchin was composing his account of the deeds and virtues of his ancestors in Anjou, his neighbor Stephen II, scion of the Blois-Chartres dynasty (arch-nemeses of the counts of Anjou), made a gift of woodland to the powerful abbey of Marmoutier near Tours.[44] The charter recording the gift set out how Stephen's benefaction followed in a tradition of piety and reverence for the abbey and its founder, Saint Martin. According to the narrative, written in the count's voice, Stephen's great-grandfather Eudes I and his brother Hugh had helped to reestablish Marmoutier after its sack by the Vikings in the ninth century:

> Following in their footsteps, my father [Thibaut III, Count of Chartres and Blois] out of love and reverence first for the glorious confessor of Christ Martin, and then of the monks living the religious life,

---

40. Suger, *Vie de Louis VI le Gros,* ed. and trans. Henri Waquet (Paris, 1929), 128–130.
41. Suger, *Vie,* 112.
42. Suger, *Vie,* 114.
43. Stephen White, *Custom, Kinship, and Gifts to Saints: The* laudatio parentum *in Western France, 1050–1150* (Chapel Hill, NC, 1988), 33.
44. *Cartulaire de Marmoutier pour le Dunois,* ed. Émile Mabille (Chateaudun, 1874), 79–82.

fully honored and augmented that same abbey from his own means. And because his father [Thibaut III of Blois and Tours] was buried there, he had so much love [for the monastery] as he did for all of Tours, that when he surrendered the same city to the Count of Anjou Geoffrey Martel, who had captured him, in his ransom, he explicitly made an exception of it [Marmoutier] and retained it in his own domain. If so far I have not protected or helped the abbey as assiduously as I ought, I have taken care not to offend it seriously; nor have I molested it much.[45]

Unlike Fulk's chronicle, with its battles and fortifications, Stephen's was not a narrative that gloried in his ancestors' martial success. The charter was nonetheless a demonstration that, even in defeat, it was of the utmost importance to uphold ancestral traditions, in this case the family's support for Saint Martin and his monks at Marmoutier. In the charter, Stephen openly disclosed his desire to be seen "following in the footsteps" (*sequens vestigia*) of his virtuous ancestors by imitating their pious deeds.

Stephen's extraordinarily effusive charter went on to explain that he was motivated to make his gift to Marmoutier because, aware of his ancestors' tradition of pious benefactions, he became concerned that he had not, in fact, upheld this tradition:

When at last my father had died, fearing that by honoring him less or being less obedient to him, I had offended him while he lived, I used to complain about it until at last after almost six years I summoned two of the monks of that monastery who were associates (*familiares*) of mine— Bernard called "the Whip" and Gausbert Louis—who often used to advise me, that I might make some gifts to Marmoutier for the soul of my father, just as my ancestors had done.[46]

45. "quorum sequens vestigia, pater meius, tum pro reverentia et amore gloriosi confessoris Christi Martini, tum pro religione in habitantium monachorum, eandem abbatiam de substantia sua honoravit admodum et augmentavit, et quia pater suus, apud eam sepultus erat, in tantum caram habuit ut cum totam Turonicam, cum civitate ipsa traderet Andegavorum comiti Gaufredo Martello, qui eum ceperat in redemptionem sui, ipsam tamen, id est abbatiam Majoris Monasterii nominatim exciperet atque sibi in proprio dominio retineret. Quam et ego hactenus si non ut debui assidue, tutatus sum, atque juvi, non multum tamen graviter offendere curavi, nec valde molestus fui." *Cartulaire de Marmoutier pour le Dunois,* 79–81. For the last line of this passage, I am following the translation of Riley-Smith, *The First Crusaders,* 128.

46. "Mortuo denique patre meo, timens ego eum minus honorando vel minus ei parendo, me ipsum quod vixerat offendisse, cum sepius inde conquerer et cum prefata post annos circiter sex accersivi duos quosdam monachorum iam dicti monasterii familiares meos Bernardum scilicet congnomento Flagellum, et Gausbertum Ludovici, qui mihi solebant frequenter suadere, ut Maiori Monasterio facere mali qui delemos in elemosinae pro anima patris mei, sicut fecerant antecessores mei." *Cartulaire de Marmoutier pour le Dunois,* 80.

Like the chronicle created by Fulk le Réchin, the charter of gift enacted by Stephen was the result of a nobleman's anxiety that he had failed to uphold family traditions. If Fulk was responding to political pressures exerted by members of his family, in particular his brother and his eldest son, Stephen's fears of failing his father were brought out in discussions with members of his wider *familia,* or household. These were the contexts in which the discourse of ancestry was conducted, where nobles, their relations, households, and familiars, decided on the behavior that best reflected the virtuous ways of their ancestors.

What Stephen's charter also shows is that satisfactory faithfulness to ancestral tradition was closely intertwined with the liturgical commemoration of the dead, something that Fulk le Réchin also hinted at when, at the beginning of his chronicle, he indicated that it would be impossible to "worthily" or "appropriately" (*digne*) describe the deeds of his earliest ancestors because he did not know where they were buried. The link is also suggested by the fact that rituals of gift or subsequent disputes over the exchange of rights between families and religious communities were often conducted over sites of ancestral burial. When Count Hugh II of Ponthieu died in 1052, his son Enguerrand II enacted a charter confirming his father's dying wishes that the *villa* of Porte be given to the abbey of Saint-Riquier. According to the copy of the document kept by the monks, the act of exchange (which they called a *traditio*) was solemnly confirmed by Enguerrand II, who held the charter he had endorsed over the abbey's altar on the very day that his father was buried there.[47] The monks of the abbey of Préaux similarly chose to petition Waleran of Meulan before his father's tomb.[48] In other documents, the heirs of a monastery's noble patron or founder are shown swearing on the tombs of their parents not only to abide by a particular grant, as Enguerrand of Ponthieu had done, but to follow their pious example. According to a narrative composed in the first decade of the twelfth century by the monks of the priory of Saint Nicholas, located near the chief fortress of the viscounts of Thouars, the funeral obsequies of Viscount Aimery, which were celebrated on 21 December 1093, saw the gathering of his two sons, Herbert II and Geoffrey. The monks recalled that Geoffrey "received the solemn promise (*per fidem acccepit*) of his brother over his father's tomb that he would never allow this place of his father's to deteriorate."[49] Both brothers would take the cross for the First Crusade, as did Rotrou III of Perche, who was in the East

47. *Recueil des actes des comtes de Pontieu,* ed. Clovis Brunel (Paris, 1930), 3–4, no. 3.

48. David Crouch, *The Image of Aristocracy in Britain, 1000–1300* (London, 1992), 245.

49. "Gaufridum fratrem suum Herbertum ne unquam hunc locum patris sui sineret deteriorari super patris sepulchrum per fidem accepit." "Chronique de Saint-Nicolas de La Chaise-le-Vicomte," ed. Elisabeth Carpentier and Georges Pon, *Revue historique du Centre-Ouest* 6 (2007): 382.

when his father, Geoffrey, died and was buried at the family's foundation of Saint-Denis at their castle of Nogent-le-Rotrou. Returning from crusade in 1099, he proceeded directly to Saint-Denis where, as the new lord, he confirmed all of the gifts to the house that had been made by his mother and father and by all of his ancestors to Saint-Denis and its mother house of Cluny. In place of the earth or instruments that might traditionally symbolize his act, he placed on the altar the palm leaves he had brought from Jerusalem.[50]

These associations between the commemoration of previous generations and the continuity of dynastic traditions such as support for religious houses are particularly significant, because while discursive records like the ones created by Fulk and by the monks of Marmoutier for Stephen are rare, documents witnessing the concern with liturgical commemoration of ancestors survive in great abundance, and from all over the medieval West. Not every gift made in expectation of intercessionary prayer for ancestors can have elicited the careful consideration of ancestral behavior and traditions that Stephen's did, but the charter is nonetheless a reminder that when nobles contemplated their ancestors or heard their names spoken or chanted in prayer, far more than just their names and the degree of their relationship may have come to mind.

In the 1096 charter of Stephen of Blois we find a nobleman concerned to uphold the traditions of his ancestors as he took the cross for the crusade. But were the two impulses in any way related? Those taking part in the First Crusade would clearly have understood that what they were doing was unprecedented in its scope and objectives, but this does not preclude the possibility that they saw taking the cross as upholding earlier traditions of noble conduct within their own families. Robert, the monk of Saint-Remi of Reims who claimed to have heard Urban II preach at Clermont, recalled in his chronicle of the crusade that the pope himself had invoked the noble preoccupation with ancestry and responsibility:

> May the deeds of your ancestors move you and spur your souls to manly courage—the worth (*probitas*) and greatness of Charlemagne, his son Louis and your other kings who destroyed the pagan kingdoms and brought them within the bounds of Christendom.... Oh most valiant soldiers, and descendants of victorious ancestors, do not fall short of, but be inspired by, the courage of your forefathers.[51]

Robert, who zealously advocated that the First Crusade was a fundamentally "Frankish" undertaking, probably included this reference to Charlemagne

---

50. *Saint-Denis de Nogent-le-Rotrou, 1031–1789: Histoire et cartulaire,* ed. Charles Métais (Vannes, 1899), 36–37, no. 10.

51. Robert the Monk, *Historia Iherosolimitana, RHC Occ.* 3: 728; trans. Carole Sweetenham as *Robert the Monk's History of the First Crusade: Historia Iherosolimitana* (Aldershot, UK, 2005), 80.

in order to further his own narrative agenda.[52] But it would be surprising if Urban II, who met many of the princely lords of the West (like Fulk of Anjou), had formerly been a monk, and was of knightly stock himself, did not make use of the prevalent discourse of ancestral virtue in his appeals to the laity to take the cross. As Jonathan Riley-Smith pointed out, in 1096 he similarly called on past dynastic examples when he exhorted Coloman I of Hungary to go to war against the antipope Clement III (Guibert of Ravenna).[53] In his letter, Urban in fact suggests that if Coloman would, in his efforts, strive to emulate his ancestor Stephen, he could hope for "whatever honor, whatever dignity your predecessor is judged to have received from our apostolic church."[54] This was quite a promise, as Stephen had been canonized by Pope Gregory VII thirteen years earlier.

At least one monastic chronicler of the crusade, Guibert of Nogent, imagined that while the expedition was under way, crusaders were stirred to great deeds by the contemplation of their ancestors' achievements. Guibert described the Duke of Normandy, Robert II Curthose, as "properly mindful of his father's military valor and noble ancestry" in battle against the Seljuk Turks at Dorylaeum in Asia Minor in 1097.[55] Robert's father was William the Conqueror, and while his fame as a crusader would be enshrined in verse and in prose in accounts of the crusade and in histories of his dynasty, in wall paintings at Westminster and in the stained-glass windows of the abbey church of Saint-Denis, he was probably the only participant in the First Crusade whose memory would not completely overshadow those of his ancestors. For most who took part, the fame and glory associated with their participation would forever change how their descendants perceived their ancestry, traditions, and responsibilities.

The Watershed

Leaving aside men like Stephen of Blois and Robert Curthose of Normandy, whose power and wealth going into the expedition ensured detailed reportage, the names of a remarkable number of crusaders are still known to us. The unique nature of the crusading enterprise, as a devotional undertaking

---

52. Matthew Gabriele, *Empire of Memory: The Legend of Charlemagne, the Franks, and Jerusalem before the First Crusade* (Oxford, 2011), 154.

53. Jonathan Riley-Smith, *The First Crusade and the Idea of Crusading* (London, 1986), 25–26.

54. "Reminiscat tunc strenuitas tua religiosi principis Stephani, qui generis tui primus a sancta Romana et apostolica Ecclesia fidei religionem suscepit, et regularis dignitatis jura permeruit.... Porro de nobis ita tuam excellentiam confidere volumus, ut quidquid honoris, quidquid dignitatis praedecessor tuus Stephanus ab apostolica nostra Ecclesia promeruisse cognoscitur." Urban II, "Epistolae et privilegia," *PL* 151, cols. 481–482.

55. Guibert of Nogent, *Dei Gesta per Francos et cinq autres textes,* ed. R. B. C. Huygens, *CCCM* 127a (Turnhout, 1996), 217; trans. Robert Levine as *The Deeds of God through the Franks* (Woodbridge, UK, and Rochester, NY, 1997), 66.

marked by numerous opportunities for the display of steadfastness and martial valor, encouraged participants and observers to record the names and deeds of those who took part. Evidence for this process comes early, from the letters of participants in the expedition who sent home lists of the names of those who died and accounts of the deeds that had been done.[56]

The listing or perhaps ritual naming of those who had taken part in the expedition continued even after the events of the expedition had been shaped into complete narratives. Brief epigrams, usually found copied at the end of manuscripts bearing narratives of the crusade expedition, either lauded particular crusaders or recalled the names of particularly prominent individuals. While some of these works were clearly written only to immortalize the greatest commanders of the expedition, perhaps as aide-memoires to those who would recount the narrative, at least two works survive that demonstrate the preservation of names on a far more local level.[57] The first, a poem generally known by its early modern title, *Versus de viris illustribus,* gives a list of lords, including men of obscure origins, from the diocese of Thérouanne who did not return from the East.[58] The second list, this one in prose, recorded those from the diocese of Limoges who "stood out" (*eminebant*) on the crusade.[59] Such lists created a new fellowship of status among the nobility of particular regions, and they may also have been useful for the purposes of recruitment for future crusades in those same regions, where the descendants of those named were unlikely to want to exclude themselves from the proud traditions founded by their ancestors.

The unprecedented geographical range of the communities involved in the prosecution of the First Crusade and the universal significance of its achievement among Latin Christians, however, also meant that the names and deeds of those involved in the First Crusade were transmitted far beyond the localities where they and their ancestors had traditionally wielded political power and influence. The primary mode for the diffusion of their names and deeds was narrative. In the aftermath of the First Crusade, attempts were made in Latin and the vernacular to create complete narrative accounts of the deeds that the

---

56. See, for instance, "Epistola I, Anselmi Ribodimonte ad Manassem archiepiscopum Remorum," in *Die Kreuzzugsbriefe aus den Jahren 1088–1100,* ed. Heinrich Hagenmeyer (Innsbruck, 1901), 144.

57. Examples of brief verses on crusade leaders include "Verses from Paris, Bibliotheque Nationale de France MS lat. 5513," ed. Nicholas Paul, in "Crusade, Memory, and Regional Politics in Twelfth-Century Amboise," *Journal of Medieval History* 31 (2005): 140–141; For the two poems, "Versus de viris illustribus" and "Venerandus Podiensis Aimarus episcopus" found in MS Stowe 56A, see H. V. Sauerland, "Aus Handschriften der Trierer Seminarbibliothek," *Neues Archiv der Gesellschaft für ältere deutsche Geschichtskunde* 17 (1895): 605–606. The text of the "Versus de viris illustribus" was also edited by C. Moeller, "Les Flamands du Ternois au royaume latin de Jérusalem," in *Mélanges Paul Frédéricq* (Brussels, 1904), 191.

58. See Heather J. Tanner, *Family, Friends, and Allies: Boulogne and Politics in Northern France and England* (Leiden, 2004), 137.

59. *Notitiae duae de praedicatione sancte crucis in Aquitania I, RHC Occ.* 5: 350–351.

crusaders (or God, acting through the crusaders) had done in the East. The earliest of these were the work of household clerics traveling in the entourage of the great princes, who took it on themselves—sometimes with the assistance of lay collaborators—to create written narratives of the expedition shortly after its conclusion.[60] A second generation of chroniclers, writing a few years after this first one, drew on both written records and the further testimony of participants they had known to produce more polished works for broader consumption. While the fruits of this second phase of writing, which rendered the crusade narrative theologically, politically, and stylistically palatable to the audiences of the West, and which included several vernacular Romance versions, were ultimately more popular than the early narratives of participants, the earlier works left an important legacy. Those who had taken part in the expedition brought back with them names and tales of men who, despite relatively low status and distance from the princely leaders of the expedition, took center stage for their deeds, bravery, and wisdom. These were men like Gouffier of Lastours, who held three modest lordships near Limoges, and who was essentially invisible on the expedition until he distinguished himself at the siege of Ma'arrat an-Nu'man in 1098. By the second decade of the twelfth century, Gouffier's name was mentioned by every Latin and vernacular crusade chronicle composed in Francophone Europe.[61] The earliest writers and copyists knew only a garbled orthography of his chief lordship (known in the Limousin as Turribus), calling him "Daturre" or "de Turre,"[62] and at most could identify him as a southerner.[63] Interest in him increased as time went on, and by the 1170s William of Tyre, writing in Palestine, would be able to say with confidence that he was "from the diocese

---

60. Peter Tudebode, *Historia de Hierosolymitano itinere,* ed. John H. Hill and Laurita L. Hill, Documents relatifs à l'histoire des croisades 12 (Paris, 1977); Raymond of Aguilers, *Le 'Liber' de Raymond d'Aguilers,* ed. John H. Hill and Laurita L. Hill and trans. Philippe Wolff, Documents relatifs à l'histoire des croisades 9 (Paris, 1969); Fulcher of Chartres, *Historia Hierosolymitana (1095–1127),* ed. Heinrich Hagenmeyer (Heidelberg, 1913); *Gesta Francorum et aliorum Hierosolymitanorum,* ed. Rosalind Hill (New York and London, 1962). See Jay Rubenstein, "What Is the *Gesta Francorum* and Who Was Peter Tudebode?" *Revue Mabillon* 16 (2005): 179–204. For the narratives more generally, see Jean Flori, *Chroniqueurs et propagandistes: Introduction critique aux sources de la Première Croisade* (Geneva, 2010).

61. For all of the references to Gouffier in the chronicles, see Riley-Smith, *The First Crusaders,* 209. The only chronicler not to note Gouffier was Fulcher of Chartres, who, having accompanied Baldwin of Boulogne to Edessa, was no longer aware of many events of the crusade.

62. According to the work's most recent editors, the correct version, Turribus, found in the Y manuscript of the chronicle of Robert the Monk, was added by a modern hand. See Robert the Monk, *Historia Hierosolimitana, RHC Occ.* 3: 847 n. 19.

63. "From the Towers" could indicate any one of hundreds of towns, castles, and lordships in western Europe. The chronicler who was his nearest neighbor, the Poitevin Peter Tudebode, knew very little about Gouffier but did include him in a list of seven southern crusaders. Peter Tudebode, *Historia,* 57.

of Limoges."[64] While Gouffier would remain best known in the lands south of the Loire, where, indeed, he may have been considered one of the great heroes of the expedition, the presence of his name in texts that circulated far beyond the Limousin was, as we will see in later chapters, a source of cultural power, the importance of which was not lost on his descendants.

Despite its immense significance for medieval society, and particularly for the military aristocracy, the value of reputation (*fama*) is not easy to quantify. It is therefore not easy to gauge the degree to which the reputation of a crusader like Gouffier of Lastours might actively enhance his own or his family's position. It could be argued that the fame earned by Gouffier or other crusading lords such as the lord of Amboise Hugh of Chaumont-sur-Loire or Arnold II of Ardres was the spark that drove the families of all three to regional power and prominence by the end of the twelfth century. It is certainly the case that the marriage alliances contracted by Gouffier's family after his return from the First Crusade show his family participating in a larger world of power than he, his brothers, or their ancestors had done before the crusade.[65]

Early, and quite dramatic, evidence of the transformation of an individual's status and reputation can be found at the royal court of the Capetian king of France Philip I. At the time of the First Crusade, the Capetians were attempting to consolidate their relatively weak claims of suzerainty over the castle lords in their immediate neighborhood.[66] Philip I did not take the cross himself, and his crusading brother, Count Hugh of Vermandois, had departed from the expedition before its conclusion. After the conquest of Jerusalem in 1099, many of the castle lords of the Île-de-France and the northwest returned. They came bearing the palm branches of pilgrims, telling stories of how frantically they had struggled and how, amid clear signs of divine approbation, they had prevailed.[67] Around Paris, as in Normandy and doubtless elsewhere, their advent was the cause of great celebration.

Now surrounded by men transformed by their fame and reputation as crusaders, the Capetian royal family took the extraordinary step of allying themselves in marriage with the new heroes, regardless of how suitable they would have appeared before the crusade.[68] The marriage between Constance, eldest daughter of King Philip I of France, and the Count of Champagne, Hugh of Troyes, having conveniently been annulled on Christmas Day 1104, at the synod

---

64. WT, 1: 354–355.

65. Gouffier's brother Guy, also a crusader, married the Norman noblewoman Mathilda of Perche, sister of his crusading colleague Count Rotrou III of Perche. Gouffier himself married Agnes, daughter of the Viscount of Aubusson. His descendants would marry into the families of the viscounts of Comborn and the lords of Born.

66. Jean Dunbabin, *France in the Making, 843–1180* (Oxford, 2000), 256–267, 295–299; Elizabeth M. Hallam and Judith Everard, *Capetian France, 987–1328,* 2nd ed. (Harlow, UK, 2001), 149–155.

67. Riley-Smith, *The First Crusaders,* 44–168.

68. For a broader consideration of this topic, see James Naus, "The French Royal Court and the Memory of the First Crusade," *Nottingham Medieval Studies* 55 (2011): 49–78.

of Soissons, Philip now granted the princess instead to a man whose weird name had never, before the crusade, been heard in the Francophone north.[69] Bohemond, born in southern Italy the illegitimate son of the Norman adventurer Robert Guiscard, was, by 1104, the lord of an independent principality in northern Syria and was renowned for his role at key points in the early history of the expedition. Not only did Philip marry his eldest daughter to this crusading hero, he promised the much younger Cecilia, still only an infant, to Bohemond's nephew Tancred, who had emerged from the expedition no less a formidable figure.[70] In contracting these alliances of marriage with Bohemond and Tancred, Philip may at one level have been attempting to create a link between his own dynasty and the new ruling houses of the crusader frontier. According to Suger of Saint-Denis, who wrote the biography of Bohemond's brother-in-law King Louis VI of France, it was the crusader's fame, and not his family's tenuous hold over their Syrian state, that constituted the Capetians' true coup.[71]

Another measure of the power of the First Crusade to shape hereditable dynastic notions of honor is the profundity of the shame and scorn earned by those who were perceived to have abandoned the crusade. Flight from the crusade, and the failure of those who had taken the vow to join it, must have been problems from the outset of the expedition. In the collective memory, however, the true cowards and traitors were those who left the army in its darkest hour, in spring 1098, when the crusaders were trapped between the citadel of Antioch and the advancing army of the *atabeg* of Mosul. Guibert of Nogent, the well-connected chronicler of the expedition who was writing within a decade of the crusade's conclusion, tellingly remarked when he reached this point in the narrative:

> I would name the towns from which they [those who fled from Antioch] came, were I not constrained by my close friendship with some members of their family to limit my remarks.[72]

By the time Guibert was writing, the negotiation of familial honor through the narrative of the crusade had already begun.

Dying and Living in the Shadow of Saint George

How the memory of the First Crusade could shape an individual's reputation and create new models of behavior can be observed most clearly in Flanders. At the time of the First Crusade, the counts of Flanders were already a

---

69. Orderic Vitalis, *Historia ecclesiastica,* ed. and trans. Marjorie Chibnall, 6: 70–71 and n. 5.
70. "Historia regum Francorum monasterii sancti Dionysii," *MGH SS* 9: 405; WT, 1: 495.
71. Suger, *Vie,* 48.
72. Guibert of Nogent, *Dei Gesta per Francos,* 217; trans. Levine, 99.

powerful dynasty, ruling a principality that lay between Capetian France and the empire and that was, in essence, a completely independent marcher kingdom. The Count of Flanders at the time of the crusade, Robert II, was the son of the fearsome Robert I the Frisian, who had violently wrested control of the county from his nephew Arnulf at the battle of Cassel in 1071. When clergy from Flanders reached Pope Urban II, complaining of Robert's tyranny, and especially his use of the *ius spolii* Urban was moved to warn him against capitalizing on his recent rise to power, which, although it had been permitted by God, was "against the will of [his] parents," dismissing with sarcastic skepticism his claim that such practices were customary.[73] Later, some time around 1089, Robert I went on pilgrimage to Jerusalem and on his return established diplomatic contact with the Byzantine emperor Alexios Komnenos. It was a measure of his power that he undertook to support Alexios in his wars against the Seljuk Turks of Anatolia, and contemporaries described him sending five hundred of his knights, a body of soldiers that would have rivaled the later Flemish contingent on the First Crusade.[74]

So formidable was the old Count Robert that it is hardly surprising to find that, in his youth, his son Robert II was identified in the *intitulatio* of his charters in terms that were, in a word, patronizing. In Bruges on 18 October 1089, most likely when his father was away on pilgrimage, Robert identified himself as "son of Robert, son of the glorious prince Baldwin."[75] Four years later, once again in Bruges, Robert invoked the pilgrimage as one of the distinguishing acts of his father's career, calling himself "Robert, son of Count Robert the Jerusalemite."[76] When, at Lille sometime before October 1096, Robert was on the point of departure with the First Crusade, he was still only *Robertus iunior.*[77]

Between October 1096 and 1100, when Robert returned to Flanders, his family, allies, and the people of Flanders would have heard only fragmentary reports of what was transpiring in the East. We know that Robert communicated at least once, early in the expedition, with his wife, Clemency, in whose care he left the county.[78] The missives of a more prolific correspondent, Anselm of Ribemont, whose lordship was in neighboring Oostrevant and Valenciennes, may give us some idea of the news that filtered back to the West.[79] From Anselm's letters, the

---

73. "Genealogia comitum Flandriae," *MGH SS* 9: 310.

74. Krijnie N. Ciggaar, "Flemish Counts and Emperors: Friends and Foreigners in Byzantium," in *The Latin Empire: Some Contributions,* ed. Krijnie N. Ciggaar and V. D. van Aalst (Hernen, Neth., 1990), 35–36.

75. *Actes des comtes de Flandre, 1071–1128,* ed. F. Vercautern, Recueil des actes des princes Belges (Brussels, 1938), 22, no. 8.

76. *Actes des comtes de Flandre,* 38, no. 23.

77. *Actes des comtes de Flandre,* 63, no. 20.

78. "Charta Clementiae Comitissae Flandriae," in *Die Kreuzzugsbriefe aus den Jahren 1088–1100,* ed. Heinrich Hagenmeyer (Innsbruck, 1901), 42–44.

79. "Epistula I, Anselmi de Ribodimonte ad Manassemarchi episcopum Remorum," in *Die Kreuzzugsbriefe,* 144–146; "Epistula II, Anselmi de Ribodimonte ad Manassemarchi episcopum Remorum," 156–160.

Flemish court, churches, and people would learn of the count's place in the center of the army at the desperate battle of Dorylaeum in Anatolia at the beginning of July 1097, his successful attack on the army of Damascus during the Foraging Battle fought near Antioch in December of that year, and his precise place in the divisions that marched out against Kerbogha of Mosul (Corbaran "prince of the knights of Persia," in Anselm's letter) on 28 June 1098.[80]

By the time Robert, along with his brother-in-law Robert of Normandy, who remained his comrade throughout the expedition, bathed himself in the waters of the Jordan, collected palm branches from the garden of Abraham in Jericho, and prepared to return home, therefore, the Count of Flanders was already famous.[81] Although no major narrative was written either by a participant on the expedition with allegiance directly to the count or by any subsequent author writing within Flanders, Robert's careful navigation of the political problems that otherwise divided the army's leadership left to him the role of quiet military hero in the early narrative accounts. Looking back on the events of the crusade from the second decade of the twelfth century, the chronicler Ralph of Caen shrewdly judged that Robert was "praised above all the other leaders of the army for his skill with the sword and spear. But he shrank from taking a leadership role. As a result, he gained much more renown than the other leaders as a soldier but much less as a leader since he avoided the worries of command."[82] Robert's own role in the propagation of his image as a crusading hero, however, was not a passive one.

Robert's return was dominated by his presentation of a major relic of Saint George, which he had acquired in the course of the expedition, to the church of Anchin. The narrative produced at Anchin reveals that upon his return the count regaled the monks with stories of his adventure and in particular of how he had safeguarded the relic through storms at sea, shipwreck, foreign islands, and encounters with barbarians. The narrative also reveals that, in the wake of its transmarine translation, the relic had been sent ahead of the count to greet him upon his arrival at the abbey; it was a triumph apparently staged, at least partly, by the count himself.[83]

Robert's surviving charters, enacted between his return in 1100 and his death in 1111, show that the count did not hesitate to refer to his part in the expedition. At Ypres within a year of his return, Robert referred to himself

---

80. "Epistula I, Anselmi de Ribodimonte," 145.

81. Fulcher of Charters, *Historia hierosolymitana*, 318–320, cited in Penelope Adair, "Flemish Comital Family and the Crusades," in *The Crusades: Other Experiences, Alternate Perspectives*, ed. Khalil I. Semaan (Binghamton, NY, 2003), 107.

82. Ralph of Caen, *The Gesta Tancredi of Ralph of Caen: A History of the Normans on the First Crusade*, trans. David S. Bachrach and Bernard S. Bachrach (Aldershot, UK, and Burlington, VT, 2005), 38.

83. *Narratio quomodo reliquiae martyris Georgii ad nos Aquicinenses pervenerunt*, *RHC Occ.* 5: 251; *Annales Aquicinctini*, *MGH SS* 16: 251–252.

as "son of Count Robert the Frisian" but added the phrase "having undertaken the course of the Jerusalem journey with desire that divine grace should show favor to me."[84] At Arras in 1106 he referred to his wife's rule over Flanders as the time when he had been away at Jerusalem "for the Lord's war" (*Dominica bella*).[85] The reputation that he had developed was noted by an annalist at Ghent, who wrote in his entry for the year 1100 "Count Robert [II] of Flanders, who had been greatly missed, returned from the way of the Lord (*via Domini*). He achieved for himself the great praise of secular knighthood."[86] He had also, of course, won great recognition as a dependable warrior for the faith, something that Urban II's successor, Paschal II, exploited in 1103, when he wrote to Robert asking him to make war against Liège, "striving to attain the celestial Jerusalem with the deeds of just knighthood (*justae militae*)."[87] For Robert, the renown won in the East had come with a title, which would grandly accompany his name in the genealogies of the great princely houses compiled by monastic authors and appear in dramatic dialogue in the *Chanson d'Antioche*. The man who departed for the East known as the "son of the Jerusalemite" had come back known as the "son of Saint George."[88]

For a lay lord, the effects of such fame can have been only salutary, but the implications for his family were potentially more complicated. Had the First Crusade, like the Norman conquest of England, consisted of a single, sustained campaign to conquer, subdue, and settle, its consequences for the families of those that had been involved would have been largely commemorative, depending on how the event would become situated within the larger conception of the family past. But the movement begun by Urban II at Clermont in November 1095 did not end with the taking of Jerusalem in July 1099, nor was it over when Robert II of Flanders left the Holy Land in 1100, by which time a massive second wave of crusaders drawn from Poitou to Bavaria had yet to begin their journey. As every anxious season passed in the nascent Latin Kingdom established by the crusaders in the East, it became clear that further help would be nearly continually required from the West. Major preaching campaigns, backed by papal indulgences for participants, were undertaken less than a decade

---

84. *Actes des comtes de Flandre*, 81. no. 26.

85. *Actes des comtes de Flandre*, 100, no. 34.

86. "Annales Blandinienses," in *Annales de Saint-Pierre de Gand et de Saint Amand,* ed. Philippe Grierson (Brussels, 1937), 33.

87. Sigebert of Gembloux, "Leodicensium epistolae adversus Paschalae papam," ed. Ernst Sackur, in *Libelli de lite* (Hanover, 1891–97), 2: 449–464, 451–452, cited in Housley, "Crusades against Christians: The Origins and Early Development, c. 1000–1216," in *The Crusades: Essential Readings,* ed. Thomas F. Madden (Malden, MA, and Oxford, 2005), 77.

88. See the verses at the end of "Gesta Francorum hierusalem expugnatium," *RHC Occ.* 3: 543; "Genealogiae Brevis Regum Francorum," *MGH SS* 13: 250; *Chanson d'Antioche,* 254, l. 7630; Ciggaar, "Flemish Counts," 38.

after the conquest of Jerusalem. Knights, castle lords, and regional princes can frequently be found taking the cross on their own or in small groups in this early period.[89] Thus, unlike the memory of an event such as the Norman conquest, the memory of the First Crusade constantly interacted with the potential for further action in imitation of its actors and in support of their achievements. What did it mean, in this context of continuous crusading possibility, as narratives of the expedition were being written and rewritten, to be the descendant of one of those who had participated in the original expedition of 1095–99? What did it mean to be the son of the "son of Saint George?"

Some sense of the burden of memory and the growing sense of responsibility that came with kinship to a renowned crusader like Robert II can be detected in a charter enacted by his son, Count Baldwin VII of Flanders, for the abbey of Saint-Bertin as he lay dying in the winter or spring of 1119. Baldwin VII succeeded his father as count in 1111 while still only a young man, only two years after the age of knighthood. The next seven years of his reign were marked by his involvement in the dangerous struggle between William Clito, son of Duke Robert II Curthose of Normandy, and his uncle, Robert's younger brother, Henry I of England, for control of Normandy. Early in his reign as count, Baldwin welcomed the young rebel William to his court in defiance of King Henry, and in September 1118 the Count of Flanders rode into battle at Bures-en-Bray in support of his Norman friend. Complications resulting from a wound received in the battle were slowly killing him when, sometime before the summer of 1119, he drew up the charter of privileges for Saint-Bertin. The dying count identified himself as "Baldwin, by the grace of God marquis of Flanders, son of Count Robert who conquered with his arms and with God's cooperation Jerusalem and the sepulcher of the Lord with the other princes of the Christian army."[90]

Baldwin was only about six years old when his father returned from the East. From that time onward, during his father's life and after his death in 1111, there were countless occasions on which his father's crusading feats might have been invoked. The young count was still surrounded by living veterans of the expedition, and at various sites, most prominently the abbeys of Anchin (where the relic of Saint George was enshrined) and Saint-Vaast, where Robert was buried, his memory was preserved in both texts and rituals.

89. Riley-Smith, *The First Crusaders,* 169–188; Mary Stroll, *Calixtus II, 1119–1124: A Pope Born to Rule* (Leiden, 2004), 441–446.

90. "Ego Balduinus, Dei gratia Flandrensium marchisus, filius Robreti comitis qui sepulcrum Domini et Jerusalem cum ceteris principibus militie christianorum, Deo cooperante, armis suis devicit." *Actes des comtes de Flandre,* 195, no. 87 (at Aire before 17 June 1119).

Following the same customs as his father, in the *intitulatio* clauses of charters of his early rule, Baldwin identified himself as the son of Robert II. On two occasions when he visited Saint-Vaast, accompanied by his mother, Robert's widow, Clemency, Baldwin would invoke the presence of his father's tomb.[91]

But it was only in 1119, on his deathbed, that the young count referred to his father as a crusader. Cut down in his twenty-eighth year, the young man despairingly considered how his own "brief and mortal life" would be remembered against the great achievements of his father. Hoping that the saints of the local churches would win some mercy for him from God, he humbly referred to his own attempts to defend "the places of the saints and those who serve them day and night against the incursions of wicked men."[92] He must have wished that like his cousin and successor Charles of Denmark, who was present with him when he enacted his deathbed charter, he had taken the cross in the year he received the belt of knighthood.[93] Had he lived a year longer, he might have joined the other princes of his rank, like Count Fulk V of Anjou, who were already preparing to undertake a new expedition just as, in the words of his charter, "the passing of my power to God is close at hand."

Baldwin's deathbed regrets were personal ones, colored not only by his own feelings about his father, which were probably complex, but also by his sense of his own limited accomplishments with regard to his lordship and his piety. But not long after his death, events were put in motion that seem to have encouraged a growing sense among the political community of Flanders that their counts should, as successors to Robert II, take the cross. In 1127, Flanders was rocked by the murder of Baldwin VII's successor, Charles, and the succession crisis that followed devolved into a bitter civil war. These events inspired the composition of two independent narratives. Walter, archdeacon of Thérouanne, and Galbert, notary of the comital church of Bruges, each wrote accounts of Charles's death and the civil war that followed between the rival successors William Clito of Normandy, the favored candidate of Louis VI of France, and Thierry of Alsace, a nephew of Robert II. In describing the matchless worth of the murdered man,

---

91. *Actes des comtes de Flandre,* 131, no. 52 (6 October 1111); 164, no. 70 (1115); Baldwin's relations with his mother were not without tension. In 1113, she (working through Lambert of Arras) forced Baldwin to respect her rights to her dowry and possessions granted to her by Robert II. In his letter to Baldwin regarding the matter, Lambert invoked the fifth commandment ("Honor your father and mother"). *PL* 162, col. 693.

92. "si, in hac brevi et mortali vita, loca sanctorum, eisque die noctusque servientes, contra pravorum hominum incursus, juxta potestatem a Deo michi concessam, tueri ac defendere non negligo, quatinus apud omnipotentis Dei misericordiam eosdem sanctos pro excessibus meis, tam in vita quam in morte, habeam intercessores." *Actes des comtes de Flandre,* 195, no. 87.

93. See Walter of Thérouanne, *Vita Karoli comitis Flandriae et vita domni Ioannis Morinensis episcopi; quibus subiungitur poemata de morte comitis Karoli conscripta et quaestio de eadem acta,* ed. Jeff Rider, *CCCM* 217 (Turnhout, 2006), 30–31.

both recalled the count's youthful career as a crusader as evidence of his character. For both authors the count's crusading was juxtaposed with his ancestry. Galbert wrote:

> His ancestors were among the best and most powerful rulers who from the beginning of the Holy Church had flourished in France, or Flanders, or Denmark, or under the Roman Empire. From their stock the pious count was born in our time and grew up from boyhood to perfect manhood, never departing from the noble habits of his royal ancestors or their natural integrity of life. And before he became count, after performing many notable and distinguished deeds, he took the road of holy pilgrimage to Jerusalem....Here he also fought strenuously against the enemies of the Christian faith.[94]

Walter was more explicit. His *Vita Karoli comitis Flandriae* closely associated Charles with his uncle Robert II, describing how, after his return from crusade, Charles proceeded directly to his uncle's court. One crusader and future count met the older crusading hero and was received with great honor.[95] This scene was followed by a biography of Robert II (a *vita* within a *vita*) called in the extant manuscripts of his work the "Remembrance of the *probitas* of Robert the Younger."[96] This narrative decision was in itself extremely telling: Walter did not need to present a model for Charles's noble behavior, and Robert was by no means the only one of Charles's ancestors who might have played this role. Earlier generations of the comital family boasted heroic figures, in particular Baldwin Iron Arm and his descendants, who provided the Flemish counts with their much-heralded link to Carolingian legitimacy. Walter's entire "Remembrance" was a meditation on Robert as a crusader, describing how he had been mindful of the decrees of the Council of Clermont, how he demanded justice for the destruction of the holy places "at the hands of the pagans," and how, in taking the sign of the cross of Christ on his shoulders, "he himself had been able to follow in his [Christ's] footsteps."[97] Having referred to Robert's fighting at

---

94. Galbert of Bruges, *De multro, traditione, et occisione gloriosi Karoli comitis Flandriarum,* ed. Jeff Rider, CCCM 131 (Turnhout, 1994), 15; trans. James Bruce Ross as *The Murder of Charles the Good, Count of Flanders* (New York, 1967), 112.

95. In fact, the earliest act that bears witness to Charles in Flanders is from 1118: *Actes des comtes de Flandre,* 197, no. 86.

96. Walter of Thérouanne, *Vita Karoli,* 30–31. The chapter headings are those of the MS, see 25.

97. "Hic est enim Robertus ille comes inclitus, superioris Roberti frisonis filius, qui audito illo sancti et omnium saecularum memoria recolendi Clarimontensis concilii decreto, de venerabili scilicet dominice passionis et resurrectionis loco a paganorum minibus eruendo et christiane fidei vendicando...et crucis eius in humeris baiulando insignia, ac ipsius etiam corporalia quo poterat sequendo vestigia, illud apostolice sedis mandatum tota fidei adimplere constantia cum aliis, quos eadem inspiraverat gratia, alacriter properavit." Walter of Thérouanne, *Vita Karoli,* 31.

Antioch and Jerusalem, and trumpeting the fact that his deeds were extensively reported in chronicles of the expedition, Walter concluded his biography by noting that "on account of the invincible constancy of his soul those Arabs and Turks called him 'the son of Saint George.'"[98] Walter noted little about the career of Robert's son Baldwin except his ill-advised war with the king of England, but he did add the detail that at Bures-en-Bray, Baldwin had been wounded in the forehead, "in that place where he was accustomed to have the sign of the life-giving cross marked upon him."[99]

Jonathan Phillips has argued that the succession crisis that followed Charles's assassination significantly disrupted recruitment for crusades, in particular for the Second Crusade, in Flanders. It is probably true that, as Phillips has suggested, numerous castellan families, who would otherwise demonstrate their enthusiasm both before and after the Second Crusade, could not take part in the crusade of 1147–51 because of the political uncertainty and real devastation caused by the tumult that followed Charles's murder and by the subsequent war between the two major claimants to the county.[100] Galbert's chronicle in particular, however, suggests that the civil war led to a careful evaluation of the meaning of the comital office and a bold restatement of the family's identity. Charles had been a model count in part because he was a worthy successor to the crusader Robert II. It followed that Charles's successor would have to fit the paradigm established by these two men. Galbert, who was by no means obviously partisan, indeed suggested that ultimately Thierry of Alsace was the better candidate, in his behavior "worthily imitating the character and customs and deeds of his predecessors."[101]

Thierry of Alsace was one of the most committed crusaders of the Middle Ages, taking the cross four times in his lifetime (in 1138, 1147, 1157, and 1165). It has often been suggested that his marriage to Sibylla of Anjou, daughter of Fulk V, Count of Anjou, and, after 1131, king of Jerusalem, was the primary motivation for these many journeys. Sibylla's family connections in the East and her own obvious dedication to the cause of the kingdom of Jerusalem, where she retired to a monastery from 1157 until her death in 1161, must have played a significant role. But it is nonetheless difficult to overlook the fact that in taking the cross Thierry was characterizing himself as part of the Flemish comital

---

98. "Ex qua laudem eius hoc solum hic satis est commemorari, quod ob invincibilem animi constantiam ab ipsis quoque Arabibus ac Turcis Georgii filius scribitur appellatus." Walter of Thérouanne, *Vita Karoli*, 31.

99. "et ex illisione modico in eo quo salutiferum crucis signum imprimi consueverat loco tumore oborto." Walter of Thérouanne, *Vita Karoli*, 33.

100. Jonathan Phillips, "The Murder of Charles the Good and the Second Crusade: Household, Nobility, and Traditions of Crusading in Medieval Flanders," *Medieval Prosopography* 19 (1998): 55–76.

101. Galbert of Bruges, *The Murder of Charles the Good*, 284.

lineage of honor and *probitas*. His transition to power had not been easy, and the early years of his rule required the careful reconstruction of relations with his towns and the castle lords, who were called the "peers" of Flanders.[102] If the chronicles of Galbert and Walter, very different historians, writing separately and with different audiences and aims in mind, are any measure, Thierry may have felt compelled to take the cross in order to truly become the Count of Flanders.

Obligations

In 1137, one year before Thierry set out on his first journey to the Holy Land, a new Capetian ruler, Louis VII, was crowned king of France. As Jay Rubenstein has shown, it was probably at Bourges, on Christmas of that year, that the new king was presented with a manuscript containing narratives of the First Crusade and the early history of the Latin Kingdom of Jerusalem.[103] The knight who made the gift for him, William Grassegals, prefaced the collection with a letter in which he admonished the new king to take the cross. Grassegals, a knight from Le Puy-en-Velay, claimed to have been a participant in the First Crusade, and he vividly imagined Christ as the "paterfamilias" and the crusaders as his "co-heirs," who, in taking the cross, were therefore following his example. Creating a link between this crusading past and the present reign of Louis, Grassegals enjoined the king to

> look in this book with the eye of reason as if in a mirror at the images of your ancestors—Hugh the Great, Robert Count of Flanders, and others—and you might follow their footsteps on the path of virtue (*vestigia passibus virtutum sequaris*). If only you might learn how necessary it is not to appear to wish to fall short of them in physical exertion and in the use of the temporal sword.... I beseech you by humble prayer that the book not be removed from your presence or from your heirs', so that you might always have these signposts to lead you to an ideal of similar goodness.[104]

Here we find the same sense of the crusaders as models of behavior and virtue that we have seen was current in Flanders. It is clear from his dedicatory letter that Grassegals hoped the king would choose to take the cross as a crusader,

---

102. Tanner, *Family, Friends, and Allies,* 187.

103. Jay Rubenstein, "Putting History to Use: Three Crusade Chronicles in Context," *Viator* 35 (2004): 151–152.

104. "Monitum Willelmi Grassegals militis," *RHC Occ.* 3: 317–318; trans. Rubenstein, "Putting History to Use," 134.

but his reference to the "temporal sword" of justice and government could also mean that the king should remember and mimic the virtues and efforts of the crusaders (such as himself) in the governance of his kingdom.

Eight years later, a further appeal to consider the deeds of the crusaders would arrive at Louis's court in the form of Eugenius III's letter *Quantum Praedecessores*. By that time, the shocking news had arrived that the county of Edessa, the first principality established by the conquests of the crusaders in the East, had fallen into the hands of the *atabeg* of Mosul, Imad ad-Din Zengi, in December 1144. This message, however, enjoined its readers not just to contemplate crusading ancestors as models of virtue, but to consider the dishonor that would result if their great labors were in vain. The only appropriate response, especially for the many lay lords who already viewed crusaders as models of virtue, was literally to follow in their footsteps as crusaders.

The sense of obligation to uphold ancestral efforts was, as we have seen, not a new one. It was invoked in criticisms like those leveled at Fulk le Réchin, who had not fulfilled his responsibilities as the defender of his patrimony, and in the anxieties of men like Stephen of Blois and the viscounts of Thouars, who wanted to be seen as committed to the support of institutions dear to their parents or ancestors. After the fall of Edessa in 1144, the Latin Kingdom of Jerusalem, like the church of Saint Nicholas of La Chaize so beloved of Viscount Aimery IV of Thouars, was in danger of "deterioration." Just as Aimery's sons Geoffrey and Herbert II felt obligated to support Saint Nicholas, it was necessary for the children and more distant descendants of crusaders to support what their ancestors had established. As the condition of the Latin Kingdom continued to deteriorate over the course of the later twelfth century, and as major expeditions like the Second Crusade of 1147–49 failed to successfully shore up its defenses, the fear that the accomplishments of early crusaders would be wiped away grew stronger. Hence, over the course of the twelfth century, ancestral involvement in the crusades became increasingly seen not only as an exemplary model of virtue to be upheld, but as a real obligation to be borne, somewhat like the crusader's cross itself. This may, at least in part, explain the substitution, noted by Purkis, of *strenuitas patruum* for *imitatio Christi* in appeals to potential crusaders by the papacy.

After 1145, Eugenius and every succeeding pope until the election of Innocent III in 1198 continued to appeal to a general sense of obligation among the descendants of crusaders not to let those achievements that their ancestors had bled and died for fade from memory and responsibility. At the same time, however, other, much more specific notions of obligation were current in western noble society. The first was the revolutionary notion of the hereditability of the crusader's votive obligation, which, although it only gradually became codified within canon law in the later thirteenth and fourteenth centuries, was already apparently in practice around the year 1200. If, as it seems, this was an idea that had originated among the nobility themselves, it may have been an outgrowth of a second notion, observable at the time of the First Crusade, that the merits of penance won by crusading activity benefited not only the individual crusaders themselves, but also their deceased kin.

Sometime between 1195 and 1196 King Béla III of Hungary heard of the crusading plans of Emperor Henry VI of Germany to launch a follow-up campaign to the inconclusive Third Crusade, which had seen the death of the emperor, Henry's father, in Anatolia in June 1190. Neither ruler would see the Holy Land. But while Henry was at least able to accompany his army as far as Messina on Sicily before succumbing to malaria in September 1197, Béla died in April 1196, without having even set out on his pilgrimage.[105] Chroniclers asserted that Béla left the kingdom to his first son, Emeric, and to his second, Andrew, a certain number of castles, large estates, and the great fortune that he had amassed in order to go on crusade. Andrew, who was still a minor, spent much of the money, using it in part to feud with his brother.[106] In late February 1198, only days after his election to the Holy See, Pope Innocent III wrote angrily to Andrew insisting that he take the cross for the next general passage, suggesting that the prince would be excommunicated and his inheritance forfeit "if the burden, having been enjoined upon you by your father and willingly taken up by you, you decline in any way when the proper time comes."[107] Although Innocent explicitly referred to the money that Béla had raised and Andrew had wasted on his military campaigns, and began his letter with the reminder that vows were matters of will and not compulsion, later decretalists saw in his letter a more general injunction that heirs of those who died without having fulfilled their crusading vows were obligated to carry them out.[108] By the fourteenth century, the letters testimonial of departing crusaders like Viscount Amaury of Lautrec explicitly absolved their children of obligations arising from their own crusading vows.[109]

---

105. James Ross Sweeney, "Hungary in the Crusades," *International History Review* 3:4 (1981): 474–475; for the background to papal relations with Hungary, see Sweeney, "*Summa potestas post Deum*—Papal *Dilectio* and Hungarian *Devotio* in the Region of Innocent III," in *The Man of Many Devices Who Wandered Full Many Ways: Festschrift in Honor of János M. Bak*, ed. Baldázs Nagy and Marcell Sebók (Budapest, 1999), 492–498.

106. *Chronica regia coloniensis*, ed. George Waitz, *MGH SS rer. Germ.* 18: 168.

107. "si onus tibi a patre iniunctum et a te sponte susceptum occasione qualibet detrectaveris." *Corpus iuris canonici*, ed. Aemilius Ludwig Richter and Emil Friedberg (Leipzig, 1879–81), 2: 590–591, 3: title xxxiv chapter 6.

108. James Brundage, *Medieval Canon Law and the Crusader* (Madison, WI, 1969), 78, 129–130; Maureen Purcell, *Papal Crusading Policy* (Leiden, 1975), 105.

109. See *Documents on the Later Crusades*, ed. and trans. Norman Housley (New York, 1996), 70–71.

Innocent's letter reveals that in the last years of the twelfth century a practice was already in place in which crusaders who died without having undertaken their journeys would transmit their votive obligations and the funding required to perform them to others. Although they are rare, examples survive that suggest that by this time the practice was widespread in continental Europe. In a dramatic scene in 1183, for instance, Henry, the Young King of England, had, on his deathbed, handed William Marshal his cloak with the sign of the cross sewn onto it, urging him to undertake the journey to Jerusalem in his stead and "pay his debts to God."[110] Henry had no heirs, so the choice of his companion, the most renowned knight of his household, may be explained by the fact that William was the individual most likely to complete the journey. The proper disposal of wealth accumulated for the purpose of crusading was certainly a concern at the time of the Fourth Crusade when, as Geoffrey of Villehardouin bitterly remembered, leading figures of the expedition like Thibaud III of Champagne and Geoffrey of Perche died before the expedition began. Both men, according to Villehardouin, made careful provisions for the use of their crusading purses, Geoffrey passing his to his brother Stephen, and Thibaud, whose heir had not yet been born, distributing his among his vassals and friends, making them swear on relics to use the money as funds for crusading only.[111]

In all of the above cases, as in the situation addressed by Innocent III in 1198, the use of funding and resources was a key part of the hereditability of crusading obligations. It was the wasting of these funds that stoked the wrath of contemporaries like Innocent, who threatened the squanderers with excommunication; Villehardouin said they "were rebuked as a result."[112] But it is likely that the sense that crusading responsibility could or should be passed along to heirs was related to another belief, that the spiritual benefits obtained by crusaders profited not only the crusaders themselves, but also their dead relatives. Evidence of such convictions can be found from the time of the First Crusade, when Herbert II of Thouars, ever careful to respect his father's memory, conferred with the bishop of Poitiers to clarify that his suffering as a crusader would benefit his father.[113]

A colorful story found in the De naturis rerum of Alexander Neckam, compiled in the last years of the twelfth century, tells of a noble youth, "the nobility of whose soul transcended the nobility of his birth," who was accustomed to

110. *History of William Marshal,* ed. A. J. Holden with English translation by S. Gregory and historical notes by David Crouch (London, 2003), 1: ll. 6891–6989.
111. Geoffrey of Villehardouin, *La conquête de Constantinople,* ed. Edmond Faral, Les classiques de l'histoire de France au Moyen Âge 17–18 (Paris, 1938–39), 1: 36–39, 46–49.
112. "et mult en furent blasmé." Geoffrey of Villehardouin, *La conquête de Constantinople,* 1: 36–38.
113. Jonathan Riley-Smith, "The Crusades, 1095–1198," in *The New Cambridge Medieval History,* vol. 4, *c. 1024–c. 1198,* pt. 1, ed. David Luscombe and Jonathan Riley-Smith (Cambridge, 2004), 539.

frequently visit his father's tomb.[114] He often wept, prayed, and gave alms in aid of the soul of his father, but when, shortly before hosting a number of his friends for a banquet, he opened the tomb, he found the ominous sign of a disgusting toad sitting on his father's throat "shamelessly pressing its feet into the neck of the dead man." It was a sure sign that his father had been a glutton. Horrified, the young nobleman swore to give up his patrimony, go to Jerusalem, and serve the poor. While the story does not explicitly invoke crusading, its apparent message was that only the most radical demonstrations of piety, such as the journey to Jerusalem, could elicit divine clemency for the awful sin of gluttony, which, the banquet setting suggests, had the potential to carry from father to son. Central to the son's remedy for the sins he and his father had committed in their lives of noble avarice was the journey to Jerusalem. In 1198, the same year that Innocent wrote to Andrew II of Hungary, a direct analogue to this fictional exemplum was played out. In that year, Frederick I of Austria, who had joined the German king Henry VI's ill-fated expedition, died. His bones were brought back to the family foundation of Heiligenkreuz to lie beside his father, Leopold VI. Leopold himself had been a crusader, a major figure on the Third Crusade, but was subsequently excommunicated by Alexander III for his imprisonment of his fellow crusader Richard I of England.[115] Commenting on the death of Leopold's son in 1198, the chronicler Otto of Saint-Blasien remarked that the young man had taken the cross "for the salvation of his father's soul."[116] This practice of crusading for the sake of parents would continue, and in his testament of 1268, William de Beauchamp, Earl of Warwick, understood that his son Walter had taken the cross and would travel to the Holy Land "on my behalf and of Isabel, his mother."[117]

When Innocent wrote to Andrew of Hungary, therefore, he was probably drawing not only on standard conventions for the transmission of money and supplies by those who were unable to fulfill their crusading vows, but on deeper convictions about the spiritual benefits of taking the cross for a crusader's dead relatives. Interestingly, in Hungary, the idea that the responsibility of taking the cross could be passed down from one generation to another

---

114. Alexander Neckam, *De naturis rerum libri duo: With the Poem of the Same Author "De laudibus divinae sapientiae,"* ed. Thomas Wright (London, 1863), 334–335.

115. John Gillingham, "The Kidnapped King: Richard I in Germany, 1192–4," *Bulletin of the German Historical Institute, London* 30 (2008): 5–34.

116. Otto of St. Blasien, *Chronica,* ed. Adolf Hofmeister, *MGH SS rer. Germ.* 47: 67; trans. Graham Loud in *The Crusade of Frederick Barbarossa: The History of the Expedition of the Emperor Frederick and Related Texts* (Farnham, UK, and Burlington, VT, 2010), 189.

117. Nicholas Harris Nicolas, *Testamenta vetusta: Being Illustrations from Wills of Manners, Customs, etc. as Well as the Descents and Possessions of Many Distinguished Families from the Reign of Henry II to the Accession of Queen Elizabeth* (London, 1826), 1: 50–51; and *MA* 1: 227.

may have been what led Béla III to take the cross in the first place. As James Ross Sweeney has shown, a few years before Béla's decision to join Henry VI on crusade, his ancestor Laszló I (d. 1095) was canonized, and traditions circulating in Hungary at the time reimagined the king, who actually died some months before the Council of Clermont, as the acknowledged leader of the First Crusade who died before he could set out.[118] The emergence of this tradition of the thwarted crusading ancestor in the context of Béla's own cross-taking suggests that he was seen as fulfilling a long-frustrated dynastic crusading obligation. This, of course, may only have made Andrew's hesitation seem so much worse, since he was ignoring his responsibility to uphold a twice-deferred ancestral desire to participate in a crusade.

Seemingly worlds away from the rough eleventh-century *habitus* of the Loire with which we began this chapter, the late-twelfth-century man of letters Guy of Bazoches was, for all his time among the dialecticians of Paris and Montpellier and the clerical office he held as the chanter of Châlons-sur-Marne, a nobleman who thought about ancestry and behavior in much the same way that Count Fulk IV of Anjou had done a century earlier.[119] Like Fulk, Guy knew his own genealogy, which he sketched out in a letter to his nephew, demonstrating their distinguished lineage, which ran all the way back to Charlemagne.[120] Among his ancestors on his mother's side he named "Baldwin of Jerusalem," by whom he meant Count Baldwin II of Hainaut, who participated in the First Crusade.

Like his ancestor Baldwin, Guy was a crusader, taking part in the Third Crusade before returning to Champagne. Was Guy's knowledge of his crusading ancestor Baldwin important to him when he decided to take the cross? This is certainly possible, for in the *Apologia* that he wrote against his detractors before he set off on crusade, he explained that there were three main forces that bound "my soul to my indestructible faith. They are the law of nature, the law of nurture, and the fear of God." By the law of nature, Guy explained, he meant his natural ability to tell right from wrong; the "law of nurture" (*jus nutriture*), however, derived from the examples provided by his noble ancestors.

118. Sweeney, "Hungary in the Crusades," 473; Gábor Klaniczay, *Holy Rulers and Blessed Princesses* (Cambridge, 2002), 187, accepts the same context for the origin of the crusading material in the legend, although dating the extant written version after 1204. For the later legend, see Laszlo Vespremy, "*Dux et Praeceptor Hierosolymitanorum,* König Ladislaus (Lasxlo) von Ungarn als Imaginarer Kreuzritter," in Nagy and Sebók, *The Man of Many Devices,* 470–477.

119. For Guy's biography, see John F. Benton, "Consciousness of Self and Perceptions of Individuality," in *Renaissance and Renewal in the Twelfth Century,* ed. Robert Benson, Giles Constable, and Carol Lanham (Cambridge, MA, 1982), 263–295.

120. *Liber epistularum Guidonis de Basochis,* ed. H. Adolfsson, Acta Universitatis Stockholmiensis, Studia Latina Stockholmiensis 18 (Stockholm, 1969), 141–142.

In describing this second "law" he pointed not only to the virtues of his own ancestors, but also to how their virtue stemmed from the nobility that they had themselves inherited:

> Since, however, it is not unknown (saving private discretion) I would assert that my parents and ancestors for the most part always lived lives of venerable honour, having been endowed with virtue and with the legacy of great reputation, not less than with the worth of their blood and the prominence of nobility that comes with worldly authority. Doubtless, if I should seek to hold such a path (*tenuere vestigia*) I would want to imitate examples of such distinction in my small measure.[121]

Defending himself against his detractors, Guy claimed, as Fulk had done in 1096, that he strove to follow the examples of his noble ancestors, one of whom he knew to have been a crusader. Guy's words are suggestive, and we might be tempted to conclude that he, like biographers of Charles the Good in Flanders or the knight William Grassegals, saw crusading as one of the central models of virtuous conduct. Guy was not a lay lord, with *honores* to defend and enlarge. He was not a knight and does not mention *probitas* among the virtues he felt he needed to carry forward from his noble ancestors. His nobility was nevertheless inherited, and if it was to be preserved, Guy knew that he needed to follow in their footsteps. Few ancestral paths can have been more clearly demarcated than the one that led to the East, and it was this path that he ultimately chose to follow.

Perhaps Guy, like many of his contemporaries, felt a sense of obligation to uphold what his ancestor Baldwin helped to establish, or felt he needed to take the cross to benefit the souls of his deceased parents and relatives. We can never know the full range of ideas and images that were prompted by a reference to an ancestor who was *Iherosolimitanus*. For some families, however, we have a greater degree of access to that world of associations. Where memorials were established, in text, material, and ritual, we are permitted a further degree of inquiry into the meaning of the crusades for nobles who, like Guy, thought about their family past. It is to those memorials that we will now turn.

---

121. "non est ambiguum quin oporteat eam sequi, cum ad utilia vel honesta deducit. Et quia luce non eget, salvo tamen privilegio temperantie, dixerim quod parentes et antecessores mei pro majori parte non minus semper extiterunt vite venerabilis honorati, virtutibus et dotibus honestatis ornati, quam genere spectabiles et eminentie potentia secularis illustres. Nimirum, si talia talium vestigia teuere studeam et exempla pro modulo meo cupiam imitari." Wilhelm Wattenbach, "Die Apologie des Guido von Bazoches," *Sitzungsberichte der Königlich Preussischen Akademie der Wissenschaften zu Berlin* (1893): 404.

❧ CHAPTER 2

Relations

It was probably with the encouragement of the English king Henry II that, in 1160, a self-styled "reading cleric" (*clerc lisant*) of the town of Caen in Normandy who called himself Master Wace started work on a rough draft of his second great vernacular historical poem, the *Roman de Rou*.[1] As a *romancier,* a writer who could transform Latin histories into vernacular verse, Wace was already renowned for his *Roman de Brut*—a retelling of Geoffrey of Monmouth's popular Latin chronicle of the kings of Britain—which he completed in 1155, the first year of Henry's reign. Five years later, with the clear expectation of royal patronage, Wace undertook a different kind of project, a narrative of the lineage of Henry's maternal ancestors the dukes of Normandy beginning with the Viking Rollo (or *Rou*). Wace began his first draft, a draft that he subsequently abandoned, with a ten-line pronouncement about how the ancestral past should be invoked. Rendered in English prose, these ten lines read:

> To remember the deeds, words, and ways of our ancestors, the felonies of the wicked and the prowess of the worthy, one should read books, accounts of deeds, and histories aloud at feasts.[2]

---

1. Françoise Le Saux, *A Companion to Wace* (Woodbridge, UK, 2005), 1–10 (for Wace himself) and 153–154 (for the order of composition). Peter Damian-Grint, *New Historians of the Twelfth-Century Renaissance: Inventing Vernacular Authority* (Woodbridge, UK, 1999), 54. And see below, 231–232.

2. "Pur remembrer des ancesurs / les feiz e les diz e les murs, / les felunies des feluns / e les barnages des baruns, / deit l'um les livres e les gestes / e les estoires lire a festes." Wace, *Roman de Rou,*

More so than others that he wrote in his early draft, these lines of verse in particular appear to have been pleasing to Wace, because he used them again when he wrote the opening lines to the third part of his work more than a decade later in 1173.[3] There he paired them with another quatrain that succinctly summed up his own role in the commemorative process. They are rendered here again in prose:

> If writings were not composed and then read and recounted by clerics, many things which transpired in times gone by would be forgotten.[4]

It was in this third book that Wace told the history of the Norman dynasty in the eleventh and twelfth centuries. While more famous to modern historians for its account of the conquest of England by William I in 1066, this book would have been no less important to the royal court in the 1170s because it recounted the stories of the glorious pilgrimage of Duke Robert I the Magnificent to Jerusalem in 1035 and of the great achievements of Robert's grandson, Henry's great-uncle Robert II Curthose on the First Crusade. These stories linked the king's ancestors to the sacred geography of the East at a time when "the business of the Holy Land" (*negocium terrae sanctae*) was becoming a major preoccupation at courts throughout the West.

Wace's ten-line opening presents us with an apparently perspicuous description of the mechanism through which narratives of ancestry and the crusading past would be related. A literate class of observers and recorders (*clers*), the guardians and transmitters of the past, referred to a combination of written and perhaps also oral sources (*livres, gestes,* and *estoires*) in order to prepare their narrative retellings or even translations (*retraits* from his *retraire*) for performance in celebratory public environments (*festes*). These performances helped to distinguish, for the edification of the current generation, the wicked ancestors (*feluns*) from the worthy (*baruns*). Following Wace, then, this would be one of the principal ways that twelfth-century men and women were reminded of the deeds of their crusading ancestors; had we access to them, these performances would provide a key to understanding the place of the crusading past within the collective memory of the medieval noble family and household.

Such claims about performances, source materials, and mnemonic personnel, however, must be treated with the greatest caution. On the one hand, as

---

ed. Anthony J. Holden and trans. Glynn S. Burgess, with notes by Burgess and Elisabeth M. C. van Houts (St. Helier, Jersey, 2002), 340–341 (my translation).

3. Wace, *Roman de Rou,* 108–109. Le Saux, *Companion to Wace,* 154, points out that both the third part of the work and the first were written in the same octosyllabic rhyming couplets, which may also have encouraged him to mine the first part when beginning the third.

4. "Si escripture ne fust feite / e puis par clers litte e retraite, / mult fussent choses ublïees / ki de viez tens sunt trespassees." Wace, *Roman de Rou,* 108 (my translation).

students of the *Roman de Rou* have long noted, Wace himself indeed selected from among a large number of different types of sources, including Latin narratives, regional chronicles, and biographies, reliable personal testimony, and his own knowledge, and it is easy to see how these might have been invoked in the terse terminology of *gestes* and *estoires*.[5] But much of what Wace had to say was also conventional. The terms he chose to denote the modes of historical retelling may have had as much to do with the sweetness of their sound as the weight of their meaning (the rhyming of *gestes* with *festes* appearing particularly convenient). That history was valuable because it was a source of moral edification was a common trope of historical narratives that could be traced back to Cicero.[6] Finally, Wace's exaltation of his own class of "reading clerics" as the chief custodians of the past referred to the same maxim that rang out in the preambles of thousands of charters documenting legal and financial transactions produced in nearly every corner of Latin Europe since the late tenth century: that the inscription of deeds in written texts is a required safeguard against the frailty of human memory and the looming threat of oblivion.

The reading cleric's desire to demarcate the contexts of ancestral storytelling and to stress his own role in the process is particularly problematic. As we saw in the previous chapter, interactions between lay households and religious communities often provided opportunities for the invocation of the ancestral past, but they were clearly not the only contexts in which family storytelling could occur. Such relations might also take place on the tournament field, at court, or in battle, when noblemen were asked to explain the pattern and origins of their heraldry.[7] In teaching a daughter her prayers, an aristocratic woman might explain her grandmother's piety. Like all free people, noble men and women referred to their ancestry when considering legal candidates for marriage, in order to defend hereditary rights and possessions, and to appropriately honor the community of their dead relatives, who, it was hoped, would in return remember the living in intercessory prayer to God and the saints. Knowledge about ancestry, therefore, did not live only or

---

5. The possible meaning of these terms has been discussed at length by Damian-Grint, *New Historians,* 209–264, esp. 263–264. See also Wace, *Roman de Rou,* "Introduction," xxx–xxxiv. Matthew Bennett, "Poetry as History? The *Roman de Rou* of Wace as a Source for the Norman Conquest," in *Anglo-Norman Studies V: Proceedings of the Battle Conference,* ed. R. Allen Brown (Woodbridge, UK, 1983), 23, 38.

6. Bernard Guenée, *Histoire et culture historique dans l'Occident médiévale* (Paris, 1980), 27–29. For its place in vernacular historiography of the twelfth century, see Damian-Grint, *New Historians,* 92.

7. Maurice Keen, "Chaucer's Knight, the English Aristocracy, and the Crusade," in *English Court Culture in the Later Middle Ages,* ed. V. J. Scattergood and J. W. Sherborne (London, 1983), 45–62, esp. 49–55, presents three cases presented to the English Court of Chivalry in which crusading is invoked as evidence of claims to particular armorial bearings.

even primarily in books, but at the interstices of parent and child, family and household, and between individuals and their friends, followers, and enemies.

Although, inevitably, the most informal and intimate manifestations of this wide-ranging discourse of social memory are lost to us, a significant body of material does survive that may grant us access, however indirectly, to images of the crusading past as it was evoked in family memory. Wace's lifetime corresponded with a great proliferation of written narratives dedicated to the ancestry of noble families. He had in fact relied on such works himself. Among the *livres* that he consulted in order to write the *Roman de Rou,* for instance, were versions of a sustained Latin dynastic history of the Norman ducal family.[8] This *Gesta Normannorum ducum,* as it came to be known, was essentially a series of continuations and revisions of a textual tradition that originated in the first decades of the eleventh century with the *De moribus et actis primorum Normanniae ducum* of the canon Dudo of St. Quentin. Until the middle of the eleventh century, Dudo's work was the only text of its kind dedicated to a princely dynasty, but by the time that Wace completed his own contribution to this program in the 1170s, at least eleven other families who were the holders of princely and seigneurial honors had had dynastic historical narratives dedicated to them, with some families the subject of multiple narratives. These family narratives were composed throughout western Europe, as far east as Poland and Austria and as far west as Catalonia and across all of continental Europe north of the Alps, including a small number that were written in Anglo-Norman Britain (see appendix 1). By the second quarter of the thirteenth century, at least four more families were the subjects of such historical enterprises. The popularity and utility of such texts, particularly those written about the families of more powerful territorial princes, are reflected in their survival in numerous manuscripts, which bear evidence of continuous revisions and continuations—over the course of more than a century.

This remarkable efflorescence of a new historiographical form was only part of a larger trend that saw a wide proliferation of writings about ancestry, including genealogies, epitaphs, and a range of other types of anecdotes and notices. These writings manifested themselves in a variety of ways. Genealogies and accounts of the origin of particular families appeared in letters, chronicles, and hagiographical tracts and as prefaces to cartularies. Writings commemorating a particular individual, such as epitaphs of verse and prose and brief *commemoratio* narratives, were copied into chronicles and inscribed on or otherwise attached to tomb monuments. *Planctus* songs

---

8. Damian-Grint, *New Historians,* 215, 223, argues that Wace referred to the *Gesta Normannorum ducum* as both *geste* and *estoire.*

lamenting the death of heroic ancestors and patrons were sung by monks and troubadours alike. The urge to narrate the familial past was strong, and whether they were writing hagiography or regional or ecclesiastical history, monastic and clerical authors like Guy of Bazoches,[9] Milo Crispin of Bec,[10] Geoffrey of Vigeois,[11] Lambert of Wattrelos,[12] and the anonymous chronicler of the abbey of Liessies[13] could not resist informing their readers of their own ancestry, connecting themselves through their kin to the events and times that they described.

References to crusaders and reflections on the crusading experience appear across all genres of genealogical and ancestral writing. All but one of the writers in the preceding list (Lambert of Wattrelos), for example, indicated that they were related to a crusader. In the longer family narratives like the one written by Wace, the presence of crusading ancestors is especially notable. Ancestors who are described as participating in holy wars against non-Christian opponents are mentioned in every surviving dynastic narrative composed after the First Crusade. They also appear together with other information relating to particular families that was embedded in larger regional and institutional histories (see appendix 2). While some texts make only brief references to crusading, in others we find extensive accounts of a crusader's experiences, and references to the implications of the crusades for the family. It is to these examples that we must turn to find the place of the crusades within family memory.

Multiple layers of transmission, translation, and the creative (but in this context also destructive) forces of literary style and authorial intervention lie between an oral tradition as it may have existed or been performed and the primarily Latin narratives that survive today. Can we use them, then, to access the collective memory of medieval families? Were all of the texts written in isolated abbeys, locked away in monastic libraries to be read only by a single community with only minimal contact with the laity, we might conclude, with Gerd Althoff, that they could not represent "a noble family's own

---

9. Guy of Bazoches, *Liber epistularum Guidonis de Basochis,* ed. Herbert Adolfsson (Stockholm, 1969), 141–142. The genealogical part of the letter is translated by Elisabeth van Houts, *Memory and Gender in Medieval Europe, 900–1200* (Basingstoke, UK, 1992), app. 6.

10. "Miraculum quod Beata Maria subvenit Guillelmo Crispino senior—ubi de nobili Crispinorum genere agitur," *PL* 150, col. 742. Milo writes proudly of a relative who died shortly after taking the cross.

11. Geoffrey of Vigeois, "Geoffroi de Breuil, prieur de Vigeois: *Chronique* (première partie)," ed. Pierre Botineau (Thesis, École des Chartes, 1968), xviii–xxiv, 134–135, 151–152. Geoffrey cites on two occasions his relationship with the three crusading brothers, Gouffier, Guy, and Gerald of Lastours.

12. *Annales Cameracenses, MGH SS* 16: 511–512.

13. *Chronicon Laetiense, MGH SS* 14: 492. The Liessies chronicler noted that his father was a crusader who had visited Constantinople.

knowledge of its origins and forefathers" but only the perspectives of the institutions where they were composed.[14] But, as we will see, the contexts for the creation and preservation of dynastic narratives were extremely diverse. What we learn from the textual and manuscript evidence about how, where, and by whom dynastic narratives were composed, and what their authors say about their reasons for writing, all suggest that these were works that would accurately reflect the collective memory of the family.

Although each surviving text was written to evoke the shared sense of ancestry in particular social and political contexts, most can be seen performing the same range of basic functions. Family histories were commemorative, helping to properly locate and commemorate ancestors for the purposes of prayer; normative, constructing models of lordship and aristocratic behavior for younger members of the family; and political, providing crucial cultural capital and what Georges Duby called the "legacy of honor" to bolster the family's cultural status and nobility. Stories about crusading ancestors played an important role in all three functions. In describing the family's contribution to well-known events from a local perspective, they also helped to shape dynastic identities that were in each case distinctive while at the same time broadly familiar and mutually intelligible throughout the community of European nobility. So important was the crusading ancestor in the construction of identity, in fact, that by the early thirteenth century the stories of crusaders remembered by their descendants were, in some cases, overwhelmed by the popularity of chivalric romance storytelling. Crusading ancestors, whose deeds and experiences had been preserved for generations in the memory of their family and household, were, in some cases, subsumed into larger archetypes of the romance hero.

Narratives and Social Memory

The comments of the authors and redactors of dynastic histories and the manuscript traditions in which their works have survived all bear witness to the diversity of individuals and environments that could contribute to the inscription of the family past. While a small minority of works were created only by a single individual or institution, the majority passed freely between monastic *scriptoria,* castral chapels, and household clergy, where they were updated, revised, or rewritten to suit new circumstances. Seeing these works as part of an ongoing process of written remembrance helps us to comprehend

---

14. Gerd Althoff, *Family, Friends, and Followers: Political and Social Bonds in Early Medieval Europe* (Cambridge, 2004), 54–59, quote at 54; and see also his "Anlässe zur schriftlichen Fixierung adligen Selbstverständnisses," *Zeitschrift für die Geschichte des Oberrheins* 134 (1986): 34–46.

both their popularity and their utility within the landscape of institutions and individuals that surrounded noble families and through which the noble household was constantly moving.

Writers, Texts, and Remembrance

The commemorative responsibilities of medieval monks, their literate culture, and the close ties of patronage (and often also of kinship) that bound them to the aristocracy made them natural centers for the collection of information relating to their noble founders and benefactors. Everywhere, but particularly in the German empire and in England, it was customary for this information, often presented as a genealogy of a founder, to be incorporated into the institution's central diplomatic and narrative productions.[15] The dynastic histories of territorial princely families, for instance those written at Alaón in Catalonia, Melk in Austria, Walden in Essex, and Vézelay in Burgundy, are known only or primarily in copies associated with the institutions where they were authored.

A similarly small number of histories, really only two, were written entirely by men who were not monks and who had, at some point in their lives, occupied positions closer to the household. Lambert of Ardres, who wrote the histories of the counts of Guines and lords of Ardres, was the priest of the Ardres family's castral church.[16] Gislebert of Mons, who narrated the deeds of the counts of Hainaut, had served in several important household capacities. Gislebert became the count's "second notary" in 1180, his "first notary" in 1184, and then served as the chancellor of Hainaut from 1178 to 1195, becoming the chancellor of Namur in 1192. Following the death of his patron and lord Count Baldwin V, Gislebert seems to have moved on to administer the family's most important ecclesiastical communities, acting as the *praepositus* to the chapters of Saint-Germain of Mons, Saint-Waudru of Mons, and Saint-Aubin of Namur.[17]

---

15. See, for example, the foundation narratives of the abbeys of Ford and Wigmore in *MA* 5: 348–355, 377–382; and Lacock in *Annals and Antiquities of Lacck Abbey: In the County of Wiltshire,* ed. W. L. Bowles and John Gough Nichols (London, 1835), app. I. For German examples, see Jörg Kastner, *Historiae fundationum monasterium: Fruhforben monasticher Institutionsgeschichtschreibung im Mittelalter,* Munchener Beitrage zur Mediävistik und Renaissance-Forschung 18 (Munich, 1974); Timothy Reuter, "Past, Present, and No Future in the *Regnum Teutonicum,*" in *The Perception of the Past in Twelfth-Century Europe,* ed. Paul Magdalino (London, 1992), 28–29.

16. For Lambert, see Leah Shopkow, introduction to *History of the Counts of Guines and Lords of Ardres* (Philadelphia, 2001), 2–3.

17. GM, vi–xxii. See also Ferdinand Vercauteren, "Note sur Gislebert de Mons, rédacteur de chartes," *Mitteilungen des Instituts für Österreichiche Geschichtsforschung* 62 (1954): 238–253.

By far the greatest number of surviving dynastic histories, however, are characterized by active circulation between the scriptoria of a region's chief monasteries and the chapels and collegiate communities associated with the ruling families themselves. The list of authors contributing to the Angevin dynastic historical tradition (*Chronica de gestis consulum Andegavorum*), for instance, which was provided in the 1170s by the text's last redactor, the monk John of Marmoutier, includes an abbot of his own house, a former chaplain of the comital family, and two other men, one of whom was probably a canon at a collegiate foundation located within a major regional stronghold.[18] The text's movement and development didn't stop there, as the only surviving medieval copy of John's chronicle, written in the late twelfth century, was kept by a chapter of canons within the Angevin comital palace in Angers.[19] Other medieval copies of the text, now lost, were kept in monastic settings and in secular institutions associated with the comital family.[20]

In Normandy, the dynastic historical tradition followed a similarly complex trajectory. It originated, as we have seen, with Dudo of Saint-Quentin, a canon in the service of the ducal household, but later in the eleventh and twelfth centuries it was most famously expanded and continued by three monks, William of Jumièges, Orderic Vitalis, and Robert of Torigni. Other anonymous versions also survive, at least one of which is thought to have been the work of a chaplain of the ducal household.[21] The situation in Flanders is similar to what we find in Normandy. Beginning with a genealogy dictated to a priest in the mid-tenth century, the tradition of genealogical writing was adopted next at Saint-Bertin, the abbey where the counts of Flanders were traditionally interred, before being copied and continued at the Benedictine abbey of Marchiennes and adapted in verse and in prose by a canon of the cathedral St. Omer. A dynastic history proper emerged around 1164, probably at Saint-Bertin, only to be copied, adapted, and continued at monastic houses around the region, most prominently the Cistercian house of Clairmarais. The same tradition was still very much alive, being continued and translated by new authors until the early fifteenth century.[22]

The easy circulation of dynastic histories among different types of communities, and their obvious appeal among secular household clergy, administrators,

---

18. *CCA*, 164. For commentary on the possible identity of the authors named by John, see *CCA*, xxvii-xxxvi.

19. For the manuscript, see Adrien Planchenault, *Cartulaire de Saint Laud d'Angers* (Angers, 1903), xv-xxi; and below, 244.

20. *CCA*, lxxiv (for a copy probably deriving from the abbey of Toussaint in Angers) and lxxvi (for a copy probably deriving from Notre-Dame de Loches).

21. Elisabeth van Houts, *Gesta Normannorum ducum: Een studie over de handschriften, de tekst, het geschiedwerk en het genre* (Groningen, 1982), 94–106.

22. *Genealogiae comitum Flandriae*, ed. Joseph Heller, *MGH* 9: 313–317.

and monks alike, also explain why it has been so difficult to assign a provenance to some texts that survive without an author or an institution with
which to anchor them. It is tempting to assign the authorship of the history
of the lords of Amboise, for instance, to a canon of the college of Saint-
Florentin located within the seigneurial castle of Amboise, but the writer also
betrays strong sympathies with the abbey of Pontlevoy, perhaps suggesting
that the text was redacted at some point by a writer from that abbey.[23] The
Historia Welforum of the Welf dukes and the so-called *Historia Reinhardsbrunnensis* of the landgraves of Thuringia bear only faint traces of loyalty to any
particular monastic house and may therefore originally have been the work
of household clergy. Both, however, would ultimately become central parts
of the historical traditions of the abbeys of Weingarten and Reinhardsbrunn,
respectively.[24]

If, in some cases, the ambiguity surrounding the authorship of dynastic
texts is the result of multiple layers of authorship in a single text, it also reveals
how similar the secular and monastic authors may have been. When it came
to the families that they wrote about, these men had similar responsibilities.
Both Lambert and Gislebert, for instance, had in common with the monk
Orderic Vitalis and the monks of Ripoll in Catalonia that they were responsible for the composition of epitaphs or other commemorative verses either
for inscription or oral performance.[25] Individual authors could also reflect the
perspectives of more than one community. Wace, for instance, the *romancier*
of the Norman ducal family whom we met at the beginning of this chapter,
was more of a courtier cleric, and not a member of the ducal household,
but he based part of his narrative on the relations of his own ancestors, one
of whom, he proudly recalled, was the chamberlain of Duke Robert I the

23. *CCA*, lvii–lviii.

24. For the copy of the *Historia Welforum* made at Weingarten (Wiesbaden, Hessische Landes-
bibliothek, Fulda MS D 11), see the description in the edition of Ludwig Weiland in *Monumenta
Welforum antiqua, MGH SS rer. Germ* 43: 8–9; and Otto Gerhard Oexle, "Welfische und staufische
Hausüberlieferung in der Handschrift Fulda D 11 aus Weingarten," in *Von der Klosterbibliothek zur
Landebibliothek: Beiträge zum zweihundertjährigen Bestehen der Hessischen Landesbibliothek Fulda,* ed.
Artur Brall (Stuttgart, 1978), 203–231. The so-called *Historia Reinhardsbrunnensis* was incorporated
into the major chronicle of the abbey of Reinhardsbrunn, which was completed between 1340
and 1349. See Stefan Tebruck, *Die Reinhardsbrunner Geschichtsschreibung im Hochmittelalter: Klösterliche
Traditionsbildung zwischen Fürstenhof, Kirche und Reich* (Frankfurt-am-Main, 2001); and *Chronica Reinhardsbrunnensis,* ed. Oswald Holder-Egger, *MGH SS* 30.1: 491.

25. For Orderic, see OV 3: 168–169, 256–258. Orderic may have learned to write epitaphs from
his teacher John of Rheims. See OV 2: xvi–xvii. For John's epitaph of Peter of Maule: OV 3: 178–179.
For Gislebert, see Ferdinand Vercauteren, "Gislebert de Mons, auteur des épitaphes des comtes de
Hainaut Baudouin IV et Baudouin V," *Bulletin de la Commission Royale d'Histoire* 125 (1959): 379–403.
LA, 600; trans. Shopkow, 118. For Ripoll, see 259–262 and 272–274.

Magnificent.[26] Wace's work is in many ways the greatest monument to social memory, combining the knowledge of centuries-old monastic chronicle traditions, memories passed down to him from his ancestors by his parents, and his own experiences and inquiries.

Like Wace, the writers, redactors, and continuators of dynastic histories often mentioned the sources, oral and written, from which they forged their narratives. Both the author of the *Historia Welforum* and the monks of Melk, who wrote of the dukes of Austria, referred to written histories and charter documents,[27] and the author of the Amboise history had access to documents pertaining to the family that were kept in the castle.[28] One of the early Angevin chroniclers, perhaps the chaplain Thomas of Loches, named official storytellers, or *relatores,* from whom he had received information about the lineage of the counts of Anjou.[29] As we will see below, the presence of such individuals in the household is attested in the work of Lambert of Ardres.

But the use of documents and the reports of official storytellers does not tell the whole story of the transmission of ideas about the past within families. As Elisabeth van Houts and others have argued, the enumeration and evaluation of particular sources by—exclusively, in this case—male historians almost certainly elides the presence of women as authorities about ancestry.[30] In some cases, the nature of the information being related and the social situation of the family make it a virtual certainty that women were the bearers of family traditions.[31] Aristocratic women frequently outlived the men they married, and this was especially true of families with patterns of active male participation in crusades.[32] Just as women could assume sole control over lordships in the absence of their husbands on crusade, in captivity, or, after their death, during the minority of their children, so the aristocratic woman and her household would then be primarily responsible for the transmission of the memories of these events to her children. Even when the conjugal unit was not disrupted, however, women could act as informants for the writers

---

26. Wace, *Roman de Rou,* ll. 3223–3225. Although this connection is based on a textual emendation first suggested by Gaston Paris, Wace's relationship to the chamberlain Turstin is now widely accepted. See Wace, *Roman de Rou,* xvii and n. 22.

27. *Historia Welforum Weingartenensis,* ed. Erich König, Schwäbische chroniken der Stauferzeit (Thorbecke, 1978), 1; *Breve chronicon Austriae Mellicense,* ed. Wilhelm Wattenbach, *MGH SS* 24: 70.

28. *CCA,* 87.

29. *CCA,* 27.

30. Van Houts, *Memory and Gender,* passim. Renée Nip, "Gendered Memories from Flanders," in *Medieval Memories: Men, Women, and the Past,* ed. Elisabeth M. C. van Houts (Harlow, UK, 2001), 124–127.

31. Van Houts, *Memory and Gender,* 71–92.

32. Theodore Evergates, *The Aristocracy in the County of Champagne, 1100–1300* (Philadelphia, 2007), 141–152. Van Houts, *Memory and Gender,* 69, makes the point that nuns tended to live longer than laywomen because of the dangers of childbirth.

of dynastic history, especially with reference to the ancestry and concomitant lands, wealth, and honor that they brought into a marriage.[33] They also acted as transmitters of knowledge about events and experiences that particularly affected their female ancestors.

Family Storytelling: Contexts and Functions

Wace, as we have seen, called for written accounts of the deeds of past generations to be "read aloud at feasts," perhaps suggesting that his *Roman de Rou* was a written analogue of what might normally have been a live adaptation of Latin chronicles into the vernacular. Further evidence explicitly linking written accounts of the dynastic past to such festive performance situations, however, is scant. Texts of the later twelfth and early thirteenth centuries do claim that the noble lords Henry the Lion of Saxony and Baldwin II of Guines asked to have texts read out loud or translated for them, but the same sources make it clear that these cases were exceptional.[34] We need not return, though, to some notion of a *séance épique*, so beloved of an earlier generation of philologists, to believe that works of history, whether in the vernacular or in Latin, existed as utterances as well as strokes of the pen.[35] The writers of dynastic historical narratives themselves clearly believed that what they were writing would be communicated, in some form, to the noble families whose ancestries they described.

In some cases, there was a clear expectation that the work would be read aloud. The anonymous author of the *Gesta principum Polonorum,* for instance, aspired to have his Latin dynastic history recited (*recitare*) "in schools or in palaces" (*in scolis vel in palatiis*) and "in schools and capitols" (*in scolis et capitoliis*).[36] John of Marmoutier, Lambert of Ardres, and the anonymous monks of Melk who

---

33. This point was originally made by Georges Duby, "The Structure of Kinship and Nobility: Northern France in the Eleventh and Twelfth Centuries," in *The Chivalrous Society,* trans. Cynthia Postan (Berkeley, 1977), 139–142. See also Van Houts, *Memory and Gender,* 78–84.

34. For Henry the Lion, see *Annales Stederbugenses auctore Gerhardo praeposito, MGH SS* 16: 230, quoted with further discussion in Klaus Nass, "Geschichtschreibung am Hofe Heinrichs des Löwen,"in *Die Welfen und ihr Braunschweiger Hof im hohen Mittelalter,* ed. Bernd Schneidmüller, 33rd Wolfenbütteler Symposion (Wiesbaden, 1995), 124–161. LA, 598–599; trans. Shopkow, 114–115.

35. For an exploration (and explosion) of the traditional understandings of the performative context of medieval epic, see Andrew Taylor, "The Challenge of Editing Sung Objects: Editing Digby 23," in *The Book Unbound: Editing and Reading Medieval Manuscripts and Texts* (Toronto, 2004), 78–104; Taylor, *Textual Situations: Three Medieval Manuscripts and Their Readers* (Philadelphia, 2002), 26–70.

36. *Gesta principum Polonorum,* 212–213, 214–215. In a general sense, this expectation should not surprise us, consonant as it was with what Mary Carruthers, *The Book of Memory: A Study of Memory in Medieval Culture,* 2nd ed. (Cambridge, 2008), 231, has called the "hermeneutical dialogue" of medieval literacy, whereby if reading did not occur aloud, "reading has not truly taken place, for the memory has not been engaged."

wrote a brief narrative of the Babenberg dukes of Austria addressed their works directly to the men whose lineage they chronicled.[37] But it was also expected that the matters mentioned in the narrative texts would be presented to the laity through other, less direct paths of transmission. The same author of the *Gesta principum Polonorum* who asked for his chronicle to be read aloud, for instance, dedicated his work not to the duke himself, but to bishops and ducal chaplains. This suggests that his work would be transmitted indirectly to Poland's noble rulers, passing first from the writer to the educated clerical courtiers, and then from the courtiers to their lay patrons. A similar expectation can be found in the history of the Amboise seigneurial family (*Gesta Ambaziensium dominorum*). The author of this text, who may have been a canon of the castral college of Saint-Florentin in Amboise, addressed his work to a "friend," explaining that the terrible political crisis that had recently befallen the family was his "very great reason for writing" (*scribendi...ista permaxima causa*).[38] The writer told his friend that the recent ills that had befallen Lord Sulpicius II of Amboise, who had been imprisoned by Count Thibaud IV of Blois, were the result of the bad advice the lord had received. The author suggested that if he had instead listened to wiser counsel, the result would have been better for him:

> and no wonder, because from the good tree are gathered good and delicious fruits, and truly upon the bad tree one finds neither excellent, nor agreeable fruit.[39]

That he should preface his narrative with a lengthy discussion about the importance of good counsel suggests that the Amboise historian understood his own project as having relevance to contemporary events. He may have hoped that his mysterious "friend," perhaps a literate member of the Amboise household, would pass along his narrative to the heirs of the imprisoned lord. Then they could listen to the examples of good and bad ancestry provided in the narrative before making further decisions that might imperil the lordship. Indeed, much of the family history deals with the relations between the lords of Amboise and their neighbors in Anjou and Blois, and so the ancestral narrative did provide crucial context for the political debacle that confronted the family. Central to this story, as we will see below, was the First Crusade.

---

37. *CCA*, 171; and see below, chapter 6; *Breve chronicon Austriae Mellicensis, MGH SS* 24: 70; LA, 598–599; trans. Shopkow, 113–115.

38. *CCA*, 74.

39. "nec mirum, quia bone arboris est bonos et suaves fructus affere; in male vero arboris fructibus nulla bonitas, nulla prorsus suavitas reperitur." *CCA*, 74.

If the anonymous historian of the family indeed understood his task as one of moral instruction, separating the good ancestral "trees" from which sprung virtuous deeds from those that yielded the more dangerous fruit, like that recently tasted by Sulpicius II, he was not alone. The Norman historian Wace, as we have seen, also wanted to help distinguish *baruns* from *feluns,* and similar sentiments can be found in many other histories. The anonymous author of the earliest version of the *Chronica de gestis consulum Andegavorum,* who wrote between 1106 and 1109, closed his work assuring his intended audience, which must have included the young Fulk V of Anjou, about the purpose of his undertaking:[40]

> To the honour, therefore, of our lords the counts (*consulem*) of Anjou, I wrote of their deeds what I understood of them, and what I believed ought to be intended for the instruction of their successors, praying that our work should be useful to the current generation for finding enjoyment in the imitation of their best ancestors.[41]

The point was made yet more poetically by the anonymous author of the history of the dukes of Poland, *Gesta principum Polonorum,* who declared in the epilogue to his first book that "already for one day we have our route surveyed, / With that behind us will our future plans be laid."[42]

Lambert of Ardres, historian of the Guines and Ardres families, was more subtle. Instead of admonishing Count Arnold II of Guines, to whom he addressed his history, to be watchful of good and bad examples, he artfully allowed the narrative itself to do this work. Lambert described how earlier generations of Arnold's family (including Siegfried, the legendary founder of the Guines dynasty, and Eustace, another distant ancestor who ruled in the first half of the eleventh century) profited greatly from listening to those who knew about the history of the family. Siegfried first claimed the *honor* of Guines and built the family's ancestral castle because of what he had "heard in his ears and received here and there from fame's shining pen and the truest testimony of genealogical writing."[43] Eustace, on the other hand, was constantly reminded of the evils that his father had perpetrated on his subjects, who Lambert imagined warning the young count that he should be mindful

---

40. On the earliest version of the *Chronica,* see Nicholas Paul, "*Origo consulum:* Murder, Memory, and the Legendary Origins of the Counts of Anjou" (in preparation).

41. "Hec ego dum in voluminibus abditis invenissem scripta, non sum perpessus infructuoso silentio tegi. Ad honorem igitur dominorum nostrorum Andegavorum consulum sicut gesta eorum agnovi conscripse et ad edificationem successorum credidi destinanda, obsecrans ut labor noster in optimorum antecessorum imitatione a modernis valeat fructum invenire." *CCA,* 67.

42. *Gesta principum Polonorum,* trans. Paul W. Knoll and Frank Schaer with a preface by Thomas N. Bisson (Budapest, 2003), 114–115.

43. LA, 566; trans. Shopkow, 59.

of his lordship and his people, lest "like your father, at some time / accursed ills should follow close behind."[44] Three further chapters of Lambert's history are devoted to a story told to Eustace by a wise old man to encourage him to avoid the mistakes his father had made.[45]

Alluding to the importance of written texts and spoken and sung admonishments to remember the good and bad ways of ancestors in the earlier part of his narrative, Lambert of Ardres presented in a later chapter the most vivid description of the performance of the ancestral past found in any dynastic history. Having narrated the history of the ancestors of the counts of Guines from their origins in the early tenth-century adventurer Siegfried the Dane through the career of the young heir to the county of Guines and the lordship of Ardres, Arnold II of Guines, Lambert described how the young man, returning to his lands from tournaments held in Flanders, often came to visit Colvida and Ardres, the major strongholds of his maternal ancestors, the lords of Ardres.[46] As the head of the religious community residing at the castle of Ardres, Lambert would have been an eyewitness to these visits, which brought the young man home from the tournament circuit, a world Lambert clearly thought frivolous, and into the heart of his ancestral home. If there was ever an opportunity for the performance of the family past, for the recollection of virtuous behavior and the reinforcement of a sense of familial identity, it was during these visits, when the older members of Arnold's household would entertain him with "adventures, fables, and histories of the ancients." But whether it was Robert of Coutances, telling stories of the Roman, Carolingian, and Arthurian past, Philip of Montgardin, who spoke of the crusaders and the exotic world of the East, or Walter of Le Clud, who knew the accounts of Tristan and Isolde, Merlin, and the Ardres family, all were concerned to help educate their youthful lord, mixing, "serious matters of morality to their narrative."[47] Walter, the narrator of family history, is said by Lambert to have been a member of the lord's household and also, as an illegitimate son of Arnold's maternal great-uncle, a member of the Ardres family. Having established the context in which a variety of narratives, including family history, would be performed, Lambert went on to describe how, around 1190, during a span of two days in which the lord and his household were detained at Ardres, they were entertained with the story of the Amboise family as told by Walter of Le Clud.[48]

---

44. LA, 571; trans. Shopkow, 67.

45. LA, 572–573. The story centers on a character named "Rainier of Boulogne," who is explicitly said to represent Eustace's father.

46. LA, 607–608; trans. Shopkow, 129–131.

47. LA, 607.

48. The storytelling is placed chronologically following the elopement of Rainaud of Dammartin and Ida of Boulogne, which happened between 1190 and 1192. See Henri Malo, *Un grand feudataire: Renaud de Dammartin et la coalition de Bouvines* (Paris, 1898), 313.

The storytelling at the castle of Ardres is central to Lambert's narrative because it serves as the fulcrum of the complex mechanism of Lambert's two-part history of the Guines-Ardres family. It was Lambert's conceit that fifty of the fifty-nine chapters of his history that followed this point are direct translations into Latin prose of the tale told by Walter of Le Clud in the vernacular. While this claim can be dismissed out of hand—Lambert himself seems to wink at the reader when he has Walter complain of the difficulties of translating, from memory, a document in Latin into the vernacular that Lambert appears to have copied directly into his text—its implications for the relationship between dynastic histories and oral performances should not.[49] Lambert's conceit was, fundamentally, that written Latin narratives like the one he had composed about the counts of Guines, and spoken oral histories like the ones performed at Ardres, were not very different.

There is no question that secular spaces provided the contexts for boasting and the advertisement of personal, hereditary honor. Just as the knights of Arthur's court gathered first in the hall, and then at the threshold of the chamber where their lord slept, sitting at the feet of their lady, to boast of their experiences in Chrétien de Troyes's romance *Yvain*,[50] it would be in the "ladies' chamber" that John II of Nesle assured John of Joinville that the two would tell the story of their bravery at the battle of Mansourah in Egypt in 1250.[51] As Evelyn Birge Vitz has shown, the more intimate spaces of private chambers and gardens were populated, in romance literature, by images of women reading, singing, and storytelling, and in these spaces they likely played an important role in the transmission of dynastic memory that was separate from, but perhaps also complementary to, that of the old men who told stories in the hall.[52] Ladies were listening, but they were also responding.

Ancestral Memories and Visits with the Monks

As we have seen, dynastic histories, whether they were originally written by monks or secular clergy, were often redacted, continued, or copied at monastic scriptoria. Monks or regular canons were responsible for the creation of the dynastic histories of the counts of Flanders, Anjou, and Nevers, the earls of Huntingdon and Northampton, the lords of Matheflon, the dukes of Austria,

---

49. LA, 617–618, trans. Shopkow, 148–149.

50. Chrétien de Troyes, *Yvain,* ed. Wendelin Foerster (Manchester, UK, 1984), ll. 42–85.

51. John of Joinville, *Vie de Saint Louis,* ed. and trans. Jacques Monfrin (Paris, 1995), 120 § 242; trans. Caroline Smith, *Chronicles of the Crusades* (New York and London, 2008), 206. For discussion of this passage in the context of the discussions surrounding crusading, see Smith, *Crusading in the Age of Joinville* (Aldershot, UK, 2006), 8–10; for a further example of performance in the hall, see 34–35.

52. Evelyn Birge Vitz, *Orality and Performance in Early French Romance* (Woodbridge, UK, 1999), 207–215. See also the example of the *Conte de Floire et Blancheflor* cited in Van Houts, *Memory and Gender,* 76–77.

the landgraves of Thuringia, the margraves of Meissen, and the counts of Barcelona, and for the writing of chronicles that included family histories of the nobility of Picardy, the Limousin, Normandy, and Champagne. In Normandy, Anjou, Flanders, and Bavaria, dynastic histories circulated among the major monastic houses of the region, where they were redacted, updated, continued, and combined with other traditions of historical writing.

If, as Lambert of Ardres claimed, family storytelling occurred in the shifting contexts of itinerant lordship, then it could have taken place at monasteries in very much the same way that it did in castle halls and palace chambers. Those very halls, like the one in the castle of Ardres, were closely related, both architecturally and functionally, to the reception halls and visitors quarters of monasteries, where the ceaselessly itinerant retinues of noble lords frequently stayed.[53] At different times during their stay at a monastery, noble guests would be read to from the books of the community's library. As Julie Kerr has shown, until at least the early thirteenth century, English Benedictine communities customarily read "words of consolation" to their guests when they were lead into the parlor.[54]

Public reading is in fact as well attested in the context of monastic hospitality as it is in purely secular environments. A notice recorded in the cartulary of the Benedictine abbey of Saint-Maur in the 1130s or 1140s described a gift of mills at Gennes made a century earlier to the monks by Count Fulk Nerra of Anjou (d. 1040).[55] The text recounts how Fulk, having departed on pilgrimage to Jerusalem in the company of his wife and son, the bishop of Angers, and many of his knights, received hospitality at Saint-Maur following the first day of their journey. "The monks," the text reads "honorably received him as the defender and master of all the homeland (*defensorem ac rectorem totius patriae*)." That night, during dinner, the assembled company listened as the *Life* of Saint Maur was read aloud. On account of the stories they had heard, the bishop and the count agreed to finance the reconstruction of the conventual buildings, which had fallen into ruin. The twelfth-century monks of Saint-Maur who consulted the cartulary learned how a dignified reception, hospitality, and storytelling could be used to gain favor and patronage. The text in this case was a life of the saint, but if the monks of Saint-Maur had also possessed a history of their guests' families, which was entertaining and complimentary while managing to point out the better

---

53. Michael W. Thompson, *The Medieval Hall: The Basis of Secular Domestic Life, 600–1600 AD* (Aldershot, UK, and Brookfield, VT, 1995), 50–74.

54. Julie Kerr, *Monastic Hospitality: The Benedictines in England, c. 1070–1250* (Woodbridge, UK, 2007), 102–104.

55. "Cartularia Sancti-Mauri," in *Archives d'Anjou: Recueil de documents et mémoires inédits sur cette province*, ed. P. Marchegay (Angers, 1843), 1.356, no. 8.

elements of ancestral behavior, would this not also have been a useful tool in courting their patronage?

The Norman monk Robert of Torigni's dual career as historian and administrator leaves open to question whether he intended his works to be used to flatter and court visitors of the ducal family to the houses of Bec, where he was a monk (1128–49) and then prior (1149–54), and Mont-Saint-Michel, where he was abbot (1154–86). While at Bec he composed a new redaction of the Norman dynastic history *Gesta Normannorum ducum*. In his magnum opus, the *Chronicon*, which he wrote at Mont-Saint-Michel, Robert bragged about his ability to attract the attention and favor of guests to the monastery. Robert related how in 1158 he had elicited rich gifts for his monastery from King Henry II of England, Duke of Normandy, while Henry was staying at the abbey.[56] He did so despite the king's reluctance, he says, by constant entreaties during dinner, finally getting what he wanted when the meal was done and the two had retired to his chamber. What form did these entreaties take? Once again, it is not clear what kind of rhetoric was required under these circumstances, but as a writer of dynastic narrative, he would certainly have had many possible stories with which to convince the reluctant king. Robert's interest in having written histories to read to guests is evidenced by his sponsorship of William of Saint-Pair's *Roman du Mont Saint Michel*, which was explicitly intended for performance before pilgrims and guests.[57]

Monasteries that acted as the burial places for one or more of a family's noble ancestors might make particularly effective settings for the performance of dynastic historical narratives. This is true even for texts that were not created at monasteries. The *Historia Welforum*, for instance, which is not thought to have been originally written in a monastery, was copied at the abbey of Weingarten, where several members of the Welf family were buried, together with that house's necrology. It has also been proposed that the earlier parts of the *Roman de Rou* of Wace were read to Henry II when the king was staying at the abbey of Fécamp in 1162 to celebrate the translation of the bodies of his ancestors Richard I and Richard II to a new location behind the main altar.[58] Dynastic narratives that were either written or copied at institutions with commemorative responsibilities served as useful instruments in

---

56. Robert of Torigni, *Chronique*, ed. Leopold Delisle (Rouen, 1872), 1:313. See Elisabeth M. C. van Houts, "Le roi et son historien: Henri II Plantagenêt et Robert de Torigni, abbé de Mont-Saint-Michel," *Cahiers de civilisation médiévale* 37 (1994): 115–118.

57. See Leah Shopkow, *History and Community: Norman Historical Writing in the Eleventh and Twelfth Centuries* (Washington, DC, 1997), 268.

58. Elisabeth van Houts, "Wace as Historian," in *Family Trees and the Roots of Politics: The Prosopography of Britain and France from the Tenth to the Twelfth Century*, ed. K. S. B. Keats-Rohan (Woodbridge, UK, 1997), 114–115. Wace, *Roman de Rou*, 152–153, l. 2242; For the king's visit, see Robert of Torigni, *Chronique*, 1: 336–337 and 5.

commemoration and to illustrate to visiting guests the continuing relationship between the abbey and the family. Saint-Bertin in Flanders, Walden
in Essex, Marmoutier in the continental Angevin domains, Weingarten in
Bavaria, and Ripoll in Catalonia all served (or claimed to serve) as necropolises for several generations of princely families. They were also all important centers for the writing and transmission of dynastic historical narratives,
and the manuscript traditions of these texts reveal how, as in the case of the
Chronica de gestis consulum Andegavorum at Marmoutier and the *Gesta comitum
Barcinonensium* at Ripoll, existing traditions could be updated to emphasize
the importance of the family's tradition of burial at the abbey.[59] Even where,
for instance at Marmoutier, claims of ancestral burial were (to the modern
eye) obviously fictive, such "imaginative" memories must have fallen at least
within the horizon of expectations of the family for them to have been
useful.[60] As was true with everything recounted in dynastic histories, these
claims must at least have been recognizable to the laity to warrant the copying, revision, and dissemination of the texts.

The use of texts in formal receptions, reading to guests, and the need for
narrative traditions to cultivate relations with the laity all potentially enrich
our understanding of monastic houses as sites for the production and preservation of dynastic historical narratives. But the ancestral discourse, with
its many possible uses, was not limited only to dedicated dynastic histories.
Other chronicles, which recorded either the history of the abbey or the
region, might also reflect the memories shared by the monastic community
and the family.

Monks well knew how to write history for their own purposes and to
their own advantage, and some of their historical projects were intended, at
least in part, for internal consumption. All of their compositions, however,
were products of a world that was closely associated with the lay nobility.
As Marjorie Chibnall pointed out, although parts of the *Historia ecclesiastica*
of Orderic Vitalis are thought to have been read aloud in the refectory of
his monastery of Saint-Evroult or on feast days, this chronicle nonetheless
reveals a great preoccupation with the world and secular affairs.[61] Orderic
had witnessed the instruction of youths by a chaplain in a noble household,
heard the songs of troubadours, and was concerned, in his history, to record
the deeds and ancestry of lay patrons of his abbey and its priories, such as the

---

59. *CCA,* 31 n. a (Enjuger), 34 n. a (Fulk Rufus), 37 n. a (Fulk the Good), 44 n. c (Geoffrey
Greymantle); for the interlinear and marginal annotations giving the date and place of interment of
the counts of Barcelona in BNF, Lat. 5132, see *GCB,* xiv–xvii.

60. For the fictitious additions to the Angevin *Chronica,* see Sharon Farmer, *Communities of Saint
Martin: Legend and Ritual in Medieval Tours* (Ithaca, NY, 1991), 89.

61. Marjorie Chibnall, "Feudal Society in Orderic Vitalis," *Anglo-Norman Studies* 1 (1978): 35–36.

knight Ansold of Maule. Even works like the chronicle of the abbey of Vézelay, with its scathing attack on the comital family of Nevers could, John O.
Ward has argued, play a role in mediation between the monks and the family.[62] The Vézelay text is particularly interesting because it is part of a larger
traditionsbuch (now MS Auxerre 227), which also contains annals, charters,
and a brief dynastic history of the counts of Nevers: a veritable communications array for the celebration, chastisement, and persuasion of the abbey's
noble antagonists. Occupying a central place in the Vézelay-Nevers discourse
of family traditions was the story of Renaud, younger son of Count William
II of Nevers, who was captured on the Second Crusade. His uncertain fate
was, to the monks, evidence of the punishment meted out to his family for
his father's crimes against the abbey.[63]

When, together with their households, members of aristocratic families
visited the chief monastic houses of their regions, they were often interact-
ing with communities that served important purposes for their dynasties.
Through their ceremonial receptions, monasteries provided ritual approbation of secular lordship, but they also often served as critical sites for the commemoration of past generations of the family in prayer. This was, of course,
especially true when these locations served as the burial places of one or more
generations of the family. Although religious communities, especially if they
were important regional cult centers, did not have to be necropolises to provide valuable prayer for the dead, the old Benedictine abbeys that served as
burial places for many generations of princely families are most often associated with the writing of dynastic narrative.

The creation of dynastic historical narrative by both household clerics and
monks and the easy movement of these texts between secular and monastic
environments are strongly suggestive of their appeal both to the nobility
and to the literate communities that created, used, and altered them. The
authors of these works hoped and expected that what they wrote would be
part of a discourse in which members of the family were active participants,
and which was seen not only as honoring and entertaining them, but also
educating them. The presence of literate clerics and *relatores* within the noble
household meant that this discourse was not tied to any particular location

---

62. John O. Ward, "Memorializing Dispute Resolution in the Twelfth Century: Annal, History,
and Chronicle at Vézelay," in *The Medieval Chronicle: Proceedings of the First International Conference on
the Medieval Chronicle,* ed. Erik Kooper (Utrecht, 1991), 269–284.

63. *Monumenta Vizeliacensia: Textes relatifs à l'histoire de l'abbaye de Vézelay,* ed. R. B. C. Huygens,
CCCM 42 (Turnhout, 1976), 423–424; trans. John O. Ward as *The Vezelay Chronicle and other Docu-
ments from MS Auxerre 227 and Elsewhere* (New York and Binghamton, NY, 1992), 164–165. See
Elizabeth Siberry, "The Crusading Counts of Nevers," *Nottingham Medieval Studies* 34 (1990): 66.

or performance context, but the movement of family members through the landscape of their ancestral residences and religious foundations provided frequent opportunities to recall certain stories and ancestors.

The Crusader in Dynastic Narrative

As they moved through their domains, visiting the palaces and fortresses their forebears had built and the churches and monasteries they had patronized and where they were buried, accompanied by their household clerics and other storytellers who told them of the deeds and customs of previous generations, noble men and women would hear about their crusading ancestors. For several reasons, the crusader might occupy a special place in ancestral narratives. Crusading was one of the few activities, including pilgrimage (with which it was largely analogous), that might take individuals far from the lands of their kindred and from which they might never return. This separation necessitated explanation and intensified the need for narrative commemoration in order that the memory of the dead might not altogether disappear. Crusading was also an activity that, to nearly all clerical and lay observers of the twelfth and thirteenth centuries, exemplified the best qualities to which a noble might aspire. It would be hard to imagine an exemplar as useful ro the clerical writers and *relatores* of the household as the crusading ancestor, nor a narrative frame as charged with potential resonance as that of the crusade. Crusades were also, as we saw in the previous chapter, the contexts in which hereditary honor was built and shattered. Whether the scene was set at the siege of Antioch in 1098, Almería in 1147, or Acre in 1190, the crusade provided universally acknowledged contexts, as recognizable as Roncevaux, for the establishment of a legacy of honor in the increasingly competitive and exclusive cultural world of nobility.

Naming and Locating the Dead

When Count Fulk IV le Réchin of Anjou set out to describe his ancestry in 1096, he commented that he could not speak "worthily" (*digne*) of his four earliest forebears because he did not know where they were buried.[64] He was clearly not alone in insisting on the location of the dead in the imagination before commemorating them in narrative, as many dynastic historians included not only the names of the religious institutions where particular ancestors were buried, but even, in the case of Gislebert of Mons, Geoffrey

---

64. *CCA*, 233.

of Vigeois, or the later chronicle of the counts of Eu, describing *where* in the church their bodies lay.[65] If, like Fulk le Réchin, an aristocrat wished to recite his lineage, and if he wanted to properly discuss the deeds of a crusader, he would want to know the location of the crusader's burial, even if that location was far beyond his geographic imagination. For communities of prayer associated with the family, such information was also critically important for the proper commemoration of the dead. So much is clear, for instance, from a brief notice copied at Saint-Julien of Tours, the purpose of which was to establish the precise information necessary for liturgical commemoration of the seigneurial family of Saint-Médard. The document twice rehearses the genealogical relationships between the individuals singled out for commemoration, and the dates and places of their death. Since one family member, Eudes, the abbot of Preuilly, died on crusade in 1101, the locations of his death and burial ("Licea," possibly Nicaea) are given, with the date of his death and information about how these details had been gathered.[66] Deaths of crusaders, then, and the circumstances of their burial, often received attention in dynastic narratives.

Two men, former rivals but cousins by marriage, Hugh of Chaumont-sur-Loire and Aimery of Courron, shared the lordship of Amboise between them at the time of the First Crusade. Both would die in the East as crusaders at different times and under different circumstances, and the family history, written around 1153, provided the Amboise family with details of their deaths and the locations of their burials. Aimery, the family narrative reported, had been wounded at the siege of Nicaea, which ended in mid-June 1097. As the army moved southwest across Anatolia, Hugh had borne Aimery, described, significantly, as "his friend," on a bier until the crusaders encamped by a bridge. It was at the entrance to the bridge that Aimery and other dead crusaders were buried, the family history added, "with honor."[67] Aimery was not buried in sacred ground, and perhaps not even in Christian territory, but it was clearly of importance to the writers of the family history that he had received a noble burial at a particular place near a recognizable landmark.

The establishment of the Latin states in the East following the conquest of Jeruslaem in 1099 created a zone for the burial and commemoration of crusaders in the East that had the advantages of both relative safety and profound sanctity. These changed circumstances meant that when Hugh of

---

65. GM, 2, 96; GV, 111; *Chronique des comtes d'Eu, RHGF* 23: 439–448.

66. Chantal Sensey, "Entre *gesta,* chronique, et nécrologe: Une *notitia memorialis* de Saint-Julien de Tours (début xii siècle)," *Journal des savants* (2006): 250–251.

67. *CCA,* 101.

Chaumont, who had been forced to make the impromptu grave for his relative Aimery, returned to the East for the second time, in 1129, with his lord, Count Fulk V of Anjou, his burial place would be more easily marked. As the Amboise family historian knew, and could relate with some pride, after Hugh's death in battle outside Damascus his body was buried on the Mount of Olives.[68] By the time of Hugh's second journey, he was probably nearing old age, and his burial in Jerusalem, the city he had helped to conquer three decades earlier, may have been his own wish, or that of his former lord, Fulk, now king of Jerusalem. In either case, the Mount of Olives provided a vivid place in the imaginary geography of Hugh's family, enabling them to think, pray, and speak of him with confidence many decades later, despite his distant burial place.

Although burial at sites of great devotional significance, like the Mount of Olives, may have been desirable for some crusaders, others might make do with places that connected them, in some way, to the communities and cult sites of their home. Such was the case with Herbert, Viscount of Thouars in Poitou, who died after a stroke or heart attack in Jaffa in May 1102, having accompanied his brother Geoffrey and their lord, William of Aquitaine, on the 1101 wave of the First Crusade.[69] The chronicler of the priory of Saint Nicholas of La Chaize, the foundation immediately adjacent to the viscount's residence, recorded that the viscount's brother Geoffrey arranged for the burial of his body in Jaffa at another church dedicated to Saint Nicholas, by the seaside. Herbert's brother also recorded his deathbed bequests, and the monks at La Chaize knew the details of his death in astonishing detail, including the hour he breathed his last (nine o'clock in the morning).[70]

As was no doubt clear to the monks of La Chaize, the connection in their narrative between the devotion demonstrated by Herbert of Thouars to Saint Nicholas in death, and the commemorative link between the burial place of the crusader in the East and that of his father in the West, created a sense that even though he lay so far away, Herbert was, commemoratively speaking, still essentially in the bosom of his family. But the larger narrative that the monks of La Chaize told about the experiences of the two brothers Herbert and Geoffrey was not on the whole a very comforting one. The La Chaize narrative stressed that the two men had acted with honor under extraordinarily difficult circumstances. As crusaders, they provided for their descendants

---

68. *CCA*, 116.

69. "Chronique de Saint-Nicolas de La Chaize-le-Vicomte," ed. Elisabeth Carpentier and Georges Pon, *Revue historique du Centre Ouest* 6 (2007): 339–391.

70. "Chronique de Saint-Nicolas," 338–339.

a model of forbearance, bravery, and righteous suffering, the qualities that nobles were clearly expected to learn from their crusading ancestors.

Taking Up the Cross

As we have seen, one of the primary aims of the writers of dynastic historical narratives was to provide moral instruction from past examples for the edification of the current generation, perhaps especially the youngest members of the family. A colorful reminder that noble youths were not always open to the lessons offered by their family history, and in particular to salutary examples of their crusading ancestors, is found in the work of Lambert of Ardres. Lambert, as we have seen, described at length both the context and the content of a narrative of the Ardres family past delivered to the young heir of Guines and Ardres, Arnold II of Guines, by a storyteller from his retinue. Among the episodes from the Ardres history of greatest importance to the storyteller Walter of Le Clud—at least in Lambert's presentation of it—was the tale of the heroism of Arnold's ancestor Arnold II of Ardres on the First Crusade. As we shall see, the crusading career of Arnold II of Ardres was a point of great pride and honor for the family, but the story that was told about him emphasized his forbearance and suffering in the imitation of Christ and the service of God. Citing Matthew 61:24, "He who wishes to come after me should deny himself and take up his cross and follow me," the scriptural passage most often associated with crusading, he moved his narrative directly from the preaching of the crusade to Arnold's arrival at Antioch, where

> the wisdom and strength of his knighthood were known and attested by all. Although one bean, as they say, in this Antiochene army, cost a gold bezant, and an ass's head sold for five shillings of Byzantine gold nevertheless he always remained strong and robust.[71]

When these lines are placed in the larger context of Lambert's history, it becomes clear that he wanted to juxtapose the kind of want and suffering that Arnold II of Ardres had experienced with the youthful follies of his descendant and namesake, Arnold II of Guines, who was the audience of this story. Although he was careful to mix his criticism with flattery and to cloak his own opinions with narrative devices that distanced the message from the messenger, Lambert's text registers disapproval of his young lord Arnold's carefree life of tournaments and chivalric indulgence.[72] Late in his

---

71. LA, 626; trans. Shopkow, 164.
72. LA, 606–607. This at least seems to be the moral of the story of Arnold's brief affair with Ida of Boulogne.

narrative, Lambert appears particularly bothered by the fact that his lord had taken the cross for the Third Crusade but failed to undertake the expedition, spending the money he had collected for the crusade for other purposes.[73] There is even, in Lambert's complex chronicle, a scene that connects the tale told about the brave crusading ancestor with the shameful performance of the contemporary young lord. When, according to Lambert, the storyteller Walter of Le Clud was finished with his narrative of the Ardres family and its crusading hero, the young Arnold II, sprang up and walked outside, clearly either bored or disinterested in the story and said, in a way that almost appears menacing, that he was no longer interested in hearing the deeds of old men but would prefer to talk of youth instead.[74]

The fear expressed by Lambert of Ardres that young men would not follow the examples of their crusading ancestors either by imitating their steadfast, virtuous piety or more specifically by taking the cross did not prevent him and other writers of family history from continuing to hold up crusaders as models for imitation. The Amboise family history, like that of Ardres, began its account of the crusade with preaching at Clermont, citing in place of Lambert's Matthew the slightly more ominous follow-on of Luke 14:27, "If anyone does not take up his cross and come after me, he cannot be my disciple." As in Ardres, memory of the crusade in Amboise focused on Antioch. This is in no way surprising, since the brutal eight-month contest for the city in northern Syria (November 1097–June 1098) was at the center of every account of the expedition; the earliest vernacular works dedicated to the crusade were dominated by what had happened at Antioch.

A discovery by Neil Wright reveals that writers of dynastic history could refer to events at Antioch and suggest models of behavior without even mentioning the crusade itself.[75] Because Count Fulk IV le Réchin of Anjou did not take the cross, the First Crusade was not mentioned in the earliest surviving version of the Angevin dynastic history, *Chronica de gestis consulum Andegavorum*. But, as Wright has shown, the author of this earliest version, writing in the immediate vicinity and at the same moment that Baudri of Bourgueil composed his crusade chronicle, used Baudri's descriptions of battle at Antioch as the stylistic base for his own depiction of the wars waged by the tenth-century Angevin count Geoffrey Greymantle against a rampaging army of Norsemen and Flemings.[76] For the Angevin author, the image

---

73. LA, 606; trans. Shopkow, 128.
74. LA, 636; trans. Shopkow, 183.
75. Neil Wright, "Epic and Romance in the Chronicles of Anjou," *Anglo-Norman Studies* 26 (2003): 177–189.
76. Wright, "Epic and Romance," 180–181.

of the crusaders at Antioch provided precisely the image of the Christian warrior that he wanted to present in his dynastic narrative.

While they may not have made such subtle use of crusade chronicles as did the anonymous Angevin historian, other dynastic history writers nonetheless demonstrate a great interest in the chronicles of the First Crusade. The Norman historian Orderic Vitalis based his own account of the First Crusade largely on the chronicle of Baudri of Bourgueil.[77] Baudri's work was also praised by the Limousin historian Geoffrey of Vigeois, who recounted the history of several noble families of the Limousin, most prominently his relatives the lords of Lastours.[78] Geoffrey was also impressed by the work of a local knight of the castle of Lastours, Gregory Bechada, who had composed his own written vernacular account, the *Canso d'Antioca,* part of which survives.[79] Walter of Thérouanne, writing of the crusading ancestor of Charles the Good of Flanders, referred to the anonymous redaction of the crusade chronicle of Fulcher of Chartres known as the *Gesta Francorum Iherusalem expuganatium.*[80] In their lengthy account of the translation to their abbey of a relic of the True Cross, which included a brief history of the lords of Hierges, the monks of Brogne referred readers to the crusade chronicle of Robert the Monk.[81] Lambert of Ardres described the performance at Ardres of two oral accounts of crusade expeditions, one of which was a version of the *Chanson d'Antioche,* while the other chronicled the history of the Latin Kingdom of Jerusalem.[82]

The instances of copying from and reference to crusade chronicles by historians of noble dynasties is striking, especially because, in nearly every case, they are the only instances in which these writers explicitly refer to other authors. On the one hand, this suggests a close relationship in the minds of the authors of ancestral narratives between their own projects and the crusade histories. Although the earliest dynastic narratives, as we have seen, predate the First Crusade by several decades, it is possible that the explosion in the number of crusade narratives in the first decades of the twelfth century inspired the subsequent proliferation of dynastic narratives. Both were accounts of princely deeds (*gesta principum* and *gesta Francorum*), and both provided models for noble conduct. Narratives of the crusades, and especially

---

77. OV 5: xiv.

78. GV, 55–56.

79. GV, 66.

80. Walter of Thérouanne, *Vita Karoli comitis Flandriae et vita domni Ioannis Morinensis episcopi; quibus subiungitur poemata de morte comitis Karoli conscripta et quaestio de eadem acta,* ed. Jeff Rider, *CCCM* 217 (Turnhout, 2006), 23, 31.

81. The Brogne text, *Quomodo sancta crux ab Antiochia allata sit in Broniense cenobium,* is unedited. The text occupies ff. 122–174v of an unnumbered MS of the Bibliothèque du Séminaire de Namur.

82. LA, 607; trans. Shopkow, 130, 165.

of the First Crusade, however, also played a more direct role in family invocations of the crusading past.

Legacies of Honor and Shame

It was clearly a mark of great prestige for families to be able to point to the name of their ancestor in the Latin and vernacular crusade chronicles. Geoffrey of Vigeois, for instance, distinguished between those that he knew had traveled to Jerusalem, those who "are renowned in the Jerusalem war" (*qui in bello Hierosolimitano memoratur*) and those, like his own ancestor Gouffier of Lastours, "of whom the history of the Jerusalem war makes mention" (*de quo mentio fit in historia Hierosolimytani belli*).[83] We encounter in Lambert of Ardres the family storyteller's rage and incomprehension that the name of Arnold II of Ardres had been left out of what was by this time perhaps the most important tradition, the *Chanson d'Antioche:*

> And yet the singer of the song of Antioch, who was led by avaricious zeal and was more desirous of the reward of temporal gain than Arnold was of human praise, suppressed the glory and tribute of praise that he deserved. . . . For Arnold, who was in strength and skill in every way a noble hero, refused to give two scarlet stockings to this same wretch, who deserves to be known by no name. So he made no mention of Arnold in his song; in this song he mixed false deeds with true ones, but nevertheless left many deeds of many praiseworthy men untouched under a blanket of silence.[84]

The lengthy tirade against the singer and the insistence on Arnold's participation are the clearest indications in any surviving text of how important crusader ancestry was deemed to be. The legacy of honor that the Ardres family derived from this crusading hero was potentially important for many reasons, but among them must have been the courtship between the young heir to the lordship, Arnold II of Guines, and Ida, the widowed Countess of Boulogne. In 1190, the same year in which he was presented with the spoken narrative of his ancestral past at the castle of Ardres, and the same year in which he was expected to depart on the Third Crusade, Arnold had attempted to woo Ida on the tournament circuit in Flanders and Hainaut.[85] Writing about Ida's family, Lambert of Ardres excitedly recalled their central

---

83. GV, 10 (Gouffier of Lastours *mentio fit in historia*), 70 (William of Aquitaine *perrexit*), 79 (Robert Curthose *memoratur*).

84. LA, 626–627, trans. Shopkow, 165.

85. LA, 604–605, trans. Shopkow, 125–126.

role in the First Crusade, and how two of the three crusading sons of another Ida of Boulogne had become the first two rulers of the crusader kingdom of Jerusalem.[86] It may have been critical, at least in the eyes of the historian, to remind not only his lord but the wider community that the Ardres lords too were descended from a famous crusader. This would contrast Arnold sharply with his rival for Ida's attention, Rainald of Dammartin. Rainald was a lord with a murky family background who could not make any such claims to crusading ancestry.[87]

Another case in which a family's crusading past was highlighted to distinguish them from their political rivals can be found in the Amboise dynastic history *Gesta Ambaziensium dominorum*. The Amboise text was, as we have seen, composed in the context of a major crisis for the dynasty. In his opening address to his "friend," the writer explained that the lord of Amboise, Sulpicius II, and his sons had recently been captured by Count Thibaud IV of Blois and thrown in prison (he later alluded to the torture of Sulpicius.)[88] In response, the dynastic history activated a powerful discourse centered on the First Crusade that reaffirmed the honor and heroism of the Amboise family while at the same time invoking the shame and dishonor of the counts of Blois.

The resonance of the siege of Antioch among the twelfth-century nobility, and especially among descendants of crusaders, was all the stronger because the story distinguished those who stood fast in the face of danger from those who abandoned their fellows and fled back to the West. Despite the attempts by some chroniclers, such as Guibert of Nogent, to limit the damage caused by the scandalous story of the "rope-dancers," who lowered themselves down through the latrines in the city walls to escape what they assumed would be certain death, no one forgot their faithlessness. The most famous of the deserters was Count Thibaud's father, Stephen II of Blois and Chartres, the crusade leader who had quietly separated himself and his companions from the main body of the Christian army at Alexandretta before abruptly heading home.[89] In some quarters, it appears that Stephen's subsequent return to the East and his death at the Second Battle of Ramla in 1102 made amends for his earlier actions. An anonymous poet from the Loire would say of Stephen that

---

86. LA, 570, trans. Shopkow, 65.

87. Rainaild would later fabricate a genealogy tracing his roots to Charlemagne, which was appended to a translation of Pseudo-Turpin. See Gabrielle Spiegel, *Romancing the Past: The Rise of Vernacular Prose Historiography in Thirteenth-Century France* (Berkeley, 1993), 93.

88. *CCA*, 129.

89. On Stephen's crusade, see James Brundage, "An Errant Crusader: Stephen of Blois," *Traditio* 16 (1960): 380–395.

in the end he "proved himself acceptable" (*satis approbatus*).[90] For enemies of the family, like the lords of Amboise, however, it was a weak spot in the family's honor that would be easy to exploit.

In its account of the crusading experiences of Aimery of Courron and Hugh of Chaumont, the Amboise family history noted that news of Aimery's death near Nicaea had been brought back to the West not by a member of the Amboise family, but by Stephen, who of course arrived in the region while the crusade was still in progress. Having already established Stephen's departure from the crusade, the Amboise family history went on to describe Hugh of Chaumont's steadfastness at the siege of Antioch:

> Hugh, having suffered in many engagements with the others, stayed in the army of God for a further two years. He was therefore in every battle and in the siege of Antioch, just as the other men, he endured many misfortunes. He never considered running away, as [did] many who had given up hope.[91]

The Amboise historian went on to explain that Hugh had played a key role in defending the walls of Antioch, being assigned, along with another lord from the Touraine region, Ralph of Beaugency, the guardianship of a certain entrance called "Bohemond's Gate."[92]

While no more is said in the family history about these events, we pick up the story in a variant manuscript of the crusade chronicle of Baudri of Bourgueil known as manuscript G.[93] In this variant manuscript, the whole affair is described in greater detail, and we learn that the night that Hugh and Ralph stood watch over Bohemond's Gate was the night of the infamous flight of many men from the walls through the latrines and out of the city.[94] G reports a conversation the next morning between Bohemond of Taranto and the two Tourainers, "those prudent men, his close friends," wherein the distinction is made explicitly between these two who stood fast and the others, many of whom were from lands near Amboise, who had fled with

---

90. See the verses in Nicholas Paul, "Crusade, Memory, and Regional Politics in Twelfth-Century Amboise," *Journal of Medieval History* 31 (2005): 141.

91. "Hugo in exercitu dei, multis erumpnis cum aliis afflictus, duobus annis post hoc permansit. Fuit enim in omnibus preliis, et in Antiochie obsidione multa infortunia, sicut alii, perpessus, nunquam de fuga, ut multi desperati, cogitavit." *CCA*, 101.

92. *CCA*, 101.

93. BNF, Lat. 5513. For an extended discussion of the relationship between this manuscript and the Amboise family, see Nicholas Paul, "Crusade, Memory, and Regional Politics in Twelfth-Century Amboise," *Journal of Medieval History* 31 (2005): 127–141. Some other interesting points about the variant version of Baudri found in this manuscript were made by Benjamin Kedar, "The Subjected Muslims of the Frankish Levant," in *Muslims under Latin Rule*, ed. James M. Powell (Princeton, NJ, 1990), 145 n. 18.

94. Baudri of Bourgueil, *Historia Jerosolimitana, RHC Occ.* 4: 65, var. 4.

Stephen. According to the G manuscript, it is Hugh and Ralph who are given the privilege of punishing those like Stephen of Blois, who, having run away, eventually returned to the crusade army in shame in 1101. Strikingly, G also revises Baudri's description of the flight of Stephen of Blois. Where Baudri had given Stephen the benefit of the doubt, believing that he had "withdrawn" from the fighting, because he was ill, the G manuscript insists that the illness was a sham and cover for his cowardice.[95] These many additions, and others, including the names of crusaders from the Touraine region, suggest that the G manuscript reflects a view of the First Crusade that is sympathetic with the Amboise family.[96]

Ancestral Romance

In Lambert of Ardres's description of storytelling inside the castle of Ardres, family history and the history of the crusades are two of the types of narratives offered to the young lord for performance. The evidence of the G manuscript strongly suggests these two narratives might not always have been separate: just as a family history would include sustained accounts of ancestors on crusade, accounts of the crusade would likely also privilege ancestral participation. But these were not the only types of narratives that the storytellers could relate. Many of the other kinds of stories that Lambert described, of the Romans and Charlemagne, of Tristan, Merlin, and Arthur, must have corresponded closely with (if they were not identical to) surviving works of epic and romance literature. The fictionalized pasts in these entertaining narratives were also not distinct from narratives of the family past. Arthur was among several potential fonts of authority from which families claimed descent and title. The history of the lords of Amboise, for instance, referred both to the Roman and Arthurian history of the Touraine region, claiming that the nearby Angevin fortress of Chinon was so named because it was founded by Arthur's seneschal Kay.[97]

The rising popularity, over the course of the twelfth century, of the new courtly literature of Arthurian romance inevitably influenced the way that the nobility understood and described the crusading past. A clear sign of this influence is the account in the *Historia Reinhardsbrunnensis*—a fragmentary text composed before 1217—of the deeds of the landgrave of Thuringia Ludwig III on the Third Crusade. The *Historia,* as we have seen, was the work of an unknown author with close links to the Thuringian family. It

---

95. Baudri of Bourgueil, *Historia Jerosolimitana, RHC Occ.* 4: 71, var. 7.
96. Paul, "Crusade, Memory, and Regional Politics," 139.
97. *CCA,* 10.

was written at a time when the Thuringian court was one of the preeminent literary centers in German-speaking lands.[98] The text's account of the landgrave's crusading deeds is among the longest reminiscences about a crusader in a local or dynastic chronicle, including details about Ludwig's journey, his arrival in the East, his role in the fighting, his death, and the return of his remains for burial in Thuringia.

According to the *Historia,* Ludwig virtually single-handedly rescued the forces besieging Acre from Saladin, restoring their morale. At one point during the fighting, the *Historia* describes how Ludwig, abandoned by his fellow crusaders in the face of a Saracen onslaught, called out for divine assistance only to see "a certain knight, of noble stature, dressed in red clothing riding a snow-white horse." The knight was recognized as Saint George, to whom Ludwig had a special devotion. The red knight planted a red banner in the earth, saying, "Under this banner you will conquer" (*Sub hoc vexillo vinces*), and then disappeared.

> Since many knights wanted to pull that banner from the ground, but were not able, the said pious prince [Ludwig] drew it out very quickly and, with a few men who returned to him, fiercely harassed the Saracens, throwing them back all the way to Saladin's tent, killing many and many more fled the field with wounds. And that banner was called "Sieghard," that is to say, "Victory."[99]

In the story of Ludwig's deeds on crusade we find the convergence of three strands of literary influence. The appearance of Saint George at a crucial moment during the battle was a familiar scene from narratives of the battle at Antioch during the First Crusade, drawing parallels between Ludwig's deeds and those of the first crusaders.[100] Saint George's words to the landgrave, on the other hand, clearly refer to Constantine's vision of the angel and the Chi-Rho symbol the night before the battle of Milvian Bridge in 312. Finally, Ludwig's success in extracting the banner with ease where other knights had failed evokes the drawing of the sword Excalibur from the stone by the

---

98. Joachim Bumke, *Courtly Culture: Literature and Society in the High Middle Ages,* trans. Thomas Dunlap (Woodstock, NY, 2000), 90.

99. "Cum ergo multi milites illud vexillum extrahere vellent et non possent, dictus pius princeps multa velocitate extrahit et cum paucis resumptis viribus, multis Sarracenorum milibus acriter instabat, et usque ad Saladini tabernaculum eos abiciens, plurimis interfectis, infinitos vulnere sauciatos semivivos campo deseruit. Et illud vexillum proprie segehard, id est victoriosum, dicebatur." *Chronica Reinhardsbrunnensis,* 546.

100. *La Chanson d'Antioche,* ed. Jan Nelson, *OFCC* 4 (Tuscaloosa, AL, 2003), 338, ll. 10928–10942.

young Arthur, a motif that first appears in early thirteenth-century works of Arthurian literature by Robert de Boron.[101]

If, as is very likely, the *Historia* reflects traditions that were current at the Thuringian court at Wartburg in the early thirteenth century, it demonstrates a shift in attitudes toward the importance of crusading deeds in the family memory. Ludwig's honor is no longer measured simply in terms of his participation, suffering, and triumph but is elaborated with details that render him more like a hero of epic or romance.

There is no doubt that the stories told about crusaders became more elaborate in their retellings. In chronicles of the First Crusade, for instance, Duke Robert Curthose of Normandy's charge at the standard-bearer of Ascalon in 1099 was transformed first into a charge at the emir of Ascalon and then into single combat with "Rouge Lion," the dread opponent of the crusaders at the battle of Antioch two years earlier.[102] The crusading feats of Robert of Normandy gradually conformed with the expectations of audiences who were accustomed to hearing about single combats between enemy leaders in romances. The introduction of romance motifs that we find in the *Historia,* however, is a more dramatic development and signals a shift that can be observed more generally away from the family commemorative traditions of the twelfth century that we have seen at work in this chapter and toward a new world dominated by motifs from courtly romance.

In chapter 1 we met Gouffier of Lastours, the Limousin lord who acquired great fame on the First Crusade. When, in 1183, Geoffrey of Vigeois composed his regional history, which included a genealogy of the Lastours family and copious details about various of its members, he referred to the deeds by Gouffier at the siege of Ma'arrat an-Nu'man, which were mentioned by numerous crusade chroniclers.[103] But around the same time that Geoffrey wrote his chronicle, or perhaps shortly afterward, a different set of traditions about Gouffier began to emerge. The troubadours Gaucelm Faidit and Guillem Magret referred to other stories about Gouffier, including one about Gouffier freeing a lion.[104] While the first text to recount the whole tale of

---

101. *Merlin and the Grail: Joseph of Arimathea, Merlin, Perceval; The Trilogy of Arthurian Romances Attributed to Robert de Boron,* trans. Nigel Bryant (Cambridge, 2001), 107–109.

102. *Gesta Francorum et aliorum Hierosolymitanorum,* ed. Rosalind Hill (New York and London, 1962), 95; Baudri, *Historia Jerosolimitana, RHC Occ.* 4: 110; *La Chanson d'Antioche, OFCC* 4: 338, ll. 10900–10909.

103. GV, 67.

104. The literary references to this tradition were catalogued first in *Chanson de la croisade contre les Albigeoise,* ed. Paul Meyer (Paris, 1879), 2: 379–380 n. 1. For further contributions, see *The Canso d'Antioca: An Occitan Epic Chronicle of the First Crusade,* ed. and trans. Carol Sweetenham and Linda Paterson (Aldershot, UK, 2003), 11–14.

Gouffier only dates to the late thirteenth or the early fourteenth century,[105] by which time it was known as far away as Italy, it is clear from the troubadour songs and a reference in the verse history of the Albigensian crusade (the *Canso de la crotzada* of c. 1228) that the story was well known south of the Loire by the early thirteenth century.[106] The story is essentially identical to that of the hero in Chrétien de Troyes's Arthurian romance *Yvain:* Gouffier, while on crusade, freed a lion from the grip of a serpent or dragon, and the lion became his devoted companion.[107]

While the story has some distinct features and is of interest in the way that it may relate to other stories about lions told by returning crusaders in the twelfth and thirteenth centuries, for our purposes here it is noteworthy as a story that essentially replaces the unique memory of Gouffier as the hero of Ma'arrat, which was proudly related by his descendants in the 1180s, with a common romance motif. Remarkably, Gouffier was not the only crusader to have his memory transformed in this way. Before the fourteenth century, two other crusaders, the knight Gilles de Chin, the lord of Berlaymont near Tournai,[108] who took the cross in the early twelfth century, and Roger de Mowbray, who died shortly after the battle of Hattin in 1187, had the same story of the lion and the serpent associated with their time on crusade.[109]

In none of these cases is there any evidence that descendants of the crusader publicized or associated themselves in any way with these stories. Neither the lords of Lastours nor those of Berlaymont, for instance, employed lions on their heraldry in the thirteenth century. The origins of the stories were not familial but regional and marked the adoption of each of these crusaders as a regional chivalric hero. In the *Historia Reinhardsbrunnensis,* for

---

105. *Notitiae duae Lemovicenses de praedicatione crucis in Aquitania, RHC Occ.* 5: 350–353; see also the preface to this edition, lxxxiv. This text is often associated with Geoffrey of Vigeois. In fact, it is more likely to have been the work of one of the two great inquisitor-storytellers, Bernard Gui or Étienne de Bourbon. For the latter's *Tractatus de diversis materiis praedicabilibus,* see Étienne de Bourbon, *Anecdotes historiques, légendes, et apologues tirés du recueil inédit d'Étienne de Bourbon,* ed. Albert Lecoy de la Marche (Paris, 1877), 188, no. 216 and n. 1.

106. *Chanson de la croisade contre les Albigeoise,* 2: 379.

107. For the story, see Arthur Gilchrist Brodeur, "The Grateful Lion: A Study in the Development of Medieval Narrative," *Publications of the Modern Language Association of America* 39:3 (1924): 485–524.

108. For the historical Gilles de Chin, see GM, 59–60; trans. Napran, 36 and n. 154. For the legend, see *L'histoire de Gilles de Chin de Gautier de Tournai,* ed. E. B. Place (Evanston, IL, 1941); Camille Liégeois, *Gilles de Chin, l'histoire et légende* (Louvain, 1903); Charity Cannon Willard, "Gilles de Chin in History, Literature, and Folklore," in *The Medieval Opus: Imitation, Rewriting, and Transmission in the French Tradition,* ed. D. Kelly (Amsterdam, 1996), 357–366.

109. "Progenies Moubraiorum, huius abbatiae fundatorum," *MA* 6.1: 320. But see "Quomodo mutatum fuit Cognomen de Albaneio in Cognomen de Mubrai," *MA* 5: 346; and Roy Gilyard-Beer, "Byland Abbey and the Grave of Roger de Mowbray," *Yorkshire Archeological Journal* 55 (1983): 61–66. And see below, 156–157.

instance, the brave deeds of Ludwig at Acre are constantly compared to the cowardice and weakness of the French, whom he struggles to rally and who ultimately abandon him on the battlefield. The allusion to Constantine at the Milvian bridge may also be a reference to the advent of the new German emperor Frederick II, whose birth name was "Constantine."[110] In either case, it is Germanness, or at least a sense of imperial, eastern Frankish solidarity, that underpins the narrative.

One of the first clear references to the story of Gouffier of Lastours and the lion is given in the context of the Albigensian crusade. The efforts of Simon de Montfort, leader of the northern French crusaders, to capture Toulouse are compared unfavorably to Gouffier's defeat of the serpent. The southern French crusading hero is thus used to undercut the legitimacy of the northerner, who was seen to be leading an illegitimate crusade against the south.[111]

Perhaps the most famous examples of literary elaboration in the ancestry of a crusading family are the origin legends associated with the ancestors of Godfrey of Bouillon and the crusading lords of Lusignan. These do not, technically, constitute the same phenomenon we have just seen, as they deal with the ancestry of crusaders—the Swan Knight from a fairy-tale kingdom in the case of Godfrey of Bouillon, and a demon/water fairy named Mélusine in the case of the lords of Lusignan—rather than with crusaders themselves. There is, however, an important similarity with the case of the lion knights mentioned above: neither the Lusignan dynasty, descendants of which ruled in Cyprus and Armenia in the thirteenth and early fourteenth centuries, nor the kings of Jerusalem nor the counts of Boulogne nor the dukes of Lower Lorraine, all of whom could claim the closest ties of kinship with Godfrey of Bouillon, identified themselves with these legends in the twelfth or early thirteenth century. While the genealogical branches of the Old French Crusade Cycle may have been influenced by the political interests of the crusading Duke Henry I of Brabant (d. 1235), whose wife Mathilda was great-granddaughter of Godfrey of Bouillon's brother Eustace III of Boulogne, there is as yet no evidence that either Henry or Mathilda sought to associate him- or herself with the legend or their crusading forebears.[112]

---

110. David Abulafia, *Frederick II: A Medieval Emperor* (Oxford, 1988), 62. For the anonymous author's reference to Frederick as Constantine elsewhere, see Tebruck, *Die Reinhardsbrunner Geschichtsschreibung,* 47.

111. This contrast was pointed out by Janet Shirley, who noted the further irony that Montfort's heraldic symbol is prominently displayed in the only surviving MS of the text. William of Tudela, *Song of the Cathar Wars,* trans. J. Shirley (Aldershot, 1996), 155.

112. Geert Classens, "Über den 'Sitz im Leben' der altfranzösischen *épopées intermédiaires,*" in *Chanson de geste im europäischen Kontext,* ed. Hans-Joachim Ziegeler (Göttingen, 2008), 15–25. My thanks to Simon John for pointing out this article. According to Anne McGee Morganstern, *Gothic Tombs of Kinship in France, the Low Countries, and England* (University Park, PA, 2000), 27–31, while

Both the Swan Knight and the Mélusine legends existed in some form before the end of the twelfth century.[113] Chroniclers in the Rhineland, and families that were distantly (and possibly fictitiously) related to the house of Boulogne, like the family of Guines, might refer to the legend of the Swan Knight in the context of Godfrey of Bouillon and his saintly mother, Ida of Boulogne.[114] There is no evidence, however, that it was embraced by Ida's or Godfrey's descendants. William of Tyre, who wrote the closest thing to an official history of the Latin Kingdom of Jerusalem and its rulers in the early 1180s had heard the story but dismissed it as rubbish.[115] Even Rainald of Dammartin, who, as we have seen, abducted the heiress of Boulogne in 1190, does not seem to have associated himself with the legend. Creating a fictional genealogy for himself, he, like most of the nobility of continental Europe, was concerned primarily with establishing his descent from Charlemagne.[116]

Much later, after the living memory of the early crusades to the East had long passed, both the Swan Knight and Mélusine traditions came to play important roles for noble dynasties. As Susan Crane has shown, by the fourteenth century, two hundred descendants of Godfrey of Bouillon were using the image of the swan in their heraldry.[117] As she notes, this ancestry had little to do with crusading: "Never mind that their genuine ancestor Godfrey had won and ruled Jerusalem; their mythical ancestor was the one they preferred for their self-representations."[118] Mélusine makes her first complete appearance in a romance entitled *La noble histoire de Lusignen*. This ancestral romance was written in 1392 for John, Duke of Berry, who used the castle of Lusignan as his residence and may therefore have seen himself as a kind of heir to the crusading Lusignans of Poitou, whose line had been extinguished since the first decade of the fourteenth century.[119]

This process of romancing the twelfth-century crusading past led to a great proliferation of traditions about historical individuals who had taken the

---

the extensive commemorative program of architecture and verse dedicated to the ducal family at the Cistercian abbey of Villers, may depict crusaders, it is silent about any family crusading lore. The numerous Brabant genealogies in verse and prose (see appendix 1) are likewise silent.

113. For a useful comparative study of both legends, see Claude Lécouteux, *Mélusine et le Chevalier au Cygne* (Paris, 1982).

114. LA, 570; trans. Shopkow, 65; Guy of Bazoches, *Liber epistularum Guidonis de Basochis,* ed. Henry Adolfsson, Acta Universitatis Stochholmensis: Studia Latina Stockholmensia 18 (Stockholm, 1969), 95. An early version of the Swan Knight story repeated as history for the counts of Boulogne is also found in a MS from the cathedral of Arras, now Arras, Bibliothèque Municipale, MS 184. It was edited in F. A. de Reiffenberg, *Le chevalier au cygne et Godefroid de Bouillon* (Brussels, 1846), 1: viiii.

115. WT, 1: 427.

116. See Spiegel, *Romancing the Past,* 93. Classens, "Über den 'Sitz im Leben'," 23–24.

117. Susan Crane, *The Performance of Self: Ritual, Clothing, and Identity during the Hundred Years War* (Philadelphia, 2002), 107–139.

118. Crane, *The Performance of Self,* 113.

119. Jean d'Arras, *Mélusine: Roman du xiv siècle,* ed. Louis Stouff (Geneva, 1974).

cross, but it signals a shift from one type of remembrance to another. The social memory of medieval noble families, which was generated through the interactions between men and women, their households, and the monastic institutions that they visited and patronized and where they were buried, was in many cases overwhelmed by the force of the chivalric imagination, which was quick to adopt heroes of the crusading past as totemic figures of regional identity, and equally quick to homogenize them, stripping them of their unique features and fitting them into preexisting stereotypes. This new, totalizing discourse had none of the functions of the stories told in the twelfth- and early thirteenth-century texts. It did not help to commemorate the dead or instruct the living or distinguish families as possessing unique identities. While it did not actively destroy the memories of all noble families, or prevent dynasties like the lords of Joinville from preserving the unique traditions of their ancestors, it may have been responsible for the disappearance of the works that celebrated those traditions. By the middle of the thirteenth century, dynastic historical narratives had all but disappeared.

This force was still quite distant when, in 1166, Wace worked on the third book of the *Roman de Rou,* in which he, the *clerc lisant,* imagined instructing King Henry II about his Norman ancestry in some festive setting. Relating the deeds of the king's crusading ancestor, the Duke of Normandy, Robert Curthose, Wace, like other writers of family histories, turned to a variety of sources. But in his account of Curthose, Wace made a startling claim, one that cannot be found in any other text describing the duke's crusading adventures. According to the *romancier,* the standard that the duke had captured at the battle of Antioch had returned with him to Normandy and was given as a gift to the abbey of La Trinité in Caen where his sister Cecilia was the abbess.[120] The implication in Wace is that it was still there for the king to see, a souvenir of his ancestor's crusading accomplishments. Whether or not this was true, and regardless of the authenticity of whatever old piece of fabric may have been kept at La Trinité, Wace's reference to such an object in the middle of his ancestral narrative is important because it points to a larger phenomenon. By the end of the twelfth century, old materials were scattered throughout the monasteries, chapels, and seigneurial residences of the West that noble families associated with the deeds of their crusading ancestors. These objects, no less than the stories that the families told, were critical elements of the mechanism through which ideas of the crusading past were transmitted and understood.

---

120. Wace, *Roman de Rou,* 200–201. See below, 231.

❧ CHAPTER 3

The Fabric of Victory

In the early months of 1183, Geoffrey, the prior of the Benedictine house of Vigeois, near Limoges, was in the process of finishing his chronicle of the churches, monasteries, and noble families of his region when the narrative of deeds and power he had been so carefully recording suddenly overtook him.[1] Having described with obvious apprehension the recent return of sinister groups of armed men in the region, who were called, among other vulgar names, *Brabansons,* Geoffrey abruptly abandoned the course of his narrative and began instead to take short notes on the events that were happening around him. That summer, Henry II of England and his younger son, Richard of Poitou, descended on the Limousin in an attempt to suppress a revolt led by Viscount Adhémar V of Limoges and the king's eldest son, Henry, known as the Young King.[2] They were accompanied by an army of Brabançon mercenaries led by a frightening man

---

1. For Geoffrey and his chronicle, see Pierre Botineau's introduction to GV. See also François Arbellot, "Étude historique et bibliographique sur Geoffroy de Vigeois," *Bulletin de la Société Archéologique et Historique du Limousin* 36 (1888): 135–161; Michel Aubrun, "Le prieur Geoffroy de Vigeois et sa chronique," *Revue Mabillon* 63 (1974): 313–326.

2. The best account of these events, which includes the background to the revolt, is that of John Gillingham, *Richard I* (New Haven, CT, 1999), 64–75. See also W. L. Warren, *Henry II* (New Haven, CT, 2000), 581, 589–593. For the mercenaries, see Hercule Géraud, "Mercadier: Les routiers au treizième siècle," *Bibliothèque de l'École des Chartes* 3:3 (1842): 422–423; J. F. Verbruggen, *The Art of Warfare in Western Europe during the Middle Ages,* trans. Sumner Willard and R. W. Southern, 2nd ed. (Woodbridge, UK, 1997), 136–137. I have also found very useful the discussion in Christian Rémy,

known only as Mercadier (The Merchant), who mercilessly ravaged the lands of the rebel lords.

By early autumn, Mercadier had begun to besiege the rebel castles south of Limoges, moving his army into the immediate vicinity of Geoffrey's house of Vigeois. The notes that Geoffrey made soon afterward describe the panic that seized the area as reports arrived that the rampaging bands were going to attack the castle of Pompadour, the ancestral stronghold of the lords of Lastours, on the same day that people from throughout the region, including Geoffrey and his monks, were gathering outside the castle at the priory church of Arnac for the Feast of Saint Pardoux.

On the vigil of Pardoux's feast, October 6, just as the evening prayers began, the alarm was raised and word spread that Mercadier, whom Geoffrey called "that prince of ruin," would begin besieging the castle at dawn. All through the night, Geoffrey wrote, monks labored to remove the liturgical apparatus (*sacramenta*) from the nearby churches and to bring them into a part of the castle known as the "tower of Gouffier" (*turrim Gulpherii*). Geoffrey, who must have been among the monks conducting this emergency operation through the night, recalled in his notes that "on that occasion, the walls of the tower were more beautifully decorated than was customary" because of certain "cloth-hangings" (*pallia*) that a "prince" of Lastours had brought back from Jerusalem.[3]

On 12 October, six days after the danger had passed, Geoffrey and his brethren were preparing to return to Vigeois when the prior was struck on the head by a stone falling from the dilapidated roof of the priory church.[4]

Lastours et les Lastours du X au XVI siècle, Mémoire de maîtrise, Université des Sciences Humaines–Strasbourg 2 (Strasbourg, 1990), 1: 49–50.

3. "Die septima ab ordinatione archiepiscopi Bituricensis, Princeps perditorum, qui vocabatur Merchaders, terram Archambaldi Combornensis usque ad Sanctum Germanum, die eiusdem Confessoris deuastauit. Post haec rediit retro in Petragorico, ut sollicitatos redderet incautos, cum in vigilia Sancti Pardulphi vespertinas laudes Arnaco persoluissemus, clamor factus est dicentium, quod iam Pompedorium obsedissent castrum, quod omnino falsum erat. Sed clamor et metus clamoris nobiles matronas de Segur, plebeiosque, qui ad festum ex vicis confluebant, longius propulsauit. Nuntii iterumque venere qui mane hostes venturos esse dicebant: Et ea nocte, quo populi sua solebant deferre vota, coeperunt Monachi diuersa Ecclesiae sacramenta auferrre, et in turrim Gulpherii deferre. Erant tunc turris parietes ornati pulchrius solito, quia pallia quaedam [quinque—some MSS] ab Hierosolymis detulerat Princeps [Principes—some MSS] de Turribus. Tempore illo matutinas processionis, caeterasque horas diei Domino largiente celebrauimus admodum honeste." GV PA, 340. For a discussion of this passage, citing all variants, see Alain J. Stocler, "À la recherche du ban perdu: Le trésor et les dépouilles de Waïfre, duc d'Aquitaine (d. 768), d'après Adémar de Chabannes, Rigord, et quelques autres," *Cahiers de civilisation médiévale* 42 (1999): 349–350. Stocler's association of the five *pallia* at Pompadour with the five *pallia* of Duke Waiffre of Aquitaine paraded at Limoges does not take into account the desire on the part of the text's later medieval and early modern copyists to see Gouffier everywhere in their text. The paraphernalia at Limoges were much more likely ducal than seigneurial. For the Waiffre banners, see below, 129 and n. 148.

4. GV PA, 340.

Allowing the other monks to proceed without him, Geoffrey convalesced at the healing shrine of Saint Pardoux with the memories of the visit to Arnac, of the panicking pilgrims and what he had seen during the dramatic night-time evacuation to the castle of Pompadour, etched (somewhat literally) on his fevered brow.[5]

At the center of Geoffrey's memory of the frightening night spent at Pompadour was a rich visual image: a number of textiles (*pallia*) that, apparently unusually, decorated the walls. For Geoffrey these objects evoked the memory of a journey to Jerusalem undertaken by of one of the lords of Lastours, a lineage to which he himself claimed kinship, and whose crusading traditions he discussed at length elsewhere in his chronicle. His statement about the *pallia* leaves us with several questions. Who was the "prince of Lastours" responsible for acquiring these objects? What were they? Why, on the night that Geoffrey saw them, were they hanging on the walls of Pompadour?

By the time that Geoffrey was writing, several men from the Lastours family had taken the cross. The most well-known by far was Gouffier I, the lord of Lastours, Hautefort, and Terrason, who, as we saw in chap. 1, had achieved widespread renown for his bravery in 1098 at the siege of Ma'arrat an-Nu'man. There it was said he had been first to climb up the ladders placed against the walls of the city, fighting against innumerable opponents even after he had lost his own helmet and shield.[6] His name was repeated by every crusade chronicler writing in the French-speaking lands, and until the early modern period he was arguably the most famous crusader from the regions south of the Loire.[7] Gouffier survived his crusade experience to return in glory and lived until about 1126, but his relatives were not as fortunate. His brother Guy II was said to have died "at Jerusalem," while his nephew Guy III and probably also his nephew's son, who was also named Guy, died on the Second Crusade.[8] Gouffier's youngest son, Olivier, must have been a relatively

---

5. Geoffrey's faith in Saint Pardoux may have been misplaced. His chronicle ends abruptly only a few months after the incident, suggesting that the wound he received may not, in fact, have healed. See Botineau's introduction to GV: "Geoffroi de Breuil, prieur de Vigeois: *Chronique* (première partie)," ed. Pierre Botineau (Thesis, École des Chartes, 1968), xxiiii–xxiv. Botineau dates the work to between Easter 1183 and Lent 1184.

6. The story of course differs slightly between the chroniclers. The only French chronicler failing to mention Gouffier was Fulcher of Chartres, who participated in the expedition but accompanied Baldwin of Boulogne to Edessa and so was absent from the main crusader army at the siege of Ma'arrat. For a complete list, see Jonathan Riley-Smith, *The First Crusaders, 1095–113* (Cambridge, 1997), 209.

7. Claude Bernard, "Un chevalier Limousin: Goufier de Lastours," *Bulletin de la Société Archéologique et Historique du Limousin* 86 (1955): 23–33.

8. GV, 9–10. Geoffrey used nearly the same construction, "obiit...Ludovicus rex perrexit," for both Guy II's son and his nephew but differentiates between the two by saying that his nephew died at Jerusalem and that he was "with Louis" and that his son died "when" the king marched to Jerusalem.

old man when he took the cross in 1178, dying in the East in 1180. Since, by Geoffrey's account, only one member of the Lastours family had returned alive from Jerusalem, it is likely that the prince whose *pallia* were on display in 1183 was the crusader Gouffier I. At the time of Geoffrey's evacuation to Pompadour, Gouffier had been dead for nearly sixty years, but among his descendants his memory was preserved not only in the fabric hanging within the tower but in the very fabric of the tower itself, which bore his name.[9]

We can be relatively sure that the *pallia* belonged to the crusader Gouffier, but what were they? Like so many of the precious objects mentioned in textual sources of the central Middle Ages, the textiles that were on display in the tower at Pompadour do not survive. They cannot be examined by art historians, and their provenance, craftsmanship, and precise relationship to other objects must remain unknown. It is unclear what type of material, precisely, was being designated by Geoffrey's Latin term *pallia,* a word that in the twelfth century could connote banners, vestments, tapestries, or some other kind of drapery.[10] Precious cloth in general, and silk in particular, was easy to carry, and would have made useful currency.[11] Silk was the language of diplomacy in the eastern Mediterranean, especially in Byzantium, and for centuries western travelers of high status were rewarded with gifts of silk.[12] Silk cloth was also used to make bags like the ones that relic collections were carried in.[13] After their return from crusading expeditions in the later twelfth century, Henry the Lion, William Marshal, and William de Mandeville would make presents to their friends and relatives of lengths of silk obtained in the East.[14]

---

9. The date of Gouffier's death cannot be established with certainty, but he was certainly active as late as 1120, when his name appears in a charter for the abbey of Dalon. See Louis Grillon, "Cartulaire de Notre-Dame de Dalon" (Master's thesis, University of Bordeaux, 1962), 22, acts nos. 52–53.

10. Charles du Fresne sieur Du Cange et al., *Glossarium mediae et infimae latinitatis* (Niort, 1883–87), 6: 113–119. For some attempts to match the Latin terminology of textiles with surviving, often fragmentary, evidence, see Mildred Budny, "The Byrhtnoth Tapestry or Embroidery," in *The Battle of Maldon, AD 991,* ed. Donald Scragg (Oxford, 1991), 263–278. My thanks to Mildred Budny for discussing textile terminology with me.

11. For cloth as a way of paying knights on an expedition, see Alan Murray, "Money and Logistics in the Forces of the First Crusade: Coinage, Bullion, Service, and Supply, 1096–99," in *Logistics of Warfare in the Age of the Crusades,* ed. John H. Pryor (Aldershot, UK, 2006), 213.

12. Anna Muthesius, "Silken Diplomacy," in *Byzantine Diplomacy,* ed. Jonathan Shephard and Simon Franklin (Aldershot, UK, 1992), 237–248.

13. E. Jane Burns, "Saracen Silk and the Virgin's Chemise: Cultural Crossings in Cloth," *Speculum* 81 (2006): 365–397, at 378. My thanks to Julia Smith for pointing this out.

14. *The Book of the Foundation of Walden Monastery,* ed. and trans. Diana Greenway and Leslie Watkiss (Oxford, 1999), 48–8; *History of William Marshal,* ed. A. J. Holden with English translation by S. Gregory and historical notes by David Crouch (London, 2002), 2:l. 18185 (although note that William took the silk back from his cousin Stephen of Evreux as he lay dying); Arnold of Lübeck, *Chronica Slavorum,* ed. J. M. Lappenberg, *MGH SS* 21: 125.

Given that the Lastours *pallia* were associated with a participant in the First Crusade, and noting Geoffrey's especially appreciative comments, we might be tempted to compare them with two extant textiles that probably returned from the East after the conquest of Jerusalem in 1099. By the end of the twelfth century, both the nearby abbey of Cadouin in Périgord and the more distant cathedral of Apt in Provence treasured what are now recognized as *tiraz* embroideries of linen, silk, and cloth of gold, which, according to inscriptions stitched into their borders, were produced in Fatimid Egypt for the vizier al-Afdal (d. 1121) and in the reign of the caliph Musta'ali (d. 1101).[15] These inscriptions are a key piece of evidence, not only of the provenance of these two textiles but also of the likely context for their movement from Egypt to France. Chroniclers of the First Crusade described with delight how, on 12 August 1099, the crusaders won a great victory over al-Afdal on the plains before Ascalon, taking the vizier's camp, including his tents and "all the goods, all the animals, and all the weapons."[16] The embroideries may well have been captured during this engagement or at the subsequent battles of Ramla (1101) and Jaffa (1103), or they may have been given as gifts to the crusaders at Antioch in 1097, when Fatimid ambassadors tried to form an alliance with the crusaders against the Seljuk Turks.[17]

Whether the Pompadour *pallia* were another in this series of Egyptian textiles brought to southwestern Francia from the East, a Byzantine silk, a personal standard, or something unrelated to the crusade that had earned its eastern associations at a later date is impossible to say.[18] But the comparison between the object that Geoffrey saw at Pompadour and the surviving silks from Apt and Cadouin reveals something fundamental about their nature. The latter two objects were almost certainly acquired in the context of the First Crusade, and by the thirteenth century the Cadouin fabric was said to have been dispatched from the East by the crusade leader Adhémar of Montheil, but both had also been the subject of radical transformation from luxury textiles into devotional objects.[19] The monks of Cadouin claimed their *tiraz*

---

15. Brigitte Delluc and Gilles Delluc, "Le suaire de Cadouin et son frère le voile de sainte Anne d'Apt (Vaucluse): Deux pièces exceptionelles d'archéologie textile," *Bulletin de la Société Historique et Archéologique du Périgord* 128 (2001): 607–626.

16. "Reversi sunt nostri ad illorum tentoria acceperunt que innumera spolia auri et argenti, omniumque bonorum ac omnium animalium genera, omniumque armorum instrumenta, quae voluerunt asportaverunt; reliqua igne consumpserunt." *Gesta Francorum et aliorum Hierosolymitanorum,* ed. and trans. Rosalind Hill (New York and London, 1962), 96 (my translation).

17. On the embassy, see Thomas Asbridge, *The First Crusade: A New History* (London, 2004), 186–187.

18. The fact that Gouffier knew the abbot of Cadouin and transacted business with him later in his life does raise the intriguing possibility that the Cadouin shroud and the Lastours *pallia* were in some way related—perhaps part of the same treasure? See "Préface," *RHC* 5: lxxxiiii.

19. For Adhémar and the Cadouin shroud, see below, 111–112.

was the shroud of Christ; the one at Apt was said to be the veil of Saint Anne. Whatever original value they had held for the westerners who found or plundered them, they could have value for the religious of Cadouin and Apt only as referents of well-known and established sacred cults. By contrast, whatever they had originally been, and however they may have been identified by the communities that traditionally held them, the textiles that Geoffrey saw on the wall of the chief fortress of the Lastours family in 1183 evoked for him only the journey to Jerusalem undertaken by the family's famous crusading ancestor nearly ninety years earlier. The value of the Lastours *pallia* lay in their special significance as commemorative objects, memorabilia of the crusade, similar to the "souvenir" of Susan Stewart's *On Longing,* which

> always displays the romance of contraband, for its scandal is its removal from its "natural" location. Yet it is only by means of its material relation to that location that it acquires value.[20]

In safeguarding and exhibiting the objects linked with a crusading ancestor, the lords of Lastours were hardly unique. References to this kind of memorabilia are rare, but scattered among the narratives and ceremonial and documentary texts of the West it is possible to identify a wide variety of objects associated with crusaders and preserved in familial and ceremonial contexts. These included sacred relics and sacramental and liturgical items; weapons and armor; jewelry and exotic animals. To collect and compare examples of these objects is to reconstruct the material framework undergirding much of the commemorative discourse surrounding the early crusades. This reconstruction, in turn, reveals more about how memory and material culture were related for the medieval nobility. More precisely, it reveals the degree to which crusaders and their relatives sought out the solid substance to which memory could be effectively affixed, and how by deliberate arrangement, exchange, disruption, and appropriation of this fabric, they hoped to alter or access the discourse of ancestry and tradition.[21] Key to understanding these processes are the nature of the material possessions that crusaders brought back with them from the East, the contexts and locations in which these materials were kept, and the rites and ceremonies that surrounded their use. Before we address the types of materials that western historical sources associated with the memories of early crusaders, it is useful to consider the commemorative power attributed to certain kinds of precious objects.

20. Susan Stewart, *On Longing: Narratives of the Miniature, the Gigantic, the Souvenir, the Collection* (Durham, NC, 1993), 135.

21. For the creation of monuments to alter "prospective memory," see Jan Assman, *Das kulturelle Gedächtnis: Schrift, Erinnerung und politische Identität in frühen Hochkulturen* (Munich, 1992), 169.

The Power and Meaning of Commemorative Material

In the world of the medieval nobility, physical matter in all its forms—terrestrial, architectural, artistic, and organic—acted as vessel and conduit for the preservation and transmission of knowledge about the family past. Territories, inasmuch as they were landscapes of lordship, were also necessarily landscapes of memory, and, like the architectural expressions of power such as the "tower of Gouffier" at Pompadour, they were closely linked to the names of those by whose right they were traditionally ruled.[22] As we will see in the next chapter, the bodies of the noble dead were often fundamental to the commemoration of ancestry, and by the early thirteenth century new and increasingly elaborate markers began to be constructed over the sites where they lay entombed. Some of these—which have been termed "tombs of kinship"—demonstrated in their design the ties of kinship between the dead, their relatives, and their ancestors.[23]

The ties of memory that bound the living to their dead and distant relatives, however, also depended on more intimate personal possessions—commemorative objects or *memorialia* (souvenirs, memorabilia) that carried with them the memories of their previous owners or bearers. The existence of this material culture of memory among the aristocracy has been demonstrated by Elisabeth van Houts, who pointed to dozens of examples of precious objects, in particular jewelry and textiles, that serve as "pegs" to fix or arrange the memory of loved ones and family members.[24] In their function and significance, these objects match the description given by anthropologists of *immeuble* or "inalienable wealth," which resists detachment from some original context, has the power to confer or affirm identity, and "acts as a vehicle for bringing past time into the present, so that the histories of ancestors, titles, or mythological events become an intimate part of who one is in the present."[25] Although *immeuble* in the sense that they remained attached to some original remembered context, the types of objects that functioned as memorabilia for crusaders and their families were personal, highly portable objects. Because they could travel over great distances, from Syria and Palestine to a family

---

22. This point is made particularly well in Frederic Cheyette, *Ermengard of Narbonne and the World of the Troubadours* (Ithaca, NY, 2001), 129–148. The role of the seigneurial landscape as commemorative was explored by Maurice Halbwachs, *Les cadres sociaux de la mémoire* (Paris, 1925; repr., 1952), 163.

23. Anne McGee Morganstern, *Gothic Tombs of Kinship in France, the Low Countries, and England* (University Park, PA, 2000).

24. Elisabeth van Houts, *Memory and Gender in Medieval Europe: 900–1200* (Basingstoke, UK, 1999), 101–106.

25. Annette B. Weiner, "Inalienable Wealth," *American Ethnologist* 12:2 (1985): 210–227, at 210. See also Weiner's *Inalienable Possessions: The Paradox of Keeping-While-Giving* (Berkeley, 1992): 36–40; and the foundational work of Marcel Mauss, "Essai sur le don: Forme et raison de l'échange dans les sociétés archaïques," *L'année sociologique* 1 (1923–24): 49, 133, and 165.

residence in the West and (in a few cases) back again, they were particularly important transmitters of memories associated with crusaders.

For the nobility of the twelfth and thirteenth centuries, commemorative objects acted as both a symbol of a person's ancestral identity and a reminder of the responsibilities of kinship and lineage. In the *Chevalier au Cygne,* one of the branches of the Old French epic cycle dedicated to the ancestry of the crusader Godfrey of Bouillon, Godfrey's grandmother Beatrix is shocked to hear that her husband and the father of her infant daughter, Ida, the mysterious Swan Knight, must leave her forever or die. As her husband prepares to leave, she appeals to him: "Lord, but leave me some souvenir (*conniscance*), either a shield or a sword or your horn, in remainder. I will keep it in remembrance of you."[26] The Swan Knight gives Beatrix his ivory horn, an object he had himself inherited from his mother, but specifies that the object is not ultimately meant for her but for her daughter Ida.[27] Beatrix later forgets the horn, keeping it locked in a high tower, undifferentiated from many other horns that she owns. The tower catches fire, a dire warning about the consequences of forgetting to pass along memory and traditions.[28] The horn is rescued from the flames by a white bird, reminding Beatrix of the Swan Knight and her obligation to safeguard the object intended for her daughter.

Subsequent episodes of the crusade cycle contrast this failure of memory and the transmission of commemorative objects with the successful communication of such items. In the *Fin d'Elias,* the poem linking the Swan Knight's story with that of his grandson Godfrey, Ida, Beatrix's daughter, discovers her elderly father close to his death at the abbey of Sainteron where he had become a monk. After their reunion he passes to her a series of objects, including the treasure amassed by his grandmother Matabrune, his armor, his shield with a cross, his hauberk, his sword, and a new, golden horn. These are intended for Beatrix's son Godfrey, the future crusade leader and first ruler of the Latin Kingdom of Jerusalem.[29] True to her saintly reputation and the care with which she has raised her sons, Ida does not forget her father's instructions, and in still another episode of the cycle, the *Chanson d'Antioche,* she is shown passing her father's weapons and his horn on to Godfrey on the eve of his departure for the crusade, saying: "Beloved son, carry these and you will be the great master of the kingdom of Outremer."[30]

---

26. "Sire, car me laisiés aucune conniscance- / U escu u espee u vocor- en balance. / Porvos le garderai, s'en avrai ramembrance." *Le Chevalier au cygne,* 108–109, ll. 4251–4260.

27. How the horn was passed to the Swan Knight from his mother is described in the "Beatrix" version of the *Naissance du Chévalier au Cygne,* 188, l. 2597.

28. *Le Chevalier au cygne,* 114–116, ll. 4444–4543.

29. *La Fin d'Elias,* 415, ll. 2297–2303.

30. *La Chanson d'Antioche,* 80, ll. 1135–1137.

The commemorative objects in the Old French crusade cycle are, at one level, a literary conceit, binding together the branches of the cycle and fore-shadowing the greatness of the family. In the images illustrating the thirteenth-century manuscript that is thought to preserve the earliest version of the cycle, a horn features prominently. It is pictured being carried by the Swan Knight's father, Lothair, hanging over Lothair and his wife as they lie in a lovers' embrace, and rescued from the burning tower by the white bird.[31] But the horn and arms passed from father to mother to son also highlight the importance of ancestral objects to an individual's identity, actions, and membership in a lineage. The horn is described in detail, suggesting that its unique appearance was an important element of its function as memorabilia, and this is underscored by the use of the word *conniscance,* used elsewhere in the crusade cycle for an armorial bearing.[32] When commemorative objects are not treated with proper respect, the great destiny of the dynasty itself is endangered. Only when one is in the possession of the correct markers of ancestry is victory assured.

The passing along of certain types of precious objects, symbols of power, and reminders of ancestry from generation to generation was not only a convention of the idealized world of the epics. For practical as well as ceremonial reasons, weapons, armor, and other items like those passed to Godfrey of Bouillon in the *Chanson d'Antioche* were preserved and inherited by young noblemen when they came of age. In the manuscript that he prepared for his children in 1166 before his departure for an expedition from which, like the Swan Knight in the *Chevalier au Cygne,* he feared that he would never return, Count Siboto IV of Falkenstein included a list of precious objects, including armor, weapons, silverware, and gaming tables, preserved at his castle at Neuburg. Among them were certain silver vessels that he forcefully stipulated "should never in any way be sold."[33] There is no reason to doubt that memorabilia, as emotive reminders of events in the past, could spur those that saw and possessed them into action. As Lambert of Ardres reminded his readers, mementos of family members killed in feuds were used to incite their relatives to revenge.[34]

The Things They Carried

At the time of the First Crusade, the European nobility already participated in a culture of resonant material possessions. Those who took part in the

---

31. The images are in BNF, MS Fr. 12558, Endleaf IV-5a, Endleaf IV-5b. See *Naissance du Chévalier au Cygne,* xxiv-v.

32. "sa conniscance fud'une qeue d'ermin." *Le Chevalier au cygne,* 88, l. 3454.

33. *Codex Falkensteinensis: Die Rechtsaufzeichnungen der Graven von Falkenstein,* ed. Elizabeth Noichl (Munich, 1978), 67, no. 104.

34. LA, 572.

early expeditions (as Godfrey of Bouillon was depicted doing in the *Chanson d'Antioche*) carried many different personal items with them, from weapons and armor to liveries, banners, and other fine materials, which served as markers and reminders of their lineage and identity. In the course of their crusading experiences, however, the meaning of this material changed, both in the eyes of the crusaders themselves and also for their families, who would henceforth associate it with the memory of the crusade. But these initial possessions were also supplemented by a wide range of new stuff that the crusaders acquired along their journeys. Pilgrims to Jerusalem had for centuries before 1099 sought souvenirs of the sites they had visited in the Holy Land, but for the crusaders the gathering of memorabilia, occurring in the context of military conquest, was fundamentally different.[35] What they selected, and how these objects were treated when they returned to the West, reveal the deep significance of the memory of crusading for the western nobility.

Relics

As Jonathan Riley-Smith observed, participants in early crusade expeditions who survived to return to their homelands were nearly always poorer in land and in coin than they had been when they set out, but they could come home fantastically rich in another kind of commodity: sacred relics.[36] Because the relics that were carried or sent home from the East by crusaders were often given as gifts to religious houses, references to their provenance and to the circumstances of their arrival appear in polyptychs, charter documents, chronicles, and, less frequently, in full *translatio* narratives. Once in the hands of these religious communities, preserved in their precious containers, relics were the objects of veneration over the course of generations, often surviving until the early modern period. Consequently, sacred relics are the items most often associated with crusaders, and they have elicited the most attention from modern commentators.

Given the great value attached to them by medieval Christians and modern historians of the Middle Ages, the pride of place awarded to relics among other material carried home by crusaders is probably not unwarranted. But although the devotional significance of these sacred objects, undeniably the sites of dialogue between eastern and western Christianities and potent reminders of Christ's humanity, is no doubt of great historical importance more generally, the exploitation of relics as instruments of memorialization

---

35. Even earlier evidence survives for the collection of purpose-made souvenirs. See André Grabar, *Ampoules de Terre Sainte* (Paris, 1958).

36. Jonathan Riley-Smith, *The First Crusade and the Idea of Crusading* (London, 1986), 122–123.

by the crusaders who obtained them and by their relatives and descendants suggests that we should treat them as only one type, albeit a particularly powerful and well-documented type, of crusade memorabilia. Before proceeding to demonstrate how a collection of crusade relics functioned in this way for one seigneurial family, however, a few things should be noted about the special significance of relics from the Holy Land to the medieval aristocracy.

The collection of relics from the East was a behavior that the early crusaders inherited directly from earlier eleventh-century pilgrims, whose retrieval of relics of the Passion, the life of Christ, the apostles, and exotic eastern saints is also thought to have helped fuel the growing obsession among the eleventh-century arms-bearing classes with the Holy Sepulchre, Jerusalem, and the Christian East more generally.[37] That relics sent from the East could direct the thoughts and concerns of western communities toward Jerusalem was well understood by those who sought to harness this devotional enthusiasm in order to recruit crusaders or to redirect crusading energies toward new targets or theaters of war. When he departed for southern Francia to begin preaching the First Crusade, Pope Urban II may have brought with him a small part of the large collection of eastern relics kept at the Lateran, reputedly sent to Rome by Constantine and Helena.[38] Ilger Bigod, a knight in the service of Bohemond of Antioch, produced a most exotic type of sacred item, hairs of the Virgin, to illustrate his stories of the adventures he had shared with Bohemond on the First Crusade and to encourage others to join in a new campaign in 1107.[39] A document probably written in the early twelfth century in support of an attack on the Byzantine empire included a lengthy list of Passion relics found in the city, relics that would ultimately, during the Fourth Crusade, be the object of looting by western crusaders.[40] Leaders of Christian military campaigns in Spain in the first decades of the twelfth century deliberately associated themselves, their projects, and their crusading institutions with the Holy Sepulchre in Jerusalem and the relics of the Passion.[41] In the second half of the twelfth

---

37. Riley-Smith, *The First Crusaders,* 31–32; Colin Morris, *The Sepulchre of Christ and the Medieval West: From the Beginning to 1600* (Oxford, 2005), 146–153.

38. H. E. J. Cowdrey, "Pope Urban II and the Idea of Crusade," *Studi medievali* 36 (1995): 737–739.

39. Eadmer, *Historia novorum in Anglie,* ed. Martin Rule, RS 81 (London, 1884), 179–80; OV 5:170–171.

40. The only attempt to catalogue the movement of relics in the wake of the Fourth Crusade is Paul Riant, *Exuviae sacrae Constantinopolitanae,* 2 vols. (Geneva, 1877–78; repr., Paris, 2004). For discussion of the plunder, see Thomas Madden and Donald Queller, *The Fourth Crusade* 2nd ed. (Philadelphia, 1997), 192–204; for Venetian relic theft, see David Perry, "Paul the Martyr and Venetian Memories of the Fourth Crusade," in *Remembering the Crusades: Myth, Image, and Identity,* ed. Nicholas Paul and Suzanne Yeager (Baltimore, 2012), 215–232.

41. William Purkis, *Crusading Spirituality in the Holy Land and Iberia, c. 1095–c. 1187* (Woodbridge, UK, and Rochester, NY, 2008), 70–71, 135–136.

century, senior royal and ecclesiastical officials in the Holy Land actively used the transmission of relics, particularly fragments of the True Cross, to help galvanize enthusiasm for a new crusade in defense of the Holy Land.[42]

Although there is evidence of a surge of interest in certain eastern saints, especially Nicholas of Myra, at some sites in the West earlier in the eleventh century, the route of the First Crusade through the Byzantine empire and the heartlands of other eastern Christian traditions seems to have inspired a particular fascination among western knights with the cults of eastern military saints, among them George, Demetrios, Mercurios, Sergios, and Bacchos, and the Theban Legion.[43] Accounts of the First Crusade demonstrate the conviction that these saints had appeared to assist the crusade army during the most difficult moments of the expedition, helping the Franks to turn the tide of battle against the Turks at Antioch.[44] The appeal of exotic military saints to the western knighthood requires little explanation, but we might wonder what it meant for so many knights to have been able to obtain and return with relics of these alien holy men, together with powerful relics of the passion of the apostles, into the old devotional landscape of their homelands. There, in the eleventh century, local holy men and martyrs might be venerated and entreated by the laity and, in a few cases, defended by laymen who acted as "advocates" for the saint's shrine, or, with the assent of the religious who guarded them, carried into battle. But for many members of the military aristocracy, especially the castellans and knights who were often in dispute with monks over possessions and customs, the local saints were just as often the fearsome allies with whose help monks threatened and punished the lay lords who opposed them.[45] The crusaders who returned from the East came back having walked in the footsteps of Christ, military saints fighting at their side, and they came back with the "proof" (the literal meaning of *pignora,* the term most commonly used to denote relics) to show for it.

---

42. Jonathan Riley-Smith, "Peace Never Established: The Case of the Latin Kingdom of Jerusalem," *Transactions of the Royal Historical Society,* 5th series, 28 (1978): 89–93; Morris, *The Sepulchre of Christ,* 223–245; Sylvia Schein, *Gateway to the Heavenly City: Crusader Jerusalem and the Catholic West (1099–1187)* (Aldershot, UK, 2005), 84–90.

43. Elizabeth Lapina, "Demetrius of Thessaloniki: Patron Saint of Crusaders," *Viator* 40:2 (2009): 93–112; the same author takes up the topic of the representation of eastern military saints in mural paintings in "The Mural Paintings at Berzé-la-ville in the Context of the First Crusade and the Reconquista," *Journal of Medieval History* 31:4 (2005): 309–326.

44. Lapina, "Demetrius of Thessaloniki," 93–94.

45. Patrick Geary, *Living with the Dead in the Middle Ages* (Ithaca, NY, 1994), 96–115. Of the use of humiliation and clamor by monks to combat their enemies, Geary writes: "These latter two measures were grounded in the physical control that the religious had over the most important sacral objects in the Christian tradition: the body of Christ and the Eucharist and the bodies of the saints" (96). For cases of princes seeking out relics to bring with them into battle, see Geoffrey Koziol, *Begging Pardon and Favor: Ritual and Political Order in Early Medieval France* (Ithaca, NY, 1992), 92.

The role that relics acquired in the Holy Land by crusaders could play in the collective memory of their descendants is most clearly illustrated by the chronicle of Lambert of Ardres. In the narrative of the Ardres family history that, according to Lambert, was performed by a member of the household of Arnold II of Guines and V of Ardres (d. 1220), a list of the relics brought back from Jerusalem and Antioch by Arnold's ancestor Arnold II of Ardres at the time of the First Crusade was used both to illustrate and to validate the deeds that Arnold had done in the East:

> When Antioch was conquered and Jerusalem, ruled by Godfrey, was liberated from the hands of the Turks with the help of the venerable lord of Le Puiset and his kindred, Arnold, having acquitted his vow, returned happily and prosperously and brought back the only thing he wanted to his church at Ardres. He carried back, indeed, a holy sign of the victory (*sacri insigne trophei*) from Jerusalem, a most precious reliquary covered over with gold and precious stones. [It contained] some of the Lord's beard, some of the Lord's cross, and some of the stone from which the Lord ascended to heaven. But from Antioch he brought a piece of the Holy Lance and relics of St. George the Martyr and many other relics of other saints. It ought to be known, moreover, that in this fight of the Antiochenes, Arnold the Old was counted as the best of the best among many nobles from many nations and peoples, for the strength of his spirit no less than for the knightly worth of his distinguished body.[46]

The integration of the sacred objects and their container, literally here a "trophy" of the victory won at Jerusalem, and the separate enumeration of items from Antioch, where Arnold's deeds were a point of special pride for the

---

46. "cum debellata fuisset a christianis Antiochia et Ierosolima, regnante Godefrido, de minibus Turcorum liberata, venerabili domino et consanguineo suo de Puteolo vel Podio sive Puio opitulante, quod solum optavit, feliciter et prospero cursu rediens et voti compos, in ecclesia sua apud Ardeam reportavit. Attulit enim sacri insigne trophei de terra Ierosolimorum, super aurum et lapidem preciosum preciosissimum sanctuarium scilicet de barba Domini, de lingo Domini, de petra super quam Dominus ascendit ad celum. De Antiochia vero attulit de lancea Domini et reliquias sancti Georgii martiris et multas alias aliorum sanctorum reliquias. Sciendum est autem, quod in hac Antiochenorum expugnatione hic Arnoldis Senex inter multos multarum nationum et gentium proceres animi virtute non minus quam prestantis corporis in milicia probitate cum primis annumeratus est primus." LA, 626; compare with Lambert of Ardres, *History of the Counts of Guines and Lords of Ardres,* trans. Leah Shopkow (Philadelphia, 2001), 164. The helpful lord *de Puteolo vel Podio sive Puio* was assumed by Heller and Shopkow to be Adhémar of Le Puy. But all three constructions more faithfully match an attempt to render the name Le Puiset, a large family many of whose members were central actors in the expedition. Lambert's use of "expugnatione ... Antiochenorum" is strongly suggestive of the contemporary evocation of the *Chanson d'Antioche* and is reminiscent of the "gesta Antiochenorum" in the poem on the siege of Acre in 1191 by Aimery Monachus, the archbishop of Caesarea. See Roger of Howden, *Chronicon,* ed. William Stubbs, RS 51 (London, 1870), 3: cv–cxxxvi.

family, are strongly suggestive of the place of such objects in the architecture of a family's identity and social status. The relics and their associated narrative were part of what elevated the descendants of Arnold II into an elite group of families who could count crusaders among their ancestors and who went to some lengths to advertise this fact. Thus while in so many of our sources the relics that returned with crusaders are only tersely said to have come "from Jerusalem," the Ardres narrative shows how from the point of view of noble families these same objects could play a potentially critical role in the transmission and illustration of the dynastic crusading past.

Other Trophies

Because of their symbolic resonance with the sacred geography of the Holy Land and their evocation of central elements in the mythic narrative of the First Crusade, the relics that returned with crusaders from the East were particularly useful instruments for the preservation and performance of crusading memory. They were not, however, the only type of crusade memorabilia. Although references in our sources to other types of crusade memorabilia are far less common than references to relics, documents written over the course of the twelfth century reveal a surprising array of treasures said to have been brought from the East by crusaders. When we catch sight of them, glimpsed by chroniclers or given as gifts to religious foundations, they almost always seem to have been treated as important dynastic, or at least familial, possessions.

The *Miracles* of Thomas Becket, witnessed and recorded by William of Canterbury at the shrine of the martyred archbishop between 1172 and c. 1179, describe the visit to Canterbury of two "Englishmen, who were great and well known to us."[47] The first of the nobles, Ralph, presented to Saint Thomas a precious stone, described as topaz, in thanks for the saint's help in curing him of an illness.[48] The provenance of such an exotic item was

---

47. "Miracula gloriosi martyris Thomae, Cantuarensis archiepiscopi," in *Materials for The History of Thomas Becket,* ed. James Craigie Robertson and J. B. Sheppard, RS 67 (London, 1875), 1: 482–483. For commentary on William's miracle collection, see Marcus Bull, "Criticism of Henry II's Expedition to Ireland in William of Canterbury's *Miracles of St. Thomas Becket,*" *Journal of Medieval History* 33:2 (2007): 107–129; and Michael Staunton, *Thomas Becket and His Biographers* (Woodbridge, UK, 2006), 51–52.

48. Topaz was a popular precious gem in the central Middle Ages, signifying to Marbod of Rennes "ardent contemplation." Marbod of Rennes (1055–1123), *De lapidibus: Considered as a Medical Treatise with Text, Commentary, and C. W. King's Translation, Together with Text and Translation of Marbode's Minor Works on Stones,* ed. John M. Riddle (Wiesbaden, 1977), 121. Yet there is still a temptation to associate this stone with the reliquary of Robert of Normandy's comrade Pagan Peverel, on which, see below, 121.

of some interest, if not to the saint, then certainly to the inquisitive William, who recorded Ralph's surprisingly detailed explanation:

> The history of this item should not be hidden from you. This stone was brought back by Robert of Normandy from Jerusalem. Dying, he left it to his heirs (*successoribus*), from whom it has come down to me [i.e., Ralph]. From me, however, the martyr wishes to transfer ownership to himself. I am indeed so greatly pleased, as one is because of human weakness, to have regained my health; I am no less pleased by the succession of such an heir.[49]

The wording of this miracle is striking in its insistence that an object brought back from the East should properly be passed down by family inheritance. Ralph felt comfortable presenting the relic to the shrine at Canterbury because Saint Thomas was a worthy heir to his ancestor's crusading legacy.

Items that, like Ralph's topaz, were obviously of an eastern provenance, were recognized to have a special value as memorabilia. So it was that when Alexander I of Scotland (r. 1107–24) wished to firmly anchor the memory of his reconciliation with the canons of St. Andrews cathedral priory, restoring to them lands that had earlier been taken from them, he ceremoniously presented to them an extraordinary collection of objects that is generally, and quite reasonably, supposed to have been acquired by a crusader.[50] According to a narrative apparently written by the prior, Robert, in the 1140s, the king made a special provision:

> As a monument of this gift, the king ordered that a splendid Arab horse, covered with a large and precious cloth, together with its own saddle and bridle and silver lance, should be led to the altar. And [in honor] of the aforesaid gift of liberties from all royal customs he also gave Turkish arms of a different style to decorate the church, which, with his own shield and saddle, are conserved until this day in the church of Saint Andrew in memory of his royal munificence. Because they are shown to people coming from so many places they are not in any way forgotten; hence it [i.e., Alexander's gift] is very often called to memory.[51]

---

49. "Lapidem hunc ne te lateat rei series, comes Neustrie Robertus Jerosolymis allatum successoribus suis moriens reliquit, a quibus ad me devolutus est. A me tandem voluit ad se martyr transferre dominion. Gratulor quidem multum, sicut est humanae fragilitatis, super hac collatione sanitatis, nec minus sucessione talis heredis." "Miracula gloriosi martyris Thomae," 482–483.

50. See A. A. M. Duncan, "The Foundation of St. Andrews Cathedral Priory," *Scottish Historical Review* 84 (2005): 1–37. Duncan suggests that the gift may have been made in 1124 *in extremis*. My thanks to Bill Aird for drawing my attention to this article.

51. "Ob cujus etiam donationis monumentum regium equum Arabicum cum proprio freno et sella et scuto et lancea argentea opertum pallio grandi et pretioso praecepit Rex usque ad altare adduci

Where did Alexander, who is not known to have been a crusader himself, obtain such exotic finery? Why was the source of the material, which would presumably have been of as much interest in St. Andrews as the story of the topaz had been to William of Canterbury, not mentioned? Previous commentaries on this passage have suggested that the Turkish arms must have returned with the Anglo-Norman realm's most famous crusader, the Duke of Normandy Robert Curthose. Since Curthose had, as far as we know, no contact (and certainly no friendly contact) with Alexander after his return from the East, the assumption is that the souvenirs of the crusade were taken when Robert was captured by his brother Henry I after the battle of Tinchebray in 1106. They would then presumably have been presented to the king of the Scots as a diplomatic gift some time later.[52]

A rather more plausible explanation for the presence of an Arab steed in Fife, however, is suggested by the close ties between the Scottish royal family and the comital family of Huntingdon.[53] The Earl of Huntingdon, Simon I of Senlis, was an enthusiastic crusader, who in fact died in the course of his second voyage to the Holy Land in 1111. A short dynastic narrative written by the monks of Crowland chronicling the successors to the saintly Earl Waltheof (d. 1076), whose body lay at the abbey, recorded that Simon had returned from his first crusade expedition (presumably the First Crusade, of 1095–99) in "favorable" or "prosperous" achievement (*prospero successu*).[54] Simon had succeeded Waltheof in the earldoms of Huntingdon and Northampton, after the execution of Waltheof for treason by William the Conqueror, by marrying Waltheof's daughter Mathilda. After Simon's death on his return journey to the Holy Land in 1111, Mathilda married David, Alexander of Scotland's youngest son, who succeeded him as king in 1124.[55] In the years between David's marriage and his succession, he

---

et de predictis donis libertatibus et consuetudinibus omnibus regalibus ecclesiam investiri arma quoque Turchensia diversi generis dedit quae cum ipsius scuto et sella in memoriam regiae munificentiae usque hodie in ecclesia Sancti Andreae conserventur quae undecunque advenientibus populis ostenduntur ne oblivione ullatenus delentur quod tam crebro ad memoriam revocatur." *Chronicles of the Picts, Chronicles of the Scots, and Other Early Memorials of Scottish History,* ed. William Forbes Skene (Edinburgh, 1867), 190. I have followed Duncan's rendering of *diversi generis*.

52. Duncan, "The Foundation of St. Andrews," 7 n. 27; William M. Aird, *Robert Curthose: Duke of Normandy, c. 1050–1134* (Woodbridge, UK, 2008), 199 n. 59.

53. For what follows, see Matthew Strickland, "Senlis, Simon (I) de, Earl of Northampton and Earl of Huntingdon (d. 1111x13)," in *Oxford Dictionary of National Biography,* online ed., ed. Lawrence Goldman, Oxford: OUP, [doi:10.1093/ref:odnb/25091]and Keith Stringer, "Senlis, Simon (II) de, earl of Northampton and earl of Huntingdon (d. 1153)," in *Oxford Dictionary of National Biography* (Oxford, 2004), doi:10.1093/ref:odnb/25092.

54. "De Judith auxore Waldevi comitis," in *Chroniques Anglo-Normandes: Recueil d'extraits et d'écrits relatifs à l'histoire de Normandie et d'Angleterre,* ed. Francisque Michel (Rouen, 1836), 2: 126.

55. Judith A. Green, *Henry I: King of England and Duke of Normandy* (Cambridge, 2006), 128–129; Green, *The Aristocracy of Norman England* (Cambridge, 1997), 122, 269, 294.

ruled as Simon's successor in Huntingdon and Northampton, suppressing the inheritance of Simon's eldest son, Simon II, in favor of his own first son with Mathilda, whom he named Henry after his friend the king of England. The St. Andrews memorial was thus most likely a collection that had passed into the possession of the royal family of Scotland through David's marriage to a crusader's widow. Even though it was technically family property, the political situation within the family meant that its presentation to the priory was as much about the erasure of the memory of the crusader Simon of Senlis as it was about the preservation of the memory of Alexander I.

Another case of the appropriation (or perhaps theft) of memorabilia brought back by a crusader by those who were not his kin is suggestive of the significance of such mnemonically charged objects to the broader community of nobility within a particular region. Writing of events that occurred in the Limousin in the mid-twelfth century, Geoffrey of Vigeois noted the death, in the year 1148, of the brothers Guy and Adhémar, who between them jointly held the viscountships of Limoges and Comborn.[56] Guy had taken the cross to join Louis VII on the Second Crusade. Before dying at Acre in 1148, Geoffrey wrote that he sent his brother

> a ring of the greatest value which he had taken with him to Jerusalem. Gouffier the elder had acquired that ring in the war for Jerusalem. The old viscount Adhémar [III] had skillfully solicited it from him.[57]

Here we encounter further memorabilia associated with the Limousin hero Gouffier of Lastours, the same crusader whose *pallia* we have seen displayed in the tower of Pompadour in 1183. Like the *pallia,* it is not clear whether the ring "of the greatest value" was of eastern provenance, or whether Gouffier had procured it from another crusader. The man credited with obtaining the ring for the Limoges family was Guy's maternal grandfather, Adhémar III, who died around 1139. It has been remarked that Adhémar, who must have been almost the same age as Gouffier of Lastours, demonstrated all of the behavior that would seem to predispose him to respond favorably to the preaching of the First Crusade, but there is no evidence that he took the cross.[58] Although it is not said precisely how Adhémar got hold of the ring, Geoffrey's adverbial combination of *callide* and *exigo* strongly suggests that in the economy of gift and theft that governed the majority of

---

56. Vincent Roblin, *Recueil des actes des vicomtes de Limoges* (Geneva, 2009), 31–32.

57. "Huic remisit annulum magni pretii supradictus frater Guido quem secum detuerat Hierosolymis. Annulum istum acquisivit Gouffier iste senior in bello Hierosolymitano quem veteranus vicecomes Ademarus callide ab eo exegit." GV, 111.

58. Marcus Bull, *Knightly Piety and the Lay Response to the First Crusade: The Limousin and Gascony* (Oxford, 1993), 252–253.

exchanges between nobles, the transfer probably fell into the latter category.[59] By the time Geoffrey was writing (1183), the ring was still remembered as having belonged to Gouffier, although at the time of the Second Crusade the ring was a possession of some significance for the viscounts of Limoges.

What value did the ring have for the Limoges family? Medieval rings had many potential functions, acting as amulets to ward off danger, symbols of status and office, love tokens, and markers of personal identity. As Elisabeth Antoine has shown, one band could hold multiple valences.[60] Diplomatic and literary evidence suggests that by the middle of the twelfth century powerful nobles were adopting the Roman practice of using ring intaglios as counterseals in their documents.[61] Seals were some of the most potent markers of personal identity available to the lay aristocracy, and even *without* unique intaglios, rings, sometimes bearing inscriptions, are described in vernacular literature as unmistakable signs of an individual's identity.[62] As such, when knowledge of a person's fate was unclear, rings were uniquely useful in communicating and confirming whether that person was alive or dead. Circumstances that would necessitate such communication were clearly extraordinary, as, for instance, when partisans of Count Charles of Flanders were pursued and murdered by the count's assassins in the castle of Bruges on 2 March 1127. That morning, Galbert of Bruges, who must have been taking refuge himself somewhere in the castle precincts, distinctly remembered Walter, castellan of Bourbourg, and Fromold the Younger entrusting their rings to religious on the scene for delivery to their female relatives.[63]

59. For gift and theft in the economy of relics, see Patrick Geary, "Sacred Commodities: The Circulation of Medieval Relics," in *The Social Life of Things: Commodities in Cultural Perspective,* ed. Arjun Appaduri (Cambridge, 1986), 169–191, esp. 172–174; and Geary, *Living with the Dead,* 195–212.

60. Elisabeth Antoine, "A Thirteenth-Century Signet Ring and Its Inscriptions: Between Identity and Power, Magic and Prophylaxis," in *De re metallica: The Uses of Metal in the Middle Ages,* ed. Robert Bork (Woodbridge, UK, 2005), 101–112. That rings inscribed with sacred or magical formulations were commonly used to ward off danger may explain the reference to one crusader, the knight Stephen of Neublans, solemnly invested with a ring ("the sign of salvation") at the same time that he took the cross. See *Recueil des chartes de l'abbaye de Cluny,* 5: 89, no. 3737. Stephen returned from crusade and took the cross again in 1120. See Constance Bouchard, *Sword, Miter, and Cloister: Nobility and the Church in Burgundy, 980–1198* (Ithaca, NY, 1987), 299, app. A.

61. For the use of ring intaglios as counterseals in the 1140s by the earls of Leicester and Chester, see David Crouch, *The Beaumont Twins: The Roots and Branches of Power in the Twelfth Century* (Cambridge, 1986), 210–211.

62. Alain Corbellari, "Le jeux de l'anneux: Fonctions et trajets d'un objet dans la littérature narrative médiévale," in *"De sensrassism": Essays in Honor of Rupert T. Pickens,* ed. Keith Busby, Bernard Guidot, and Logan E. Whalen (Amsterdam, 1994), 157–167, notes, citing Shishemi Sasaki, "Annel et seel: De Béroul et du Lancelot au roman de Tristan en prose," *Miscellania Mediaevalia: Mélanges offerts à Philippe Ménard,* ed. J. C. Fauchet, A. Labbé, et al. (Paris, Champion, 1998), 2: 1203–1212, that in *Tristan* the contemporary Anglo-Norman poet Béroul often rhymed *anel* (ring) with *seel* (seal).

63. Galbert of Bruges, *De multro, traditione, et occisione gloriosi Karoli comitis Flandriarum,* ed. Jeff Rider, *CCCM* 131 (Turnholt, 1994), 27, 39.

The long-distance travel and the especially vicious interconfessional warfare associated with the crusades, of course, created a setting that was yet
more turbulent and uncertain than that violent morning in Bruges. Hence
it is probably not surprising that there is abundant evidence of rings being
sent from East to West. In 1206, Henry of Flanders sent his chaplain Daniel de Scausin as a messenger from Constantinople to his brother Philip of
Namur in Flanders bearing two rings, "one of emerald and the other a ruby,"
together with three lengths of samite and a large number of relics from the
Bucoleon palace. The items arrived shortly before Henry and Philip's elder
brother Count Baldwin IX of Flanders, who had disappeared in battle a year
previously, was finally declared dead. They could have signaled either the
death of Baldwin or the passing of the county of Flanders to his daughter
Jeanne, or both.[64] The codicil added to the testament of the Earl of Stafford
as he lay dying on Rhodes on his return journey from Jerusalem in 1386 was
also largely concerned with transmitting various rings to his family, although
on this occasion the five recipients were all women.[65]

A striking visual example of a ring functioning in this way, as a message of
death from the crusading frontier, is to be found in the cycles of images created
around the shrine of Saint Elisabeth of Hungary in the church dedicated to her
in Marburg. As we will see in chapter 4, central to the narrative of Elisabeth's
saintly life was the death in 1227 of her husband, Landgrave Ludwig IV of
Thuringia, while on crusade with Emperor Frederick II. Both the reliefs encas-
ing her reliquary shrine and the stained-glass windows in the choir depict a scene
with two returning crusaders clothed in mail armor and carrying pilgrim's staves
and a bag of bones presenting Elisabeth with a ring. A passage in the *Vita* composed for Elisabeth by Dietrich of Apolda in the later thirteenth century describing Ludwig's departure on crusade makes clear the ring's intended function:

> And when, by turns necessity urged and opportunity compelled him
> to go, last of all the man of faith showed to his sorrowful wife a ring,
> which he used for his personal seal, saying: "My sister, this ring bearing
> the image of the lamb of God with a banner is evidence of my life and
> it is the proof of my death."[66]

---

64. Riant, *Exuviae*, 2: 74, no. 23, citing Aubert Le Mire [Miraeus] and Jean François Foppens,
Continens codicem donationum piarum, diplomata Belgica, donationes Belgicas et notitiam ecclesiarum Belgii
(Brussels, 1723), 174. Many of the relics named in the letter from Henry to Philip can be identified
in an inventory of the treasury of Saint-Aubin of Namur drawn up a decade later. "Inventarium
ecclesiae St. Albini Namurcensi, Ann. 1218," in *Organ für christliche Kunst*, vol. 13, ed. F. Baudri Jahrg
(Cologne, 1863): 41–44.

65. Nicholas H. Nicolas, *Testamenta vetusta: Being Illustrations from Wills of Manners, Customs, etc.
as Well as the Descents and Possessions of Many Distinguished Families, from the Reign of Henry II to the
Accession of Queen Elizabeth* (London, 1826), 1: 118–120.

66. "Cumque discedi ab invicem compelleret necessitas et urgeret opportunitas, in fine omnium
annulum, quo pro secreto sigillo utebatur, vir fidelis coniugu meste protulit dicens: 'Soror mea,

The use of finger rings as markers of personal identity may be related to the fact that rings were often equipped with the apparatus to make seal impressions.[67] But unlike seal matrices, which were customarily destroyed after the death of the individual whose identity they replicated, or more rarely buried with that individual's body, the life of rings as commemorative objects continued after the death of their owners.[68] This continuity made rings particularly important for passing on notions of hereditary power and office and dynastic identity from one generation to another. As Logan E. Whalen has noted of the use of the ring in Marie de France's lays *Fresne* and *Milun,* "For Marie the object serves to connect the past to the present, a symbol of narrative continuity."[69] The inquest of the possessions of Count Eudes of Nevers, drawn up by his executors after his death in Acre in 1266 while on crusade, presents evidence of rings in a crusading context being preserved as heirlooms.[70] Eudes had taken no fewer than thirteen rings with him on crusade. Most of these, including the eleven "rings of Le Puy," must have been simply ornamental jewelry, and the dying count gave several as gifts to his knights.[71] Two, however, were distinguished from the rest and appear to have been entrusted for transport to Hugh Augerant. The first, a ring "which the duke had given to the count," must refer to a ring given to Eudes by his father, Duke Hugh IV of Burgundy, a veteran of the crusade of 1239 who survived his son.[72] The second, the executors said, "should be for the heirs of Nevers."[73]

All of these examples suggest that the dispatch of the ring from brother to brother was likely a strategy for ensuring that Adhémar of Limoges knew and believed that his brother Guy was truly dead, and that the vice comital *honores* and office were now his alone. It is no less important, however, that for Geoffrey of Vigeois, writing in 1183, the ring was still also associated with the earlier journey of the lord of Lastours to Jerusalem. Like the relics kept in

annulus hic sculpturam agni dei cum vexillo habens veritatis mandatorum meorum, indicium est viteque mee et mortis argumentum.'" Dietrich of Apolda, *Die Vita der heiligen Elizabeth,* ed. Monika Rener (Marburg, 1993), 67.

67. For seals and identity, see Brigitte Bedos-Rezak, "Medieval Identity: A Sign and a Concept," *American Historical Review* 105:5 (2000): 1489–1533.

68. For burial of matrices, see Martin Aurell, *Les noces du comte: Mariage et pouvoir en Catalogne (785–1213)* (Paris, 1995), 93 n. 1.

69. Logan E. Whalen, *Marie de France and the Poetics of Memory* (Washington, DC, 2008), 84.

70. M. Chazaud, "Inventaire et comptes de la succession d'Eudes, comte de Nevers (Acre, 1266)," *Mémoires de la Société des Antiquaires de France,* 4th series, 2 (1871): 164–206. For discussion of the text see Jaroslav Folda, *Crusader Art and the Holy Land: From the Third Crusade to the Fall of Acre* (Cambridge, 2005), 356–358.

71. Chazaud, "Inventaire et comptes," 195; Walter Cahn, *The Romaneque Wooden Doors of Auvergne* (New York, 1974), 150, sees this reference as possible evidence of the goldsmithing industry in the Auvergne.

72. Michael Lower, *The Barons' Crusade: A Call to Arms and Its Consequences* (Philadelphia, 2005), 42.

73. "Item messier Hug[ues] Augerant en porte l'enel que li dux avoit doné le conte, en l'enel qui deit ester as oirs de Neverz." Chazaud, "Inventaire et comptes," 195–196.

Ardres, it was still a trophy, a token of sacred victory. The strong identification between the ring and its crusading past makes it tempting to associate Guy's possession of the ring with the fact that it was he, and not his brother, who decided to join the Second Crusade. Given that the two brothers had, according to Geoffrey, held their lordship "equally," it seems unlikely that it was a coincidence that the ring was in the possession of the younger brother, who also happened to have been the crusader in the family. What happened to the ring after it was sent to Adhémar IV of Limoges is not clear, but it is worth noting that, for both Adhémar's family and the lords of Lastours to whom the ring formerly belonged, "the war for Jerusalem," which the ring still evoked in 1183, remained imperative. When Guy of Limoges took the cross in 1147, he did so in the company of the nephew of Gouffier of Lastours.[74] When Guy's nephew, Adhémar V, followed in his uncle's footsteps and took the cross, he was part of a small group of Limousin noblemen who departed for Jerusalem in 1178 that included Gouffier's youngest son, Olivier.[75] The powerful memory of the crusade that bound the ring to Jerusalem also, it seems, bound these families to each other.

Context and Control

The fate of the ring of Gouffier of Lastours after its return to the West in 1148 is unknown, but as we have seen from the examples of the relics at Ardres, the horse and arms at St. Andrews, and the gemstone at Canterbury, it is often possible to discover the locations in which relics and other commemorative objects that returned to the West were kept. The crusaders who selected and either carried or sent the items knew well that the environment in which crusade memorabilia was preserved was of critical importance to the role that these objects could play and the meanings they might hold both during and after their lifetimes. Items deemed to be sacred, in particular, had the ability to profoundly alter the devotional landscape of a region and were therefore objects of potentially great value not only to families but also to the religious institutions that offered to provide an appropriate liturgical setting for their veneration. It is perhaps unsurprising, then, to find that control over sacred memorabilia was disputed, but it was also the case that some crusaders not only carefully determined where their relics should be kept but also

---

74. GV, 179. Guy IV of Lastours identifies himself in a charter witnessing his departure on crusade with Adhémar as "Wido de Turribus, filius Widonis qui Jrosolimis [sic] perrexit." Roblin, *Recueil des actes,* 206, no. 86.

75. For the list of those who "ascenderunt Hierosolymam" during the Octave of the Feast of Saint Martial in 1178, see GV, 177. For the "cheerful" reception of Adhémar upon his return from Jerusalem at Christmas 1179, see GV, 180.

interceded to dictate the ritual contexts in which their memorabilia would be preserved and interpreted by future generations.

Monastic Communities

A number of factors, not unlike those that inspired laymen to take the cross in the first place, could determine where those same crusaders would choose to place the material remainders of their experiences of holy war. Personal devotional attachment to, or the regional power and reputation of, particular old and established religious communities might mean that crusaders would feel inclined to make gifts to these institutions, perhaps in thanks for their survival of the ordeal. We may get some idea of the extent of such gifts from the chronicler at the venerable old Benedictine monastery of Saint-Maixent in Poitou. The writer, who presented the narrative of the First Crusade in great detail, noted that the relics that had been given to his own house by the crusader Peter Fasin were among a wave of such objects "sent from Jerusalem to many places."[76]

Thoughts of the familiar sacred geography of their homelands may also have been what led crusaders in fear for their lives or at the point of death to commit the sacred objects they had collected to the most prominent communities and shrines in their homelands. Hence we find the Breton knight Riou of Lohéac, who died in the East with the First Crusade, sending the "certain parts of the Lord's Cross and of the Sepulcher of the Lord and of other holy places" he had collected to the Benedictine abbey of the Holy Savior at Redon through another man named Simon of Ludron.[77] Similar gifts of relics were made on behalf of Raymond IV of Saint-Gilles and Stephen II of Blois-Chartres to the Benedictines at La Chaise-Dieu and Saint-Pierre-le-Vif by their chaplains, Arbert and Alexander.[78] Such a mode of transmission was apparently common enough that by the middle of the thirteenth century the chronicler Alberic of Trois-Fontaines was spreading the story that the "Lord's Shroud" enshrined at Cadouin had originally been sent to the cathedral of Le Puy by the dying papal legate to the First Crusade, Adhémar of Montheil. Alberic claimed that the shroud had been accompanied by letters of authentication and was carried by one of the legate's assistant chaplains. When

---

76. "Eodem anno allatae sunt reliquiae de Jerusalem in pluribus locis, et apud nos a quodam nomine Petro Fasin." *Chronique de Saint-Maixent, 751–1140,* ed. and trans. J. Verdon (Paris, 1979), 171.

77. *Cartulaire de l'abbaye de Redon,* 318, no 366.

78. *AS,* Aprilis iii, 330; Geoffroy de Courlon claimed that Stephen's chaplain, Alexander, had been a priest at Saint-Loup de Naud, in the region of Sens. It is likely in this case that it was the chaplain, and not his lord, who decided the fate of the sacred objects. Geoffroy de Courlon, *Le livre des reliques de l'abbaye de Saint-Pierre-le-Vif de Sens,* ed. Gustave Julliot and Maurice Prou (Sens, 1887), 20.

the canons of Le Puy rejected the gift (according to the report of Alberic of Trois-Fontaines, a Cistercian) the chaplain returned to his native diocese of Bourges and brought the relic to the Cistercians at Cadouin.[79]

Crusaders who granted their relics (and their bodies) to the grand old Benedictine and Augustinian communities or, later, to new reformed houses may have found in the austerity and holy detachment of these institutions a sense of purity and sanctity. They had good reason to hope that their names and their holy labors would be remembered by the monks when the relics were venerated or paraded on feast days.[80] When Henry of Ulmen gave the *staurotheke* reliquary he had taken from Constantinople after the sack of the city by the crusaders in 1204 to the house of Augustinian canonesses of Saint-Nicholas at Stuben four years later, he explicitly established an anniversary with a *refectio* for himself, his mother, and his wife, Ermengard.[81] When the same crusader gave another relic he had acquired to the chapter of Saint-Pantaleon in Cologne, he received in return the grant of a hereditary prebend, which could only be held by his descendants. The charter drawn up at Saint-Pantaleon, in fact, was to become a hereditary object, and whoever carried it had the power to resolve disputes among Henry's heirs as to the true holder of the prebend.[82] In relinquishing a powerful hereditary possession, Henry and his family gained another.

With the weight of tradition and considerable ritual force behind them, monastic houses could make powerful allies for a donor and his family. One of the more famous translations to follow the First Crusade was that of the major relic of Saint George (an arm and part of his rib cage) that Count Robert II of Flanders presented to the abbey of Anchin as part of his triumphal return to Flanders.[83] While it was hardly an ancient institution, Anchin was politically very important. The gift of land that had enabled the original foundation of the abbey by the archbishop of Cambrai was made in 1079 by Anselm of Ribemont, the lord of Oostrevant and crusader who, in helping to

---

79. Alberic of Trois-Fontaines, *Chronica,* ed. Paul Scheffer-Boichorst, *MGH SS* 23: 824. For the problems associated with the *translatio* narrative of the Cadouin shroud, see "Préface," *RHC* 5: lix–lxiii.

80. William Durand (d. 1296) wrote that the contents of treasuries should be displayed on solemn feast days "in memory of their being offered to the church, namely, in memory of those that offered them to that church." *The "Rationale Divinorum Officiorum" of William Durand of Mende,* trans. Timothy M. Thibodeau (New York, 2007), 45. My thanks to Cynthia Hahn for this reference.

81. *Exuviae,* 82. no. 31; *Urkundenbuch zur Geschichte der jetzt die Preussischen Regierungsbezirke Coblenz und Trier bilenden mittelrheinischen Territorien,* ed. Heinrich Beyer, Leopold Eltester, and Adam Goerz (Coblenz, 1865), 2: 275, no. 235.

82. *Exuviae,* 96, no. 36. See also *Chronica regia coloniensis,* ed. George Waitz, *MGH SS rer. Germ.* 18: 228.

83. *Narratio quomodo reliquiae martyris Georgii ad nos Aquicinenses pervenerunt, RHC Occ.* 5: 251; *Annales Aquicinctini, MGH SS* 16: 503.

found Anchin, may have been attempting to assert himself politically before his powerful neighbors, the counts of Flanders and Hainaut.[84] Anselm himself did not return from the expedition, dying outside the walls of Tell Arqua in Lebanon in 1099. Thus Robert's gift, with its triumphal ceremonial setting, may have been an attempt to assert greater Flemish authority over the strategically placed abbey and to subvert whatever political influence the lords of Oostrevant were building on his border.

We might expect that a returning crusader's gift of a precious relic, like a gift of land, could establish a cooperative relationship that benefited both the institution and the crusader's family. At the Benedictine abbey of Redon in Brittany, for instance, the gift of relics made by the crusader Riou of Lohéac seems to have inspired Riou's living relatives to make further grants in his memory to the abbey.[85] Strikingly, however, there is no surviving evidence that the gift of a crusade-related object to a powerful, independent religious house like Redon, Anchin, or Saint-Maixent resulted in long-lasting relations between the abbey and the family. Nor are objects alienated in such ways associated with lasting traditions of participation in the crusades by particular families. Some Benedictine houses, like Ripoll in Catalonia, Liessies in Picardy, and Andres in Guines, actively considered themselves the guardians of the bodies and memories of particular crusading families, but in none of these cases was a transfer of relics or other commemorative objects (other than the crusaders' bodies) known to have occurred. The capricious nature of devotional patterns and the often uneasy political relationships between such houses and noble families made it difficult to ensure that a mutually beneficial relationship between a family and an independent religious house would last into a second generation, to say nothing of a third or a fourth.

The way the monks of Anchin referred to their relic of Saint George in texts, for instance, is suggestive of this. The relic was obviously a highly prized asset for the community, which, to judge by its library, maintained an avid interest in the crusades and in anti-Islamic polemical literature through the thirteenth century.[86] Clearly, the monks of Anchin did not wish to totally dissociate the object from the glorious conquest of Jerusalem or from the crusading hero Robert II of Flanders. Over the course of the twelfth century,

---

84. See Jean-Pierre Gerzaguet, *L'abbaye d'Anchin de sa fondation (1079) au xiv siècle: Essor, vie, et rayonnement d'une grande communauté bénédictine* (Villeneuve d'Ascq, 1997), 59.

85. *Cartulaire de l'abbaye de Redon,* 318, no 366.

86. For the library at Anchin, see Joseph Hippolyte-Romain Duthilloeul, *Catalogue déscriptif et raisonné des manuscrits de la bibliothèque de Douai* (Douai, 1846), 327–332. The abbey had copies of Josephus (s. xii, no. 832), the *Gesta Francorum Hierusalem expugnatium,* the chronicles of Fulcher of Chartres and Gilo of Paris, and the *Histoire de Mahomet* attributed to Hildebert of Lavardin (s. xii–xiii, no 838).

however, the abbey became increasingly distant from the Flemish comital family. By 1174, the abbey's chroniclers were, in the eyes of Jean-Pierre Gerzaguet, making positively "anti-Flemish" remarks.[87] Strikingly, when the monks composed a history of their abbey in the second half of the twelfth century, they added a new detail to the story of the relic. Describing Robert's gift of the relic, the *Historia monasterii Aquicinctini* began with the claim that the relic "was transmitted (*transmissum est*) by Anselm count of Ribemont to the church of the Holy Savior [i.e., Anchin]."[88] Robert, the *Historia* explained, was merely the bearer of Anselm's gift, bringing it from Lydda and presenting it to the abbot and the monks upon his return. The Count of Flanders, whom the *Historia* may have attempted to slight with faint praise, calling him *miles emeritae militiae,* was thus shifted from center stage to the role of messenger. If the memory of the gift itself was so mutable, the presence of the great relic of Saint George cannot be said to have effected a permanent alliance between the abbey and the crusader's descendants.[89]

Another useful example of the disputes that could arise between families and independent religious communities that claimed control of a crusader's memorabilia is provided by the narratives composed at the old Benedictine abbey of Brogne (in what is today the Belgian province of Namur). The monks of Brogne treasured until at least the early modern period a relic of the True Cross that, according to their traditions, had been brought to them from Jerusalem by Manasses of Hierges. Manasses traveled to the East in 1142 and served as the constable of Queen Melisende of Jerusalem, to whom he was related, from 1143 to 1152.[90] Returning from the East in 1158, Manasses lived as lord of Hierges until 1176, when, according to the monks of Brogne, he made a deathbed conversion to the monastic life and gave his relic of the Cross to the abbey.[91] The texts at Brogne also record, however, that Manasses' son Heribrand, upon receiving explicit instructions from his dying father to bring the portion of the Cross to the abbey, refused to surrender it.[92] It was this defiance of the monks and his father's wishes, the monks suggested, that

---

87. Gerzaguet, *L'abbaye d'Anchin,* 263, makes a convincing argument based not only on the monks' chronicles but also on the entries in their necrology.

88. *Historia monasterii Aquicinctinae,* ed. Johann Heller, *MGH SS* 14: 586.

89. A monk of Anchin did, however, note the details of the death and burial of Philip of Flanders during the Third Crusade. Sigebert of Gembloux, *Chronica,* ed. L. C. Bethmann, *MGH SS* 6: 427.

90. The biography of Manasses has been reconstructed by Hans Eberhard Mayer, "Manasses of Hierges in East and West," *Revue Belge de philologie et d'histoire* 66 (1988): 757–766. This complements the earlier study of C.-G. Roland, "Un croisé ardennais: Manassès de Hierges," *Revue historique ardennaise* 14 (1907): 197–212.

91. A modern history of the abbey records the suspiciously simple epitaph found on Manasses' tomb as *Vir nobilis Manasses.* Eugéne de Marmol, "L'abbaye de Brogneou de Saint Gérard," *Annales de la Société Archéoloqique de Namur* 5 (1857–58): 264.

92. "Notae Bronienses," *MGH SS* 24: 27.

led to the son's swift demise, only forty days after his father. The constable's brother, Henry, wisely conceded to the monks' demands and handed over the relic. Satisfied with their victory, and after receiving a gift of ten sous from Heribrand's wife to pay for a feast in his memory, the monks allowed his body to be buried in the abbey beside his father and his mother, Alice.[93]

For the abbey of Brogne, the possession of the True Cross relic, a gift from the constable of the crusader kingdom, was treated as a major coup. The separate entries dedicated to Manasses and his wife in the Brogne obituary both invoke the gift.[94] Moreover, a little more than a decade after the abbey's acquisition of the object, we find evidence of its association both with the Holy Land and crusading. A charter recording the 1189 visit of James of Avesnes to Brogne on the eve of his departure for the East, where he died one of the great heroes of the Third Crusade, described him providing the funds to keep two candles perpetually lit before the relic.[95] It is not difficult to imagine that the possession of such a sacred object, especially during the early decades of the thirteenth century, when crusading enthusiasm reached a fever pitch in the Ardennes, had the same salutary effect on Brogne as the acquisition of other Passion relics had on religious houses throughout the West after the sack of Constantinople by the Fourth Crusade.

By making gifts of what they found in the East to powerful religious communities and popular saints' shrines, returning crusaders won thanks and prayer and, in the narratives and liturgies of the monks, confirmation of their status and piety. But as the story from Brogne suggests, there was also resistance among some noble families to alienating objects of such profound significance to them. Indeed, a remarkable number of returning crusaders chose *not* to give away the items they brought home with them. Jewelry, weapons, armor, and sacred objects could be kept as personal possessions and even worn, but they could also be entrusted to communities with special relationships to the lord and the household, particularly castral chapels and proprietary collegiate churches. In some cases, these were communities already in place within a family's domains, and in others they were purposely created after a crusader's return. The fact that so many crusaders placed their memorabilia in these environments is striking evidence of the attempt to retain control over the material fabric of crusading memory. It is also in the

---

93. "L'obituaire de l'abbaye de Brogne ou de Saint-Gérard, de l'ordre de Saint-Benoît," ed. Joseph Barbier, *Analectes pour servir à l'histoire ecclésiastique de la Belgique* 18 (1882): 202–203. For the relic, which was embedded in 1505 in a new cross reliquary that now resides in the cathedral of St. Aubin in Namur, see N.-J. Aigret, *Histoire de l'église et du chapitre de Saint-Aubin à Namur* (Namur, 1881), 57–58 and n. 4.

94. "Obituaire de l'abbaye de Brogne," 293–294, 334.

95. Mayer, "Manasses of Hierges," 766.

context of these more intimate and proprietary spaces that we find the best evidence of objects at the center of family traditions.

Chapels and Proprietary Collegiate Churches

Whether at rest at a residence, fortress, or palace or on the move, medieval nobles always had access to their own, proprietary sacred spaces and the communities of clergy attached to them. The most immediate and intimate of these spaces was known as the "chapel." Derived, as C. Stephen Jaeger has pointed out, from the area of the Frankish royal palace where the major relic of Saint Martin, his *cappa* was kept, the "chapel" (*capella*) of the high medieval nobility designated a variety of spaces set aside for the saying of masses by household clergy (chaplains, *capellani*) within the domestic environment.[96] When, as was often the case, the household was on the move, *capella* would designate the religious personnel and sacramental equipment that traveled with it, which were sometimes collectively housed in a specially made tent.

Like other household officials, chaplains were extensions of a lord's public persona, and by the twelfth century their presence in the retinue of a powerful man or woman had probably become indicative of seigneurial power and noble status.[97] The chapels consecrated inside the walls of castles and palaces, and the colleges of canons founded exclusively for the purposes of noble families, often worked closely with secular lords as arms of their administration. Chaplains presumably came from a variety of different backgrounds, and many must have received their training at monasteries or cathedral chapters to which they may have retained some ties of loyalty. So much was acknowledged by the Picard noblewoman Countess Eleanor of Saint-Quentin in an agreement with the abbot of Saint-Nicolas des Prés in 1200. The countess explained that while the chaplain serving her in the chapel she constructed inside the castle of Ribemont might owe secondary loyalties to the abbot of Saint-Nicolas, "I and my successors ought to appoint the chaplain in the said chapel."[98]

As we have already seen, the gifts of relics to religious houses in the West postmortem reveal that after the death of crusaders it was often their chaplains who were entrusted with the sacred objects they had acquired. By safeguarding these relics, and the narratives that were attached to them,

---

96. C. Stephen Jaeger, *The Origins of Courtliness: Civilizing Trends and the Formation of Courtly Ideals: 939–1210* (Philadelphia, 1985), 20–23.

97. David Crouch, *The Image of Aristocracy in Britain, 1000–1300* (London, 1992), 292–293.

98. "Ego et successores mei debemus in dicta capella capellanum instituere." *Cartulaire de l'ancienne abbaye de Saint Nicolas,* ed. Henri Stein (Saint-Quentin, 1884), 57.

household chaplains played a major role in preserving and potentially shaping the memories of their lords. Just as the *capella* of the Frankish kings had
served as a repository for the relic of Saint Martin, the chapels of the nobility,
with their almost complete subjection to the families of their lords, made
excellent sites for the preservation of a family's most precious memorabilia.
It was in his palace chapel of Sainte-Croix, for instance, that William VI of
Montpellier installed the relic of the True Cross that he had brought back
from Jerusalem, as he was setting out, once again, for the East with the Second Crusade.[99]

A notice recorded by the Augustinian canons of Toussaints in Angers
describes the chapel of the Holy Savior in the Angevin comital castle of
Langeais, which they were given as a gift by Count Fulk V of Anjou in
1118.[100] The chapel contained a fragment of the Holy Sepulchre and a part
of the manger in which Christ lay, both of which had been brought back
from Jerusalem by Count Fulk III Nerra (d. 1040), who was remembered
in the Toussaint cartulary in language redolent of the crusade. Recalling not
only the relics but the many privileges that Fulk III had bestowed on the
chapel, the canons of Toussaint concluded "he is to be imitated" (*imitandus
est*). Indeed, while he ultimately granted control over the chapel of Langeais
and its lucrative rights to the canons of Toussaint, Fulk's great-grandson Fulk
V, as we will see, later made his own gift of powerful commemorative material obtained in the East to a small proprietary community within the castle
at Angers.

In 1199 control of the castle of Langeais passed into the hands of Robert
of Vitré, whose brother Andrew II was an enthusiastic crusader.[101] Having
already served for a year in the East in 1187, Andrew took the cross again in
1209 for the Albigensian crusade. Shortly before departing, Andrew founded
his own community of Sainte-Madeleine at Vitré. When, on 19 November
1249, Andrew's son Andrew III drew up his testament at Damietta in Egypt,
where he was with the forces of King Louis IX's first crusade, he asked that
the cross that he had carried with him in his chapel and "all of the ornaments
of that chapel" be sent back to his father's chapel at Vitré.[102]

99. Jonathan Phillips, *The Second Crusade: Extending the Frontiers of Christendom* (New Haven,
CT, 200), 114. For the location of the palace and the chapel, see Jacqueline Gaille, "Urban Expan-
sion in Languedoc from the Eleventh to the Fourteenth Century: The Example of Narbonne and
Montpellier," in *Urban and Rural Communities in Medieval France: Provence and Languedoc, 1000–1500*,
ed. Kathryn L. Ryerson and J. Drendel (Leiden, 1998), 57–60.

100. François Comte, *L'abbaye de Toussaints d'Angers* (Angers, 1985), 146–148, no. 102.

101. Judith Everard and Michael Jones, eds., *The Charters of Duchess Constance of Brittany and Her
Family, 1171–1221* (Woodbridge, UK, 1999), 196–197.

102. "Cartulaire de Laval et de Vitré," ed. Arthur Bertrand de Broussillon, in *La maison de Laval,
1020–1605* (Paris, 1895), 1: 256.

In some cases, the "ornaments" of a crusader's chapel may have included the crusade memorabilia of earlier generations. As he prepared to depart on the Third Crusade in 1190, Count Philip of Flanders and his wife, Mathilda of Portugal, arranged that they should both be buried at the Cistercian abbey of Clairvaux.[103] In a gesture signaling his friendship and even subjection to the Cistercians, Philip granted to the monks his chapel, the portable sacred equipment that he was planning to take with him on crusade, only to receive it back from them in gift.[104] The document recording this transaction listed all of the fineries of Philip's chapel, including candelabra, basins and flasks of silver, a golden chalice, liturgical vestments, altar cloths, and three crosses. One of the crosses he would keep as his own, and his gift to Clairvaux also made an exception of "a reliquary (*filacterium*) with which the *Pax* [ritual kiss of peace] is given, which I leave to my successors just as I have had it from my predecessors."[105] The 1190 charter of donation does not specify what relics were kept in the *filacterium,* but the traditions of the monks of Clairvaux held that the reliquary was made of gold and that it contained parts of the wood of the Holy Cross, the sponge, the thorns, and the manger, and that it was originally the property of Count Robert II of Flanders, "who was among those who captured Jerusalem and Antioch together with Godfrey of Bouillon and many other barons."[106]

Possession of sacred objects, including relics but also the liturgical vestments and vessels needed to perform religious rites, was the fundamental requirement, besides access to land and funds, that was needed either to found or to rededicate a church or monastery. Hence when Arnold I of Ardres, father of the crusader Arnold II and a veteran of the Norman conquest of England, wished to found a new church beside his stronghold at Ardres, he had to travel to the chief shrines in the region to buy or beg small parts of the major relics they guarded with which to endow his new foundation.[107] Like many lords in the eleventh and twelfth centuries, Arnold I was interested not only in patronizing existing religious communities but also in developing new, proprietary sacred space close to or even within the walls of the castle that was also his residence. The new collegiate church that he founded at Ardres in 1069 would be totally identified with his successors as lords of

103. *Recueil des chartes de l'abbaye de Clairvaux,* ed. Jean Waquet (Troyes, 1950), 359, no. 289.

104. A similar gift of a chapel on the eve of a crusader's departure was made by the Angevin castellan Robert of Sablé to Saint-Serge d'Angers. See Jacques Boussard, *L'Anjou sous Henri II Plantagenet et ses fils, 1151–1204* (Paris, 1938), 28 n. 3.

105. "filacterium parvum cum quo pax defertur, quod, sicut ab predecessoribus meis habeo, ita successoribus relinquo." *Recueil des chartes de l'abbaye de Clairvaux,* 358–359, no. 288.

106. Charles Lalore, *Le trésor de Clairvaux du xiie au xviiie siècle* (Troyes, 1875), 22.

107. LA, 618; trans. Shopkow, 150.

Ardres. According to Lambert of Ardres, from the outset it was specifically intended to provide the clergy to staff the chapel inside the family's castle at Ardres. Until at least the late twelfth century, this church served as a place of burial, nuptials, and perhaps also baptism for members the Ardres family.[108]

When Arnold II returned from Jerusalem (or, as the dynastic history says, "from Antioch," the site that dominated his family's memory of his travels) it is not surprising to find that it was to the collegiate church that he gave his relics. By keeping them in this intimate environment he was able to strengthen the spiritual center of the household and ensure that his memorabilia would remain at the center of the devotional theater that surrounded the family. The Ardres dynastic narrative in Lambert's chronicle describes how Arnold II, on the point of death, had brought to him the cross pendant "that he had brought back from the Lord's tomb" containing one hair of Christ's beard. Dying shortly afterward, Arnold II was buried in the church of Ardres beside his wife and the relics collected by himself and his father.[109]

To reformers, proprietary collegiate churches like the one at Ardres were not to be tolerated. Indeed Lord Baldwin of Ardres himself (d. 1147) was persuaded at one point to surrender his control over the Ardres collegiate church to the nearby monastery of Capella, only to have his successors lobby vigorously for its return to seigneurial provostship.[110] A nearby seigneurial collegiate church of five canons was founded by Baldwin of Licques, who intended to keep the position of provost for himself.[111] After Baldwin of Licques and his four sons died on the First Crusade, the church was taken over by the Premonstratensian order.[112] For families that demonstrated support for the crusade movement, itself closely allied with sentiments of reform, maintaining control over these religious communities in the face of such pressure must have been difficult. But in those places, as at Ardres, where collegiate churches survived, persisting in their guardianship of family crusade memorabilia, they became important focal points for dynastic tradition.

---

108. LA, 637–638 (marriage), 600–601 (burial, and especially the sense that members of the Ardres family should always be buried at Ardres); for a general discussion of the college based mainly on Lambert, see Georges Coolens, "Arnoul I d'Ardres et son chapitre," *Bulletin de la Société Académique des Antiquaires de la Morinie* 20 (1967): 576–636.

109. LA, 628

110. LA, 630–633, 637.

111. LA, 580–581.

112. Although it is only mentioned by Lambert of Ardres, the existence of Robert's collegiate church at Licques can be confirmed by references to several canons of Licques in documents of the early to mid-twelfth century. See, for instance, the obit for *Willermi de Liscques canonici* in Thomas Duchet, *Cartulaires de l'église de Térouanne,* 312 (6 March). For a brief discussion of the college, based mainly on the evidence of Lambert, see Georges Coolens, "Le chapitre de Licques et la croisade," *Bulletin de la Société Académique des Antiquaires de la Morinie* 21 (1967): 33–45.

Stopping in Apulia on his way to the Holy Land in 1097, Count Robert II of Flanders met his brother-in-law Roger Borsa, from whom he solicited a gift of relics. He was given a small collection of precisely the kind of sacred objects that fascinated crusaders: hairs of the Virgin and parts of the bodies of Saints Matthew and Nicholas. These he sent back to his wife, Clemency, to whom he had entrusted his domains upon departure, with explicit instructions that they be used to reconsecrate the collegiate church at Watten in honor of the blessed Virgin.[113] Watten had been a foundation close to Robert's family since the 1070s, when Robert's grandmother had admonished her son, Robert I, to take the church and its canons under his protection. Complete with its new collection, Watten would continue to receive the patronage and protection of the comital family. In the later eleventh and twelfth centuries, the counts of Flanders had no dynastic mausoleum, so it is worth noting that in 1168, two years after returning from his fourth and last crusading venture in the Holy Land, Robert's nephew and successor as Count of Flanders, Thierry of Alsace, was buried at the site his aunt had refounded around his uncle's crusade memorabilia. Lamenting the death of Count Thierry, the chronicler Lambert of Wattrelos observed the parallel turn to Watten by both men after their return from crusades:

> Count Thierry of Flanders, a powerful warrior, being advanced in age, after many dangerous trials and after several outstanding labors of his own doing—for the noble man went back to Jerusalem four times, and returning back from his journey, by God's providence, he satisfied his wish to see Jerusalem—and with all the land having been quieted in peace with the succession of his son, this year he was overtaken by death. . . . He was buried however by his children with honor at the church of the Blessed Virgin Mary at Watten, which his uncle Count Robert had built after his return from Jerusalem.[114]

According to Lambert of Ardres, the nobility of Flanders saw Watten as something of a model proprietary church. Arnold I had modeled his own collegiate church on the example of Watten, as had the unfortunate lord of Licques.[115]

---

113. "Charta Clementiae comitissae Flandriae," ed. Heinrich Hagenmeyer, in *Kreuzzugsbriefen,* 142–143, no. 7.

114. "Theodericus comes Flandriae, strenuus armis, provectus aetate, post plurima periculorum certamina postque praeclaros nonnullos actuum suorum labores- nam Ierusalem quater vir nobilis repetiit, rursusque iter suum, Domino providente, Ierusalem cupiens invisere satagebat- omnique terra iam sedata concordiam cum fillis ordinatam, hoc anno praeventus morte, felix princeps dormitionis diem a Domino foelix foeliciter accepit. Sepelitur tandem a filiis suis circa epiphaniam honorifice in ecclesia beatae Mariae semper virginis Wathinensi, quam struxit comes Robertus avunculus suus rediens Hierusalem." Lambert of Wattrelos, *Annales Cameracenses, MGH SS* 16: 544.

115. LA, 581.

The Anglo-Norman knight Robert "Pagan" Peverel, who acted as standard-bearer to Duke Robert Curthose of Normandy, similarly used the relics he had acquired to refound a college of canons. Like Watten, Pagan's foundation of Barnwell in Cambridgeshire also seems to have become part of the mechanism of family tradition. Pagan returned to England in 1103,[116] but it was not until nine years later, when, according to the late thirteenth-century *Liber memorandorum ecclesie de Bernewelle,* he was contemplating his own mortality, that he had either the means or the motivation to find a home for the gold- and topaz-encrusted reliquary he had brought back with him from the East. Pagan decided to relocate the canons of Barnwell priory, promising to augment their number to thirty (twenty more than were installed at Ardres) in the thirty years he believed he had yet to live.[117] On that occasion, he presented the canons with his reliquary. It was an eminently sensible decision, long considered, and it proved effective in sustaining the name and reputation of this obscure crusader.

According to the Barnwell chronicler, Pagan had also established a family tradition. One of Pagan's sons, William, "following in his father's footsteps," (*sequens uestigia patris*) was said to have lavished further gifts of lands on the priory before departing with the armies of the Second Crusade for the Holy Land, where he died without heirs.[118] The lordships of the Peverels, together with the responsibility for the patronage of Barnwell, passed through the marriage of William's sister Alice to a family of lords named Pecche. As Christopher Tyerman has noted, this family continued to have a striking devotion to the Holy Land. Alice's son Gilbert was forced to mortgage much of his property in order to finance his participation in the Third Crusade.[119] Despite the fact that his father went missing in the East and was presumed dead, and that the subsequent litigation to regain the family's lands lasted until 1237, Alice's grandson Hamo continued the family tradition. In 1241, presumably while on crusade with Thibaud of Champagne and Richard of Cornwall, Hamo Pecche, remembered fondly by the canons as among the last noble patrons of Barnwell priory, died in the Holy Land.[120]

The memorabilia preserved in proprietary institutions was not limited to sacred objects. In the epitaph he wrote for his great-grandfather Geoffrey III

---

116. See Susan Edgington, "Pagan Peverel: An Anglo-Norman Crusader," in *Crusade and Settlement: Papers Read at the First Conference of the Society for the Study of the Crusades and the Latin East and Presented to R. C. Smail,* ed. Peter Edbury (Cardiff, 1985), 90–93.

117. *Liber memorandorum ecclesie de Bernewelle,* ed. J. W. Clark (Cambridge, 1907), 41; for the early history of Barnwell, see also *MA* 6.1: 83.

118. *Liber memorandorum,* 48.

119. Christopher Tyerman, *England and the Crusades, 1095–1588* (Chicago, 1988), 216.

120. *Liber memorandorum,* 48.

of Joinville (d. 1188), John of Joinville recalled how during his own crusade campaign (1248–54) he made a special journey to the Hospitaller castle of Krak des Chevaliers to collect his uncle Geoffrey V's shield.[121] The shield had remained in Syria since Geoffrey's death there around 1204, and Joinville brought it back with him when he returned from crusade. He placed the object at the collegiate church of Saint-Laurent adjacent to the castle of Joinville. Saint-Laurent, which his great-grandfather had founded around 1180, occupied a position of extraordinary intimacy with the family. John's father, Simon, remembering how the canons had come into the castle to say mass for him when he had broken his leg and could not go to the church, went so far as to officially decree in 1231 that no chapel should be built by any of his successors in the castle of Joinville, "because we have the said church as our chapel."[122]

The chapel of Saint-Laurent was a particularly appropriate place for the family's crusade memorabilia. In 1277 John deposited the contents of his chapel at Saint-Laurent, including the relics of Saints George, John Chrysostom, and Stephen, the latter of which he is known to have been given on crusade by the prince of Antioch, Bohemond VI.[123] After his great friend the crusading king Louis IX of France, whose biography he wrote, was canonized, John also obtained permission to have a chapel installed at Saint-Laurent dedicated to the saintly king and crusader. Later in his life, he requested relics of Louis for this chapel and had visions of his friend standing happily near it.[124]

The shield of Geoffrey V of Joinville was not the relic of a saint, but its commemorative function in the collegiate church was nonetheless partly sacramental. John placed his uncle's shield at Saint-Laurent, he said, "so that one might pray for him," and then, revealing the power of the object as a peg for family memories, his thoughts turned abruptly to the story of how, because of the *prouesse* he demonstrated on crusade, his grandfather Geoffrey IV

---

121. "Épitaphe composée par Joinville," in *Histoire de Saint Louis, Credo, et lettre à Louis X,* ed. Natalis de Wailly, 4th ed. (Paris, 1872), 544–547; for discussion, see Caroline Smith, *Crusading in the Age of Joinville* (Aldershot, UK, and Burlington, VT, 2006), 173; the text of the epitaph is translated by Smith in John of Joinville and Geoffrey of Villehardouin, *Chronicles of the Crusades* (New York and London, 2008), 346–347.

122. "ecclesia beati Laurencii de Joinvilla ab antecessoribus meis privilegiata est quod in castro de Jonvilla capela a successoribus nostris edificari non potest, sed dictam ecclesiam habebimus in perpetuum pro capella." Jules Simmonet, *Essai sur l'histoire et la généalogie des sires de Joinville (1008–1386)* (Langres, 1876), 126; John himself made a similar decree in 1273. Champollion Figeac, *Documents historiques inédits: Tirés des collections manuscrites de la Bibliothèque royale et des bibliothèques des départements* (Paris, 1841), 1: 626.

123. Simmonet, *Essai sur l'histoire,* 233; Figeac, *Documents historiques,* 1: 627.

124. John of Joinville, *Vie de Saint Louis,* ed. and trans. Jacques Monfrin (Paris, 2005), 377–378, §§ 766–767.

(d. 1190) had won from Richard the Lionheart the right for himself and his descendants to quarter their arms with those of the Angevin royal house.[125] When he died in 1317 at the age of at least ninety-two, John of Joinville was buried among all of his family's crusade memorabilia in the church of Saint-Laurent.[126]

Ceremonial

In its intimate, familial setting, the shield of Geoffrey of Joinville, like the relics that accompanied it, could be visited, touched, adored, and used to beg for personal intercession. But there is also evidence that on certain occasions crusade memorabilia could become part of more public, paraliturgical performances or rituals of power. Narrative sources most frequently describe sacred objects brought from the East being used to celebrate or ceremonially receive the returning crusaders who had been responsible for their translation. The monk of Anchin who described the translation of the relics of Saint George by Count Robert II of Flanders wrote that the count, returning from Jerusalem in 1100, was greeted by a great crowd from the monastery, led by the abbot who carried with him the relics that the count had apparently sent ahead of his return.[127] A monastic chronicler at Saint-Amand in Flanders similarly recalled how the crusader Walter of Warignies, returning home in 1179 with a *staurotheke* reliquary containing two pieces of the True Cross, "was received by us with a procession in joy and exultation."[128] Arnold of Lübeck, describing the return of Henry the Lion from the East in 1173, mentioned honorable receptions in Hungary, at the imperial court where "he was joyfully received on his arrival (*adventu*) on account of his safe [return]," and finally at his capital of Brunswick, where he decorated the cathedral with relics in precious gold and silver containers, and the churches "with the best cloth-hangings (*palliis*), and finely made chasubles and dalmatics."[129] When William de Mandeville, whom the monks of Walden in Essex described as "that illustrious man, third advocate [after his father and grandfather] of our house," returned from crusade in 1178, he came first to Walden. There, as one of the monks recalled in the priory's chronicle, written in 1203,

---

125. "Ly dis sires de Joinville [ie Jean] mist l'escu à saint Lorans pour ce qu'on proit pour lui, ouquel escu apert la prouesse doudit Jofroi en l'onnour que li rois Richars d'Aingleterre ly fist en cequ'il parti ses armes à seues." Figeac, *Documents historiques,* 1: 547.

126. For the probable dates of his birth and death, see Smith, *Crusading,* 47.

127. *Narratio quomodo reliquiae martyris Georgii ad nos Aquicinenses pervenerunt,* 251.

128. "1179 Crux gemina quae apud nos est, duobus in locis de cruce domini Salvatoris habens, a Gualtero nobili milite de Wariniaco de Iherusalem allata et ecclesie nostra oblata, a nobis est cum processione suscepta in gaudio et exultatione." *Annales Elnonenses maiores, MGH SS* 5: 15.

129. Arnold of Lübeck, *Chronica Slavorum,* 125.

we met him in ordered procession wearing albs and copes, singing in chorus words that came from the heart, "Blessed is he that comes in the name of the Lord." He made his way to the high altar with great joy and when he had prostrated himself there the prior gave his blessing. After receiving this, he rose and then knelt to make an offering of precious relics in an ivory box, relics which he had acquired in the land of Jerusalem or had received as a gift from the Emperor at Constantinople or from the Count of Flanders. Then he rose and stood before the altar, and the prior in a loud voice followed by the others began the hymn "Te Deum laudamus." Leaving the church, the earl went directly into the chapter-house to be greeted by everyone there, and to give and receive from each one the kiss of peace. When they had enjoyed pleasant, friendly conversation, he was escorted to his lodging where a splendid banquet was sumptuously provided for him and his men. When he departed from there he visited some friends and relations who were delighted by his success.[130]

The arrival of the returned crusader was clearly a memorable event. Peter, abbot of Saint-Bertin, even created his own independent narrative—an "elegantly styled treatise," in the words of William of Andres—of how he and his monks received Count Philip of Flanders upon his return from the East in 1179.[131]

The scenes evoked in these accounts, and in the Walden chronicle in particular, show that the crusader's return, and the presentation of relics to local religious communities, was performed in the style of the ceremonial receptions, or *adventus,* that celebrated the arrival of royal and princely figures at the chief town, churches, and monasteries of their domains.[132] As public performances of power, friendship, and subjection, receptions were potentially powerful demonstrations of the legitimacy of the honored ruler or visitor.[133] Like all such rituals, however, they had to be carefully curated. Their public nature made them open to protestation and contesting interpretations. Thus while eminently useful, they were also, to use Philippe Buc's term,

---

130. *The Book of the Foundation of Walden Monastery,* 59.

131. The work does not survive. See William of Andres, *Chronicon Andrensis,* ed. Johann Heller, *MGH SS* 24: 712.

132. David A. Warner, "Ritual and Memory in the Ottonian Reich: The Ceremony of Adventus," *Speculum* 76:2 (2001): 255–283; Susan Boynton, *Shaping a Monastic Identity: Liturgy and History at the Imperial Abbey of Farfa, 1000–1125* (Ithaca, NY, 2006), 127–135, 242–244 (app. 3); Zbigniew Dalewski, *Ritual and Politics: The History of a Dynastic Conflict in Medieval Poland* (Leiden, 2008), 13–40.

133. Koziol, *Begging Pardon and Favor,* 133–134; and Koziol, "England, France, and the Problem of Sacrality in Twelfth-Century Ritual," in *Cultures of Power: Lordship, Status, and Process in Twelfth-Cenutry Europe,* ed. Thomas N. Bisson (Philadelphia, 1995), 147.

"dangerous."[134] This placed the performers of such ceremonies in a position of considerable power. The monks of Saint-Florent near Saumur, for instance, effectively argued at the court of Fulk IV of Anjou that the count should pay them 100 sous per annum to cover the expenses of properly greeting and feasting the count when he was received at the abbey every year to celebrate the feast of the translation of holy Florent.[135]

If, as Geoffrey Koziol has argued, the *adventus* ceremony was one of the ritual mechanisms exploited by eleventh-century princes to consolidate their authority and face down the rising threat from the castle lords below them, these rulers must have watched with interest as the honor was extended to more modest lords like Guy II of Rochefort as they returned from crusade.[136] According to the chronicle of the abbey of Morigny, the abbot of that community rushed to greet Guy as he entered the region, kissing him "as was appropriate for the occasion" and promising him a most honorable reception, complete with processions, if he would come to stay as a guest at Morigny. After the monks had received him *honorificentissime,* he passed to his castles, where he lovingly took back into his care those who came out to greet him. These were only the first such scenes, which were played out throughout the region as Guy was received at other religious houses.[137] For those who had not joined the expedition, the experience of this joyous homecoming, which was said to feature solemn liturgical processions and public acclamations, represented the fundamental framework around which the memory of the crusade would be formed. Like the stories told by the crusaders and the objects that they carried, the celebration of their return would not be forgotten.

Among those living in the Île-de-France at the time of the return of the surviving first crusaders was a boy of about nine or ten years named Fulk. The younger son of the Count of Anjou, Fulk was raised partly in the household of his mother, Bertrada, who around the time of his birth had fled Anjou and eloped with King Philip I of France. After the death of his brother (in 1107) and father (in 1109) Fulk succeeded them as Count

---

134. See Philippe Buc, *The Dangers of Ritual: Between Early Medieval Texts and Social Scientific Theory* (Princeton, NJ, 2001); Geoffrey Koziol, "The Dangers of Polemic: Is Ritual Still an Interesting Topic of Historical Study?" *Early Medieval Europe* 11:4 (2002): 367–388; Buc, "The Monster and the Critics: A Ritual Reply," *Early Medieval Europe* 15:4 (2007): 441–454; Christina Pössel, "The Magic of Early Medieval Ritual," *Early Medieval Europe* 17:2 (2009): 111–125.

135. Josèphe Chartrou, *L'Anjou de 1109 à 1151: Foulque de Jérusalem et Geoffroi Plantagenêt* (Paris, 1928), 348–350.

136. Geoffrey Koziol, *Begging Pardon and Favor,* 138–139; more recently, Zbigniew Dalewski cites the ceremonial return of Vladimir II from crusade in 1148 (described by Vincent of Prague) as an example of *adventus.* Dalewski, *Ritual and Politics,* 26, citing *Annales Bohemorum Vincentii Pragensis,* ed. Josef Emler, in *Fontes rerum Bohemicarum* (Prague, 1874), 2: 419.

137. *La chronique de Morigny,* 41. See Riley-Smith, *The First Crusaders,* 144–145.

Fulk V of Anjou. Twice in his lifetime, first in 1120 and then in 1129, Fulk would take the cross and travel to the Holy Land, the second time to rule the kingdom of Jerusalem as husband to its heiress, the queen Melisende. After his accession to the crown of Jerusalem in 1129, Fulk would not return home again, but this did not prevent him from sending material to Anjou. Shortly after his accession as king in Jerusalem, Fulk sent an object back to the West. A ceremonial guide composed several decades later, probably around the year 1200, describes how the count acquired and then transmitted to the canons of the chapter of Saint-Laud at Angers an object that is called an "ivory tau" *(thau eboreum)*.[138] What was written about this object reveals how a crusader like Fulk V of Anjou hoped that the material he collected would be kept and used by subsequent generations of his family.

The chapter of Saint-Laud was associated with a chapel of the same name located within the castle of Angers, and the canons owed strict obedience to the Count of Anjou and his family.[139] In the late twelfth or early thirteenth century a manuscript was produced at Saint-Laud that contained descriptions of the rituals observed by the canons, including the rite of initiation for new canons and the instructions for the ceremonial reception of the Count of Anjou at Angers. It is this second text that contains the extraordinary instructions for the use of the "ivory tau":

> When a count who has been newly created, and also when he has returned from a lengthy pilgrimage or from a long absence, comes to the church, and no less when he is attended by the countess and their children, he will be solemnly received in procession by the chapter and the priests of Saint Laud. And he will be received by the dean or by whoever is the chief prior of the same church with the Gospels and the censer, taking similarly to the said count in the same reception the ivory Tau which Fulk, king of Jerusalem and count of Anjou had from the sultan of Babylon when Christ elevated the same Fulk to the crown of Jerusalem. Indeed I, Guy of Athée, with all the chapter of the church and with the clergy, have often received the count of Anjou in this way. And the said king Fulk gave to our church the said Tau that we might thus receive counts, and he began this and he wished it to signify that

---

138. Antiquarians wrongly assumed that the tau might have been a reliquary of the fragment of the True Cross that the canons also possessed. Although no further mention of the tau was made in medieval documents, the records of the chapter do mention the theft, in 1596, of "small ivory images which surrounded the ivory crozier" of Saint-Laud. ADML, G 916, f. 329.

139. Jacques Isolle, *Les anciennes chapelles du chateau d'Angers et les origines du chapitre de Saint-Laud* (n.p., on deposit at ADML, dated 1945–64).

the counts of Anjou above all other churchmen are the lords and abbots of the church of Saint Laud.[140]

If, as the author of the ritual text, Guy of Athée, claimed, it was Fulk V himself who dictated the use of the tau in the reception ceremony, what was he hoping to achieve by it, and why did he choose this distinctive object as its centerpiece? Fulk was clearly a ruler who understood the importance of ceremonial. Around the time of his first expedition, he agreed to continue paying the monks of Saint-Florent the 100 sous established by his father to cover the cost of his ceremonial reception at their abbey.[141] The list of occasions on which the Saint-Laud ceremony should be conducted includes new investitures, the traditional *adventus,* and the return from "a long pilgrimage," which would include a crusade.

The Saint-Laud ceremony quite explicitly created a theater of power in which the castle and its functionaries (the canons of Saint-Laud) performed their subjection to the count. The canons believed, naturally, that the ceremony was mainly about their community, and if this was the case the tau may have been intended to act as a kind of crozier or rod of office for the count in his capacity as their ceremonial abbot. But in choosing the tau as a symbol for use in processions, Fulk may have had a more deliberate meaning in mind—one specifically associated with his status as a crusader king.

For western Christians, the Greek letter tau was understood to be an analogue of the sign of the cross, but the exegetical origins of this association gave it a very particular meaning. Because tau is the Greek numerical symbol of the number 300, Origen and later patristic writers, including Augustine, associated it with the small force of three hundred men that Gideon had led to victory against the Midianites (Judges 7:4–7).[142] The battle was thus a victory of the sign of the cross (300 = tau = the Holy Cross) over the enemies of God. At least one chronicler of the First Crusade, Guibert of Nogent, com-

---

140. "Comes vero qui de novo creatus fuerit cum ad ecclesiam venerit processionaliter recipientur a capitulo et ecclesiasticis solemniter sancti laudi et quotiescumque a peregrinatione longa sive absentia redierit idem comes: quod etiam cum comitissa eorumque liberis observibitur et recipientur a decano sive ab illo qui primus erit prior eiusdem ecclesia cum texta turribulo et aqua benedicta, tradens dicto comiti similiter in dicta receptione thau eboreum quod fulco rex Jerusalem Andegavensium comes dicta ecclesiam dedit, quod habuit a Sodanno Babylonia cum ipse in regem Jerusalem ipsam fulconem sublimavit. Ego vero Guido de Athenis cum toto capitulo ecclesia et clercis pluries comitem Andegavorum ita recepit. Et ideo dictus folco rex dictum thau ecclesia nostra dedit ut nos ita comites reciperemus. Et hac praecepit et voluit ad significationem quod comites andegavenses pro omnibus ecclesii sunt domini et abbas ecclesia sancti laudi." *Cartulaire du chapitre de Saint-Laud d'Angers,* ed. Adrien Planchenault (Angers, 1903), 4–5, no. 3.

141. See above, n. 133.

142. Origen, *Homilies on Judges,* trans. Elizabeth Ann Dively Lauro, Fathers of the Church 119 (Washington, DC, 2010), 115–117; Augustine, *Exposition on the Book of Psalms,* trans. A Cleveland Coxe (Grand Rapids, MI, 1979), 295.

pared Gideon's small army to the crusaders, who likewise faced impossible odds, and made a direct parallel between the crusader's cross and the tau.[143] The connection between the tau and the crusader's cross was reaffirmed by Innocent III both in 1202 and in 1215, and the so-called Children's Crusade adopted the tau as its badge in preference to the cross.[144]

While, more generally, the tau was closely associated with crusading and leadership of the Christian people in arms, for Guy of Athée and the canons of Saint-Laud, the tau was also a straightforward reminder of the count's elevation by Christ to be the king of Jerusalem.[145] Notes for sermons written at Saint-Laud in the later thirteenth or fourteenth centuries, which contrast the "King of Jerusalem" and the "Sultan of Babylon," strongly suggest that the effectiveness of the tau as memorabilia was still preserved long after control of Angers had been wrested from Fulk's descendants by the Capetian kings of France in the early thirteenth century.[146]

The Souvenir in Context

With the tau of Saint-Laud we see crusade memorabilia in action. Not only had the object itself been especially selected by the count, probably for its resonance as a reminder of the crusade effort in the East, but its location and the context in which it was to be used had also been dictated by him. His selection of Saint-Laud, a community of canons with absolute loyalty to his family, was, as we have seen, representative of the choices made by many other returning crusaders who chose to keep the materials they acquired on crusade within their dynastic control. This control in turn fostered the use of objects as memorabilia and placed memories associated with the crusades at the center of a family's dynastic identity. Perhaps thinking of the triumphant ceremonies that had greeted returning first crusaders, Fulk also elected to have the ivory staff head he sent from Jerusalem used in ceremonies, including

---

143. Guibert of Nogent, *Dei Gesta per Francos et cinq autres texts,* ed. R. B. C Huygens, *CCCM* 127a (Turnhout, 1996), 321; trans. Robert Levine as *The Deeds of God through the Franks* (Woodbridge, UK, and Rochester, NY, 1997), 248–249.

144. Gary Dickson, *The Children's Crusade: Medieval History, Modern Mythistory* (Houndmills, Basingstoke, UK, and New York, 2008), 104–105, 114–115.

145. The tau symbol was also associated with crusaders through Ezekiel's vision of the marking of the elect in Ezekiel 9:4–6. Ann Derbes, "The Frescoes of Schwarzheindorf, Arnold of Wied, and the Second Crusade," in *The Second Crusade and the Cistercians,* ed. Michael Gervers (New York, 1992), 145; see also Daniel F. Callaghan, "The Tau Cross in the Writings of Adhémar of Chabannes," in *In the Year 1000: Religious and Social Response to the Turn of the First Millennium,* ed. Michael Frassetto (New York, 2002), 63–71.

146. Here the tau should not be confused with the relic of the True Cross associated with Saint-Laud. See Jean Michel Matz, "Religion et politique à la fin du Moyen Âge: La Vraie Croix de Saint-Laud d'Angers," *Annales de Bretagne et des pays de l'Ouest* 94:3 (1987): 241–263.

adventus and the accession of new counts. This ceremony associated his tri-umph in Jerusalem with the power of his descendants in the future.

Fulk's elegant use of his crusading souvenir as a symbol of his dynasty's God-given strength brings us back to the scene presented at the beginning of this chapter, that of the *pallia* of Lastours and their display on the walls of the castle of Pompadour in the autumn of 1183. We know from Geoffrey of Vigeois, whose chronicle betrays an avid interest in liturgical practice and the use of sacramental objects, how important ritual items and performances were as accessories to the exercise of power in the Limousin. Like other Bene-dictine houses in western Francia, most famously the French royal abbey of Saint-Denis, the abbey of Saint-Martial in Limoges possessed military banners symbolizing the advocacy of the territorial princes (in this case the dukes of Aquitaine) for their patron Martial.[147] Describing the liturgical rites of Saint-Martial, Geoffrey noted in his chronicle the five banners associated with Duke Waiffre of Aquitaine, supposedly gifts to Saint Martial from Pepin the Short, which were among the centerpieces of processions in Limoges.[148] Geoffrey also described how, in 1172, the new duke of Aquitaine, Richard, Count of Poitou, was presented with the ring of Saint Valerie when he arrived in Limoges.[149]

In the tense years 1182–83, as unrest began to shake the region and the armies of Henry II, his sons Richard and Henry the Young King, and the hordes of mercenaries appeared, Geoffrey noticed how banners and other ceremonial cloths were being used in the contest between royal authority and local identity. He described the raising and lowering of the banners of the king and the Viscount of Limoges over the castle of Pierre-Buffière, and how in 1182, a year before the Young King's insurrection against his father, the prince attempted to use sacramental cloth to literally inscribe himself in the devotional consciousness of the Limousin.[150] Arriving at Limoges, where he was greeted by a crowd of dancing monks, he presented the abbey of Saint-Martial with a new altar frontal on which was ornately (if immodestly)

---

147. Carl Erdmann, *The Origin of the Idea of Crusade,* trans. Marshal Baldwin and Walter Goffart (Princeton, NJ, 1977), 35–56; Daniel F. Callahan, "Eleanor of Aquitaine, the Coronation Rite of the Duke of Aquitaine, and the Cult of Saint Martial of Limoges," in *The World of Eleanor of Aquitaine: Literature and Society in Southern France,* ed. Marcus Bull and Catherine Léglu (Woodbridge, UK, 2005), 34.

148. GV, 129; the five banners are also mentioned in an early thirteenth-century description of the treasury of Saint-Martial. H. Duplès-Agier, "Le trésor de Saint-Martial de Limoges au XIIIe siècle," *Bibliothèque de l'école des chartes* (1860), 32. For the banners, see Callahan, "Eleanor of Aqui-taine," 34 n. 42.

149. Callahan, "Eleanor of Aquitaine," 29–30, believes that Limoges had become the center of ducal ceremonial by this time.

150. For the banners at Pierre-Buffière, see GV PA, 333.

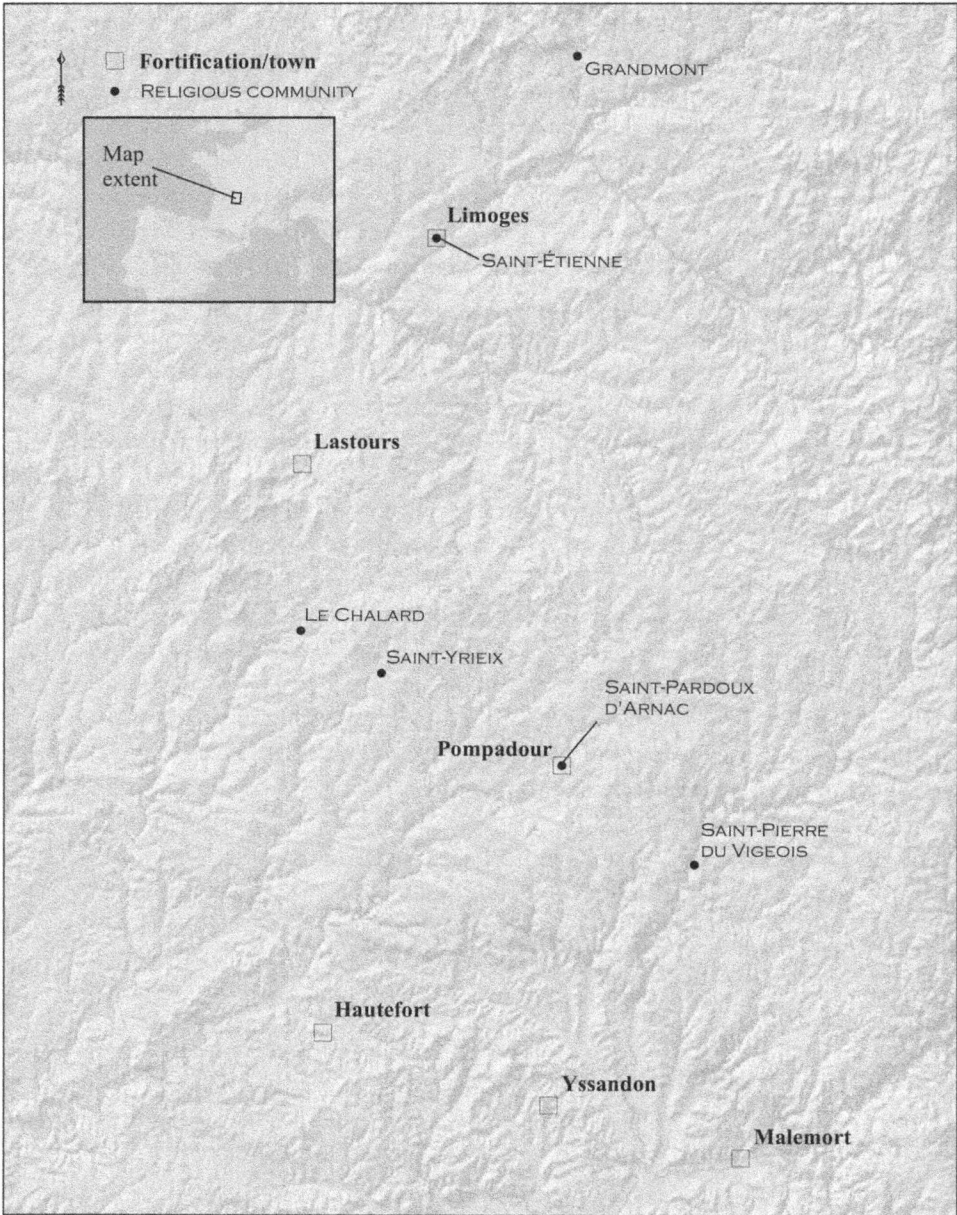

Within the map:

Fortification/town
Religious community

Map
extent

GRANDMONT

Limoges
SAINT-ÉTIENNE

Lastours

LE CHALARD
SAINT-YRIEIX

SAINT-PARDOUX
D'ARNAC

Pompadour

SAINT-PIERRE
DU VIGEOIS

Hautefort

Yssandon

Malemort

MAP 1. Sites of preservation and display of crusade memorabilia in the Limousin before 1183

written "King Henry."[151] This was the visual marker that Saint-Martial was his new base, from which he would recruit supporters and, in early 1183, begin to devastate his father's lands.

Crusading played a key role in the strategy that the Young King used against his father and brother. Like the other nobles and crowned heads of Europe, all three men were under considerable pressure from within and without their domains to take the cross and help defend the kingdom of Jerusalem from the onslaught of Saladin. According to the chronicler Roger of Howden, when he heard that his father and brother were on their way to Limoges, the Young King first withdrew to the nearby town of Le Dorat. Then, in a surprise move, he suddenly returned to Limoges and seized the initiative by placing his hands over the body of Saint Martial and vowing to take the cross as a crusader.[152] It was checkmate; Henry II could do little else for the moment but publicly demonstrate his enthusiasm for his son's decision and promise to assist him in fulfilling his vow.

As Henry the Young King shrewdly realized, the Limousin was a region where the memory of the crusades and commitment to the continued crusading enterprise had not waned since the time when so many of the region's knights and lords had headed for Jerusalem in 1096 (see map 1). While the kings of England, France, and Aragón had hesitated, the Viscount of Limoges, Adhémar V, and a number of other Limousin knights had traveled to the Holy Land in 1178.[153] Writing a few years later, the troubadour Bertran de Born gives a clear sense of how the Limousin nobility felt about the royal inaction in the face of repeated calls for help from the East. In two *sirventes* addressed to Marquis Conrad of Montferrat, who was at the time defending the city of Tyre from Saladin, Bertran contrasted Conrad's bravery and steadfastness with the dithering of Richard, who was by then king of England, and Philip Augustus of France, both of whom "took the cross but they don't say a word about going!"[154] Although both rulers were, according to Bertran's second song, still promising to depart on crusade, their inaction had deeply damaged enthusiasm for the expedition: "I would have been

---

151. GVPA, 331. For discussion of comparable examples, see Nicholas Vincent, "Pilgrimages of the Angevin Kings of England, 1154–1272," in *Pilgrimage: The English Experience from Becket to Bunyan,* ed. Colin Morris and Peter Roberts (Cambridge, 2002), 20 and n. 32.

152. Roger of Howden, *Chronicon,* 2: 276.

153. Roblin, *Recueil des actes des vicomtes de Limoges,* 210. Their number included Aymeric Brun, one of the knights responsible for the translation of the relic of the holy oil of Saydanya to the monastery of Altavaux. See Paul Devos, "Les premières versions occidentales de la légende de Saidanaia," *Analecta Bollandiana* 65 (1947): 259–272.

154. Bertran de Born, *The Poems of the Troubadour Bertan de Born,* ed. and trans. William D. Paden (Berkeley, 1986), 416–417.

there in Saladin's [siege of] Tyre, but I gave up when the counts and dukes, the kings and princes dawdled so."[155]

Bertran is an excellent source for evidence of the mentality of the Limousin nobility, and his songs perfectly complement the chronicle of the monk Geoffrey of Vigeois. Like Geoffrey, Bertran was related to the Lastours family. His daughter Aimeline was married to Seguin, a grandson of one of the brothers of the famous crusader Gouffier of Lastours.[156] Bertran's brother, Constantine, with whom he vied for control of the Lastours family's castle of Hautefort, was married to Gouffier's granddaughter.[157] Deferring to the far greater fame of the Lastours lords, Constantine and his wife, Agnes, named their son Gouffier. In 1183, Bertran was near the center of events, joining the revolt against Henry II in early summer, only to be driven from his stronghold of Hautefort by Henry's son Richard on 30 June.

Voicing both resistance to royal overlordship in the Limousin and disappointment in the failure of the Angevin royal family to come to the aid of the Holy Land, Bertran's songs may provide the key to the use of the Jerusalem *pallia* as commemorative objects in the castle of Pompadour in 1183. By displaying their crusade memorabilia in preparation for a siege of their castle, the Lastours family reminded the royal agents in the region of their prominence among the southern nobility and of their commitment to the crusading cause. Elsewhere in the events noted by Geoffrey of Vigeois, we may, indeed, see a pattern of the use of such objects in this way. Geoffrey recorded that during an earlier outbreak of violence in 1177, when royal mercenaries ravaged the countryside of Yssandon from their stronghold at Malemort, they were confronted by a popular uprising led by the abbot of Saint-Martial, who carried with him a relic of the True Cross brought from Jerusalem in 1168 by William Vidal.[158] More recently, in the early summer of 1183, while Henry II was fighting Bertran de Born and the other rebels south of Limoges, the king celebrated Pentecost at the church of Saint-Yrieix, an institution of great local significance that was virtually the center point of the lands of the Lastours family. There, according to Geoffrey, he expressed an interest in the saint (Aredius), learned about his life, and made gifts to the church.[159] The relics of Aredius had apparently been removed at the outbreak of the fighting, because later in the summer (August 25) Geoffrey describes the bishop of Limoges, Sébrand Chabot, returning them to the church, where they were placed in a

155. Bertran de Born, *The Poems,* 416–417.
156. Bertran de Born, *Poésies complètes de Bertran de Born,* ed. Antoine Thomas (Toulouse, 1888), xv.
157. Bertran de Born, *The Poems,* 15–16.
158. GV, 172.
159. GV PA, 330.

new shrine. The solemn procession included the four male heirs of the Las-tours lordship and the heads of the two other religious communities, Vigeois and Le Chalard, where the crusader Gouffier was buried. The most senior of the Lastours men, one of two named Gouffier who were present, carried the relics and cloth-hangings (*pallia*) that the deacon of Saint-Yrieix had brought back from Jerusalem, after joining the Viscount of Limoges, the lord of Lastours, and other members of the Limousin nobility on crusade in 1178.[160]

Carrying objects from one recent journey to Jerusalem in procession to reclaim their local cult center and festooning the walls of their castle with tex-tiles brought back from the First Crusade, the lords of Lastours sent a political message to the family's enemies about the age and nobility of their lineage and their independence from foreign Angevin overlordship. Unlike their enemy Henry, the king of England, duke of Normandy, and count of Anjou, the Lastours lords could be proud of a crusading tradition that they, like many other families in the region, had upheld. They were not English, not Norman, nor were they Angevins or Poitevins. They were the lords of Lastours, and they were crusaders. The objects displayed in their tower connected them to a tradition of nobility and sacrifice that made the Angevins, who fought among themselves as Jerusalem suffered, only more alien and illegitimate.

---

160. GV PA, 339. Geoffrey specifies that the translation and rededication of Saint Yrieix occurred on the same day as the death of Archbishop Christian I of Mainz, which was 25 August 1183.

❧ CHAPTER 4

Missing Men

The fixed point at the center of the crusading imaginary, the site that crusaders sought to recover and protect, was the sepulchre of Jesus Christ in Jerusalem, an empty tomb. The Holy Sepulchre was, for the crusaders, the symbol of their Lord's triumph over suffering and death. Illustrating the importance of the site to the memory of the First Crusade is the fact that the anonymous *Gesta Francorum et aliorum Hierosolymitanorum,* perhaps the earliest surviving narrative of the First Crusade, is found copied in an early twelfth-century manuscript together with materials for a liturgical celebration of the Sepulchre. Visual schematics—lines representing the site's dimensions—follow the liturgy, accompanied by verses of prophylactic magic promising that the very lines themselves are enough to protect those who see them against sudden death.[1]

However much it may have represented the transcendence over earthly death hoped for in Christian devotion, the centrality of this burial place in the imagination is nonetheless also a reminder of the paramount importance of death and burial in medieval Christian culture. Indeed, while devotional hopes and fears relating to the fate of the resurrected body and soul after death were central to the impulse that drove crusade recruitment, cultural concerns about

---

1. BAV, Reg. Lat. 572. The text of the *Gesta* (ff. 1–64v) is followed by a description of the holy places (ff. 64v–66v) and then the *Missa in veneratione sancti sepulcri* (ff. 66v–7) and verses of prophylactic magic with the dimensions of the sepulchre (f. 67).

the integrity, preparation, inhumation, and commemoration of the body while it awaited resurrection led crusaders, their families, households, and communities to worry about the fate of those who died far from home while on crusade.

We have seen how, in remembering their crusading kin, medieval noble families recalled crusaders' triumph and honor, treasuring objects that acted as trophies and reminders of the sacred victories and sacrifices of their ancestors. Even after disastrous expeditions in 1101, 1147–49, and 1190–92, which took the lives of many nobles and were treated in some quarters with criticism, works associated with the nobility generally refrained from criticizing crusades, which were still depicted as the highest expression of nobility and piety. Family histories do not conceal, however, the profound difficulties and tragedies that crusading could cause. Chief among these was the problem of the vast distances and poor communications separating crusaders from their communities. Distance, combined with the extreme dangers of crusade campaigns, meant that the families and households of many crusaders associated crusading with fear, loss, and above all uncertainty regarding the fate of their kin on crusade. Although families adopted a variety of strategies to try to combat the problem of death at great distance, the memories that lingered in courts and households were haunted by doubts and ambiguities. The death of crusaders undoubtedly affected the whole family and household, but the burden of commemorative responsibilities most frequently fell on women.

Death, Distance, and Memory

Concerns about death, distance, and memory are woven throughout the letters and chronicle accounts of those who participated in crusades to the East. The first note of this uncertainty was sounded by the crusader Anselm of Ribemont in the letter he wrote to Archbishop Manasses II of Reims after the arrival of the crusade armies outside of Antioch in late November 1097. Anselm's main concern was to present news of the expedition, but as he concluded his message, he turned his mind to those whose company he had lost, the crusaders, including members of his own household, who had died between Nicaea and Antioch. He presented Manasses, and "everyone whom this letter reaches," with a list of the dead, including information about how, when, and where they had died, and asked for prayers for these fallen men. He assured Manasses that they had not died in vain, because "in certainty, we have acquired two hundred cities and castles for the Lord."[2]

---

2. "Epistula I, Anselmi de Ribodimonte ad Manassem archiepiscopum Remorum," in *Die Kreuzzugsbriefe aus den Jahren 1088–1100,* ed. Heinrich Hagenmeyer (Innsbruck, 1901), 144–146.

Although the turning point of the expedition, the siege and battle before Antioch, was yet to come, in 1097 Anselm was already concerned that the names of those who had died in the East should be known to their friends and families thousands of kilometers away. By the time that Anselm wrote a second letter to Manasses in July 1098, the number of dead had increased significantly.[3] They included those who had starved to death or were killed in combat, some horribly like Roger of Barneville, whose death Anselm explicitly mentioned. Only recently Roger's body had been dismembered and decapitated in full view of the crusading host, his head put on a spike.[4] Anselm closed his letter by once again imploring the archbishop and the canons of Reims to pray for those who had been killed.

Participants in the expedition who composed chronicles of their experiences joined Anselm in worrying about the commemoration of the dead. Fulcher of Chartres, who settled in the East and traversed the territory where so many crusaders had died and were buried, admonished the readers of his chronicle to remember that:

> It is very beneficial to those who have died in the Lord when the faithful who are still alive, hearing of the good and pious deeds of their forebears, bless the souls of the departed and in love bestow alms with prayers on their behalf whether they, the living, knew the departed or not.[5]

When the Poitevin cleric Peter Tudebode, who, like Fulcher, had been a crusader, revised a rudimentary account of the First Crusade that was circulating in the West in the first decade of the twelfth century, he added a description of how he had buried his brother, the knight Arvedus, in the city of Antioch shortly after its conquest, when the crusaders were themselves besieged within the city. Recording precisely where his brother's body lay, he wrote: "We beg all those who read and hear this to give alms and say prayers for his soul and for the souls of all the dead who died on this journey to Jerusalem." He also remembered how, as he was burying his brother's body, his thoughts turned to his own mortality, and how he had "greatly feared death by decapitation."[6]

---

3. "Epistula II, Anselmi de Ribodimonte ad Manassem archiepiscopum Remorum," in *Die Kreuzzugsbriefe*, 156–160.

4. There were numerous accounts of Roger's death. See Thomas Asbridge, *The First Crusade: A New History* (New York and London, 2004), 212–213.

5. Fulcher of Chartres, *Historia hierosolymitana (1095–1127): Erläuterungen und einem Anhange*, ed. Heinrich Hagenmeyer (Heidelberg, 1913), 116; trans. Martha Evelyn McGinty as *The Chronicle of the First Crusade* (Philadelphia, 1941), 57.

6. Peter Tudebode, *Historia de Hierosolymitano itinere*, ed. John Hugh Hill and Laurita L. Hill, Documents relatifs à l'histoire des croisades 12 (Paris, 1977), 72.

The remarks of Anselm, Fulcher, and Tudebode reveal a variety of concerns associated with death on crusade, namely that crusaders who died so far away should be remembered in prayer, that they should receive a Christian burial at a site that might be recognized by later generations, and that their bodies would not be dismembered or otherwise violated by their non-Christian adversaries. These concerns must, to some degree, have been assuaged by the widespread belief, in evidence from the time of the First Crusade until at least the fourteenth century, that death in the course of crusading expeditions brought with it the possibility of the crown of martyrdom. The language of martyrdom was applied by chroniclers to crusaders in general and by participants to particular individuals whose deaths they witnessed. This was, unsurprisingly, true for a number of crusaders whose deaths were described as particularly horrific, such as Roger of Barneville, although martyrdom was also associated with crusaders of great renown, such as Anselm of Ribemont himself.[7]

In the *Chanson de Jérusalem* branch of the Old French Crusade Cycle, the spiritual reward earned by the crusaders was directly connected to the protection of their remains and provision of Christian burial. The poem describes how, after the climactic battle on the plain of Ramla, in which the crusaders finally defeated the forces of their enemy Cornumarant and secured the safety of Jerusalem, great numbers of Christian dead lay unburied, commingled with the bodies of their Saracen enemies. What was liable to happen when bodies fell into enemy hands on the crusading frontier is not left to the imagination, for the crusaders are described ripping Cornumarant's heart from his corpse.[8] Riding out to survey the Ramla plain, however, the Christians found that while the bodies of the dead Muslims were snatched away by demons, a single great lion carried the Christian dead away to prepare them for burial.[9] The symbolism here can hardly be clearer: Christ had taken the care for the crusader dead directly into his own hands.[10]

The experiences of those who joined crusade expeditions in the twelfth century, however, did not correspond with this reassuring image. A rising sense of anxiety over the dead and the missing can be detected, for example, in Odo of Deuil's chronicle of the French experience on the Second

---

7. "Epistula Manasses Remorum archiepiscopi ad Lambertum Atrebatensem episcopum," in *Die Kreuzzugsbriefe,* 176.

8. *La Chanson de Jérusalem,* ed. Nigel R. Thorpe, *OFCC* 6 (Tuscaloosa, AL, 1992), 257, ll. 9858–9864.

9. *La Chanson de Jérusalem,* 255, ll. 9794–9801.

10. The same scene is imagined after Roncescalles in the *Pseudo-Turpin Chronicle.* It is the archangel Michael who bears away the souls of Roland and the Christian dead. See Ronald Walpole, *The Old French Johannes Translation of the Pseudo-Turpin Chronicle: A Critical Edition* (London, 1976), 170, laisse lxii, lines 9–18.

Crusade. Odo described how the army of the Capetian king Louis VII proceeding from Constantinople into Asia Minor followed a trail of unburied corpses from the German contingent immediately ahead of them.[11] The leader of the German party, Conrad III, revealed himself to be overwhelmed when he explicitly asked his Capetian colleague for assistance in burying the dead.[12] Odo remembered how, after the French were defeated in their first major engagement, he and the other survivors took refuge and waited for any word of their companions, many of whom were never seen again.[13] He was thinking of men like William II of Nevers, who, as Constance Bouchard has shown, still could not be sure in 1153 if his brother might still be alive and in captivity, even though the king had declared him dead in 1148.[14]

A participant in the next disastrous march through Asia Minor, led by the emperor Frederick Barbarossa as part of the Third Crusade in 1190, described how the corpses of dead crusaders that had been hastily buried along the side of the road were subsequently dug up and desecrated. He quoted the second verse of Psalm 79: "They have given the dead bodies of your servants to be meat for the fowls of the air: the flesh of your saints for the beasts of the earth."[15] The same verse inspired the anonymous poet of the "Lamentum lacrymabile," a verse meditation on the dead of the Second Crusade that was still being copied in the early thirteenth century, to write that "their bodies, having been cut down, lie unburied and in the water, food for the birds, left scattered about for wild animals."[16] Although derived from scripture, the reality of such scenes can be confirmed, for instance by the reports of the chronicler Ibn al-Athir, who described how the bones of those who died at the battle of Hattin in 1187 still covered the ground when he visited it two years later.[17]

The two poetic visions—of the bodies of crusaders recovered and buried by the lion of Christ in the *Jérusalem* and dispersed, submerged, and

---

11. Odo of Deuil, *De profectione Ludovici VII in Orientem,* ed. and trans. Virginia Gingerick Berry (New York, 1948), 46–47. See Jonathan Phillips, *The Second Crusade: Extending the Frontiers of Christendom* (New Haven, CT, 2007), 199.

12. Odo of Deuil, *De profectione,* 98–99, 114–115.

13. Odo of Deuil, *De profectione,* 122–123.

14. Constance Bouchard, *Sword, Miter, and Cloister: Nobility and the Church in Burgundy, 980 to 1198* (Ithaca, NY, 1987), 347 n. 198, citing *RHGF* 15: 496 (for the letter) and *Le premier cartulaire de l'abbaye cistercienne de Pontigny (XII-XIII siecles),* Collection des documents inédits sur l'histoire de France 14 (Paris, 1981), 122–124 (for the charters of William II).

15. *The Crusade of Frederick Barbarossa: The History of the Expedition of the Emperor Frederick and Related Texts,* trans. Graham A. Loud (Farnham, UK, and Burlington, VT, 2010), 88.

16. "Lamentum lacrymabile super his qui in expeditione Jerosolimitana diversis mortibus," *PL* 155, cols. 1095a–1098b.

17. *The Chronicle of Ibn al-Athir for the Crusading Period from al-Kamil fi'l Ta'rikh,* pt. 2, trans. D. S. Richards (Farnham, UK, and Burlington, VT, 2010), 324.

consumed in the "Lamentum"—illustrate the disparity between the idea and reality of death on crusade. As Caroline Bynum has noted, precisely the same distinctions between bodies broken and consumed and bodies whole and protected emerged in hagiographical texts of the later thirteenth century, where the bodies of saints are miraculously protected from loss or dissection while the bodies of their oppressors are devoured or lost, left to lie unburied in an unknown location.[18] By insisting that the bodies of crusaders would be protected and recovered, the *Jérusalem* poet may have been suggesting that the dead crusaders were martyrs, and while this idea was accepted in many circles in the twelfth and thirteenth centuries, it did nothing to ease the anxiety of noble crusaders about what would become of their bodies. One outgrowth of this anxiety was the foundation, later in the course of the Third Crusade, of the new military order of Saint Thomas of Acre, whose stated function was in part to ensure that crusaders and other pilgrims received a Christian burial.[19] Another, as we will see, was the growing custom of repatriating the remains of dead crusaders. Neither of these practices, however, could do anything to solve the problem of crusaders who disappeared, many into captivity. Canon lawyers would eventually agree that five years was an acceptable period to wait before declaring a crusader dead, but it was not unheard-of for men to return from the East after more than three decades.[20]

For the clearest sense of what the death and disappearance of crusaders meant to the communities of the West, however, we must turn to the narratives created in the orbit of medieval noble families in the twelfth and early thirteenth centuries. In these sources, alongside what might be considered the more predictable accounts of the glory and heroism of crusading ancestors, are a surprising number of references to death, disappearance, the burial and transportation of bodies and body parts, and novel rituals of commemoration, including the transmission and use of memorabilia by crusaders. Despite this interest in death, and although the authors clearly believed crusading to have been a meritorious activity, dynastic histories and related texts, including epitaphs and commemorative songs composed for dead crusaders, do not assume the dead to have been martyrs. The sources written close to noble families offer images of what would have been considered "better" deaths

---

18. Caroline Bynum, *The Resurrection of the Body in Western Christianity, 200–1336* (New York, 1995), 313 n. 127.

19. Alan Forey, "The Military Order of St. Thomas of Acre," *English Historical Review* 92 (1977): 481–503.

20. James Brundage, "The Crusader's Wife Revisited," *Studia Gratiana* 14 (1967): 241–252; see Theodore Evergates, *Feudal Society in Medieval France: Documents from the County of Champagne* (Philadelphia, 1993), 120–121 (for the case of Renaud II of Dampierre); and Jacques Paviot, *Projets de Croisade (v. 1290–v. 1330)* (Paris, 2008), 35–43 (for the case of Roger of Stanegrave).

in the East—those that followed more closely the norms expected of dying noble men and women in the West and that generated a fixed sense of the body's location and preparedness for resurrection. They also describe what were, from the point of view of the noble family, worst-case scenarios. Overall, they demonstrate the great challenge that crusading posed to the medieval aristocratic culture of death and commemoration. In order to understand this challenge, it is first necessary to establish the principal elements of that culture of death.

Noble Death

In chapter 1 we saw how moments of death and burial represented important opportunities for families to gather and reaffirm their commitment to the traditions of their forebears. More generally, the rituals of aristocratic death were of central importance for the restructuring of a family's identity and for renegotiating relations between members of the family and the wider community. As we will see, the most vivid descriptions of these rituals are in vernacular works of the early thirteenth century, but the culture that they describe was hardly new. Earlier texts, especially the abundant and discursive charter evidence from northwestern Francia, reveal that at the time of the First Crusade the more powerful noble families participated in elaborate funeral rites in which the relatives of the deceased gathered together and met with members of religious communities to ensure both intercessory prayer for the dead and continuities of lordship and patronage. The ideal noble death, already sought at the time of the First Crusade, engaged the dying and their families in a lengthy process of preparation, ritual disposition of the body, and the beginnings of what was intended to be perpetual commemoration.

Fulk IV le Réchin, Count of Anjou (d. 1109)

The death and burial of Count Fulk le Réchin of Anjou in April 1109 provides a well-documented example from the generation of the earliest crusaders. Unlike some families of princely and seigneurial rank, the counts of Anjou had, until they became rulers of England, no central family necropolis; their bodies were entombed at a variety of institutions around their domains. This did not mean, however, that they considered burial to be any less important. The burial of several members of a family, sometimes over multiple generations, together at one site projected a powerful sense of that family's dynastic identity and of the continuity of their power and traditions. While the importance of such sites cannot be overlooked, however, the existence of such necropolises as Liessies, Ripoll, and Andres, where monks saw the burial of members of particular noble families as customary, should not lead us to overlook the fact that all burials in and around a family's lands, regardless of whether they were at sites of earlier family entombments, might be selected for reasons relating to kinship and could further dynastic political purposes.[21] Fulk IV's choice of burial place, the priory of La Trinité in Angers (called l'Évière), is a case in point. Although Fulk was the first of his family to be buried at L'Évière, the priory was a dependency of La Trinité in Vendôme, a powerful abbey founded by his ancestor Geoffrey II Martel (d. 1060), who had ruled Vendôme in right of his younger sister Adéle for nearly twenty years. The priory maintained close connections to its mother house, and thus to the memory of the comital dynasty in the golden age of its ascendancy. Fulk ensured that while his body would lie in Angers, the capital of the family's *honor,* his memory would be preserved in the prayers of the monks in Vendôme, where his predecessor Geoffery II, the house's founder, was also remembered. A notice of the mother house in Vendôme recorded that as Fulk was dying he conceded back to the abbey all of the rights that his ancestor had granted and that he or intervening generations had usurped, and confirmed the abbey in possession of all that previous generations of counts had given.[22] The count's deathbed concessions were later confirmed by his daughter Ermengard, Dutchess of Brittany, and Geoffrey Caiaphas, a canon of Saint-Laud in Angers who had served as Fulk's secretary.[23]

On the day of the count's death, 14 May 1109, Fulk's son and daughter attended his funeral procession, which began in the cathedral church of Saint Maurice in Angers. In an act that was apparently part of the ceremonial, brother and sister proclaimed their hatred of bondage and freed their serf Benedict.[24] According to the priory's house chronicle, Fulk was buried "with the greatest honor" at l'Évière, a turn of phrase that may have been associated either with the dignity of the ceremonial, the quality of the monument erected over the count's tomb, or both.[25] Each year, the monks would celebrate the count's anniversary, just as they did those of their founder

---

21. Michel Lauwers, *La mémoire des ancêtres, le souci des morts: Morts, rites, et société au Moyen Âge* (Paris, 1997), 294–301. For monastic claims to dynastic burial, see *Chronicon Laetiense, MGH SS* 14: 495 (for Liessies); *Gesta comitum Barcinonensium,* ed. Lluís Barrau Dihigo and Jaume Masso Torrents, Croniques Catalanes 2 (Barcelona, 1925; repr., 2007), 15 (for Ripoll); William of Andres, *Chronicon Andrensis,* ed. Johann Heller, *MGH SS* 24: 730 (for Andres).

22. *Cartulaire de l'abbaye cardinal de La Trinité de Vendôme,* ed. Charles Metais (Paris, 1893–97), 2: 190–191, no. 422.

23. *Cartulaire du chapitre de Saint-Laud d'Angers,* ed. Adrien Planchenault (Angers, 1903), 13.

24. *Cartulaire du chapitre de Saint-Laud d'Angers,* 12–13.

25. "Chronicon Vindocinense seu Aquaria," in *Chroniques des églises d'Anjou,* ed. Paul Marchegay and Émile Mabille (Paris, 1869), 172.

(Geoffrey Martel) and his father (Fulk Nerra), which they observed with the same dignity as that given to their own abbot.[26]

The case of Fulk le Réchin also demonstrates how the concern of a deceased noble's descendants to honor the memory of their ancestor fueled a continuing dialogue between the family and its associated religious communities. However honorable the count's commemoration had been at l'Évière, the tomb monument was apparently soon considered insufficient. The first half of the twelfth century saw the appearance for the first time in western France—indeed in the lands of Fulk's descendants—of lavish tomb monuments with figural representations of the deceased. It must have been in reference to a particularly early example (now lost) of such tomb architecture that Fulk's son Fulk V referred when, in 1124, together with his "sweetest wife," Eremburga of Maine, and their son Geoffrey, he conceded fishing rights in the River Maine in Angers to the monks of l'Évière. In recognition of the gift, the monks agreed to pray for their souls on their anniversaries, both in the main church at Vendôme and in the priory at Angers, with as much solemnity as for their own abbots. The charter documenting the transaction also stipulated, however, that the monks would improve the monument to the count's father, Fulk IV, and make it "as good, if not better, than that of [Eremburga's father] Count Elias of Maine, who is buried in the abbey of La Couture."[27] Present among the group was a young man named Guillaume of Passavant, a contemporary and perhaps a friend of their son Geoffrey. Guillaume was the future bishop of Le Mans, whose cathedral church would one day exhibit one of the finest early figural tomb monuments, which was dedicated to the same Geoffrey, the future Geoffrey V the Fair, Count of Anjou, after his death in 1151 at the age of only thirty-eight.[28]

The monument erected for Fulk at L'Évière is lost to us, and the precise details and ceremonies performed in his memory remain obscure, but what we can see of the count's death suggests the potentially great significance of the rituals surrounding death, burial, and commemoration for the nobility at the time of the First Crusade. Fulk's son's demand, fifteen years after his father's death, for a better monument at L'Évière, like the one that lay above his father-in-law's tomb, also shows that over the course of the twelfth century

---

26. *Cartulaire de l'abbaye cardinale de la Trinité de Vendôme,* 1: 191–192 n. 1 (citing the necrology of La Trinité).

27. "praeterea tumbam Fulconis comitis, qui in monasterio vestro Andegavis sepultus jacet, vestro sumptu talem facietis, si non meliorem, qualis est tumba Heliae, Cenomanensis comitis, qui in monasterio de Cultura sepultus est." *Cartulaire de l'abbaye cardinale de la Trinité de Vendôme,* 2: 235–236. Count Elias of Maine's tomb was drawn by Gaignières; see Jean Adhémar, "Les tombeaux de la collection Gaignières (première partie)," *Gazette des beaux arts,* 6th series, 84 (1974): 20, no. 58.

28. John Phillip O'Neill, ed., *Enamels of Limoges: 1100–1350* (New York, 1996), 98.

the competition for status among noble families was only making the culture of death more elaborate.[29] Such competition probably explains the rapid proliferation of incised stone slabs and recumbent effigies in monastic chapter houses, church choirs, and ultimately the chantries of the later Middle Ages.[30] While these stone monuments are striking visual evidence, they tell only part of the story of the lavish pageantry of death and commemoration. As Michel Lauwers has pointed out, this culture had both religious and secular elements, the latter of which were the subject of repeated complaints by moralists of the twelfth and thirteenth centuries.[31]

William Marshal, Earl of Pembroke (d. 1219)

An early thirteenth-century text, the metrical *Histoire* of the life of William Marshal, Earl of Pembroke, presents what it describes as the ideal noble death as it was perceived by the knightly classes of the Francophone northwest. Having recounted the life of the famous man, the greatest knight of them all, the anonymous author of the *Histoire* turned to the earl's final days as he succumbed to illness at his manor Caversham.[32] As he lay dying over the course of several days, the earl was visited in turn by members of his family and the heads of local religious communities, each of whom played a key role at his bedside. While his daughters sang and danced him a *rotrouenge,* his son led the household knights in a constant vigil by his bed. The abbot of Notley, an Augustinian community that supplied the earl with his household chaplains, promised him commemoration in the prayers of the canons, while the abbot of Reading offered him absolution for his sins. The arrangements that the earl made from his deathbed included the formal, testamentary disposition of his property, decided with his family gathered around him, and specific benefactions to Notley and Reading. But his long, lingering death also allowed him to distribute his own fine robes to the knights in his service. All the while he was comforted by the presence of his dear friend John of Earley.

29. David Crouch, *The Birth of Nobility: Constructing Aristocracy in England and France, 900–1300* (Harlow, UK, 2005), 162–167.

30. Rachel Dressler, "Steel Corpse: Imagining the Knight in Death," in *Conflicted Identities and Multiple Masculinities: Men in the Medieval West,* ed. Jacqueline Murray (New York, 1999), 135–168; H. A. Tummers, *Early Secular Effigies in England* (Leiden, 1980); Kurt Bauch, *Das mittelalterliche Grabbild: Figürliche Grabmäler des 11 bis 15 Jahrhunderts in Europa* (Berlin, 1976); Henriette Jacob, *Idealism and Realism: A Study of Sepulchral Symbolism* (Leiden, 1954); Frank A. Greenhill, *Incised Effigial Slabs: A Study of Engraved Stone Memorials in Latin Christendom, c. 1100 to c. 1700,* 2 vols. (London, 1976).

31. Lauwers, *La mémoire des ancêtres,* 345–351.

32. For commentary, see David Crouch, *William Marshal: Knighthood, War, and Chivalry, 1147–1219,* 2nd ed. (London, 2002), 207–216.

To the anonymous author of the *Histoire,* William Marshal's final moments were also his finest, a theater of noble death perfectly performed by the dying man and the whole cast that surrounded him:

> My lords, it is the very truth that in this world the Marshal experienced many fine and splendid adventures. His dying was the best amongst them, as you will hear shortly. All those of you who ever rejoiced in the great deeds you heard that he had done, will rejoice in that too.[33]

The earl lay in a room with all of the doors and windows open, clasping the cross, surrounded by his family, and receiving final absolution. The performance did not end there. The earl's body was carried in a cortege toward London, escorted by a host of other barons. When it reached Westminster, a funeral mass was sung, and a vigil with a "magnificent display of candles and a magnificent service" was held before the body was interred in the Temple church. Even the place of the tomb in the church was just as "the Marshal had willed it with his own voice."[34]

William Marshal's was not the only model of death available for pious noblemen. Some, more concerned about the consequences of their lives of power and violence than was William, chose to enter religious life in old age.[35] For many knights and barons, however, William Marshal's was the ideal way to die in an aristocratic society, in which, as the thirteenth-century Cypriot knight Philip of Novara would say, "The good death is everything" (*la bone fin va tous*).[36] He was surrounded by friends and family, with enough time to take counsel and make appropriate pious benefactions, to decide on the disposition of his estates and personal possessions. He also had the time and strength to dictate some of the ceremonial elements of his own obsequies and burial. Finally, his death at one of his favorite manors and the transport of his body to fixed points where it would be met by other nobles before the gathering together of a wide community of mourners at the site of burial offered numerous opportunities for the inscription of his memory in the landscape of his own domains. The Temple church in London, where a fine marble effigy would surmount his tomb, was two days' ride from his lands, and in the central city in the kingdom, where his descendants would often visit.

---

33. *History of William Marshal,* ed. A. J. Holden with English translation by S. Gregory and historical notes by David Crouch (London, 2003), 1: 447, ll. 18897–18904.

34. *History of William Marshal,* 1: 545, l. 19043.

35. For discussion, see Jonathan Lyon, "The Withdrawal of Aged Noblemen into Monastic Communities: Interpreting the Sources From Twelfth-Century Germany," in *Old Age in the Middle Ages and the Renaissance: Interdisciplinary Approaches,* ed. Albrecht Classen (Göttingen, 2007), 143–170 and 145, for the phenomenon in France and Spain.

36. Philip of Novara, *Les quatre âges de l'homme,* ed. Marcel de Fréville (Paris, 1888), 92.

William Marshal was also a crusader, having taken the cross to redeem a vow made by his lord and tutee Henry the Young King shortly before his death in 1183.[37] Because of his biographer's curious and inexplicable aversion to discussing the details of his two-year sojourn in the Holy Land, crusading is not often associated with William Marshal's career and identity. The biographer does reveal, however, that as the earl lay dying, memories of his crusading past were very much on his mind; it was a past he wished to memorialize in his death.[38] It was on his deathbed that he revealed that while in the Holy Land he had promised his body to the Templars after his death. The promise was presumably made with the expectation that he might die in the East, where in the 1180s the Templars and the Hospitallers were chiefly responsible for the burial of crusader dead. Although he had survived, returned home, and, in the remaining thirty years of his life, founded and endowed numerous religious foundations, he did not intend to break his promise and thus upheld the connection forged with crusading institutions and experiences in his memory.

According to his biographer, William Marshal also took steps to ensure that his crusading deeds would not be forgotten; he asked his son to fetch a length of silk he had acquired in the Holy Land so that it could be used as a winding sheet and a cover for his bier.[39] Although the poem does not make this clear, he may also have intended it as decoration for his tomb, as his testament specified was the purpose of a length of samite he entrusted to his nephew for transportation to the tomb of King John.[40] William knew that the site of his remains, the most potent physical reminder of his life and achievements, would play a central role in the preservation of his memory. By festooning the coffin or sarcophagus with oriental silk he was taking steps to ensure that his adventures in the East would be included in whatever narrative was constructed around him.

Possession of the Crusader's Body

The loss of the cloth-hangings and polychromy that once decorated the burial places of the medieval nobility, and the widespread destruction and

---

37. *History of William Marshal,* 1: ll. 7275–7301.
38. The same emergence of a crusader's past at or after the moment of their death seems to occur in the *Chronicon montis Sereni*. Describing the funeral obsequies of Conrad of Meissen, who had led a campaign against the pagan Wends in 1147, the Augustinian canons of Petersberg, where Conrad had retired, noted using the well-worn words of Matthew 19, that because he had once "taken up his cross," there was no doubt that Conrad was a disciple of Christ. See *Chronicon montis sereni,* ed. Ernestus Ehrenfuchter, *MGH SS* 23: 150–151.
39. *History of William Marshal,* 3: ll. 18179–18260.
40. *Rotuli litterarum clausarum in Turri londinensi asservati,* ed. G. Eyre and A Spottiswoode (London, 1833–34), 1: 603a. See Sidney Painter, *William Marshal: Knight Errant, Baron, and Regent of England* (Baltimore, 1933), 203–204.

reconfiguration of their tombs in the modern era, have rendered our knowledge of these monuments relatively limited. From what has survived, no consistent iconography can be detected in tomb architecture that explicitly marked out an individual as a crusader. There is abundant evidence, however, that steps were taken to underscore the importance of particular noblemen as crusaders in the memorial architecture that housed their remains. Evocations of crusading can be found in the reliefs and commemorative verses on the bronze doors of the mausoleum of Bohemond of Taranto (d. 1111);[41] in the images on the kinship tomb of Henry II of Brabant in the Cistercian house of Villers (d. 1248);[42] in the epitaphs that adorned the tombs of Eustace of Boulogne (d. 1123) at Cluny,[43] Ramón Berenguer IV of Barcelona (d. 1164) at Ripoll,[44] the kinship tombs of Thibaud of Champagne (d. 1201) in his palatine chapel of Saint-Étienne in Troyes,[45] and of Jean of Eppes (d. 1293) in Saint-Vincent of Laon;[46] and in the hilt of the sword, thought to be of eastern origin, depicted in the tomb effigy of Jean d'Alluye (d. 1248) in the Cistercian house of La Clarté Dieu.[47]

Even in the absence of surviving tomb architecture referring explicitly to the crusades, there are clear indications that a crusader's remains could play a special role in the structuring of family and community memory. The decision of the Limousin crusader Gouffier of Lastours to break with family tradition and have his body interred at the small collegiate church of Le Chalard located near his domains, for instance, led the canons of that community to rewrite key events in the history of their foundation, focusing attention on the relationship between their founder, the hermit Geoffrey of Le Chalard, and the crusader Gouffier.[48] In a dramatic dialogue drawing rhetorical and stylistic force from the exchange between Phaeton and Helios in the second book of Ovid's Metamorphosis, the *Vita beati Gaufredi Castaliensis,* composed

41. Jean Flori, *Bohémond d'Antioche: Chevalier d'aventure* (Paris, 2007), 293–300.

42. Anne McGee Morganstern, *Gothic Tombs of Kinship in France, the Low Countries, and England* (University Park, PA, 2000), 30–31.

43. Phillips, *The Second Crusade,* 30–31.

44. Jose Morgades y Gili, "El sepulcro de D. Ramón Berenguer IV, conde de Barcelona," *Boletín de la Real Academia de la Historia* 26 (1895): 484–485; and see below, 272–274.

45. Morganstern, *Gothic Tombs,* 13–15.

46. Robert Wyard, *Histoire de l'abbaye de Saint Vincent de Laon* (Saint-Quentin, 1858), 263–265.

47. Helmut Nickel, "A Crusader's Sword: Concerning the Effigy of Jean d'Alluye," *Metropolitan Museum Journal* 26 (1991): 123–128.

48. A. Lecler, "Le tombeau de Gouffier de Lastours," *Bulletin de la Société Archeologique et Historique du Limousin* 32 (1885): 113–116; Geoffroi Tenant de La Tour, *L'homme et la terre de Charlemagne à Saint Louis: Essai sur les origines et les caractères d'une féodalité* (Paris, 1943), 368–369. Tenant refers to the epitaph as reconstructed by Bonaventure, with anachronistic spelling and the inclusion of the lordship of "Nexon." The epitaph as copied by Lecler does not contain these elements. The epitaph is no longer legible.

sometime in the middle of the twelfth century, imagined Gouffier and Geoffrey discussing the relative merits of the crusade.[49] The crusader is heard to say
to his friend: "I will be your servant, however undeserving, devoted and faithful in whatever way I can be; I myself and all that is mine I give to you, waiting
on your every need, and furnishing whatever your counsel should contrive."[50]

The closeness of the two men in the *Vita* mirrored the physical proximity
of Gouffier's tomb to the shrine where Geoffrey's body was guarded as a holy
relic in the late eleventh-century church.[51] The creation of such a rhetori-
cally sophisticated work about the relationship between the crusading lord
of Lastours and the holy hermit Geoffrey at the time when Gouffier's son
Guy was taking the cross for the Second Crusade may have been intended
to remind the family of the variety of ways that they (as crusaders) were tied
and indebted to the blessed Geoffrey's community of Chalard. Gouffier's
presence at Chalard also had longer-term consequences for the family's relationship with this small college. According to an inscription (now illegible)
that once ran around a tomb monument in the church, Gouffier, his sons,
and other members of the family had chosen burial at Le Chalard.[52] The
monument on which the inscription was found, an incised slab depicting a
knight bearing the arms of Lastours and a lady under a Gothic canopy,[53] can
be dated on stylistic grounds to the late thirteenth or early fourteenth century.[54] Because the inscription, even when it was still legible, was already damaged, and because miniature shields of metal inlay that probably displayed the
lady's arms are now missing, the monument is difficult to interpret. At least
one other memorial marking the burials of multiple generations of a single
family, that of the viscounts of Comborn at the abbey of Aubazine, was
constructed during this period (c. 1298), and it therefore seems likely that
the incised slab was meant to represent an inhumation of multiple Lastours

---

49. For a reconstruction of the chronology of the *Life,* see J. Becquet, "Les chanoines réguliers
du Chalard," *Bulletin de la Société Archéologique et Historique du Limousin* 98 (1971): 154–172.

50. "Ego famulus tuus ero, licet indignus, devotus tamen et fidelis in quantum potero; omnia
mea et me ipsum tibi dedam, sumptum per omnia tibi subministrans, consiliis que tuis parere paratus
ubique." "Vita beati Gaufredi Castaliensis," ed. Auguste Bosvieux, *Mémoires de la Société des Sciences
Naturelles et Archeologiques de la Creuse* 2 (1862): 94.

51. For the church, see Xavier L'Hermite, "Le prieuré du Chalard, étude architecturale," *Bulletin
de la Société Archéologique et Historique du Limousin* 131 (2003): 37–71.

52. Lecler, "Le tombeau de Gouffier de Lastours," 115–116. Another slab now located in the
floor of the upper church, and almost totally effaced, still clearly bears the arms of Lastours. Multiple
burials by members of the family would seem, then, to have occurred at Le Chalard.

53. For the arms, see Alfred de Froidefond de Boulazac, *Armorial de la noblesse du Périgord* (Périgeux, 1891), 1: 296.

54. See, for comparison from the monuments reproduced in Greenhill, *Incised Effigial Slabs,* 113,
Eudes de Montfaucon and his wife, Aelide de Gallardon, confidently dated to 1299 in Magny-les-
Hameaux, Yvelines. My thanks to Dirk H. Breiding for his thoughts on the slab.

family members at Chalard, beginning with Gouffier and his wife, Agnes of Aubusson.[55]

There is abundant evidence that the burial sites of crusaders, like that of Gouffier at Le Chalard, were revisited and reconstructed by later generations of their families. We know, for instance, that over the course of the thirteenth and fourteenth centuries, lavish new tomb monuments were erected over the bodies of the First Crusade veteran Duke Robert Curthose of Normandy (d. 1136), at Saint Peter's abbey in Gloucester (now Gloucester Cathedral),[56] and the Catalan crusader Count Ramón Berenguer IV of Barcelona (d. 1164), at Saint Mary of Ripoll.[57] In 1219 the lord of Coucy, Enguerrand III, ordered the monks of Nogent-sous-Coucy to "honorably translate" the body of his crusading ancestor "that noble man of happy memory" Thomas of Marle (d. 1130) to a new and more prominent position in the choir of the reconstructed abbey church of Nogent-sous-Coucy.[58] As we have seen, John of Joinville's epitaph for the tomb of his great-grandfather Geoffrey (d. 1188), which he placed at the Cistercian abbey of Clairvaux some time after his return from Louis IX's first crusade in 1254, mentioned not only Geoffrey's own crusade but the crusading feats of every subsequent generation of the Joinville lineage through himself.[59] It was also at Clairvaux that the Count of Flanders, Philip of Alsace, was buried after his death in the East in 1191. We have frustratingly few details about the "chapel of the Count of Flanders" built at Clairvaux and decorated with the rich liturgical adornment

---

55. For the Comborn monument at Aubazine, see *Corpus des inscriptions de la France médiévale*, vol. 4, *Limousin: Corrèze, Creuse, Haute-Vienne, Poitiers* (Paris, 1977), 1112. Although it is not known who commissioned the slab at Le Chalard, the lord of Lastours from 1291 to 1354 was Gouffier V, the last of his line, whose son was declared legally incompetent. It is possible, then, that the tomb monument was the work of Gouffier V's father, Ramnulphe, whose interest in the crusading ancestor was evident in his decision to name his son after his famous ancestor, whose name had not been used by heirs of the Lastours lordship for generations. It could also have been produced by Gouffier V himself, in the hopes of preserving the name of his lineage as the lordship passed through his sister Agnes to a nephew from the family of knights known as the "de Champagne." For the end of the Lastours lineage, see the testament of Gouffier V in the *Histoire des vicomtes et de la vicomté de Limoges* (Paris, 1873), 1: 392–398. Another possibility is the family of Gouffier's wife, Agnes of Aubusson. In 1281, the last viscount of Aubusson died, and his testament records a bequest of 100 livres "for the journey overseas, to transport Peter, his brother, and his knights in the first general passage (*in primo generali passagio*)." Testament de Renaud d'Aubusson, ADHV 5 F/K pièce n. 5 (transcribed from a seventeenth-century copy from the archives of the abbey of Blessac).

56. Charles Wendell David, *Robert Curthose, Duke of Normandy* (Cambridge, MA, 1920), 189 n. 89.

57. Morgades y Gili, "El sepulcro de D. Ramón Berenguer IV"; and see below, 272.

58. Toussaints Duplessis, *Histoire de la ville et des seigneurs de Coucy* (Paris, 1728), 150, no. 35.

59. Natalis de Wailly, *Jean, sire de Joinville: Histoire de Saint Louis, Credo, et lettre à Louis X* (Paris, 1874), 154–157; trans. Caroline Smith in *Chronicles of the Crusades* (New York and London, 2008), 346–347.

Philip gave from his own chapel as he departed on crusade, but the continuing significance of Philip's tomb to his successors can nonetheless be
demonstrated. It was to Philip's chapel at Clairvaux that first his nephew
Baldwin, and then his grandson Guy of Dampierre, went before they
departed on crusade in 1202 and 1270 respectively.[60]

As the site around which rights of lordship and spiritual commitment were
ritually renegotiated and the power and identity of a family was restated,
the aristocratic body was the precious keystone supporting the weight of
the noble house. Even more than most, however, the bodies of crusaders
were objects of honor and sacrality to be treasured, and it was for this reason
later generations returned to them, ensuring that they were appropriately
enshrined and that the deeds of the crusaders were known.

Well might these few families celebrate their possession of crusader dead,
for to take the cross for the crusading frontier was to risk forfeiting every
element of noble death, including, most catastrophically, the loss of the noble
body. For a small minority of those who died on crusade expeditions, such
as Alvisus, bishop of Arras, on the Second Crusade,[61] or King Louis IX of
France, who died in a fashion nearly identical to William Marshal while on
his second crusade to Tunis in 1270,[62] the "good death" was still possible.
For countless others, including the nameless and unrecognizable corpses that
fed the burbot of the Nile, or those who had their hands and feet hacked off
before being decapitated during that king's first campaign to Egypt, it was
not.[63] In the aftermath of the battle of Mansourah in February 1250, Joinville
recalled that he had seen many people "seaching for their friends among
the dead. But I did not hear that anyone was found."[64] Looking back on the
events of the Fourth Crusade, Geoffrey of Villehardouin would say only of
the crusade leader Count Thibaud III of Champagne that "of all the men in

60. *De Oorkonden der Graven van Vlaanderen (1191- aanvang 1206)*, ed. Walter Prevenier (Brussels, 1966), 509–512, no. 243. Thomas Coomans, "Cistercian Nuns and Princely Memorials: Dynastic Burial Churches in the Cistercian Abbeys of the Medieval Low Countries," in *Sépulture, mort, et représentation du pouvoir au Moyen Âge*, ed. Michel Margue (Luxembourg, 2000), 691.

61. Odo of Deuil, *De profectione*, 44–47; *Historia monasterii Aquicintini*, ed. Johann Heller, *MGH SS* 14: 588; Phillips, *The Second Crusade*, 189.

62. Jacques le Goff, *Saint Louis* (Paris, 1996), 298–300.

63. For John of Joinville's description of bodies floating in the river, identifiable as Christians only if they were uncircumcised, see John of Joinville, *Vie de Saint Louis*, ed. and trans. Jacques Monfrin (Paris, 2005), 142–144 §§ 289–291; trans. Caroline Smith in *Chronicles of the Crusades*, 217–218. For other reports of the dismemberment of the bodies of the dead after Mansourah, see Matthew Paris, *Chronica maiora*, ed. H. R. Luard, RS 57 (London, 1872), 5: 160.

64. Joinville, *Vie de Saint Louis*, 144 § 290.

this world he made the finest end."[65] But Thibaud, like William Marshal, had died at home in bed, surrounded by his family and vassals, and was buried with splendor, having not yet set out on his pilgrimage.

If their bodies could be recovered, the families of deceased crusaders might at least perpetuate their memory and have access to a tomb as a point of family cohesion and commemoration. Transportation of human remains, usually the bones or disemboweled corpse of the crusader, was possible, but only with financial means, manpower, and a safe opportunity, and only if the crusader died en route or close to a seaport. Without access to long-distance transport, the bodies of crusaders recovered by their fellow Christians might be buried locally. Many of the dead, however, were simply lost, and their fellow soldiers, who benefited from little leadership, poor communications, and who were often themselves in danger for their lives, might issue conflicting reports of their colleagues' fates upon their return to the West. It is this last scenario, the worst noble families might endure, that was recalled in the dynastic histories of the families of Hainaut and Ardres.

Disappearances

Baldwin of Mons

Among the informants who provided Albert, canon of the cathedral church of Aachen, with the wealth of detail that he used to ornament the lengthy narrative of the First Crusade he composed sometime in the 1120s, was one or perhaps a group of crusaders who had remained in the East in the first years after the conquest of Jerusalem in 1099.[66] This source helped Albert to construct his account of the events in the fraught period in August 1105 when King Baldwin I of Jerusalem successfully fought off an invading army from Fatimid Egypt that had made camp at Yibna (later known to the crusaders as Ibelin), only a few days' march away from Jerusalem and the kingdom's chief port of Jaffa.[67] Albert described how, in early spring of the following year, the king counterattacked, ravaging the land around the Fatimid stronghold at Ascalon. The coda to this triumphal royal narrative, however, was a disturbing story of loss, doubt, and trauma.

Albert related how, as the Frankish knights attacked the plains of Ascalon, the horse ridden by the squire of the young Flemish nobleman Arnulf of Oudenaarde had bolted, carrying him into the nearby foothills. His lord,

---

65. Geoffrey of Villehardouin, *La conquête de Constantinople,* ed. and trans. Edmond Faral (Paris, 1938), 1: 38 § 37; trans. Caroline Smith in *Chronicles of the Crusades,* 12–13.
66. For the sources of Albert's chronicle, see Albert of Aachen, *Historia Ierosolimitatna: History of the Journey to Jerusalem,* ed. and trans. Susan B. Edgington (Oxford, 2007), xxvi–xxviii.
67. Albert of Aachen, *Historia Ierosolimitana,* 705–717.

concerned according to Albert, about both his horse and his boy, went to look for them, somewhat foolishly, on foot and unarmed. Neither man returned alive. The squire, according to Albert, was never seen again, although his horse, which returned to the crusader's camp covered in blood, was interpreted as a sign of some frightful end. It came to light that Arnulf had been ambushed and killed, his body decapitated, and his head taken as a prize inside the walls of Ascalon. The body was returned to Jerusalem, where, Albert's source told him, it was buried with honor but much sadness in the church of St. Mary in the valley of Josaphat. Among the mourners who wept at the burial of the noble boy, Albert's source remembered one in particular: "The noble wife of Count Baldwin of Hainaut also wept over him with bitterest tears (*amarisimus lacrimis*), because he was a comrade and fellow traveler of hers who had come down from distant Gaul to worship in Jerusalem."[68] She was probably still in Jerusalem when, following a formal request by the king to the emir of Ascalon, the boy's head was returned three days later. A note attached to his hair indicated that the gesture was not one of sympathy, but a warning not to attempt another attack.

The countess of Hainaut whom Albert described was Ida of Louvain, wife of the crusader Count Baldwin II of Hainaut. What was she doing in Jerusalem in early 1106, and what was it that made Albert's source remember her in such great distress during the burial rites for her decapitated Flemish friend? Albert was the only chronicler, either of the crusade expedition itself or of the early history of the kingdom, to mention Ida, but her husband, a great territorial prince, had not gone unrecorded. Albert of Aachen and Guibert of Nogent knew that after the fall of Antioch in July 1098, he had been chosen along with the French magnate Hugh the Great of Vermandois to undertake a diplomatic mission to Constantinople. Along the way, however, the two were ambushed, and, according to Guibert,

> in a certain place, the Turks attacked them; those who had horses nearby escaped; those who were not close enough to their horses were carried away as captives, or were slain by the sword. We are not at all certain yet about the unfortunate fate that befell the count of Mons.[69]

Albert was likewise uncertain about Baldwin's fate:

> [The Turks] shot Baldwin, who was travelling slightly in front of Hugh, so they say, full of arrows. Some declare it is true that they led him away

68. Albert of Aachen, *Historia Ierosolimitana*, 714–717.

69. Guibert of Nogent, *Dei Gesta per Francos et cinq autres textes*, ed. R. B. C. Huygens (Turnhout, 1996), 243; trans. Robert Levine as Guibert of Nogent, *The Deeds of God through the Franks* (Woodbridge, UK, and Rochester, NY, 1997), 102.

alive and captive, but it is not known to this very day what death that very noble and Christian prince suffered.[70]

The circumstances of Ida's husband's disappearance were similar to those that led to the death of Arnulf and his squire. In Albert's narrative, at least, it may have been at the funeral obsequies in the valley of Josaphat that she at last realized the likely fate suffered by her husband.

Working only with the information provided by crusade chroniclers we might assume, as Albert himself may have done on the basis of what his sources told him, that Ida had taken the cross and traveled to the East with her husband. Such participation by women in the expedition was extremely rare but not unknown, and another Ida, the dowager marchioness of Austria, marched alongside Welf IV of Bavaria in the crusade of 1101.[71] A further source survives, however, that both broadens our knowledge of the travels of Ida of Louvain and her husband Baldwin of Hainaut and suggests the depths of trauma that might be experienced by families of those who, like Baldwin, died far away on crusade.

In 1197, almost exactly a century after Baldwin's disappearance on the road from Antioch to the Byzantine frontier, a cleric named Gislebert who had served as chancellor to Baldwin V of Hainaut set out to write the history of his former lord's family. The account he provided of Baldwin II's experiences on the First Crusade was extensive, beginning with a history of the city of Jerusalem and the True Cross and, when he finally reached the events of the First Crusade, including an account of Baldwin's brave deeds at the siege of Antioch.[72] He explained, in terms similar to those used by Guibert of Nogent and Albert of Aachen, the uncertain fate of the count on his diplomatic mission to Byzantium, writing: "In that same battle Count Baldwin of Hainault perished, but it is unknown to this day how he succumbed to misfortune."[73] At this point, however, Gislebert turned his attention from the count to Countess Ida:

> It also ought not to be passed over in silence that Countess Ida heard about the death of her lord and, as she was uncertain if he had been killed or was being held captive, esteeming God and her husband, she unhesitatingly went to those regions with great effort and heavy expenses. Because of this, she, previously unsure about her husband, returned even more uncertain.[74]

---

70. Albert of Aachen, *Historia Ierosolimitana,* 342–343 (I have modified the translation slightly.)

71. Jonathan Riley-Smith, *The First Crusaders: 1095–1131* (Cambridge, 1997), 149 (for Havide of Chiny), 213 (for Ida of Austria).

72. GM, 44–45.

73. GM, 44–45.

74. GM, 45; trans. Laura Napran as Gislebert of Mons, *Chronicle of Hainaut* (Woodbridge, UK, 2005), 30.

Here, in the twenty-seventh chapter of Gislebert's chronicle, we find the key to Ida of Hainaut's presence in Jerusalem in 1106. For a century, the Hainaut family had preserved the memory of how, seven years after her husband's disappearance, she had gone to the East to search for him. Unlike the crusade chroniclers, who insisted that the count must have died, Gislebert preserved the sense of doubt and ambiguity that had returned with her.

He also recorded another detail, which compounded the bleak situation of the comital family after the First Crusade. Immediately after he recorded the story of Ida's sorrowful pilgrimage to Jerusalem, Gislebert chose to include the tale of another ill-fated journey:

> This pious wife [i.e., Ida of Louvain] often went to Rome for the sake of prayer. Accordingly, when she was returning through the Ardennes from a pilgrimage, where she had allods near the church of Saint-Hubert, the count of Chiny attacked her violently, wishing to capture her. She fled to the church of Saint-Hubert, where she remained for some time until she could cross safely from there into Hainaut.[75]

"Out of thanks and friendship," which she owed to the monks of Saint-Hubert, Gislebert explained, she granted to them rights to lands in their vicinity, part of which they already controlled thanks to gifts by Ida's mother-in-law, the Countess Richilde. It had been further stipulated, moreover, that the abbot of Saint-Hubert would act as the chaplain of the counts of Hainaut every Christmas, Easter, and Pentecost, bringing with him on these occasions two full barrels of wine of the Lieser (*vino Leasure*).[76]

Gislebert's decision to relate the story of Ida's near abduction and her subsequent friendship with the abbey of Saint-Hubert after describing her husband's disappearance is particularly notable because it represented a rearrangement of events in the family past. In fact, it was not Baldwin's widow, but his mother, Richilde, who had nearly been abducted by Count Arnold II of Chiny and who had taken refuge with the monks of Saint-Hubert. The monks of Saint-Hubert knew this, for the story was recorded in the chronicle that they called their *Cantatorium,* written in 1106.[77] But Gislebert's version of the story can hardly have been a simple mistake. Gislebert was not mistaking Ida for Richilde, since he described Ida's gift of thanks to the monastery as supplemental to the one the earlier countess had made. Moreover, Gislebert, who had for years been a member of the comital household, must have witnessed the thrice-annual ceremony of wine giving and the

---

75. GM, 45; trans. Napran, 30 (translation slightly modified).
76. GM, 46.
77. *La chronique de Saint-Hubert dite Cantatorium,* ed. K. Hanquet, Recueil des textes pour servir a l'étude de l'histoire de Belgique (Brussels, 1906), 134.

guest chaplaincy of the abbot, a ceremony that to his understanding commemorated the incident. What he described was thus most likely what the
comital family themselves believed to have been the sequence of events. It
was certainly the way the story was being told a century later, when Baldwin
of Avesnes repeated it, with further elaboration, in his chronicle of c. 1280.[78]
The story of Richilde's near abduction became associated with Ida's plight
after her husband's disappearance.

Gislebert's (and later Baldwin of Avesnes's) retelling of the story reveals
that almost a century after his disappearance, a memory of Baldwin's participation in the crusade survived among his household and descendants that
was more complex and more painful than the one known more generally in
the medieval West. To the writers of crusade narratives and songs, Baldwin
II was remembered as one of the heroes of the First Crusade and would,
together with all of the others who died on the expedition, have been considered a martyr in some quarters. As a leading member of the expedition, his
memory was associated with the ultimate triumph of the conquest of Jerusalem. His name was read out in lists of the crusade's noble commanders,[79]
and in genealogies that circulated among those more distant from him in
time and in degrees of kinship, he was named "the Jerusalemite."[80] For his
family, however, the story was different. While, like other families, Baldwin's
descendants were eager to claim this legacy of honor, they had not forgotten
the depth of loss and fear experienced by his widow, and the friendship of
those communities that had stood together with the countess and her young
son, Baldwin III.

Baldwin of Ardres

A thread of loss, sadness, and uncertainty associated with the experience of
crusading runs through Lambert of Ardres's chronicle of the Guines and
Ardres families. His narrative includes stories of an illegitimate son of Arnold
I of Ardres (d. 1094) named Anselm who "went off, arrived, and stayed in the
lands across the sea," most likely as a crusader. Having been captured by the
"Saracens," he escaped and returned to Ardres "after many years" but was so
changed by his experiences (he was said to have apostasized) that he preferred
to return to the East rather than stay at home, where he was "hateful to his

---

78. Kervyn de Lettenhove, *Istore et chroniques de Flandres d'après les textes de divers manuscrits* (Brussels, 1880), 2: 570.

79. See the verses edited in Nicholas L. Paul, "Crusade, Memory, and Regional Politics in
Twelfth-Century Amboise," *Journal of Medieval History* 31:2 (2005), 141.

80. *Liber epistularum Guidonis de Basochis,* ed. H. Adolfsson, Acta Universitatis Stockholmiensis,
Studia Latina Stockholmiensis 18 (Stockholm, 1969), 141–142. See above, 52.

Christian relatives."[81] Lambert paints a vivid picture of a mother, Gertrude of Aalst, "crushed, broken, and weighed down" by the sadness she carried for years, until she died an old woman, over the death of her son in the East many years before.[82]

Lambert's chronicle also contains two reminiscences of the confusion that surrounded the fate of a participant in the Second Crusade, who, like the Count of Hainaut, was named Baldwin and who, like the other Baldwin, also disappeared. The bi-lineal conceit of Lambert's narrative presents the event first from the point of view of the living count Arnold II's paternal family, the counts of Guines, and then from the perspective of his mother's household in Ardres. Of chief concern to the Guines narrative was a crisis of succession: the lord of Ardres left behind no male heir, and in his absence the lordship was contested between his provost and his son-in-law. Into this tense situation came the rumors

> now that Baldwin, the lord of Ardres, had perished of hunger at Sata-
> lieh, now that he had drowned in the sea, now that he was slain by the
> blades of Christ's enemies, but whether this or that, in the end that he
> was dead and buried beyond any hope of returning.[83]

Members of the father's household were apparently less concerned with Baldwin's precise fate, and more interested in establishing that he was actually dead and would not return.

When, later in his history, Lambert returned to the story of the crusader's disappearance as told by the narrator of the Ardres family past, he presented an account that was both more focused and more detailed, and that reveals quite different concerns from those of the Guines version. Baldwin, according to the Ardres storyteller Walter of Le Clud, was with the forces of the French king Louis VII when they reached Satalieh on the southern coast of Asia Minor. To those familiar with the crusade, this fact signaled that he had survived the harrowing rearguard actions fought by Louis VII as he attempted to move his army across Anatolia, battles in which many other men had already disappeared.[84] Walter noted that the army was starving, but that Baldwin had died not from hunger but disease. It was at his own request that his body was thrown into the sea. This was the reason he "never again appeared before his people."[85]

---

81. LA, 615; trans. Shopkow, 144 and n. 389.
82. LA, 628: trans. Shopkow, 168.
83. LA, 593; trans. Shopkow, 105.
84. Phillips, *The Second Crusade,* 201–203.
85. LA, 634; trans. Shopkow, 178.

As recorded by Lambert, Walter's story restored a degree of agency and dignity to the chaotic and troubling circumstances of Baldwin's disappearance. In the narrative, the family confronted the deeply troubling fact that Baldwin's body had been thrown into the sea. The promise of Revelations 20:13 that the sea would give up "the dead that were in it" notwithstanding, nonseafaring medieval Christians greatly feared the prospect of death at sea, precisely because of the implied loss of the body and the absence of a commemorative site.[86] Well into the early modern period, open water was, in the words of Robert A. Houston, "a shifting, abstract, potentially dangerous medium."[87] It was also full of monsters that would consume the bodies of the dead.[88]

The disposal of dead bodies in the sea was a strategy adopted by medieval soldiers and travelers to prevent the spread of disease, and it seems likely that, with or without his consent, Baldwin's body was committed to the depths for this reason.[89] When, in the early stages of the Third Crusade's siege of Acre, disease carried off many of those present, we hear from the eyewitness Roger of Howden that their bodies were thrown into the sea.[90] Those whose bodies were disposed of in this manner included Roger's fellow Yorkshireman Nigel de Mowbray, whose father Roger (d. 1188) was buried just up the coast at Tyre.[91] Like the descendants of Baldwin of Ardres, the heirs to the honor of Mowbray and their associated communities faced the lack either of a body or a location with which Nigel's memory might be associated. Narratives of the Mowbrays written much later, probably in the fourteenth century, at the family foundations of Byland and Newburgh reveal an interesting divergence from Roger of Howden's account. The monks of Byland and Newburgh explained that Nigel had been buried at sea because he had died at sea. They also added that he was buried in a container bearing an inscription (or possibly containing an epitaph) describing "what kind of man he was."[92] Like the claim that Baldwin of Ardres had chosen his mode of burial,

---

86. Jean Delumeau, *La peur en Occident (XIVe-XVIIIe siècles): Une citée assiégée* (Paris, 1978), 49–62. For Delumeau's ideas in the crusading context, see Caroline Smith, "Saints and Sinners at Sea on the First Crusade of Saint Louis," in *Crusades: Medieval Worlds in Conflict,* ed. Thomas F. Madden, Vincent Ryan, and James Naus (Farnham, UK, and Burlington, VT, 2010), 161–172.

87. R. A. Houston, *Punishing the Dead? Suicide, Lordship, and Community in Britain, 1500–1830* (Oxford, 2010), 218.

88. Christopher Daniell, *Death and Burial in Medieval England, 1066–1550* (New York, 1997), 98.

89. This was the explanation for the burials at sea witnessed by Felix Fabri in 1480. They were, however, no less disturbing to the pilgrim passengers. Nicole Chareyron, *Pilgrims to Jerusalem in the Middle Ages,* trans. W. Donald Wilson (New York, 2005), 55.

90. [Roger of Howden], *Gesta regis Henrici secundi Benedicti abbatis,* ed. William Stubbs, RS 49 (London, 1867), 2: 149.

91. Roger of Howden, *Chronica,* ed. William Stubbs, RS 51 (London, 1868–71), 2: 325.

92. The somewhat nonsensical rendering of Byland's chronicle of its founders ("Nigellus, cruce signatus, obiit in Mare Graeco, in dolio, in mare projectus, continente, qualis vir fuerit"; for which, see

the image of Nigel de Mowbray's body accompanied by written signifiers of his nobility maintained for the family an air of dignity around his altogether undignified end.

As in Hainaut, the consequences of the crusader's disappearance in Ardres were political as well as emotional and commemorative. Turning to events not hinted at in the Guines history, the Ardres narrative of Baldwin's disappearance described how in 1176, thirty years after any news had been heard about his fate, an individual emerged, dressed as a monk, who claimed to be the missing crusader.[93] While some members of the family, following the current lord of Ardres, refused to accept the story, others, including the narrator of the Ardres family history, Walter of Le Clud, who was an illegitimate son of the missing man, actually went to see him to find out for themselves. After such a long absence, the narrator claims that neither he nor others that had known his father could be sure, when they had met with him, whether he was who he claimed to be. It was only when he was revealed to be a thief, said Walter, that they knew he was truly a "tramp" (trutannum) and not the long-lost crusading lord.[94]

The dire consequences that a crusader's disappearance could have on a noble family, however, which are only hinted at in the Ardres account, can be illustrated using other examples. Both nearby in Flanders, after Count Baldwin IX of Flanders, who had been among the leaders of the Fourth Crusade, was taken prisoner by the Bulgarian tsar Kaloyan in April 1205, and as far away as Spain, after the death of Alfonso I of Aragón at the battle of Fraga in the Muslim-held Ebro Valley in 1134, serious political disturbances were caused by the appearance, decades later, of pretenders falsely claiming to be the missing men.[95] In the former case, twenty years of uncertainty about the fate of the missing lord passed, while in Aragón forty-three years elapsed since the king's death, which had been transformed in the popular imagination as having occurred in the course of a journey to Jerusalem.

MA 5: 346) can be rendered comprehensible by comparison to the equivalent text from Newburgh ("Nigellus, cruce signatus, ivit in Terram Sanctam, obiit in Mare Graeco, et projectus fuit in mare; in dolio continebatur scriptum qualis vir erat"; in "Progenies Moubraiorum, huius abbatiae fundatorum," MA 6: 320). It is clear that in Yorkshire he was thought to have died at sea.

93. LA, 634–635; trans. Shopkow, 178–180.
94. LA, 634; trans. Shopkow, 180.
95. R. L. Wolff, "Baldwin of Flanders and Hainaut, First Latin Emperor of Constantinople, His Life, Death, and Resurrection, 1172–1225," Speculum 27:3 (1952): 281–322; Marcelin Defourneux, "Louis VII et les souverains Espagnols: L'enigme du 'Pseudo-Alphonse'," in Estudios dedicados a Menéndez Pidal (Madrid, 1950–62), 6: 647–661; Antonio Ubieto-Arteta and Federico Balguer Sánchez, "L'aparición del falso Alfonso el Batallador" and "Alusiones de los trovadores al Pseudo-Alfonso," Argensola 9 (1958): 29–47; Thomas N. Bisson, "The Rise of Catalonia: Identity, Power, and Ideology in a Twelfth-Century Society," in Medieval France and Her Pyrenean Neighbours: Studies in Early Institutional History (London and Ronceverte, WV, 1989), 146–147. And see below, 284–285.

Reclaiming the Dead

The cases outlined above illustrate the traumatic impact that the loss of a crusader's body could have on a family and household. Robbed of the rituals of death and burial and the body that would enable appropriate commemoration, families faced both emotional and political consequences. The narrative texts that usually acted as vehicles for commemorative tradition, containing epitaphs and information about an ancestor's place of burial, recorded instead the consequences of uncertainty. Given the potential familial trauma and real political dangers a family faced when normal commemorative systems failed, it is unsurprising to find that individuals, their families, and familial institutions went to great lengths to recover what they could of crusaders' bodies and to fix their memory with greater certainty. As we saw in chapter 2, the memory of those who died in the East could, to some extent, be preserved in narratives that would explain to their family members the circumstances of their death and the location of their burial.

Whether it was near a landmark like the bridge outside of Nicaea where Aimery of Courron's body lay, at the church of Saint Nicholas in Jaffa where Herbert of Thouars had been interred by his brother, or on the Mount of Olives where Hugh of Chaumont awaited bodily resurrection, knowledge of the location of a crusader's burial helped his family to comprehend and cope with his faraway death. A clear sense of a crusader's burial place helped not only to direct prayers said for the dead at a distance but could also guide travelers on their way to visit the dead in the East. In 1211, for example, Wilibrand of Oldenburg paid such a visit to the tomb of his uncle who had died of disease at Antioch on the Third Crusade, and who was buried in a grotto near the church of Saint Peter. It could not have been very difficult for Wilibrand to find his uncle's tomb, as it was near the place that the leader of the expedition, Emperor Frederick I Barbarossa, had been buried after he drowned crossing a river in Anatolia.[96]

Habeant corpora

By the time of the Third Crusade, most powerful princes, who traveled with great entourages of followers and supporters and who had access to greater financial resources, did not follow Frederick in finding their final resting places in the East. Since the mid-eleventh century at least, the practice of separating and burying the viscera from dead bodies to preserve them and

---

96. J. C. M. Laurent, *Peregrinatores medii aevi quatuor: Burchardus de Monte Sion, Ricoldis de Monte Crucis, Odoricus de Foro Iulii, Wilbrandus de Oldenborg* (Leipzig, 1864), 186–187.

facilitate transportation was in use throughout medieval Christendom.[97] The custom was most famously adopted to preserve the body of King Louis IX of France for its long journey to Paris after his death at Tunis in 1270.[98] The case of Louis IX was in no way ordinary, however. Those who were with the king, who died in the odor of sanctity, may already have been thinking of his remains as relics.[99] The extraordinary lengths to which noble and knightly families went to recover the bodies of crusaders reflected more basic concerns, first with the retrieval of the body from possible danger or pollution at the hands of non-Christians, and second with the reestablishment of a locus of commemoration for the dead crusader.

Those who fought on the frontiers of religious conflict wanted to ensure that their bodies, the vessels in which they would find redemption and resurrection, would be safely buried in Christian soil. A charter of the Spanish nobleman Gonzalo Salvadorez, written at the moment of his "readiness for battle against the Moors," demanded that, if he died in Muslim lands, his body should be "borne to Oña and buried there with my kinsfolk." "If my vassals and retainers do not carry me [to the abbey of Oña] in the event of my death," he added, "they are nothing worth, like a traitor who kills his lord."[100] The striking comparison between abandonment of the body and betrayal gives a clear sense of Gonzalo's apprehension. The Spaniard's concern is echoed, in the eastern theater of war, by the dying commands of Baldwin of Boulogne, second ruler of Jerusalem, who ordered that

> if he should die they should never bury his lifeless body in any grave in this land of the Saracens, lest it should be an object of mockery and derision to the gentiles, but with all the skill and exertion they could muster they should carry his corpse back to the land of Jerusalem and bury it next to his brother Godfrey.[101]

If the medieval rituals of death were, as Danielle Westerhof has suggested, strategies to contain the sense of "exclusion from the community, being forgotten and isolated," which death entailed, it is easy to see why crusaders would fear death and the loss of their bodies in alien landscapes.[102] So

---

97. Elizabeth A. R. Brown, "Death and the Human Body in the Later Middle Ages: The Legislation of Boniface VIII on the Division of the Corpse," *Viator* 12 (1981): 228.

98. Brown, "Death and the Human Body," 231–233; Jacques le Goff, *Saint Louis* (Paris, 1996), 298–310.

99. M. Cecilia Gaposchkin, *The Making of Saint Louis: Kingship, Sanctity, and Crusade in the Later Middle Ages* (Ithaca, NY, 2008), 28–30, 140–141.

100. Quoted in Richard Fletcher, *The Quest for El Cid* (London, 1989), 137.

101. Albert of Aachen, *Historia Ierosolimitana,* 866–867.

102. Danielle Westerhof, *Death and the Noble Body in Medieval England* (Woodbridge, UK, 2008), 31.

strongly, in fact, did Christians feel about the matter that when in 1299 Pope Boniface VIII harshly condemned what was then the popular aristocratic practice of dividing the body for multiple burials, he explicitly made an exception for those who died in non-Christian territory.[103]

This concern would at least partly explain the apparent spread of the practice of repatriating the remains of crusaders in the last decades of the twelfth century, when it appeared for the first time that the survival of the Latin states in the East might be in jeopardy. Excepting, for the moment, the claim made by the *Historia Welforum Weingartenensis* that the bones of Duke Welf IV of Bavaria were transported from Cyprus, where he died in 1101, to Weingarten for burial, repatriation appears to have become common only in the last decades of the twelfth century. Geoffrey of Vigeois, writing in 1183–84, reported that members of local seigneurial families in the Limousin who died on journeys to the Holy Land in the late 1160s and 1170s were being carried home by their kin and companions.[104] Before his departure with the armies of the Third Crusade, Philip of Flanders appears to have arranged in advance for his body to be transported for burial to Clairvaux in the event of his death in the East.[105] While Philip's selection of a burial site was undoubtedly a reflection of his and his wife's devotion to the Cistercian order, Clairvaux might have seemed particularly reassuring as a final destination given the dangers that he knew a buried corpse might face in the East. Indeed, when Philip took the cross in 1190, he knew that the convent of Mary and Martha at Bethany, where his mother Sibylla was buried, had been sacked and conquered by Saladin.[106]

The idea of repatriation may have granted some crusaders peace of mind that their tombs would not be lost, their bodies not desecrated, and their memories not forgotten, but it was to the crusaders' families and the communities where the recovered remains were eventually interred that the lasting benefit of such costly and difficult undertakings really accrued. By 1200, the abbeys of Weingarten in Bavaria and Reinhardsbrunn in Thuringia could boast that they had acquired the bones of Welf IV of Bavaria (d. 1101) and Ludwig III of Thuringia (d. 1191) respectively.[107] According to narratives of

---

103. Brown, "Death and the Human Body," 221; for Saint Louis as an exception, see 231–232.

104. GV, 172 (for the transportation of the bones of the wife of William Vidal) and 179 (for the recovery of the body of Olivier of Lastours).

105. *Recueil des chartes de l'abbaye de Clairvaux,* ed. Jean Waquet (Troyes, 1950), 359, no. 289. See above, 118.

106. Robert of Torigni, *Chronique,* ed. Leopold Delisle (Rouen, 1872–73), 1: 325. For Saladin's attack on the abbey, see Jonathan Riley-Smith, *The Crusades: A History,* 2nd ed. (New York, 2005), 58.

107. The story of the repatriation of Welf's body, which does not appear in the *Genealogia Welforum* of c. 1126 and is not mentioned by Ekkehard of Aura, first emerges in the *Historia Welforum*. In the thirteenth century, it was being proudly repeated in other memorials at Weingarten. See "Codex

the two families, the bones of each man were recovered from Cyprus, where
their flesh was buried separately. It is probably significant that in each case the
story of the transportation of the crusader's bones is the final act of the narrative of his crusading accomplishments. In this way, Weingarten and Reinhardsbrunn, both of which were the locations of dynastic mausolea, became
part of the crusading story for the community around them, including the
family.

The *Historia Reinhardsbrunnensis*'s account of the recovery of the body
of Ludwig III of Thuringia underscores the potential difficulties associated
with the transportation of human remains over large distances. The anonymous author of the *Historia* described how, after the body of Ludwig III
of Thuringia was prepared for transport on Cyprus, the ship carrying the
landgrave's bones and his faithful companions was caught in a terrible storm.
When the sailors who crewed the ship discovered that they were carrying the
bones of the prince in the hold, they demanded that Ludwig's men throw the
remains overboard. Risking their lives before the angry crew, the Thuringian
crusaders pretended to throw the bones into the sea, making a show of weeping to fool the sailors. In fact, what they threw were only stones, and in their
dissimulation they protected the precious cargo so that it could be carried
to Reinhardsbrunn. There, on Christmas Eve 1191, the bones of Ludwig III
"were placed with greatest reverence near the tombs of his ancestors."[108]

The ability to present a confident, triumphant narrative about a crusader's
death in the East while at the same time preserving that crusader's remains
for commemoration may have been particularly important for the descendants of Welf IV and Ludwig III, whose siblings, children, and grandchil-
dren would take the cross for further crusade expeditions.[109] Neither
the tomb of Welf IV nor that of Ludwig III survives in its original state,
but the tomb slabs of the landgraves of Thuringia, rebuilt after a fire in the
fourteenth century, do have the distinction of being the unique example of
sepulchral architecture in which a consistent visual symbol (the scallop shell
usually associated with pilgrimage to Compostela) was used to mark out
crusaders to the East.[110]

---

maior traditionum Weingartensium," ed. Paul Friedrich Stalin, in *Festgruss zum 400 Jahrestag der Stiftung der Universität Tübingen im Jahre 1877* (Tübingen, 1877), 25–47; "Necrologia sanctimonialium
Weingartensium," ed. F. L. Baumann, *MGH Necrologia Germaniae* 1 (Berlin, 1888), 230.

108. *Chronica Reinhardsbrunnensis,* ed. Oswald Holder-Egger, *MGH* 30.1: 546–547.

109. Welf IV's grandson Welf VI joined Conrad on the Second Crusade, and his great-grandson
traveled to the East in 1172. Ludwig III's brother Herman I joined Henry VI's expedition in 1197, and
his nephew Ludwig IV of Thuringia died early in the expedition of Emperor Frederick II in 1227.

110. Ernst Schubert, "Drei Grabmäler des Thüringer Landgrafenhauses aus dem Kloster
Reinhardsbrunn," in *Skulptur des Mittelalters: Funktion und Gestalt,* ed. Friedrich Möbius and Ernst
Schubert (Weimar, 1987), 219, 221.

Like the relics of saints, the bodies of crusaders were valuable enough commodities for medieval religious institutions to make fictive discoveries and translations. The most obviously fictive claim to the body of a crusader was made by the monks of Byland, who, by the early fourteenth century, had constructed not only a tomb but an elaborate narrative tradition surrounding the return of their founder, Roger de Mowbray, who had in fact died in the East in 1188, a year after his capture by Saladin at the battle of Hattin.[111] Roger of Howden, who had been to the East, was also from Yorkshire and probably knew Roger's son the crusader Nigel would be able to report upon his return that Roger de Mowbray was dead and buried in Tyre. But the confusing circumstances regarding Roger's death—his capture, ransom, release, and subsequent death in the mayhem in Tyre—and the fact that Roger's son Nigel also died on crusade and was buried at sea shortly afterward created a situation at least as complicated as that of Baldwin of Ardres on the Second Crusade, and it is easy to understand why more than one tradition might have persisted in the Honor of Mowbray.

Other probably fanciful tales of the recovery of crusaders' remains, like the one told about the body of the Earl of Salisbury, William Longespée II, after the battle of Mansourah in February 1250, give us a sense of the often-contradictory attempts by western aristocratic society to deal with the disappearance of so many men on crusading expeditions. The carnage that resulted from Louis IX's disastrous attack on the town of al-Mansourah was widely reported. Many knights fleeing the town, including the king's own brother Robert of Artois, drowned trying to cross a river, and John of Joinville remembered seeing Robert's chamberlains at the water's edge searching in vain for their lord's body.[112] According to numerous accounts, including that of the contemporary chronicler Matthew Paris, the bodies that did not just disappear in the river were dismembered either during or after the battle.[113] From the standpoint of aristocratic commemorative culture, Mansourah was a nightmare, and the surviving crusaders themselves were obviously shaken. One year after the battle, while the surviving crusaders were still in the East, Eudes of Châteauroux preached two sermons in memory of those who had fallen.[114] They are unique in the corpus of surviving sermons associated with crusading. Around the same time the king made arrangements for the return

---

111. Roy Gilyard-Beer, "Byland Abbey and the Grave of Roger de Mowbray," *Yorkshire Archeo-logical Journal* 55 (1983): 66.

112. Joinville, *Vie de Saint Louis,* 144 §290.

113. Matthew Paris, *Chronica maiora,* 5: 153.

114. Peter Jackson, *The Seventh Crusade, 1244–1254: Sources and Documents* (Aldershot, UK, and Burlington, VT, 2007), 170–173.

and burial of the remains of earlier crusaders, who had been killed in 1239 and whose heads were said to decorate the gates of Cairo.[115]

Letters to the West after the battle described how one of the English crusading contingent, William Longespée II, had greatly distinguished himself in the battle before being killed. Longespée, whose life and legend were the subject of a close study by Simon Lloyd, had made careful preparations for his own burial and commemoration before his departure.[116] In the immediate aftermath of the crusade, however, there was no indication that his body was recoverable. A vernacular song written about his death at Mansourah, the *Chanson du bon William Longespée,* which may have been based on the accounts of Walter Giffard, one of Longespée's companions who escaped, describes, for instance, how he fought on as his limbs were hacked off one by one, finally collapsing in a pile of Christian corpses.[117]

As the song composed about his death and the long sections dedicated to him in the chronicle of Matthew Paris testify, Longespée was something of an English national hero. But Lloyd noted with some consternation that despite Longespée's instructions before his departure there is no evidence that any member of his family made any attempt to have him commemorated liturgically.[118] How can this be explained? While Lloyd considered several possibilities, including the existence of some dark family secret about William that would have made his family turn away from him, there is a potentially much simpler explanation. It starts with a question: What happened to his body?

Although Matthew Paris himself seems to have accepted that most of those killed at Mansourah were mutilated, their bodies beyond recovery, he had a heartening anecdote about the fate of Longespée's remains. Paris, who was writing within three years of the battle, and for whom Longespée was a major heroic figure, reported that when envoys of Louis IX met with the sultan of Egypt, the sultan announced that he had had the bones of Longespée "excellently and elegantly" entombed and that they had wondrous properties.[119] Grudgingly, the French emissaries accepted that William must indeed have been a most noble knight, and they took the bones with them back to Acre for burial. For Paris, this story served as a final detail in his

---

115. Joinville, *Vie de Saint Louis,* 230–232, 256, §469, §518; trans. Smith, in *Chronicles of the Crusades,* 261, 274–275.

116. Simon Lloyd, "William Longespée II: The Making of an English Crusading Hero" [Parts 1 & 2], *Nottingham Medieval Studies* 35 (1991): 41–69 and 36 (1992): 79–125.

117. "Chanson du bon William Longespée," ed. Tony Hunt, in Lloyd, "William Longespée II," 120–121.

118. This is in contrast to Robert of Artois, who was commemorated despite the lack of remains. The reasons for this, as Lloyd shows, were obviously a political attempt by Louis to remove any sense of Robert's role in the disaster.

119. Matthew Paris, *Chronica maiora,* 5: 342.

presentation of Mansourah as a French debacle and of Longespée as a heroic martyr. None of the dozens of other sources that describe William's death, however, make this claim, suggesting that it was either optimistic lore brought back by a returning crusader or Paris's own invention.

If Longespée's family did not have his body or know its location, and if they in fact knew that, as the *Chanson du bon William* claimed, it had been badly mutilated, how would they preserve his memory? There is very little evidence to suggest that under such circumstances crusaders could be commemorated liturgically. As we have seen, after Mansourah an anniversary sermon was preached for the dead crusaders by Eudes of Châteauroux, and Louis IX ensured that anniversary masses were said for his brother, but outside of Louis's own family and his royal influence, I know of only one charter, dating from the First Crusade, that asks for commemoration in prayer of a crusader whose precise place of burial and day of death was not known.[120] Liturgical commemoration, then, may not have been an option for crusaders who disappeared or whose remains could not be traced.

This does not mean, however, that Longespée was forgotten by his family. "Attempts," Lloyd wrote, "to underline his memory can certainly be found at particular monastic houses of the family's connection." Lloyd cites the chronicles of Barlongs, Waverly, Bradenstoke, and most prominently the Book of Lacock, the major memorial of the house where Longespée's mother, Ela, was abbess and in which "Longespée II is the real hero of the piece."[121] Longespée's mother was also mentioned in the context of his death in the chronicle of Matthew Paris. On the night before her son's death, she was reported to have had a vision of her son ascending into heaven accompanied by angels.[122] When the news finally arrived from the East six months later that he had been killed, she announced the vision she had kept silent about for so long.[123]

The story of Ela's vision and her six months of stoic silence was intended to highlight her piety, but it might also serve as a useful metaphor for a phenomenon underlying other cases we have encountered in this chapter. Behind the world of our male chroniclers like Matthew Paris and the largely male liturgical apparatus that usually handled the commemoration of the noble dead lay the commemorative structures that operated within the family and household, structures that we only rarely glimpse, and in which women are

---

120. Christopher Tyerman, *England and the Crusades, 1095–1588* (Chicago, 1988), 37, citing "Cartulary of the Cluniac Priory of Montacute," in *Two Cartularies of the Augustinian Priory of Bruton and the Cluniac Priory of Montacute,* ed. H. C. Maxwell-Lyte, Somerset Record Society (London, 1894), 184–185, nos. 167–168.

121. Lloyd, "William Longespée II," 86.

122. Matthew Paris, *Chronica maiora,* 5: 153–154.

123. Matthew Paris, *Chronica maiora,* 5: 173.

likely to have played a central role. We have already seen, in the case of Ida of Louvain's journey to Jerusalem, that when the normal culture of death and commemoration was disrupted, women could come suddenly and dramatically to the forefront. Even in the chronicle of Lambert of Ardres, where the story of the disappearance of Baldwin of Ardres on the Second Crusade was described through reference mainly to male actors, a female family member probably played a crucial role. At the moment that the impostor appeared in Ardres claiming to be Baldwin, Ardres was in the possession of the missing crusader's niece Christina. Walter, the storyteller who recounted the tale, was likely to have been a member of Christina's household.

Women, Household, and Memory

Historians of the crusades have advanced conflicting arguments about the impact of the crusade movement on the lives of women in western Europe.[124] On the one hand, using legal evidence, it is possible to understand the precarious position in which women found themselves when their husbands, fathers, or brothers were away on crusade.[125] It is also difficult to ignore, however, the prominent examples of women, usually from the princely aristocracy, like Ermengard of Brittany, Adela of Blois, Clemency and Sibylla of Flanders, and Blanche of Champagne, who were able to hold their lordships as a result of the absence or death of their husbands on crusade.[126] What all of these women, regardless of the power or influence they gained or lost, had to contend with, however, was the commemorative responsibility enjoined on them by the crusading commitments of their men.[127] Some sense of the variety of ways that these responsibilities could manifest themselves has been provided in the examples we have encountered already in this chapter. There is, however, one final example of the traumatic effects of crusading death on the noble family that, at least for the period after 1250, stood as the archetype

---

124. See in general Natasha R. Hodgson, *Women, Crusading, and the Holy Land in Historical Narrative* (Woodbridge, UK, 2007), 108–117.

125. Tyerman, *England and the Crusades*, 209–215.

126. Kimberly LoPrete, *Adela of Blois: Countess and Lord (c. 1067–1137)* (Dublin, 2007), 94–231; Thérèse de Hemptinne, "Les épouses de croisés et pèlerins flamands au xie et xiie siècle: L'éxample des comtesses de Flandre Clémence et Sibylle," in *Autour de la première croisade: Actes du Colloque de la Society for the Study of the Crusades and the Latin East (Clermont-Ferrand, 22–25 juin 1995),* ed. Michel Balard (Clermont-Ferrand, 1996), 83–95.

127. For the general responsibilities incumbent on the wives of men captured by Muslims in Spain, see Martin Aurell, *Les noces du comte: Mariage et pouvoir en Catalogne (785–1213)* (Paris, 1995), 96–97. For widows more generally, see Bernard Jussen, "Challenging the Culture of *Memoria*: Dead Men, Oblivion, and the 'Faithless Widow' in the Middle Ages," in *Medieval Concepts of the Past: Ritual, Memory, Historiography,* ed. Gerd Althoff and Johannes Fried (Cambridge, 2002), 215–231.

of the female experience of crusading death and distance for nobles across Latin Christendom. It is the story of Saint Elisabeth of Thuringia.

The *Historia Reinhardsbrunnensis,* as far as we can tell from the portion that was copied into the fourteenth-century chronicle of Reinhardsbrunn, was finished before 1217, the year of the death of Ludwig III's brother and successor Herman as Landgrave of Thuringia.[128] The story of Ludwig III's crusade and the near loss of his bones at sea was probably well known at the family's great hall of Wartburg, where, in 1220, Herman's son Ludwig IV married the Hungarian princess Elisabeth. In 1227, Ludwig IV followed his father (who joined Henry VI's abortive crusade of 1197) and uncle in taking the cross for an expedition to the East from which he, like his uncle, did not return alive.

As was the case for Ida of Hainaut and the family of Ardres, Ludwig's death had profound consequences for Elisabeth. Ludwig's brother Heinrich immediately seized control of Thuringia as regent for Elisabeth's infant son Herman II, denying to the landgravine her dowry and attempting to force her into exile.[129] Tellingly, the dangerous situation only stabilized once Ludwig's remains had been returned for burial at Reinhardsbrunn. It was at the abbey, over the body of the dead crusader, that Elisabeth and her brother-in-law reached a settlement that would allow her an income and residence within the family's domains.[130] The landgravine's relief upon the arrival of her husband's remains was later recalled by her handmaid Isentrud, who remembered her uttering the prayer "Lord, thank you for mercifully consoling me with the much desired bones of my husband."[131]

Elisabeth, who had been renowned for her piety even before her husband's death, lived the remaining four years of her life as an ascetic caring for the poor, and she was quickly canonized in 1235. Although they have attracted hardly any scholarly attention, Ludwig's crusading experiences and death played a central part in the hagiographical texts and art objects associated with his widow. It would be wrong to say that these works, which were written and crafted to establish the landgravine's sanctity and to locate her cult politically and devotionally, can be used to paint an accurate picture of the impact of Ludwig's death on his family and household. They do, however,

---

128. Stefan Tebruck, *Die Reinhardsbrunner Geschichtschreibung im Hochmittelalter* (Frankfurt, 2001), 45–80.

129. Lori Pieper, *Saint Elisabeth of Hungary: The Voice of a Medieval Woman and Franciscan Penitent* (N.p., 2007), 113–125.

130. Anja Petrakopoulos, "Sanctity and Motherhood: Elisabeth of Thuringia," in *Sanctity and Motherhood: Essays on Holy Mothers in the Middle Ages,* ed. Anneke B. Mulder-Bakker (New York, 1995), 263–264.

131. Albert Huyskens, *Quellenstudien zur Geschichte der heilige Elisabeth, Landgräfin von Thuringen* (Marburg, 1908), 124; trans. in Kenneth Baxter Wolfe, *The Life and Afterlife of St. Elizabeth of Hungary: Testimony from Her Canonization Hearings* (Oxford, 2011), 204.

reveal a profound sympathy among the wider community for the suffering and uncertainty that the death of a crusader could generate within a family.

Elisabeth's confessor, the inquisitor Conrad of Marburg, whose shadow looms large over the canonization inquiry, was not apparently interested in the landgrave's crusade and its effects on his widow. But Ludwig's departure, the arrival of news of his death, and the return of his remains were all dominant themes in the earliest artistic productions associated with her cult. Both the reliefs on the golden reliquary shrine that contained Elisabeth's relics and the stained-glass windows of the choir of the church in Marburg that was erected to house them feature cycles of images dedicated to Elisabeth's life.[132] Three of the eight scenes depicted on the shrine deal with Ludwig's crusade and its consequences. Both the shrine and the windows vividly portrayed both the landgrave taking his leave from Elisabeth and the arrival of messengers bearing the news of his death. In both the gold reliefs and the painted glass, pilgrims wearing the sign of the cross (hence returning crusaders) present Elisabeth with a ring (see figures 1 and 2). On the shrine, one of the returning crusaders carries what appear to be the landgrave's bones.

When, in the later thirteenth century, Dietrich of Apolda created the first sustained *Vita* of Saint Elisabeth, he dedicated the better part of two books, out of a total of eight, to the landgrave's death and the return of his remains.[133] Much of Dietrich's *Vita* was concerned with how the landgravine, even though she was dispossessed and without protection, was still able to honorably restore the remains of her husband to the abbey of Reinhardsbrunn, where he would lie beside his ancestors. Within this larger narrative, however, were emotional scenes, like the landgrave's tearful departure and the moment when Ludwig's mother, Sophie of Wittelsbach communicated the news of his death to her daughter-in-law. The scene may well be pure fiction, but the moment that it captures was clearly of the greatest importance in the narrative of Elisabeth's life as popularly understood. In Dietrich of Apolda's *Vita,* it begins a lengthy section of the life concerned solely with the retrieval and burial of Ludwig's body.

As in the accounts of fateful news arriving in the dynastic histories of Hainaut and Ardres, there was at first some uncertainty, but when it is clear that the landgrave is definitely dead, and not captured, she cries out in anguish: "He is dead, dead, and the world and everything that is sweet in the world is

---

132. For the shrine, see Andreas Köstler, *Die Ausstattung der Marburger Elisabethkirche: Zur Ästhetisierung des Kultraums im Mittelalter* (Berlin, 1995), 21–23. For the windows, see Monika Bierschenk, *Glasmalereien der Elisabethkirche in Marburg* (Berlin, 1991), 186, 191, and pls. 73, 408, and 464.

133. Dietrich of Apolda, *Die Vita der heiligen Elizabeth,* ed. Monika Rener (Marburg, 1993), 61–82, bks. 4–5.

FIGURE 1. Returning crusaders present Elisabeth of Thuringia with her husband's ring. An early artistic representation associated with the cult of Saint Elisabeth, on the golden reliquary shrine containing her relics. Shrine of Saint Elisabeth, Saint Elisabeth's Church, Marburg. Richard Hamann and Heinrich Kohlhaussen, *Der Schrein der heiligen Elizabeth zu Marburg* (Marburg, 1921), pl. 49.

dead to me!"[134] The high melodrama of this scene, written some sixty years after the events it describes, was not a faithful record of the actual events

---

134. "Mortuus;- mortuus et michi mundus et omne, quod in mundo blanditur." Dietrich of Apolda, *Die Vita der heiligen Elizabeth,* 70.

FIGURE 2.   Returning crusaders present Elisabeth of Thuringia with her husband's ring. Depiction on a stained-glass window in the choir of Saint Elisabeth's Church, Marburg. Photo: Art Resource.

after the death of Ludwig IV, but neither was it a fanciful product of Dietrich of Apolda's imagination. In fact, the very earliest reference to an oral or textual tradition of any kind associated with the life of the saint appears in a miracle story dated to 1232. Mathilda of Biedenkopf, a fifty-year-old woman who had been blind in her left eye for three years swore that while on her way to the tomb of Saint Elisabeth "she heard men singing in the German tongue of the mournful separation of blessed Elisabeth and her husband Landgrave Ludwig on the journey to the Holy Land." The song so greatly affected Mathilda that she began to weep, and as the tears flowed her vision was restored.[135] This miracle story is important for two reasons, for not only does it posit the existence of a very early narrative tradition—possibly *Minne* or courtly lyric—dedicated to the effects of the crusade on Elisabeth, but it also suggests that the suffering endured by Elisabeth in Ludwig's absence

---

135. Huyskens, *Quellenstudien zur Geschichte der heilige Elisabeth*, 225.

and following his death far away were central elements in how other *women* understood her sanctity.

Dyan Elliott has argued that Elisabeth's emotional attachment to her husband in the *Vita* of Dietrich of Apolda and elsewhere is "most unusual" of holy matrons, but it is possible that there is something very specific at work in these traditions.[136] Elisabeth was not just another holy woman whose husband had died; to those who flocked to her cult, like Mathilda of Biedenkopf, she represented the archetypal widow of the crusader, suffering much more from the distance and uncertainty of Ludwig's crusade.[137]

Laments sung in the voices of women about their separation from crusaders appear in Occitan, Old French, and Middle High German lyric.[138] As works composed by male authors within the highly stylized traditions of secular lyric and courtly love, their appeal to any "real" sentiment is easily dismissed. What the miracle of Mathilda of Biedenkopf suggests, however, is that the challenges posed by the experience of crusading, in particular the combination of death and distance that stood out so sharply in the dynastic histories of the twelfth century, were no less acute by the end of the thirteenth. These challenges were understood particularly clearly by women, who, like Elisabeth, were often responsible for containing the potential damage that crusading death could do to the family's rituals of death and traditions of burial. These rituals and traditions, they knew, were not only necessary for the appropriate liturgical commemoration of the dead but also fundamental to the family's continuity and identity.

---

136. Dyan Elliott, *Proving Woman: Female Spirituality and Inquisitional Culture in the Later Middle Ages* (Princeton, NJ, 2004), 86 and n. 5.

137. For Elisabeth as model, see Petrakopoulos, "Sanctity and Motherhood," 278.

138. William E Jackson, *Ardent Complaints and Equivocal Piety: The Portrayal of the Crusader in Medieval German Poetry* (Lanham, MD, 2003), 77–92.

❧ CHAPTER 5

Opening the Gates

The numerous, well-publicized pilgrimages undertaken by members of European princely dynasties in the century before the First Crusade have not escaped the attention of modern historians.[1] For those interested in the motivations of the earliest crusaders, these even earlier journeys are seen as a part of the pattern of behavior, along with support for movements of religious reform and for local monastic institutions, that demonstrates a strong belief on the part of the arms-bearing classes in the promise of penitential reward.[2] Logistically, the experience of pilgrims in the eleventh century probably dictated the roads that the crusaders would follow and the arrangements they would make for the care of their families and estates. Intellectually, pilgrimage provided the conceptual framework through which the crusaders understood their undertaking. Indeed, what makes the comparison between the First Crusade and the earlier pilgrimages of the eleventh-century nobility so apparently appropriate is the fact that

---

1. Carl Erdmann, *The Origin of the Idea of Crusade,* trans. Marshall W. Baldwin and Walter Goffart (Princeton, NJ, 1977), 362; Paul Alphandéry and Alphonse Dupront, *La chrétienté et l'idée de croisade* (Paris, 1954–59), 9–42, esp. 10–14; Matthew Gabriele, *An Empire of Memory: The Legend of Charlemagne, the Franks, and Jerusalem before the First Crusade* (Oxford, 2011), 79–93.

2. M. Bull, *Knightly Piety and the Lay Response to the First Crusade: The Limousin and Gascony* (Oxford, 1993), 204–217; Jonathan C. Riley-Smith, *The First Crusaders: 1095–1131* (Cambridge, 1997), 23–29.

among those who made the pilgrimage to Jerusalem before 1095 were the parents or more distant ancestors of those who would achieve great fame in the first decades of the twelfth century as the liberators and rulers of the Holy Land. Some of these pilgrimages, especially those that featured violence or distress on the part of the participants, seem very much to prefigure the subsequent crusade.[3]

But modern historians were not the first to view the eleventh-century pilgrimages to Jerusalem in the light of the First Crusade. The conquest of Jerusalem in 1099 caused twelfth-century historians to rediscover these earlier journeys and to rewrite them radically in the light of the extraordinary events that had transpired in the East. Even within the first decade of the expedition, when the chroniclers of the crusade were at work explaining it to their audiences, this process of rediscovery and reinterpretation was already under way. Guibert of Nogent, who sought to create a narrative sensitive to the "motives and needs" that had brought about the expedition, noted in his chronicle that Count Robert I of Flanders, called "the Frisian," who was the father of one of the most prominent crusade heroes, Count Robert II of Flanders, had undertaken a pilgrimage to Jerusalem in 1083, twelve years before the First Crusade.[4] According to Guibert, the count's wealth and generosity had enabled him to observe and inquire about events in the city. One day, after the whole population of Jerusalem had met together in the "temple of Solomon," Robert was received as a guest "by an old, wise man, who had led a virtuous life by Saracen standards."[5] The man explained to the count that certain celestial signs had been interpreted to mean that an army of Christians would come and conquer the lands held by the Muslims. Prophecies like the one told to Robert, Guibert explained, were to be taken very seriously and carefully contemplated, for "the emperor Heraclius, through this kind of study, foresaw that a circumcised race would rise up against the Roman empire, but he was unable through this method to foresee that it would not be the Jews but the Saracens who would do this."[6]

---

3. Einar Joranson, "The Great German Pilgrimage of 1064–5," in *The Crusades and Other Historical Essays, Presented to Dana C. Munro by His Former Students,* (New York, 1928), 3–56. On the dangers faced by pilgrims to the Holy Land, see Alice-Mary Talbot, "Byzantine Pilgrimage to the Holy Land from the Eighth to the Fifteenth Century," in *The Sabaite Heritage in the Orthodox Church from the Fifth Century to the Present,* ed. Joseph Patrich (Leuven, 2001), 100–101. I am indebted to Alexandra Cuffel for referring me to the Talbot article.

4. Guibert of Nogent, *Dei gesta per Francos et cinq autres textes,* ed. R. B. C. Huygens (Turnhout, 1996), 391–320.

5. Guibert of Nogent, *Dei gesta per Francos,* 319.

6. Guibert of Nogent, *Dei gesta per Francos,* 320–321; trans. Robert Levine as *The Deeds of God through the Franks* (Woodbridge, UK, and Rochester, NY, 1997), 138. Guibert refers to a tradition first reported by Fredegar: *Chronicarum qui dicuntur Fredegarii Scholastici libri IV cum continuationibus,* ed. Bruno Krusch, *MGH Scriptores rerum Merovingicarum* 2 (Hanover, 1888), 154.

Robert I of Flanders had in fact undertaken a pilgrimage to Jerusalem in the late 1080s, and Guibert claimed to have heard the story about the prophecy from one of the count's companions.[7] The prophecy that he repeated was actually quite complex: it also foretold how the Christians would one day be driven from the Holy Land. But as Guibert himself made clear, the story was important because it foretold and explained the success of the First Crusade. Prophecy and other literary techniques of foreshadowing placed the crusade within the unfolding of salvation history, a tradition rooted in the prophetic relationships between the Old and New Testaments and resulting in a view of the past that looked for prophecies and antecedents to explain historical events.[8] Tales of pilgrimages and prophecies foretelling the coming of the crusaders subsequently appeared in all manner of narratives associated with the First Crusade.

The abuse of Christian pilgrims and the desecration of holy sites by Jerusalem's "pagan" overlords were central themes in the preaching of the First Crusade and still resonated in the minds of chroniclers of the expedition working in the first decade of the twelfth century.[9] This narrative context, in turn, prepared the way for later chroniclers, who asserted that prominent early crusaders had been among those thwarted or harassed on pilgrimages. The Spanish vernacular epic of the crusade, *Gran Conquista de Ultramar*, attributed the story to three knights who were stopped before they could enter the holy city.[10] In northern Europe, such stories were usually attributed to the leader of the "People's Crusade," Peter the Hermit, and appeared in the chronicles of Albert of Aachen and the *Chanson d'Antioche*, eventually making their way into William of Tyre's chronicle of the Latin Kingdom of

---

7. Charles Verlinden, *Robert Ier le Frison, comte de Flandre: Étude d'histoire politique* (Paris, 1935), 151–166; Krijnie Ciggaar, "Flemish Counts and Emperors: Friends and Foreigners in Byzantium," in *The Latin Empire: Some Contributions,* ed. V. D. van Aalst and K. N. Ciggaar (Hernen, 1994), 35–38. Verlinden dated the pilgrimage to some time between 1086 and 1089. Robert was back in Flanders by the beginning of 1090.

8. J. M. Powell, "Myth, Legend, Propaganda, and History: The First Crusade, 1140–c. 1300," in *Autour de la première croisade: Actes du Colloque de la Society for the Study of the Cruasdes and the Latin East (Clermont-Ferrand, 22–25 juin 1995),* edited by Michel Balard (Paris, 1996), 129.

9. Guibert of Nogent, *Dei gesta per Francos,* 100–101; Robert the Monk, *Historia Iherosolimitana, RHC Occ.* 3: 727–728; Baudri of Bourgueil, *Historia Jeroslimitana, RHC Occ.* 4: 11–15; Urban referred to these themes in his letter to the laity of Flanders, "Epistula Urbani II papae ad omnes fideles in Flandria commorantes," in *Die Kreuzzugsbriefe aus den Jahren 1088–1100: Eine Quellensammlung zur Geschichte des ersten Kreuzzuges,* ed. Heinrich Hagenmeyer (Innsbruck, 1901), 136–137; Marcus Bull, "Views of Muslims and Jerusalem in Miracle Stories," in *The Experience of Crusading,* vol. 1, *Western Approaches,* ed. Marcus Bull and Norman Housley (Cambridge, 2003), 34–36.

10. *La Gran Conquista de Ultramar,* ed. Louis Cooper (Bogota, 1979), 1: 357–359. My thanks to Carole Sweetenham for pointing out this reference.

Jerusalem.[11] In Italy, Caffaro of Genoa attributed such an experience to the first ruler of the crusader capital, Godfrey of Bouillon himself.[12]

However fanciful, these stories about Peter and Godfrey are nonetheless important for what they demonstrate about the fashioning of crusade narrative. Within a short time of the conquest of Jerusalem, new narrative episodes related to the people and places in the history of the crusade were being generated or collected and then interposed or interlaced into the broader well-known narrative of the crusade in such a way as to emphasize or explain some part of that narrative. In this way, the First Crusade story demonstrated the same characteristics as other narratives of tremendous mythic power and cultural significance in the Middle Ages. Like the life of Christ and other central stories from the biblical tradition, or the stories of King Arthur (*matière de Bretagne*), Charlemagne (*matière de France*), and William of Orange, the story of the First Crusade formed the center of a narrative cycle.[13] To use the formulation of Peter Happé, the basic characteristic of a core story within a narrative cycle is its capacity to "generate other material which reflects back upon it," material which "functions as a means of enhancing the central matter, however indirectly."[14]

By the last decade of the twelfth century, an early vernacular account of the First Crusade ending with the crusaders' miraculous victory at the siege of Antioch, known as the *Chanson d'Antioche,* had already begun to manifest its cyclic force. Like a magnet, it drew in related materials, which were rendered gradually into separate books or "branches" within the cycle. One branch (*Les Chétifs*) told of a group of knights captured in northern Syria; another (*Jérusalem*) related the story of the establishment of the Latin Kingdom of Jerusalem after the conquest of the city in 1099. Soon afterward other materials, relating the youth and legendary ancestry of Godfrey of Bouillon, were also incorporated. This material was added in several stages, beginning with

11. Albert of Aachen, *Historia Ierosolimitana,* ed. and trans. Susan B. Edgington (Oxford, 2007), 2–5; *Chanson d'Antioche,* ed. Jan A. Nelson, OFCC 4 (Tuscaloosa, AL, 2003), 57–59; WT, 1: 124–127.

12. Caffaro di Caschifelone, "De liberatione civitatum orientis," ed. Luigi Belgrano, in *Annali Genovesi di Caffaro e de'suoi continuatori dai MXCIX al MCCXCIIII* (Genoa, 1929), 99–101. The story was also repeated by Guy of Bazoches and then by Alberic of Trois-Fontaines. See *Chronica Alberici monachum trium fontium,* ed. Paul Scheffer-Boichorst, MGH SS 23: 803.

13. For the process of "cyclification," see the essays in *Transtextualities: Of Cycles and Cyclicity in Medieval French Literature,* ed. Sarah Sturm-Maddox and Donald Maddox (Binghamton, NY, 1996); for the process whereby copyists created cyclical manuscripts, see Maurice Delbouille, "Dans un atelier de copistes: En regardans de plus près les manuscrits B1 and B2 du cycle épique de *Garin de Monglane,*" *Cahiers de civilisation médiévale* 3 (1960): 14–22; see also Madeleine Tyssens, *La geste de Guillaume d'Orange dans les manuscrits cycliques* (Paris, 1967); Luke Sunderland, *Old French Narrative Cycles: Heroism between Ethics and Morality* (Woodbridge, UK, 2010).

14. Peter Happé, *Cyclic Form and the English Mystery Plays: A Comparative Study of the English Biblical Cycles and Their Continental Iconographic Counterparts* (Amsterdam and New York, 2004), 16.

Le Chévalier au Cygne and *Enfances Godefroi,*[15] but before 1218 it included three other branches.[16] What emerged by the end of the thirteenth century was a long cycle of narrative poetry, called by its American editors the "Old French Crusade Cycle," and comprising, in its most extensive manuscript, twelve branches total.[17] Episodes chronologically antecedent, succeeding, and contemporary surrounded the well-known crusade narrative in the *Chanson d'Antioche,* foreshadowing, explaining, and in some senses glossing the events of the First Crusade. As new material was added, old material was revised so that each episode and character could become interlaced into the broader narrative.

It should not surprise us that much of the early material that was textually woven together with the *Chanson d'Antioche* dealt with ancestry and genealogy. As Donald Maddox and Sara Sturm-Maddox have suggested, the literary cycle itself mirrored other cycles: "among them various configurations of the liturgical calendar, the human life cycle, the *translatio imperii,* the generations within a lineage, the successive reigns of a line of monarchs, the phases of a dynasty, and even the eschatalogical paradigm of universal history itself."[18] The processes of narrative interlace, episodic generation, and episodic cyclification, through which episodes were woven together to form a cycle of events, characters, and motifs referring back and forth to each other through time, were common to both epic cycles and dynastic historical narratives. This was in part because the normative discourse of ancestry (which, as we saw in chapter 1, sought to locate models from the past against which current or recent behaviors might be compared and contrasted) naturally led writers of dynastic history to adopt the techniques of foreshadowing and internal reference used in epic cycles. But it was also because the narratives of the dynastic and epic pasts actually intersected, for instance at those mythic moments when noble dynasties acquired their regalian or seigneurial

---

15. Geoffrey M. Meyers, "The Manuscripts of the Cycle," in *La naissance du Chevalier au cygne,* ed. Emmanuel Mickel Jr. and Jan A. Nelson, *OFCC 1* (Tuscaloosa, AL, 1977), xv. Of the complexity of various manuscript traditions, Meyers wrote: "One must conclude that there were probably as many attempts at a unified poem as there are cyclical manuscripts." He lists fifteen complete manuscripts, three fragments, and numerous references to manuscripts that are now lost (lx-lxv). The last episode to be added from the genealogical branch of the cycle was *La Fin d'Elias,* written between 1198 and 1218. *La Chanson d'Antioche,* ed. Jan A. Nelson, *OFCC 4* (Tuscaloosa, AL, 2003), 29. For cyclification and the crusade narrative, see David Trotter, *Medieval French Literature and the Crusades (1100–1300)* (Geneva, 1988), 131.

16. *"Le Chevalier au Cygne" and "La Fin d'Elias,"* ed. Jan Nelson, *OFCC 2* (Tuscaloosa, AL, 1985), xxvi-xxviii.

17. Meyers, "The Manuscripts of the Cycle," xiii-lxxxviii; and Keith Busby, *Codex and Context: Reading Old French Verse Narrative in Manuscript* (Amsterdam and New York, 2002), 1: 253–278.

18. Sara Sturm-Maddox and Donald Maddox, "Cyclicity and Medieval Literary Cycles," in Sturm-Maddox and Maddox, *Transtextualities,* 5.

rights. Whether the family's rights were thought to have been acquired through victory against non-Christian enemies or from service rendered to Charlemagne, Arthur, or another popular font of authority, these moments invited the writers of dynastic history to interweave the family's ancestors with broader epic narratives about the past.

When the writers and performers of dynastic history set about their work forging the family pasts of their patrons in the twelfth century they were working in a world and for a community that had been transformed by the First Crusade. Drawing from a common store of motifs and images, they recast the stories of their families' pilgrim ancestors, using these stories not only to prefigure and explain the coming of the First Crusade but also to place these eleventh- and twelfth-century episodes within a larger context of salvation history. The most important and most widely employed image in this dynastic crusading discourse was that of the closed gate of Jerusalem, the *porta clausa,* which required demonstrations of piety, humility, and often also bravery before the pilgrims could access the city and its sacred sites. Identification of this motif not only informs our understanding of how noble families perceived the purpose and place of crusading within historical tradition but also offers a useful cipher for interpreting some of the more opaque rhetoric and ritual of crusade recruitment in use at the end of the twelfth century.

Pilgrim Forefathers

At some time between 1198 and 1219, *remanieurs* who were assembling manuscripts of the Old French Crusade Cycle introduced a new episode to bridge awkward gaps that had emerged between different narrative elements in the genealogical branches of the cycle.[19] This new work, *La Fin d'Elias,* tells the story of the latter years of the life of Godfrey of Bouillon's maternal grandfather, Helyas, the Swan Knight, as he founds and constructs the castles and religious foundations later associated with the family of the historical Godfrey of Bouillon. The middle section of the narrative tells the story of one of the Swan Knight's companions, Pons, the provost of the Ardennes, who carries the standard of Bouillon and fights heroically in the wars against the Saxons. Feeling guilt for the many deaths that he has caused in battle,

---

19. The *Fin d'Elias* was introduced primarily to explain how the plot of the Saracen Cornumarant to travel to the West and poison Godfrey of Bouillon before the First Crusade was foiled. By sending the priest Gerart of Sainteron to the East, the *Fin d'Elias* explains how Gerart and Cornumarant met, allowing Gerart to recognize Cornumarant when he later travels in disguise to Bouillon to poison the young duke in the *Retour de Cornumarant. "Le Chevalier au cygne" and "La Fin d'Elias,"* 394, ll. 1433–1451, where the connection is made explicit.

he joins the priest Gerart in Sainteron, and together with a whole company from Bouillon they depart on a pilgrimage to Jerusalem to achieve absolution for their sins.

Evoking scenes familiar from the departure of crusading armies in the late twelfth century, the poem depicts the party of pilgrims receiving a blessing for their journey directly from the pope ("Milo") "so that if we should die on the journey," they say, "we might achieve salvation."[20] Passing through Italian port cities crowded with warships, transports, and merchant ships, the pilgrim company arrives in Acre, where they unload their warhorses and palfries. As the audience is introduced to the geography of the Syrian coastline, familiar from crusade narratives, they are repeatedly reminded that at one time these cities were not in Christian hands:

> My lords at that port [Acre], which I have told you about, the Persians and the Arabs held the whole kingdom. The Christians had nothing, not Acre, not Caesarea, nor Jaffa either. When the Saracens had seized that kingdom, all belonged to them. When our good pilgrims arrived, the workhorses and the warhorses were unloaded from the ship and the barons mounted and then took to the road. In those days the land was held by the Saracens, their dominion extended to the *Braccium sancti Georgi*. No one could go to the Sepulchre without paying a tribute of silver or fine gold.[21]

According to the tale, the visit of the pilgrims from Bouillon happens to correspond with the coronation of Cornumarant, the young heir of Jerusalem, at the Feast of Apollo. The poem's description of how "all of the pagans and barbarians were ordered to come for the celebration," which was to be held first in the "Temple of Apollo" and then in the Templum Salamonis, is reminiscent of the scene encountered by Count Robert I the Frisian of Flanders in the story of Guibert of Nogent. As the pilgrims are caught up in the crowd headed for the city, they find themselves presented with a frightening obstacle:

> All came straight to the Golden Gate early in the morning. That gate was guarded by sixty bedouin. Each one was wearing a double-meshed

---

20. "Se morons en la voie, s'arons salvatïon." *"La Fin d'Elias,"* 389, ll. 1231–1240.

21. "Signour a cel termine que je vous conte ci / Tenoient tout cel regne parsant et Arrabi; / N'il avoit Crestïen, tout s'en erent fuï / A Acre n'a Cesare ne a Jafe autresi / Quant Sarracin avoient tout cel regne saisi. / Or furent arivé no gentil pelerin; / De la nef furent trait et ceval et roncin / Et li baron i montent, s'aquellent lor cemin, / A icel jour tenoient la tiere Sarrasin, / Desi al Brac Saint Jore ert tout a aus aclin: / Nus n'aoit au Sepucre que n'en fust faite fin, / Se n'estoit par treü u d'argent u d'or fin." *"Fin d'Elias,"* 390, ll. 1290–1301.

hauberk and wore on the left of the belt a steel blade. They noticed our pilgrims, who came down the path, at the entrance to the gate. They judged them to be paupers and they swore to Mahomed, Tervagant, and Jupiter that nevermore will [the pilgrims] see their relatives, that today they would be killed if at the end to their journey they could not pay two hundred ounces of fine gold and all of the silk that one pack horse could carry.[22]

Without waiting for their reply, the guards inform the pilgrims that they will be tied to a central pillar in the Templum Salamonis (al-Aqsa Mosque) and used as target practice during the celebrations for Cornumarant's coronation. Although threatened with this gruesome fate, the pilgrims are defiant, only to be spared by the prince Cornumarant, who recognizes their nobility and allows them to stay to witness his coronation and to venerate the holy sites of Calvary, the Holy Sepulchre, and Bethlehem.

As is explicitly stated in the text, the entire pilgrimage episode was included to explain why, later in the cycle, one of the pilgrims is able to recognize Cornumarant when he travels in disguise to the court of Godfrey of Bouillon.[23] But the pilgrimage episode in *La Fin d'Elias* is also important because it introduces the city of Jerusalem and its holy sites into the narrative of the cycle for the first time. It was, therefore, among the most potent cyclic images anticipating the later conquest of the city by the crusaders, and its rendering of the experiences of Jerusalem pilgrims before the First Crusade was designed to appeal to a wide audience. Although *La Fin d'Elias,* unlike other branches of the Old French Crusade Cycle, is not known to have been drawn from narrative traditions associated with any particular family, it nonetheless depicts a scene of pre-crusade pilgrimage that can be found in several other narratives associated with three powerful princely dynasties: Anjou, Normandy, and Flanders-Hainaut.

Anjou

One of the earliest narratives of a pre-crusade pilgrim found in the dynastic histories is also, in some ways, the most spectacular. Count Fulk III Nerra of Anjou (d. 1040) may have gone to Jerusalem as many as four times

---

22. "Tout droit a Portes Ores vinrest a 1 matin / Cele porte gardeoient LX Beduïn. / Cescuns avoit vestu le hauberc doblentin / Et a costet senestre caint le branc acerin. / Nos pelerins coisirent ki vinrent le cemin, / A l'entrer de la porte les prisent li frarin. Et jurent Mahoumet, Tervagant, et Jupin / Que ja mais ne veront ne parent ne cousin. Ancui seront pendu, si en ert faite fin, / S'il ne puent paier CC onces d'or fin / Et de pales roés tout cargieit 1 roncin." *"Fin d'Elias,"* 391, ll. 1295–1324.

23. See above, n. 19.

in his lifetime,[24] but it was his third pilgrimage, undertaken in 1035, that was described in the greatest detail in the family history.[25] Precisely when the account of his journey entered the Angevin dynastic narrative tradition (*Chronica de gestis consulum Andegavorum*) is impossible to say with certainty. It appears in all extant versions, including the first redaction, and may thus have been the work of either the original anonymous author (working around 1107) or the first redactor, who wrote shortly after the death of Count Geoffrey the Fair in 1151.[26]

The account begins with Fulk Nerra's departure on pilgrimage, first to Rome, where he met the pope, and then to Constantinople, where he encountered another pilgrim prince, Duke Robert of Normandy. Subsequently, Fulk was led under guard to the city of Jerusalem, only to find his way barred by a closed gate:

> He could not, however, enter the gate of the city, where in order to gain entry, pilgrims were violently compelled to give up their money. When he had paid the fee both for himself and for other Christians who were lingering in the area of the gate and unable to enter, he and these others went swiftly into the city.[27]

Having resolved the problem of this closed gate, the account goes on, he was immediately faced with another. The gates of the church of the Holy Sepulchre were also locked. The guards, who did not realize that Fulk was a nobleman, mocked him and said that "no one might wish to be able to reach the Sepulcher, unless he would urinate on it and the cross of the Lord."[28] This was a profound challenge for a man of faith, but the sly Fulk concocted a solution. He asked for a dried wineskin, filled it with "the best wine," and placed it between his thighs. He then proceeded barefoot to the Sepulchre and let the wine pour out over the holy tomb. The trick worked, the guards were fooled, and the count and his pilgrims approached the Holy Sepulchre, weeping with joy.[29] Having covered the Sepulchre with his wine and tears,

---

24. Bernard S. Bachrach, "The Pilgrimages of Fulk Nerra: Count of the Angevins 987–1040," in *Religion, Culture, and Society in the Early Middle Ages,* ed. Thomas F. X. Noble and John J. Contreni (Kalamazoo, MI, 1987), 205–217.

25. *CCA,* 50.

26. *CCA,* xxix–xxx.

27. "Portam tamen urbis intrare non valuit, ad quam peregrini ut intrarent violenter suas pecunias dare urgebantur. Dato autem pretio tam pro se quam pro aliis christianis ad portam sibi prohibitam morantibus urbem celeriter cum omnibus intravit." *CCA,* 50.

28. "Nempe cognito quod vir alti sanguinis esset, deludendo dixerunt nullo alio modo ad sepulcrum optatum pervenire posse, nisi super eum et crucem dominicam mingeret." *CCA,* 51.

29. *CCA,* 51.

Fulk kneeled down as if to kiss the stone and actually bit out a chunk of it to bring home with him.

At the center of the Angevin story is the image of Jerusalem in the time before the First Crusade as a city of locked and barred gates, where hopeful pilgrims are forcibly restrained from visiting the holy places. While contact with the Cross and the Sepulchre are permitted only after an extraordinary public demonstration of humility, Fulk achieves access to the city both for himself and, significantly, *for all of the other Christian pilgrims,* through a demonstration of noble largesse. On its own, the story seems absurd, dominated by the wineskin-urination trick the count is forced to play to avoid desecrating the holiest site in the Christian world. But it nevertheless underscores widely held perceptions about the experiences of earlier generations of pilgrims to Jerusalem. The repetition of particular motifs—including the obstruction of the pilgrim's progress at the gate of Jerusalem (and here also at the gate of the Sepulchre), the persecution of pilgrims, and the pilgrim's eventual triumph over these obstacles, however humbled—links the Angevin story to the pilgrimage narrative in *La Fin d'Elias* and to stories found in other dynastic narratives.

Normandy

In the same year that Fulk Nerra made his difficult third pilgrimage to Jerusalem, another of the most powerful princes of the West, Duke Robert I the Magnificent of Normandy (r. 1027–35), also embarked on a penitential journey to the Holy Land from which he, unlike Fulk, would not return. The Angevin *Chronica* actually claimed that the two met in Constantinople and were being led through imperial territory by men from Antioch, but that Robert died in Bithynia before Fulk "was led under guard (*sub conductu*) to Jerusalem," suggesting that the duke's death occurred before he reached Jerusalem.[30] The Norman dynastic chronicler William of Jumièges, in his Latin dynastic history, *Gesta Normannorum ducum,* asserted that, to the contrary, the duke had died on the return journey and that he spent no less than eight days shedding tears over the Holy Sepulchre. Otherwise, however, William's account of Robert's journey was remarkably brief.[31]

In the decades after 1099, redactions and adaptations of the *Gesta Normannorum ducum,* and one text composed independently of it, reveal that the narrators of dynastic history in Normandy became steadily more interested in the duke's pilgrimage. These writers added new episodes to the story and

---

30. *CCA,* 51.
31. *GND,* 2: 82–83.

revised each other's additions. What they chose to add and revise reveals the changing attitude toward pilgrimage narratives over the course of the twelfth century. In Normandy, Duke Robert's pilgrimage was a noble adventure, demonstrating the wit, restraint, and sagacity of the pilgrim, and his dignified end. It also presented a space in which to rewrite some uncomfortable aspects of the First Crusade.

Working between 1114 and 1120, an anonymous monk of Battle Abbey began his biography of William the Conqueror, the *Brevis relatio de Guillelmo nobilissimo comite Normannorum,* by establishing William's rightful rule over the duchy of Normandy. The narrative begins with an explanation of how William's father, Duke Robert I, chose his illegitimate son as his heir before setting out on pilgrimage for Jerusalem in 1035.[32] Initially, the Battle Abbey monk presented few details of the journey, asserting that Robert had died returning from Jerusalem and that he was buried with honor at Nicaea in a tomb that bore witness to his virtues with "certain images with his likeness" (*quedam signa similia*).[33] The Battle Abbey author also indulged, however, in a brief bawdy anecdote that he hoped would illustrate Robert's goodness and his willingness to suffer injuries for the love of God. Once on his journey Robert had come to a certain place where *musellae* (the gate tax demanded of pilgrims) and tribute were demanded from him and from all of the poor who were in his company. Having paid the tribute both for himself and for everyone, the duke waited for his men to make the crossing "when one of the pagans who had been accepting the *musellas* became angry with him and, lifting up his cudgel mightily, struck him on the back."[34] The duke immediately urged his men not to avenge the offense, because "for the gas that it released from my belly, I am happier for the blow that he gave me than if he had given me a great treasure." Like the Angevin narrative of the pilgrimage of Fulk Nerra, the *Brevis relatio* account is basically a humorous tale, and likewise its humor is based on a more general assumption about the violence and difficulties faced by pilgrims to the East. Robert, like Fulk, provides passage through the difficult and dangerous journey for poor pilgrims who would be helpless and in danger without his protection and largesse.

---

32. "The *Brevis relatio de Guillelmo nobilissimo comite Normannorum,* Written by a Monk of Battle Abbey" ed. and comm. Elisabeth M. C. van Houts, in *Chronology, Conquest, and Conflict in Medieval England,* Camden Miscellany 34 (5th series, 10) (London, 1997), 1–48.

33. "The *Brevis relatio,*" 26.

34. "Quadam namque die contigit eum uenire ad quondam locum ubi musellas et tributum debebat pro se et pro pauperibus qui in eius comitatu errant, persoluere. Dum itaque ibi cum suis hominibus expectaret donec omnes pauperes quos secum ducebat transire fecisset quidam de paganis qui eas musellas accipiebant iratus contra eum, arepto fuste fortiter, supra dorsum percussit illum." "The *Brevis relatio,*" 26.

Working at roughly the same time as the monk of Battle Abbey who wrote the *Brevis relatio,* another anonymous writer was creating a new version (redaction B) of the *Gesta Normannorum ducum* of William of Jumièges.[35] While it is not known where the redaction was confected, it appears to have been written in the service of an author or community in search of patronage, as all of its interpolations highlight the noble virtue of generosity.[36] Among the most colorful interpolations of redaction B is an episode associated with Robert I's pilgrimage to Jerusalem. The *Gesta Normannorum ducum,* like the *Brevis relatio,* suggested that Robert reached Jerusalem, but the added episode in redaction B focused on Robert's visit to the Byzantine capital of Constantinople. Employing a narrative motif popular in Scandinavian and Old French texts, the story related how Robert had impressed the Byzantine emperor with his great wealth and indifference to the sophistication of the Constantinopolitan court.[37] When the mule Robert rode into Constantinople cast off one of its horseshoes, which the duke had ordered to be cast from gold instead of iron, Robert and his men paid no attention to the costly article, refusing to turn back and pick it up. While in the city, he likewise refused to accept the sumptuous gifts and food offered by the emperor and sat, uninvited, beside him. Enraged, the emperor at first cut off the group's access to food markets, but amazed at the resourcefulness and humility that they subsequently demonstrated in feeding themselves, he agreed to reopen the markets to them, "saying that the Franks were skilled in every enterprise, and that no one could match their cunning."[38]

Such ostentatious rejection of Byzantine largesse and imperial dignity contrasts sharply both with what is known about the nature of European and Scandinavian relations with Byzantium in the eleventh century and more specifically with the numerous reports of gift giving that accompanied the arrival of the leaders of the First Crusade in Constantinople in 1096–97.[39] Both the writers and audiences of the Norman dynastic texts would immediately have been reminded of how the Byzantine emperor Alexios Komnenos had beguiled the crusade leaders with gifts and then extracted

---

35. Elisabeth van Houts, "Introduction," *GND,* 1: lxi–lxv (author), cxxiii–cxxiv (text).

36. *GND,* 1: lxv.

37. For the story, see Elisabeth M. C. van Houts, "Normandy and Byzantium in the Eleventh Century," *Byzantion* 55 (1985): 544–549.

38. *GND,* 2: 82–85.

39. For the background, see Jonathan Shepard, "The Uses of the Franks in Eleventh-Century Byzantium," *Anglo-Norman* Studies 15 (1992): 275–305. For the First Crusade, see Anna Komnene, *Alexiad,* trans. E. R. A. Sewter and rev. Peter Frankopan (London, 2005), 292–294; and for the western sources, see Alan V. Murray, "Money and Logistics in the Forces of the First Crusade: Coinage, Bullion, Service, and Supply," in *Logistics of Warfare in the Age of the Crusades,* ed. John Pryor (Aldershot, UK, and Burlington, VT, 2006), 243–244.

from them oaths of loyalty in his palace. References to the food markets and the limited availability of food,[40] the failure to acknowledge the emperor's legitimacy by sitting on his throne,[41] and the refusal to participate in the gift exchange, with its concomitant obligations, are all direct echoes of tense moments in the negotiations between the crusade leaders and the emperor as the crusaders passed through Byzantine territory on their way east.[42] Unlike what actually happened in 1097, when all but one of the crusade leaders, Count Raymond IV of Saint-Gilles, took oaths of fidelity to the emperor and accepted his money, food, and largesse, in this story, the duke is not cowed by imperial majesty and emerges with his honor intact and with the emperor bearing witness to his wisdom.[43]

In the second half of the twelfth century, the Norman dynastic narrative tradition, with its increasingly elaborate stories of the pilgrimage of Duke Robert the Magnificent, found new life in vernacular verse histories of the ducal family. The first of these was the *Roman de Rou* of Wace, written between the mid-1160s and the early 1170s for Henry II of England. Among the sources Wace drew on were the *Brevis relatio* and redaction B of the *Gesta Normannorum ducum*. Both the *Brevis relatio*'s story of the violent gatekeeper and redaction B's tale of the golden horseshoes were included in Wace's work, although with significant alterations. Wace removed, for instance, the bawdy humor of the monk of Battle Abbey and moved the gatekeeper story from "pagan" lands to a much earlier stage of the pilgrimage in Burgundy. Wace expanded on the anti-Byzantine sentiment in redaction B of the *Gesta Normannorum ducum,* telling a story about the duke's largesse that played on knowledge of a particular statue in the city that was the subject of commentary by crusaders.[44] But Wace also greatly elaborated on the latter part of Robert's pilgrimage through Muslim-held territory to Jerusalem, shifting

---

40. Murray, "Money and Logistics," 229–250.

41. This detail echoes the story related by Anna Komnene, *Alexiad,* 291, of the crusader in the company of Godfrey of Bouillon and Baldwin of Boulogne who likewise sat beside the emperor, only to be rebuked by Baldwin for his bad behavior.

42. Although the two stories are different, it is also possible that the Norman diffidence was an echo of traditions surrounding Charlemagne's pilgrimage to the East, or that both responded to the same uncomfortable memory of western knights serving as Byzantine mercenaries. See "Descriptio qualiter," in *Die Legende Karls des Grossen im 11 und 12 Jahrhundert,* ed. Gerhard Rauschen (Leipzig, 1890), 109–111; Gabriele, *An Empire of Memory,* 52–53.

43. Thomas Asbridge, *The First Crusade: A New History* (London, 2004), 110–113.

44. Wace, *Roman de Rou,* 173, l. 3159; Robert of Clari, a participant in the Fourth Crusade, described a copper statue clad in a "golden mantle" near one of the gates of the city. An inscription on the statue read: "All they that tarry in Constantinople for one year ought to have a mantle of gold, even as I have." Robert of Clari, *Conquest of Constantinople,* trans. Edgar Holmes McNeal (New York, 1969), 108.

the focus of the story away from Constantinople and toward the holy city that was the duke's destination.

Wace began with a vigorous response to the Angevin tradition that Robert had died upon leaving Constantinople by suggesting that he had merely fallen ill after his departure from the city. Wace, who described the duke as having "taken the cross" for his pilgrimage, recounted how he hired a cortege of "Saracen" bearers to carry him onward.[45] Encountering a Norman pilgrim who was on his way home, Robert says: "Tell my friends and the people in my country that, alive and well, I am having myself carried to paradise by devils; pagans, who are carrying me to the Lord God, have raised me up shoulder high."[46] Arriving at the gates of Jerusalem, however, Robert found his progress halted by a familiar problem. "At that time," Wace wrote,

> ... throughout the entire kingdom of Syria the power lay in pagan hands. No pilgrim could enter Jerusalem to pray without giving a bezant or the equivalent in gold or silver before doing so. There were many people in that region to whom entry to the gate was forbidden; because they could not get hold of any bezants they remained outside the gates.[47]

Enter Duke Robert of Normandy, who swears that he will pay not only for himself but, like Fulk Nerra in the previous account, for all of the pilgrims. The local Muslim commander is so astonished at this show of charity that, ashamed, he presents Duke Robert with three days' profits from the entrance fee and is even more astonished when Robert immediately distributes this money to the poor.[48] Both of Wace's interpolations were either unknown or rejected by his contemporary and rival Benoît de Sainte-Maure, whose *Chronique des ducs de Normandie* included a reference to Robert's largesse but left out the image of the closed gate.[49]

Flanders-Hainaut

In the Low Countries, a narrative tradition emerged that, like those of *La Fin d'Elias* and the dynastic histories of Anjou and Normandy, imagined a Jerusalem pilgrim barred from entering the city in the decades before the First Crusade. The pilgrim was Count Robert I the Frisian of Flanders, the same

45. Wace, *Roman de Rou,* 195.

46. Wace, *Roman de Rou,* 170–173, ll. 3144–3148.

47. Wace, *Roman de Rou,* 172–173, ll. 3151–3166.

48. Wace, *Roman de Rou,* 173, ll. 3203–3204.

49. See Benoît de Sainte-Maur, *Chronique des ducs de Normandie,* ed. Francisque Michel (Paris, 1844), 2: 573–576, ll. 31686–31778.

man Guibert of Nogent described receiving a prophecy of the conquest of Jerusalem twelve years before the First Crusade. Although the story of Robert the Frisian's pilgrimage described in the dynastic narratives of the Low Countries is comparable in some ways to Norman and Angevin traditions, it also contains unique features that may offer a key to the popularity and significance of the "closed-gate story." For this reason, the political context of the appearance of the motif must be addressed in greater detail.

If, as Guibert of Nogent claimed, the story he told of the Muslim prophecy of the conquest of Jerusalem had come directly from one of Count Robert the Frisian's companions, then it is possible that the tradition was known in the comital household in the first decades of the twelfth century. But if this was the case, the story of the Muslim prophecy was not repeated in either of the two earliest histories of the comital family, an expanded and narrativized genealogy written in 1120 and the first narrative history proper, written in 1164 and known by its early modern title, *Flandria generosa.*[50] The latter text was exceptionally popular, and was the subject of numerous redactions and continuations, eventually forming the basis for widely disseminated vernacular adaptations. It was in one of the earlier Latin redactions of the *Flandria generosa,* the so-called B version—probably written between 1191 and 1193—that the story of Robert I's pilgrimage reemerged, fully incorporated into the dynastic history.[51]

The B version's story concerning Count Robert's pilgrimage was interpolated into the text between the description of his violent rise to power and his son's distinction "for his praiseworthy military service" on the First Crusade:

> After a few years [i.e., following his seizure of power] the same Robert [I the Frisian] of Flanders went to Jerusalem, which then was possessed by the Saracens. And when he wished to enter the gate of the city, the gate closed itself suddenly. Seeing this, he was seized by a great fear, understanding this not to be an auspicious sign for him. He went

---

50. "Genealogia regum Francorum comitumque Flandriae," and "Flandria generosa" in *Genealogiae comitum Flandriae,* ed. L. C. Bethmann, *MGH SS* 9: 308 and 313–325.

51. See Bethmann's introduction to the "Flandria Generosa," *MGH SS* 9: 315. The B version is published in the notes to the *MGH* edition. On this version, and the textual tradition in general, see Jean-Marie Moeglin, "Une première histoire nationale Flamande," in *Liber largitorius: Études d'histoire médiévale offertes à Pierre Toubert par ses élèves,* ed. Dominique Barthélemy and Jean-Marie Martin, Hautes études médiévales et modernes 84 (Geneva, 2003), 455–476. Although the complete MSS of the B version are all of a later date, the text definitely existed in the later twelfth century, when it was used by the monk Andrew of Marchiennes in his *Historia regum Francorum.* For the sake of brevity, the text of what he copied was not included in the *MGH* edition of the *Historia regum Francorum* (*MGH* 26: 204–212, it should appear at p. 208) but appears in BAV, Reg. Lat. 838, one of the earlier manuscripts of Andrew's chronicle. My thanks to James Naus for obtaining the digital images of this MS, which confirm the early circulation of the "Flandria generosa" text and its pilgrimage narrative.

therefore to a certain hermit, living near the city, whom he had heard to be holy and religious, in order to make confession for his sins. Having heard his confession, therefore, the holy man enjoined to him the penitence for his nephew Arnulf, whom he had killed, and he said to him that if he wished to have the good favour of God, he should return Flanders to his nephew Baldwin, from whom he had taken it. That man (Robert), however, greatly fearing the portent of the gate, but agreeing with the hermit's advice, came to the gate, which opened of its own accord for him. When, however, he had passed through the city, he stayed in the house of a very powerful Saracen. He heard from Saracen astrologers and from others that Jerusalem was soon to be captured by the Christians. It would be captured not long afterward, in the thirty-ninth year of King Philip. Robert, however, having returned from the journey to Jerusalem, gave back Douai to Baldwin of Hainaut because of his great fear.[52]

Written at the time of the reunification of the counties of Flanders and Hainaut after the marriage of Count Baldwin V of Hainaut and Countess Marguerite of Flanders in 1169, the story looks back over a century to the last time that the two honors had been joined. The pilgrim-count of the story, Robert I, was in fact born the younger son of Baldwin V of Flanders, whose eldest, Baldwin VI, not only was the heir to Flanders but, through his marriage to Richilde, the dowager countess of Hainaut, was also able to briefly unite the two powerful counties of Flanders and Hainaut after his father's death in 1067. After Baldwin VI died only three years later, in 1070, his own son Arnulf's claim to Flanders and Hainaut was challenged by his uncle Robert the Frisian. At Cassel in 1071, Robert crushed an army led by

---

52. "Post paucos annos idem Robertus Iherusalem abiit, quam tunc possidebant Sarraceni. Cumque portam civitatis vellet intrare, porta se clausit spontanea. At ille hoc videns, nimio timore correptus est, intellegens hoc sibi non esse prosperum prodigium. Abiit ergo inde ad quondam eremitam, prope civitatem manentem, quem audierat virum esse sanctum et religiosum, ut faceret confessionem peccatorum suorum. Audita ergo vir sanctus illius confessione, inuinxit ei poenitentiam de Arnulfo nepote suo, quem occiderat, et dixit ei, ut si vellet Deum habere propitium, Balduino nepoti suo rederet Flandriam, quam abstuleret ei. Ille autem nimis timoratus de portae prodigio, annuit eremitae consilio, venit ad portam quae ultro aperta est ei. Cum autem in civitate degeret, in domo cuiusdam perpotentis Saraceni audivit ab astrologis Sarracenorum et diversis, Iherusalem in proximo capiendo esse a cristianis; quae capta est non multo post, 39 anno Philippi Regis. Robertus autem reversus de itinere Iherusalem, Duacum timore nimio reddidit Balduino comiti Hainoniensi." "Flandria generosa," *MGH SS* 9: 323 n. 23**. For the inclusion of the story in later vernacular adaptations, see the *Reimchronik von Flanderen,* ed. Eduard Kausler (Tübingen, 1840), 69. Another account of Robert's pilgrimage, including the story of the Saracen astrologer but without the closed-gate motif, was copied at the end of the chronicle of the foundation of the abbey of Anchin in a fifteenth-century MS of Anchin (now Bibliothèque Municipale de Douai, MS 827); see *Monumenta Aquicinctina, MGH SS* 14: 592.

Arnulf and his brother Baldwin, killing Arnulf and others of his commanders and seizing Flanders by force.[53]

Other additions to the B version include material relating to the collegiate churches of Saint-Peter at Lille[54] and Saint-Donatien at Bruges,[55] as well as a note about the fate of Baldwin of Mons on the First Crusade.[56] If all of these additions represent the work of a single redactor, that individual would appear to have been both close to the count's court and sympathetic to Hainaut. Like the contemporary Hennuyer chronicler Gislebert of Mons, the redactor probably had a dim view of Robert the Frisian's aggression and his murder of his nephew.[57] But in order to acknowledge the changed political situation in Flanders and Hainaut in the later twelfth century, the writer artfully added the narrative mechanism of the closed-gate story, through which Count Robert I could ultimately earn forgiveness for his crimes, giving back a part of what he had seized to his nephew Baldwin of Hainaut, creating amity between Flanders and Hainaut, and opening the way for their reunion in the late twelfth century. The story also effectively redirected attention away from the darkest period in the relations between Flanders and Hainaut toward the glorious crusading future, in which future counts of Flanders (beginning with Robert's son) would redeem the reputation of their lineage by following in the footsteps of their maternal (Flanders) and paternal (Hainaut) ancestors, both of whom had taken the road to Jerusalem.

The Closed Gate

Common to all dynastic traditions of eleventh-century pilgrim forebears written after the First Crusade is the narrative motif of a closed or barred gate. It is likely that pilgrims traveling to Jerusalem in the eleventh century had to pay fees for entry or travel at different points in their journey, as perhaps pilgrims of all ages and in all lands do. Pilgrims could also certainly encounter difficulties, as did those who joined the German expedition of 1064, but these were not said to have involved tolls or restricted access to

---

53. For Robert I's rise to power, see Verlinden, *Robert Ier le Frison,* 27–72.

54. "Flandria generosa," *MGH SS* 9: 319 n. 9*. The thirteenth-century Ordinary of Saint-Peter at Lille reveals a strong liturgical and commemorative association with the comital family, including instructions to sings psalms "for the count" at particular feasts. E. Hautcoeur, *Documents liturgiques et necrologiques de l'église collégiale de Saint-Pierre de Lille* (Lille and Paris, 1895), 59.

55. "Flandria generosa," *MGH SS* 9: 313 n. 24**.

56. "Flandria generosa," *MGH SS* 9: 322 (the addition is taken from Herman of Tournai, chap. 33).

57. GM, 6.

holy places.[58] As the earliest version of the pilgrimage of Duke Robert the Magnificent suggests, closed gates were as likely to be found in Burgundy as in Palestine. Since most of the sources that describe this phenomenon postdate the pilgrimages they describe by a marked interval of time, during which period the First Crusade conquered Jerusalem, it may be safe to credit the popularity of this motif more to the literary imagination of the twelfth century than to any remembered experience from the eleventh.

The obstacle elicits a variety of heuristic approaches, each highlighting the noble qualities of the Jerusalem travelers, but the stories from Anjou, Normandy, and Flanders all point to humility. What we see in the dynastic narratives appears, therefore, to be a variation on a folk motif catalogued using the typologies first developed by Stith Thompson in the early twentieth century. Examples of the motif "hero must suffer humiliation in order to enter by the city gate" are found in Spanish and Talmudic traditions, as well as in Arthurian literature.[59] From the examples cited above, however, it is evident that the motif also had a particular appeal and utility in family storytelling. In Anjou, associated with the story of Fulk's clever use of the wineskin, it was included in every surviving redaction of the dynastic historical tradition. In Normandy, even writers who attempted to eliminate the vulgar elements of earlier traditions maintained the scene of the pilgrim before the gate, eventually rendering a version quite close to that given in the Angevin texts. Wace, the writer who championed the motif in the text he created for Henry II, chose to contrast the scene of Duke Robert I of Normandy offering payment so that pilgrims could be admitted to Jerusalem with the earlier added image of him carried toward the city by non-Christian bearers. In Flanders, the gate became the redemptive mechanism for the unification of Flanders and Hainaut. So central was the image of the pilgrims before the gate that it was even included in that storehouse of popular crusading lore, the Old French Crusade Cycle. The inclusion of the motif in *La Fin d'Elias,* a work with a wider diffusion that was not limited to one court, monastery, or even region, suggests a shared resonance within the noble classes more generally.

What made the motif so resonant? In the political imaginaries of medieval princes and their encomiasts, city gates of any kind were redolent of the symbolic language of triumphal rulership that still dominated discourses and

---

58. *Annales Altahenses maiores, MGH SS* 20: 815–817. The story of the embattled German pilgrims in fact ends with the *opening* of the gates of the city by their savior, the Fatimid caliph al-Mustansir.

59. Stith Thompson, *Motif-Index of Folk-Literature: A Classification of Narrative Elements in Folktales, Ballads, Myths, Fables, Mediaeval Romances, Exempla, Fabliaux, Jest-Books, and Local Legends,* rev. and enl. ed. (Copenhagen, 1955–58), 509 g. H1553.3; Anita Guerreau-Jalalbert, *Index des motifs narratifs dans les romans arthuriens français en vers: xiie-xiiie siecles* (Geneva, 1992), 109.

performances of power.[60] Triumphal entry through the gates of cities and buildings was as often invoked in the rites of the liturgical calendar as it was in the *adventus* of kings, princes, and bishops.[61] Entry into Jerusalem, the critical moment in the pilgrimage episodes, was evoked every year in Palm Sunday processions, which would have been familiar to every performer and audience of the dynastic narratives or *La Fin d'Elias*. For these audiences, however, what mattered was not simply that this gate opened by Christ was closed by non-Christians in the eleventh century, but that it would eventually be reopened by the crusaders.

The conquest of Jerusalem by the crusaders represented, from the earliest surviving accounts of the expedition, an opening of the gates that had for a long time been closed to pilgrims, and that were associated with unfair exactions demanded from them. Describing the moment that the crusaders overcame the defenses of the city on 15 July 1099, the anonymous author of the text known as the *Gesta Francorum* reminded his readers of the difficulties that their forebears had encountered as pilgrims before the very same gates: "The Amir who held the Tower of David surrendered to the count [Raymond IV of Saint-Gilles] and opened for him the gate where the pilgrims used to pay taxes."[62] Reworking this basic narrative, Guibert of Nogent added further details, invoking the name of the hated tax and juxtaposing this earlier frustration with the purifying massacre of the city's inhabitants:

> Thus the satrap, after a pact had been agreed upon between them, opened for him the gate through which the pilgrims used to pass when they entered Jerusalem, and where they were cruelly and unfairly compelled to pay tribute, which was called *musellae*. When the Provencals, that is, the army of the Count of Saint-Gilles, and all the others had entered the city, a general slaughter of the pagans took place.[63]

In exhortations that were intended to celebrate the Feast of the Liberation of Jerusalem (15 July) at the abbey of Santa Maria de Ripoll in Catalonia, knights (*milites*) in particular were enjoined as follows:

---

60. As Michael McCormick has shown, triumphal rulership extended long after the end of effective Roman power in the West. Although his study concentrated on the revivals and uses of imperial triumph in the early Middle Ages, it should be noted that for lay princes of northern Europe a recognized official entry into urban centers may have had increased significance in an age when those centers became increasingly powerful in their own right and difficult to control. Michael McCormick, *Eternal Victory: Triumphal Rulership in Late Antiquity, Byzantium, and the Early Medieval West* (Cambridge, 1986).

61. For the adventus, see Geoffrey Koziol, *Begging Pardon and Favor: Ritual and Political Order in Medieval France* (Ithaca, NY, 1992), 133–134, 138–139.

62. *Gesta Francorum et aliorum Hierosolymitanorum*, 91.

63. Guibert of Nogent, *Dei gesta per Francos*, 280; trans. Levine, 131.

Look! No enemies guard the gate of Jerusalem! No-one closes what has been opened through Christ's labours! None of the faithful is required to pay any tribute to enter! Oh happy month of July, that on its sixteenth day entrance was given by the Son of Light to that city where the sun of justice shone out everywhere and the power of the darkness vanished.[64]

But like an episode in a narrative cycle, the closed-gate motif in the dynastic histories not only anticipated the coming of the First Crusade, linking the pilgrims of the eleventh century with their crusader descendants; it also acted as a bridge between the crusaders of the twelfth century and yet more distant predecessors from the mythic past. These predecessors likewise extended the narrative across salvation history, from the time of the crusaders back to Christ's triumphal entry. Central among these predecessors was the seventh-century Byzantine emperor Heraclius (d. 641).

Heraclius's defeat of the Sassanian king Khosrau II in 627 and his restoration of the major relic of the True Cross to Jerusalem two years later,[65] deeds that had been celebrated in the Latin liturgy as the Feast of the Exaltation of the Cross (14 September) since the early ninth century,[66] had obvious resonance with the objectives and experiences of the crusaders.[67] The similarities between Heraclius's achievements and those of the crusaders, especially the recovery on both occasions of the True Cross, were clear enough for two crusade chroniclers, Fulcher of Chartres and Guibert of Nogent, to invoke the emperor's name in their narratives.[68] Over the course of the twelfth century, the two narratives became gradually intertwined in a process of cyclification, with Heraclius becoming a prefatory episode in the history of the

---

64. "Ecce portam Iherosolimitanam nullus custodit hostis, nemo claudit quam per uestrum laborem Christus aperuit, nullus tributum nisi fidei ab intrantibus requirit. Felix mensis ille quintilis, xvi illa feria ipsius qua filio lucis datus est ingressus civitatis, ex qua sol iusticie undique refulsit et potestas tenebrarum evanuit." John France, "The Text of the Account of the Capture of Jerusalem in the Ripoll Manuscript, Bibliothèque Nationale Latin 5132," *English Historical Review* 103 (1988): 653.

65. See Jan Willem Drijvers, "Heraclius and the *Restitutio crucis:* Notes on Symbolism and Ideology," in *The Reign of Heraclius (610–641): Crisis and Confrontation,* edited by Gerrit J. Reinink and Bernard H. Stolte (Leuven, 2002), 175–190.

66. Barbara Baert, *A Heritage of Holy Wood: The Legend of the True Cross in Text and Image,* trans. Lee Preedy (Leiden and Boston, 2004), 140–141.

67. Although Andrea Sommerlechner's study "Kaiser Herakleios und die Rückkehr des Heiligen Kreuzes nach Jerusalem: Überlegungen zu Stoff- und Motifgeschichte," *Romische historische Mitteilungen* 45 (2003): 319–360, relates primarily to the reception and adaptation of the Heraclius legend within imperial modes of representation, hers is the most thorough survey of the narrative and ritual references to the emperor in the medieval West.

68. For the knowledge of Heraclius in the West, see Sommerlechner, "Kaiser Herakleios"; Stephan Borgehammar, "Heraclius Learns Humility: Two Early Latin Accounts Composed for the Celebration of *Exaltatio Crucis,*" *Millennium* 6 (2009): 145–201; Baert, *A Heritage of Holy Wood.*

First Crusade. Arnold of Lübeck's account of the armed pilgrimage of Duke
Henry the Lion of Bavaria and Saxony to the East in 1172 recalled the duke's
visit to the city of Heraclea,

> which in the language of the Turks is called *Rakilei* and in our tongue
> *Eraclia,* which the prince of the Jerusalemites (*princeps Ierosolimitanus*)
> Heraclius held. He killed Chosroes, who had captured Jerusalem and
> taken away the cross of the Lord into captivity.[69]

When, at some point in the same decade, Archbishop William of Tyre composed his *Historia transmarinis partibus,* his opening lines invoked both Heraclius and Charlemagne, but it was the former whose name was attached to
the enormously popular Old French translation of William's work, which
was known as the *Estoire d'Eracles empereur.*[70]

Significantly, however, the clearest manifestation of the narrative correla-
tion between the emperor Heraclius and the crusaders appears in a dynastic
history. In the twenty-third chapter of the *Chronicon Hanoniense,* Gislebert
set out to describe the deeds of the first crusader Count Baldwin II Hainaut:

> In those days Jerusalem and the holy cities of Armenia, Syria, and part
> of Greece as far as the arm of St. George were held by the gentiles,
> having been occupied by them. Thus were many men of the Roman
> empire and the kingdom of France eager to aid the eastern churches;
> among that group was Baldwin count of Hainault, a man powerful in
> war, well meaning in his actions, [and] most liberal in alms. He decided
> to join with them.[71]

These introductory statements are followed by a history of Jerusalem, beginning with a discussion of the several theories of the origin of the city's
name, and including the destruction of the Temple by Nebuchadnezzar, the
account of the city in the books of the Maccabees and Josephus's chronicles,
and the coming of Jesus Christ, who "glorified it by his conversion, his

---

69. "Qui iuxta linguam Turcorum dicitur Rakilei, in nostra lingua Eraclia, quam princeps Iero-
solymitanus Eraclius olim tenebat, qui occidit Cosdroe, qui Ierosolymam ceperat et lignum Domini
in captivitatem asportaverat." Arnold of Lübeck, *Chronica Slavorum,* ed. J. M. Lappenberg, *MGH SS*
21: 122.

70. *L'estoire de Eracles empereur et la conqueste de la terre d'Outremer,* ed. Académie des Inscriptions
et Belles Lettres, *RHC Occ.* 2: 1. For a comparison of William's chronicle and the Old French version, see J. H. Pryor, "The Eracles and William of Tyre: An Interim Report," in *The Horns of Hattin:
Proceedings of the Second Conference of the Society for the Study of the Crusades and the Latin East,* ed. B. Z.
Kedar (Jerusalem, 1992), 270–293; Peter Edbury, "The Lyon *Eracles* and the Old French Continuations of William of Tyre," in *Montjoie: Studies in Crusade History in Honour of Hans Eberhard Mayer,* ed.
B. Z. Kedar, J. S. C. Riley-Smith, and R. Hiestand (Aldershot, UK, 1997), 139–154.

71. GM, 37; trans. Laura Napran as *The Chronicle of Hainaut* (Woodbridge, UK, 2005), 24–25.

miracles, and by his tomb."[72] To Gislebert, the two most salient episodes in the Christian history of the city of Jerusalem before the First Crusade were the discovery of the Holy Cross by Constantine's mother, Helena, and its recovery and restoration to Jerusalem by the emperor Heraclius. The emperor's martial deeds were recounted in detail by Gislebert:

> Therefore, when [Heraclius] had subjugated the heathens, he went to Persia with a Christian army, came all the way to the shrine at which the treacherous Khusrau was waiting, and discovered him sitting on a golden throne. Heraclius advised him to become a Christian so that he might receive the kingdom of Persia from his hand. But he did not wish to be converted, and immediately Heraclius drew his sword and cut off his head and caused his son, a child, to be baptised, received from the sacred font and conceded the kingdom of Persia to him, having received hostages from him so he would be further subject to him. Heraclius brought back to Jerusalem the Lord's cross which Khusrau had carried away, and put it in the Lord's sepulchre, as is read publicly at the Feast of the Exaltation of the Holy Cross throughout churches. And so for a long time the kingdom of Persia was subject to the power of Constantinople, and the religion of the Christian faith flourished in Jerusalem and many Eastern cities, until God was offended by the sins of Christians, and the error of the heathen grew strong again, and the heathens left their territories and came to the Lord's sepulchre, and took Armenia, Syria, and part of Greece almost all the way to that sea which is called the Bosporus.[73]

Gislebert's history of Jerusalem is framed with nearly identical statements about the spread of the "gentiles" into Christian lands. Therefore, although they were actually pagan Persians, the "gentiles" defeated and driven from Jerusalem by Heraclius were directly equated with the Muslims that the crusaders sought to defeat. Baldwin of Hainaut and his companions are, therefore, following directly in the footsteps of Heraclius.

Because, as Gislebert said, the story was already widely known from being read aloud at the Feast of the Exaltation of the Cross, he did not go into detail about exactly how the emperor had returned the cross to Jerusalem. The best-known Latin account of Heraclius and the cross is the one given by Hrabanus Maurus in the collection of homilies that he addressed to the Carolingian king Lothar I (d. 844).[74] It describes how Heraclius, having

---

72. GM, 37; Napran, 24–25.
73. GM, 40; trans. adapted from Napran, 24–25.
74. Hrabanus Maurus, "Homiliae," *PL* 110, cols. 131–134.

FIGURE 3.   Heraclius is humbled before the gates of Jerusalem. Lower register of a miniature from the Sacramentary of Mont-Saint-Michel. New York, Pierpont Morgan Library M.641 f. 155v. Photo courtesy Pierpont Morgan Library.

vanquished Khusrau and retrieved the cross, brought it to Jerusalem with the intention of installing it in the church of the Holy Sepulchre. Arriving at the city gates in his imperial splendor, mounted on a fine palfrey, he found that stones miraculously flew down and blocked the city gate. An angel appeared, accompanied by a flaming cross in the sky, and explained that when Christ had entered these same gates on Palm Sunday, he wore neither the purple nor the imperial diadem, nor did he require a horse for transportation. When, humble and penitent, stripped of his imperial garb, Heraclius once again attempted to enter, the stones blocking the gateway miraculously rose, clearing his path.

The popularity of the story was already on the rise on the eve of the First Crusade, when, for instance, it was the subject of a miniature in the Mont-Saint-Michel Sacramentary (see figure 3). From the miniature, it is clear that the "stones" (*lapides*) that blocked the emperor's way in Hrabanus's account had become a closed gate by the later eleventh century. Barbara Baert has suggested this simple image of a prince humbled before a gate was a powerful evocation of the vision of the eastern gate of the Temple and hence the Golden Gate (Porta Aurea) of the city in Ezekiel 44:1–2:[75]

> And he brought me back to the way of the gate of the outer sanctuary, which looked towards the east: and it was shut. And the Lord said to me: This gate shall be shut, it shall not be opened, and no man shall pass through it: because the Lord God of Israel hath entered in by it, and it shall be shut for the prince.[76]

As Baert has also shown, this trivalent association between the Golden Gate of Jerusalem, the gate of Heraclius, and the closed gate of Ezekiel exercised a powerful hold over the imagination of twelfth-century crusaders and settlers in the Latin Kingdom of Jerusalem, who would open the gate only on Palm Sunday and the Feast of the Exaltation.[77]

It is in this story of Heraclius, "the prince" humbled before Jerusalem, that we find the origin of the closed-gate motif so often applied to eleventh-century visitors to Jerusalem. Heraclius, as a protocrusader from the distant past, presents a model and prefiguration not only of the crusaders themselves but of pilgrims to Jerusalem before the First Crusade. His story is a reminder that access to the city is available only to those who are sufficiently penitent. As they are mocked, threatened, and abused before the gates of the city, the pilgrim ancestors from Anjou, Normandy, and Flanders and the imagined group from Bouillon demonstrate enough true piety and humility to visit the Sepulchre for themselves. They also demonstrate a desire to end the challenges that pilgrims faced, to open the gates of the city for all pilgrims, and

---

75. Baert, *A Heritage of Holy Wood*, 175–76. Biblical commentators (who mainly followed Jerome on Ezekiel) did not gloss the passage from Ezekiel as an explicit reference to Heraclius, but such an interpretation may well not have been, in their eyes, allegorical (as was for instance the passage's relevance to the Annunciation) but literal. See Jerome, "Commentariorum in Ezechielem," *PL* 25, cols. 427–430; Hugh of Saint-Cher, *In Libros Prophetarum Ezechielis, Danielis, Oseae, Joelis, Amos, Abdiae, Jonae, Michae, Nahum, Habacuc, Sophoniae, Aggaei, Zachariae, Malachae, et Machabaeuorum I* (Venice, 1754), 5: 136–137; and *Bibliorum Sacrorum cum glossa ordinaria* (Venice, 1603), 5: 1435. An association between the Ezekiel passage and Heraclius is, however, strongly suggested by the juxtaposition of an image of Heraclius and the tetramorph seraph of Ezekiel in the enamels of Godefroid de Claire of Huy. See Wilhelm Neuss, *Das Buch Ezechiel in Theologie und Kunst bis zum Ende des 12. Jahrhunderts* (Münster, 1912), 237.

76. "Et convertit me ad viam portae sanctuarii exterioris quae respiciebat ad orientem et erat clausa et dixit Dominus ad me porta haec clausa erit non aperietur et vir non transiet per eam quoniam Dominus Deus Israhel ingressus est per eam eritque clausa principi." Ezekiel 44:1–2. (Note that different versions of the vulgate disagreed about where the sense of the second verse ended and the third began.)

77. Baert, *A Heritage of Holy Wood*, 176–178. Ezekiel's closed gate was also associated with the virginity of Mary; see Gail McMurray Gibson, "*Porta haec clausa erit:* Comedy, Conception, and Ezekiel's Closed Door in the *Ludus coventriae* Play of Joseph's Return," *Journal of Medieval and Renaissance Studies* 8 (1976), 137–156.

to free those trapped there, a desire that was also attributed to Heraclius by one twelfth-century chronicler.[78]

It would not be until the advent of the First Crusade, however, with its severe levels of suffering and sacrifice, and the many deaths and endless horrors experienced along the harrowing journey, that the gates would truly be opened to all pilgrims.

The Keys

The identification and elucidation of the closed-gate motif helps us to understand how the medieval nobility, and the great princely dynasties in particular, understood the place of the crusades within their own dynastic histories. But it may also help us to understand how and why elements of this imagery were invoked in other contexts. If, as I have argued, the power and significance of the motif was understood by the *remanieurs* of the Old French Crusade Cycle, it can hardly have escaped the attention of popes and preachers, who increasingly used inherited familial obligations and the language of kinship in their attempts to encourage the nobility to take the cross. Among the model crusade sermons written by thirteenth-century crusade preachers, for instance, we find repeated analogues between the crusader's cross and the key that will open the gates to Jerusalem and thus also to paradise. With reference to Isaiah 13:2 ("Hoist a sign on a cloudy mountain, raise your voice, lift up your hand so that the nobles may go through the gates"), the veteran preacher James of Vitry identified the cross as the sign that had to be lifted up in order to open the "gates."[79] Here, the gates were interpreted as the hearing and sense of James's listeners, but he quickly added that "the cross is the key that opens the gates of paradise," calling crusaders "key-bearers" (*clavigeri*).[80] Virtually the same scriptural passages and interpretations were employed by Gilbert of Tournai, who wrote that "the cross is in fact the key to heaven, that opened the gates of paradise." Gilbert of Tournai also described those marked with the cross as bearing the sign that would permit them to enter, like paupers admitted to a feast, "and so the crusaders truly walk through the gate of paradise without rejection."[81]

In 1184, when the political and military situation in the Latin Kingdom of Jerusalem had reached its lowest ebb as Saladin united the Islamic Near

---

78. OV, 3: 60–61.

79. Christoph Maier, *Crusade Propaganda and Ideology: Model Sermons for the Preaching of the Cross* (Cambridge, 2000), 104–105.

80. Maier, *Crusade Propaganda and Ideology*, 105–106.

81. Maier, *Crusade Propaganda and Ideology*, 186–187.

East and prepared for a direct assault on the crusader states, an embassy was dispatched from the East to the courts of western Christendom to seek assistance.[82] Central to the strategy of the Latin Kingdom's earlier requests for aid from the West was the transmission of relics, particularly relics of the Passion such as pieces of the True Cross, in an attempt to focus the minds of the European military aristocracy on the need for a new crusade. In a clear sign of the desperate position in which the Latins in the East found themselves in 1184, however, the leaders of the mission, the patriarch of Jerusalem, and the masters of both the Temple and the Hospital brought with them not relics but the keys to the Holy Sepulchre, the banner of the kingdom of Jerusalem, and another set of keys, variously reported as the keys to the city of Jerusalem itself or to the Tower of David.[83] These items were presented to various potential crusaders, including King Philip Augustus of France and King Henry II of England.

What did this solemn offer signify? To most modern commentators, the presentation of the banner and the keys represented an offer of the crown of Jerusalem to any of the ambitious rulers who might protect the kingdom. As we have seen, however, keys could have their own associations with crusading without symbolizing the right to rule the city of Jerusalem. If we think about the keys in this way, it was also potentially of profound importance that the patriarch of Jerusalem, the chief ambassador who, according to accounts of his visit to England, presented the keys and banner prostrate and weeping before the king and his court, was named Heraclius. The significance of this name was certainly not lost on contemporaries in the East.[84] The keys, as presented by "Heraclius of Jerusalem," constituted a serious challenge to the western nobility not only to uphold the traditions established by earlier crusaders but to include themselves in the great cycle of narrative centered on Jerusalem, which included the crusaders, their pilgrim predecessors, Heraclius, and Christ.

---

82. See below, 210–212.

83. Ralph of Diceto, "Ymagines," in *Radulfi de Diceto decani Lundonensis opera: The Historical Works of Master Ralph of Diceto,* ed. William Stubbs, RS 68 (London, 1876) 2: 32–33; Gervase of Canterbury, *The Historical Works of Gervase of Canterbury,* ed. William Stubbs, RS 73 (London, 1879–80), 1: 325, 373; Gerald of Wales, *Opera,* ed. J. S. Brewer, RS 21 (London, 1861–91), 5: 360–363 and 8: 202–212. The master of the Templars, Arnold of Torroja, died in Verona in September 1184. See Jonathan Phillips, *Defenders of the Holy Land: Relations between the Latin East and the West, 1119–1187* (Oxford, 1996), 257.

84. The chronicler Ernoul, in his account of contemporary events in the Holy Land after the failure of Heraclius's mission in the West, compared Heraclius the emperor with Heraclius the patriarch, ultimately deciding that both had failed to secure the cross for Jerusalem. See Bernard Hamilton, "William of Tyre and the Byzantine Empire," in *Porphyrogenita: Essays on the History and Literature of Byzantium and the Latin East in Honour of Julian Chrysostomides,* ed. Charalambos Dendrinos et al. (Aldershot, UK, 2003), 219–220.

Gates Left Unopened

No monarch would answer Patriarch Heraclius's last call for help. Within two years both the True Cross and the city of Jerusalem had fallen into the hands of Saladin. And when a new expedition, the Third Crusade, failed to imitate Emperor Heraclius and recover either the city or the symbol, plans were put in place almost immediately for a new expedition to try to regain the Holy Sepulchre. Although the Fourth Crusade was not formally preached until 1198, in the pontificate of Innocent III, planning for the new crusade was probably under way as early as 1194.[85]

Among the regions that demonstrated the most enthusiastic response was Flanders, where Baldwin IX, count of the united Flanders and Hainaut, together with two of his brothers, Henry and Eustace, his wife, and most of the Flemish nobility, took the cross.[86] Baldwin had a strong sense of his own family's crusading traditions. He had watched his uncle Philip take the cross at Ghent in 1190 to depart for an expedition from which he would not return. Two dynastic histories, the B version of *Flandria generosa,* complete with its account of Robert I's Heraclius-like humbling before the gates of Jerusalem, and the *Chronicon Hanoniense* of Gislebert of Mons, which emphatically associated Heraclius with the deeds of the crusaders, had been written during the reign of his father, Baldwin V of Hainaut. Baldwin V was also a patron of vernacular literature, and at some point in the mid-1180s he helped a clerically trained writer named Walter of Arras to complete a long romance on the life of the emperor Heraclius. Walter had begun his *Eracles* some time earlier under the patronage of Thibaud V of Blois (d. 1190). His earlier books dealt with the youth and adventures of young Heraclius, but the third part, completed under Baldwin's patronage, followed the story of the Holy Cross, from its discovery by Helena to its recovery after Heraclius's martial triumphs over the Persians. In the romance *Eracles,* the emperor's experiences before the gates of Jerusalem are described in the greatest detail. Walter's interest in the story can be compared to that of the later writer Otte, who translated and adapted the *Eracles* into Middle High German in the 1230s.[87] In their treatment of the story of Heraclius, the Persians, and the cross, the difference between the two writers is striking.

85. Vincent Ryan, "Richard I and the Early Evolution of the Fourth Crusade," in *The Fourth Crusade: Event, Aftermath, and Perceptions; Papers from the Sixth Conference of the Society for the Study of the Crusades and the Latin East, Istanbul, Turkey, 25–29 August 2004,* ed. Thomas F. Madden (Aldershot, UK, 2008), 3–14.

86. Jean Longnon, *Les compagnons de Villehardouin: recherches sur les croisés de la quatrième croisade.* (Geneva, 1978), 137–140, 175–177: Baldwin, his brothers Henry and Eustace, and nephew Thierry and wife, Marie.

87. Otte, *Eraclius,* ed. Winfried Frey (Göppingen, 1983).

According to Karen Pratt, who conducted a comparative structural analysis of the two poems, where Walter dedicated 92 lines of verse to the story of Helena, Otte left out the matter entirely, elaborating instead on the battle scenes, which are all longer than Walter's. In Walter's romance, the miracle of the closed gates is treated in 271 lines, making it the longest episode in the whole book. In Otte's work, this episode (which while not a battle was still a good story) warranted a mere 56 lines.[88]

Clearly, the court of the counts of Flanders-Hainaut was a place where the closed-gate motif was particularly resonant. It may even explain, in part, the urgency with which Count Philip of Flanders responded to the loss of Jerusalem and the cross in 1187. But is it also possible that after these failures, and especially after the failure of Heraclius's expedition, that the motif took on new associations? According to the English chronicler Roger of Howden, in the year 1188, messengers sent by the king of France to the court of the Byzantine emperor Isaac Comnenus reported that they had heard a number of wondrous and disturbing stories during their stay in Constantinople.[89] Among them was the prophecy of "Daniel the Constantinopolitan prophet" that the year when the Feast of the Annunciation fell on Easter Sunday "the Franks would restore the promised land." The messengers also reported that "a certain old Greek from Astralix" had said to them that the prophecy that is written on Constantinople's Golden Gate would soon be fulfilled. The gate, they said, had not been opened for more than two hundred years. The prophecy inscribed on the gate read: "When King Flavus [or "a blond/golden-headed king"] comes from the West, then will I open by myself." "And then," the messengers explained, "the Latins will rule and hold power in the city of Constantinople."[90]

This prophecy, with its striking resemblance to the closed-gate motif associated with Jerusalem, was reported by a writer who is not thought to have lived later than 1201. He could not even have imagined that three years later, after an extraordinary sequence of events, a fleet of Latin crusaders would indeed conquer Constantinople. At the head of one of the largest contingents of that army was Baldwin, Count of Flanders-Hainaut, who had been raised in a world of stories and songs that reinforced the relationship between his

---

88. Karen Pratt, *Meister Otte's "Eraclius" as an Adaptation of "Eracle" by Gautier d'Arras*, (Göppingen, 1987), tables 1 and 2, 135–139.

89. Roger of Howden, *Chronica*, ed. William Stubbs, RS 51 (London, 1868–71), 2: 355–356.

90. "quidam Graecus senex de Astralix dixit eis, quod implebitur prophetia quae scripta est in porta aurea, quae non fuit aperta ducentis annis retro, scilicet 'Quando veniet rex Flavus Occidentalis, tunc ego per me ipsam aperiar;' et tunc Latini imperabunt et dominabuntur in civitate Constantinopolitana." Roger of Howden, *Chronica*, 2: 345. I thank Thomas Madden for sharing his thoughts on the prophecy and his forthcoming study of the Golden Gate.

own crusading ancestors, the Byzantine emperor Heraclius, and a troubled pilgrim-ancestor who, like Heraclius, had been humbled before the gate of Jerusalem. Baldwin was elected the first Latin emperor of Constantinople, but he did not fulfill the prophecy by marching triumphantly through the Golden Gate. Instead, according to the Byzantine chronicler Niketas Choniates, it was the Byzantine population of the city that threw itself on the locked gate in its headlong flight from the looting, conquering, vengeful crusaders.[91]

---

91. Niketas Choniates, *O City of Byzantium: The Annals of Niketas Choniates,* ed. and trans. Harry J. Magoulias (Detroit, 1984), 313. Niketas also noted bitterly that it was through the Golden Gate that he himself withdrew from the city (324).

Conclusions

The three eldest sons of the Count of Hainaut were in their late teens when, one September day in 1190, they traveled with their parents to Ghent, where their uncle, their mother's brother Count Philip of Flanders, was about to depart on the Third Crusade.[1] In Ghent, the family watched as Philip, already marked with the sign of the cross, received the purse and the staff, the symbols of pilgrimage presented to crusaders upon their departure. Producing fifty silver marks, Philip gave forty to his wife, Mathilda, ceremonially entrusting to her the governance and protection of Flanders. For Philip, the rite of passage was nothing new—he had taken the cross once before in 1177—but for the children of his sister's family, the ritual exchange of objects, the gift of money, and the departure of their uncle for Italy, where he would join the kings of France and England in their bid to halt the conquest of the Latin Kingdom of Jerusalem by Saladin, may have marked their formal introduction into the practical realities of the crusades to the Holy Land.

Philip's purse- and staff-taking ceremony may have been the first time that the Hainaut children had actually seen one of their kin depart on crusade, but it was not the first time a member of their family had done so. Four of

---

1. GM, 167; trans. Laura Napran as *The Chronicle of Hainaut* (Woodbridge, UK, 2005), 136. Napran concludes that Gislebert's date for the ceremony is more reliable than the one given by the continuators of Sigebert of Gembloux. See Napran, 167 n. 463.

the previous five men who had called themselves counts of Flanders had taken the cross, including Philip's father, Thierry, who did so four times. One countess, Philip's mother, Sibylla, had in fact died in the Holy Land, where her father had once ruled as king. Even before the First Crusade (which had, among its many princely leaders, ancestors on both their father's and mother's side) an earlier maternal forebear, Count Robert I of Flanders, had undertaken a pilgrimage to Jerusalem and assisted the Byzantine emperor in his campaign against the Seljuk Turks in Asia Minor, behavior that very much foreshadowed the coming of the crusades.

If, as well as being heirs to their ancestors' titles, lands, and nobility, the Hainaut children were the heirs to a legacy of crusading involvement, it was a legacy that they did not fail to uphold. The day came in 1200, five years after their father's death and ten years after watching Philip's purse- and staff-taking ceremony, when Baldwin, the eldest of the Hainaut children and heir to both Flanders and Hainaut, his wife, Marie, his younger brothers Henry and Eustace, and his nephew Thierry all took the cross and became crusaders, leading a substantial portion of the Flemish nobility on the Fourth Crusade.[2] The pattern did not end with them: Baldwin's grandson Guy of Dampierre would take the cross twice, in 1248 and 1270, accompanied on the second occasion by his own son Robert of Béthune.[3]

Was this pattern a result of a "family tradition" of crusading? Because a tradition is really "a series of creative acts that are only partially predictable," it is impossible to say what precisely led Guy, Baldwin, Philip, or any of their predecessors to decide for themselves to take the cross.[4] In the past five chapters, however, we have seen that their decisions and actions took place in the context of powerful discourses and an elaborate cultural system that at least conditioned their creative acts to make them much more predictable. Like many others, this family inhabited a landscape that was thick with ancestral memories of all kinds. Each new generation, like the teenagers who went to watch Philip's departure in Ghent, was raised to believe that its worth (*probitas*) depended largely on its ability to maintain and defend the best of what its ancestors had accomplished and acquired. In a variety of contexts, those accomplishments and acquisitions would have been explained to new generations as narrative.

2. Geoffrey of Villehardouin, *La conquête de Constantinople,* ed. Edmond Faral, (Paris, 1938), 1: 10–13; Donald Queller and Thomas Madden, *The Fourth Crusade: The Conquest of Constantinople, 1201–4* (Philadelphia, 2001), 15.

3. Victor Louis Marie Gaillard, *Expedition de Gui de Dampierre à Tunis, en 1270* (Ghent, 1833), 11.

4. John D. Niles, *Homo Narrans: The Poetics and Anthropology of Oral Literature* (Philadephia, 1999), 173.

When they were in Ghent, the Hainaut children may, for instance, have been educated and entertained at Philip's palace, the Gravensteen, with stories about their maternal ancestors in the same way that their neighbor and acquaintance Arnold of Guines had listened to stories of his maternal crusading ancestors when visiting his maternal stronghold of Ardres. The crusading efforts of these ancestors would make most sense to the Hainaut children in the context of what they knew about Robert II's father, Robert I, who had been prevented from entering Jerusalem by its ominously closed gates in 1089. A century later, those gates were closed again, and it was clearly necessary for a crusader like Phillip to assume the role of Robert II and serve God with humility in order to see them reopened.

When they traveled within their domains and beyond to neighboring Flanders and Artois the children of the Hainaut family would pass familiar religious communities like Clairmarais, Hasnon, Marchiennes, and Anchin, where texts relating to their maternal ancestors were actively being copied, redacted, and continued. When they visited these communities, they would hear stories of their model ancestors who had acted as the abbey's benefactors, including Philip's father, Thierry, his predecessor Charles the Good, and even Robert II, the "Son of Saint George" himself. At Anchin, they could see the relic that resonated so well with Robert's epithet, but because it was no longer in the family's control, the relic of Saint George may not have been as important to them as the objects that they treasured in their proprietary churches and chapels. While at Ghent, for instance, the children could have seen the phylactery with its relics that Robert II had brought back from Jerusalem, and that Philip intended to take with him to the East.

Somewhat surprisingly for Flanders, a comparatively well-documented region in the twelfth century, no charter document survives that witnesses the moment that Philip of Alsace took the cross in Ghent. The details of the count's departure come down to us only because somewhere on the edges of that scene, perhaps standing near the Count of Hainaut, his wife, and their young children was their faithful retainer and notary, Gislebert of Mons, who only five years later would describe the ceremony, together with much of their family history, in his *Chronicon*.[5] The cleric Gislebert may have been responsible for telling the Hainaut children about how their paternal ancestor Baldwin II had disappeared in the course of the First Crusade, and how his wife had gone to look for him. Perhaps, for the children, the tragic story from their father's family was easily overlooked, considering the glories

---

5. At the time of the Ghent ceremony, Gislebert was traveling with the count acting in his capacity as chancellor to draw up Balwin V's charters. See Charles Albert Duivivier, *Chartes inédits concernant les comtes de Hainaut, 887–1207* (Brussels, 1093), 150–152, no. 74.

associated with the crusaders on their mother's side. But the story of death and distance would haunt them again when, in the course of the Fourth Crusade, Baldwin's wife, Marie, died in Acre and then, several months later, Baldwin himself disappeared into captivity in Bulgaria.

In practice, most families were not like the counts of Flanders. There were countless reasons why members of a noble family, even those that celebrated and revered ancestors who were crusaders, would choose not to respond to calls to take the cross. Jonathan Phillips has attempted to explain why, for instance, so many families from Flanders and the surrounding region did not, unlike their count, Thierry, take the cross for the Second Crusade as their ancestors had for the First.[6] Phillips has concluded that as a result of the war and unrest in Flanders following the murder of Charles the Good, many families were simply not in a position, either financially or politically, to join a crusade. No matter how shining an example their ancestors had set, crusading was not to everyone's tastes. Lambert of Ardres's remarks about the wasted crusading resources of the young lord Arnold II of Guines suggest that in some cases aristocratic youths preferred to spend their time and money on the tournament field and in courts of love rather than risking their lives and fortunes in perilous enterprises abroad.

Sometimes, however, crashing failures are more revealing to us than quiet traditions of success. For instance, while our evidence for the mechanisms of crusading memory in Flanders is unequivocal, the dynastic histories written in Flanders are, in many ways, the least forthcoming about the crusading past. This may be because the writers felt that the oral traditions surrounding the deeds of Robert, Charles, Thierry, Sibylla, and Philip were so strong that they did not bear repeating. Regardless of why this may have been true in Flanders, elsewhere it is clear that the stories and rituals associated with the family crusading past became more elaborate and significant when traditions were in danger of being abandoned.

The final two chapters are case studies of the heirs of two noble dynasties who ultimately failed to lead crusades despite repeated appeals to them during a period of great crisis on the crusading frontiers in the East and in Spain. As the crisis deepened, appeals from without were supplemented by appeals from within their domains, and the resulting discourse offers us an intimate look at the operation of family memory in the context of the crusades.

---

6. Jonathan Phillips, "The Murder of Charles the Good and the Second Crusade: Household, Nobility, and Traditions of Crusading in Medieval Flanders," *Medieval Prosopography* 19 (1998): 55–76.

PART II

*Two Count-Kings and
the Crusading Past*

🍎 CHAPTER 6

The Fire at Marmoutier

In January 1153 a twenty-year-old prince named Henry sailed to England from the port of Barfleur in the duchy of Normandy to press his claim to the English crown.[1] By November that year he had forced his rival Stephen, son of the Count of Blois and a daughter of William the Conqueror, who had ruled of much of England for the previous nineteen years, to acknowledge him as the successor to the kingdom. At Westminster Abbey a treaty was drawn up to this effect, and at about the same time the prior of that house, Osbert de Clare, composed a poem in honor of the dynamic leader whose accession as Henry II was now assured.[2] The poem begins:

> Illustrious duke of Normans and count of Angevins, judge of Poitevins, and defender of the Tourangeaux, at whose command the swords of men of Maine are all unsheathed. The English people crowding round

---

1. For the accession of Henry II, see Emilie Amt, *The Accession of Henry II in England: Royal Government Restored* (Woodbridge, UK, 1993); Edmund King, "The Accession of Henry II," in *Henry II: New Interpretations,* ed. Christopher Harper-Hill and Nicholas Vincent (Woodbridge, UK, 2007), 24–46; G. J. White, *Restoration and Reform, 1153–1165: Recovery from Civil War in England* (Cambridge, 2000); John D. Hosler, *Henry II: A Medieval Soldier at War, 1147–1189* (Leiden and Boston, 2009).

2. The best edition of the text is Osbert of Clare, *The Letters and Poems of Osbert of Clare,* ed. E. W. Williamson (Oxford, 1929), 130–132.

ANCESTRY OF HENRY II OF ENGLAND

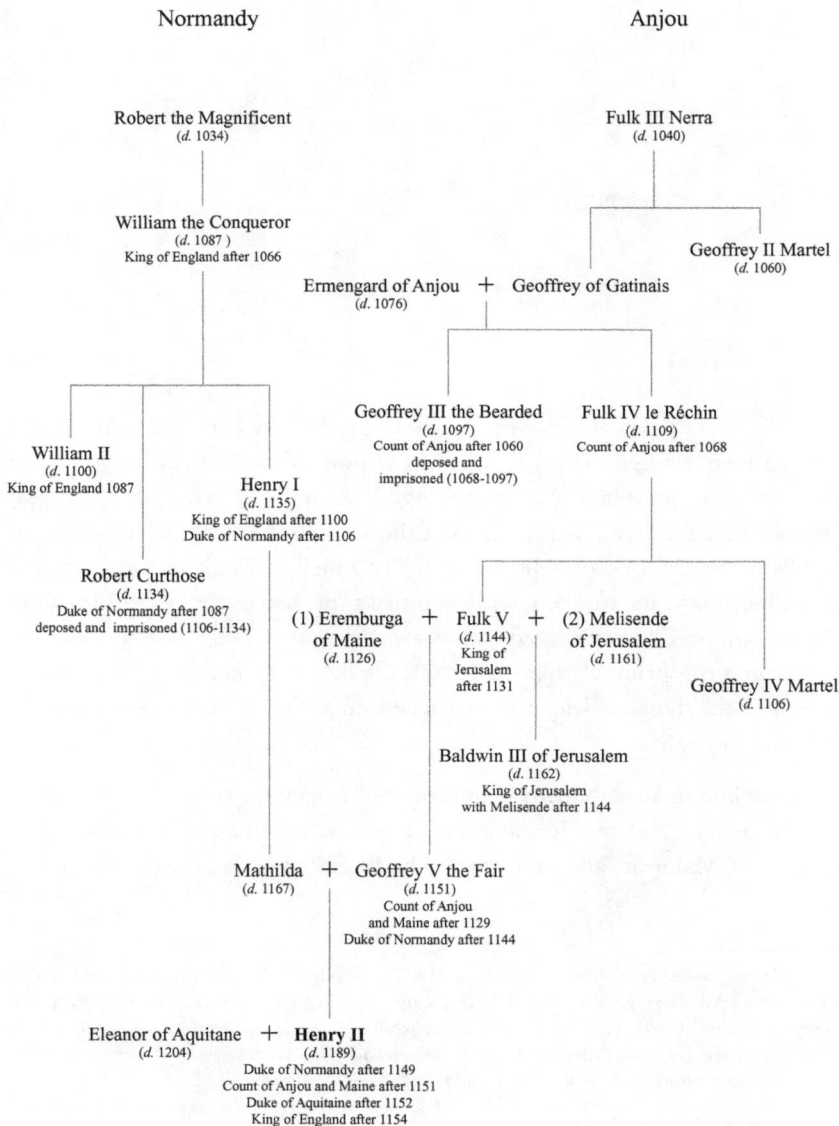

Normandy   Anjou

Robert the Magnificent
(*d.* 1034)

Fulk III Nerra
(*d.* 1040)

William the Conqueror
(*d.* 1087)
King of England after 1066

Geoffrey II Martel
(*d.* 1060)

Ermengard of Anjou + Geoffrey of Gatinais
(*d.* 1076)

Geoffrey III the Bearded
(*d.* 1097)
Count of Anjou after 1060
deposed and
imprisoned (1068-1097)

Fulk IV le Réchin
(*d.* 1109)
Count of Anjou after 1068

William II
(*d.* 1100)
King of England 1087

Henry I
(*d.* 1135)
King of England after 1100
Duke of Normandy after 1106

Robert Curthose
(*d.* 1134)
Duke of Normandy after 1087
deposed and imprisoned (1106-1134)

(1) Eremburga + Fulk V + (2) Melisende
of Maine   (*d.* 1144)   of Jerusalem
(*d.* 1126)   King of   (*d.* 1161)
                  Jerusalem
                  after 1131

Geoffrey IV Martel
(*d.* 1106)

Baldwin III of Jerusalem
(*d.* 1162)
King of Jerusalem
with Melisende after 1144

Mathilda + Geoffrey V the Fair
(*d.* 1167)   (*d.* 1151)
                  Count of Anjou
                  and Maine after 1129
                  Duke of Normandy after 1144

Eleanor of Aquitane + **Henry II**
(*d.* 1204)   (*d.* 1189)
                            Duke of Normandy after 1149
                            Count of Anjou and Maine after 1151
                            Duke of Aquitaine after 1152
                            King of England after 1154

CHART 1. Ancestry of Henry II of England

rejoice at being given peace. For you the heavenly host exults [when] God hears of your victory. Since you are grandson to that great king, by whom all of the laws were made, now you carry that name of his, good omens smile on you.[3]

After ninety-eight years of domination by continental princely dynasties, primarily that of the dukes of Normandy, but recently also of the counts of Blois-Chartres and Boulogne, the idea of a ruler from across the *mare Anglicum* was not a new one. It was nonetheless important to Osbert that he demonstrate how the lineage and dynastic traditions of Henry's paternal ancestors, the counts of Anjou, would complement the Norman ancestry that he claimed through his mother, Mathilda, a daughter of Henry I. The accession of the young Henry brought a welcome return to the peace and justice associated with earlier Norman kings and a new alliance with the vast continental domains of the Angevins, which included not only the three counties of Anjou, Maine, and Touraine but also the duchy of Aquitaine, which Henry held by right of his wife, Eleanor (see chart 1).

To Osbert, the legacy of Henry's paternal ancestors was especially useful in calling to mind the responsibilities that would face the young king once he had been crowned. Remarking that even the distant "kings of Jerusalem praise you as is fitting," Osbert specified that he meant "your uncle and grandfather, to whom the faithless succumbed."[4] The reference was to Henry's paternal grandfather (*avus*), Fulk V of Anjou, who traveled to the East twice, first as a crusader in 1120 and then again in 1129 to become king of Jerusalem through his marriage to Melisende, daughter of King Baldwin II. His paternal uncle (*patruus*), Fulk's son Baldwin III, was the reigning sovereign of the crusader kingdom. To Osbert, the significance of Henry's ties of kinship with the ruling house of Jerusalem was twofold. The prior drew on the image of the Holy Sepulchre defended by Henry's relatives as a model for how Henry should rule in England, a "new Jerusalem":

> On account of your kindred, Christ the king retains his place, and the beauty of the Holy Sepulchre will not be destroyed by blind error. You have been taught by this example: now the temple of God everywhere should be restored by you, because the poor, who have been robbed,

---

3. "Dux illustris normannorum / et comes Andegavorum / Pictavorum damnator / Turonorum propugnator / cuius nutu vibrant enses / populi Cenomannenses / Anglorumque plebs turbata / gratulatur pace data / tibi coetus coeli plaudit / te victorem Deus audit / quum sis nepos magni regis / per quem stetit summa legis / illius iam praefers nomen / cuius tibi ridet omen." Osbert of Clare, *The Letters and Poems of Osbert of Clare,* 130.

4. "Reges Jerosolymorum / te condecorant decorum / tui patruus et avus / quibus cedit quisque pravus." Osbert of Clare, *The Letters and Poems of Osbert of Clare,* 131.

were weeping. You should found a new Jerusalem, and you will clean this whole kingdom of those filthy ones who are the slaves of idols, who kill many in the pursuit of silver.[5]

Events in the East were also meant to instruct Henry in another way. Reporting that good news of the conquest of Ascalon by Henry's uncle Baldwin III had just reached him, Osbert suggested the role that Henry might play in future conquests in the Holy Land:[6]

> With their praise resounds good news: that Ascalon is captured and Babylon shall be destroyed and Damascus conquered. These things are next for you who even now are celebrated there.[7]

The poem of Osbert de Clare reveals how even at this early stage in the career of the Angevin ruler, speculation had already begun as to whether active participation in crusade campaigns would be a feature of Henry's rule. At the same time, however, Osbert openly contrasted the opportunity for glorious Christian conquest in the East with the need for justice, the protection of the poor, and the restoration of the church in England after years of lawlessness. The problem of how to balance these competing responsibilities—the defense of the Holy Land on the one hand and the maintenance of justice and order at home on the other—was a subject of debate at Henry's court for most of his thirty-five-year reign.

Henry's reign saw a dramatic deterioration in the strength and safety of the Latin polities in the East.[8] Beginning in the later 1160s, the position of relative confidence that the kingdom enjoyed at the time of Henry's coronation gradually disappeared as the Zengid emir of Damascus and Aleppo, Nur al-Din, began his campaign to consolidate his power over all the lands between the Euphrates and the Nile. Despite a concerted attempt by the Latins in the East to stop the Zengid takeover of Egypt, this objective was achieved in

---

5. "Rex Christus per genus tuum / sic conservat locum suum / sepulchrique sancti decus / haud delebit error caecus / Hec edocutus es exemplo / ut ubique Dei templo / per te iam sit restauratum / Quod lugebat plebs ablatum / Jerusalem novam fundas / hocque regnum totum mundas / a spurcitiis eorum / servi qui sunt idolorum / et argentum ambientes / multas occiderunt gentes." Osbert of Clare, *The Letters and Poems of Osbert of Clare,* 131–132.

6. Ascalon was captured on 19 August. It is reasonable to assume news of this event would have reached England around the time of the treaty between Henry and Stephen.

7. "Fama sonat laude bona / capta quod sit Ascalona / Babylonque confundetur / et Damascus capietur / Hicque proximi sunt tibi / qui sic nunc triumphant ibi/ tribulantur Saraceni / immense dolore pleni / Et exultant Christiani / cultus casu iam profani." Osbert of Clare, *The Letters and Poems of Osbert of Clare,* 131.

8. For the history of the Latin Kingdom in the 1160s and 1170s, see Bernard Hamilton, *The Leper King and His Heirs: Baldwin IV and the Crusader Kingdom of Jerusalem* (Cambridge, 2000). The account of diplomacy that follows owes much to the work of Jonathan Phillips, *Defenders of the Holy Land: Relations between The Latin East and the West, 1119 –1187* (Oxford, 1996).

1169. Archbishop William of Tyre recalled the anxiety with which the Latins of the East greeted news of these events:

> The wise men of the kingdom began to realize that the subjugation of Egypt by the Turks had been a serious injury to us and that our situation had become materially worse. By sailing out from Egypt with his large fleet, Nureddin, our most powerful enemy, could effectively shut in the realm and blockade all the coast cities by land and sea with his two armies. Still more to be dreaded was the fact that he could hinder the passage of pilgrims on their way to us, or even refuse the permission to pass at all.[9]

The Near Eastern Islamic empire created by Nur al-Din, which would be ruled shortly thereafter by his former general, Saladin, was now in a position to launch large-scale assaults on the kingdom of Jerusalem, governed from 1174 by King Baldwin IV, who suffered from leprosy. The crisis reached its zenith when the massed armies of the kingdom of Jerusalem were destroyed by Saladin on 4 July 1187 at the battle of Hattin. Within five months the greater part of the kingdom, including the capital of Jerusalem, had fallen to Saladin.

Although he repeatedly made agreements stating his intent to lead a crusade, supported the expeditions of several of his vassals, and, it was claimed, raised an immense sum of money to be spent in aid of the Holy Land, Henry did not take the cross until January 1188, after news of the disaster at Hattin had reached the West but with the fate of Jerusalem still unknown. When he died at the castle of Chinon in Anjou in July 1189, Henry's many promises and solemn vow to undertake the pilgrimage were left unfulfilled, and the cash he had set aside for this purpose was not enough to defend Jerusalem. His many hesitations and ultimate failure as a crusader can be contrasted with the enthusiasm of his sons Henry, who took the cross shortly before his early death (he was twenty-eight) in 1183, and Richard, who did so both before and independently of his father in 1187 and who was quick to organize and then lead the Third Crusade soon after his accession in 1189.[10]

---

9. WT, 1:926; trans. Emily Atwater Babcock and A. C. Krey as *History of the Deeds Done beyond the Sea* (New York, 1943), 2:360.

10. For Richard's cross-taking in 1187, see William of Newburgh, *Historia rerum Anglicarum,* ed. Richard Howlett, in *Chronicles of the Reigns of Stephen, Henry II, and Richard I,* RS 82 (London, 1884–89), 1: 271; Ralph of Diceto, *Radulfi de Diceto decani Lundonensis opera: The Historical Works of Master Ralph of Diceto,* ed. William Stubbs, RS 68 (London, 1876), 2: 50; Gervase of Canterbury, *The Historical Works of Gervase of Canterbury,* ed. William Stubbs, RS 73 (London, 1879–80), 1: 389; Gerald of Wales, *Opera,* ed. J. S. Brewer, RS 21 (London, 1861–91), 8: 239–240.

Neither the contemporary chroniclers of his reign nor modern scholars agree about whether Henry II ever really wanted or intended to become a crusader, or if the *negotium terrae sanctae* was only a political card to be played periodically in his contest with France for continental hegemony or in order to extricate himself from ecclesiastical censure after the murder by his knights of Thomas Becket, the archbishop of Canterbury, in 1170.[11] So large and sophisticated were his court and administrative apparatus that Henry II himself, like other medieval rulers, can often seem subsumed by them.[12] Because of this, and because, unlike his great-grandfather Count Fulk IV of Anjou, Henry did not choose to compose an *apologia,* the king's own intentions and desires with regard to the Holy Land remain elusive. The sources we have do not speak to Henry's personal motives, but to the wider discourse of crusading at Henry's court and beyond. They reveal how the case for a crusade was put to Henry, by whom it was made, and in what contexts.

As Osbert de Clare had anticipated, Henry's dynastic traditions and ties of kinship to the ruling dynasty of Jerusalem would, at critical moments, occupy a central place in the crusading discourse of his court and in the appeals directed to him by the papacy and representatives of the beleaguered Latin Kingdom of Jerusalem. Most strikingly, as we saw in chapter 5, in 1185 the patriarch of Jerusalem, Heraclius, himself journeyed to England and, according to a contemporary observer at the court, reminded Henry of his precise genealogical relationship to the leper king Baldwin IV. The letter that Heraclius carried from Pope Lucius III constantly returned to themes of ancestry:

> Since all of your ancestors have from times long past shone in glory of arms and nobility of soul above other territorial princes, and the people of faith knew in them a protector from adversity, it is presumed that deservedly and freely not only the merits of the crown but also the inheritance of ancestral values are passed to you. . . .
>
> . . .
>
> and just as your glorious and noble predecessors freed [the Holy Land] from the power of great numbers of unbelievers and from great

---

11. For the principal contributions to the debate, see Hans Eberhard Mayer, "Henry II of England and the Holy Land", *English Historical Review* 97 (1982): 721–739; Christopher Tyerman, *England and the Crusades: 1095–1588* (Chicago, 1988): 36–56; Phillips, *Defenders of the Holy Land;* Alan Forey, "Henry II's Crusading Penances for Becket's Murder," *Crusades* 7 (2008): 153–164.

12. Similar problems inspired Jacques le Goff to ask of the French king Louis IX: "Lous a-t-il été un individu? Et en quell sens?"; and later: "Saint Louis a-t-il-existé?" Jacques Le Goff, *Saint Louis* (Paris, 1996): 22, 314.

danger, so [Saladin] has brought it back under the yoke of execrable tyranny.

. . .

And so that the outpouring of His [blood] in this region should be exalted, you should add to the powerful work of He who for you chose to be mocked in that same land, following in the footsteps of your ancestors who snatched it from the jaws of the Prince of Darkness.[13]

By at least 1185, at the time of greatest need, the Roman pontiff and the eastern ambassadors had adopted the rhetoric of tradition and dynastic responsibility in the petitions they put to Henry. But in doing so, they were only joining their voices to a polyphony of opinions about ancestry and crusading tradition that had surrounded Henry since his youth and that had found new and more sophisticated modes of expression in the literature produced at his court and in his domains in the 1160s and 1170s. In order to understand how the letters and embassies dispatched to Henry were interpreted by the king and his courtiers, we must restore them to the context of dynastic discourse that surrounded the king.

One of the voices that spoke to the king of his family's past belonged to a monk of the abbey of Marmoutier named John. John composed for Henry a history of his paternal ancestors the counts of Anjou, actually a greatly revised and expanded version of the *Chronica de gestis consulum Andegavorum*. At its center was a striking new narrative image of his grandfather Fulk V watching the burning ramparts of the abbey of Marmoutier. This chapter will show how this image was intended to catch the king's attention as he traveled through his domains, and what it was supposed to tell him about his ancestry, his responsibilities, and his identity.

John was not the only writer to provide Henry with a narrative of his crusading ancestry, but his courtly style and the fact that what he wrote was grounded in the rituals and traditions of power that had surrounded Henry since childhood suggest that his work might have been particularly persuasive. The manuscript context of the sole medieval copy of John's *Chronica* may also be a sign of its continued relevance or proximity to the Angevin

---

13. "Cum cuncti praedecessores tui, prae ceteris terrae principibus, armorum gloria et animi nobilitate longe retro claruerunt; eosque fidelium populus habere in sua didicerit adversitate patronos; merito ad te, non tam regni sed paternarum virtutum haeredem, quadam securitate praesumpta recurritur... et quam gloriosi et nobiles praedecessores tui a dominio gentis incredulae multis laboribus et periculis exemerunt, rursus nefando tyranny nequissimi dominio subjugetur... et ut eius confusio in hac parte tollatur, qui pro te in ipsa terra voluit haberi ludibrio, operam adhibeas efficacem quatenus praedecessorem tuorum vestigia subsecutus, quam ipsi de principis tenebrarum faucibus eripuerunt." [Roger of Howden], *Gesta regis Henrici secundi Benedicti abbatis,* ed. William Stubbs (London, 1867), 1: 333. The letter was also printed in *PL* 201, col. 1312A.

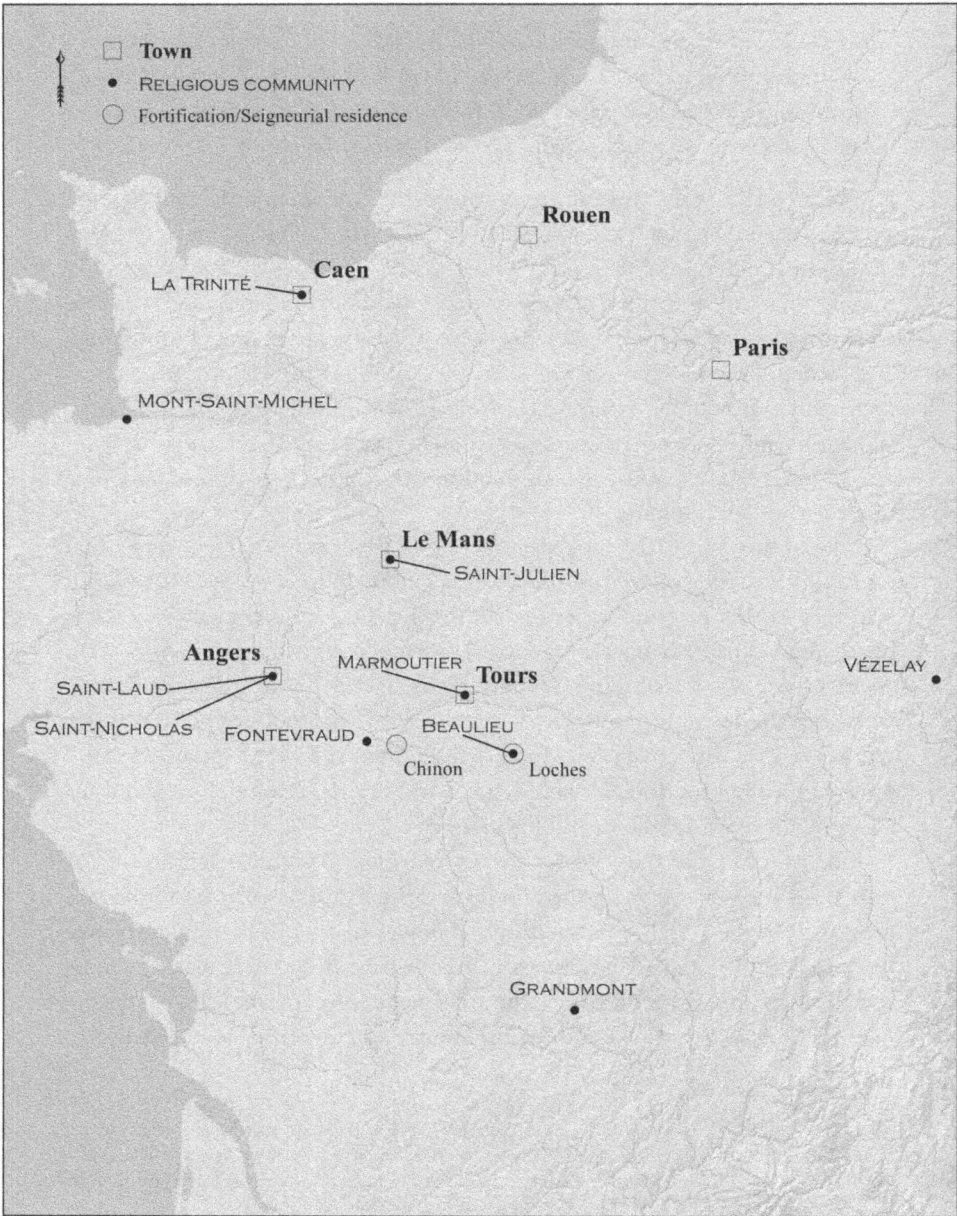

MAP 2. Sites of dynastic commemoration in Henry II's domains

dynasty. The chaotic later years of Henry's reign, and his death in 1189 while planning for a crusade was still under way, make it nearly impossible to determine what impact, if any, the *Chronica* had on Henry's actions or his dynastic imaginary. But the behavior of his son Richard, the famous leader of the Third Crusade, may suggest that John of Marmoutier was successful in associating crusading with a specifically Angevin identity in the ruling house.

Sites and Rites of Memory

Since his childhood days growing up in his father's domains, Henry moved in a landscape where disparate commemorative traditions of his crusading ancestors were preserved by a variety of communities.[14] At particular times in the liturgical year and in concert with rituals established by Henry's ancestors, these memories were invoked through the procession or presentation of relics and other commemorative objects. In many cases, the same communities that acted as the guardians of the traditions also housed the remains of preceding generations of the Angevin comital family (see map 2).

The abbey church of Saint-Nicholas in Angers was the burial place of two of Henry's most renowned ancestors, Count Geoffrey II Martel of Anjou (d. 1060) and his namesake, the much-beloved and widely eulogized Geoffrey IV Martel the Younger (d. 1106). Saint-Nicholas was also the site of feasts and rites that evoked the crusades and the deeds of earlier Angevin counts in the East. As abbot Noël of Saint-Nicholas wrote to his friend Joël of La Couture in the last decade of the eleventh century, the monks celebrated a special feast in memory of Count Fulk Nerra of Anjou's wondrous retrieval of the relics of Nicholas from Myra on his return from pilgrimage to Jerusalem, and his son Geoffrey Martel's gift of yet more relics of the same saint, earned through an appreciation of his great military valor by the German emperor Henry III.[15] Each year, on 10 February, the monks of Saint-Nicholas of Angers marked the anniversary of Pope Urban II's 1096 visit to rededicate

---

14. Henry spent only brief periods of his youth being educated in England. By the later 1140s, he may have accompanied his father on campaign in Normandy. We can occasionally catch sight of him in his youth in Anjou: *Recueil des actes de Henry II roi d'Angleterre et duc de Normandie: Concernant les provinces françaises et les affaires de France,* ed. Léopold Delisle and rev. Élie Berger (Paris, 1909–27), 1: 6–7, 8–9. It has been observed that although Henry did not often come to Anjou, those times when he did were some of the most crucial in his career. See Noël-Yves Tonnerre, "Henri II et l'Anjou," in *Plantagenêts et Capétiens: Confrontations et héritages,* ed. Martin Aurell and Noël-Yves Tonnerre, Histoires de famille: La parenté au Moyen Âge 4 (Turnhout, 2006), 211–225 (the remark is at 214).

15. "Miraculum sancti Nicolai Andegavi" [from BNF, MS Lat. 12611 s. xii], *Catalogus codicum hagiographicorum latinorum antiquiorum saeculo xvi qui asservantur in Bibliotheca nationali Parisiensi* (Brussels, 1893), 3: 159–160. For commentary, see Yvonne Mailfert, "Fondation du monastère bénédictin de Saint-Nicholas d'Angers," in *Bibliothèque de l'École des Chartes* 92 (1931): 43–61.

their new church and preach the crusade, offering those who joined in their celebrations a remittance of a seventh of their penance. The date 10 February also marked the anniversary of the translation of the body of Count Geoffrey Martel to the nave of the new church, where he lay in presumably greater splendor and in much-increased visibility.

At the heart of Angers was the comital palace, which housed both the *aula comitis* and the residence where a visiting count and his family would stay. The palace was obviously of some importance to Henry, since, according to Ralph of Diceto, he refurbished it in the "splendor befitting a king."[16] Within the palace complex was the collegiate church of Saint-Laud. This was a community with extremely close ties to the comital family and household, and in the early twelfth century its members held offices in the count's household and administration.[17] When Henry and his family returned to Angers from a long absence or from a pilgrimage, the canons of Saint-Laud were instructed to process out to meet him, ringing bells and carrying holy water, and to present the count with the ivory tau sent to them by Henry's grandfather Fulk V.[18] As we saw in chapter 3, this tau was directly associated by the canons of Saint-Laud with Fulk's status as defender of the Holy Sepulchre. The deacon of Saint-Laud, Guy of Athée, remembered how "that same Fulk had [the tau] from the sultan of Babylon, when Christ elevated him to be king of Jerusalem."[19] The tau evoked the honor Fulk had brought on his family in Anjou, and, especially in this ceremonial context, it briefly figured the Count of Anjou as the leader of a crusading army, bearing before him the sign of Gideon.[20]

The canons of Saint-Laud remembered Henry as a generous benefactor who had recognized the importance of the objects given to them by Fulk V. In their necrology, they recorded how he had given a new reliquary for the "most precious piece of the living cross that his venerable

---

16. Ralph of Diceto, *Opera,* 1: 292.

17. For the college, see *Cartulaire du chapitre de Saint-Laud d'Angers,* ed. Adrien Planchenault (Angers, 1903), v–ix. In 1116 the count's chancellor was Guibert of Saint-Laud, see Josèphe Chartrou, *L'Anjou de 1109 à 1151: Foulque de Jérusalem et Geoffroi Plantagenêt* (Paris, 1928), 109 (and no. 12). Another canon of Saint-Laud, Geoffrey Caiaphas, was the chaplain and scribe of Fulk le Réchin. *Cartulaire de Saint-Laud d'Angers,* nos. 8, 13, 18, 23, 24, 55, 60, 61, 62, 75, 104.

18. *Cartulaire de Saint Laud,* 4–5 (no. 3). For the origins of the relic and its transmission to Anjou, see Jonathan Riley-Smith, "King Fulk of Jerusalem and the 'Sultan of Babylon,'" in *Montjoie: Studies in Crusade Hisory in Honour of Hans Eberhard Mayer,* ed. Benjamin Kedar and Jonathan Riley-Smith (Aldershot, UK, 1997), 55–66. See also Riley-Smith, *The First Crusaders, 1095–1131* (Cambridge, 1997), 182.

19. "quod habuit a sodanno Babilonie, quando Christus in regem Jerusalem ipsum Fulconem sublimavit." *Cartulaire de Saint-Laud,* 5.

20. See above, 127–128.

uncle Fulk, then count of Anjou, had brought from Jerusalem."[21] A fragment of a liturgical manuscript written at Saint-Laud in the later Middle Ages reveals that the story of the "King of Jerusalem and the Sultan of Babylon" was used in sermons on the text of *Vexilla regis prodeunt,* the hymn of Venantius Fortunatus sung at Easter and the Feast of the Exaltation (14 September).[22]

To the east of Angers, near the important frontier castle of Loches, was the abbey of Beaulieu (*Belli Locus*).[23] By the early twelfth century, the foundation of Beaulieu was associated primarily with the pilgrimages of Henry's ancestor Fulk Nerra (d. 1040) to Rome and Jerusalem.[24] The monks claimed that Fulk had entrusted them with relics of saints Chrysanthus and Daria, gifts to Fulk from Pope Sergius IV, a lamp and oil associated with the miracle of the Holy Fire in the church of the Holy Sepulchre in Jerusalem, and, most importantly, a piece of the Holy Sepulchre itself.[25] Dramatic stories of Fulk's pilgrimage to Jerusalem, which included the account of his confrontation with the "Syrians" (*Suriani*) who guarded the Sepulchre, were present in the dynastic narrative traditions that had circulated in the Touraine since Henry's youth, and these same traditions would ultimately be incorporated into the abbey's liturgy.[26] The parts of Fulk's remains dispatched back to Anjou after his death returning from his final pilgrimage to Jerusalem were buried at Beaulieu, where, at some point, an effigy of the count was constructed to lie over them.[27] Decades later, monks in Anjou would continue to comment on the association between the place of the count's burial with the objective of his last journey.[28] After the conquest of Jerusalem by the First Crusade, the office for the Holy Sepulchre was celebrated on 15 July to mark the anniversary of

21. Chartrou, *L'Anjou,* 204. The True Cross relic may have been sent with the ivory tau or perhaps returned with the count to Anjou after his earlier crusade of 1120.

22. Angers, Bibliothèque Municipale, MS 252 (243) f. 1v.

23. Bernard Bachrach associates the name *Belli locus* with the battle of Conquereil, but it is notable that the liturgy of the monks suggests the abbey was called Bellus Allodus. See Bernard Bachrach, *Fulk Nerra, the Neo-Roman consul, 987–1040: A Political Biography of the Angevin Count* (Berkeley, 1993), 101.

24. *CCA,* 50–51.

25. *CCA,* 51.

26. For the stories associated with Beaulieu, see above, 178–180; *CCA,* 50–51; *Histoire de Fulk Nerra, comte d'Anjou suivie par l'office du Saint-Sépulchre de l'abbaye de Beaulieu,* ed. Alexandre de Salies (Paris 1874), 529–533. Although see Louis Halphen, *Comté d'Anjou au xi siècle* (Paris, 1906), xi, who argues that the office as it survives cannot be dated with any confidence before the fifteenth century.

27. The effigy does not survive but was drawn by Roger Gaignières. See Halphen, *Comté d'Anjou,* 234–236; Bachrach, *Fulk Nerra,* 244–246.

28. "Miraculum sancti Nicolai Andegavi," 160.

the capture of Jerusalem by the First Crusade, further conflating Fulk's fateful pilgrimage with the efforts of his namesake and descendant.[29]

Another institution that encouraged the association between Henry's crusader and pilgrim ancestors was the chapel of Saint-Saveur at Langeais. Upon his return from one of several journeys to Jerusalem, Fulk III Nerra founded a chapel inside the important stronghold of Langeais, west of Loches, between Tours and Angers. As we saw in chapter 3, by the time of Henry's grandfather Fulk V, the chapel was said to house relic fragments of the manger where Christ had lain when he was born and of the Holy Sepulchre itself.[30] The canons of the Augustinian abbey of Toussaint in Angers, who successfully gained control of the chapel at some point during Fulk V's rule, had cleverly used it as a focus of their appeals to family tradition. When they had praised Fulk V as surpassing Cato in the rigor of his justice and Job in his beneficence and endurance, they also explicitly described the pilgrimage of Fulk Nerra, whose deeds "were to be imitated," as a response to the injunction to "take up the cross" in Matthew 16:24. Traveling the road east from Angers to Loches, therefore, Henry II would pass two fragments of the Holy Sepulchre that flanked Tours, both brought back by his ancestor Fulk III, the protocrusader who struggled before the gates.

If the traditions that Count Fulk le Réchin had established following Urban's visit in 1096 were still followed, then a visit by a count to Tours on Palm Sunday would feature the procession of the golden flower (most likely the Golden Rose) presented to Fulk by Urban, which Fulk had decreed should always be carried before the count during Palm Sunday processions out of "remembrance and love" for the architect of the First Crusade.[31] After 1099, of course, this juxtaposition of an object from the time of the preaching of the First Crusade and the Palm Sunday liturgical processions—themselves

---

29. Sylvia Schein, *Gateway to the Heavenly City: Crusader Jerusalem and the Catholic West* (Aldershot, UK, 2005), 30–31.

30. François Comte, *L'abbaye de Toussaints d'Angers* (Angers, 1985), 146–148, no. 102.

31. *CCA*, 238; the visit was also recalled by the monks of Saint Aubin; *Cartulaire de l'abbaye de Saint-Aubin d'Angers,* ed. Arthur Bertrand de Broussilon (Paris, 1903), 363 (act no. 889). As Charles W. Jones, *Saint Nicholas of Myra, Bari, and Manhattan* (Chicago, 1978), 214–215, has pointed out, a sermon of Hildbert of Lavardin ("Sermones," *PL* 171, cols. 751–752) confirms that the ceremonies at Saint Nicholas were still associated with Urban's visit years later. What had happened to the flower by the time of Henry's boyhood is unclear, but one historian has suggested that it was the inspiration for the golden broom (*planta genesta*) that Henry's father, Geoffrey the Fair, reportedly wore on his helmet. Jim Bradbury, "Fulk le Réchin and the Origins of the Plantagenets," in *Studies in Medieval History Presented to R. Allen Brown,* ed. Christopher Harper Hill et al. (Woodbridge, UK, 1989), 27–42.

echoes of Christ's entry into Jerusalem—would have the count symbolically entering Jerusalem not only in imitation of Christ but also of the crusaders.[32]

A site of great significance for Henry for its numerous associations with his parents was the cathedral church of Saint-Julien at Le Mans. Henry, as the canons of Saint-Julien recalled in the *Acta pontificum Cenomannis,* had actually been baptized in the cathedral a few weeks after his mother, Mathilda, stopped near Le Mans to give birth on 5 March 1133.[33] On that occasion she had honored the canons with a *pallium,*[34] a gift matched by other liturgical garments and hangings *(dorsalia* and *tapetii)* given to the canons upon her death.[35] On one of his many return visits to Le Mans, Henry would have had the opportunity to view these hangings, and beneath them the tomb where the body of his father, Geoffrey, had lain since his death on 7 September 1151. The tomb was topped by a magnificent plaque with his father's image rendered in Limoges enamels. Included in the panoply of dynastic objects preserved at Le Mans were others invoking Henry's dynastic links with the East. At the time of the accession of his grandfather Fulk V to the royal dignity of Jerusalem, William of Bures, the knight who arrived as *nuncio* bringing the offer of the crown to the Angevin count, had left at Saint-Julien relics of the True Cross, a *pallium,* and a precious banner called a *transartat* hung on hammered metal crossbars and worth nine silver marks.[36]

Although a much more recent foundation than the other devotional sites, the double monastery at Fontevraud, founded in 1101 on the south bank of the Loire only a few miles west of the castle of Chinon by the reformer Robert Arbrissel, was among the most important for Henry's Angevin ancestors.[37] Ermengard of Anjou, dowager duchess of Brittany and daughter of Fulk IV le Réchin, was the recipient of the only surviving letter from Robert Arbrissel.[38] Her brother, Fulk V, attended Robert's funeral and the dedication of the abbey church by Calixtus II. As part of his final preparations for departure to take up the crown of the crusader kingdom, Fulk met with all of his children at Fontevraud to confirm the privileges of the abbey.[39] Fulk and the Angevin

---

32. Easter processions held in Tours in the thirteenth century are described in *Rituel de Saint Martin de Tours,* ed. A. Fleuret (Paris, 1899–1901), 49–52; for commentary, see Sharon Farmer, *Communities of Saint Martin: Legend and Ritual in Medieval Tours* (Ithaca, NY, 1991), 297.

33. *Actus pontificum Cenomannis in urbe degentium,* ed. Gustav Busson and André Ledru (Le Mans, 1903), 432.

34. *Actus pontificum Cenomannis,* 432. In imitation of the "noble matron" who was the founder of a certain monastery earlier in the same text (405)?

35. *Actus pontificum Cenomannis,* 433.

36. *Actus pontificum Cenomannis,* 430.

37. *Trésor des chartes de l'abbaye royale de Fontevraud,* ed. Archives Nationales (Paris, 1992), 19.

38. Bruce L. Venarde, *Robert of Arbrissel: A Medieval Religious Life* (Washington, DC, 2003), 68–79.

39. Chartrou, *L'Anjou,* 372–373.

contingent that he brought with him to the East (which included for a time his sister Ermengard) apparently instilled in the ruling dynasty of Jerusalem a respect for Fontevraud.[40] At some point before her death in the 1170s, perhaps while Fulk's sister, Mathilda, was abbess (r. 1149–55), Fulk's sister-in-law Ivetta, who was the abbess of Saint-Lazarus in Bethany, sent to Fontevraud a pix containing relics.[41] It was inscribed:

> Abbess Ivetta of Saint Lazarus of Bethany, daughter of King Baldwin [II of Jerusalem] placed these precious relics in this sacred little container and sent them to the holy convent of Fontevraud. . . . She asks that, for such a gift, when they should hear of the day of her death, they should write it into the obituary and celebrate it, together with the anniversaries of her parents, in the general chapter.[42]

The Angevin tradition of support for Fontevraud was continued by Henry, his wife, Eleanor, and their children. After Henry's burial at the abbey under the supervision of his son Richard in 1189, Fontevraud became a dynastic mausoleum, where descendants of Eleanor and Henry would be entombed until the mid-thirteenth century.

The castles, churches, and monasteries of Anjou, Maine, and the Touraine were not the only sites in Henry's domains with links to the East or to the crusading past. Numerous other institutions, such as Holy Trinity in Caen and Grandmont in the Limousin, were in possession of Passion relics, some of them associated with Jerusalem. But nowhere outside the Angevin heartland (Anjou-Touraine-Maine) do we find narratives or rituals associating such relics either with Henry's family, as at Fontevraud, or with a prominent crusading ancestor or pre-crusade pilgrim, as at Le Mans, Angers, Fontevraud, and Loches. As we saw in chapter 3, other memorabilia associated with the First Crusade certainly circulated in Normandy and the Limousin, but there they pertained to other families and were not present in the contexts or

---

40. Ermengard was the likely transmitter of the Angevin enthusiasm for Fontevraud. Although the details are very sketchy, evidence from both East and West seems to confirm that Ermengard spent at least part of her time in the East as a nun at the convent of Saint Anne in Jerusalem. The itinerary and chronology provided in Philippe Carrer, *Ermengarde d'Anjou: L'autre duchesse de Bretagne* (Spézet, 2003), 249–253, are largely speculative.

41. For Ivetta and Saint Lazarus, see Hans Eberhard Mayer, *Bistümer, Klöster, und Stifte im Königreich Jerusalem, Monumenta Germaniae Historica: Schriften* 26 (Stuttgart, 1977), 243–257.

42. "Iuditha abbatissa beati Lazari de Bethania, filia regis Balduini reposuit has pretiosas reliqias in hoc sacro loculo, et misit eas sacro conventui Fontis-Ebraldi etc. Rogans, ut pro tanto munere, obitus sui diem, cum illum audierint, in Martyrologiis scribant et in publico conventu concelebrent, et anniversarios parentus suorum similiter." Inscription transcribed by Jean de Mainferme, in *Clypeus nascentis Font-Ebraldensis oridinis* (Paris, 1684–92), 2: 233–234.

environments that would help foster a connection between Henry and past crusaders from Normandy or Aquitaine.

Outside of the Angevin domains, moreover, the crusading past was more complicated. Normandy, which was Henry's maternal inheritance, and the Aquitainian lands he ruled together with his wife, Eleanor, had been strong in crusading enthusiasm since 1095, but neither offered Henry an easy link with past dynastic crusading glory. The princely dukes of both territories, Robert Curthose of Normandy and William IX of Aquitaine, had participated in the First Crusade. The expedition undertaken by William in 1101, however, had ended in defeat and rumors of shameful conduct, establishing a tradition that might be seen to have been inherited by his daughter Eleanor, whose participation in the Second Crusade would come to be associated with that expedition's disastrous conclusion.[43] Curthose, on the contrary, had won great renown in the East but upon his return had chosen to challenge his brother's succession to the English crown as Henry I. Since, as we have seen in the poem of Osbert de Clare, Henry I was the model ruler presented to his grandson for imitation, it was not possible to invoke the crusading feats of Curthose without also reviving memories of the disputed succession and subsequent civil war.

Thus it was primarily to the traditions maintained within and related to the Angevin domains that those around Henry and perhaps also the king himself turned when considering the crusading past. It was to the master of this realm of crusading memory that appeals for help from the East and from Rome began to be dispatched in the 1160s.

The Invocation of Tradition

As had been the case since its inception after the conquest of Jerusalem by the First Crusade in 1099, the survival of the Latin Kingdom in the 1160s rested on the ability of the settlers to summon aid from the West. The Anglo-Norman and Blésois rulers of England, unlike the Capetians of France, had not undertaken to lead or sponsor an expedition to the Holy Land and had shown only casual interest in the military orders.[44] There were several reasons for contemporaries to believe that Henry might be different. By the second year of Henry's reign, as Emily Amt has shown, it was already clear that

---

43. For the association between William's failure as a crusader and his sexual profligacy, see GV, 70–71. For the earliest traditions about Eleanor, see Daniel Power, "The Stripping of a Queen: Eleanor in 13th-Century Norman Tradition," in *The World of Eleanor of Aquitaine: Literature and Society in Medieval France,* ed. Marcus Bull and Catherine Léglu (Woodbridge, UK, 2005), 127–128.

44. Phillips, *Defenders of the Holy Land,* 173.

the military orders could rely on him, as they had not been able to rely on his mother or any of his Norman ancestors, as a great patron and benefactor. Under Henry, the Templars received royal alms and were allowed to keep the lands granted to them by Stephen, on which they did not have to pay the customary Danegeld.[45] Moreover, there is evidence that in 1159, before the crisis began to unfold in the East, Henry and the crusade veteran Louis VII were planning to campaign in Spain, where they were intent, according to a letter of Pope Adrian IV, on "expanding the frontiers of the Christian people, fighting the barbarity of the pagans, and subjugating under the yoke and rule of the Christians the apostate peoples and those who hide and will not receive the truth of the Catholic faith."[46]

In considering potential targets for their letters and embassies requesting aid, the Latins of Outremer and the papacy may also have considered, as had Osbert de Clare, Henry's ties of kinship with the royal house of Jerusalem, but reference to this fact is conspicuously absent from their early appeals. The most common reminders of the situation in the East came in the form of papal bulls. Following the example (and quite often the text) of *Quantum praedecessores,* the letter issued by Eugenius III in 1145 and 1147 in response to the fall of Edessa in 1144, the crusade bulls issued by Alexander III in 1165, 1166, 1169, and 1181 retained the references to the efforts, zeal, and suffering of "our" or "your" fathers, while also invoking the language of fraternity and adding details of the most recent grim news from the East. The bull of 1181 curiously added to *patres* the listener's *genitores,* a term that in the context of dynastic history was often linked to very distant and legendary ancestry.[47] In his 1165 reissue of *Quantum praedecessores,* Alexander was shrewd enough to remove his predecessor's reference to "powerful warriors of the kingdom of France and also those of Italy," a phrase that would certainly have stung a rival of the Capetians like Henry.[48] But these letters were intended for a

---

45. Amt, *The Accession of Henry II in England,* 103–109.

46. "ad dilatandos terminos populi Christiani, ad paganorum barbariem debellandam, et ad gentes apostatrices, et quae catholicae fidei refugiunt nec recipiunt veritatem, Christianorum jugo et ditioni subdendas." Adrian IV, "Epistolae et privilegia," *PL* 188, cols. 1615–1617. Adrian writes to Louis VII, who planned to undertake the expedition "simul cum charissimo filio nostro Henrico illustri Anglorum rege." See Phillips, *Defenders of the Holy Land,* 174; Anne Duggan, "*Servus servorum Dei,*" in *Adrian IV, the English Pope, 1154–1159: Studies and Texts,* ed. Brenda Bolton and Anne Duggan (Aldershot, UK, and Burlington, VT, 2003), 191–192.

47. Alexander III, "Epistolae et privilegia," *PL* 200, cols. 1294–1295. *Cor Nostrum,* Jan., 1181: "that land, for which our fathers and progenitors shed their own blood in the conflicts which they once had with the gentiles." For the sense of *genitor* as "progenitor," see its use in the dynastic history of the counts of Anjou, *Chronica de gestis consulum Andegavorum,* where it is used to describe the earliest (and legendary) ancestors of the counts.

48. Eugenius III, "Epistolae et privilegia," *PL* 180, cols. 1064–1066 at 1064.

general audience, and their appeal to a shared crusading past was understandably vague.

In 1166 and 1169 two embassies from the Latin East traveled to the West in search of aid and with the hopes of inspiring Christendom's most powerful lords to take the cross. The primary target of the first embassy, led by the master of the Hospital, Gilbert of Assailly, was the proven crusade enthusiast Louis VII of France, but the embassy, or at least its message, is likely to have reached Henry. In 1166, Henry celebrated Easter (24 April) with his court at Angers and there held a meeting with Louis.[49] A visit like this by the French king to one of the centers of the Angevin domains was extraordinary in itself, but it is also worth noting that if Louis celebrated Holy Week with Henry, he would have been present for the processions of the golden flower and the tau of Saint-Laud. His journey into and around Anjou provided numerous potential rendezvous with Angevin dynastic traditions and Henry's kinship with the ruling dynasty of Jerusalem. Indeed, the primary subject of their discussion was apparently how to aid the Holy Land.[50] A few weeks after the Easter meeting with Louis, at a conference with ecclesiastical prelates from his continental holdings, Henry began to collect a levy in aid of the Holy Land in concert with a similar action taken by Louis in France.[51]

The second embassy, led by Archbishop Frederick of Tyre, one of the leading ecclesiastical figures of the kingdom of Jerusalem, was directed toward a named group of rulers and nobles that included Henry, the crowned heads of France, Germany, and Sicily, and the territorial princes of Flanders, Champagne, and Blois. Jonathan Phillips, who conducted a detailed study of Frederick's embassy, noted that all of these men were members of dynasties with significant crusading traditions.[52] It would therefore seem reasonable to conclude that those traditions would be at the center of the appeal for their assistance in the East. But apart from the inclusion of the general language of past sufferings and accomplishments common to the papal crusading letters, there is no evidence in either the correspondence surrounding these legations or the narrative descriptions of them that the ties of kinship of the English king were invoked. By contrast, as Phillips has shown, the letters borne by Frederick in 1169 carried explicit invocations of the ties of kinship between

---

49. Robert of Torigni remembered that the conference was in Normandy and at Lent, but John of Salisbury, who traveled to Angers to meet with Henry and wrote about it shortly afterward, dates it to Easter: Robert of Torigni, *Chronique,* ed. Léopold Delisle (Rouen, 1872–73), 359; John of Salisbury, *The Letters of John of Salisbury,* ed. J. W. Millor, H. E. Butler, and C. N. L. Brooke, (Oxford, 1986), 2: xxviii and no. 166 (99). See also Marcel Pacaut, *Louis VII et son royaume* (Paris, 1964), 199.

50. Robert of Torigni, *Chronique,* 359.

51. Gervase of Canterbury, *The Historical Works,* 198.

52. Phillips, *Defenders of the Holy Land,* 178–179.

the Capetian dynasty and the ruling family of Antioch.[53] Phillips has also argued that part of the appeals to Louis focused on the growing association, sponsored mainly by the monks of the royal abbey of Saint-Denis, between the Capetian dynasty and Charlemagne, who had been reimagined by this time as Louis's crusading ancestor.[54]

A Visit to Paris

This focus on French leadership was reinforced when, in November 1169, Henry met with papal representatives, Louis VII, Frederick of Tyre, and the man who had once been Henry's friend but was by this time his bitter enemy, the archbishop of Canterbury, Thomas Becket, in Paris.[55] This gathering, one of the great scenes in the drama of Henry and Thomas, is known to us primarily through a letter written by Thomas himself and the account of one of his biographers, Herbert of Bosham, who was a member of the archbishop's household.[56] These two narratives, one recounted through the lens of Becket's subsequent murder, place the quarrel between Henry and Thomas center stage, but an attempt at reconciliation between the two men was only one of the matters on the agenda for the Paris conference. The broader objective was to bring about the conditions necessary for a crusade, conditions that included peace between Henry and Louis, a settlement of competing claims to the county of Toulouse by Henry's twelve-year-old son Richard and Raymond V of Saint-Gilles, as well as a reconciliation between Henry and the archbishop Thomas.[57]

While Becket waited impatiently in the city of Paris itself, Henry undertook a pilgrimage to the abbey church of Saint-Denis.[58] Arriving on 16 November, he and Louis spent two days at Saint-Denis, where, according to Becket, they discussed political matters, including Toulouse and Henry's

---

53. Phillips, *Defenders of the Holy Land,* 181.

54. Phillips, *Defenders of the Holy Land,* 191–192.

55. Robert William Eyton, *Court, Household, and Itinerary* (Dorchester, UK, 1878), 131; Pacaut, *Louis VII et son royaume,* 200–201.

56. Herbert of Bosham, "Vita Sancti Thomae," *Materials for the History of Thomas Becket,* ed. James Craigie Robertson, RS 67 (London, 1875–85), 3: 445–446; *The Correspondence of Thomas Becket,* ed. Anne Duggan (Oxford, 2000), 2: 1047, no. 243.

57. The dispute in the south centered on the succession to the county following the death of Count William IV of Toulouse in 1094. His daughter Philippa married William IX of Aquitaine, who claimed the county through right of his wife, but the territory was seized by William IV's brother Raymond IV of Saint-Gilles. See Fredric Cheyette, *Ermegard of Narbonne and the World of the Troubadours* (Ithaca, NY, 2001), 4.

58. Henry's status as a penitent was highlighted by both Becket and Bosham, but while Becket presented Henry II as feigning a pilgrim's piety, Bosham assumed that the king was indeed plagued by guilt at his earlier treatment of Becket. Frank Barlow, *Thomas Becket* (London, 1986), 193–194.

desire to have the young Richard educated at Louis's court. Since Becket
and his biographer were barred from attending the meeting, no chronicler
was present who can relate to us the reaction of Henry II upon visiting the
royal abbey, but we know what he saw. At Saint-Denis the English king was
confronted with a center of dynastic identity and royal authority unlike any
that existed at the time. Under the inspired administration of Suger from
1122 to 1155 and his successor, Odo of Deuil, Saint-Denis had become architecturally unique as a site of early experimentation in the Gothic style but
also presented a vehicle for the projection of dynastic power in which royal
legitimacy was closely intertwined with images and rituals of the crusading
tradition.

The narrative of the dynastic past that underlay the iconographic and
commemorative program of Saint-Denis associated the Capetians with the
earlier Carolingian and Merovingian royal dynasties, many of whose rulers
were entombed beneath the abbey's floor.[59] Among the most prominent
tombs visible at the time of Henry's November visit would thus have been
those of Louis's own father, Louis VI, and the Carolingian king Charles the
Bald, whose burial before the high altar was advertised by Suger with a new
large cross marking its position. Inscriptions added by Suger to the high altar
also reminded visitors that the original decorations of the Dionysian altar
and the collection of relics inside it had been transferred from the imperial
treasury on the orders of Charles himself.[60] For Henry's Angevin ancestors,
the Carolingians were considered a crucial touchstone of authority, from
whom they claimed to have received their lands and titles.[61] By the time of
Henry's visit, however, the Capetians had begun to claim their own special
status as successors to the Carolingian dynasty. If earlier generations of counts
of Anjou had argued independence from Capetian overlordship as a consequence of the origin of their rights in Carolingian times, the Capetians,
assisted by the monks of Saint-Denis, were now prepared to argue that they,
as successors to Charlemagne, could claim authority over Anjou and every
other principality in the former west Frankish Carolingian *regnum.*

---

59. For Suger and the creation of dynastic traditions at Saint-Denis, see Gabrielle Spiegel, *The Chronicle Tradition of Saint Denis: A Survey* (Brookline, MA, 1978), 44–45; and Spiegel, *The Past as Text: The Theory and Practice of Medieval Historiography* (Baltimore, 1997), 85; Andrew W. Lewis, *Royal Succession in Capetian France: Studies on Familial Order and the State* (Cambridge, MA, 1981), 104–122, argued that Capetian "dynasticism" linking the royal family to the Carolingians began in earnest only in the reign of Philip Augustus. Lewis notes that writers in Anjou were making genealogical connections between Capetians and Carolingians before the royalist writers (like Suger and Odo) did so (268 n. 13), citing *CCA,* 31 and *Chroniques des églises d'Anjou,* ed. Paul Marchegay and Émile Mabille (Paris, 1869), 21.

60. Suger, *Oeuvres complètes de Suger,* ed. Albert Lecoy de la Marche (Paris, 1867), 196–197.

61. See *CCA,* 24–31.

Since at least the first decade of the twelfth century, traditions had been developing that imagined Carolingian kings first as pilgrims and then crusaders to the Holy Land. A historical work written in the Touraine, but closely associated with the dynastic traditions of Henry's father's family and probably known to Henry, recalled a time when

> the Persians and many other Saracens who had invested Constantinople laid waste to Greece. Coming to their aid, Charles the Bald conquered the Persians with a great army and put to flight the Saracens and liberated the royal city with the kingdom of Greece. . . . Returning from Constantinople with many relics, Charles gave them to many churches in his kingdom.[62]

At Saint-Denis, similar traditions that refigured Charlemagne as the leader of a Frankish crusade to the Holy Land were adapted and integrated into the texts and artworks associated with the Capetian dynasty. The monks of Saint-Denis were the guardians of the French war banner Oriflamme, associated since the later eleventh century with the standard of Charlemagne and said to have been carried by him on his legendary crusade to Jerusalem.[63] Oriflamme had been presented to Louis VII at Saint-Denis upon his departure on crusade in 1147. When Henry and Louis discussed the possibility of a new crusade in 1169, they were in the presence of the flag that waited to be presented ritually to the crusading *rex Francorum* once more and that marked the king of France as the undisputed defender of Christendom.

The church's new ambulatory, no doubt the most striking feature to a visiting pilgrim in 1169, used innovative architectural techniques to allow large stained-glass windows to be installed in its radiating chapels. In one of the westernmost of these chapels was a single large window composed of fourteen panels all dedicated to the theme of crusading and explicitly addressing a Capetian and Frankish royal tradition of crusading originating with Charlemagne.[64] In its lower registers, the window depicted Charlemagne responding

---

62. "Post hec, Perse aliique Saraceni multi Constantinopoli, obsederunt, Greciam vastaverunt; ad cuius succursum Karolus Calvus cum magno exercitu pergens Persas devicit, Saracenos fugavit, urbem regiam cum regno Grecie deliberavit . . . Karolus a Constantinopoli cum lulti reliqiis rediens, quas diversis ecclesiis sui regni posuit." *CCA,* 20.

63. Oriflamme was in fact the standard of the French Vexin. E. M. Hallam, *Capetian France, 987–1328,* 2nd ed. (Harlow, UK, 2001), 154, 241. The earliest text that makes this claim is the *Descriptio qualiter Karous Magnus;* for the *Descriptio* and its links to the Capetian court, see Matthew Gabriele, "The Provenance of the *Descriptio qualiter Karolus Magnus:* Remembering the Carolingians in the Entourage of King Philip I (1060–1108) before the First Crusade," *Viator* 39:2 (2008): 93–117.

64. See Elizabeth A. R. Brown and Michael W. Cothren, "The Twelfth-Century Crusading Window of Saint Denis: *Praeteritorum enim recordatio futurorum est exhibitio,*" *Journal of the Warburg and Courtauld Institutes* 49 (1986): 1–40. While Brown and Cothren preferred an attribution of the window to Suger's successor Eudes of Deuil, both Jonathan Phillips and Lindy Grant associate the

to a call for help from the Byzantine emperor and riding to the aid of Con-stantinople.[65] Reading upward, a viewer would then be led through the twelve images of the chief episodes of the First Crusade. Among these twelve, only two depicted named figures: the first, Count Robert II of Flanders as he routed a large army of Turks (*Parthi*) after the capture of Nicaea, and the second, Duke Robert Curthose of Normandy attacking the standard-bearer of the Egyptian emir at the battle of Ascalon in 1099. These images, which may have been closely juxtaposed in the window's original design, depicted two men who were, at different times, presented to Louis and Henry as exem-plary crusading ancestors.[66]

When Henry and Louis emerged from their two days of political discus-sions, they met with Becket and his associates at Montmartre, another site associated with Saint-Denis, located halfway between the king's encampment and Becket's. There, the conversation centered on reconciliation between the English king and his archbishop, and although the matter was not resolved, Henry swore an oath regarding his intentions to settle the matter. As John of Salisbury recalled, the king invoked his uncle Amalric, the king of Jerusalem, in his oath, reminding the assembly not only of the chief purpose behind their efforts for peace, but also invoking his dynastic responsibilities and fam-ily ties with the Holy Land.[67]

The real progress that was made, including agreement on Easter 1171 as the date of departure for a new crusade, was dashed when, on 29 December 1170, four of Henry's knights murdered Becket in his cathedral. But while the murder of Becket upset plans for an immediate expedition, the terms of penance to which Henry subsequently agreed with representatives of the Roman church at Avranches in May 1172 put them solidly back on course. Henry promised to subsidize two hundred knights to serve with the Templars in the Holy Land, to take the cross himself before Easter 1173, and to lead a crusade of no less than three years in duration.[68] This plan, too, would have

---

window with Suger. See Jonathan Phillips, *The Second Crusade: Extending the Frontiers of Christendom* (New Haven, CT, 2007), 122–124; and Lindy Grant, *Abbot Suger of St-Denis: Church and State in Early Twelfth-Century France* (New York, 1998), 158.

65. Charlemagne carries the "Dragon Banner," which Brown and Cothren convincingly show to be a long-standing sign of divinely inspired kingship, but which would, for Henry, have obvious evocations of the Draco Normannicus, the standard borne by dukes of Normandy, most famously at the battle of Hastings.

66. Brown and Cothren, "Crusading Window"; for their reconstructions, see pls. 7a, 12, and 13 (for commentary, see p. 16).

67. John of Salisbury, *The Letters of John of Salisbury*, 2: 694–695.

68. Phillips, *Defenders of the Holy Land*, 214–215; it was specified that the king's crusade could be redirected toward Iberia if the situation were more pressing. See also Forey, "Henry II's Crusading Penances," who argues that Henry was not to take the cross *for* three years but *within* three years of Easter 1173.

to be abandoned when at Easter 1173, the proposed date for the taking of the cross, Henry's sons rose in rebellion against him.

The contradictory and incomplete nature of the surviving evidence makes it impossible to know whether or not Henry intended to fulfill his promise. But even if he did not intend to, it is important to remember that his contemporaries, who either saw or heard about his great public announcements of contrition and intent to take the cross at Avranches, may have believed his sentiments to be genuine. His very real desire to make amends for the death of Becket, the solemn and public nature of his promise, and the favorable state of affairs in his kingdom between Avranches and the uprising of 1173 may have convinced observers in his lands that in the years 1172 and 1173, Henry was better prepared and better placed to lead a successful crusade than at any other time in his reign and was indeed about to take the cross.

The Problematic Norman Narrative

Between Gilbert of Assailly's embassy of 1166 and the uprising of Henry's sons in 1173 writers in both the Norman and Angevin domains undertook the second great wave of dynastic historical writing of Henry's reign. More generally, the king's thirty-five-year rule corresponded with both what has been termed the "golden age" of English medieval historiography and the rise of vernacular romance literature in England and on the continent.[69] But within this broader efflorescence of writing devoted to pasts both real and fabulous was a subset of works all of which were dedicated to Henry's maternal and paternal ancestors. Our first evidence of a concern to create such narratives appears in a letter of Robert of Torigni, abbot of Mont-Saint-Michel and author of a redaction of the *Gesta Normannorum ducum,* to Gervaise, prior of Saint-Cénery-la-Gere, dated to 1151. In the letter, Robert asks Gervaise for help in the creation of a narrative of recent Norman history, prefaced by a complete genealogical history of the Angevin dynasty from the founder, Enjuger, down to Geoffrey le Bel and also including a genealogical history of the counts of Maine down to Geoffrey's mother, Countess Eremburga.[70]

While no text matching the description provided by Robert survives, no fewer than six works devoted primarily to dynastic affairs were composed during Henry's reign. The first two, the poem of Osbert de Clare and the

---

69. Antonia Gransden, *Historical Writing in England (c. 500–1307)* (London, 1996), 219. On the possible connections between Henry's court and the patronage of Arthurian literature, see now Martin Aurell, "Henry II and Arthurian Legend," in *Henry II: New Interpretations,* ed. Christopher Harper Bill and Nicholas Vincent (Woodbridge, UK, 2007), 362–394; see also the essays in Simon Meecham-Jones and Ruth Kennedy, eds., *Writers of the Reign of Henry II* (Houndmills, Basingstoke, UK, 2006).

70. Robert of Torigni, "Epistola ad Gervaise priorem Saint-Serenici," *PL* 202, cols. 1307–1310.

Genealogia regum Anglorum of Aelred of Rievaulx, were written in 1153–54, at some point before Henry's coronation.[71] Then, for about the first decade of Henry's rule, we know of no new dynastic compositions. From the later 1160s to the mid-1170s, however, four new works emerged, written in both Latin and the vernacular, in verse and in prose, between sites in Normandy and the Touraine: the *Draco Normannicus* of Stephen of Rouen, the *Roman de Rou* of Wace, the *Chronique des ducs de Normandie* of Benoît de Sainte-Maure, and a new redaction of the *Chronica de gestis consulum Andegavorum* by John of Marmoutier. These four works had in common that they were all based on preexisting dynastic historical traditions relating either to the ducal house of Normandy or to the comital family of Anjou and were therefore working from a base of stories that Henry may already have known. The latter three were all explicitly addressed to Henry himself.

The Latin poem *Draco Normannicus,* written in 1169 by a monk of Le Bec named Stephen of Rouen, and the two vernacular dynastic romances, the *Roman de Rou,* completed around 1173 by Wace, and the *Chronique des ducs de Normandie,* composed a few years later by the Tourangeau *romancier* Benoît de Sainte-Maur, were all primarily accounts of Henry's Norman ancestry. All three relied on versions of the Latin prose narrative *Gesta Normannorum ducum,* the chronicle tradition initiated in the first decades of the eleventh century in the work of Dudo of Saint-Quentin and continued into the early twelfth century by Orderic Vitalis and Robert of Torigni.

In their shared debt to these earlier dynastic historical traditions, however, Stephen, Wace, and Benoît also faced the common problem of how to locate the crusades within Norman dynastic history. A Norman hero, Duke Robert Curthose, featured prominently in the First Crusade, and his deeds were fondly remembered by participants. At least three different copyists of the anonymous crusade narrative known as the *Gesta Francorum,* all of whom may have been working in England, altered their manuscripts to privilege the duke's place in the expedition.[72] But Curthose was a controversial figure. His absence on crusade had provided the opportunity for his younger brother, Henry's grandfather, to successfully seize the throne as Henry I in 1100. Upon his return from the East, Curthose mounted a challenge to his brother's succession, only to be comprehensively defeated at Tinchebrai in 1106 and subsequently imprisoned for the remaining twenty-eight years of

---

71. Aelred's work was produced chiefly to demonstrate how Henry, through his maternal grandmother, "that most saintly lady Queen Margaret of Scotland," was a descendant of all the Anglo-Saxon kings going back to Woden and also a relative of Aelred's former patron David I of Scotland.

72. See the comments of Rosalind Hill in *Gesta Francorum et aliorum Hierosolymitanorum,* ed. and trans. Rosalind Hill (London and New York, 1962), xxxix–xl.

his life.[73] At the time of Orderic and Robert of Torigni's continuations and redactions of the *Gesta Normannorum ducum,* Robert Curthose, while imprisoned, was still alive, and his son William Clito was Henry's mortal enemy on the continent.[74] Robert was therefore a potentially threatening figure. Hence Orderic, who elsewhere demonstrated a great interest in the expeditions to the East and who had undoubtedly spoken to returning veterans of the expedition, included only passing references to the First Crusade and gave no account of Robert's deeds or experiences.[75] Robert of Torigny, who added an entirely new book to the *Gesta Normannorum ducum,* contributed little more.

By the middle of the twelfth century, writers of Anglo-Norman history in England had developed a strategy for negotiating the problem of Curthose on crusade.[76] The English historians William of Malmesbury and Henry of Huntingdon both seized on a story told by returning crusaders but not repeated in the most well-known chronicles of the expedition, that Robert had been the first choice among the leaders of the First Crusade to be offered the crown of Jerusalem after the conquest of the city on 15 July 1099.[77] In their retelling, Robert had shamefully rejected the crown that had been divinely ordained for him, to return to England, where, appropriately enough, his efforts met with failure, imprisonment, and ultimately death.[78] To Henry of Huntingdon, Robert's ill-fated decision was inspired by greed and anxiety that his younger brother would succeed in England, while William claimed that it came out of fear of the "insoluble difficulty" of the crusader kingdom.

Apparently unaware of these English histories, Stephen of Rouen, whose work was not addressed to the king and does not seem to have been intended for reading beyond Le Bec, made no reference whatsoever to crusading either in his narrative poem or in any of the other works attributed to him.[79] The

---

73. William M. Aird, *Robert Curthose: Duke of Normandy, c. 1050–1134* (Woodbridge, UK, 2008), 197–244; Warren Hollister, *Henry I* (New Haven, CT, 2001), 183–191, 204–208; Judith A. Green, *Henry I: King of England and Duke of Normandy* (Cambridge, 2006), 89–94.

74. Aird, *Robert Curthose,* 245–273.

75. For Orderic as a crusade historian, see OV 5: xiii–xix and 4–191.

76. See the commentary on this story in Björn Weiler, "The *Rex renitens* and the Medieval Idea of Kingship, ca. 900–ca. 1250," *Viator* 31 (2000): 1–42.

77. Without explicitly depicting the crusade leaders offering Robert the crown of Jerusalem, Gaimar imagines Robert as their superior, delegating lands and authorities (including royal authority) in the East before returning home. Geoffrey Gaimar, *Estoire des Engleis,* ed. and trans. Ian Short (Oxford and New York, 2009), 312–313.

78. William of Malmesbury, *Gesta regum Anglorum: The History of the English Kings,* ed. Rodney M. Thompson and Michael Winterbottom (Oxford, 1999), 1: 702–704; Henry of Huntingdon, *Historia Anglorum, the History of the English People,* ed. and trans. Diana Greenway (Oxford, 1996), 442–443. See also Rodney M. Thompson, *William of Malmesbury* (Woodbridge, UK, 1987), 178–188.

79. A reference to Robert Curthose's deeds on the First Crusade may have occurred somewhere in the hundred verses missing from chapters 31–32 in the single extant *Draco* manuscript, but if so it

problem of Curthose's reputation as a crusader and achievements on the expedition was thus avoided, if somewhat awkwardly, through total disregard for the First Crusade or any subsequent discussion of crusading in the context of either the comital family of Anjou or the peace negotiations between Henry II and Louis VII in 1169.

By contrast, Wace dedicated forty lines of his third book to an account of the great deeds of Robert Curthose in the East. Wace was careful to place Robert at the major engagements, naming the conquests of Nicaea, Antioch, and Jerusalem. To Wace, however, his fame and great reputations were mainly

> a result of the standard which he knocked down, where Kerbogha fought, and the pagans whom he killed and the banner he conquered, which he later gave to the church his mother had founded at Caen.[80]

Wace here took up the tradition, found in most chronicles of the First Crusade and depicted, as we have seen, in the window at Saint-Denis, that Robert had captured the standard of the emir of Ascalon at the battle of Ascalon in 1099. But through reference to Kerbogha of Mosul, universally known as Corbagan in the Francophone West, Wace transposed the scene to the more famous battle before Antioch in the summer of 1098.[81] While accounts by contemporaries or participants nearly all agreed that the banner had been given to the church of the Holy Sepulchre in Jerusalem, Wace located it at the *abbaye aux dames* of the Holy Trinity at Caen, where Robert's sister Cecilia was abbess from 1112 and where she and their mother, Mathilda, were buried.

Although he seems to have had access to William of Malmesbury's *Gesta regum Anglorum,* Wace did not make any reference to the tradition of Curthose as a candidate for the crown of Jerusalem.[82] Together with his unique claims about Robert's crusading feats, this decision should be seen as part of Wace's more favorable treatment of Robert in general. Wace expressed sympathy with Robert's cause and condemned as dishonorable all of those

---

was not summarized in the chapter headings, which survive. Stephen of Rouen, *Draco Normannicus,* ed. Richard Howlett, in *Chronicles of the Reigns of Stephen, Henry II, and Richard I,* RS 82 (London, 1894–99), 2: 648–649; Stephen is also thought to have been the author of poems dedicated both to Geoffrey Martel and to Henry II, but these works, unlike that of Osbert de Clare, do not make any reference to the deeds or career of Fulk V and thus the family's crusading legacy. See *Draco Normannicaus, Le "Dragon Norman" et autres poèmes d'Etienne de Rouen,* ed. Henri Omont (Rouen, 1894), 215–218. Stephen, *Draco Normannicus,* 640, did refer briefly to the pilgrimage of Duke Robert the Magnificent of Normandy and his death in Nicaea.

80. Wace, *Roman de Rou,* ed. Anthony J. Holden and trans. Glynn S. Burgess, with notes by Elizabeth M. C. van Houts (St. Helier, Jersey, 2002), 200–201.

81. The claim that Robert had faced Kerbogha at Antioch had first been made by William of Malmesbury, *Gesta regum Anglorum,* 1: 702–703. No reference to the banner is made, however.

82. Wace, *Roman de Rou,* xxx.

Norman and English barons who deserted his side before the battle of Tinchebrai in 1106.[83] In fact, Robert's status as a crusading hero and his stance as a rebel are actually in some sense combined, as when Robert's supporters in Normandy say to him: "You who have been to the Holy Sepulcher should instruct us all, teach us and educate us."[84] These controversial sentiments were expressed late in the third book of the *Roman de Rou,* at a time when Wace already knew that the royal patronage he had enjoyed was being withdrawn, and the task of setting in romance the Norman dynastic history had been passed on to Benoît de Sainte-Maure.[85] That Benoît, a native and probably also a resident of the Touraine, should have been entrusted with this task is striking; it suggests that if Normans could not be trusted to write Norman history, perhaps an Angevin could do better.

Benoît's version of Henry's maternal ancestry was much more conservative than that of Wace, and his work is often seen as nothing more than a straight translation into vernacular verse of the *Gesta Normannorum ducum.* In treating the place of the First Crusade within his work, however, Benoît revealed himself to be neither radical nor unoriginal. Benoît, who probably had access to what Wace had written (the two had apparently met), did not repeat Wace's claims about the capture of the standard either at Antioch or elsewhere. He did choose to include the story of Robert's *grant folie:* his decision to turn down the crown of Jerusalem.[86] But Benoît was also ready to praise Robert's crusading career, and here he diverged from his sources, offering a description of the preaching of the crusade by Urban II and the worthiness of the expedition undertaken by "dukes, princes, counts, and castellans: all the flower of the West."[87] Robert earned "from his very great valor" the nickname "Robert the Good of Normandy," and Benoît proclaimed:

> I've never heard of greater deeds at any time than I have from the men who were there with him.[88]

It was thus only with Benoît's compromise that Duke Robert could finally emerge as a crusading ancestor in the Norman dynastic narrative tradition.

---

83. Wace, *Roman de Rou,* 207–220.

84. Wace, *Roman de Rou,* 209.

85. Françoise Le Saux, *A Companion to Wace* (Woodbridge, UK, 2005), 275–278.

86. Benoît de Sainte-Maur, *Chronique des ducs de Normandie,* ed. Francisque Michel (Paris, 1836–44), 3: 353; on the relationship between Wace and Benoît, see Peter Damian-Grint, "*En nul leu nel truis escrit:* Research and Invention in Benoît de Sainte-Maur's *Chronique des ducs de Normandie,"* *Anglo-Norman Studies* 21 (1999): 11–30.

87. "Duc, prince e conte e chastelain / E tote la flor d'Occident." Benoît, *Chronique,* 3: 314.

88. "C'unc n'i ou cors de chevalier / Nul plus del suen i fust preisiez / Ne honorez ne essauciez; / E en por sa très grant valor / L'apelerent tuit li plusor / Le bon Robert de Normandie. / Ja plus haut ovre n'ert oie / A nul jor mais, si cum je qui, / D'ome que i fu la de lui." Benoît, *Chronique,* 3: 316.

That compromise presented him as a crusading hero, but a tragically flawe-
done:

> I have already told you of the journey to Jerusalem; henceforth never
> a day comes that someone does not say that of the better men was he
> the best and the blossom. And thus by his great simplicity, by his trans-
> gression, by his idleness, he lost land, he lost honour, and he lost all his
> worth. That caused the shame and the great suffering that so greatly
> will yet again befall him.[89]

Even with the rehabilitations and revisions of Wace and Benoît, Robert
Curthose could not be freed entirely from the mire of controversy that surrounded his rebellion against Henry I. He could certainly not be discussed as
a crusader without reference to his later failings, and any rituals or traditions
with which he may have been associated, for instance at Holy Trinity in Caen,
were not widely recognized and may even have been actively suppressed.[90] A
very different set of images and emotions could be invoked through reference
to Henry's paternal ancestors, whose crusading glory would have been well
known to Henry through the rituals he witnessed as a child, long before he
ever traveled to Normandy. These Angevin ancestors were the subject of an
ambitious new historical treatment by John of Marmoutier.

John of Marmoutier

Nothing is known about the writer who, in the *proemia* of his works, called
himself "brother John of Marmoutier, most humble of monks and lowest of
priests" beyond what can be deduced from the histories attributed to him.
According to Louis Halphen and Rénee Poupardin's analysis of the surviving manuscripts of the various redactions of the *Chronica de gestis consulum
Andegavorum,* the first evidence of John's activity as a historian would seem

---

89. "Qui arrere vos est contée / Del eire de Jerusalem / Où unques jor ne vint cil hoem / Qui
ne deist que des meillors / Ert-ce li mieudres e la flors. / Eissi par sa grant simplece, / Par son forfait,
par sa perece, / Perdi terre, perdi honor / E perdi tote sa valor / Ce fu damage e granz dolors; / Uncor
r'avendra as plusors." Benoît, *Chronique,* 3: 363–364.

90. No other text from Holy Trinity at Caen mentions the banner won by Curthose on crusade,
which would have represented a great prize for the abbey. It must be noted, however, that by the thirteenth century the legitimacy of Angevin rule was secure enough for Curthose to be reintroduced as
a crusading ancestor, and at the court of Henry III and Eleanor of Provence his deeds were sung and
painted in chambers at the Tower of London, Winchester Castle, and Clarendon. See Simon Lloyd,
"King Henry III, the Crusade, and the Mediterranean," in *England and Her Neighbours, 1066–1453:
Essays in Honor of Pierre Chaplais,* ed. Michael Jones and Malcolm Vale (London, 1989), 102–106.

to be a series of notes written in the margin of Paris BNF MS Lat. 6006.[91] These notes served as the basis for John's subsequent rewriting of the *Chronica,* which was addressed to Henry. Besides the notable excision of certain passages, the new *Chronica* essentially amplified the preexisting text, adding color and dramatic flair to speeches, inserting brief notes on the burial place of each count, and interpolating several lengthy passages. After completing this work, John went on to write a biography of Henry's father, Geoffrey the Fair, addressed to Guillaume de Passavant, the bishop of Le Mans who had presided over both the burial of Geoffrey in his cathedral church of Saint-Julien and the erection of Geoffrey's impressive tomb.[92] A reference to the death of Henry's brother William (d. 1164) in the *proemium* to the *Chronica,* and the date of the death of Guillaume de Passavant (1186), establish the basic chronological boundaries for John's two major compositions, although, as we will see, it may be possible to place the *Chronica* in a more specific context.

Sharon Farmer and C. Stephen Jaeger have argued that John of Marmoutier's works demonstrate an interest in the internal motivations of laymen and the cultivation of virtuous conduct, two features that are usually associated with "courtly" romance literature. Although John wrote in Latin and about more recent events, while the traditionally "courtly" and chivalric texts written in the orbit of Henry II were composed in the vernacular and set in the distant past, Jaeger identified the figure of Geoffrey the Fair in John's biography as approaching "the chivalric knight in full flower."[93] The impulse toward romance is also evident in the first of John's lengthy interpolations in the *Chronica,* a narrative describing how Enjuger fought to defend the honor of his godmother against an imposing enemy named Guntrand at the court of a Carolingian king that, substituting an Arthurian setting for a Carolingian one, echoes episodes from the *Chevalier de la Charette* of Chrétien de Troyes.[94] John's style rendered the *Chronica* potentially more relevant and interesting, and therefore potentially more influential for the comital family, who, as we saw in chapter 2, had always been its intended audience.

Of critical importance to our understanding of John's own apparent motives and intentions is his inclusion of much material relating to particular institutions and locations in Anjou and the Touraine. The pervasive

---

91. *CCA,* ix–xvii. The main texts in MS Lat. 6006 are the second redaction of the *Chronica* by Brito of Amboise together with the *Liber de compositione castri Ambaziae* and the *Gesta Ambaziensium dominorum.*

92. For the dating, see *CCA,* xl, lxxxiv. The order of composition can be established by John's remark to Guillaume de Passavant: "Et cum multorum aliorum principum historias collegerimus ...". *CCA,* 178.

93. C. Stephen Jaeger, *The Origins of Courtliness: Civilizing Trends and the Formation of Courtly Ideals, 939–1210* (Philadelphia, 1985), 205.

94. Chrétien de Troyes, *Le roman du Chevalier de la Charette,* ed. Prosper Tarbé (Geneva, 1977).

references to Tours and to the abbey of Marmoutier in John's additions led Sharon Farmer to see him as an agent of Saint-Martin within Henry's court, who sought patronage both for his abbey and the shrine of Martin at Tours at a time when dynastic interest in the saint's cult was apparently waning.[95] As Farmer has noted, John's insistence in the *Chronica* that the four earliest counts of Anjou—Enjuger, Fulk Rufus, Fulk the Good, and Geoffrey Greymantle—were all buried in the church of Saint-Martin at Tours is particularly telling in this regard.[96] We know that in 1096, Fulk IV le Réchin did not know where these four counts were buried,[97] and John's own notes indicate that he had evidence that Geoffrey Greymantle, at least, was buried at Saint-Aubin.[98] The contention that all four of the earliest counts were at Tours was apparently then a fabrication intended explicitly for Henry.

In attempting to cultivate what he presented as older Angevin devotional attachment to Saint Martin, John stressed the importance of Henry's Angevin ancestry and admonished him not to neglect the traditions associated with it. Shining through both of John's works is his passionate partisanship for the Angevin heartlands of Anjou and the Touraine, whose people (*gentem*), as he wrote in his biography of Geoffrey the Fair, "are strengthened by their magnanimous and warlike princes and by the terror that they arouse in the surrounding nations."[99] The distinction between the traditional Angevin dominions and their new Anglo-Norman possessions is reinforced near the end of the same work, where John imagines Geoffrey, on his deathbed, forbidding his son Henry from introducing any of the alien customs of England or Normandy into "the lands of his consulate," by which he must mean Anjou, Touraine, and possibly Maine.[100] Indeed, in the *proemium* of the work he addressed to the king, John applied a classical turn of phrase he had seen elsewhere to praise Henry for not neglecting the traditions of his father.[101] John's desire to privilege the Angevin lands also included a careful suppression of those elements of history that might call into question the loyalties

---

95. Farmer, *Communities of Saint Martin*, 88–95, and on the decline in Angevin largesse, 72, table 2.

96. *CCA*, 31 n. a (Enjuger), 34 n. a (Fulk Rufus), 37 n. a (Fulk the Good), 44 n. c (Geoffrey Greymantle).

97. *CCA*, 233.

98. *CCA*, 44 n. c.

99. "Andegavorum gentem magnanimis et bellicosis principibus valuisse et terrori extitisse circumfusis nationibus celebre percognitum est." *CCA*, 176.

100. "Henrico heredi suo interdixit ne Normannie vel Anglie consuetudines in consulatus sui terram vel e converso, varie vicissitudinis alternatione, permutaret." *CCA*, 224.

101. "Tu solus consiliarios patris tui familiaritate et sodalitate perreniter servas." *CCA*, 171. The words were really those of Sidonius Apollinaris but had been adapted by the author of the *Gesta Ambaziensium dominorum*, with reference to the strength of the relationship between Hugh I of Amboise and his lords Fulk V of Anjou and Thibaud IV of Blois. See *CCA*, 113–114.

of Angevin lords to an English monarch. As Richard Barton has observed, a long and detailed account of the battle of Alençon, where a great defeat had been handed to Henry I by Fulk V of Anjou, was not included in John's new history.[102]

Central to the dynastic identity that John of Marmoutier sought to project was, as Farmer has shown, a devotion to Saint Martin, but allied with this was a devotion to the Holy Sepulchre, its liberation, and protection. Set against the backdrop of the deepening crisis in the East and the rising rhetoric of crusade at the court, and expressed through the medium of John's courtly dynastic narrative, the images and stories associated with the Holy Land and with crusading would have the potential to elicit powerful responses.

The attachment of Henry's Angevin ancestors to the Holy Sepulchre during the long period of its captivity was highlighted in John's work in two supplementary stories relating to the foundation of the abbey of Beaulieu, where, as we have seen, the memory of how Count Fulk Nerra had translated relics of the Passion and a piece of the Sepulchre itself was celebrated in the liturgy. The first of these supplemented the story of Fulk Nerra's pilgrimage to Jerusalem that was already in the *Chronica,* recounting how upon his return Fulk had chosen the first abbot of Beaulieu and how, in addition to all those things necessary for the liturgy, he had given them a piece of the True Cross and "the portion of the Lord's Sepulcher which he had, by himself through divine favor, bitten off miraculously."[103] John described these gifts as the seeds planted by Fulk, which, watered by the wise doctrines of the abbot, had produced a bountiful harvest in the form of a thriving monastic community.[104] This artfully wrought analogy implied that it was the responsibility of pious lords to obtain sacred relics in order to ensure the fruitful propagation of religion in their domains.

The second story about Beaulieu, the so-called Legend of the Death of Crescentius, likewise involves Fulk's pilgrimage and the acquisition of further relics of Daria and Chrysanthus in Rome on his return journey from Jerusalem. The legend refers to actual events that occurred in Rome in 998, when Pope Gregory V requested the assistance of Emperor Otto III to rescue him from the depredations of the local despot named Crescentius.[105]

---

102. Richard Barton, "Writing Warfare, Lordship and History: The *Gesta Consulum Andegavorum*'s Account of the Battle of Alençon," *Anglo-Norman Studies* 27, ed. John Gillingham (2005): 46–47 and n. 78. Barton suggested that John had not yet seen it but would find it later for incorporation into his *Historia Gaufredi.*

103. "et insuper portionem de ligno dominice cruicis necnon et quod de Domini sepulchro mirabiliter, sibi favente divinitate, ipse momorderat." *CCA,* 143. See above, 179–180.

104. *CCA,* 144.

105. For the original story, see *Die Chronik des Bischofs Thietmar von Merseburg und ihre Korveier Überarbeitung,* ed. Robert Holtzmann, *MGH* n.s. 9 (1935; repr., 1980), 167–168.

At some point in the later eleventh or early twelfth century a rival version of these events emerged at the Angevin abbey of Saint-Florent-les-Saumur that claimed that it had not been Otto III, but Fulk Nerra of Anjou who had saved a pope from a man named Crescentius.[106] According to the monks, this occurred during Fulk Nerra's pilgrimage to the Holy Land in the first decade of the eleventh century, and thus they changed the name of the pope to Sergius IV.[107] The story as it appears in the St. Florent text is very brief. Fulk is on his return journey from Jerusalem when he comes to Rome, which is suffering from the depredations of evil men led by Crescentius. Fulk instructs Renier, his archer, to take aim at a particular window in a tower. Renier successfully slays Crescentius, and Sergius is returned to safety. The story contains few details, save the mention of Renier's excellent shot through the window.

The version of this story found in John of Marmoutier's *Chronica* is much more extensive and differs substantially from the one recorded at St. Florent.[108] In John's version, Fulk is summoned by Sergius, who asks him for military assistance, not to save just him, but to save all of the Christian pilgrims whose lives have been endangered. Fulk replies that he will assist the pope, but that first he must undertake his own pilgrimage to Jerusalem. Upon his return, Fulk prepares to deal with the problem of Crescentius, but he is bothered by what he refers to as the "sin of murder and the crime of premeditation" (*peccato homicidii et sceleris excogitati*), and the pope replies: "I absolve you from the sin and, as is fitting, I will recompensate you with worthy gifts." Fulk calls up his forces, which include not one, but four archers, who are called the Prompti. With perfect aim they slay Crescentius, and Fulk returns to the Lateran, "where the pope with all of the clergy and people of Rome were saying masses and orations for him."[109] Fulk is paraded through Rome preceded by all of the clergy, ringing bells and chanting the *Te Deum*. When Fulk asks what is necessary to expiate his sins, the pope responds that because Crescentius was "an enemy of God," no expiatory act is required.[110] As a reward for his services, Fulk is given the bodies of saints Daria and Chrysanthus, which he installs upon his return to Anjou in his new church of Beaulieu-les-Loches. Many of the new elements of the story— the war against the *inimicus Dei*, the question of violence and absolution, the protection of pilgrims, and the triumphal entry into the liberated holy

---

106. *Chroniques des églises d'Anjou*, xxv (introduction), 273–274 (text).

107. The *Historia Sancti Florentii* was probably compiled in the mid-twelfth century from texts written around 1070. See *Chroniques des églises d'Anjou*, xxv (introduction), 273–274 (text).

108. *CCA*, 144–147.

109. *CCA*, 147.

110. *CCA*, 147.

city—could have provoked associations with crusading. As we will see, however, in the likely context of the text's composition, the story may also have
been intended to resonate in other ways.

The moment of greatest importance to Henry's connection with the Holy
Land occurred after the gates of the Holy Sepulchre, the Templum Domini,
and the city of Jerusalem itself had finally been opened by the forces of
the First Crusade, when in 1127 Henry's grandfather Fulk V accepted the
offer made to him by Baldwin II of Jerusalem to marry Baldwin's daughter
Melisende and take up the crown of Jerusalem. In the second redaction of
the Anjou *Chronica,* which was compiled in the mid-twelfth century by
Brito of Amboise, the fact of Fulk's rule over the Latin East was added rather
awkwardly to the dynastic history. Lacking much basic information about
his reign, Brito provided an outline of the genealogy of Fulk's predecessors,
showing how he was related by marriage to the dynasty of Antioch, and
hence to both Robert Guiscard and the counts of Poitou. Brito wrote that
Fulk ruled "manfully; he made the Damascenes and the Ascalonites pay him
tribute, and before Raymond [of Poitiers] married the daughter of Bohemond [II, Constance of Antioch,] he maintained the principality of Antioch
through great labor against the Turks and without doing it any harm."[111]

John transformed what was essentially an afterthought in the dynastic
history into a central moment for the Anjou family and their relations with
the institutions in their domains. John added a detailed account of Fulk's
departure, at the center of which was the ceremony of his cross-taking at
Tours.[112] By focusing on this ceremony, John reminded Henry that when
his grandfather traveled to the East, he not only was taking up the crown
of Jerusalem but was also a crusader fulfilling a crusading vow. According
to John's narrative, Fulk V traveled to the city of Tours at the time of Pentecost so that "in the way of many pilgrims, he might receive the sign of
the Holy Cross from the archbishop."[113] When the ceremony was over, and
Mass had been celebrated, Fulk and his fellow knights and those who would
share his table departed. But as they left, Fulk and two priests who were
with him turned to gaze at the distant monastic complex of Marmoutier. As
they looked, the three men saw flames leaping toward the battlements of the

---

111. "Mortuo Balduino rege, Fulco rex Jerusalem regnum viriliter rexit. Damascenos Ascaloni-
tasque sibi tributarios effecit diuque antequam Raimundus filiam Buamundi duceret, Antiochenum
principatum maximo labore contra Turcos absque ullo dampno manu tenuit." *CCA,* 70–71.

112. The full text of the story is included as part of the *Additamenta* in *CCA,* 161–162. A nearly
identical, although slightly less polished copy of the story was included in the text "De rebus gestis in
Majori-monasterio saeculo II," *ASOB,* 6.2: 395–405. Since the dating or nature of the original work
is unknown, it is impossible to say if this version of the text is earlier or later than John's *Chronica.*

113. *CCA,* 161.

THE FIRE AT MARMOUTIER

monastery, now "consuming the very foundations," now "overcoming the
ramparts." The count, in shock, ordered his men to ride immediately to the
monastery to find out what was happening. The men rode off and returned,
saying that "they had neither seen nor heard anything of such matters."
Perplexed, Fulk discussed the matter with the two priests, who offered their
interpretation as follows:

> "Lord, the honourable vision which you had has been presented to you
> on account of the business which you have undertaken, the solemnity
> of the present matter, the holy place in which the divine portent has
> appeared to you. For, inspired by the Holy Spirit, you have had the
> sign of the Lord placed upon you today, the same day that the Holy
> Spirit descended upon the apostles in fire, and it is appropriate that it
> should be shown to descend upon Marmoutier, the community that
> lives aflame with that Spirit." The illustrious man, pleased by the wor-
> thy interpretation of the honourable vision, without hesitation went
> the next day and told his vision to the community, and he asked that
> he might be made a brother himself and participant in their services.
> Thereafter he held that place and its inhabitants in great reverence.[114]

John's story utilizes the image, most famously deployed on the western portal
of the Madeleine at Vézelay, of the crusader as apostle and the signing with
the cross as the blessing with divine fire at Pentecost.[115] The story locates
this expression of divine favor, however, at Tours and Marmoutier, and the
cross-taking and Fulk's subsequent vision become the context for the count's
honorary inclusion in the community.

If the purpose of this story was, as seems likely, to encourage Henry not
to neglect the traditions of his esteemed ancestor Fulk V, its rhetorical effectiveness would depend to a large degree on the king's feelings about his own
obligations to take the cross. If crusading was a possibility, or even a likeli-
hood, then Henry would be more likely to see himself reflected in the actions
of his forebear. If, on the contrary, crusading was impossible or had been
abandoned, the invocation of such a glorious but now unrepeatable moment

---

114. "Domine, inquit, digna satis visio pro negotio que cepistis, pro sollempnitate presenti, pro
loci reverentia in quo apparuit vobis divinitus ostensus est. Nam et vos, Spiritu Sancto inspirante,
dominicum signum vobis hodie imposuistis et ipse Spiritus Sanctus hodierna die super apostolos in
igne descendit, et locus Majoris Monasterii dignus est in que idem se demonstret descendere, quem
tamen conventus eodem Spiritu inflammatus cohabitat'. Placuit viro illustri digna digne visionis
interpretatio, nec moratus in crastino eo venit, visionem conventui refert, fratrem se et participem
beneficii rogat effici. Locum illum et eius incolas cum digna reverentia deinceps habuit." *CCA*, 162.

115. For the identification of the Vézelay portal with the crusade, see Adolf Katzenellenbogen,
"The Central Tympanum at Vézelay: Its Encyclopedic Meaning and Its Relation to the First Crusade," *Art Bulletin* 26:3 (1944): 141–151, esp 148–151.

would seem foolish or even dangerous to John and his community. With this in mind, is it possible to provide any clearer context for John's composition?

The dating of John's work depends entirely on the interpretation of John's good wishes for Henry in the *proemium*. The valediction establishes that Henry's brothers were dead and that some of his children were of age, and suggests, in its use of the future active participle *dimissurus,* that he had begun the process of associating them with their own lands:

> You, fifteenth in [the line] of your ancestors the counts of Anjou, who, following the death of your brothers, rule alone (*monarchiam tenes*). With God's help you distribute [this power] happily among your children.

That he really was doing so "happily" (*feliciter*) is reinforced in John's wish for Henry to "prevail, my lord king, together with your children, with grow-ing and rising fortune according to your wishes."[116] The process by which Henry allotted lands and titles to his heirs was certainly under way by 1170 and lasted until the revolt of his heirs in 1173, after which point any hope of an easy and ordered succession was effectively lost.[117]

Within this time frame is an even narrower window in which it may have seemed likely that the king was going to take the cross. The period between Henry's reconciliation with the church at Avranches in May 1172 and the scheduled date for his taking the cross at Pentecost 1173 has been described as a time of great strength and confidence for Henry and his family, his "moment of triumph" and *annus mirabilis.*[118] In the previous year, Henry had extended his dominion over Ireland.[119] During that summer, relations with Louis VII had warmed enough to allow Henry's eldest son, Henry (known as the Young King), to finally marry the Capetian princess Margaret, and the two were crowned in August at Winchester. Meanwhile, Henry had negoti-ated for his youngest son, John (then aged seven), to be betrothed to Alice, daughter of Humbert III of Savoy, an alliance that would potentially add the transalpine county of Maurienne to the Angevin empire.[120] At the same time, Henry masterfully resolved the political tensions in the south, reconcil-ing the dispute between the Count of Toulouse and the king of Aragón.[121] In

---

116. "Vale, domine mi rex, et cum filiis tuis, crescentibus prosperis ad vota successibus, polle." *CCA,* 171.

117. W. L. Warren, *Henry II* (New Haven, CT, 2000), 110–111.

118. Kate Norgate, *England under the Angevin Kings* (London and New York, 1882), 2: 130–133; Warren, *Henry II,* 117; Richard Barber, *Henry Plantagenet,* 2nd ed. (Woodbridge, UK, 2001), 166.

119. Warren, *Henry II,* 114–115.

120. Warren, *Henry II,* 117.

121. Warren, *Henry II,* 117.

February 1173 Raymond of Saint-Gilles did homage to Henry and Richard for Toulouse, ending their long-standing conflict.[122]

In the midst of this wave of successes, Henry spent December in his paternal domains of Maine and Anjou, holding his Christmas court, together with Eleanor, at the castle of Chinon.[123] Chinon, a favored location for the king and his family, and the castle where he would return to die in 1189, was located in the absolute heart of what his great-grandfather Fulk le Réchin had described as the *honor* of the counts of Anjou. Situated on the banks of the Vienne, it was almost equidistant on an east-west axis between Angers and Tours, and on a north-south axis between Le Mans and Poitiers.[124] It was within easy reach of the rich monasteries of Bourgueil and Marmoutier and the strategically important castles of Loches, Saumur, and Loudun.

It was almost certainly within the context of this *annus mirabilis* and probably related to Henry's journeys through Anjou and the Touraine at the time of the Feast of the Nativity that John of Marmoutier composed a radically new version of the *Chronica de gestis consulum Andegavorum,* which he dedicated to the king. If John's work really was a court text and intended for court performance or presentation, then the king's Christmas court of 1172 at Chinon would have provided the perfect opportunity. Henry's public commitments at Avranches and the resolution of disputes within his domains may have made it appear to many observers that he was more likely than ever to take the cross.

Within this context, John's narrative directed him to consider his Angevin ancestors and the two religious communities in the Touraine associated with their earlier journeys to the Holy Land, Beaulieu and Marmoutier. Like Fulk Nerra, Henry would be helping to defend the church against the "enemies of God," keeping open the way of pilgrimage to the Holy Sepulchre. Following this example, he could rest assured that such actions would earn him great rewards, including absolution for the homicide committed by four overeager "men at the ready" (*prompti*), which weighed heavily on him in 1172.[125]

122. Robert of Torigni, *Chronique,* 2: 34.

123. Roger of Howden, *Gesta regis Henrici secundi,* 1: 35; and *Chronica,* ed. William Stubbs, RS 51 (London, 1868), 2: 41.

124. For the significance of Tours to Henry II and Richard, and the contests for control of the episcopal see, see Ralph V. Turner and Richard Heiser, *The Reign of Richard Lionheart: Ruler of the Angevin Empire, 1189–1199* (Harlow, UK, 2000), 84.

125. While several aspects of the story of the killing of Crescentius are suggestive of the murder of Becket, the two are not perfectly in parallel. Both the accounts of Becket's murder and the story of Crescentius, for instance, linger on the details of the slain men's wounds. While Becket's five wounds are famously said to parallel Christ's, however, the four shots received by Crescentius strike him in his chest, torso, and groin.

But the most powerful rhetorical element of John's call to tradition was the inclusion of the story of the Pentecostal fire at Marmoutier. By fixing his narrative of how Henry's grandfather had earned divine favor by taking the cross and defending the kingdom of Jerusalem at the point in the liturgical calendar when Henry himself was expected to depart on crusade, he was able to direct the king's attention geographically toward Tours and Marmoutier. If the king would take up the responsibilities of a crusader in imitation of his Angevin ancestor, he might be inclined to do so at Tours, bringing the city and its religious establishments back to the center of his devotional imagination and fixing their place in dynastic tradition and ceremonial.

Reception

I have argued that the Christmas court of 1172 at Chinon represents the most likely context for the presentation or performance of John's work, but is there any evidence that Henry and his family were ever aware of John's composition? Can we see any way that the stories collected and expertly rewritten by John in the new and fashionable style might have influenced the ideas or behavior of Henry and his family? While it is impossible to determine with certainty that Henry was ever aware of John's work, the textual history of the *Chronica* suggests both that it was of continued relevance to an institution close to the Angevin dynasty in the last decades of the twelfth century and that it may have been associated in particular with the Angevin crusading tradition.

Only one medieval exemplar of John's *Chronica* survives, found copied in a composite codex now in a private collection.[126] The codex, which has been described by both Léopold Delisle and Adrien Planchenault, can be codicologically divided into three parts (see table 1). The first part, consisting of two quires, represents the unique copy of a poem in Old French on the life of Saint Silvester and the discovery of the True Cross by Saint Helena written in a hand of the early thirteenth century. On the final two folios of the second quire, which were left blank by the original copyist of the poem, several different hands copied a variety of texts relating to the lands and privileges of Saint-Laud. The second part of the codex, consisting of eight complete quires, is the text of John of Marmoutier's *Chronica* written in a hand of the twelfth century.

In the process of copying this text, the scribe apparently skipped a few lines relating to the foundation of La Trinité of Vendôme by Count Geoffrey Martel. To remedy this, a small strip of parchment was sewn between

---

126. At the time of writing, the codex itself was not available for examination, and so the text can be consulted only in the microfilm ADML, 1 MI 28.

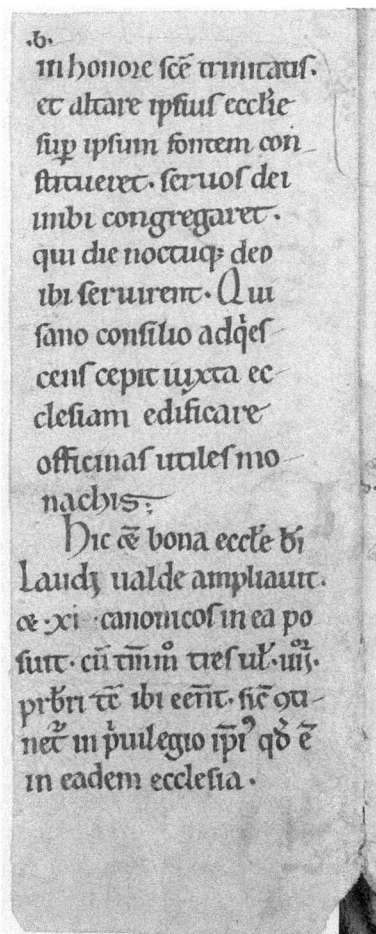

FIGURE 4. A small strip of parchment describing the endowment of the college of Saint-Laud in the castle of Angers, sewn between two folios of John of Marmoutier's *Chronica de gestis consulum Andegavorum*. Cartulary of Saint-Laud, ff. 57v and 58r. ADML 1 Mi 28. ©collection particulière/Archives départmentales de Maine-et-Loire. Photo courtesy Archives départmentales de Maine-et-Loire.

folios 57 and 58 (see fig. 4). Here, the missing lines of the Vendôme foundation were supplied. Below them, the scribe has written a description of how Geoffrey Martel also enlarged the possessions of the community of Saint-Laud, installing eleven canons and three or four priests. Strikingly (for John's text does not elsewhere refer to specific documents), the inserted lines relating to Saint-Laud refer the reader to the relevant charter (*privilegium*), "which is in the same church."[127] As if in response to this prompt, the text of

127. *CCA,* 150–151.

Table 1   Cartulary of Saint-Laud, Composite Codex (xii^ex^-xiii^in^)[1]

I. ff. 1–14 [I^vi^, II^viii^]	1. Old French poem on the life of Saint Silvester and the discovery of the True Cross (ff. 1r-12v)
	2. Records of gifts and privileges to Saint- Laud (ff. 12v-14v)
II. ff. 15–72 [7 complete quires +1 add. folio (f. 72)]	1. John of Marmoutier, *Chronica de gestis consulum Andegavorum* (ff. 15r-71v) (Parchment strip with Saint-Laud narrative, sewn between ff. 57v and 58r)
	2. Privileges and customs of Saint-Laud
	a. Oath taken by new canons of Saint-Laud of Angers to the count, the countess, and their children (f. 71v)
	b. Alexander III (1172): letter instructing monks how to resolve disputes (f. 72r)
	c. Geoffrey le Bel: act placing canons under authority of his court (f. 72r-72v)
	d. Guy of Athée: ceremony of the "ivory tau" of Saint-Laud (f. 72v)
	e. Fulk IV: authorization of the transfer of a part of the wood of Fouilloux (f. 72v)
III. ff. 73–99 [I^viii^, II^viii^, III^viii^, IV^viii^]	1. Cartulary of Saint-Laud (ff. 73r-99v)

[1]This description is based on my analysis of the microfilm 1 MI 28 held at the Archives Départementales de Maine-et-Loire in Angers and on Adrien Planchenault, *Cartulaire du de chapitre Saint-Laud d'Angers (actes du xi et xii siècle) suivie de la vie de Saint Silvestre et l'invention de la Sainte-Croix* (Angers, 1903), xiv-xxii. Planchenault's description essentially follows that of Léopold Delisle, "Notice sur un manuscript de Saint Laud d'Angers appartenant à M. le Marquis de Villoutreys," *Bibliothèque de l'École des Chartes* 59 (1898): 533–549. At the time of writing, the manuscript itself was not available for consultation. My codicological division of the manuscript must therefore be provisional.

the dynastic narrative was followed by a series of four customs and privileges of Saint-Laud, beginning with the oath of obedience to the Count of Anjou and his family taken by new canons of Saint-Laud, at the bottom of the final folio containing the narrative and continuing onto one additional folio. To this collection of texts was then added (at a very early date, according to Léopold Delisle) a cartulary of eleventh- and twelfth-century acts relating to Saint-Laud, among which was the very *privilegium* of Geoffrey Martel named in the parchment strip.[128]

The three parts of the codex are connected by their references to the Saint-Laud community's rituals, cult objects, privileges, and possessions. The

128. Although the codex was rebound in the sixteenth century, Delisle believed that the three texts had been "réunies de toute ancienneté," and cited a reference to the MS in a dispute in the chapter on 8 April 1477. To settle their dispute, the canons referred to a *Liber cronicarum in pergameno confectus, in quo quidem libro tractatur de actibus ecclesie necnon de Gestis per comites seu Duces Andegavie quondam factis.* Léopold Delisle, "Notice sur un manuscript de Saint Laud d'Angers appartenant à M. le Marquis de Villoutreys," *Bibliothèque de l'École des Chartes* 59 (1898): 534. It is also unclear what value the codex might have had after the conquest of Anjou by the French king Philip Augustus in the first decade of the thirteenth century, for which see John Baldwin, *The Government of Philip Augustus: Foundations of French Royal Power in the Middle Ages* (Berkeley, 1986), 194–195.

canons appear to have combined two preexisting works, the poem on the True Cross and John of Marmoutier's *Chronica,* with their own cartulary. The canons made the poem and the dynastic narrative their own, adding a reference to themselves and their privileges on the parchment strip, and copying texts related to their community in the available blank folios following the poem and the chronicle. The result was a codex suffused with the identity of Saint-Laud and loudly advertising both the community's loyalty to the comital family and its possession of the relic of the True Cross. That the canons believed that John's text would be useful to them, either ceremonially or in their interactions with members of the comital family, demonstrates its continued relevance beyond the immediate context of its composition at Marmoutier. The juxtaposition of John's *Chronica* with the poem of the True Cross and text of the ceremony featuring the tau of Fulk V, moreover, suggests that at least one group of readers was aware of the potential significance of John's added passages to the fostering of the dynastic crusading tradition.

Response?

The presence of John's work in this ritual context at Saint-Laud in Angers provided for the possibility of numerous further encounters between Henry and his family and the narrative and the traditions John was attempting to cultivate. These repeated contacts reminding Henry of the importance of Saint Martin's cult and of his community near Tours may explain the lavish gift of 1,000 pounds of silver Henry promised to Marmoutier in the testament prepared at Waltham while he waited to cross the English Channel in February 1182.[129] Although the amount pledged to Marmoutier was less than what was promised to Grandmont, which was then his preferred site of burial, or Fontevraud, his actual final resting place, it was still impressive, equaling the amount promised to the powerful abbey of Cluny; it was the same amount set aside for all of the rest of the churches in Anjou combined. But could the existence of a coherent Angevin dynastic narrative that privileged the place of Henry's crusading ancestor Fulk V have had any effect on the discourse of crusade, responsibility, and princely identity at Henry's court?

---

129. For the testament, see *Recueil des actes de Henry II roi d'Angleterre et duc de Normandie: Concernant les provinces françaises et les affaires de France,* ed. Léopold Delisle and rev. Élie Berger (Paris, 1909–27), 2: 219, doc. 612; for discussion, see Warren, *Henry II,* 559; Forey, "Henry II's Crusading Penances," 161; Anne Duggan, "Diplomacy, Status, and Conscience: Henry II's Penance for Becket's Murder," in *Forschungen zur Reichs-, Papst- und Landesgeschichte: Peter Herde sum 65. Geburtstag von Freunden, Schülern und Kollegen dargebracht,* ed. Karl Borchardt and Enno Bünz (Stuttgart, 1998), 1: 286; Christopher Tyerman, *England and the Crusades, 1095–1588* (Chicago, 1988), 54–56.

In the same testament that so richly rewarded Marmoutier, a vast sum of 5,000 pounds was earmarked for the defense of the Holy Land, supplemented by 5,000 pounds each for the crusading institutions of the Temple and the Hospital and the religious houses of the kingdom of Jerusalem. In 1182, of course, these lavish promises may have been meant in some measure to compensate for Henry's lack of action, his failure to take the cross. Testaments could in any case be revised and were not always followed. Before Henry could demonstrate to his contemporaries or posterity his intentions regarding the agreement reached at Avranches in 1172, all chances of a crusade were upset in March 1173 when his sons Henry and Richard, at the instigation of their mother, Eleanor, rose against him in open revolt. The intended date for Henry's departure passed as he fought to bring his sons to heel. Neither the Latins of the East nor their indefatigable supporter, Alexander III, would give up the hope that Henry might still be encouraged to lead a crusade. More embassies and letters followed, and as Saladin's onslaught against the kingdom of Jerusalem intensified and succession to the throne of the kingdom broke down, in 1184 the patriarch of Jerusalem Heraclius himself crossed the sea. Receiving adequate help "neither from the Lord pope, nor the Roman emperor, nor from the king of the Franks," he went to see Henry, meeting with the king at Reading on 29 January 1185.[130]

A number of contemporary chroniclers, including Ralph of Diceto, Gerald of Wales, Gervase of Canterbury, and Roger of Howden, offered accounts and interpretations of the patriarch's visit.[131] All reported that the patriarch had offered the king the keys to the Holy Sepulchre, the banner of the kingdom of Jerusalem, and another set of keys, variously reported as the keys to the city of Jerusalem itself or to the Tower of David. The chroniclers infused the scene with gesture and emotion. According to Gerald of Wales, the patriarch came *humiliter* and, weeping and wailing, prostrated himself before the king.[132] According to Ralph, it was the king and his assembled court who wept and sighed at this sight.[133]

In the context of what is known about the language and imagery of dynastic crusading memory in the twelfth century, the scene that unfolded at Reading is particularly striking. A representative from the East named "Heraclius" offered Henry the royal standard ("the standard of the kingdom and the banner of war," as Gerald of Wales wrote) and keys that would

---

130. Ralph of Diceto, *Opera*, 2: 32.

131. Ralph of Diceto, *Opera*, 2: 32–33; Gervase of Canterbury, *Works*, 1: 325, 373: Gerald of Wales, *Opera*, 5: 360–363 and 8: 202–212.

132. Gerald of Wales, *Opera*, 8: 203, 5: 360–361.

133. Ralph of Diceto, *Opera*, 33.

symbolically unlock the gates of the holy city and its shrines. As we have seen in chapters 3 and 4, these objects carried particular resonance as symbols of triumphal leadership (the banner) and the protection of pilgrims (the keys). Presented with these symbols by "Heraclius of Jerusalem," the king could not have helped but understand them at least in part in the light of the cycle of crusading memory that invoked Christ, Heraclius, the difficult pilgrimages of his ancestors Robert the Magnificent of Normandy and Fulk Nerra of Anjou, and the triumphal wars of his grandfather Fulk V, memories that were reinforced by the legends repeated at Beaulieu, the triumphal processions at Angers, and the texts composed for him in Normandy, Anjou, and the Touraine.

The chroniclers of Henry's court offered their own interpretations. Ralph saw the banner and keys as memorials (*memorialia*) of the birth, passion, and resurrection of Jesus Christ, to which the king showed appropriate deference. To Gerald they represented an official offer of the crown of Jerusalem from the clergy and populus of the kingdom—an offer the king ultimately declined by failing to immediately take the cross. But in the contemporary year-by-year account of Henry's reign known as the *Gesta regis Henrici secundi*, Henry's courtier Roger of Howden offered a unique and much more detailed interpretation of the patriarch's visit.[134] Howden, who may have been writing shortly after the event, related how Heraclius had brought the royal banner of Jerusalem and the keys to the Sepulchre, the city, and the Tower of David. He echoed Gerald's sentiment that this constituted an offer of the crown, but added that the offer was made because the kingdom was Henry's "by the hereditary right of his predecessors."[135] He then embarked on a brief history of the First Crusade and the early Latin Kingdom of Jerusalem in order to demonstrate that this was really the case. In his account of the crusade, the only act of martial valor Roger reported was the killing of Kerbogha, "the enemy of the cross of Christ," by Robert of Normandy in single combat (*duello*). The crusade account ends with the offer of the crown to Robert and his refusal, both because "he did not want it" and because news had reached him of the death of his father. But "by the equitable judgment of God," Robert was denied the ability to take the English crown, having refused the kingdom of Jerusalem.[136] Roger described how Fulk V of Anjou had become king of Jerusalem, demonstrating the relationship

134. The passage is discussed at length in John Gillingham, "Roger of Howden on Crusade," in *Richard Coeur de Lion: Kingship, Chivalry, and War in the Twelfth Century* (London and Rio Grande, 1994), 141–153.

135. Roger of Howden, *Gesta regis Henrici secundi*, 1: 328.

136. Roger of Howden, *Gesta regis Henrici secundi*, 1: 329–330.

between Henry and Baldwin IV of Jerusalem. At the end of this account, Roger copied the letter of Pope Lucius III to Henry, with its repeated invocations of his ancestral crusading traditions.

The way that Roger chose to record the patriarch's embassy to Henry reveals the vivid and contested discourse of kinship and tradition within Henry's court. Roger's presentation of Robert of Normandy as both hero and shameful villain matches that given by Benoît de Sainte-Maure and may even have been intended to foreshadow Henry's own subsequent rejection of what he perceived as Heraclius's offer of the crown. Roger's belief, shared by his fellow courtier Gerald of Wales, that the embassy really *did* constitute an offer of the kingdom, is also striking, because, as Christopher Tyerman has observed, there is no evidence that the patriarch had been empowered to make such an offer.[137] If the offer was explicit, other chroniclers might have suppressed it precisely because of its uncanny echo of the story of Robert of Normandy. On the other hand, we must consider the possibility that Roger's interpretation, linked as it is in his narrative with his demonstration of the kinship between Henry and Baldwin IV of Jerusalem, was inspired by a new awareness of the importance of the Angevin dynastic history, which in turn may have been generated by John of Marmoutier's *Chronica*. Roger, not a dynastic chronicler, but an English courtier clerk, was not in a position to take sides in debates about the relative importance of Henry's identity as king of the English, duke of the Normans, or count of the Angevins. He did not, in the end, understand the correct relationship between Henry and Fulk, making the latter the king's uncle rather than his grandfather.[138] How the king may have interpreted the patriarch's gesture is not revealed either in his subsequent correspondence or in the reports of conversations he had about the matter afterward.[139]

In March, Henry convened a weeklong meeting of his barons in Clerkenwell to discuss whether or not to he should take the cross. By this time, the tide of opinion had turned firmly against the possibility of a crusade. The reluctance of the barons, his sons' continued defiance and their alliance with the cunning Philip II Augustus of France, and the possibility that once in the East Henry would become enmeshed in a disintegrating Latin kingdom rendered the crusading cause nearly hopeless. It was not until after the disaster at Hattin on 4 July 1187, when the massed armies of Jerusalem were destroyed by Saladin, and the return of Jerusalem to Muslim hands, that Henry could

---

137. Tyerman, *England and the Crusades*, 51.
138. Roger of Howden, *Gesta regis Henrici secundi*, 331.
139. Gerald of Wales, *Opera*, 207–208.

once again be moved to take the cross, in January 1188.[140] This gesture, however sincere, was fruitless as new conflict erupted between Henry and the formidable alliance of his son Richard and Philip Augustus.[141]

In evaluating the impact of dynastic memories and traditions, and in particular the work of John of Marmoutier on these traditions, there is one last event to consider. We have seen that Henry's son Richard was among the first of the European princes to take the cross in 1187. He did so, as was noted by nearly every chronicler of the day, at Tours.[142] After his father's death, Richard aggressively pursued the cause of the Latin East, successfully negotiating peace with Philip Augustus so that the two could jointly lead an expedition to the Holy Land. The joint departure point of the expedition, where the two leaders met for the last time in July 1190 to agree terms before setting off, was the abbey church of Vézelay, itself a place of important ritual significance for its associations with the preaching of the Second Crusade.[143]

While at Vézelay, the two kings undoubtedly made final ritual commitments to reaffirm their crusading status, but before doing so, both had already engaged in their own separate departure ceremonies in their own domains. As Richard would have been well aware, Philip's ceremony was performed at Saint-Denis, a site that, as Richard would have known since his youth, was specially prepared for such acts. "Following," according to the French royal chronicler Rigord, "the ancient kings of the Franks," Philip received the banner Oriflamme, and like his father, he received the staff and purse of the pilgrim from the archbishop, William of Reims.[144] Set against this French example, which was imbued with powerful dynastic and regalian significance, Richard must have considered very carefully where he would enact his own purse- and staff-taking ceremony. Any one of numerous important administrative centers and popular shrines, such as Westminster, Caen, Fontevraud, or even Grandmont, might have been chosen. But like his great-grandfather Fulk V, whose departure had been blessed by the tongues of Pentecostal fire, Richard received the purse and staff, as he had received the cross, at Tours from the hands of the archbishop.[145] The poet Ambroise, who was with Richard, remembered the moment when "King Richard was at Tours, with

140. Roger of Howden, *Chronicon,* 344–345.

141. Warren, *Henry II,* 607–630.

142. The significance of Tours as a site of dynastic crusading tradition was not lost on John Gillingham, *Richard I* (New Haven, CT, 1999), 87.

143. Roger of Howden, *Gesta regis Henrici secundi,* 2: 92–93.

144. *Oeuvres de Rigord et de Guillaume le Breton,* ed. Henri François Delaborde (Paris, 1882), 1: 98–99.

145. Roger of Howden, *Chronica,* 3: 36; Ambroise, *A History of the Holy War: Ambroise's "Estoire de la Guerre Sainte,"* trans. Marianne Ailes and Malcolm Barber (Woodbridge, UK, 2003), 2: 34.

all his armor and all the accoutrements of war."[146] He described the streets of the city teeming with crusaders and their siege machines and ladies young and old, fair and plain, weeping at the moment of the official departure of the crusade. Richard I is remembered as the greatest crusader-king of England, but he very deliberately departed on crusade as the Count of Anjou.

---

146. Ambroise, *A History of the Holy War,* 2: 34.

❧ CHAPTER 7

Triumph at Ripoll

Stopping at the city of Perpignan in December 1194, the ruler known through his intitulature as "Alfonso, king of Aragón, count of Barcelona, and marquis of Provence" prepared his testament.[1]

1. Although Jordi Ventura's study of the life and reign of this important ruler, *Alfonso el Cast: El primer comte-rei* (Barcelona, 1961) is clearly insufficient, it is still the only monograph dedicated to the count-king. Still valuable is Joan F. Cabestany's short biography of Alfonso, "Alfons el Cast," in *Els primers comtes-reis: Ramon Berenguer IV, Alfons el Cast, Pere el Catòlic*, ed. Percy E. Schramm, Joan F. Cabestany, and Enric Bagué (Barcelona, 1960), 55–99. By far the best accounts of Catalonia in this period, and on which much of this chapter has been grounded, are those of Thomas Bisson. See the relevant sections of Thomas N. Bisson, *The Medieval Crown of Aragón: A Short History* (Oxford, 1986), 35–57; and Bisson, "The Rise of Catalonia: Identity, Power, and Ideology in a Twelfth-Century Society," in *Medieval France and Her Pyrenean Neighbours: Studies in Early Institutional History* (London and Ronceverte, WV, 1989), 125–152, esp. 140–152 (originally published as "L'Essor de la Catalogne: Identité, pouvoir, et idéologie dans une société du XIIe siècle," *Annales: ESC* 39 [1984]: 454–479); and Bisson, *The Crisis of the Twelfth Century: Power, Lordship, and the Origins of European Government* (Princeton, NJ, 2009), 499–514. For his trans-Pyrenean policies and lands, see Ramon d'Abadals i de Vinyals, "À propos de la domination de la maison comtale de la Barcelone sur le Midi français," *Annales du Midi* 76 (1964): 315–345. Also useful is Fredric Cheyette, *Ermengard of Narbonne and the World of the Troubadours* (Ithaca, NY, 2001). For Alfonso's death and testament, see Ventura, *Alfonso el Cast,* 266–279. The text of the will was first published by Próspero de Bofarull y Mascaró in *Los condes de Barcelona vindicados* (Barcelona, 1836), 1: 216–227; for more recent editions, see *Els testaments dels comtes de Barcelona i dels reis de la Corona d'Àrago: De Guifré Borrell a Joan II,* ed. Antoni Udina i Abelló (Barcelona, 2001), 117–127, and the analytical edition found in *Alfonso II Rey de Aragón, Conde de Barcelona y Marqués de Provenza: Documentos, 1162–1196,* ed. Ana Isabel Sanchez Casabón (Zaragoza, 1995), 808–820, no. 628. On testaments in Catalonia, see Nathaniel L. Taylor, "Testaments,

Declaring himself to be of sound mind, he named his executors, elected his place of burial, and then proceeded to establish his temporal and spiritual legacies, dividing the lands he ruled among his heirs and making dozens of gifts to shrines, churches, and religious communities in his own dominions and beyond. Alfonso was only forty years old, and although he died two years later, there is no reason to believe that he was yet in ill health. It is likely that his decision to create a testament at this moment was related to the pilgrimage that he subsequently undertook across the Iberian Peninsula to the shrine of Santiago de Compostela the following summer, during which journey Alfonso intended to gather forces and allies for a massive assault on the Almohad Muslim powers that had begun to threaten the Christian frontier in Spain. The testamentary process involved many difficult decisions, and they required Alfonso to weigh the memory of past friendships and strategies against the new concerns and challenges that confronted him. In doing so, Alfonso openly acknowledged that in at least one important respect he stood in contravention of long-standing dynastic tradition.

In both the testament itself and a brief codicil added shortly before his death two years later in April 1196, Alfonso tried to balance the traditions of his maternal ancestors of the royal house of Aragón with those of his father's family, who ruled the trans-Pyrenean federation of Catalan counties under the domination of the comital house of Barcelona.[2] The fortunes of the two families had been united with the marriage in 1137 of Alfonso's father, Count Ramón Berenguer IV of Barcelona, to his mother, Petronilla, heiress to the kingdom of Aragón (see chart 2).[3] The man drawing up his testament at Perpignan in 1194 bore the same name as his mother's uncle, Alfonso I "the Battler" of Aragón, although he had in fact been born Ramón Berenguer. The adoption of the new name, which occurred immediately after his father's death in 1164, while Ramón was still a minor and his mother served as regent of his kingdom, is suggestive of the tensions that were already present at the

publication de testaments, et ordre public en Catalogne et en Languedoc (IX-XII siècle)," *Annales du Midi* 118 (2006): 447–451. Alfonso's will is also discussed in Taylor's doctoral dissertation, "The Will and Society in Medieval Catalonia and Languedoc, 800–1200" (PhD diss., Harvard University, 1995), app. B, 353–356. My thanks to Adam Kosto for pointing out Dr. Taylor's work.

2. For the codicil, see *Els testaments dels comtes de Barcelona,* 127–132; *Alfonso II Rey de Aragón,* 852–853, no. 656.

3. For the marriage and its implications, see William Clay Stalls, "Queenship and Royal Patrimony in Twelfth-Century Iberia: The Example of Petronilla of Aragón," in *Queens, Regents, and Potentates,* ed. Theresa M. Vann (Denton, TX, 1993), 49–61 (at 49–54). For the nature of Petronilla's authority, see *Liber feudorum maior: Cartulario real que se conserva en el Archivo de la Corona de Aragón,* ed. Francisco Miquel Rosell (Barcelona, 1945), 1: nos. 7, 16, and 17; Antonio Ubieto-Arteta, *Historia de Aragón: Creación y desarrollo de la Corona de Aragón* (Zaragoza, 1987), 93–173; and Martin Aurell, *Les noces du comte: Mariage et pouvoir en Catalogne (785–1213)* (Paris, 1995), 361–380.

ANCESTRY OF ALFONSO II OF ARAGÓN

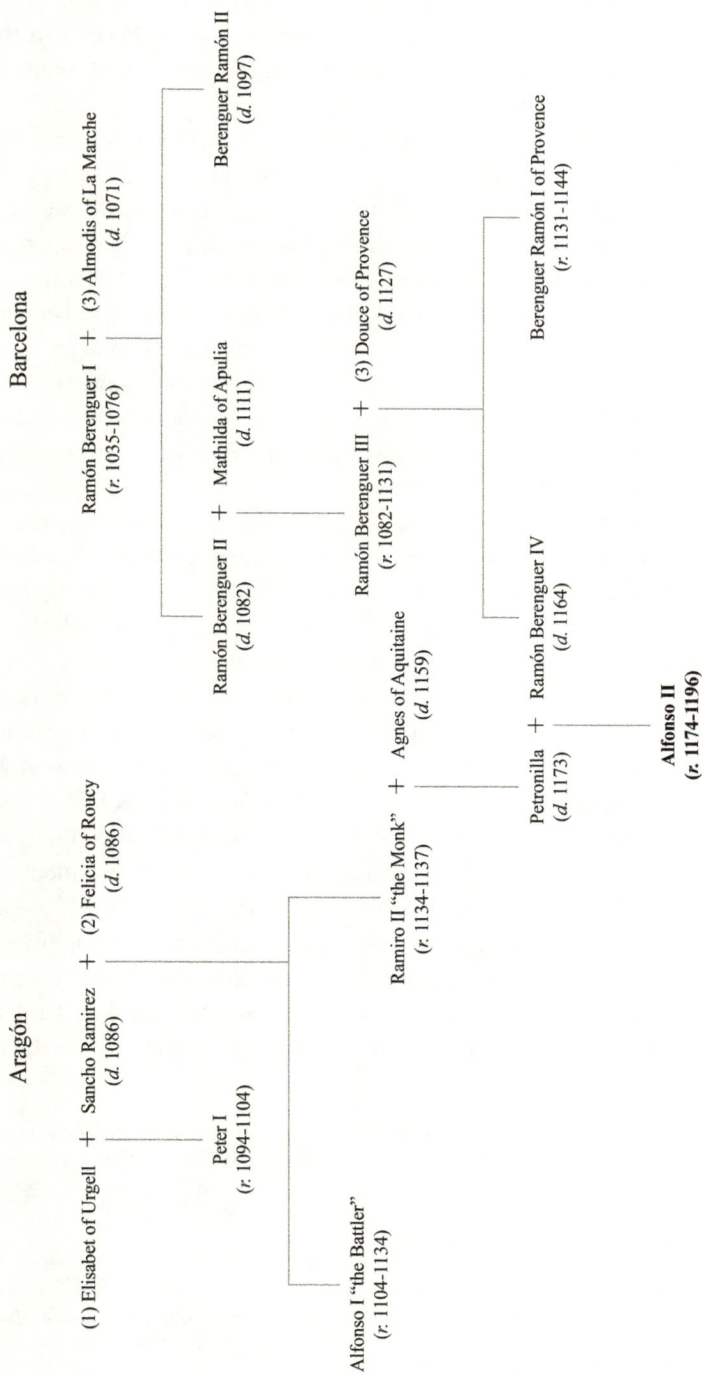

Aragón

Barcelona

(1) Elisabet of Urgell + Sancho Ramírez + (2) Felicia of Roucy
(d. 1086)   (d. 1086)

Ramón Berenguer I + (3) Almodis of La Marche
(r. 1035-1076)   (d. 1071)

Berenguer Ramón II
(d. 1097)

Peter I
(r. 1094-1104)

Ramón Berenguer II + Mathilda of Apulia
(d. 1082)   (d. 1111)

Alfonso I "the Battler"
(r. 1104-1134)

Ramón Berenguer III + (3) Douce of Provence
(r. 1082-1131)   (d. 1127)

Ramiro II "the Monk" + Agnes of Aquitaine
(r. 1134-1137)   (d. 1159)

Berenguer Ramón I of Provence
(r. 1131-1144)

Petronilla + Ramón Berenguer IV
(d. 1173)   (d. 1164)

Alfonso II
(r. 1174-1196)

CHART 2. Ancestry of Alfonso II of Aragón

birth of the new unified realm (or "Crown") of Aragón-Catalonia.[4] The onomastic realignment of the eight-year-old Alfonso was by no means a complete acquiescence to Aragonese identity, and at Perpignan thirty-two years later symbolic acts of deference were still required to maintain parity between his two inheritances.

Passing on his lands and titles in his testament, the count-king largely followed the example set by his parents. Alfonso proclaimed that his eldest son, Peter, would inherit, as he had, the royal and comital titles of Aragón and Barcelona, together with the counties of Roussillon, Cerdanya, Conflent, and Pallars, which along with some others constituted what Alfonso called *tota Cathalonia*.[5] The troublesome jewel of Provence, which had been a concern of his father's family since 1112,[6] he bestowed on his younger son Alfonso, just as his grandfather had once given it to his own younger son Berenguer Ramón in 1131.[7] As his mother's grandfather Sancho Ramirez of Aragón had done in the case of his youngest son, Ramiro, Alfonso II encouraged his own youngest, Ferrand, to become a monk.

Another decision, of no less significance in maintaining the symbolic parity between Barcelona and Aragón, concerned where Alfonso would be buried. The Benedictine abbeys of San Juan de la Peña in Aragón and Santa Maria de Ripoll in Catalonia had, at different times, served as the burial places for multiple generations of his maternal and paternal ancestors respectively.[8] As Alfonso was keenly aware, another precedent had been established by his predecessor and namesake, Alfonso I, who had chosen the Augustinian house of Jesus of Nazareth located within the precincts of the castle of Montearagón for his burial. Established to fulfill a role somewhat like the one Saint-Laud performed for the counts of Anjou, Montearagón was closely associated with the administration of the Aragonese royal chapel, and members of the royal family served as abbot during and after Alfonso's reign.

Had he chosen any of these communities as his final resting place, Alfonso might be seen as definitively promoting one dynastic identity over the other, upsetting the balance that he and his parents had worked hard to maintain. He would also have been out of step with fashion. Over the course of

---

4. The *avertacio sacramental* of the testament of Ramón Berenguer IV published in October 1162, for instance, indicates that he had left all of his *honorem de Aragone et Barchinona* to "filio suo maiori Raymundo." *Els testaments dels comtes de Barcelona*, 104.

5. *Els testaments dels comtes de Barcelona*, 114; *Alfonso II Rey de Aragón*, 817.

6. Martin Aurell, *Les noces du comte*, 391–396.

7. *Els testaments dels comtes de Barcelona*, 97.

8. Burials at San Juan included Ramiro I, Sancho Ramirez, and Peter I. See *Crónica de San Juan de la Peña*, ed. Antonio Ubieto-Arteta, Textos medievales 4 (Valencia, 1961), chap. 16; trans. Lynn H. Nelson as *The Chronicle of San Juan de la Peña: A Fourteenth-Century Official History of the Crown of Aragón* (Pittsburgh, 1991), 17, 25, 55.

Alfonso's reign, the new, much stricter, reformed orders of monks and nuns had found favor with secular rulers at the expense of the older and more traditional Benedictine houses and cathedral chapters.[9] Among contemporary territorial princes and sovereigns, Leopold V of Austria (d. 1194), Philip of Flanders (d. 1168), and Henry II of England (d. 1189) had opted for burial at the reformed houses of Heiligenkreuz, Clairvaux, and Fontevraud respectively, and both Heiligenkreuz and Fontevraud became new dynastic mausolea. A few decades later, Louis IX of France would establish an important Capetian mausoleum in the Cistercian house of Royaumont. In the 1170s and 1180s, Alfonso showed himself to be a great supporter of the Cistercians, offering gifts, privileges, and protection to Santa Maria de Poblet,[10] and also to the daughter community of Granselve at Valldaura that came to be known as Santes Creus.[11]

For reasons of political expediency, princely chic, and devotional predilection, the Cistercians were a logical choice, and thus it seems hardly surprising that in 1194, in the very first act of his testament, Alfonso decreed that his body, a gift to the Lord God and to the Blessed Virgin Mary, should be buried at the Cistercian house of Santa Maria de Poblet.[12] Poblet had been founded in 1151 by Alfonso's father, Ramón Berenguer IV, and although the monks did not display any perceptible ritual association with the comital dynasty before Alfonso's death, his testament ensured a close bond between the house and the dynasty in the future. In addition to the count-king's body, Poblet would also receive his crown, and it was to Poblet that Alfonso's youngest son, Ferrand, was entrusted for his novitiate.[13] When the testament was

9. See Constance Bouchard, *Sword, Miter, and Cloister: Nobility and the Church in Burgundy, 980–1198* (Ithaca, NY, 1987), 87–246, esp. 138.

10. *Diplomatari de Santa Maria de Poblet I: 960–1177*, ed. Agusti Altisent (Barcelona, 1993), gift of a Saracen Meferiz Avinimel, 280–281, no. 369 (c. 1170); protection and concessions, 284–285, no. 375 (1170); gift of a *villa* of Vimbodi, 327–328, no. 436 (1172); protection from vassals, 334–335, no. 446 (1173–75); gift of Abraham son of Solomon of Barbastro, 383–384, no. 519 (1175); gift of a *villa* of Cepolla near Valencia to establish a daughter-house of Poblet, 404, no. 548 (1176).

11. *Diplomatari del monestir de Santa Maria de Santes Creus (975–1225)*, ed. Joan de Papell i Tardiu (Barcelona, 2005). Santes Creus had been founded in 1158 through gifts of land to Granselve by William Ramón Montcada. An initial grant by Alfonso in 1166 of pasture rights to the abbot and monks of Valldaura was followed by privileges in the houses they held in Barcelona in 1168 (222, no. 133) and Tortosa (242–243, no. 234), rights to pasture and protection for their animals in 1170 (230–231, no. 141), extraordinary powers in local legal disputes in 1173 (256, no. 162), and the transfer to the monks both of unfree men in 1181 (301, no. 201) and the rights to lordship over numerous vassals.

12. *Diplomatari de Santa Maria de Poblet*, 127–128, no. 140. The foundation was acknowledged to be under papal protection by Eugenius III in November, 1152 (136–137, no. 152). In 1176, the same year that he first discussed election of sepulchre at Poblet (405 [1176]), he also made a gift of a *funduq* at Tortosa (411–412, no. 560 [1176]), a gift of a man of Barcelona named Benencasa (412, no. 561 [1176]), and a gift of the pastures and the whole port of Peguera and Angostrina, which they had earlier been given by a group of knights (417–418, no. 570 [1176]).

13. *Els testaments dels comtes de Barcelona*, 114; *Alfonso II Rey de Aragón*, 817.

ceremonially announced at the cathedral of Zaragoza after Alfonso's death, the choice would have come as no surprise to the monks of Poblet, with whom Alfonso had been privately negotiating his burial since 1176.[14]

Alfonso's testament also reveals, however, that the decision for burial at Poblet was not unproblematic. Later in the document, as he announced the many pious benefactions that would be made to the churches, monasteries, and shrines of his kingdom, Alfonso turned to the abbey of Santa Maria de Ripoll, where lay the bodies of his father, grandfather, and numerous other relatives, including the founder of the house and *progenitor* of the Catalan comital dynasties, Guifré I (d. 897), the first ruler of the Spanish march. Like only a handful of other institutions among the dozens mentioned, including Poblet, the military orders of the Temple and the Hospital, and the Canons of the Holy Sepulchre in Jerusalem, and the Hospitaller convent of Sigena, the monks of Ripoll were promised gifts of land and outright lordship rather than money. The rich benefactions to Ripoll, including all of the mills at Ribes (north of Ripoll along the river Freser), the entire *honor* of the episcopal city of Barbastro, and additional lands at Monzón, were expressly given *in recompensacione sepulture mee*.[15]

What was meant by this enigmatic stipulation? In later (undated) negotiations with Ripoll over the details of his father's testamentary benefactions, Alfonso's son Peter revealed that his father had initially indicated to him a preference for Ripoll, and that he had only become aware of his father's change of heart at the end of his life.[16] This might suggest that in 1194 the monks of Ripoll were unaware of Alfonso's selection of Poblet, and that *recompensacione* was owed because the monks had prepared an elaborate tomb monument for the king to be located beside those that had already been constructed for his ancestors. Or it might reflect the fears that Alfonso's choice of Poblet would result in Ripoll being forgotten by his descendants. A sense of abandonment was still being expressed at Ripoll a decade later, when the monks recalled how "forsaking (*relinquens*) the burial place of his fathers (*patrum suorum*) [Alfonso] ordered that he should be entombed at Poblet."[17]

---

14. *Diplomatari de Santa Maria de Poblet,* 405, no. 549.

15. Although both Alfonso's will and its *avertacio sacramental* clearly give the *honorem Barbastro* to Ripoll, the later reference to the gift in a charter of Alfonso's son Peter II referred only to "some vineyards" in Barbastro. This disappointing outcome for the abbey might be compared with the difficulties experienced by the nuns of Sigena in realizing the lands given to them by Alfonso in 1188. See Luis Garcia-Guijarro Ramos, "The Aragonese Hospitaller Monastery of Sigena: Its Early Stages 1188–c. 1210," *Hospitaller Women in the Middle Ages,* ed. Anthony Luttrell and Helen J. Nicholson (Aldershot, UK, and Burlington, VT, 2006), 122.

16. Pere Pujol y Tubau, "Mudança en la elecció de sepultura per la rey Alfons I," *Boletín de la Real Academia de Buenas Letras de Barcelona* 7 (1913): 86–89.

17. *GCB,* 15.

Between the monks' regret and the king's apologetic attempt to make good the wrong he had done them, one senses that the debt owed by Alfonso to Ripoll was greater than just the price of a carved stone sarcophagus.

Because the archives of Ripoll were completely destroyed by fire in 1835, we cannot know when or how often Alfonso may have visited the abbey. From scattered references to visits in documents that have survived elsewhere, it is clear that Ripoll could be on the count-king's itinerary when he was traveling to Perpignan, a journey he undertook nearly annually. There are strong reasons to believe that Alfonso would have been drawn to Ripoll. His courts were frequented by troubadours, and he was both the composer and the dedicatee of songs of love and war. Ripoll was famous for its schools of music and poetry. The abbey was the conduit through which the new musical culture of Saint-Martial of Limoges was introduced to the courts and cloisters of Christian Iberia. Around the time Alfonso was knighted in 1174, at least one great author of secular love songs was completing the autograph of his erotic collection.[18] Work was then beginning on Ripoll's great western portal, the "bible in stone" that was a marvel of Romanesque sculpture, featuring many martial as well as bucolic scenes. A monk named Arnaldus had just returned from the shrine of Saint James at Compostela carrying a manuscript copy of the *Historia Turpini,* which told how the emperor Charlemagne had been the first to take the cross for the crusade in Spain.[19]

Perhaps most importantly, however, the community that Alfonso was leaving behind had, since the time of his paternal grandfather, Ramón Berenguer III, focused its considerable artistic and cultural resources in an ongoing campaign to honor his ancestors who were the counts of Barcelona. This effort reached its climax during the count-king's own lifetime, when the monks produced works of poetry, music, and prose memorial texts, including a dynastic history, the *Gesta comitum Barcinonensium,* that traced the count-king's lineage to Guifré I. According to the new story told by the monks, that founding figure had, in his adventurous youth, seduced the daughter of a Count of Flanders. As everyone knew, the counts of Flanders were descendants of Charlemagne, and so Alfonso was directly descended from that great emperor, the first Iberian crusader.

Following the landmark arguments of Thomas N. Bisson, a number of historians, including Stefano Maria Cingolani, have concurred that the program

---

18. See Peter Dronke, "The Interpretation of the Ripoll Love Songs," *Romance Philology* 33 (1979): 14–42.

19. *Historia Karoli Magni et Rotholandi ou Chronique de Pseudo-Turpin,* ed. C. Meredith-Jones (Geneva, 1972), 36. On the earliest extant manuscript example of the Pseudo-Turpin, see Manuel C. Díaz y Díaz, *El Códice Calixtino de la Catedral de Santiago: Estudio codicólogico y de contenido* (Santiago de Compostela, 1988), esp. 45–49; for its transmission to Ripoll, 77–81.

of commemorative writing undertaken at Ripoll after the death of Ramón Berenguer IV should be interpreted in the political context of the uneasy union of Catalonia and Aragón during the reign of Alfonso II, and the count-king's attempts to distinguish himself from his Capetian rivals.[20] For Bisson, Ripoll's commemorative and dynastic texts were a powerful expression of the simple principle expressed in numerous contemporary chronicles composed on either side of the Pyrenees: "Power is justified by heroism against the Saracens; legitimacy is dispensed by Charlemagne and his successor kings."[21] Greatly amplifying these arguments, and drawing on Marisa Melero Monero's persuasive political readings of the sculptural program of Ripoll's great western portal,[22] Nikolas Jaspert has presented Ripoll's attempts to legitimate Alfonso II as encompassing both textual and sculptural programs and, significantly, the importation of the *Historia Turpini* to Ripoll's scriptorium from Compostela in 1173.[23] For Jaspert, the program at Ripoll drew on biblical and Carolingian images of divinely sanctioned rulership, which placed Alfonso II's ancestors in a tradition of Christian warriors that included Joshua, Charlemagne, and the knights who participated in the First Crusade.[24]

But the dynastic discourse at Ripoll, with its tight focus on holy war in Iberia, must not be seen only as a consequence of the birth pangs of the Crown of Aragón. Alfonso II was a contemporary of the Angevin ruler Henry II. Both lived through the crisis of the Latin Kingdom of Jerusalem, and Alfonso witnessed a comparable crisis unfold on his own frontier as the powerful Almohad dynasty rose to prominence in al-Andalus. Like Henry, he received appeals and admonishments to take the cross and was mocked and chided when he did not. As had been the case with Henry, much of this discussion was conducted with reference to his family's past. Just as we have seen in the case of Henry, the place of the crusades within the dynastic memory of Alfonso II was contested between multiple communities, each

---

20. Thomas Bisson, "The Origins of Catalonia," 133–140; Stefano Maria Cingolani, "'Seguir les vestígies dels antecessors': Llinatge, reialesa i historiografia a Catalunya des de Ramon Berenguer IV a Pere II (1131–1285)," *Anuario de estudios medievales* 36:1 (2006): 201–240.

21. Thomas Bisson, "Unheroed Pasts: History and Communication in South Frankland before the Albigensian Crusades," *Speculum* 65:2 (1990): 297.

22. Marisa Melero Monero, "La propagande politico-religieuse du programme iconographique de la façade de Sainte-Marie de Ripoll," *Cahiers de civilisation médiévale* 46:2 (2003): 135–157.

23. Nikolas Jaspert, "Historiografía y legitimación carolingia: El monasterio de Ripoll, el Pseudo-Turpín y los condes de Barcelona," in Klaus Herbers, ed., *El Pseudo-Turpín: Lazo entre el culto jacobeo y el culto de Carlomagno,* Actas del VI Congreso Internacional de Estudios Jacobeos (Santiago de Compostela, 2003): 297–315; and, Jaspert, "Karolingische Legitimation und Karlsverehrung in Katalonien," in *Jacobus und Karl der Grosse: Von Einhards Karlsvita zum Pseudo-Turpin,* ed. Klaus Herbers (Tübingen, 2003), 127–161.

24. Jaspert, "Historiografía y legitimación," 314–315.

deriving its authority from different kinds of objects, texts, and rituals. The traditions within these communities mediated between Alfonso himself and the messages that he received both from within his own realm and from outside authorities like the pope. As I have argued was true in the case of the Angevin dynasty, where one voice, that of John of Marmoutier, came to occupy a position of particular importance as the crisis of the crusade deepened, so too can Ripoll's narrative of Alfonso's dynastic crusading past be seen to have informed his actions at the very end of his life. It may even explain the decision he made about his place for burial.

Oliba's Memory Machine

Although little can be said with certainty about the origins of the monastery of Santa Maria de Ripoll, the traditions of the monks maintained that it was founded in 888, eighty-seven years after Louis the Pious had led a military campaign to Catalonia reestablishing the Frankish frontier and conquering the old Roman port known as Barcino.[25] The monks maintained that their founder and early benefactor was a man named Guifré, the powerful lord who governed this frontier zone in the name of geographically (and increasingly also diplomatically) distant Carolingian emperors.[26] Guifré's massive marcher province comprised the territories that would form the counties of Urgell, Barcelona, Gerona, Osona, Conflent, and Cerdanya. In founding first the abbey of Santa Maria, and then the nearby nunnery of San Joan des Abadesses, Guifré may have been intending to provide anchors to help settle the Christian frontier. The fact that his son, Rodolph, became abbot of Ripoll while a daughter, Emma, was abbess of San Joan also implies their potential political utility. When Guifré died in 897, Ripoll received what would prove to be its greatest benefaction: his body.

---

25. Two cartularies of the abbey's records, one apparently of the thirteenth century, are lost. See Henri Stein, *Bibliographie générale des cartulaires français ou relatifs à l'histoire de France* (Paris, 1907), 439, no. 3208. Narratives of the abbey's history, both in the earlier and the later Middle Ages, are often problematic and based either on narrative accounts or on later copies of documents, making the authenticity of their claims difficult to verify. Ramón Abadal i de Vinyals, *Els primers comtes Catalans* (Barcelona, 1958), 130, is cautious about accepting many elements of the foundation narrative, of which the earliest surviving copy is a confirmation on the occasion of the third consecration of the church in 977. See Federico Udina Martorell, *El archivo condal de Barcelona en los siglos ix-x: Estudio crítico de sus fondos,* Consejo superior de investigaciones científicas: Escuela de estudios medievales textos 18 (Barcelona, 1951), 107–109, doc. 5.

26. Roger J. H. Collins, "Charles the Bald and Wifrid the Hairy," in *Charles the Bald: Court and Kingdom*, ed M. T. Gibson and Janet L. Nelson, 2nd ed. (London, 1990), 185–188; Ramon de Abadal i Vinyals, *Els temps i el regiment del comte Guifred el Pilós* (Barcelona, 1989). On the early period in general, see Jonathan Jarrett, *Rulers and Ruled in Frontier Catalonia, 880–1010: Pathways of Power* (London, 2010).

Guifré's patrimony was divided among his sons, with Guifré II inheriting Urgell, Barcelona, and Osona, while both Besalú and Cerdanya passed to Miro II. Over the course of the tenth and eleventh centuries, the configuration of landholding was further divided, with cadet branches of the family assuming the titles of counts of Urgell, Besalú, and Cerdanya as independent lordships. For at least a generation, association with the attitudes and practices of Guifré, the font of their legitimacy, may have been especially desirable, and this would explain why two of his sons elected for burial alongside their father at Ripoll. Without any documentary evidence, it cannot be ruled out that the abbey continued to receive patronage from Guifré's descendants after the death of his children. But in terms of what the monks themselves could later claim about the noble patrons whose bodies and souls were under their care, it seems that a tradition of burial at Ripoll did not continue among members of this kin-group through the later tenth century.

By the middle of the eleventh century, however, we begin to see evidence of Ripoll's emergence as a place of significance for the Catalan nobility. Both Count Bernard Tallaferro (d. 1020) of Besalú and his son William (d. 1052) entrusted the care of their remains and immortal souls to the abbey, over which they also claimed lordship as "counts" of Ripoll. The growing interest in Ripoll at this time can be directly attributed to the efforts of the dynamic abbot Oliba (c. 971–1046). Born into one of the prominent branches of Catalan nobility descended from Guifré I, he first ruled as Count of Berga before becoming a monk (1002) and then abbot (1008) of Ripoll and Sant Miquel de Cuixà, eventually also holding the episcopal see of Vic from 1018. It is during Oliba's abbacy that we begin to find substantial evidence of Ripoll as a site of commemoration and liturgical intercession for the Catalan nobility. At the same time, and again thanks mainly to Oliba, Ripoll became one of the major cultural and intellectual centers of its day. New types of commemorative texts produced by the abbey, which glorified the abbey's benefactors and highlighted bonds of kinship between them, were shaped in sophisticated poetic forms.[27] Hence, although he died more than a century before holy war became a consistent theme in the politics of the Iberian Peninsula and before the monks of Ripoll produced their most important dynastic commemorative monuments for the comital house of Barcelona, Oliba's legacy is crucial

---

27. For Ripoll as a center of cultural production, see Rudolf Beer, "Die Handschriften des Klosters Santa Maria de Ripoll," *Sitzungsberichte der Kaiserlichen Akademie der Wissenschaften* 154:3 (1907) and 158:2 (1908); trans. Pere Barnils as "Los manuscrits del monastir de Santa María de Ripoll," *Boletín de la Real Academia de Buenas Letras de Barcelona* 36 (1909): 137–520; Michel Zimmerman, *Écrire et lire en Catalogne (ix-xii siècle)* (Madrid, 2003), 1: 469–72; Richard Donovan, *Liturgical Drama in Medieval Spain* (Toronto, 1958), 97.

to understanding the developments that would subsequently occur over the course of the twelfth century.[28]

In a letter that he wrote to his successors as abbots of Ripoll toward the end of his life, Oliba admonished the monks that would come after him to pay close attention to the office for their dead brethren.[29] But what Oliba had instituted at Ripoll went far beyond the simple reciting of names in the chapter. According to the records kept by the monks in the later twelfth and thirteenth centuries, it was Oliba himself who first instituted the custom of the *refección,* a special meal enjoyed by the monks to mark anniversaries, most often those of benefactors.[30] It was also through Oliba's agency that Ripoll joined with other Benedictine houses as far-flung as Fleury on the Loire in sending and receiving mortuary rolls of the dead, with entries for particularly beloved or important figures written artfully in verse. Notably, although Oliba did not want monks to neglect the commemorations of their brothers (or himself, after his death), lay aristocrats occupied a prominent place in the abbey's commemorative concerns.

Sant Miquel de Cuixà, another Catalan abbey that was reformed and transformed by Oliba in the early eleventh century, had been the final home of the saintly doge of Venice, Peter Orseolo (d. 987), who died and was buried at the abbey at about the time of Oliba's religious profession. According to the *Life* of Orseolo, it was Oliba who nurtured the cult of this famous prince, constructing a new tomb for him in the church at Cuixà to which his remains were solemnly translated.[31] The only surviving copy of the *Life* itself was copied in the twelfth century at Ripoll, suggesting that the cult of this lay prince continued to be of importance to monks of both houses.

Both Oliba himself and the monks of his two scriptoria at Ripoll and Sant Miquel de Cuixà cultivated the art of commemoration of the dead, experimenting with different forms of commemorative composition both in verse and in prose.[32] In 1018, the abbot himself composed a series of verses

28. For another account of the place of Ripoll in Catalan historiography in this period more broadly, see Miguel Coll i Alentorn, "La historiografia catalana en el període primitiu," *Estudis Romànics* 3 (Barcelona, 1951–52): 180–195.

29. *Diplomatari i escrits literaris de l'abat i bisbe Oliba,* ed. Eduard Junyent and Anscari M. Mundo (Barcelona, 1992), 340–341, no. 23.

30. M. S. Gros i Pujol, "El *Libre de refeccions* del monestir de Santa Maria de Ripoll," *Studia monastica* 46:2 (2004): 365–378 (at 366–367). Guifré's anniversary was celebrated in the fourth week of Lent.

31. *Vita beati petri urseoli ducis venetiarum et dalmatiarum, ASOB,* 5: 860.

32. Years before his conversion, while he was still a young man and Count of Berga, Oliba was present at the drafting of a document confirming an endowment to the church of Saint Peter of Besalú by Miró, count-bishop of Girona. Someone involved in the transaction seems to have decided to render it partly in verse, employing for the protocol lines of Paulinus of Aquileiea's hymn for the feast of Saint Peter ad Vincula. Verses were also inserted praising Miró's dead brother Sunifred. Did

dedicated to the descendants of Guifré I, who were believed to have been buried at Ripoll.[33] This composition, which has been described as a serial epitaph,[34] served as a powerful message to the local nobility descended from Guifré I, particularly the counts of Cerdanya and Besalú, of the importance of the abbey to their ancestors, and posited the existence of a family tradition of burial at Ripoll.[35] Within two years, this attempt to revive Ripoll as a center for dynastic commemoration scored its first success when the Count of Besalú, Bernard Tallaferro, chose Ripoll as his place of sepulchre. This count, in turn, was honored with his own epitaph,[36] and when his son William followed suit in 1052, a new composition lauded the deeds, mores, and memory of both father and son together.[37] Whenever possible, the monastic poets liked to make connections between generations, showing the sons following in their father's honorable footsteps.

Whether all of these verse epitaphs were intended to play some part in the liturgy of commemoration, to be read on anniversaries or at *refecciónes,* or to be displayed or performed for visitors to the abbey is not clear, although the decision to record them in writing and their survival suggest that their functionality was long in duration. One of the longest and most impressive commemorative texts composed during Oliba's abbacy was quite clearly meant to be performed. Ninety-two lines of hendecasyllabic verse written as an abecedarian acrostic, beginning, "The mournful song of all the people / you now carry to our ears with a sympathetic heart" (*Ad carmen populi flebile cuncti / Aures nunc animo ferte benigno*), were composed for Count Ramón Borrell of Barcelona (d. 1017). They lamented the count's passing, praising him as a builder of castles, benefactor, and popular leader.[38] As would many of the later compositions either written or copied in Ripoll's scriptorium, the verses invoke the sound of the performance of funeral hymns, not only in the opening but also in the closing lines, asking the listener to "carry the hymn sweetly with God's help" (*Ymnum ferte deo dulciter almo*).

The commemorative literature produced at Ripoll during Oliba's abbacy praised the lay nobility above all for their contributions to the material fabric

---

this reflect a particular predilection of the young Oliba, or demonstrate the use of song in the ceremonial of land transactions? *Diplomatari i escrits literaris de l'abat i bisbe Oliba,* 5 and n.

33. *Diplomatari i escrits literaris de l'abat i bisbe Oliba,* 305–307.

34. *Diplomatari i escrits literaris de l'abat i bisbe Oliba,* 306–307.

35. The manuscript in which these verses were copied (no. 57 of Ripoll's library before the fire) associated them with another composition praising the abbey and its abbots (*In laude monasterii Rivipullense*). *Diplomatari i escrits literaris de l'abat i bisbe Oliba,* 307–308. n. 3.

36. Nicolau d'Olwer, L., "L'escola poetica de Ripoll en els segles X–XIII," *Anuari del Institut d'Estudis Catalans* 6 (1915–20): 30 n. 3

37. Nicolau d'Olwer, "L'escola poetica de Ripoll," 35 n. 10.

38. Nicolau d'Olwer, "L'escola poetica de Ripoll," 27–30 n. 2.

of both the church more generally and the abbey church at Ripoll in particu-lar.[39] In making such contributions, the counts were following in the foot-steps of their ancestor Guifré I. In anticipation of the campaign to rebuild and rededicate the church at Ripoll the central figure of Guifré was remembered primarily as a builder, who "constructed this house and enlarged the build-ings at great expense."[40] When the new abbey church was finally finished, complete with a (now-lost) series of wall paintings, the dedication ceremony, which took place on 15 January 1032, was attended by William I of Besalú, Guifré II of Cerdanya, Ermengol II of Urgell, and Berenguer Ramón I of Barcelona and Osona.[41] All four were direct descendants of Guifré I, and all were thus present to see his tomb in the new conventual complex and to hear Oliba's description of him as the abbey's founder. The occasion thus enforced the importance of Ripoll to the Catalan nobility while reminding the families of their relations to one another.

The period of Oliba's cultural and political renewal of Ripoll and the rise of the monastery as a center of dynastic commemoration for the nobility coincided with a period of instability on the frontier between the Chris-tian kingdoms and principalities of northern Iberia and Muslim al-Andalus, under the control of the caliph at Cordoba. In the last decades of the eleventh century, the Cordoban commander al-Mansur launched a series of devastat-ing attacks on major Christian sites in the north, sacking Barcelona in 985 and Compostela in 997. Over the succeeding decades the caliphate of Cor-doba gradually disintegrated into a patchwork of independent states, or Taifa kingdoms, offering an opportunity for the Christian powers in the north to exert their authority through raids, the exaction of regular tribute payments (*parias*), and much more rarely conquest and domination.[42]

The monks of Ripoll would have been well aware of these wars, which not only presented new dangers and responsibilities for the noble men and women whose patronage they courted, but which also provided rich new sources of revenue for those nobles who were the beneficiaries of the *parias*.[43]

---

39. Ramón Borrell: "Nam sacrata Dei templa beavit / Donis eximiis et decoravit / Et clerum patrie fovit honeste / O Borrelle magis inclite presul." Nicolau d'Olwer, "L'escola poetica de Ripoll," 29. Bernard Tallaferro and William of Besalú: "Sumptibus hanc multis ditare domum studuere." Nicolau d'Olwer, 35.

40. "Conditur hic primus Guifredus marchio celsus / qui comes atque potens fulsit in orbe manens. Hancque domum struxit et structam sumptibus auxit." *Diplomatari i escrits literaris*, 305.

41. On the evidence of Romanesque wall painting at Ripoll, see Emilia Tarraco, "La pintura mural romànica en el monastir de Ripoll," in *Miscellània in homenatge a Joan Ainaud de Lasarte* (Bar-celona, 1998), 161–169.

42. Joseph O'Callaghan, *Reconquest and Crusade in Medieval Spain* (Philadelphia, 2004), 166–167.

43. For the value of the *parias* in lay patronage for ecclesiastical and monastic centers, see Charles Julian Bishko, "Liturgical Intercession at Cluny for the King-Emperors of Leon," *Studia Monastica* 7 (1961): 53–76.

The impact of the warfare on the nobility can be read clearly in the repeated references to battle against the Sarraceni, Agareni, *barbari,* and Moabiti in the charters of the eleventh century.[44] Charters of the counts of Barcelona tell a story of success in these conflicts, with one act of 1058 proclaiming:

> Christ took pity on the city [of Barcelona], which he recovered for the faithful after expelling the noxious gentiles, and by hereditary succession he gave it to the Christian counts. From their line or natural genealogy came the glorious count and marquis Ramón Berenguer IV. He is made warrior and wall of the Christian people, and by his victory, with the help of Christ, they are made his tributaries.[45]

The charters of the counts of Urgell, beginning with the lament of Sancha of Urgell over the death of her husband, Ermengol III, at the siege of Barbastro in a charter of 1065,[46] documented the hazards of the ongoing campaigns fought by the men of the Urgell family to "liberate" both cities[47] and "the Christian people" from the *infidelios hereticos sarracenos.*[48] Ripoll's early eleventh-century sacramentary, which contained the liturgies of the Mass *pro exercitu ad bellum contra paganos* and the Mass *contra paganos,* suggests a role for the abbey in the prosecution of campaigns against Muslims.[49]

It is striking that while conflict, war against Islam or the enemies of Christ, was mentioned in the charters of this period, it is not a central theme in the narratives and poetry authored by the monks who likely wrote those same charters. While, in the commemorative works, particular figures might be singled out for their martial strength or leadership, neither holy war nor an unholy enemy was required to legitimize military prowess. The only reference to wars against a non-Christian foe in any of the commemorative writing of Ripoll before the twelfth century occurs in the long elegy to Ramón Borrel of Barcelona, which mentions that he "overthrew the barbarians and destroyed their shrines / consecrating with care the temples of God." This is a clear counterpoint to his image elsewhere in the poem as a

---

44. For several examples, see Jesús Alturo i Perucho, "La historiografia catalana del període primitiu," in *La historiografia catalana,* ed. Albert Balcells (Barcelona, 2004), 30–33.

45. "Sed etiam Christus misereri paratus predictam urbem postea recuperavit fidelibus, expulsis pestiferis gentilibus, et per successionem hereditatis tradidit christianis comitibus de quorum linea vel genealogie naturali venit gloriosus comes ac marchio Raimundus Berengarii. Factus est propugnator et murus christiani populi et per victoriam cum adjutorio Christi, facti sunt ei tributarii, pagani christianorum adversarii." Cited with French translation in Aurell, *Les noces du comte,* 266–267.

46. Jaime Villanueva, *Memorias cronológicas de los condes de Urgell,* ed. Cristian Cortés and rev. Eduardo Corredera Gutiérrez (Balaguer, 1976), 301–303.

47. Villanueva, *Memorias cronológicas,* 313.

48. Villanueva, *Memorias cronológicas,* 308.

49. *Sacramentarium Rivipullense,* ed. Alejandro Olivar (Madrid, 1964), 224, no. 392; 225, no. 394.

builder and benefactor of Christian churches.[50] The fact that the doge Peter Orseolo had cleared the Adriatic of Muslim pirates merited only a passing reference in his *Life*.[51]

Within the space of two generations, all of this would change. In the mid-twelfth century, the machinery of dynastic commemoration constructed by Oliba to draw attention to his abbey and fund its reconstruction was restarted and refocused squarely on the comital house of Barcelona, the branch of the extended Catalan kin-network that had achieved almost complete hegemony over all of the Catalan counties. As we will see, in their attempt to place their community at the spiritual and ceremonial center of the new polity forged by the conquests of the counts of Barcelona, the monks of Ripoll seized on the counts' leadership of the crusades in eastern Iberia to construct an image of legitimate rulership and warrior piety.

The Catalan Counts and the Crusade in Spain

The process whereby the wars waged by Christians against Muslims in Spain became programmatic campaigns of self-conscious reconquest cloaked in the intellectual and spiritual mantle of crusade ideology was slow, piecemeal, and is still incompletely understood.[52] However the history of this process is written, it is clear that the Barcelona comital dynasty and its Catalan kindred were at its forefront. In the 1080s and 1090s the Catalan nobility was a central part of Pope Urban II's plan first to capture and then defend the ancient episcopal see of Tarragona in the southern Ebro Valley region.[53] Urban's first appeal came in 1089 and was addressed to Berenguer Ramón of Barcelona, Ermengol of Urgell, Bernard William of Besalú, and "all other nobles and potentates, either clerics or laymen, from the regions (*provinciae*) of Barcelona and Tarragona."[54] Urban entreated these three men and their followers to aid in the reconquest of Tarragona, promising that assistance in the campaign would be rewarded with a remission of sins similar to that gained by a visit to a shrine "in Jerusalem or in other places." Urban had good reason to believe that the Catalan nobility would respond to his invocation of the efficacy of penitential pilgrimage. According to a rough catalogue compiled by Michel

---

50. See above, 262 n. 38.

51. Guido Grandi, *Vita del glorioso prencipe S. Pietro Orseolo Doge di Venezia* (Venice, 1733), 46–47.

52. See O'Callaghan, *Reconquest and Crusade,* 1–22; William Purkis, *Crusading Spirituality in the Holy Land and Iberia c. 1095–c. 1187* (Woodbridge, UK, and Rochester, NY, 2008), 120–138.

53. Urban II, "Epistolae et privilegia," *PL* 151, cols. 302–303; *Papsturkunden in Spanien I: Katalanien,* ed. Paul Kehr (Berlin, 1926), 287. For the Tarragona campaign in general, see Lawrence McCrank, "Restoration and Reconquest in Medieval Catalonia: The Church and Principality of Tarragona, 971–1177" (Phd diss., University of Virginia, 1974).

54. Urban II, "Epistolae et privilegia," *PL* 151, cols. 302–303.

Zimmermann, the number of known pilgrims departing Catalonia for Jerusalem more than doubled over the course of the eleventh century.[55] They included the heads of two of the most powerful comital families: Ermengol II of Urgell and William II of Besalú. Belief in the special efficacy of penitential pilgrimage in the expiation of profoundly sinful behavior can also be demonstrated, for instance, by the pilgrimage undertaken by Peter Ramón of Barcelona to the shrine of Saint James at Compostela for the sin of murdering his stepmother, Almodis of La Marche, in 1071.[56]

Peter's stepmother had married his father Ramón Berenguer I in 1052. He was her third husband, following her earlier marriages to Hugh V of Lusignan and Pons of Toulouse.[57] Almodis was a wealthy and powerful heiress and a conduit for reform ideas, and her marriage to Ramón Berenguer marked a significant step in the Barcelona family's political strategy of hypergamy and their introduction into circles of intense support for the Gregorian reform movement. As Jonathan Riley-Smith has noted, "a feature of her offspring from three husbands is how many of them were committed supporters of papal reform and the crusade."[58] One of the twin sons that resulted from her marriage to Ramón Berenguer was almost certainly a participant in the First Crusade, although the significance of his participation was completely overshadowed by the circumstances that led him to undertake this extreme penance: his murder of his twin brother in 1082 on a mountain pass near Girona.[59]

After the fratricide, subsequent generations of the Barcelona comital family did not take the cross for Jerusalem, but they quickly emerged as leaders of the crusade in Spain. As early as 1114, Count Ramón Berenguer III led a combined crusading force from Barcelona, southern France, and Pisa to capture Ibiza and Mallorca.[60] This expedition brought the Count of Barcelona fame as a conqueror and brought the struggle of the Catalans on the eastern coast and in the Ebro Valley back into the view of the papacy. In the succeeding decades, the counts of Barcelona in particular received guidance and

55. Michel Zimmermann, *Écrire et lire en Catalogne: ix-xii siècles* (Madrid: Casa de Velazques, 2003), 2: annex 20, 1200–1209.

56. *GCB*, 7.

57. Aurell, *Les noces du comte,* 257–280.

58. Jonathan Riley-Smith, *The First Crusaders, 1095–1131* (Cambridge, 1997), 46.

59. Bofarull y Mascaró, *Los condes,* 134–135. Later traditions suggested that the count was then forced by his brother's former supporters to receive judgment for his crime at the court of Alfonso VI of Léon-Castille; see Bofarull y Mascaró, *Los condes,* 117–118, citing a document now edited in *Liber feudorum maior,* 1: 270–271. See Nicholas Paul, "The Fruits of Penance and the Laurel of the Cross: Poetics of Crusade and Conquest in the Memorials of Santa Maria de Ripoll," in *A Storm against the Infidel,* ed. Iben Fonnesberg-Schmidt and Torben K. Nielsen (Leiden: Brill, forthcoming).

60. Bernard F. Reilly, *The Contest of Christian and Muslim Spain, 1031–1157* (Oxford,1992), 176.

support in the form of papal letters and indulgences in their campaigns against Tortosa and the hinterlands of Tarragona, which affirmed the equivalence of their efforts in Iberia to what the crusaders had accomplished in the East.[61] Although he fought only in Spain and the Balearics, Ramón Berenguer III also demonstrated his support for the crusading efforts in the East by becoming a fully professed Templar brother on his deathbed in 1131.[62]

In the same year that Ramón Berenguer III died in the habit of a Templar, his neighbor Alfonso "the Battler," ruler of Aragón and Navarre, claimant to the title *Imperator totius Hispaniae,* and no less a fearsome conqueror of Muslim territory, drew up the infamous testament in which he divided all of his lands among the Templars, the Hospitallers, and the Canons of the Holy Sepulchre. Alan Forey has suggested that Alfonso was motivated, at least in part, by a desire to encourage the Templars to take up military positions in Spain, a move they had earlier refused to make.[63] When the "emperor" Alfonso died in 1134, his testamentary terms plunged the kingdom of Aragón into a crisis that passed from the hands of Alfonso's brother Ramiro II, who briefly emerged from his life as a monk long enough to father a daughter. Both kingdom and crisis passed to the young Count Ramón Berenguer IV after his betrothal to Ramiro's one-year-old daughter, Petronilla, in 1136.[64] The subsequent negotiations between Ramón Berenguer IV and the institutions of the crusader kingdom of Jerusalem lasted for seven years but ultimately resulted in both the successful militarization of the Templars in Spain and a close alliance between the count and the Temple.[65] As Forey has demonstrated, both parties profited from this partnership: the count finding victory after victory with the Templars by his side, and the order winning enormous grants from the lands they conquered together.[66]

Ramón Berenguer IV's most famous conquests were achieved as part of the wide-ranging assault by Latin Christian forces in the Near East, the Baltic, and Iberia that is now known as the Second Crusade (1147–49). A week

61. Paul Kehr, *Das Papsttum und der katalanische Prinzipat bis zur Vereinigung mit Aragon* (Berlin, 1926), 54–67. Nikolas Jaspert, "*Capta est Dertosa: Clavis Christianorum;* Tortosa and the Crusades," in *The Second Crusade: Scope and Consequences,* ed. Jonathan Philips and Martin Hock (Manchester, UK, 2001), 92. For the campaigns, see Reilly, *The Contest,* 178–179.

62. Riley-Smith, *The First Crusaders,* 163.

63. Alan Forey, *The Templars in the Corona de Aragón* (London, 1973), 8. For a different view of Alfonso's intentions, see Elena Lourie, "The Will of Alfonso I, 'El Batallador,' King of Aragon and Navarre: A Reassessment," *Speculum* 50 (1975): 635–651.

64. Aurell, *Les noces du comte,* 369–371.

65. It should be noted that the count's attraction to the military order dated to the period before he became embroiled in the testamentary negotiations. See Forey's discussion in *The Templars,* 16, of his promise to serve with the Templars for one year as soon as they became involved in the Iberian theater.

66. Forey, *The Templars,* 20–26.

before the successful siege of Lisbon by a combined force of Portuguese and crusaders in 1147, Ramón Berenguer IV aided Alfonso VII of León-Castile in the capture of Alméria, and in the following two years Ramón led a combined force of Catalan nobles, Templars, and Hospitallers in the conquest of Tortosa, Lleida, Fraga, and Mequinenza.[67] Like his father, Ramón Berenguer IV was the object of direct papal support and attention; in 1148 Eugenius III promulgated a crusade bull in his aid that opened the way for the capture of Tortosa. So great was the count's fame as a crusader that in the years after the Second Crusade the troubadour Marcabru marveled at how "the Marquis and they of the Temple of Solomon" had rendered Iberia the true *lavador* or washing place for the prosecution of effective and successful penitential warfare.[68]

In 1143, in the document announcing his alliance with the Templars and their full mobilization in eastern Iberia, Ramón Berenguer IV revealed two critical components to his own understanding of the meaning and purpose of the wars that he was waging in Spain. First, in describing the body of brother-knights that would accompany him in his campaigns "for the defeat, overcoming, and expulsion of the race of Moors and the exaltation of the holy Christian faith and religion," he noted specifically that their efforts "to defend the western church which is in Spain" were inspired by the earlier efforts of "the *militia* of the Temple of Solomon in Jerusalem, which defends the eastern Church."[69] Not only the papacy, but Ramón himself therefore understood his campaigns to be completely equivalent to crusades in the East. Later in the charter the count granted the Templars a string of castle lordships, substantial revenues from Zaragoza and Huesca, and the right to one-fifth of all conquered territories. Forey argued that "there is no doubt" that these opulent gifts were meant as a final recompensation to the Templars for what they were owed in Alfonso I's testament. This makes it all the more striking that in this 1143 charter, unlike in earlier correspondence, Ramón Berenguer made no reference to the dead king or his testament. Instead, he invoked a different motivation for his generosity and his friendship with the knights. He made the gift, he said, "for the good of the soul of

67. For the conquests of Alméria and Tortosa, see John Bryan Williams, "The Making of a Crusade: The Genoese Anti-Muslim Attacks in Spain, 1146–1148," *Journal of Medieval History* 23:1 (1997): 29–53; Reilly, *The Contest,* 214–215; O'Callaghan, *Reconquest and Crusade,* 46; Jaspert, "*Capta est Dertosa,*" 90–110; Lucas Villegas-Aristizábal, "The Anglo-Norman Intervention in the Conquest and Settlement of Tortosa, 1148–1180," *Crusades* 8 (2009): 63–129.

68. Linda Paterson, "Syria, Poitou, and the *Reconquista* (or Tales of the Undead): Who Was the Count in Marcabru's *Verse del lavador*?" in Phillips and Hock, *The Second Crusade,* 133–149.

69. d'Albon, *Cartulaire,* 204–205 CDI IV 93–99 doc. 43; trans. Forey, *The Templars,* 23.

my father, who was a knight and a brother of that very *militia,* under whose rule and in whose habit he gloriously finished his life."[70]

Return to Ripoll

In considering how else he might imitate his father, who had gloriously ended his life as a knight of Christ, Ramón Berenguer IV must also have considered his father's decision to become the first of his line since the days of the distant ancestor Guifré to choose the abbey of Santa Maria de Ripoll for burial. Although it is impossible to know precisely what motivated Ramón Berenguer III's choice of Ripoll, there were several reasons why this community in particular might have been important both to the count himself and to his family. From 1071 the abbey had been under the control of Saint Victor of Marseilles in the county of Provence, a major force for reform in the south. Ripoll would serve as a useful trans-Pyrenean conduit for the count, who had secured Provence after his marriage to Douce, heiress of Provence, Millau, and Gevaudan in 1112, and whose wars of Christian reconquest were being waged with the assistance of reforming popes.

Since counts Ramón Berenguer III and his son made no secret of their admiration for what had been achieved in the crusading conquest of the Holy Land, it is also potentially significant that Ripoll represents one of the few monastic communities in the West for which a liturgy survives celebrating the conquest of Jerusalem in 1099. A group of texts, which John France identified as evidence of this liturgy, were written or copied at Ripoll in the early twelfth century and were structured around a specially prepared narrative account of the capture of Jerusalem in the last three quires of a manuscript of the chronicle of Raymond of Aguilers.[71] The lection-narrative of the conquest is followed by three short homiletic exhortations on the significance of the crusade, addressed (respectively) to fellow monks, Jews, and knights, and finally by a hymn with the refrain *Iherusalem exulta!* These texts, intended for performance on the Feast of the Liberation of Jerusalem (15 July), returned time and again to the spiritual rewards promised to those who endured the perils of penitential warfare, and to their ultimate success.

---

70. "ad salutem anime patris mei qui fuit miles ac frater sancte iamdicte milicie, in cuius regula et havitu gloriose vitam finivit." d'Albon, *Cartulaire,* 204.

71. For the MS, see appendix 3. For editions of the relevant texts, see John France, "The Text of the Account of the Capture of Jerusalem in the Ripoll Manuscript, Bibliothéque Nationale (Latin) 5132," *English Historical Review* 103:408 (1988), 643–657. Referring to another manuscript (British Library Add. 8927) containing *Lectiones in festivitate S. Jerusalem ad vesperas; lectiones de historia ubi capta fuit Hierusalem,* France suggested that the Ripoll texts were intended to be used for the same feast. For a (partial) description of MS 8927, see Fulcher of Chartres, *Historia Hierosolymitana (1095–1127): Mit Erläuterungen und einem Anhange,* ed. Heinrich Hagenmeyer (Heidelberg, 1913), 96.

During Ramón Berenguer III's rule, which saw the gradual application of crusading ideologies and institutions to holy war in eastern Iberia, the performance of this liturgy at Ripoll would have provided a critical reminder of the great spiritual benefits and stunning victories won by those who fought in the service of the cross.

A final reason for the allure of Ripoll to the twelfth-century counts of Barcelona lay in its potential significance within Catalonia. By the time of Ramón Berenguer III's death, the careful marriage strategies of his ancestors had culminated in the domination by the comital house of Barcelona of the Catalan counties of Osona, Girona, Cerdanya, and Besalú. For twelfth-century observers, this concentration of power would come to be seen as more than just hegemony: it was the reconstruction of the Spanish march as it had once been ruled by Guifré I. What community could be more important to the dynasty that had achieved this reconstitution of the Carolingian march than the one where the memory of the original *Marchio comes* was preserved?

In order to ensure that the logic of this mutually beneficial association was well understood both by the dynasty and throughout the region after the death of Ramón Berenguer III, Ripoll was tasked with once again activating the machinery of commemoration that had apparently lain dormant since the middle decades of the eleventh century. A chronicle written at Ripoll in 1147 demonstrates that the twelfth-century community remembered quite clearly what Oliba had accomplished in terms of building and beautifying the monastery through his relationships with the most powerful princely families.[72] It may have been in the spirit of those old programs that the monks of Ripoll prepared new memorials for Ramón Berenguer III, including a carved stone sarcophagus with an inscribed epitaph accompanying scenes of the count's death, the translation of his body to Ripoll, the mourning of his knights and subjects, and his burial.[73] Only fragments of the sarcophagus survive, but their carvings attest to a sophisticated program of funerary decoration and ostentatiously advertised Ripoll as a center of commemorative ritual.

The efforts of the monks were not in vain. In 1141, exactly ten years after his father's death, Ramón Berenguer IV granted to Ripoll the lordship of Molló "just as it had been held by the counts of Besalú," and elected to be buried at Ripoll beside his father. He was perhaps thinking of the comparatively prosperous Ripoll and its elaborate memorials when, in 1157, he lamented that the abbey of San Juan de la Peña, "which is held above all

---

72. The memory of what Oliba had accomplished was still central to how a writer in 1147 understood the history of the abbey: "Brevis historia monasterii Rivipullensi," ed. Petrus de Marca, in *Marca Hispanica sive limes Hispanicus* (Paris, 1688), cols. 1298–1299.

73. For the tomb and its epitaph, see Bofarull y Mascaró, *Los condes,* 2: 175–176.

other monasteries of Aragón because of its great antiquity and reputation and because there are the bodies of the kings of Aragón," had fallen into "poverty and misery."[74] En route to a diplomatic meeting with Emperor Frederick Barbarossa at Turin in early August 1162, Ramón Berenguer IV fell ill and, as he lay dying, dictated his testament to his seneschal William Ramón of Montcada.[75] His wishes, as they were afterward ceremonially decreed in the Aragonese capital of Huesca, began with the gift of his body for burial at the abbey of Santa Maria de Ripoll. Together with his body, he named the gift, earlier promised to the abbey, of the lordship of Molló, which lay north and east of the abbey toward Perpignan. According to his wishes, Ramón Berenguer's body was transported back to Catalonia, where it joined his father's remains for burial at Ripoll.

In taking possession of Molló, the monks made a copy onto a single sheet of vellum of the fiscal surveys of the land the count had held there and the relevant revenues and payments owed for it. On the reverse of their copy of the fiscal accounts, the monks copied another text, a description of a gift made by Ramón Berenguer IV to the abbey at some point in the last ten years of his life, which demonstrates not only Ripoll's preservation of the count's memory but the count's own interest in how his memory should be preserved. Presenting Ripoll with lands and a church in the vicinity of Zaragoza, the count had instructed Gausfred, the last abbot to be appointed by Saint Victor of Marseilles, that his own anniversary and those of his mother and father ought to be celebrated by the monks in their songs and masses, and that on those days the community might enjoy such bountiful refections as they did on the Feast of Saint Luke.[76]

Precisely how the count's memory was celebrated at Ripoll was of the greatest importance both for Ripoll and perhaps Catalonia more generally. The two-year period of regency by his widow, Petronilla of Aragón, followed by the succession of her son Ramón Berenguer (who ruled as Alfonso II) as the heir to both Catalonia and Aragón, was a period of uncertainty about how the confederation of Catalan counties would fare in the union with Aragón. Ripoll had reason to fear that it would lose the prominence that it had gained if the new ruler's attention moved west, toward the Aragonese heartland around Huesca, or even south, toward the frontier. By maintaining

---

74. *Papsturkunden in Spanien II: Navarra und Aragón,* ed. Paul Kehr (Berlin, 1928), 402 n. 84.

75. *Els testaments dels comtes,* 103–106; John C. Shideler, *A Medieval Catalan Noble Family: The Montcadas 1000–1230* (Berkeley, 1983), 106–107.

76. The original parchment is now BNF, MS Lat. 5132, ff. 105 and 107. See appendix 3. By comparison, Raymond's neighbor William of Montpellier, in his testament of 29 September 1172, founded an anniversary for himself on the feasts of Saints Cosmas and Damian. See *Layettes du trésor des chartes,* ed. Alexadre Teulet (Paris, 1863–1909), 1: 100–103, no. 237.

the memory of young Alfonso II's father and grandfather, and linking them to the founder, Guifré I, the monks of Ripoll hoped to permanently anchor the dynasty at Ripoll.

Given the lavish monument erected for Ramón Berenguer III, and the major program of rebuilding and sculpting Ripoll's great western portal, which is usually dated to the 1160s and 1170s, it is safe to assume that the sarcophagus erected for Ramón Berenguer IV was a work of the finest craftsmanship.[77] The tomb itself does not survive, having been partially destroyed during the sack of the monastery by French revolutionary troops in 1794, before its final destruction in the fire of 1835. According to the description of the nineteenth-century antiquarian Josep Maria Pellicer i Pagés, Ramón Berenguer IV's body had been placed in a wooden coffin decorated with an image of the count seated with a scepter and a sword.[78] This coffin had subsequently been decorated with silver, which was the object of the French soldiers. According to some descriptions, the tomb itself appeared to have been reconstituted in the fourteenth century, probably in the reign of Peter IV "the Ceremonious," and so the effigy that it bore, which featured the arms of Catalonia, probably did not reflect the original ornamentation. The epitaph inscribed on the tomb, however, which followed the same three-line pattern as the verses dedicated to his father, was probably original:[79]

A duke was I by my mother, a king from my wife, a marquis by my father. While I lived my span I smashed the Moor with hunger and war, and without loss I upheld the laws of the Lord.[80]

This inscription, with its clear focus on the count's crusading victories, resonates with the other textual memorials created at Ripoll after the count's death. These included two brief commemorative works known as the *Planctus* and the *Epitafium,* devoted to the memory of Count Ramón Berenguer IV, and the dynastic history of the counts of Barcelona, the *Gesta comitum Barcinonensium.*

The first of these, and the one most clearly written for use immediately after the count's death, is the *Planctus* in his memory, which begins: *Mentem meam laedit dolor.* (Sadness strikes my mind.) Although it is in poor condition,

---

77. For an example of contemporary tomb architecture, see Elizabeth Valdez del Alamo, "Lament for a Lost Queen: The Sarcophagus of Doña Blanca of Nájera," *Art Bulletin* 78 (1996): 311–333.

78. Josep Pellicer i Pagés, *Santa Maria del Monasterio del Ripoll* (Mataró, 1888), 124–125.

79. The epitaph was copied into a late fourteenth-century genealogy of the kings of Aragón. See Jean-Pierre Jardin and Georges Martin, "*Generatio regum Aragonum:* Une variante médiévale inédite de l'histoire des rois d'Aragon," *Cahiers de linguistique hispanique médiévale* 22 (1999): 180.

80. "Dux ego de matre, rex coniuge, marchio patre / Marte, fame fregi Mauros, dum tempore degi / et sine iactura tenui Domini sua iura."

possibly as a result of frequent consultation, the single sheet of vellum bearing the *Planctus,* which was later incorporated into a miscellaneous manuscript including numerous other important commemorative and dynastic texts, exhibits, as will become clear, many details that render it invaluable for understanding the commemorative rituals at Ripoll. The second commemorative text is the somewhat misleadingly entitled *Epitafium,* a lengthy prose work written on a single sheet of parchment. Seen by some early modern observers hanging on the outside of the count's tomb, it was at some point placed inside with his remains, where it was rediscovered in 1803.[81] The text laments the dead man's passing and offers prayers for him but was written as a direct address with frequent exhortations, suggesting that it was meant to be read aloud.[82] It is tempting, therefore, to conclude that the *Epitafium* was also intended for performance, perhaps in a different setting from the *Planctus,* such as a *refección* honoring the count's memory on his anniversary. The reference to "this tomb" (*hoc sepulchre*) in the text's opening lines sets a scene near the monument itself.[83]

In both the *Planctus* and the *Epitafium* Ramón Berenguer IV was remembered primarily for his crusading conquests and steadfastness in the holy war against Islam. Beginning with a pastoral lament about the dimmed hues of the Catalonian countryside after the passing of his great light, the *Planctus* rapidly moves to a vision of the count as an epic warrior who "destroyed one thousand lines of Muslim men."[84] It then turns into an annotated list of his greatest conquests, including Almería, which he took "with keels" (*cum carinis*), and Lleida and Fraga, which he was thought to have captured in one day (*sub simul luce*). One version of the hymn asserted that the count's wars had been prosecuted under a crusading banner; those who had previously been knaves or thieves were adorned with "the laurel of the cross" (*crucis lauro*) while in the count's service. The count's fame as a crusader, which was in fact extraordinarily widespread, was said to have won the admiration of the kings of France and England, the favor of the emperor, and the friendship of the kings of Castile.[85]

A much longer work, meditating not only on the count's life but on the significance of his death for the monks of Ripoll and the wider community,

81. "Epitafium," ed. Enrique Flores, in *España sagrada* 81 (Madrid, 1819): 466–470; Baluze copied the original text in BNF, Baluze MS 107, f. 461.

82. Baluze's copy also bore the title "Epitafium" but was headed "Oratio"; see Beer, "Die Handscriften," 26.

83. "Epitafium," 466.

84. The best edition of the *Planctus* is that of Nicolau d'Olwer, "L'escola poètica de Ripoll," 36–37.

85. For an invocation of Ramón Berenguer IV, "who does not leave off fighting the pagans," in a genealogy of castellans from Picardy, see the *Genealogiae scriptoris Fusniacenses, MGH SS* 13: 256.

the *Epitafium* nonetheless remained fixated on the count as a Christian warrior. The list of conquered cities appears again, and some of the text appears to play on the tomb inscription, calling him a

> king of peace, prince of justice, duke of truth and equity, chaste warrior of the Christian faith, powerful wager of war against the Saracens and unbelievers, whose arrows never fell short, whose shield was never turned aside in war, and whose lance was never turned away.[86]

The *Epitafium* also features two other striking elements. The first, hinted at in the chasteness (*intemerate*) of the count in the previous passage, is the sense of sanctity the address attempts to cultivate. At several points, the *Epitafium* refers to "clear miracles" that the count's body performed on its journey from Piedmont to Ripoll and then afterward with great regularity while in situ in the monastery.[87] The count is presented to the listener as requiring not intercession but celebration as an example of piety: "Sing! Because now he has received his penny for the considerable labour that he has done in the vineyard of the Holy Church."[88] If the count was a saint, however, he was also an explicitly triumphant one. The language of victory and triumph pervades the *Epitafium,* in its treatment of both the count himself, who is described repeatedly as *victoriosissimus* and *triunfator,* and his achievements, which are described as triumphs. At the emotional closing of the text, the listener is even asked to consider that the count's death and heavenly reward, followed by the burial of his remains at Ripoll, are in fact "what he so greatly desired for so long: having conquered his enemies he has achieved a secure triumph (*securum triunfum*)."[89] The ultimate triumph, then, was the return of the count's body to Ripoll for burial.

Although it may have been written as late as 1184, the first redaction of the dynastic history *Gesta comitum Barcinonensium,* like the *Planctus* and the *Epitafium,* is generally associated with the period after the death of Ramón

---

86. "His certe rex pacis, princeps justitiae dux veritatis et aequitatis, armiger intemerate fidei christianae, contra Sarracenos et infideles debelator fortis, cuius sagita numquam abiit retrorsum, nec declinavit clypeus eius in bello, et eius numquam est aversa hasta." "Epitafium," 466.

87. "In obitu etiam suo claruit miraculis tam in Italia quam per totam Provinciam, necnon per totum iter dum corpus eius ad monasterium Rivipullense aferretur, ubi et jusu ipsius adhuc viventis in Ecclesia in hoc sepulcro honorifice tumulatum requiescit ibique sepe et sepissime evidentibus crebris claruit mirculis." "Epitafium," 466.

88. "Cantate quod iam denarium recepit pro quo tanto labore in vinea Sanctae Ecclesiae laboravit." "Epitafium," 469.

89. "Hodie certe iste Victoriosissimus Princeps et Dominus Raymndus Berengueri obtinuit quod tanto tempore estuabat desiderio: hodie devictis hostibus securum obtinuit triunfum." "Epitafium," 468.

Berenguer IV, the last of the Barcelona counts mentioned in the narrative.[90] The *Gesta comitum Barcinonensium* is in fact an account of the three prominent families of Barcelona, Urgell, and Besalú, all of whom traced their lineage to Guifré I, with whom the narrative begins. The *Gesta comitum* charts the seemingly inexorable rise of the Barcelona counts, culminating in their ultimate hegemony and the restoration of Guifré's Carolingian patrimony in the reign of Ramón Berenguer III and celebrating the God-given victories of Ramón Berenguer IV. As we have seen, in the early eleventh century the monks at Ripoll had sought to emphasize ties of lineage between generations of their patrons, the counts of Besalú, and to remind these counts of their descent from Guifré I. While the *Gesta comitum* was an altogether more ambitious enterprise than anything that had previously been created at Ripoll, the monks responsible for its composition shared some of the strategies of their forebears.

In the days of Oliba's abbacy, when the abbey was being rebuilt and rededicated, Ripoll's poets had portrayed Guifré as a builder and patron to encourage the support of the counts of Besalú. After the death of Ramón Berenguer IV, in order to secure the continued attention of the new count-king and perhaps also to secure funding for a new, intricately carved western portal, the monks reimagined Guifré as a conqueror and holy warrior. This process of transformation had begun somewhat earlier. A description of Guifré as the one who "[expelled] the Saracens, who were at that time the inhabitants of the land" appeared for the first time in the *Brevis historia monasterii Rivipullensis,* a chronicle composed at the abbey in 1147.[91] This reference, however terse, marked the first association between Guifré and the wars against the Muslims in any surviving text. The *Gesta comitum* provided a complete and colourful legend, which associated the regalian authority of the counts with their role in the expulsion of the Muslims from Catalonia. The narrative included an assurance by the *rex Francorum* that if Guifré "and those who were with him managed by themselves to expel the Agarenes from his [the king's] frontier, the *honor* of Barcelona would pass into his power (*dominium*) and to all of his descendants forever."[92]

With the power and identity of the family predicated on this victory over the unbelievers, the dynastic history looked forward to the time of Ramón

90. For the traditional dating (1162–84), see *GCB,* xxii; for the revised, narrower dating of 1180–84, see *Gestes dels comtes de Barcelona i Reis d'Aragó,* ed. Stefano Maria Cingolani, Monuments d'Historia de la Corona d'Aragó 1 (Valencia, 2008), 29. See also Jaume Aurell, "From Genealogies to Chronicles: The Power of the Form in Medieval Catalan Historiography," *Viator* 36 (2005): 235–264, esp. 241–251.

91. "Brevis historia monasterii Rivipullensis," col. 1295.

92. *GCB,* 5.

Berenguer III and Ramón Berenguer IV, who, like Guifré, ruled the whole of the Spanish March, and who would carry the triumphal conquest forward in the Balearics, the Ebro Valley, and beyond.[93] While his father's brief conquest and devastation of the towns of Mallorca was a notable victory, it was Ramón Berenguer IV's career as a crusader that received the most attention. Narrating the count's more famous victories in much the same way as they were described in the *Planctus* and the *Epitafium,* the *Gesta comitum* indulged in a detailed account of how, at Alméria, he had faced down an army of twenty thousand Saracens with only fifty-two companions, audaciously fixing his tents beside the walls.[94] In the course of his conquests, which included the taking of Tortosa, Lleida, and Fraga in 1148 and 1149, of Mount Siurana and the castles along the banks of the Ebro River from Tortosa to Zaragoza, he was said to have "erected as many as three hundred churches and even more altars for Christ."[95]

There can be no doubt that upholding the legitimacy of Alfonso's paternal and maternal inheritance was a major concern of Ramón Berenguer IV throughout his reign. Like the troubadour Bertran de Born, who referred to Alfonso's "vulgar, upstart family" (*bas paratges sobrissitz*) and argued that Aragón rightly belonged to the king of Navarre, the count-king's enemies could question both his father's nobility and the awkward succession that followed the death of the Battler.[96] Building on the valuable arguments of Bisson, Cingolani, Monero, and Jaspert, two additional observations must be made that may help us to understand both the form and the potential impact of the Ripoll program. As was the case in the Angevin empire, claims to the dynastic crusading past in the Crown of Aragón were not limited to one institution or community. Like their fellow Benedictines at Marmoutier, the monks of Ripoll actively competed with other communities to create an image of the dynastic past that was resonant, relevant, and useful for their prince. Moreover, as in Henry II's domains, the discourse about the crusading past was shaped in response to pressures from both without and within, by papal admonishment, and, perhaps just as importantly in Alfonso's southern world, by troubadour lyric.

---

93. *GCB,* 8.

94. *GCB,* 8.

95. "plurima castra circa litus Iberi amnis a Tortosa usque Cesaraugustam cepit, et Christi ecclesiam usque ad trecenta et eo amplius altaria dilatauit." *GCB,* 8.

96. Bertran de Born, *The Poems of the Troubadour Bertan de Born,* ed. and trans. William D. Paden (Berkeley, 1986), 269–271; for the background to Bertran's attitudes toward Alfonso, see Patricia Harris Stablein, "Menace and Delight: The Catalan Image in the Poetry of Bertran de Born," in *Studia in honorem Profesor M. de Riquer* (Barcelona, 1988), 3: 453–464.

Only when the Ripoll memorial program has been put into these contexts does it become clear that the program under way at the abbey was not
just one of dynastic legitimation and the reassertion of the community's
importance to the dynasty, but also an attempt to respond to a growing crisis
within Catalonia and Aragón over the failure of Alfonso II to follow in the
footsteps of his ancestors and undertake the leadership responsibilities of a
major crusading offensive in Spain.

Competition

The sites where dynastic and crusading memory were intertwined in ritual,
narrative, and song included religious communities where Alfonso's ancestors were buried and others that sought creatively to ally themselves with
the triumphs of past generations (see map 3). Montearagón, near the Aragonese capital of Huesca, held the tomb of Alfonso's great-uncle Alfonso I
"the Battler." Alfonso II was well aware of this locus of the dynastic past, and
he honored the memory of "my uncle the King Alfonso who lies in peace
in the church of Jesus of Nazareth at Montearagón," when in March 1175
he granted a privilege for the men of the fortress.[97] From 1170 the abbot
of Montearagón was Alfonso's half brother Berenguer, an illegitimate son
of Ramón Berenguer IV, and even after Alfonso's death the abbey remained
close to the family.[98] When Berenguer was forced to relinquish the abbey
in 1205, the abbacy was taken up by Alfonso's son Ferrand.[99] Montearagón
was not only associated with the memory of the great warrior Alfonso I, but
with the crusading movement of reconquest itself. In July 1089, when he
officially placed the community under the protection of the Holy See, Urban
II noted that King Sancho Ramirez (d. 1094) and his son Peter (d. 1104) had
chosen to honor the name of Jesus of Nazareth with a new church because
"many victories were reported against the Saracens when they invoked his
name."[100]

Another site that competed with Ripoll as a point of access to the crusading past was the church of San Vincente de Roda, seat of the embattled
episcopal see of Roda–Barbastro. For the first half of the twelfth century, the
canons of Roda, headed by their bishop Ramón, had been engaged in a vicious

97. *Documentos de Montearagón (1058–1205),* ed. Dolores Barrios Martínez (Huesca, 2004),
153–154, nó. 79.

98. For his career, see Elaine Graham-Leigh, "Hirelings and Shepherds: Archbishop Berenguer of
Narbonne (1191–1211) and the Ideal Bishop," *English Historical Review* 116:469 (2001): 1083–1084.

99. María Dolores Cabré, "Cinco documentos de Infante Don Fernando Abad de Montearagón," *Argensola* 39 (1959): 239–258.

100. *Documentos de Montearagón,* 28, no. 5.

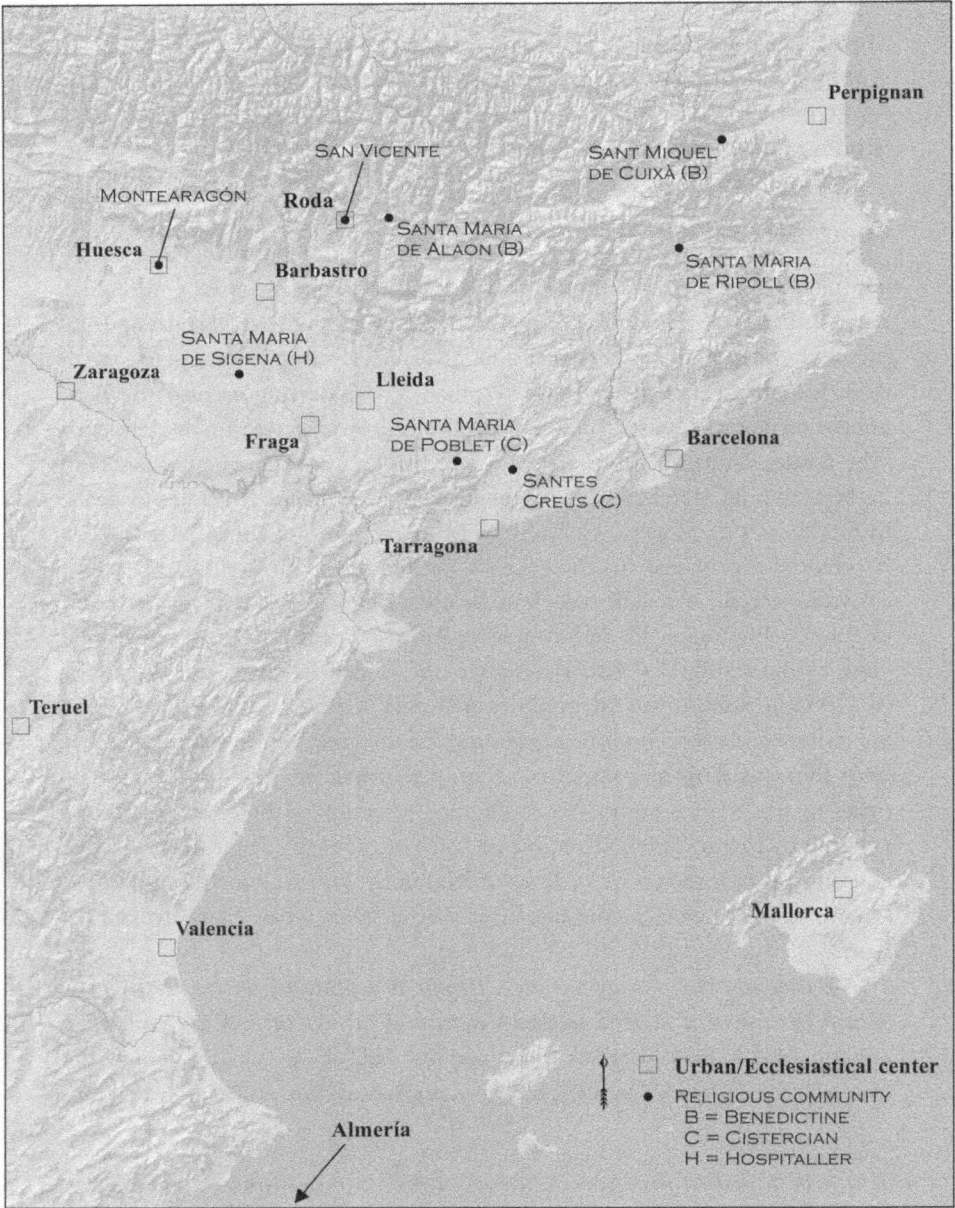

Map 3. Sites of dynastic commemoration in the Crown of Aragón-Cataloni.

struggle to assert its rights and territories against the neighboring Aragonese see of Jaca-Huesca. The conflict continued even after the death of Ramón in exile from his see in 1126.[101] In the mid-twelfth century, the canons of Roda energetically engaged in a campaign of writing and ritual to enhance the status of their church in the eyes of their new ruler Ramón Berenguer IV.

Central to their efforts was the development of the cult of their dead bishop as Saint Ramón of Barbastro. According to the *Vita* of the bishop, which was divided into *lectiones* to be read aloud on his feast day (21 June) at Roda, when

> King Alfonso of Aragón, who was powerful, warlike, triumphant, and generous, proposed to enter Iberia with an enormous Christian army and do battle with the infidels and foreign Agarenes, he wished to have the aforesaid prelate of God with him as a companion, that he might strengthen him and his army by divine exhortations and provide assistance with frequent prayer.[102]

This expedition against the Spanish and North African Muslims, who are described using the biblical terms Moabitae (Moabites) and Malachae (Amalekites), is the climactic moment in the *Vita* of Saint Ramón. It is upon the army's triumphal return to Huesca that Ramón dies, stricken by an illness contracted while on campaign. On balance, it is the image of Ramón as companion to the Aragonese conqueror and effective weapon in the war against Islam that stands out from among the more common tropes of episcopal sanctity repeated in his *Vita* and the office for his feast. As the guardians of the relics of this tireless advocate of holy war and close friend to new king Alfonso's cherished ancestor, the canons of Roda effectively positioned themselves as valuable allies, particularly if the new king were to undertake wars like those of his predecessor.

Two other productions of the Roda scriptorium suggest that the canons may have been in competition with the monks of Ripoll. Like Ripoll, Roda was also a community with an interest in the First Crusade. Although written in a Provençal dialect probably originating in the Limousin, the *Canso d'Antioca,* a vernacular epic narrative of the First Crusade, was copied in the

---

101. For the controversy, see Damian Smith, *Innocent III and the Crown of Aragón* (Aldershot, UK, 2004), 205–207.

102. "Interea Rex Aragonum Ildefonsus, armipotens, bellicosus, triumphator, magnanimous propsuit dum ingenti Christicolarum exercitu Hiberiam penetrare, Agarenos alienigenas atque infidels potenter expugnare. Qui praefatum Dei Praesulem secum voluit habere comitem ut se atque exercitum suum roboraret divinitus exortando, adiuvaret frequenter orando." Jaime Villanueva, *Viage literario,* vol. 15 (Madrid, 1851): 316–317. The manuscript from which this text derives is Archivo de la Catedral de Lérida, Codices de Roda, Rc-0029, dated by the archivists of Lérida to 1191.

twelfth century at Roda and kept in the chapter's library.[103] Moreover, it was at Roda, and not at Ripoll, that the earliest songs in praise of Ramón Berenguer IV's conquests were sung. A poem or hymn composed at Roda referring to the count as if he were still alive heralded his victories:

> New joy flashes over the world, the earth fills again with elation. Let glory be to Christ the King! New light bursts out from the sun, shines more bright than all the stars; it is unlike any other. Look how the enemy phalanxes fall! No enemy causes him to tremble; he scorns all those opposed to him. The palisades of the gentiles fell while the signs of the faithful were strengthened by you, Count of Barcelona, Prince of Aragon, Duke of Tortosa and King of Lleida, you have betook of the royal throne. The army of heaven should sing to God, since no human eloquence is sufficient. Let the court of heaven be opened by Christ! Oh what a wonder of God![104]

The metaphorical comparison of the count's appearance to the rising of a new sun might be compared to the withering of the landscape at the count's death described in the Ripoll *Planctus*. Other echoes between the texts created at Ripoll and those at Roda might also be identified, for instance, the common image of the count destroying serried ranks of the enemy (*falanges* in the Roda poem, *seras* in the *Planctus*), or the playful transformation of the triple title of prince-count-marquis.[105] Both institutions guarded the relics of men they deemed to be saints, whose sainthood was associated with the dynasty's past and with the reconquest, and both possessed unique traditions, one liturgical, the other literary, relating to the First Crusade. Hence it is not surprising to find that they competed for the appropriate *laudes comitis*.

Crisis of Crown and Crusade

In terms of collective expectation, papal admonition, dynastic precedent, and military necessity, the case of Alfonso II and the crusade in Spain is comparable

---

103. Carol Sweetenham and Linda Paterson, introduction to *Canso d'Antioca: An Occitan Epic Chronicle of the First Crusade* (Aldershot, UK, 2003), 17–24.

104. "Fulgent nova per orbem gaudia / nova mundum replet letitia/ unde Christo Regi sit gloria. / Novus solis emicat radius / nitens omni sidere clarius / cui non est similis alius / Cedunt ecce falanges hostium/ nullus pavet hostilem … / tempnit quisque sibi contrarium. / Tracta cadunt septies (septa) gentilium / solidantur signa fidelium / per te Chomes Barchinonensium. / Idem Princeps Aragonensium / Dux Tortosae, Rex Illerdensium / penetrasti regale solium. / … Psallat Deo celi milicia / Quod nequid humana facundia / Solvat Christo coelestis curia / O quam mira Dei." Dolores Porta, "El poema de Roda en honor de Ramón Berenguer IV," *Argensola* 44 (1960): 298.

105. The Roda poem transforms the prince–count–marquis into new titles associated with his conquests, the Ripoll *Epitafium* rechristens him the "king of peace, prince of justice, duke of truth and equity."

to that of the Angevin king Henry II and the crusades to the Holy Land. Like Henry, Alfonso was beset on numerous occasions by external wars, internal revolts, and the need to maintain his rule in regions separated from one another by a substantial geographic barrier, in the latter's case the Pyrenees. Like his Angevin counterpart, Alfonso's rule coincided with the descent of the Latin Kingdom of Jerusalem into crisis in the face of Saladin's conquests, and while he was never apparently encouraged to take the cross for the Holy Land, the effects of these defeats on the morale of all Latin Christians cannot be underestimated. Only a few years after the fall of Jerusalem, Christian powers in Spain were confronted by the emergence of a new threat, the North African Almohad dynasty, whose defeat of Alfonso VIII of Castile at Alarcos in 1195, the year before Alfonso's death, was in some ways comparable to the Christian defeat at Hattin in 1187.[106]

After the death of Ramón Berenguer IV in 1162, the launching of a new crusading offensive under the banner of Aragón-Catalonia was initially delayed by the ten-year minority of the new ruler, who did not end his "tutelage" under his father's seneschal William Ramón II Montcada and Archbishop William of Barcelona until he was knighted, at the age of sixteen, in January 1174.[107] It was of course not impossible for wars to be waged by the king's regents and nobles during his minority, and following the assertions of later medieval and early modern chroniclers, historians long assumed that near the end of his minority Alfonso did indeed lead major expeditions across the southern Aragonese frontier.[108] Between 1169 and 1172, there was undoubtedly fighting in the south, leading to the capture of some new territories and the establishment of new Christian settlements, such as Teruel, first founded in 1171. But it is unclear what role, if any, the boy-king or even his advisers, who had profited greatly from the campaigns waged by his father, were seen to have had in these campaigns. The cautious note sounded by Joaquín Miret i Sans regarding the actual extent and duration of these conquests may be supplemented with the observation that their real aim may not have been to take the beckoning prize of Valencia, but rather to exact *parias* payments from the Valencian ruler Ibn Mardanish, who found himself facing a much greater threat from the Almohads farther south.[109] *Fueros,* or

106. The seriousness of the defeat was noted by writers as far away as the Low Countries. *Genealogiae scriptoris Fusniacenses, MGH SS* 13: 256.

107. Shideler, *The Montcadas,* 107–113, citing (for the terms of the regency) *Viage literario* 19: 290–291, no. 30.

108. The claim is made in *The Chronicle of San Juan de la Peña,* 53–54. It is not cited in any of the chronicles written in Catalonia (at Ripoll) in the later Middle Ages. For commentary, see Bisson, "The Rise of Catalonia," 146 and n. 67.

109. Miret i Sans, "Itinerario del Rey Alfonso I," *Boletín de la Real Academia de Buenas Letras de Barcelona* 2 (1903): 268; O'Callaghan, *Reconquest and Crusade,* 51.

royal charters, might be granted to any new settlements that resulted from the border fighting, but they are not evidence of a concerted effort. No crusade bull was issued for the conquest of Valencia like the ones that had encouraged Ramón Berenguer IV and his supporters to take Tortosa.

It was only in 1179, five years after Alfonso had achieved his majority, that he was prepared to undertake a major campaign against Valencia. In the intervening time, the young ruler had concluded a marriage alliance with Castile by marrying Sancha, daughter of Alfonso VII, and then fought off an invasion by Sancho VI of Navarre. In 1179, Alfonso and his brother-in-law Alfonso VIII of Castile concluded the treaty of Cazola, which designated Denia and Jativa, as well as Valencia, as the targets of future Aragonese conquest.[110] Around the same time, Alfonso may even have mounted a small expedition against Murviedro.[111] But to the continuing threats from Navarre (and increasingly also Castile) was added the danger of open war between his brother Peter (also known as Ramón Berenguer), who held the county of Provence from him as a fief, and the powerful house of Toulouse. Intrigues associated with the latter conflict ultimately led to Peter's assassination in 1181 and necessitated direct intervention by the king in the unstable political world of Languedoc.[112]

Trouble was also brewing in the heartlands of Alfonso's realm. In his reconstruction of the attempts by Alfonso II to impose new, more centralized, bureaucratic, and impersonal forms of government on the nobility of Aragón-Catalonia, Thomas Bisson identifies a "crisis of Catalonia" beginning with the time of Alfonso's majority and lasting through the first decade of the reign of his son and successor, Peter II.[113] This crisis was essentially the king's failure to enforce either new royal statutes or the old *Usatges de Barcelona,* codified during the reign of his father, on a recalcitrant nobility. First in 1173 and then again in 1188 Alfonso attempted to promulgate and then enforce an "instituted peace" on his barons, but on both occasions his efforts failed. For Bisson, the resistance of the nobility to Alfonso's efforts represented principally a defense of the traditional rights and customs of the banal seigneurie against the encroachment of royal justice and vicarial enforcement. But Bisson also suggested that there may have been another element stirring discontent among the nobles, noting of the violence and discontent that followed

---

110. *Liber feudorum maior,* 1: 48–51, nos. 34 and 35.

111. Miret i Sans, "Itinerario," 409; Caruana, "Itinerario," 118, who notes that a charter for the Templars at Huesca in August provides the "unica correría contra moros que tenemos probaba documentalmente."

112. Abadal i Vinyals, "À propos de la 'domination,'" 315–345. Frederic Cheyette, *Ermengard of Narbonne,* 331.

113. Bisson, *The Crisis of the Twelfth-Century,* 499–514.

the first peace of 1173 that "two decades had passed since the lord-prince had led the barons in lucrative campaigns against the Muslims" and adding that the king's campaigns to restore Provence did not produce a "compensating frontier."[114] For those noble families, like the Montcadas and the counts of Urgell, that had reaped enormous profits from the many conquests of Ramón Berenguer IV, this period of peace may have come as a great disappointment.

It was this particular facet of Alfonso II's failure of lordship—his failure to lead a crusade as his father had done—that lay behind many of the barbed insults of one enemy, the troubadour Giraut del Luc. Giraut mocked what he presented as the king's overfamiliarity with both Muslims and Jews, alleging that he happily wore Jewish robes and spoke in friendly Arabic phrases "to those who confound God."[115] In a more serious accusation, he also suggested that Alfonso was undermining the work of reconquest itself, selling back the castle of Polpís, recently captured by the Templars, to its Muslim overlords:

> Happy are the men from beyond the Nile! Because their faith has such a noble supporter, the fief of their ancestors, which had been conquered by the Brothers, he sold back to them (but not for much considering the wealth that was there.) God! What joy is there in Valencia, because Polpís returns to the king of Morocco whose power mocks us? We have never seen more wickedness from the Jewish law, and Barbary rejoices.[116]

He returned to the sale of Polpís in another song, in which he compared the count-king unfavorably with his forebears:

> Great injustice comes to those who accuse him of anything, so I'll say that he never conquered Mediona by deception, nor robbed the merchants of Girona, nor took Polpís from the Templars of Ascalon. The king only carries crown and crozier on account of his ancestor, about whom everyone speaks.[117]

114. Bisson, *The Crisis of the Twelfth-Century,* 501.

115. "Li sarrazin de Fraga e d'Aytona / l'an enseignat cum entr'els si razona: / *salem alec,* volon que lor respona, / per *valica zalem,* cui Dieus confona; / mas bels arnes li presta Na Maimona / quan viest la çupa ab l'obra salamona." Martí de Riquer, "El trovador Giraut del Luc y sus poesías contra Alfonso II de Aragón," *Boletín de la Real Academia de Buenas Letras de Barcelona* 23 (1950): 238–240, and for an explanation of the anti-Jewish and anti-Muslim rhetoric, see n. 40.

116. "Gauch n'ant las gens d'outra.l Nil /car lor fai taut gen socors / c'us feus de lor ancessors / c'avion conquist li fraire / vendet, mas ges non pres gaire / vas q'era grans la ricors. / Dieus! Cal gaug n'ant part Valenssa, car Polpitz torn'en tenenssa / del rei marrochin, qui fai son esquern delai! / Et anc tant gran descrezenssa / non vim pois la leis ebraia / e Barbara.is n'apaia." Forey, *The Templars,* 26–27. For the Polpís incident, see discussion in Riquer, "El trovador," 217–220; and Forey, *The Templars,* 29.

117. "Mout fai fran tort qui de ren l'ochaisona c'anc ab engan non conquis Mediona, ni fetz raubar mercadiers a Girona, ni tolc Polpitz als templiers d'Escalona. / Aitals reis deu portar croz e corona / de part son avi, don totz lo mons rassona." Riquer, "El trovador," 238.

The terms and images employed in Giraut's political songs are important in that they openly contrast the kind of crusading conquest conducted by Alfonso's predecessors, his father Ramón Berenguer IV and his great-uncle Alfonso the Battler, who worked in concert with the Templars, with the war for *parias* and profit waged in the absence of crusading rhetoric in Iberia.[118] Living in harmony with Muslims, and entering into agreements with them, were seen to be in fundamental opposition to crusading ideology, and by sparing the Muslims in Spain, he was providing succor to their counterparts in the East whom the armies of the Third Crusade (1189–92) were at that moment engaging in desperate conflict.

A bizarre but nonetheless serious challenge to Alfonso's rule, which was likewise linked with criticism in the lyrics of the troubadours, was also founded on unfavorable comparisons between the count-king and his ancestors. In the winter of 1178–79, a man appeared claiming to be the long-dead Alfonso I "the Battler."[119] These events caused Alfonso II to dispatch his half brother Berenguer, the abbot of Montearagón (where the body of the real Alfonso I was buried), and the bishop of Lleida to Louis VII of France with a letter asking for the French king's assistance in apprehending the impostor, who by "plots and deceit" was causing a revolt within his kingdom. The letter carried by the bishop was written in a panicked voice, repeatedly expressing in the superlative the falsehood of the charlatan, who was manifestly *not* "king Alfonso my uncle," but just "some old man."[120] Given the delicate nature of the Aragonese-Catalonian union and the poor quality of the king's relations with his nobles, a contestation of the count-king's legitimacy is perhaps not surprising. But a later annalist writing on the Aragonese frontier gave a clear indication of the impostor's motives and the nature of his challenge:

> In Era 1219 (1181) there came a certain blacksmith and he said: "I am lord Alfonso, who captured Zaragoza and Calatayud and Daroca" and he was received in some places with great honour and with great ceremony. And he said many things which seemed to be true about the past and what he had done. He was captured by lord Alfonso [II] and

---

118. Alfonso's liberality was also compared unfavorably with his father's by his enemy Guillem de Berguedà. *Poesies de Guillem de Berguedà,* ed. Marti de Riquer (Barcelona, 1996), xxiii.2.10. "Reis, si fos vius lo pros coms, vostre paire/ non feira pas, per mil marcs de deniers/ la Marquesa far fondejar ni traire/ aissi cum faitz vos e vostres archiers."

119. Marcelin Defourneux, "Louis VII et les souverains Espagnols: L'enigme du 'Pseudo-Alphonse'," in *Estudios dedicados a Menéndez Pidal* (Madrid, 1950–62), 6: 647–661; Antonio Ubieto-Arteta and Federico Balguer Sánchez, "L'aparición del falso Alfonso el Batallador" and "Alusiones de los trovadores al Pseudo-Alfonso," *Argensola* 9 (1958): 29–47; Bisson, "The Rise of Catalonia," 146–147.

120. The letters were originally published in *RHGF* 15: 71, nos. 223 and 224.

afterwards it was known that it was not in fact him, and he was hanged with great dishonour before the city of Barcelona.[121]

What fueled the appearance of the rival king pseudo-Alphonso I in 1178–79 was the memory of the days of great conquests, and perhaps also a hope that those days might return. It was probably not irrelevant to the Battler's place in popular memory that Alfonso I, like his father and grandfather before him, had died in battle against the Muslims. A much later chronicler, commenting on the popular memory of the Battler, noted that while some believed he had died in battle before Fraga, others believed that following the battle he had undertaken a journey to Jerusalem, an idea that was probably generated by the king's attachment to the crusading military orders and the canons of the Holy Sepulchre.[122]

To Alfonso's critics, like Bertran de Born, the execution provided an easy metaphor for how the count-king had rejected the good rulership and traditions of his forebears: "He hanged his ancestor, and so he destroys himself and damns himself to hell." (*E pendet son ancessor / per qu.is destrui et enferna.*)[123] But in doing away with the impostor, was Alfonso trying to somehow erase or deny the past, or was he simply attempting to wrest control of the present?

To Secure a Triumph

By the late 1180s, Alfonso's struggles with his barons and the house of Toulouse began to ease as the lords of Provence and the Midi eventually submitted to his overlordship.[124] At the same time, both the dire situation in the Holy Land and the Almohad threat in Iberia inspired an energetic new pope, Clement III (r. 1187–91), to reanimate the crusading cause among the Spanish rulers. Crusading had probably never been far from the mind of Alfonso himself. Documentary evidence suggests that in 1185 the king staged an abortive siege of Valencia, accompanied by allies like Roger II Trencavel that he had won in his wars with the house of Toulouse.[125] He did not take the cross for the Third Crusade (he would not have been invited to do so), but in 1188, as the preparations for that expedition were well under way, he participated in the formal dedication of the foundation of the Hospitaller convent of Sigena by his wife, Sancha. Sancha claimed that her inspiration for

121. Antonio Floriano, "Fragmento de unos viejos anales (1089–1196)," *Boletín de la Real Academia de la Historia* 94 (1929): 153–154.

122. For the development of the legend, see Ubieto-Arteta and Sánchez, "La aparición," 30–32.

123. Bertran de Born, *The Poems*, 331; see Stablein, "Menace and Delight," 462.

124. Cabestany, "Alfons el Cast," 70.

125. Cheyette, *Ermengard of Narbonne,* 334–335 and n. 11.

founding and supporting the house had come from the frequent entreaties of a brother knight who had subsequently died at the battle of the Springs of Cresson—indelibly linking the house with contemporary anxieties about the course of the holy war at home and abroad.[126] By this time, news had arrived in Catalonia of the catastrophe at Hattin and the loss of Jerusalem, events recorded with great anxiety in the annals kept at Ripoll.

In the same year, Pope Clement dispatched a crusading bull to the Christians of Spain equating in the clearest possible terms the war in the peninsula with the struggle of the Third Crusade in the East and setting up similar systems for the collection of crusading tithes as were being deployed in England and France.[127] Two years later, the pope addressed a new version of the letter directly to Alfonso's subjects reminding them of the benefits he had offered, and pleading with them to assist the king in preparing for a crusade. In closing, he added a specific injunction to the people, nobles, and prelates to help them understand why it was important for their king to undertake the proposed expedition:

> And be diligent in carrying forward the persecution and extermination of the pagans, that he [Alfonso] might depart from you, and so that the same king of illustrious memory, by following in the footsteps of his ancestors, might return with the others with praise for the strength of his glorious deeds.[128]

This appeal to dynastic tradition, with its image of the king returning in triumph, is not found in other letters directed to the rulers of Spain.[129] The pope's message was personal, it pointed to the glorious path trodden by Alfonso's ancestors. The community best placed to lead the king down that path was Ripoll, and it is therefore not surprising that it was precisely at this moment that the monks began to gather together their songs and stories about the crusading past in order to shape a clear and urgent call for action.

It was probably during or shortly after Clement's pontificate that the monks of Ripoll began to copy a series of letters related to the dire situation

---

126. See García-Guijarro Ramos, "The Aragonese Hospitaller Monastery of Sigena," 119.

127. See O'Callaghan, *Reconquest and Crusade,* 57–58.

128. "uobis iterato mandamus et mandano precipimus, quatinus predictum regem in suo iamdicto proposito confirmetis et sic absque intermissione studeatis in persecutionem et exterminium paganorum inducere, ut et id uobis cedat in laudem et ipse rex illustris memorie pro genitorum suorum uestigiis inherendo, strenuitate suorum actum se ipsum reddat inter ceteros gloriosum." *Documentos de Montearagón,* 220–221, no. 135.

129. See, for instance, the lengthy crusading letter to Sancho of Navarre edited in Fidel Fita Colomé, "Bulas históricas del reino de Navarra en los postreros años del siglo XII," *Boletín de la Real Academia de la Historia* 26 (1895): 418–420 (no. 1).

that was unfolding in both the East and the West. The first was the letter written in Tarsus by the German contingent of the Third Crusade announcing the death of Frederick Barbarossa by drowning in the river Saleph as his armies crossed Anatolia.[130] Although the newsletter is a straightforward account of the emperor's sudden and unexpected death and does not have any apocalyptic overtones, it communicated the sense of urgency and even emergency in the state of affairs in the Holy Land. The second document, by contrast, is a thundering prophetic tract predicting a series of terrible calamities as a result of a rare conjunction of the planets in 1186. Apparently a translation of an originally Hebrew prophecy by an author known only as Johannes Toletanus, the 1186 letter was disseminated throughout the Latin West.[131] It has long been speculated that the text was seen to prophesy the victories of Saladin over the armies of Jerusalem.[132] But the version of the letter copied at Ripoll, which represents one of the earliest extant examples of the text, differs significantly from others in that it specifically predicts that the calamities will befall Muslims and Jews and will cause havoc, disorder, and the end of their religion:

> The greatest imaginable war will come about, and there will be an effusion of blood as an unbroken flood in the lands of the East and likewise in parts of the West, and doubt and ignorance will fall among the Jews and Saracens. And thus they will leave the inner sanctums of the synagogues and mosques, and thus their belief will be destroyed... by God's labors.[133]

---

130. "Italienische Quellen über die Taten Kaiser Friedrichs I," in *Italien und der Brief über den Kreuzzug Kaiser Friedrichs I,* ed. and trans. Franz-Josef Schmale, Ausgewählte Quellen zur deutschen Geschichte des Mittelalters, Freiherr vom Stein-Gedächtnisausgabe 17a (Darmstadt, 1986), 372–382.

131. Dorothea Weltecke, "Die Konjunktion der Planeten im September 1186: Zum Ursprung einer globalen Katastrophenangst," *Saeculum* 54 (2003): 179–212; my thanks to Charles de Miramon for pointing out several useful works on this letter. Richard Southern, "Aspects of the European Tradition of Historical Writing: History as Prophecy," in *History and Historians: Selected Papers of R. W. Southern,* ed. R. J. Bartlett (Oxford and Malden, MA, 2004), 57. Since the tenth century Ripoll had been a leading center for the production and dissemination of astronomical and astrological works. See Gemma Puigvert i Planagumà, *Astronomia i astrologia al Monestir de Ripoll: Edició i estudi dels manuscrits científics astronomico astrològics del Monestir de Santa Maria de Ripoll* (Bellaterra, 2000), 27–38.

132. See Hermann Grauert, "Meister Johann von Toledo," *Sitzungsberichte der Königlichen Bayerischen Akademie der Wissenschaften* (1901): 111–325; for the continuing significance of the letter into the thirteenth century, see Fritz Baer, "Eine jüdische Messiasprophetie auf das Jahr 1186 und der dritte Kreuzzug," *Monatsschrift für Geschichte und Wissenschaft des Judetums* (1926): 113–122. For the best summation of the sense of apocalyptic anxiety that had fallen over the West at this time, see Robert of Auxerre, *Chronicon,* ed. Oliver Holder-Egger, *MGH SS* 26: 249.

133. "ostendens maximum futurum bellum et effusione sanguinis perpetue fluvium in terra orientis et similiter in parte occidentis et cadet dubietatis et ignorantia inter iudeos et sarracenos. donec relinquit penitus sinagogis et mehumerias. et eorum secta ... nisu dei anullabitur." BNF, MS Lat. 5132, f. 106.

The third document copied by the Ripoll monks in this period was a let-ter of a pope "Clement" (presumably Clement III) addressed to the "king of France and to all the prelates of the Church." This letter, unknown outside of the copy made at Ripoll, is likewise a prophetic warning to all Christians that Saint Paul has appeared in Rome on Laetare Sunday, foretelling that "the Lord will come and with him his sword to strike down those who do not know him and subject all the nations to divine vengeance and the anger of the Almighty" and that "on the day of the Ascension the anger of the Lord will rise over the people of Jerusalem, and *stone will not be left on stone* [Mark 13:2] in the cities of the wicked."[134] The Sunday on which the vision was said to have occurred was the fourth Sunday in Lent, known for its Introit *Laetare Iherusalem*. In the twelfth century, the day was associated with the Feast of the Liberation of Jerusalem, with which it shared liturgical elements. It was also the day that Frederick I had chosen to hold his "Court of Jesus Christ," at which he initiated recruitment and preparations for the Third Crusade.[135]

A Guide to Victory

The three letters comprising this doom-laden dossier can today all be found in a single composite codex, Paris, Bibliothèque nationale de France, MS Lat. 5132. The codex (described in appendix 3) contains four distinct col-lections of texts, all written in hands of the twelfth and thirteenth centuries. It is not known exactly how these collections may originally have been configured; one of them (part 3: ff. 82–93) was probably added by Étienne Baluze, the secretary of Pierre de Marca who was responsible for moving manuscripts from Ripoll to Paris in the seventeenth century. Three of the collections, however, are unmistakably the products of the Ripoll scripto-rium. The extraordinary range of material found in these three collections would typically classify them as "miscellaneous," but the process by which they were developed is very similar, as is the nature of some of the mate-rial they came to encompass. It is possible that these three collections were originally part of one book, but even if they were not, they reveal a concern on the part of the monks of Ripoll, beginning in the later twelfth century, with the accumulation of texts associated with celebration, commemora-tion, and holy war.

---

134. See appendix 4.
135. For the significance of *Laetare Iherusalem* Sunday in the crusader period, see Sylvia Schein, *Gateway to the Heavenly City: Crusader Jerusalem and the Catholic West (1099–1187)* (Aldershot, UK, 2005), 116.

The three collections were formed around parts of three different twelfth-century fragments. The three core texts are, first, a narrative of the conquest of Jerusalem by the First Crusade that is accompanied by the liturgy for the Feast of the Liberation of Jerusalem (ff. 1–25); next, the *Altercatio,* between Athanasius and Arius (ff. 26–81); and finally, the *Life* of the saintly prince Peter Orseolo (ff. 94–110v). The Ripoll scribes filled their blank spaces and unused folios with texts relating to the dynasty, including the *Gesta comitum Barcinonensium,* a poem about the life of the adventurer Rodrigo Diaz de Vivar (El Cid), and the letter concerning the death of Frederick Barbarossa. A final section of new material included the abbot Gausfred's instructions for the celebrations of special *refecciónes,* the folios denoting the lands given to the abbey by Ramón Berenguer IV in return for his burial at the monastery and his instruction for the celebration of his anniversary, and the *Planctus* in his memory. The *Planctus* was accompanied, on the last folio of the manuscript, by simple musical notation, anticipating future performance. It shares its single side of vellum with another hymn, arguably one of the greatest Latin verse compositions of the twelfth century, Hildebert of Lavardin's song on the Trinity, *Alpha et Omega, magne Deus.*[136] Two other hymns to the Virgin and one to the Trinity were also included, accompanied by musical notation. In addition, the copyists filled an entire side of vellum with a piece of sophisticated musical technology, polyphonic *conductus* beginning: *Cedit frigus hiemale.* This paraliturgical celebratory song invokes at once the coming of summertime, the "triumphal cross through which man is liberated from death," and the suffering of Christ at the hands of the Jews.[137]

The extraordinary project of remembering, collecting, copying, and creating to which the miscellaneous codex bears witness has led some observers to see it as a direct expression of the abbey's distinct character, a codicological equivalent of the complex sea of images carved on Ripoll's great western portal in the early 1170s, or as a marker of Ripoll's success in its struggle for independence from Saint-Victor of Marseilles, which was achieved in some measure in 1171.[138] The collection undoubtedly reflects the abbey's long tradition as a cultural center and would probably have been impossible with-

---

136. This hymn was also in use by the Augustinians of Toulouse in the twelfth century; see *Manuscrits de la Bibliothèque de Toulouse,* ed. Auguste Molinier (Paris, 1883), 94 (description of MS 162, f. 74v); *Lateinische Hymnen des Mittelalters,* ed. Franz-Joseph Mone (Freiburg, 1853–55), 1:24–20, no. 11.

137. For the music at Ripoll in regional context, see Higini Anglés, *Música a Catalunya fins al segle XIII* (Barcelona, 1935), 252–260. Anglés dates *Cedit frigus* in the Ripoll MS to the early thirteenth century but nonetheless associates it with Alfonso's reign.

138. The abbey's campaign for independence is chronicled in a series of papal letters once preserved in the abbey's archive that are now known only through the summaries and transcriptions of Roque de Olzinellas. See *Papsturkunden in Spanien I,* 120–125.

out the efforts of the abbot Gausfred, to whose leadership we should probably look for Ripoll's twelfth-century renaissance and ultimate independence
from Marseilles. But the form and nature of the materials that were included
in the collection and their close juxtaposition with one another suggest a
more specific purpose or unifying theme girding the collection together.

The materials in the manuscript anticipated a celebration of victory, a
triumph, like the ones promised in the letter of Clement III to the people of
Aragón. The prophetic texts foretold that the critical time for a great battle
had come; events in the East and Saint Paul's message in Rome underlined
both the seriousness of the situation and the assuredness of victory over the
unbelievers. The dynastic history and the *Planctus* for Ramón Berenguer
provided the examples of past generations, the obligation to fulfill tradition,
and the reminder of what was possible. The music, the customs, and instructions for feasts prepared the way for the commemorations that would follow
as the ruler fulfilled his dynastic destiny. As the editors of the *Gesta comitum
Barcinonensium* have noted, the monks who compiled the manuscript also left
plenty of blank space, for instance at the end of the dynastic history, for the
continuation of the dynasty's glorious story and the incorporation of new
texts recording the victory that they were sure was soon to follow.[139]

Triumph Deferred

After the death of Clement III in 1191, Celestine III (r. 1191–98), who
had earlier in his career (as Cardinal Hyacinth) served as papal legate to the
Crown of Aragón under both Ramón Berenguer IV and Alfonso II, struggled
to make peace between the Spanish sovereigns and to make possible a crusade expedition. He wrote to the military orders, enjoining them to assist
the sovereigns, and then, in 1193, directly to Alfonso himself, praising him
for his zealous devotion, but complaining that some Christian powers were
still engaging in truces with the Muslims and thereby hampering efforts at
a united front.[140] In December 1194, perhaps considering an expedition to
be imminent, Alfonso drew up his testament. Second only to his final resting place of Poblet, the greatest beneficiaries in Alfonso's testament were
the crusading orders of the Hospital and the Temple.[141] As was customary

---

139. *GCB*, xiii. For another, absolutely contemporary example of this practice, see Adam Kosto,
"*The Liber Feudorum maior* of the Counts of Barcelona: The Cartulary as an Expression of Power,"
Journal of Medieval History 27 (2001): 1–22.

140. *Documentos de Montearagón,* 223–224, no. 148.

141. Assessing the exact value of Alfonso's gifts to Poblet, the Hospital, the Temple, and Ripoll is
difficult, since all three were in land, but the special value attached to them may have been implicit
in the decision to assign them all rights and lordships in perpetuity instead of gold.

among all who hoped to enter confraternity with the brothers of the Temple *post mortem,* he made the symbolic gift of all of his arms and armor together with "a good horse."[142] Following the crusading cause of the military orders came Rome, where Alfonso made donations of silver and gold chalices to the churches of Saint Peter and Saint Paul in addition to providing the pope with gold to ornament his chapel.

If Alfonso could imagine how the gold of his Spanish *morabetinos* would look ornamenting the chapel of Celestine III, his imagination became more vivid as his gaze turned even farther eastward to Jerusalem. In his gifts to the holy sites in Jerusalem, Alfonso revealed how the holy geography of the East was linked to that of his own domains, and to the possibility of future crusades:

> I leave to the church of the Holy Sepulchre of the Lord, through the hands of the prior and convent of the Sepulchre, after the death of Dalmacius of Palol, the *villa* of Palafrugell and the *villa* of Lofredo with all appurtenances in order to support five priests: one at the great high altar as leader, another before the altar of the Sepulchre of the Lord, another before the altar of the Virgin Mary in Josaphat, another before the altar of the Nativity in Bethlehem. Until such a time as the land of Jerusalem should, by the grace of the Holy Spirit, be recaptured by the Christians, those priests should be maintained by my executors in the churches dedicated to the Holy Sepulchre that lie in my own lands.[143]

Later in his testament, Alfonso returned to those same altars where he envisioned his priests one day saying masses, endowing each altar with chalices of silver and gold.[144]

In July 1195, with the Spanish monarchs still failing to agree to a peace between them, Alfonso VIII of Castile foolishly took the field on his own against the Almohad commander Abu Yusuf Yaqab al-Mansur near Alarcos.

---

142. On the ritual and practical significance of the transfer of arms to the Temple, see Jochen Schenk, "Forms of Lay Association with the Templars," *Journal of Medieval History* 34 (2008): 82.

143. "Dimitto ecclesie Sancti Dominici sepulcri villam de Palafrugello et villam de Lofredo, post obitum Dalmacii de Palaciolo cum suis terminis et pertinenciis, ad stabiliendum per manum prioris et conventu sepulcri v sacerdotes imperpetuum: unus ante altare maius in capite, alium ante altare Dominici Sepulcri, alium ante altare Sancte Crucis, alium ante altare Virginis Marie in valle Josaphat, alium ante altare Nativitatis in Bethleem, qui utique sacerdotes stabiliantur a predictis manumissoribus meis per ecclesias Sepulcri in terra mea de redditibus predicatarum villarum usque dum terra Iherosilimitana per graciam Sancri Spiritus a christianis sit recuperata." *Els testaments dels comtes de Barcelona,* 107–108; *Alfonso II Rey de Aragón,* 810. A "Dalmace of Palol" (*Dalmacius de Palaciolo*) appears in Alfonso's fiscal documents and may have held an administrative position. See Bisson, *The Fiscal Accounts of Catalonia under the Early Count-Kings,* 186, 191.

144. *Testaments dels comtes de Barcelona,* 110; *Alfonso II Rey de Aragón,* 813.

By nightfall, 18 July, the Castilian army had been annihilated, and many nobles and bishops lay dead. As the news of Hattin had shocked Henry II of England and his sons, word of what had happened at Alarcos was deeply distressing to Alfonso II and the other Spanish monarchs and prelates. In the aftermath of the battle, it was the count-king who took the initiative. Following the itinerary reconstructed by Antonio Ubieto Arteta, one month after the battle Alfonso visited the site where Alfonso I had founded the confraternity of Belchite, the first military order in Spain, and confirmed the possessions of its new masters, the Templars.[145] By October, while in Jaca, to the north of Huesca, he made a gift of the chapel of Saint Nicholas in the royal palace of Huesca to Montearagón, reaffirming that institution's association with his dynasty and its authority within the royal court. In the next month, he traveled south to Zaragoza, where he confirmed the rights of the Hospitallers to one-fifth of the spoils of conquest from the Muslims. Then he set off on a pilgrimage to Santiago de Compostela.

The purpose of this pilgrimage was explained by the monks of Ripoll in a continuation of the *Gesta comitum Barcinonensium,* which, although it was written after Alfonso's death, was still recorded with the other miscellaneous materials they had prepared for his triumph:

> Since there was still at that time discord between all of the kings of Spain, the aforesaid Alfonso, who was prescient in all good things, conceived in his heart to visit the shrine of Saint James and to call together all of the other kings in the vicinity to him one by one, so that a pact of friendship might be made between them in order to combat the Agarenes. In carrying out this proposal he was peaceably and honourably received by those kings and by all those magnates in their territories, and thus he led them, with the greatest nobility and strength, through his kingdom. By divine will, he joined with certain of the kings in a pact of love; others he was unable to bring together even with the greatest and best acts.[146]

To the monks, the king's intentions had been right, and his strategy sensible. By beginning his crusade with a pilgrimage to Compostela, he was following in the footsteps not of his immediate predecessors, but of Charlemagne, the very font of legitimate authority himself. It was the Charlemagne of the *Historia Turpini,* the text copied in the Ripoll scriptorium in 1173, who first combined the way of Saint James with the crusade, and Alfonso, in anticipa-

---

145. Antonio Ubieto-Arteta, "La peregrinación de Alfonso II de Aragón a Santiago de Compostela," *Estudios de la Edad Media de la Corona de Aragón* 5 (1952): 438–452.

146. *GCB,* 14–15.

tion of his own triumphal conquests, had followed suit. Unfortunately for the count-king, the other Spanish sovereigns were not forthcoming with their aid. Within a year of his return from his failed bid for Christian unity, Alfonso was dead. He had not, as he had hoped twenty-five years earlier, conquered Valencia, and so his body was buried at Santa Maria de Poblet. The shift in burial practice was decisive: no member of the count-king's family would be buried at Ripoll again. For the dynasty, and the abbey that had so assiduously constructed a crusading future from the family's past, triumph was deferred.

In the case of the dynasty, the deferral was only temporary. On 16 July 1212, Alfonso's son Peter II, together with his father's quarrelsome colleagues Alfonso VIII of Castile and Sancho VII of Navarre, won an overwhelming victory against an Almohad force at Las Navas de Tolosa. It was the beginning of a new century of crusading for Alfonso's heirs, the count-kings of Aragón-Catalonia, which would see nearly all of the eastern coastline of the Iberian Peninsula, together with the Balearic Islands, conquered and consolidated as possessions of the Crown.

Ripoll was not, as far as we know, the site of any victory celebrations; what survives from its library does not indicate further interest in triumphal liturgies or elegiac commemorative song. Because no crowned head rested within its cloister, Ripoll would not be favored as a "royal abbey," as would Cistercian Poblet and Santes Creus and Hospitaller Sigena. But in other ways, Ripoll may be seen to have succeeded. In the thirteenth and fourteenth centuries, Ripoll also continued to flourish as a center of other types of cultural production, in both Latin and the vernacular. The abbey's scriptorium produced several heavily glossed copies of the *Alexandreis* of Walter of Chatillon, and the monks may also have been responsible for the fourteenth-century *chansonnier* kept in their library.[147] Ripoll's interest in the Alexander legend, copied and glossed while the knights of Catalonia conquered and ruled parts of Greece, suggests an ongoing preoccupation with the continuing crusading effort in Iberia and beyond, as does its copy of a collection of crusade sermons by Bertrand de La Tour and possession of a description of the Holy Land from the mid-fourteenth century.[148] After 1200, royal patronage presumably depended on the cultural output of the monastery, which maintained its relevance to the count-king and the court. But Ripoll's life as a prestigious

147. Lola Badia, *Poesia catalana del secolo XIV: Edicio i estudi del Cançoneret de Ripoll* (Barcelona, 1983).

148. ACA, MS Ripoll 187. For the sermons, see Christoph T. Maier, *Crusade Propaganda and Ideology: Model Sermons for the Preaching of the Cross* (Cambridge, 2000), 78. For the description of the Holy Land pilgrimage, see Lluis Cifuentes i Comamala, *La ciència en català a l'Edat Mitjana i el Renaixement,* 2nd ed. (Barcelona, 2006), 259.

necropolis was not over. In the blank spaces of various folios from Ripoll's triumphal commemorative manuscript we find charters demonstrating the abbey's continued vitality as a landowner and as a commemorative community. On the reverse of the folio containing the funeral elegies for Ramón Berenguer IV, for instance, we find a charter of the bailiff of the royal palace, Bernard of Dons, electing for burial at Ripoll in 1218.[149]

Most importantly, however, through at least the middle of the fourteenth century, the abbey did not lose its reputation as a preeminent site of dynastic commemoration and cultural production. Neither the manuscript nor the dynastic history of the counts included in the manuscript compiled in anticipation of the triumph of Alfonso II was abandoned, but rather continued until the end of the reign of James I (d. 1276). James himself acknowledged the special significance of the abbey when, on 11 July 1270, he forgave the monks the repayment of debts to the Jews of Besalú and Puigcerda specifically because "the monastery of Ripoll was founded and constructed by our predecessors and many of the bodies of our ancestors have been buried in the same monastery."[150] When vernacular historiography began to flourish at the court of James I and his son Peter III, it was to the monks of Ripoll that chroniclers such as Bernat Desclot turned for their materials. The abbey's reputation as the premier site of dynastic commemoration continued into the reign of Peter IV "the Ceremonious," who ordered the monks to assemble materials for a new dynastic history.[151] In 1366, we find the king angrily writing to the abbey to demand the return of his journal, which the monks may have borrowed to continue their historiographical work.[152] Throughout this time, however far the count-kings' crusading ambitions ranged, to Sicily, Athens, or Africa, they did not forget the monks of Ripoll, who guarded the story of the origins and formation of their crusading past.

---

149. f. 110v. See appendix 3 below.

150. "Cum monasterium rivipollense fuerit per predecessares nostros fundatum et constructum et multa corpora nostrorum predecessorum in ipso monasterio honorabiliter sint sepulta." Joaqim Miret i Sans, *Itinerari de Jaume I el Conqueridor* (Barcelona, 1918; repr., 2007 with prologue by Maria Teresa Ferrer I Mallol), 505.

151. Nelson, *The Chronicle of San Juan de la Peña*, xiv. Aurell, "From Genealogies to Chronicles," 249–251, attributes the lasting influence of the *Gesta comitum* to its effective genealogical form.

152. For the letter, see Amédée Pagès, "Recherches sur la chronique Catalane attribuée á Pierre IV d'Aragón," *Romania* 18 (1889): 238–239 n. 3.

Epilogue

Henry II of England and Alfonso II of Aragón had a great deal in common. Both men were born with the hopes of accession to royal crowns, a dignity claimed, in both cases, by right of their maternal ancestry. Even when both did accede to these weighty honors, however, they could not ignore the legacies of their fathers, through whom both traced their lineage back to adventurers of the Carolingian age. But in neither case was the nobility of paternal ancestry associated wholly with the distant past. Of increasing significance during the course of their reigns was the fact that their ancestors had taken the cross as crusaders and had led successful crusade expeditions.

Both Alfonso and Henry received appeals from within their lands and from outside to lead crusades. In those appeals, their crusading ancestry played a dominant role. Papal missives to both men mentioned the achievements of crusading forebears and encouraged them to follow in the footsteps (*vestigia subsequere* or *inherere*) of these earlier crusaders. This kind of imagery, as we saw in chapter 1, was, for noblemen who came of age in the middle of the twelfth century, deeply enmeshed in the very concept of nobility itself, and in particular with the sense of responsibility that was shared among lords from across the West to uphold the worthiness, or *probitas*, of earlier generations.

Henry and Alfonso were itinerant rulers, and their ceaseless circuit of princely wandering took them through landscapes rich with objects, ceremonies, and textual traditions of poetry and prose that linked them to the crusading past, to their ancestors, and to Jerusalem. The presence of these souvenirs, and the continuing relationships between the rulers and the communities that guarded them, help us to understand why the calls to take the cross could not simply be ignored. The importance of the dynastic crusading past is underlined by the fact that monks from two communities, Marmoutier in the Touraine and Ripoll in Catalonia, attempted to use the figure of the crusading ancestor as part of sophisticated programs intended to reconfigure the political identity of their lords. For the two old Benedictine abbeys, following in the footsteps of worthy crusading ancestors was one way to redefine their lords in the image of their forebears, the counts of Anjou and Catalonia. Even if the ultimate aim of these strategies was to attract attention and ensure continued patronage for the monks, by helping their count-kings see themselves as royal count-crusaders, they nonetheless had potentially far-reaching implications for the political identity of the Angevin empire and the Crown of Aragón-Catalonia.

Both men died without having acquitted themselves of the crusading responsibilities that were seen as incumbent on them. There is good reason to believe, however, that in the northern as in the southern case, the discourse of family crusading tradition that had manifested itself in poetry, history, and ceremony was not without result. Where Henry and Alfonso had faltered, their sons and successors would find spectacular success. Richard I of England and Peter II of Aragón would lead major crusade campaigns in 1190 and 1212 respectively, both achieving success and lasting fame for their accomplishments. It is tempting to look at them as evidence for the persistence of family memory, which, if correctly cultivated, would result in long-lasting traditions of active participation in crusade campaigns.

The apparent endurance of crusading enthusiasm in these two families at the dawning of the thirteenth century, however, may obscure the fact that some things were also changing. Most notably, after the first quarter of the thirteenth century, the age of the great dynastic narrative works devoted to the lineage of noble families was over. Aside from the short works that continued to be written for the descendants of founders of religious houses, and with the exception of the much later narratives written at Parcé for the lords of Matheflon and at Foucarmont for the counts of Eu, new productions tended to be purely genealogical and nonnarrative. Noticeably absent are the dynamic household religious chroniclers like Lambert of Ardres and Gislebert of Mons and their anonymous colleagues in Amboise, Anjou, Normandy, Thuringia, and Bavaria. Gone are the days when dynastic historical narratives were busily circulated between monasteries, chapels, and collegiate churches, so much the better to intercept the itinerant lords and their families.

At the same time, the language of ancestral crusading efforts and the vestiges of crusading ancestors that we find in use during the reigns of Henry and Alfonso cannot be found in the general letters of Pope Innocent III (r. 1198–1216). While Innocent, as we saw in chapter 1, was the pope who codified the idea that a crusader's votive obligations were hereditable, his vision of the crusade was far grander and more complex than his predecessors. For Innocent, the crusade encompassed not just the nobility but all of Christian society, and it was grounded in pragmatic concerns like fundraising. In the wake of Innocent's pontificate, troubadours might still sing to their aristocratic audiences of family obligations, but the mendicant friars who were trained to preach the cross to a wider audience do not seem to have adopted noble lineage and crusading ancestry, subjects that might have alienated some of their listeners, as major themes for their sermons.

Nobility itself was also changing. Avatars of noble conduct, among which ancestors may have been the most important, lost some of their significance as the ideal forms of conduct in the noble *habitus* were codified in guides of chivalric behavior and in ever more elaborately crafted works of romance literature, to which the guides were closely related. The places where noble conduct in the form of chivalric behavior and courtly manners was learned and performed also shifted toward new centers of cultural influence: the royal courts. The growth of increasingly powerful and centralized monarchies in England and France had profound effects on the regional aristocracies. In the first quarter of the thirteenth century the nobility of Anjou, Flanders, and Catalonia (lands where, as we have seen, ancestral discourses of crusading flourished) were all violently subjected to the power of the Capetian dynasty and northern French political influence more generally. The thirteenth century would see, in the career of King Louis IX of France, the clearest expression of crusading as a royal and even a "national" responsibility. Although by no means running counter to earlier crusading ideology, changes in aristocratic spiritual predilections also occurred in the same period, signaled by Henry and Alfonso's choices for burial in reformed monastic communities. Cistercians and Franciscans, it seems, were generally less interested in writing dynastic histories.

The decline in the writing of new family histories did not mean, however, that the nobility of this new age was any less concerned about its ancestry. Heraldry, elaborate tomb monuments, and the proliferation of genealogies in the later Middle Ages testify to the contrary. Crusading ancestors were no less important to John of Joinville, the lords of Pecche, and the earls of Warwick in the fourteenth and fifteenth centuries than they had been to the families of Ardres and Amboise in the twelfth. As the living memory of twelfth-century crusading slipped away and was replaced by literary imagination and chivalric pageantry, a new crusading era, born in the aftermath of the Third Crusade, began, populated by new heroes who fought in new landscapes.

As the memories of the earlier crusaders faded or were transformed, however, the mechanisms that noble families had developed in this earlier period—the vibrant, living traditions based on storytelling and memorabilia that would preserve and celebrate the memories of their crusading forebears, give the same cyclical form to the ebb and flow of successive generations and expeditions, and rescue from oblivion those lost on the distant frontiers—continued. It was at least partly due to the efficiency and durability of these mechanisms that the nobility remained the lifeblood of the crusade movement long after royal governments and broader Christian society considered crusades impracticable and undesirable. In memory and in action, the nobility kept crusading alive.

🐌 APPENDIX 1 Dynastic Narratives and Crusading Memory

NOBLE FAMILY	NARRATIVE TEXT	AUTHOR	DATE	PATRON/ DEDICATEE	EDITION
1	Amboise†				
	Gesta Ambaziensium dominorum‡	Anon., probably canon of Saint-Florentin of Amboise	c. 1153		*CCA*, 74–132
	Liber de compositione castri Ambaziae‡	Anon., probably canon of Saint-Florentin of Amboise	c. 1150		*CCA*, 1–24
2	Angoulême†				
	Historia pontificum et comitum Engolismensium‡	Anon.	c. 1159		Boussard (1957)
3	Anjou†				
	[Chronicle of Fulk le Réchin] *Fragmentum historiae Andegavensis + Gesta Andegavensium peregrinorum*‡	Fulk IV le Réchin, Count of Anjou	1096x1098		*CCA*, 232–246; *RHC Oc* c. 5: 345–347; see Paul, "The Chronicle of Fulk le Réchin" (2007)
	Chronica de gestis consulum Andegavorum	Anon.	1109	Fulk V of Anjou† (?)	*CCA*, 25–73
	Chronica de gestis consulum Andegavorum (Redactions)	Thomas, prior of Notre-Dame of Loches, household chaplain	c. 1150		
	Chronica de gestis consulum Andegavorum (Redactions)‡	Robin (unknown) and Breton of Amboise, probably canon of Saint-Florentin of Amboise	c. 1150–72		*CCA*, 25–73, in notes
	Chronica de gestis consulum Andegavorum (Redaction 3+4)‡	John, monk of Marmoutier (OSB)	1172–73	Henry II of England†	*CCA*, 25–73, in notes
4	Austria†				
	Breve chronicon Austriae Mellicensis‡	Anon., monks of Melk (OSB)	1177–94	Leopold VI of Austria†	*MGH SS* 24: 69–71
5	Barcelona†				
	Gesta comitum Barcinonensium (redaccio primitiva)‡	Anon., monks of Ripoll (OSB)	1162–84	Alfonso II of Aragón-Catalonia† (?)	Barrau Dihigo and Massó Torrents (1925)

(Continued)

	NOBLE FAMILY	NARRATIVE TEXT	AUTHOR	DATE	PATRON/DEDICATEE	EDITION
6	Bogen†	De advocatis Altahensis‡	Herman, abbot of Niederaltaich	c. 1273		MGH SS 17: 373–376
7	Brabant†	Chronica de origine ducum Brabantiae‡	Anon., monk(s) of Afflighem	1294–1312		MGH SS 25: 405–413
8	Crispin†	"Miraculum quod Beata Maria subvenit Guillelmo Crispino senior—ubi de nobili Crispinorum genere agitur"‡	Milo Crispin, monk of Bec	c. 1149		PL 150, cols. 735–744
9	Eu†	Chronique des comtes d'Eu‡	Anon., monk(s) of Foucarmont (Cit.)	1390	Philip of Artois:	RHGF 23: 439–448
10	Flanders†	Genealogiae comitum Flandriae‡	Lambert, canon of St. Omer; Anon., monk of Saint-Bertin (OSB)	1120, cont.–1128		MGH SS 11: 308–313
		Flandria generosa (numerous redactions and continuations)‡	Anon., monks of Saint-Bertin, Marchiennes (OSB), Hasnon (OSB), Ghisle, Clairmarais (Cit.)	1164, cont.–1194, 1214		MGH SS 11: 313–334
11	Guines+Ardres†	Historia comitum Ghisnensium‡	Lambert, priest of Ardres (magister)	c. 1206	Arnold II of Guines†	MGH SS 24: 550–642
12	Hainaut–Flanders†	Chronicon Hanoniense‡	Gilbert, prévot of Saint-Waudru, chancellor of Hainault	1197	Baldwin IX of Flanders, VI of Hainaut (?)†	Vanderkindere (1904)
13	Huntingdon–Northampton†	"De Juditha Uxore Waldevi comitis," in Vita et passio Waldevi comitis‡	Anon., monk of Crowland, w/ Ingulphe, abbot of Crowland and notes of Orderic Vitalis, monk of Saint-Evroult (?)	c. 1200		Michel (1836)
14	Mandeville†	Liber de Fundacione cenobii de Waldena‡	Anon., monk(s) of Walden	c. 1203		Greenway and Watkiss (1999)

	NOBLE FAMILY	NARRATIVE TEXT	AUTHOR	DATE	PATRON/ DEDICATEE	EDITION
15	**Mark**	*Chronica comitum de Marka*	Levold of Northoff, canon of Liége	1357–58		*MGH Rerum Germanicarum scriptores, nova series 6*
16	**Mathefelon†**	*Chronique de Parcé*	Gregory, priest of Saint Paul of Parcé	(s. xiii?)		de Berranger (1953)
		[First continuation]‡	Joseph, priest of Saint Paul of Parcé and John, priest of Saint Martin of Parcé	1323–55	Fulk of Mathe-flon, bishop of Angers (preached the crusade, 1333)	
17	**Nevers†**	*Origo et brevis historia Nivernensium comitun*‡	Hugh of Poitiers, monk of Vézelay (OSB)	1160		CCCM 42
18	**Normandy†**	*De moribus et actis primorum Normannorum ducum*	Dudo, canon of Saint-Quentin	c. 1015		Lair (1865)
		Gesta Normannorum ducum	William, monk of Jumièges	c. 1070		Van Houts (1992–95)
		Gesta Normannorum ducum (Redaction)‡	Orderic Vitalis, monk of Saint-Evroult	1109–14		Van Houts (1992–95)
		Gesta Normannorum ducum (Redaction)‡	Robert of Torigny, monk of Le Bec (OSB)	c. 1139		Van Houts (1992–95)
		Roman de Rou‡	Wace, canon of Rouen (*magister, clerc lisant*)	1160–73	Henry II of England†	Holden (2002)
		Chroniques des ducs de Normandie	Benoît of Sainte-Maure, canon of Tours(?)	1172–89	Henry II of England†	Fahlin (1951–67)
19	**Ribagorça† Pallars**	[Chronicles of Alaón]‡	Anon., monks of Santa Maria i Sant Pere d'Alaón (OSB)	1072–1154		Abadal i de Vinyals (1955)

NOBLE FAMILY	NARRATIVE TEXT	AUTHOR	DATE	PATRON/ DEDICATEE	EDITION
20 Thuringia†	De ortu principum Thuringiae‡	Anon., monks of Reinhardsbrunn (OSB)	c. 1227		Tebruck (2001)
	Historia Reinhardsbrunnensis‡	Anon., household cleric of Herman I of Thuringia (?)	1198–c. 1217		MGH SS 30: 542–588
21 Vendôme	Origo comitum Vindocinensium	Anon.	c. 1068		RHGF 11:31
22 Warenne (Surrey)†	Chronica monasterii de Hida juxta Wintonam‡	Eustace of Boulogne, chaplain of King Stephen and chancellor of William IV of Warenne	1157–59	William IV and Isabelle of Warenne?	Edwards (1866)
23 Welf (Bavaria and Saxony)†	Historia Welforum‡	Anon., household cleric of Welf VI	1167–74	Welf VI†	König (1938)
	Chronicae principum Brunsvicensium fragmentum	Anon.	c. 1277		MGH SS 30.1, 22–26

† indicates known crusading activity by family/individual
‡ indicates references to crusading in text

	NOBLE FAMILY	NARRATIVE TEXT	AUTHOR	DATE	PATRON/DEDICATEE	EDITION
1	Avesnes†	*Chronicon Laetiense*‡	Anon., monk of Avesnes (OSB), member of Walcourt family?	c. 1206		*MGH SS* 14: 487–502
2	Champagne (var. families)†	*Chronica*‡	Alberic, monk of Trois Fontaines (O. Cist.)	1227–51		*MGH SS* 23: 631–950
3	Courtenay	*Fundationis et fundatorum coenobio*	Anon., monk(s) of Ford (O. Cist.)	c. 1340		*MA* 5: 377–82
4	Limousin (var. families)†	*Chronicon*‡	Geoffrey, prior of Vigeois (OSB)	c. 1184		Botineau (1968)
5	Mortimer	*Fundationis et fundatorum historia*	Anon., Augustinian canons of Wigmore	comp. 1360–70	Edmund Mortimer, 3rd Earl of March?	*MA* 5: 348–355
6	Nevers†	*Chronicon Vizeliacensis*‡	Hugh of Poitiers, monk of Vézelay (OSB)	1160		*CCCM* 42
7	Normandy (var. families)†	*Historia ecclesiastica*‡	Orderic Vitalis, monk of Saint-Evroult (mother-house of Saint Mary Maule) (OSB)	1130s		Chibnall (1969–80)
8	Peverel/Pecche†	*Liber memorandorum ecclesie de Bernewelle*‡	Anon., Augustinian canons of Barnwell	comp. c. 1296		Clark (1907)
9	Salisbury†	*Fundatorum historia*‡	Anon., Augustinian canonesses of Lacock	1275, revised before 1357		Bowles and Gough Nichols (1835), app. 1
10	Thuringia†	*Chronica Reinhardsbrunnensis*‡	Anon., monks of Reinhardsbrunn (OSB)	c. 1349		*MGH SS* 24: 514–656

† indicates known crusading activity by family/individual

‡ indicates reference to crusading in text

❧ APPENDIX 3

Description of Paris, BNF, MS Lat. 5132

Description: Paris, Bibliothèque Nationale de France, MS Lat. 5132. [See also descriptions in RISM B/IV 1: 410; Rudolf Beer, "Die Handschriften des Klosters Sancta Maria de Ripoll," in *Sitzungsberichte der Kaiserlichen Akademie der Wissenschaften, philosophisch-historische Klasse* 158:2 (1908), 59–64; trans. Pere Barnils as "Los manuscrits del monastir de Santa María de Ripoll," *Boletín de la Real Academie de Buenas Letras de Barcelona* 36 (1909): 343–355; Sabine Philipp-Sattel, *Parlar bellament en vulgar: Die Anfänge der katalanische Schriftkultur im Mittelalter* (Tübingen, 1996), 91–92; Edelstandt du Méril, *Poésies populaires latines* (Paris, 1847), 302–306; Michel Zimmerman, *Écrire et lire en Catalogne: ix-xii siècle* (Madrid, 2003), 2: 978.]

The codex is a composite miscellany of Santa Maria de Ripoll written principally in hands of s. xii-xiii[in] in long lines with marginal and interlinear notes to s. xiv. Contrary to the assertion of Miguel Coll i Alentorn, "La historiografia catalana en el període primitiu," *Estudis Romànics* 3 (1951–52): 186–187, the same hand does not appear to have written several of the literary texts.

The codex came to the royal library, where it received its current binding, through the collection of Étienne Baluze (1630–1718). It contains 110 parchment folios with 2 blank paper flyleaves (there is an error in the numbering of the folios: f. 80 was not marked, but it is not an added leaf, as it completes the quire begun on f. 74). f. 1 = 305 mm x 222 mm. Three components (Jerusalem narrative and liturgy, *Altercatio fidei Catholicae, Gesta vel obitus domini Petri*), served as base for later texts, which were written in blank spaces and continued (where necessary) onto additional folios (e.g., f. 25). Both because of differences in the condition of its parchment and because of its lack of thematic resonance with the rest of the MS, it seems unlikely that the Sermons of Chromace of Aquileia (ff. 82–93) were originally part of the codex. This part of the MS may have been added by Baluze.

Contents

Part One, ff. 1–25 [I⁸ II⁸ III⁸ +1 add. folio (f. 25)]

ff. 1–8 Jerusalem narrative based on the crusade chronicle of Ramón of Aguilers (quire marked V)

ff. 9–16 Jerusalem narrative (quire marked VI)

ff. 17–19v Jerusalem narrative (to 17r) and homilies or exhortations on conquest of Jerusalem

> f. 19v–20 exhortation *Pen sate karrissimi*
>
> ff. 20–20v exhortation *Vos autem miseri iudei*
>
> ff. 20v–21 exhortation *Vos inquam militem*
>
> ff. 21–21v *Hierusalem laetare* [all texts ed. John France, "An Unknown Account of the Capture of Jerusalem," *English Historical Review* 87: 345 (1972): 771–783] (xii^{in}), see Joseph Lemarié, *Le breviaire de Ripoll* (Abadia de Montserrat, 1965)

ff. 21v–23 *In honore semper virginis marie sermo* [See *Revue bénédictine* 77 (1967): 388]

ff. 23v–25v *Gesta comitum Barcinonensium—redaccio primitiva* (f. 25 has been added) [*Gesta comitum Barcinonensium,* ed. Lluís Barrau Dihigo and Jaume Massó Torrents (Barcelona, 1925; repr., 2007)]. The editors identified seven hands, determined from style and content to be working between 1162 and 1184 (hands 1 & 2) to s. xiii but before 1276 (hand 7).

Part Two, ff. 26–81 [I⁸ II⁸ III⁸ IV⁸ V⁸ VI⁸ VII⁸]

ff. 26–79v *Altercatio fidei Catholicae* [see Maria Eugenia Ibarburu Asurmendi, *De capitibus litterarum et aliis figuris: recull d'estudis sobre miniatura* (Barcelona, 1999), 141–143]

ff. 79v–80v *Carmen campi doctoris* [*Carmen campidoctoris: O poema latino del Campeador,* ed. A. Montaner (Madrid, 2001)]. The editors date the hand of the poem to 1181–90.

ff. 80v–81v Letter regarding the death of Frederick Barbarossa on the Third Crusade in <*Credentes sanctitatem veneram* … > [ed. Franz-Josef Schmale, "Italienische Quellen über die Taten Kaiser Friedrichs I," in *Italien und der Brief über den Kreuzzug Kaiser Friedrichs I* (Darmstadt, 1986), 372–382]

Part Three, ff. 82–93 (I¹²)—[later addition]

ff. 82–93v Sermons VIII and IX of Chromace of Aquileia [ed. R. Étaix and J. Lemarié, *Chromatii Aquileiensis opera* (Turnhout, 1974)]

Part Four, ff. 94–110v [I⁸ II⁸ +1 add. folio (f. 106)]

f. 94 Charter of donation to Ripoll and election of sepulchre at Ripoll of Raimundus de Porciano, 1211

f. 94v–102v *Gesta vel obitus domini Petri ducis venetiae atque dalmaciae* [ed. in *Acta Sanctorum ordinis sancti Benedicti, Saec. V,* 878–888]

ff. 102v–104v Customs instituted by Abbot Gausfred (abbot at Ripoll 1153–69) in 1157, including a *refección* in honor of the Virgin, on Saturdays, on which the brothers are entitled to a *ferculum* of cheese or spicy eggs

f. 105 Payments to Ripoll from the *honor* of Molló (comarca of Ripollés) c. 1160–61 [ed. Thomas Bisson, *Fiscal Accounts of Catalonia under the Early Count-Kings (1151–1213)* (Berkeley, 1984), 56–88]

f. 105v (ll. 1–4) *De duodecim abusiones claustri;* (ll. 4ff.) Abbot Gausfred relates the establishment by Count Ramón Berenguer IV in 1162 of bountiful *refecciónes,* prayers, and masses on the anniversaries of his mother and father and, when he has died, on his own anniversary.

f. 106 Prognostication of Johannes Toletanus for 1186; Letter of "Clement" to the *rex Francorum* [single leaf]

f. 106v (ll. 1–25) Copy of charter of sale by Peter of Palad, his wife, Alda, and their son Peter of land and rights in Villallobent to the monks of Ripoll, dated 26 August 1207; (ll. 25ff.) *Ave virgo gloriosa sponsa dei* (with musical notation) [ed. Guido Maria Dreves, *Analecta hymnica medii aevi,* 46, 182]

f. 107 (continues 105v)

f. 107v (continues f. 105) Notice of 1150 stating the revenues and customs owed to the counts of Barcelona from the *honor* of Molló [ed. Bisson, *Fiscal Accounts,* 27–28]

f. 108 Original notice of Abbot Gausfred concerning vestments (undated)

f. 108v (ll. 1–12) Letter of Oleguer of Tarragona to Ramón of Ausona [ed. *PL* 172, col. 1359]; (ll. 12ff.) letter of Ivo of Chartres to Olrich [ed. *PL* 162, cols. 160–162]; *Vox clarescat, mens pergetur* (with *Lauda, Sion* melody)

f. 109 (ll.1–15) Canon 17 of the Council of Chalcedon; *Lunis procer et sub mense* [ed. Du Méril, *Poésies populaires latines du Moyen Âge,* 305; *Salve virgo regia* (with Aquitanian notation)

f. 109v *Cedit frigus hiemale* (with musical notation)

f. 110 (ll. 1–10) *In laude Raimundi Berenguerii* (with musical notation); Hildebert of Lavardin, *De Sancta Trinitate* or *Alpha et Omega* [ed. A. Brian Scott, *Carmina minora* (Leipzig, 1969), 47–53]

f. 110v continuation of *Alpha et Omega;* (ll. 5ff) [Gift of a *refeccion* and election of sepulchre at Ripoll by Bernard of Dons, *baiulus* of the palace, 1218]

Letter of "Clement" in Paris, BNF, MS Lat. 5132, f. 106

Clemens episcopus servus servorum Dei dilectis in Christo filiis illustri regi francorum et huniversis prelatis ecclesie ad quos litere iste per[vene]rint salutem et apostolicam benedictionem. Notificamus vobis quod vas eleccionis beatus paulus apostolus iam in humana condolens infirmitate cuidam bono et s[anctis]sime opinionis viro religioso in urbe romana facie ad faciem aparuit in vigilia dominice qua cantatur 'letare iherusalem' dicens: 'heu ecce dominus veniet et gladius eius cum eo ad percuciendum gentes que eum non noverunt et ulcio divina et ira omnipotentis nationes subvertet huniversas. Erit enim in mano ventus teribilis in signum future perditionis *et qui faciat bonum non est usque ad unum* [Ps. 13:1]'. Revelatam itaque sanctissimi viri fide non prestita pro somnio habebamus visionem, verum id indubitanter teneatis quod in die resurreccionis coro decantante *hec dies quam fecit dominus* et volente dicere *exultemus* [Ps. 11:24], audita est vox terribilis dicens: 'exultatio vestra dolor et luctus et iratus est dominus et accensus est furor eius in die ascensionis ira Dei ascendet super populum Israel et non remanebit lapis super lapidem in civitatibus impiorum'. Inde est quod dilectis in Christo filiis per apostolica scripta mandamus et quantum in nobis est consulimus quatinus a peccatis resipi[s]centes orationibus et ieiuniis insistatis crucem domini recipientes corda vestra crucifigatis ut diem ire sue possitis securius expectare.

✒ BIBLIOGRAPHY

Manuscripts

Angers, Archives Départmentales de Maine-et-Loire, 1 Mi 28 (microfilm of the Cartulary of Saint-Laud).
Angers, Archives Départmentales de Maine-et-Loire, G 916.
Angers, Bibliothèque Municipale, MS 252 (243).
Barcelona, Arxiu de la Corona d'Aragó, MS Ripoll 187.
Limoges, Archives Départmentales de la Haute-Vienne, 5 F/K.
Namur, Bibliothèque du Séminaire de Namur, unnumbered MS of the abbey of Brogne.
Paris, Bibliothèque Nationale de France, MSS Lat. 5132, 6218, 6006.
Rome, Bibliotheca Apostolica Vaticana, MSS Reg. Lat. 572, 838.

Primary Sources

Actes des comtes de Flandre, 1071–1128. Edited by Ferdinand Vercautern. Recueil des actes des princes Belges. Brussels, 1938.
Actus pontificum Cenomannis in Urbe Degentium. Edited by Gustav Busson and André Ledru. Le Mans, 1903.
Adrian IV. "Epistolae et privilegia." *PL* 188, cols. 1361–1640.
Alberic of Trois-Fontaines. *Chronica.* Edited by Paul Scheffer-Boichorst. *MGH SS* 23: 631–950.
Albert of Aachen. *Historia Ierosolimitana: History of the Journey to Jerusalem.* Edited and translated by Susan B. Edgington. Oxford, 2007.
Alexander Neckam. *De naturis rerum libri duo: with the Poem of the Same Author "De laudibus divinae sapientiae."* Edited by Thomas Wright. London, 1863.
Alfonso II Rey de Aragón, Conde de Barcelona y Marqués de Provenza: Documentos, 1162–1196. Edited by Ana Isabel Sanchez Casabón. Zaragoza, 1995.
Ambroise. *A History of the Holy War: Ambroise's "Estoire de la Guerre Sainte."* Edited and translated by Marianne Ailes and Malcolm Barber. 2 vols. Woodbridge, UK, 2003.
Anna Komnene. *Alexiad.* Translated by E. R. A. Sewter and revised by Peter Frankopan. London, 2005.
Annales Altahenses maiores. Edited by Wilhelm de Giesebrecht and Edmund L. N. ab Oefele. *MGH SS* 20: 772–824.
Annales Aquicinctini. MGH SS 16: 503–506.
Annales Cameracenses. MGH SS 16: 509–554.
Annales de Saint-Pierre de Gand et de Saint Amand. Edited by Philippe Grierson. Brussels, 1937.
Annales Elnonenses maiores. MGH SS 5: 17–20.

Annales Stederbugenses auctore Gerhardo praeposito. MGH SS 16: 197–231.
Archives d'Anjou: Recueil de documents et mémoires inédits sur cette province. Edited by Paul Marchegay. Angers, 1843.
Arnold of Lübeck. *Chronica Slavorum.* Edited by J. M. Lappenberg. *MGH SS* 21: 100–250.
Augustine. *Exposition on the Book of Psalms.* Translated by A. Cleveland Coxe. Grand Rapids, MI, 1979.
Baudri of Bourgueil. *Historia Jerosolimitana. RHC Occ.* 4: 5–111.
Benoît de Sainte-Maure. *Chronique des ducs de Normandie.* Edited by Francisque Michel. 3 vols. Paris, 1836–44.
Bertran de Born. *Poésies complètes de Bertran de Born.* Edited by Antoine Thomas. Toulouse, 1888.
——. *The Poems of the Troubadour Bertan de Born.* Edited and translated by William D. Paden. Berkeley, 1986.
Bibliorum Sacrorum cum glossa ordinaria. 6 vols. Venice, 1603.
The Book of the Foundation of Walden Monastery. Edited and translated by Diana Greenway and Leslie Watkiss. Oxford, 1999.
Breve chronicon Austriae Mellicensis. Edited by Wilhelm Wattenbach. *MGH SS* 24: 69–71.
Brevis historia monasterii Rivipullensi. Edited by Petrus de Marca. In *Marca Hispanica sive limes Hispanicus,* cols. 1298–1299. Paris, 1688.
"The *Brevis relatio de Guillelmo nobilissimo comite Normannorum,* Written by a Monk of Battle Abbey." Edited with commentary by Elisabeth van Houts. In *Chronology, Conquest, and Conflict in Medieval England,* 1–48. Camden Miscellany 34 (5th series, 10). London, 1997.
Caffaro di Caschifelone. *De liberatione civitatum orientis.* Edited by Luigi Belgrano. In *Annali Genovesi di Caffaro e de'suoi continuatori dai MXCIX al MCCXCIIII.* Genoa, 1929.
The Canso d'Antioca: An Occitan Epic Chronicle of the First Crusade. Edited and translated by Carol Sweetenham and Linda Paterson. Aldershot, UK, 2003.
Cartulaire de l'abbaye cardinal de La Trinité de Vendome. Edited by Charles Métais. 6 vols. Paris, 1893–97.
Cartulaire de l'abbaye de Redon en Bretagne. Edited by Aurélien Marie de Courson de Villeneuve. Paris, 1863.
Cartulaire de l'abbaye de Saint-Aubin d'Angers. Edited by Arthur Bertrand de Broussillon. 3 vols. Paris, 1903.
Cartulaire de l'ancienne abbaye de Saint Nicolas. Edited by Henri Stein. Saint-Quentin, 1884.
"Cartulaire de Laval et de Vitré." Edited by Arthur Bertrand de Broussillon. In *La maison de Laval, 1020–1605: Étude historique accompagnée du cartulaire de Laval et de Vitré,* 1: 20–270. Paris, 1895.
Cartulaire de Marmoutier pour le Dunois. Edited by Émile Mabille. Chateaudun, 1874.
Cartulaire de Sainte-Croix d'Orleans (814–1300). Edited by Eugène Jarry and Joseph Thillier. Paris, 1906.
Cartulaire du chapitre de Saint-Laud d'Angers. Edited by Adrien Planchenault. Angers, 1903.
La Chanson d'Antioche. Edited by Jan Nelson. *OFCC* 4. Tuscaloosa, AL, 2003.
La Chanson de Jérusalem. Edited by Nigel R. Thorpe. *OFCC* 6. Tuscaloosa, AL, 1992.

Chanson de la croisade contre les Albigeoise. Edited by Paul Meyer. 2 vols. Paris, 1879.

"Chanson du bon William Longespée." Edited by Tony Hunt. In Simon Lloyd, "William Longespée II: The Making of an English Crusading Hero (Part II)," *Nottingham Medieval Studies* 36 (1992): 103–121.

Chartes inédites concernant les comtes de Hainaut, 887–1207. Edited by Charles Albert Duvivier. Brussels, 1903.

"Le Chevalier au cygne" and "La Fin d'Elias." Edited by Jan A. Nelson. OFCC 2. Tuscaloosa, AL, 1985.

Chrétien de Troyes. *Le roman du Chevalier de la Charette.* Edited by Prosper Tarbé. Geneva, 1977.

——. *Yvain.* Edited by Wendelin Foerster. Manchester, UK, 1984.

Chronica regia coloniensis. Edited by George Waitz. *MGH SS rer. Germ.* 18. Hanover, 1880.

Chronica Reinhardsbrunnensis. Edited by Oswald Holder-Egger. *MGH SS* 30.1, 514–656.

Chronicarum qui dicuntur Fredegarii Scholastici libri IV cum continuationibus. Edited by Bruno Krusch. *Monumenta Germaniae historica: Scriptores rerum Merovingicarum* 2. Hanover, 1888.

The Chronicle of Ibn al-Athir for the Crusading Period from al-Kamil fi'l Ta'rikh. Pt. 2. Translated by D. S. Richards. Farnham, UK, and Burlington, VT, 2010.

The Chronicle of San Juan de la Peña: A Fourteenth-Century Official History of the Crown of Aragón. Translated by Lynn H. Nelson. Pittsburgh, 1991.

Chronicles of the Crusades. Translated with an introduction and notes by Caroline A. Smith. London and New York, 2008.

Chronicles of the Picts, Chronicles of the Scots, and Other Early Memorials of Scottish History. Edited by William Forbes Skene. Edinburgh, 1867.

Chronicon Laetiense. Edited by Johann Heller. *MGH SS* 14: 487–502.

Chronicon montis sereni. Edited by Ernestus Ehrenfuchter. *MGH SS* 23: 130–226.

Die Chronik des Bischofs Thietmar von Merseburg und ihre Korveier Überarbeitung. Edited by Robert Holtzmann. Hanover, 1935; reprint, 1980.

La chronique de Morigny. Edited by Léon Mirot. Paris, 1912.

La chronique de Saint-Hubert dite Cantatorium. Edited by Karl Hanquet. Recueil des textes pour servir a l'étude de l'histoire de Belgique. Brussels, 1906.

Chronique de Saint-Maixent, 751–1140. Edited and translated by Jean Verdon. Paris, 1979.

"Chronique de Saint-Nicolas de La Chaize-le-Vicomte." Edited by Elisabeth Carpentier and Georges Pon. *Revue historique du Centre Ouest* 6 (2007): 339–391.

Chronique des comtes d'Eu. RHGF 23: 439–448.

Chroniques des comtes d'Anjou et des seigneurs d'Amboise. Edited by Louis Halphen and Renée Poupardin. Paris, 1913.

Chroniques des églises d'Anjou. Edited by Paul Marchegay and Émile Mabille. Paris, 1869.

Codex Falkensteinensis: Die Rechtsaufzeichnungen der Graven von Falkenstein. Edited by Elizabeth Noichl. Munich, 1978.

"Codex maior traditionum Weingartensium." Edited by Paul Friedrich Stalin. In *Festgruss zum 400 Jahrestag der Stiftung der Universität Tübingen im Jahre 1877,* 25–47. Tübingen, 1877.

Corpus des inscriptions de la France médiévale. Vol. 4, *Limousin: Corrèze, Creuse, Haute-Vienne, Poitiers.* Paris, 1977.

Corpus iuris canonici. Edited by Aemilius Ludwig Richter and Emil Friedberg. 2 vols. Leipzig, 1879–81.

The Correspondence of Thomas Becket. Edited by Anne Duggan. 2 vols. Oxford, 2000.

Crónica de San Juan de la Peña. Edited by Antonio Ubieto-Arteta. Textos medievales 4. Valencia, 1961.

The Crusade of Frederick Barbarossa: The History of the Expedition of the Emperor Frederick and Related Texts. Translated by Graham A. Loud. Farnham, UK, and Burlington, VT, 2010.

Dietrich of Apolda. *Die Vita der heiligen Elizabeth.* Edited by Monika Rener. Marburg, 1993.

Diplomatari del monestir de Santa Maria de Santes Creus (975–1225). Edited by Joan de Papell i Tardiu. Barcelona, 2005.

Diplomatari de Santa Maria de Poblet I: 960–1177. Edited by Agusti Altisent. Barcelona, 1993.

Diplomatari i escrits literaris de l'abat i bisbe Oliba. Edited by Edouard Junyent and Anscari M. Mundo. Barcelona, 1992.

Documentos de Montearagón (1058–1205). Edited by Dolores Barrios Martínez. Huesca, 2004.

Documents liturgiques et necrologiques de l'église collégiale de Saint-Pierre de Lille. Edited by Édouard Hautcoeur. Lille and Paris, 1895.

Documents on the Later Crusades: 1274–1580. Edited and translated by Norman Housley. New York, 1996.

Eadmer. *Historia novorum in Anglie.* Edited by Martin Rule. RS 81. London, 1884.

L'estoire de Eracles empereur et la conqueste de la terre d'Outremer. RHC Occ. 2.

Eugenius III. "Epistolae et privilegia." *PL* 180, cols. 1013–1641.

Fiscal Accounts of Catalonia under the Early Count-Kings (1151–1213). Edited by Thomas Bisson. 2 vols. Berkeley, 1984.

"Fragmento de unos viejos anales (1089–1196)." Edited by Antonio Floriano. *Boletín de la Real Academia de la Historia* 94 (1929): 133–162.

Fulcher of Chartres. *Historia Hierosolymitana (1095–1127): Mit Erläuterungen und einem Anhange.* Edited by Heinrich Hagenmeyer. Heidelberg, 1913.

——. *The Chronicle of the First Crusade.* Translated by Martha Evelyn McGinty. Philadelphia, 1941.

Galbert of Bruges. *The Murder of Charles the Good, Count of Flanders.* Translated by James Bruce Ross. New York, 1967.

——. *De multro, traditione, et occisione gloriosi Karoli comitis Flandriarum.* Edited by Jeff Rider. *CCCM* 131. Turnhout, 1994.

Genealogiae breves regum Francorum. MGH SS 13: 249–725.

Genealogiae comitum Flandriae. Edited by L. C. Bethmann. *MGH SS* 9: 302–336.

Genealogiae scriptoris Fusniacenses. MGH SS 13: 251–255.

Geoffrey Gaimar. *Estoire des Engleis.* Edited and translated by Ian Short. Oxford and New York, 2009.

Geoffrey of Vigeois. *Chronica Gaufredi prior Vosiensis: Pars altera.* Edited by Philippe Labbé. In *Novae Bibliothecae manuscriptorum librorum, tomus secundus rerum Aquitanicarum praesertim bituricensium uberrima collectio…opera ac studio,* 330–342. Paris, 1657.

——. "Geoffroi de Breuil, prieur de Vigeois: *Chronique* (première partie)." Edited by Pierre Botineau. Thesis, École des Chartes, 1968.

Geoffrey of Villehardouin. *La conquête de Constantinople*. Edited by Edmond Faral. 2 vols. Les classiques de l'histoire de France au Moyen Âge 17–18. Paris, 1938–39. For a translation of this work, see *Chronicles of the Crusades*, trans. Caroline A. Smith (London and New York, 2008), 5–135.

Geoffroy de Courlon. *Le livre des reliques de l'abbaye de Saint-Pierre-le-Vif de Sens*. Edited by Gustave Julliot and Maurice Prou. Sens, 1887.

Gerald of Wales. *Opera*. Edited by J. S. Brewer. 8 vols. RS 21. London, 1861–91.

Gervase of Canterbury. *The Historical Works of Gervase of Canterbury*. Edited by William Stubbs. 2 vols. RS 73. London, 1879–80.

Gesta Andegavensium Peregrinorum. *RHC Occ.* 5: 345–347.

Gesta comitum Barcinonensium. Edited by Lluís Barrau Dihigo and Jaume Massó Torrents. Croniques Catalanes 2. Barcelona, 1925; reprint, 2007.

Gesta Francorum et aliorum Hierosolymitanorum. Edited by Rosalind Hill. New York and London, 1962.

Gesta Francorum hierusalem expugnatium. *RHC Occ.* 3: 491–543.

The "Gesta Normannorum ducum" of William of Jumièges, Orderic Vitalis, and Robert of Torigni. Edited and translated by Elisabeth van Houts. 2 vols. Oxford, 1992–95.

Gesta principum Polonorum. Translated by Paul W. Knoll and Frank Schaer with a preface by Thomas N. Bisson. Budapest, 2003.

Gestes dels comtes de Barcelona i Reis d'Aragó. Edited by Stefano Maria Cingolani. Monuments d'Historia de la Corona d'Aragó 1. Valencia, 2008.

Gislebert of Mons. *La chronique de Gislebert de Mons*. Edited by Léon Vanderkindere. Brussels, 1904.

——. *Chronicle of Hainaut*. Translated by Laura Napran. Woodbridge, UK, 2005.

La Gran Conquista de Ultramar. Edited by Louis Cooper. 4 vols. Bogota, 1979.

Guibert of Nogent. *Dei Gesta per Francos et cinq autres textes*. Edited by R. B. C. Huygens. *CCCM* 127a. Turnhout, 1996.

——. *The Deeds of God through the Franks*. Translated by Robert Levine. Woodbridge, UK, and Rochester, NY, 1997.

Guillem de Berguedà. *Poesies de Guillem de Berguedà*. Edited by Marti de Riquer. Barcelona, 1996.

Guy of Bazoches. *Liber epistularum Guidonis de Basochis*. Edited by Herbert Adolfsson. Acta Universitatis Stockholmiensis, Studia Latina Stockholmiensis 18. Stockholm, 1969.

Henry of Huntingdon. *Historia Anglorum, the History of the English People*. Edited and translated by Diana Greenway. Oxford, 1996.

Herbert of Bosham. "Vita Sancti Thomae." Edited by James Craigie Robertson. In *Materials for the History of Thomas Becket*, edited by James Craigie Robertson and J. B. Sheppard, 3: 155–534. RS 67. London, 1877.

Hildebert of Lavardin. "Sermones." *PL* 171, cols. 339–964.

Histoire de Fulk Nerra, comte d'Anjou suivie par l'office du Saint-Sépulchre de l'abbaye de Beaulieu. Edited by Alexandre de Salies. Paris, 1874.

L'Histoire de Gilles de Chin de Gautier de Tournai. Edited by E. B. Place. Evanston, IL, 1941.

Historia Karoli Magni et Rotholandi ou Chronique de Pseudo-Turpin. Edited by C. Meredith-Jones. Geneva, 1972.

Historia monasterii Aquicinctinae. Edited by Johann Heller. *MGH SS* 14: 584–982.

Historia Welforum Weingartenensis. Edited by Erich König. Schwäbische chroniken der Stauferzeit. Thorbecke, 1978.

History of William Marshal. Edited by A. J. Holden with English translation by S. Gregory and historical notes by David Crouch. 3 vols. London, 2002–6.

Hrabanus Maurus. "Homiliae." *PL* 110, cols. 9–468.

Hugh of Saint-Cher. *In Libros Prophetarum Ezechielis, Danielis, Oseae, Joelis, Amos, Abdiae, Jonae, Michae, Nahum, Habacuc, Sophoniae, Aggaei, Zachariae, Malachae, et Machabaeuorum I.* 8 vols. Venice, 1754.

"Inventarium ecclesiae St. Albini Namurcensi, Ann. 1218." In *Organ für christliche Kunst,* vol. 13, edited by F. Baudri Jahrg, 41–44. Cologne, 1863.

"Italienische Quellen über die Taten Kaiser Friedrichs I." Edited and translated by Franz-Josef Schmale. In *Italien und der Brief über den Kreuzzug Kaiser Friedrichs I,* 372–382. Ausgewählte Quellen zur deutschen Geschichte des Mittelalters, Freiherr vom Stein-Gedächtnisausgabe 17a. Darmstadt, 1986.

Jean d'Arras. *Mélusine: Roman du xiv siècle.* Edited by Louis Stouff. Geneva, 1974.

Jerome. "Commentariorum in Ezechielem." *PL* 25, cols. 15–490.

John of Joinville. "Épitaphe composée par Joinville." In *Histoire de Saint Louis, Credo, et lettre à Louis X,* edited by Natalis de Wailly, 544–547. 4th ed. Paris, 1872. For a translation of this work, see *Chronicles of the Crusades,* trans. Caroline A. Smith (London and New York, 2008), 346–348.

———. *Vie de Saint Louis.* Edited and translated by Jacques Monfrin. Paris, 1995. For a translation of this work, see *Chronicles of the Crusades,* trans. Caroline A. Smith (London and New York, 2008), 141–336.

John of Salisbury. *The Letters of John of Salisbury.* Edited by J. W. Millor, H. E. Butler, and C. N. L. Brooke. 2 vols. Oxford, 1986.

Die Kreuzzugsbriefe aus den Jahren 1088–1100. Edited by Heinrich Hagenmeyer. Innsbruck, 1901.

Kreuzzugsdichtung. Edited by Ulrich Müller. Tübingen, 1979.

Lambert of Ardres. *Historia comitum Ghisnensium.* Edited by Johann Heller. *MGH SS* 24: 550–642.

———. *History of the Counts of Guines and Lords of Ardres.* Translated by Leah Shopkow. Philadelphia, 2001.

Lambert of Wattrelos. *Annales Cameracenses. MGH SS* 16: 509–554.

"Lamentum lacrymabile super his qui in expeditione Jerosolimitana diversis mortibus." *PL* 155, cols. 1095a–1098b.

Lateinische Hymnen des Mittelalters. Edited by Franz-Joseph Mone. 3 vols. Freiburg, 1855.

Layettes du trésor des chartes. Edited by Alexandre Teulet. 5 vols. Paris, 1863–1909.

Liber feudorum maior: Cartulario real que se conserva en el Archivo de la Corona de Aragón. Edited by Francisco Miquel Rosell. 2 vols. Barcelona, 1945.

Liber memorandorum ecclesie de Bernewelle. Edited by J. W. Clark. Cambridge, 1907.

Manuscrits de la Bibliothèque de Toulouse. Edited by Auguste Molinier. Paris, 1883.

Marbod of Rennes. *De lapidibus, Considered as a Medical Treatise with Text, Commentary, and C. W. King's Translation, Together with Text and Translation of Marbode's Minor Works on Stones.* Edited by John M. Riddle. Wiesbaden, 1977.

Matthew Paris. *Chronica maiora.* Edited by H. R. Luard. 7 vols. RS 57. London, 1872.

"Miracula gloriosi martyris Thomae, Cantuarensis archiepiscopi." In *Materials for the History of Thomas Becket,* edited by James Craigie Robertson and J. B. Sheppard, 1: 137–546. RS 67. London, 1875.

"Miraculum quod Beata Maria subvenit Guillelmo Crispino senior—ubi de nobili Crispinorum genere agitur." *PL* 150, cols. 735–744.

"Monitum Willelmi Grassegals militis." *RHC Occ.* 3: 317–318.

Monumenta Vizeliacensia: Textes relatifs à l'histoire de l'abbaye de Vézelay. Edited by R. B. C. Huygens. *CCCM* 42. Turnhout, 1976.

La naissance du Chevalier au Cygne. Edited by Emmanuel J. Mickel Jr. and Jan A. Nelson. *OFCC* 1. Tuscaloosa, AL, 1977.

Narratio quomodo reliquiae martyris Georgii ad nos Aquicinenses pervenerunt. RHC Occ. 5: 248–252.

Niketas Choniates. *O City of Byzantium: The Annals of Niketas Choniates.* Translated by Harry J. Magoulias. Detroit, 1984.

Notae Bronienses. MGH SS 24: 1–27.

Notitiae duae Lemovicenses de praedicatione crucis in Aquitania. RHC Occ. 5: 350–353.

"L'obituaire de l'abbaye de Brogne ou de Saint-Gérard, de l'ordre de Saint-Benoît." Edited by Joseph Barbier. *Analectes pour servir à l'histoire ecclésiastique de la Belgique* 18 (1882): 289–336.

Odo of Deuil. *De profectione Ludovici VII in Orientem.* Edited and translated by Virginia Gingerick Berry. New York, 1948.

Oeuvres de Rigord et de Guillaume le Breton. Edited by Henri François Delaborde. 2 vols. Paris, 1882.

The Old French Johannes Translation of the Pseudo-Turpin Chronicle: A Critical Edition. Edited by Ronald Walpole. London, 1976.

De Oorkonden der graven van Vlaanderen (1191–aanvang 1206). Edited by Walter Prevenier. Brussels, 1966.

De Oorkonden der graven van Vlaanderen (juli 1128–setember 1191). Edited by Adriaan Verhulst and Thérèse de Hemptinne. Brussels, 2009.

Orderic Vitalis. *Historia ecclesiastica.* Edited and translated by Marjorie Chibnall. 6 vols. Oxford, 1969–80.

Origen. *Homilies on Judges.* Translated by Elizabeth Ann Dively Lauro. Fathers of the Church 119. Washington, DC, 2010.

Osbert of Clare. *The Letters and Poems of Osbert of Clare.* Edited by E. W. Williamson. Oxford, 1929.

Otte. *Eraclius.* Edited by Winfried Frey. Göppingen, 1983.

Otto of St. Blasien. *Chronica.* Edited by A. Hofmeister. *MGH SS rer. Germ.* 47.

———. *The Chronicle of Otto of St. Blasien, 1187–1197.* Translated by Graham Loud. In *The Crusade of Frederick Barbarossa: The History of the Expedition of the Emperor Frederick and Related Texts,* 173–192. Farnham, UK, and Burlington, VT, 2010.

Papsturkunden in Spanien I: Katalanien. Edited by Paul Kehr. Berlin, 1926.

Papsturkunden in Spanien II: Navarra und Aragón. Edited by Paul Kehr. Berlin, 1928.

Peter Tudebode. *Historia de Hierosolymitano itinere.* Edited by John H. Hill and Laurita L. Hill. Documents relatifs à l'histoire des croisades 12. Paris, 1977.

Philip of Novara. *Les quatre âges de l'homme.* Edited by Marcel de Fréville. Paris, 1888.

"Progenies Moubraiorum, huius abbatiae fundatorum." *MA* 6: 320–321.

"Quomodo mutatum fuit Cognomen de Albaneio in Cognomen de Mubrai." *MA* 5: 346–347.

Ralph of Caen. *The "Gesta Tancredi" of Ralph of Caen: A History of the Normans on the First Crusade.* Translated by David S. Bachrach and Bernard S. Bachrach. Aldershot, UK, and Burlington, VT, 2005.

Ralph of Diceto. *Radulfi de Diceto decani Lundonensis opera: The Historical Works of Master Ralph of Diceto.* Edited by William Stubbs. 2 vols. RS 68. London, 1876.

Raymond of Aguilers. *Le 'Liber' de Raymond d'Aguilers.* Edited by John H. Hill and Laurita L. Hill and translated by Philippe Wolff. Documents relatifs à l'histoire des croisades 9. Paris, 1969.

Recueil des actes de Henry II roi d'Angleterre et duc de Normandie: Concernant les provinces françaises et les affaires de France. Edited by Léopold Delisle and revised by Élie Berger. 4 vols. Paris, 1909–27.

Recueil des actes des comtes de Pontieu. Edited by Clovis Brunel. Paris, 1930.

Recueil des chartes de l'abbaye de Clairvaux. Edited by Jean Waquet. Troyes, 1950.

Recueil des chartes de l'abbaye de Cluny. Edited by Auguste Bernard and Alexandre Bruel. 6 vols. Paris, 1876–1903.

Reimchronik von Flanderen. Edited by Eduard Kausler. Tübingen, 1840.

Rituel de Saint Martin de Tours. Edited by A. Fleuret. Paris, 1899–1901.

Robert of Auxerre. *Chronicon.* Edited by Oswald Holder-Egger. *MGH SS* 26: 219–276.

Robert de Boron. *Merlin and the Grail: Joseph of Arimathea, Merlin, Perceval; The Trilogy of Arthurian Romances Attributed to Robert de Boron.* Translated by Nigel Bryant. Cambridge, 2001.

Robert of Clari. *Conquest of Constantinople.* Translated by Edgar Holmes McNeal. New York, 1969.

Robert the Monk. *Historia Iherosolimitana. RHC Occ.* 3: 721–882.

——. *Robert the Monk's History of the First Crusade: Historia Iherosolimitana.* Translated by Carol Sweetenham. Aldershot, UK, 2005.

Robert of Torigni. *Chronique.* Edited by Léopold Delisle. 2 vols. Rouen, 1872–73.

——. "Epistola ad Gervaise priorem Saint-Serenici." *PL* 202, cols. 1307–1310.

Roger of Howden. *Gesta regis Henrici secundi Benedicti abbatis.* Edited by William Stubbs. 2 vols. RS 49. London, 1867.

——. *Chronica.* Edited by William Stubbs. 4 vols. RS 51. London, 1868–71.

Rotuli litterarum clausarum in Turri londinensi asservati. Edited by G. Eyre and A Spottiswoode. 2 vols. London, 1833–34.

Sacramentarium Rivipullense. Edited by Alejandro Olivar. Madrid, 1964.

Saint-Denis de Nogent le Rotrou, 1031–1789: Histoire et cartulaire. Edited by Charles Métais. Vannes, 1899.

The Seventh Crusade, 1244–1254: Sources and Documents. Edited and and translated by Peter Jackson. Aldershot, UK, and Burlington, VT, 2007.

Sigebert of Gembloux. *Chronica.* Edited by L. C. Bethmann. *MGH SS* 6: 268–474.

——. "Leodicensium epistolae adversus Paschalae papam." Edited by Ernst Sackur. In *Libelli de lite,* 2: 449–464. Hanover, 1892.

Stephen of Rouen. *Draco Normannicus.* Edited by Richard Howlett. In *Chronicles of the Reigns of Stephen, Henry II and Richard I,* 2: 589–702. RS 82. London, 1899.

Suger. *Oeuvres complètes de Suger.* Edited by Albert Lecoy de la Marche. Paris, 1867.

——. *Vie de Louis VI le Gros.* Edited and translated by Henri Waquet. Paris, 1929.

Els testaments dels comtes de Barcelona i dels reis de la Corona d'Árago: De Guifré Borrell a Joan II. Edited by Antoni Udina I Abello. Barcelona, 2001.

Trésor des chartes de l'abbaye royale de Fontevraud. Edited by Archives Nationales. Paris, 1992.

Urban II. "Epistolae et privilegia." *PL* 151, cols. 283–552.

Urkundenbuch zur Geschichte der jetzt die Preussischen Regierungsbezirke Coblenz und Trier bilenden mittelrheinischen Territorien. Edited by Heinrich Beyer, Leopold Eltester, and Adam Goerz. 2 vols. Coblenz, 1845–74.

"Versus de viribus." Edited by C. Moeller. In "Les Flamands du Ternois au royaume latin de Jérusalem," *Mélanges Paul Frédéricq,* 191. Brussels, 1904.

The Vezelay Chronicle and Other Documents from MS Auxerre 227 and Elsewhere. Translated by John O. Ward. New York and Binghamton, NY, 1992.

"Vita beati Gaufredi Castaliensis." Edited by Auguste Bosvieux. *Mémoires de la Société des Sciences Naturelles et Archéologiques de la Creuse* 3 (1862): 75–160.

Vita beati Petri Urseoli ducis venetiarum et dalmatiarum. ASOB 5: 847–860.

"Vita et passio Waldevi comitis." Edited by Francisque Michel. In *Chroniques Anglo-Normandes: Recueil d'extraits et d'écrits relatifs à l'histoire de Normandie et d'Angleterre,* 2: 99–142. Rouen, 1836.

Wace. *Roman de Rou.* Edited by Anthony J. Holden and translated by Glynn S. Burgess with notes by Elisabeth van Houts. St. Helier, Jersey, 2002.

Walter of Thérouanne. *Vita Karoli comitis Flandriae et vita domni Ioannis Morinensis episcopi; quibus subiungitur poemata de morte comitis Karoli conscripta et quaestio de eadem acta.* Edited by Jeff Rider. CCCM 217. Turnhout, 2006.

William Durand. *The "Rationale Divinorum Officiorum" of William Durand of Mende: A New Translation of the Prologue and Book One.* Translated by Timothy M. Thibodeau. New York, 2007.

William of Andres. *Chronicon Andrensis.* Edited by Johann Heller. *MGH SS* 24: 684–773.

William of Malmesbury. *Gesta regum Anglorum: The History of the English Kings.* Edited by Rodney M. Thompson and Michael Winterbottom. 2 vols. Oxford, 1999.

William of Newburgh. *Historia rerum Anglicarum.* Edited by Richard Howlett. In *Chronicles of the Reigns of Stephen, Henry II, and Richard I,* 1: 20–408, 2: 415–502 RS 82. London, 1884–85.

William of Saint-Pair. *Roman du Mont-Saint-Michel.* Edited by Paul Redlich. Marburg, 1894.

William of Tudela. *Song of the Cathar Wars.* Translated by Janet Shirley. Aldershot, UK, 1996.

William of Tyre. *History of the Deeds Done beyond the Sea.* Translated by Emily Atwater Babcock and A. C. Krey. 2 vols. New York, 1943.

——. *Chronique.* Edited by R. B. C. Huygens with Hans Eberhard Meyer and Gerhard Rosch. CCCM 63. 2 vols. Turnhout, 1986.

Secondary Works

Abadal i de Vinyals, Ramon d'. *Els primers comtes Catalans.* Barcelona, 1958.

——. "À propos de la domination de la maison comtale de la Barcelone sur le Midi français." *Anales du Midi* 56 (1964): 315–345.

——. *Els temps i el regiment del comte Guifred el Pilós.* Barcelona, 1989.

Abulafia, David. "Invented Italians in the Courtois Forgeries." In *Crusade and Settlement: Papers Read at the First Conference of the Society for the Study of the Crusades and the Latin East and Presented to R. C. Smail,* edited by Peter W. Edbury, 135–147. Cardiff, 1975.

Adair, Penelope. "Flemish Comital Family and the Crusades." In *The Crusades: Other Experiences, Alternate Perspectives,* edited by Khalil I. Semaan, 101–114. Binghamton, NY, 2003.

Adhémar, Jean. "Les tombeaux de la collection Gaignières (première partie)." *Gazette des beaux arts*, 6th series, 84 (1974): 4–192.

Aigret, N.-J. *Histoire de l'église et du chapitre de Saint-Aubin à Namur.* Namur, 1881.

Aird, William M. *Robert Curthose: Duke of Normandy, c. 1050–1134.* Woodbridge, UK, 2008.

Airlie, Stuart. "The Aristocracy." In *The New Cambridge Medieval History,* vol. 2, *700–900,* edited by Rosamund McKitterick, 431–450. Cambridge, 1995.

Alphandéry, Paul, and Alphonse Dupront. *La chrétienté et l'idée de croisade.* 2 vols. L'évolution d'humanité, synthèse collective 38 and 38b. Paris, 1954–59.

Althoff, Gerd. "Anlässe zur schriftlichen Fixierung adligen Selbstverständnisses." *Zeitschrift für die Geschichte des Oberrheins* 134 (1986): 34–46.

——. *Family, Friends, and Followers: Political and Social Bonds in Early Medieval Europe.* Cambridge, 2004.

Alturo i Perucho, Jesús. "La historiografia catalana del període primitiu." In *Historia de la historiografia catalana,* edited by Albert Balcells, 19–38. Barcelona, 2004.

Amt, Emilie. *The Accession of Henry II in England: Royal Government Restored.* Woodbridge, UK, 1993.

Anglés, Higini. *Música a Catalunya fins al segle XIII.* Barcelona, 1935.

Antoine, Elisabeth. "A Thirteenth-Century Signet Ring and Its Inscriptions: Between Identity and Power, Magic and Prophylaxis." In *De re metallica: The Uses of Metal in the Middle Ages,* edited by Robert Bork, 101–112. Aldershot, UK, 2005.

Arbellot, François. "Étude historique et bibliographique sur Geoffroy de Vigeois." *Bulletin de la Société Archéologique et Historique du Limousin* 36 (1888): 135–161.

Asbridge, Thomas. *The First Crusade: A New History.* London, 2004.

Aubrun, Michel. "Le prieur Geoffroy de Vigeois et sa chronique." *Revue Mabillon* 63 (1974): 313–326.

Aurell, Martin. *Les noces du comte: Mariage et pouvoir en Catalogne (785–1213).* Paris, 1995.

——. "Henry II and Arthurian Legend." In *Henry II: New Interpretations,* edited by Christopher Harper Bill and Nicholas Vincent, 362–394. Woodbridge, UK, 2007.

Bachrach, Bernard S. "The Pilgrimages of Fulk Nerra, Count of the Angevins, 987–1040." In *Religion, Culture, and Society in the Early Middle Ages: Studies in Honor of Richard E. Sullivan,* edited by Thomas F. X. Noble and John J. Contreni, 205–217. Kalamazoo, MI, 1987.

——. *Fulk Nerra, the Neo-Roman Consul, 987–1040: A Political Biography of the Angevin Count.* Berkeley, 1993.

Badia, Lola. *Poesia catalana del secolo XIV: Edicio i estudi del Cançoneret de Ripoll.* Barcelona, 1983.

Baer, Fritz. "Eine jüdische Messiasprophetie auf das Jahr 1186 und der dritte Kreuzzug." *Monatsschrift für Geschichte und Wissenschaft des Judetums* 70 (1926): 113–122.

Baert, Barbara. *A Heritage of Holy Wood: The Legend of the True Cross in Text and Image.* Translated by Lee Preedy. Leiden and Boston, 2004.

Baldwin, John. *The Government of Philip Augustus: Foundations of French Royal Power in the Middle Ages.* Berkeley, 1986.

Barber, Richard. *Henry Plantagenet.* 2nd ed. Woodbridge, UK, 2001.

Barlow, Frank. *Thomas Becket.* London, 1986.

Barthélemy, Dominique. "L'État contre le lignage: Une thème a développer dans l'histoire des pouvoirs en France aux xi, xii, et xiii siècles." *Médiévales* 5:10 (1986): 37–50.

——. *The Serf, the Knight, and the Historian.* Translated by Graham Robert Edwards. Ithaca, NY, 2009.

Barton, Richard E. *Lordship in the County of Maine, c. 890–c. 1160.* Woodbridge, UK, 2004.

——. "Writing Warfare, Lordship, and History: The *Gesta Consulum Andegavorum*'s Account of the Battle of Alençon." *Anglo-Norman Studies* 27 (2005): 32–50

——. "Aristocratic Culture: Kinship, Chivalry, and Court Culture." In *A Companion to the Medieval World,* edited by Carol Lansing and Edward English, 500–524. Malden, MA, 2009.

Bar-Yosef, Eitan. "The Last Crusade? British Propaganda and the Palestine Campaign, 1917–18." *Journal of Contemporary History* 36:1 (2001): 87–109.

Bauch, Kurt. *Das mittelalterliche Grabbild: Figürliche Grabmäler des 11 bis 15 Jahrhunderts in Europa.* Berlin, 1976.

Bautier, Robert-Henri. "La collection des chartes de croisade dite 'Collection Courtois'." *Comptes-rendus des séances de l'Academie des Inscriptions et Belles Lettres* (1956): 382–86.

Becquet, J. "Les chanoines réguliers du Chalard." *Bulletin de la Société Archéologique et Historique du Limousin* 98 (1971): 153–172.

Bedos-Rezak, Brigitte. "Medieval Identity: A Sign and a Concept." *American Historical Review* 105:5 (2000): 1489–1533.

Beer, Rudolf. "Die Handschriften des Klosters Santa Maria de Ripoll." *Sitzungsberichte der Kaiserlichen Akademie der Wissenschaften, philosophisch-historische Klasse* 155: 3 (1907) and 158: 2 (1908). Translated by Pere Barnils as "Los manuscrits del monastir de Santa María de Ripoll," *Boletín de la Real Academia de Buenas Letras de Barcelona* 5 (1910): 137–170, 230–278, 299–320, 329–365, 492–520.

Bennett, Matthew. "Poetry as History? The *Roman de Rou* of Wace as a Source for the Norman Conquest." In *Anglo-Norman Studies,* vol. 5, *Proceedings of the Battle Conference,* edited by R. Allen Brown, 21–39. Woodbridge, UK, 1983.

Benton, John F. "Consciousness of Self and Perceptions of Individuality." In *Renaissance and Renewal in the Twelfth Century,* edited by Robert Benson, Giles Constable, and Carol Lanham, 263–295. Cambridge, MA, 1982.

Bernard, Claude. "Un chevalier Limousin: Goufier de Lastours." *Bulletin de la Société Archéologique et Historique du Limousin* 86 (1955): 23–33.

Bierschenk, Monika. *Glasmalereien der Elisabethkirche in Marburg.* Berlin, 1991.

Birge Vitz, Evelyn. *Orality and Performance in Early French Romance.* Woodbridge, UK, 1999.

Bishko, Charles Julian. "Liturgical Intercession at Cluny for the King-Emperors of Leon." *Studia Monastica* 7 (1961): 53–76. Reprinted in Charles Julian Bishko, *Spanish and Portuguese Monastic History: 600–1300* (London, 1984), chap. 8.

Bisson, Thomas N. *The Medieval Crown of Aragón: A Short History.* Oxford, 1986.

——. "The Rise of Catalonia: Identity, Power, and Ideology in a Twelfth-Century Society." In *Medieval France and Her Pyrenean Neighbours: Studies in Early Institutional History,* 125–152. London and Ronceverte, WV, 1989. Originally published as "L'Essor de la Catalogne: Identité, pouvoir, et idéologie dans une société du XIIe siècle," *Annales: Économies, sociétés, civilisations* 39 (1984): 454–479.

——."Unheroed Pasts: History and Communication in South Frankland before the Albigensian Crusades." *Speculum* 65 (1990): 281–308.

——. *The Crisis of the Twelfth Century: Power, Lordship, and the Origins of the European Government.* Princeton, NJ, 2009.

Bofarull y Mascaró, Próspero de. *Los condes de Barcelona vindicados.* 2 vols. Barcelona, 1836.

Borgehammar, Stephan. "Heraclius Learns Humility: Two Early Latin Accounts Composed for the Celebration of *Exaltatio Crucis.*" *Millennium* 6 (2009): 145–201.

Bouchard, Constance. *Sword, Miter, and Cloister: Nobility and the Church in Burgundy, 980–1198.* Ithaca, NY, 1987.

Boussard, Jacques. *L'Anjou sous Henri II Plantagenet et ses fils, 1151–1204.* Paris, 1938.

Boynton, Susan. *Shaping a Monastic Identity: Liturgy and History at the Imperial Abbey of Farfa, 1000–1125.* Ithaca, NY, 2006.

Bradbury, Jim. "Fulk le Réchin and the Origins of the Plantagenets." In *Studies in Medieval History Presented to R. Allen Brown,* edited by Christopher Harper Hill et al., 27–42. Woodbridge, UK, 1989.

Brodeur, Arthur Gilchrist. "The Grateful Lion: A Study in the Development of Medieval Narrative." *Publications of the Modern Language Association of America* 39:3 (1924): 485–524.

Brown, Elizabeth A. R. "Death and the Human Body in the Later Middle Ages: The Legislation of Boniface VIII on the Division of the Corpse." *Viator* 12 (1981): 221–270.

Brown, Elizabeth A. R., and Michael W. Cothren. "The Twelfth-Century Crusading Window of Saint Denis: *Praeteritorum enim recordatio futurorum est exhibitio.*" *Journal of the Warburg and Courtauld Institutes* 49 (1986): 1–40.

Brundage, James. "An Errant Crusader: Stephen of Blois." *Traditio* 16 (1960): 380–395.

——. "The Crusader's Wife: A Canonistic Quandary." *Studia Gratiana* 12 (1967): 425–442.

——. "The Crusader's Wife Revisited." *Studia Gratiana* 14 (1967): 241–252.

——. *Medieval Canon Law and the Crusader.* Madison, WI, 1969.

Buc, Philippe. *The Dangers of Ritual: Between Early Medieval Texts and Social Scientific Theory.* Princeton, NJ, 2001.

——. "The Monster and the Critics: A Ritual Reply." *Early Medieval Europe* 15:4 (2007): 441–454.

Budny, Mildred. "The Byrhtnoth Tapestry or Embroidery." In *The Battle of Maldon, AD 991,* edited by Donald Scragg, 263–278. Oxford, 1991.

Bull, Marcus. *Knightly Piety and the Lay Response to the First Crusade: The Limousin and Gascony.* Oxford, 1993.

——. "Views of Muslims and Jerusalem in Miracle Stories." In *The Experience of Crusading,* vol. 1, *Western Approaches,* edited by Marcus Bull and Norman Housley, 13–38. Cambridge, 2003.

—— "Criticism of Henry II's Expedition to Ireland in William of Canterbury's *Miracles of St. Thomas Becket.*" *Journal of Medieval History* 33 (2007): 107–129.

Bumke, Joachim. *Courtly Culture: Literature and Society in the High Middle Ages.* Translated by Thomas Dunlap. Woodstock, NY, 2000.

Burns, E. Jane. "Saracen Silk and the Virgin's Chemise: Cultural Crossings in Cloth." *Speculum* 81 (2006): 365–397.

Busby, Keith. *Codex and Context: Reading Old French Verse Narrative in Manuscript.* 2 vols. Amsterdam and New York, 2002.

Bynum, Caroline. *The Resurrection of the Body in Western Christianity, 200–1336.* New York, 1995.

Cabestany, Joan F. "Alfons el Cast." In *Els primers comtes-reis: Ramon Berenguer IV, Alfons el Cast, Pere el Català,* edited by Percy E. Schramm, Joan F. Cabestany, and Enric Bagué, 55–99. Barcelona, 1960.

Cabré, María Dolores. "Cinco documentos de Infante Don Fernando Abad de Montearagón." *Argensola* 39 (1959): 239–258.

Cahn, Walter. *The Romanesque Wooden Doors of Auvergne.* New York, 1974.

Callahan, Daniel F. "The Tau Cross in the Writings of Adhémar of Chabannes." In *In the Year 1000: Religious and Social Response to the Turn of the First Millennium,* edited by Michael Frassetto, 63–71. New York, 2002.

———. "Eleanor of Aquitaine, the Coronation Rite of the Duke of Aquitaine, and the Cult of Saint Martial of Limoges." In *The World of Eleanor of Aquitaine: Literature and Society in Southern France,* edited by Marcus Bull and Catherine Léglu, 29–36. Woodbridge, UK, 2005.

Carraz, Damien. "Mémoire lignagère et archives monastiques: Les Bourbouton et la commanderie de Richerenches." In *Convaincre et persuader: Communication et propagande aux XIIe et XIIIe siècles,* edited by Martin Aurell, 465–502. Poitiers, 2007.

Carrer, Philippe. *Ermengarde d'Anjou: L'autre duchesse de Bretagne.* Spézet, 2003.

Carruthers, Mary. *The Book of Memory: A Study of Memory in Medieval Culture.* 2nd ed. Cambridge, 2008.

Caruana, Jaime. "Itinerario de Alfonso II de Aragón." *Estudios de Edad Media de la Corona de Aragón* 7 (1962): 73–298.

Catalogus codicum hagiographicorum latinorum antiquiorum saeculo xvi qui asservantur in Bibliotheca nationali Parisiensi. 3 vols. Brussels, 1893.

Chareyron, Nicole. *Pilgrims to Jerusalem in the Middle Ages.* Translated by W. Donald Wilson. New York, 2005.

Chartrou, Josephe. *L'Anjou de 1109 à 1151: Foulque de Jérusalem et Geoffroi Plantagenêt.* Paris, 1928.

Chazaud, M. "Inventaire et comptes de la succession d'Eudes, comte de Nevers (Acre, 1266)." *Mémoires de la société des antiquaires de France,* 4th series, 2 (1871): 164–206.

Cheyette, Frederic. *Ermengard of Narbonne and the World of the Troubadours.* Ithaca, NY, 2001.

Chibnall, Marjorie. "Feudal Society in Orderic Vitalis." *Anglo-Norman Studies* 1 (1978): 35–48.

Cifuentes i Comamala, Lluis. *La ciència en català a l'Edat Mitjana i el Renaixement.* 2nd ed. Barcelona, 2006.

Ciggaar, Krijnie N. "Flemish Counts and Emperors: Friends and Foreigners in Byzantium." In *The Latin Empire: Some Contributions,* edited by Krijnie N. Ciggaar and V. D. van Aalst, 33–62. Hernen, Neth., 1990.

Cingolani, Stefano Maria. "'Seguir les vestígies dels antecessors': Llinatge, reialesa i historiografia a Catalunya des de Ramon Berenguer IV a Pere II (1131–1285)." *Anuario de estudios medievales* 36 (2006): 201–240.

Classens, Geert. "Über den 'Sitz im Leben' der altfranzösischen *épopées intermédiaires.*" In *Chanson de geste im europäischen Kontext,* edited by Hans-Joachim Ziegeler, 15–25. Göttingen, 2008.

Coll i Alentorn, Miguel. "La historiografia catalana en el període primitiu." *Estudis Romànics* 3 (1951–52): 139–196.

Collins, Roger J. H. "Charles the Bald and Wifrid the Hairy." In *Charles the Bald: Court and Kingdom,* edited by M. T. Gibson and Janet L. Nelson, 169–188. 2nd ed. London, 1990.

Colomé, Fidel Fita. "Bulas históricas del reino de Navarra en los postreros años del siglo XII." *Boletín de la Real Academia de la Historia* 26 (1895): 417–459.

Coolens, Georges. "Arnoul I d'Ardres et son chapitre." *Bulletin de la Société Académique des Antiquaires de la Morinie* 20 (1967): 576–636.

———. "Le chapitre de Licques et la croisade." *Bulletin de la Société Académique des Antiquaires de la Morinie* 21 (1967): 33–45.

Coomans, Thomas. "Cistercian Nuns and Princely Memorials: Dynastic Burial Churches in the Cistercian Abbeys of the Medieval Low Countries." In *Sépulture, mort, et représentation du pouvoir au Moyen Âge,* edited by Michel Margue, 683–734. Luxembourg, 2000.

Constable, Giles. *Crusaders and Crusading in the Twelfth Century.* Aldershot, UK, 2008.

Corbellari, Alain. "Le jeux de l'anneux: Fonctions et trajets d'un objet dans la littérature narrative médiévale." In *"De sens rassim": Essays in Honor of Rupert T. Pickens,* edited by Keith Busby, Bernard Guidot, and Logan E. Whalen, 157–167. Amsterdam, 1994.

Cowdrey, H. E. J. "Pope Urban II's Preaching of the First Crusade." *History* 55 (1970): 177–188. Reprinted in *The Crusades: Essential Readings,* ed. Thomas Madden (Oxford, 2005), 15–29.

———. "Pope Urban II and the Idea of Crusade." *Studi medievali* 36 (1995): 721–742.

Crane, Susan. *The Performance of Self: Ritual, Clothing, and Identity during the Hundred Years War.* Philadelphia, 2002.

Crouch, David. *The Beaumont Twins: The Roots and Branches of Power in the Twelfth Century.* Cambridge, 1986.

———. *The Image of Aristocracy in Britain, 1000–1300.* London, 1992.

———. *William Marshal: Knighthood, War, and Chivalry, 1147–1219.* 2nd ed. London, 2002.

———. *The Birth of Nobility: Constructing Aristocracy in England and France, c. 900–c. 1300.* London and New York, 2005.

———. "Courtliness and Chivalry: Colliding Constructs." In *Soldiers, Nobles, and Gentlemen: Essays in Honor of Maurice Keen,* edited by Peter Coss and Christopher Tyerman, 32–48. Woodbridge, UK, 2009.

Dalewski, Zbigniew. *Ritual and Politics: The History of a Dynastic Conflict in Medieval Poland.* Leiden, 2008.

Damian-Grint, Peter. *"En nul leu nel truis escrit:* Research and Invention in Benoît de Sainte-Maur's *Chronique des ducs de Normandie." Anglo-Norman Studies* 21 (1999): 11–30.

———. *The New Historians of the Twelfth-Century Renaissance: Inventing Vernacular Authority.* Woodbridge, UK, 1999.

Daniell, Christopher. *Death and Burial in Medieval England, 1066–1550.* New York, 1997.

David, Charles Wendell. *Robert Curthose, Duke of Normandy.* Cambridge, MA, 1920.

Defourneux, Marcelin. "Louis VII et les souverains Espagnols: L'enigme du 'Pseudo-Alphonse'." In *Estudios dedicados a Menéndez Pidal,* 6: 647–661. Madrid, 1956.

Delbouille, Maurice. "Dans un atelier de copistes: En regardans de plus près les manuscrits B1 and B2 du cycle épique de *Garin de Monglane.*" *Cahiers de civilisation médiévale* 3 (1960): 14–22.

Delisle, Léopold. "Notice sur un manuscript de Saint Laud d'Angers appartenant à M. le Marquis de Villoutreys." *Bibliothèque de l'École des Chartes* 59 (1898): 533–549.

Delluc, Brigitte, and Gilles Delluc. "Le suaire de Cadouin et son frère le voile de sainte Anne d'Apt (Vaucluse): Deux pièces exceptionelles d'archéologie textile." *Bulletin de la Société Historique et Archéologique du Périgord* 128 (2001): 607–626.

Delumeau, Jean. *La peur en Occident (XIVe–XVIIIe siècles): Une citée assiégée.* Paris, 1978.

Derbes, Ann. "The Frescoes of Schwarzheindorf, Arnold of Wied, and the Second Crusade." In *The Second Crusade and the Cistercians,* edited by Michael Gervers, 141–154. New York, 1992.

Devos, Paul. "Les premières versions occidentales de la légende de Saidanaia." *Analecta Bollandiana* 65 (1947): 245–278.

Díaz y Díaz, Manuel C. *El Códice Calixtino de la Catedral de Santiago: Estudio codicológico y de contenido.* Santiago de Compostela, 1988.

Dickson, Gary. *The Children's Crusade: Medieval History, Modern Mythistory.* Houndmills, Basingstoke, UK, and New York, 2008.

Dressler, Rachel. "Steel Corpse: Imagining the Knight in Death." In *Conflicted Identities and Multiple Masculinities: Men in the Medieval West,* edited by Jacqueline Murray, 135–168. New York, 1999.

Drijvers, Jan Willem. "Heraclius and the *Restitutio crucis:* Notes on Symbolism and Ideology." In *The* Michael McCormick*: Crisis and Confrontation,* edited by Gerrit J. Reinink and Bernard H. Stolte, 175–190. Leuven, 2002.

Dronke, Peter. "The Interpretation of the Ripoll Love Songs." *Romance Philology* 33 (1979): 14–42.

Duby, Georges. "The Structure of Kinship and Nobility." In *The Chivalrous Society,* translated by Cynthia Postan, 134–148. Berkeley, 1977.

Du Cange, Charles du Fresne sieur, et al. *Glossarium mediae et infimae latinitatis.* 10 vols. Niort, 1883–87.

Duggan, Anne. "Diplomacy, Status, and Conscience: Henry II's Penance for Becket's Murder." In *Forschungen zur Reichs-, Papst- und Landesgeschichte: Peter Herde sum 65. Geburtstag von Freunden, Schülern und Kollegen dargebracht,* edited by Karl Borchardt and Enno Bünz, 1: 265–290. Stuttgart, 1998.

——. "*Servus servorum Dei.*" In *Adrian IV, the English Pope, 1154–1159: Studies and Texts,* edited by Brenda Bolton and Anne Duggan, 181–210. Aldershot, UK, 2003.

Dunbabin, Jean. *France in the Making, 843–1180.* 2nd ed. Oxford, 2000.

Duncan, A. A. M. "The Foundation of St. Andrews Cathedral Priory, 1140." *Scottish Historical Review* 84 (2005): 1–37.

Duplès-Agier, H. "Le trésor de Saint-Martial de Limoges au XIIIe siècle." *Bibliothèque de l'École des Chartes,* 4th series, 1 (1855): 28–35.

Duplessis, Toussaints. *Histoire de la ville et des seigneurs de Coucy.* Paris, 1728.

Duthilloeul, Hippolyte Romain Joseph. *Catalogue descriptif et raisonné des manuscrits de la bibliothèque de Douai.* Douai, 1846.

Edbury, Peter W. "The Lyon *Eracles* and the Old French Continuations of William of Tyre." In *Montjoie: Studies in Crusade History in Honour of Hans Eberhard Mayer,* edited by Benjamin Z. Kedar, Jonathan Riley-Smith, and Rudolf Hiestand, 139–154. Aldershot, UK, 1997.

Edgington, Susan. "Pagan Peverel: An Anglo-Norman Crusader." In *Crusade and Settlement: Papers Read at the First Conference of the Society for the Study of the Crusades and the Latin East and Presented to R. C. Smail,* edited by Peter Edbury, 90–93. Cardiff, 1985.

Elliott, Dyan. *Proving Woman: Female Spirituality and Inquisitional Culture in the Later Middle Ages.* Princeton, NJ, 2004.

Erdmann, Carl. *The Origin of the Idea of Crusade.* Translated by Marshall W. Baldwin and Walter Goffart. Princeton, NJ, 1977.

Evergates, Theodore. *Feudal Society in Medieval France: Documents from the County of Champagne.* Philadelphia, 1993.

———. *The Aristocracy in the County of Champagne, 1100–1300.* Philadelphia, 2007.

Eyton, Robert William. *Court, Household, and Itinerary of King Henry II.* Dorchester, UK, 1878.

Farmer, Sharon. *Communities of Saint Martin: Legend and Ritual in Medieval Tours.* Ithaca, NY, 1991.

Fletcher, Richard. *The Quest for El Cid.* London, 1989.

Flori, Jean. *Bohémond d'Antioche: Chevalier d'aventure.* Paris, 2007.

———. *Chroniqueurs et propagandistes: Introduction critique aux sources de la Première Croisade.* Geneva, 2010.

Forey, Alan. *The Templars in the Corona de Aragón.* London, 1973.

———. "The Military Order of St Thomas of Acre." *English Historical Review* 92 (1977): 481–503.

———. "Henry II's Crusading Penances for Becket's Murder." *Crusades* 7 (2008): 153–164.

France, John. "The Text of the Account of the Capture of Jerusalem in the Ripoll Manuscript, Bibliothèque Nationale Latin 5132." *English Historical Review* 103 (1988): 640–657.

———. *Victory in the East: A Military History of the First Crusade.* Cambridge, 1994.

Freed, John B. *The Counts of Falkenstein: Noble Self-Consciousness in Twelfth-Century Germany.* Transactions of the American Philosophical Society, n.s. 74:6. Philadelphia, 1976.

———. "Reflections on the Medieval German Nobility." *American Historical Review* 91:3 (1986): 553–575.

Froidefond de Boulazac, Alfred de. *Armorial de la noblesse du Périgord.* 2 vols. Périgeux, 1891.

Gabriele, Matthew. "The Provenance of the *Descriptio qualiter Karolus Magnus:* Remembering the Carolingians in the Entourage of King Philip I (1060–1108) before the First Crusade." *Viator* 39 (2008): 93–117.

———. *An Empire of Memory: The Legend of Charlemagne, the Franks, and Jerusalem before the First Crusade.* Oxford, 2011.

Gaposchkin, M. Cecilia. *The Making of Saint Louis: Kingship, Sanctity, and Crusade in the Later Middle Ages.* Ithaca, NY, 2008.

García–Guijarro Ramos, Luis. "The Aragonese Hospitaller Monastery of Sigena: Its Early Stages, 1188-c. 1210." In *Hospitaller Women in the Middle Ages,* edited by Anthony Luttrell and Helen J. Nicholson, 113–152. Aldershot, UK, 2006.

Geary, Patrick J. *Living with the Dead in the Middle Ages.* Ithaca, NY, 1994.

———. "Sacred Commodities: The Circulation of Medieval Relics." In *The Social Life of Things: Commodities in Cultural Perspective,* edited by Arjun Appaduri, 169–191. Cambridge, 1986.

Géraud, Hercule. "Mercadier: Les routiers au treizième siècle." *Bibliothèque de l'École des Chartes* 3:3 (1842): 417–443.

Gerzaguet, Jean-Pierre. *L'abbaye d'Anchin de sa fondation (1079) au xiv siècle: Essor, vie, et rayonnement d'une grande communauté bénédictine.* Villeneuve d'Ascq, 1997.

Gibson, Gail McMurray. "*Porta haec clausa erit:* Comedy, Conception, and Ezekiel's Closed Door in the *Ludus coventriae* Play of Joseph's Return." *Journal of Medieval and Renaissance Studies* 8 (1976): 137–156.

Gillingham, John. "Roger of Howden on Crusade." In John Gillingham, *Richard Coeur de Lion: Kingship, Chivalry, and War in the Twelfth Century,* 141–153. London, 1994.

———. *Richard I.* New Haven, CT, 1999.

———. "The Kidnapped King: Richard I in Germany, 1192-4." *Bulletin of the German Historical Institute, London* 30 (2008): 5–34.

Gilyard-Beer, Roy. "Byland Abbey and the Grave of Roger de Mowbray." *Yorkshire Archeological Journal* 55 (1983): 61–66.

Grabar, André. *Ampoules de Terre Sainte.* Paris, 1958.

Graham-Leigh, Elaine. "Hirelings and Shepherds: Archbishop Berenguer of Narbonne (1191–1211) and the Ideal Bishop." *English Historical Review* 116 (2001): 1083–1102.

Grandi, Guido. *Vita del glorioso prencipe S. Pietro Orseolo Doge di Venezia.* Venice, 1733.

Gransden, Antonia. *Historical Writing in England (c. 500–1307).* London, 1996.

Grant, Lindy. *Abbot Suger of St-Denis: Church and State in Early Twelfth-Century France.* London, 1998.

Grauert, Hermann. "Meister Johann von Toledo." *Sitzungsberichte der Königlichen Bayerischen Akademie der Wissenschaften* (1901): 111–325

Green, Judith A. *The Aristocracy of Norman England.* Cambridge, 1997.

———. *Henry I: King of England and Duke of Normandy.* Cambridge, 2006.

Greenhill, Frank A. *Incised Effigial Slabs: A Study of Engraved Stone Memorials in Latin Christendom, c. 1100 to c. 1700.* 2 vols. London, 1976.

Grillon, Louis. "Cartulaire de Notre-Dame de Dalon." PhD diss., University of Bordeaux, 1962.

Gros i Pujol, Miquel S. "El *Llibre de refeccions* del monestir de Santa Maria de Ripoll." *Studia Monastica* 46 (2004): 365–377.

Guenée, Bernard. *Histoire et culture historique dans l'Occident médiévale.* Paris, 1980.

Guerreau-Jalabert, Anita. *Index des motifs narratifs dans les romans arthuriens français en vers: xiie-xiiie siècles.* Geneva, 1992.

Halbwachs, Maurice. *Les cadres sociaux de la mémoire.* Paris, 1925; reprint, 1952.

Hallam, Elizabeth M., and Judith Everard. *Capetian France, 987–1328.* 2nd ed. Harlow, 2001.

Hamilton, Bernard. *The Leper King and His Heirs: Baldwin IV and the Crusader Kingdom of Jerusalem.* Cambridge, 2000.

———. "William of Tyre and the Byzantine Empire." In *Porphyrogenita: Essays on the History and Literature of Byzantium and the Latin East in Honour of Julian Chrysostomides,* edited by Charalambos Dendrinos et al., 219–233. Aldershot, UK, 2003.

Happé, Peter. *Cyclic Form and the English Mystery Plays: A Comparative Study of the English Biblical Cycles and Their Continental Iconographic Counterparts.* Amsterdam, 2004.

Hemptinne, Thérèse de. "Les épouses de croisés et pèlerins flamands au xie et xiie siècle: L'éxample des comtesses de Flandre Clémence et Sibylle." In *Autour de la première croisade: Actes du Colloque de la Society for the Study of the Crusades and the Latin East (Clermont-Ferrand, 22–25 juin 1995),* edited by Michel Balard, 83–95. Paris, 1996.

Hodgson, Natasha R. *Women, Crusading, and the Holy Land in Historical Narrative.* Woodbridge, UK, 2007.

Hollister, Warren. *Henry I.* New Haven, CT, 2001.

Hosler, John D. *Henry II: A Medieval Soldier at War, 1147–1189.* Leiden and Boston, 2009.

Housley, Norman. "Crusades against Christians: Their Origins and Early Development c. 1000–1216." In *The Crusades: Essential Readings,* ed. Thomas F. Madden, 69–97. Malden, MA, and Oxford, 2005.

———. *Contesting the Crusades.* Malden, MA, and Oxford, 2006.

Houston, Robert A. *Punishing the Dead? Suicide, Lordship, and Community in Britain, 1500–1830.* Oxford, 2010.

Huyskens, Albert. *Quellenstudien zur Geschichte der heilige Elisabeth, Landgräfin von Thuringen.* Marburg, 1908.

Jackson, William E. *Ardent Complaints and Equivocal Piety: The Portrayal of the Crusader in Medieval German Poetry.* Lanham, MD, 2003.

Jacob, Henriette. *Idealism and Realism: A Study of Sepulchral Symbolism.* Leiden, 1954.

Jaeger, C. Stephen. *The Origins of Courtliness: Civilizing Trends and the Formation of Courtly Ideals, 939–1210.* Philadelphia, 1985.

Jardin, Jean-Pierre, and Georges Martin. "*Generatio regum Aragonum:* Une variante médiévale inédite de l'histoire des rois d'Aragon (et une source non identifiée de Lucio Marineo Sículo)." *Cahiers de linguistique hispanique médiévale* 22 (1998–99): 177–225.

Jarrett, Jonathan. *Rulers and Ruled in Frontier Catalonia, 880–1010: Pathways of Power.* London, 2010.

Jaspert, Nikolas. "*Capta est Dertosa: Clavis Christianorum;* Tortosa and the Crusades." In *The Second Crusade: Scope and Consequences,* edited by Jonathan Philips and Martin Hock, 90–110. Manchester, 2001.

———. "Historiografía y legitimación carolingia: El monasterio de Ripoll, el Pseudo-Turpín y los condes de Barcelona." In *El Pseudo-Turpín: Lazo entre el Culto Jacobeo y el Culto de Carlomagno; Actas del VI Congreso Internacional de Estudios Jacobeos,* edited by Klaus Herbers, 297–315. Santiago de Compostela, 2003.

———. "Karolingische Legitimation und Karlsverehrung in Katalonien." In *Jacobus und Karl der Grosse: Von Einhards Karlsvita zum Pseudo-Turpin,* edited by Klaus Herbers, 127–161. Tübingen, 2003.

Jones, Charles W. *Saint Nicholas of Myra, Bari, and Manhattan.* Chicago, 1978.

Joranson, Einar. "The Great German Pilgrimage of 1064–1065." In *The Crusades and Other Historical Essays, Presented to Dana C. Munro by His Former Students,* edited by Louis Paetow, 3–56. New York, 1928.

Kastner, Jörg. *Historiae fundationum monasterium: Fruhforben monasticher Institutionsgeschichtschreibung im Mittelalter.* Munchener Beitrage zur Mediävistik und Renaissance-Forschung 18. Munich, 1974.

Katzenellenbogen, Adolf. "The Central Tympanum at Vézelay: Its Encyclopedic Meaning and Its Relation to the First Crusade." *Art Bulletin* 26 (1944): 141–151.

Kedar, Benjamin. "The Subjected Muslims of the Frankish Levant." In *Muslims under Latin Rule,* edited by James M. Powell, 135–174. Princeton, NJ, 1990.

Keen, Maurice. "Chaucer's Knight, the English Aristocracy, and the Crusade." In *English Court Culture in the Later Middle Ages,* edited by V. J. Scattergood and J. W. Sherborne, 45–62. London, 1983.

Kerr, Julie. *Monastic Hospitality: The Benedictines in England, c. 1070–c. 1250.* Woodbridge, UK, 2007.

King, Edmund. "The Accession of Henry II." In *Henry II: New Interpretations,* edited by Christopher Harper-Hill and Nicholas Vincent, 24–46. Woodbridge, UK, 2007.

Klaniczay, Gábor. *Holy Rulers and Blessed Princesses: Dynastic Cults in Medieval Central Europe.* Cambridge, 2002.

Knobler, Adam. "Holy Wars, Empires, and the Portability of the Past: The Modern Uses of Medieval Crusades." *Comparative Studies in Society and History* 48:2 (2006): 293–325.

Köstler, Andreas. *Die Ausstattung der Marburger Elisabethkirche: Zur Ästhetisierung des Kultraums im Mittelalter.* Berlin, 1995.

Kosto, Adam. *"The Liber Feudorum maior* of the Counts of Barcelona: The Cartulary as an Expression of Power." *Journal of Medieval History* 27 (2001): 1–22.

Koziol, Geoffrey. *Begging Pardon and Favor: Ritual and Political Order in Early Medieval France.* Ithaca, NY, 1992.

——. "England, France, and the Problem of Sacrality in Twelfth-Century Ritual." In *Cultures of Power: Lordship, Status, and Process in Twelfth-Century Europe,* edited by Thomas N. Bisson, 124–148. Philadelphia, 1995.

——. "The Dangers of Polemic: Is Ritual Still an Interesting Topic of Historical Study?" *Early Medieval Europe* 11:4 (2002): 367–388.

Lalore, Charles. *Le Trésor de Clairvaux du xiie au xviiie siècle.* Troyes, 1875.

Lapina, Elizabeth. "The Mural Paintings at Berzé-la-ville in the Context of the First Crusade and the Reconquista." *Journal of Medieval History* 31 (2005): 309–326.

——. "Demetrius of Thessaloniki: Patron Saint of Crusaders." *Viator* 40 (2009): 93–112.

Lauwers, Michel. *La mémoire des ancêtres, le souci des morts: Morts, rites, et société au Moyen Âge.* Paris, 1997.

Leclerc, A. "Le tombeau de Gouffier de Lastours." *Bulletin de la Société Archéologique et Historique du Limousin* 32 (1885): 113–116.

Lécouteux, Claude. *Mélusine et le Chevalier au Cygne.* Paris, 1982.

Le Goff, Jacques. *Saint Louis.* Paris, 1996.

Le Saux, Françoise. *A Companion to Wace.* Woodbridge, UK, 2005.

Lester, Anne. "A Shared Imitation: Cistercian Convents and Crusader Families in Thirteenth-Century Champagne." *Journal of Medieval History* 35:4 (2009): 353–370.

Lettenhove, Kervyn de. *Istore et chroniques de Flandres d'après les textes de divers manuscrits.* 2 vols. Brussels, 1879–80.

Lewis, Andrew W. *Royal Succession in Capetian France: Studies on Familial Order and the State.* Cambridge, MA, 1981.

L'Hermite, Xavier. "Le prieuré du Chalard, étude architecturale." *Bulletin de la Société Archéologique et Historique du Limousin* 131 (2003): 37–71.

Liégeois, Camille. *Gilles de Chin: L'histoire et la légende.* Louvain, 1903.

Lloyd, Simon. *English Society and the Crusade, 1216–1307.* Oxford, 1988.

——. "King Henry III, the Crusade, and the Mediterranean." In *England and Her Neighbours, 1066–1453: Essays in Honor of Pierre Chaplais,* edited by Michael Jones and Malcolm Vale, 97–119. London, 1989.

——. "William Longespée II: The Making of an English Crusading Hero." [Parts 1 & 2] *Nottingham Medieval Studies* 35 (1991): 41–69 and 36 (1992): 79–125.

Longnon, Jean. "Sur les croisés de la quatrième croisade." *Journal des savants* 2:2 (1977): 119–127.

——. *Les compagnons de Villehardouin: Recherches sur les croisés de la quatrième croisade.* Geneva, 1978.

Lo Prete, Kimberly. *Adela of Blois: Countess and Lord (c. 1067–1137).* Dublin, 2007.

Lower, Michael. *The Barons Crusade: A Call to Arms and Its Consequences.* Philadelphia, 2005.

Lyon, Jonathan. "Cooperation, Compromise, and Conflict Avoidance: Family Relationships in the House of Andechs ca. 1100–1204." PhD diss., University of Notre Dame, 2004.

——. "The Withdrawal of Aged Noblemen into Monastic Communities: Interpreting the Sources from Twelfth-Century Germany." In *Old Age in the Middle Ages and the Renaissance: Interdisciplinary Approaches to a Neglected Topic,* edited by Albrecht Classen, 143–169. Göttingen, 2007.

Mack, Merav. "A Genoese Perspective of the Third Crusade." *Crusades* 10 (2011): 45–62.

Mailfert, Yvonne. "Fondation du monastère bénédictin de Saint-Nicholas d'Angers." *Bibliothèque de l'École des Chartes* 92 (1931): 43–61.

Malo, Henri. *Un grand feudataire: Renaud de Dammartin et la coalition de Bouvines.* Paris, 1898.

Marmol, Eugéne de. "L'abbaye de Brogne ou de Saint Gérard." *Annales de la Société Archéologique de Namur* 5 (1857–8): 225–286,

Martindale, Jane. "Secular Propaganda and Aristocratic Values: The Autobiographies of Count Fulk le Réchin of Anjou and Count William of Poitou, Duke of Aquitaine." In *Writing Medieval Biography, 750–1250: Essays in Honour of Professor Frank Barlow,* edited by David Bates, Julia Crick, and Sarah Hamilton, 143–159. Woodbridge, UK, 2006.

Matz, Jean Michel. "Religion et politique à la fin du Moyen Âge: La Vraie Croix de Saint-Laud d'Angers." *Annales de Bretagne et des pays de l'Ouest* 94 (1987): 241–263.

Mauss, Marcel. "Essai sur le don: Forme et raison de l'échange dans les sociétés archaïques." *L'année sociologique* 1 (1923–24): 30–186.

Mayer, Hans Eberhard. *Bistümer, Klöster, und Stifte im Königreich Jerusalem*. Monumenta Germaniae Historica: Schriften 26. Stuttgart, 1977.

——. "Henry II of England and the Holy Land." *English Historical Review* 97 (1982): 721–739.

——. "Manasses of Hierges in East and West." *Revue Belge de philologie et d'histoire* 66 (1988): 757–766.

McCormick, Michael. *Eternal Victory: Triumphal Rulership in Late Antiquity, Byzantium, and the Early Medieval West*. Cambridge, 1986.

McCrank, Lawrence. "Restoration and Reconquest in Medieval Catalonia: The Church and Principality of Tarragona, 971–1177." Phd diss., University of Virginia, 1974.

Meecham-Jones, Simon, and Ruth Kennedy, eds. *Writers of the Reign of Henry II*. New York and Basingstoke, UK, 2006.

Maier, Christoph. *Crusade Propaganda and Ideology: Model Sermons for the Preaching of the Cross*. Cambridge, 2000.

Melero Monero, Marisa. "La propagande politico-religieuse du programme iconographique de la façade de Sainte-Marie de Ripoll." *Cahiers de civilisation médiévale* 46 (2003): 135–157.

Miret i Sans, Joaquín. *Itinerari de Jaume I el Conqueridor*. Barcelona, 1918. Reprint, 2007 with prologue by Maria Teresa Ferrer I Mallol.

——. "Itinerario del Rey Alfonso I de Cataluña, II en Aragón." *Boletín de la Real Academia de Buenas Letras de Barcelona* 2 (1903): 257–278.

Moeglin, Jean-Marie. "Une première histoire nationale Flamande: *L'Ancienne chronique de Flandre* (XIIe-XIIIe siècles)." In *Liber largitorius: Études d'histoire médiévale offertes à Pierre Toubert par ses élèves*, edited by Dominique Barthélemy and Jean-Marie Martin, 455–476. Hautes Études Médiévales et Modernes 84. Geneva, 2003.

Morgades y Gili, Jose. "El sepulcro de D. Ramón Berenguer IV, conde de Barcelona." *Boletín de la Real Academia de la Historia* 26 (1895): 477–486.

Morganstern, Anne McGee. *Gothic Tombs of Kinship in France, the Low Countries, and England*. University Park, PA, 2000.

Morris, Colin. *The Sepulchre of Christ and the Medieval West: From the Beginning to 1600*. Oxford, 2005.

Morsel, Joseph. "Inventing a Social Category: The Sociogenesis of the Nobility at the End of the Middle Ages." In *Ordering Medieval Society: Perspectives on Intellectual and Practical Modes of Shaping Social Relations*, edited by Bernhard Jussen and translated by Pamela Selwyn, 200–240. Philadelphia, 2001.

Morton, Nicholas. *The Teutonic Knights in the Holy Land, 1190–1291*. Woodbridge, UK, 2009.

——. "The Defence of the Holy Land and the Memory of the Maccabees." *Journal of Medieval History* 36 (2010): 275–293.

Murray, Alan. "Money and Logistics in the Forces of the First Crusade: Coinage, Bullion, Service, and Supply, 1096–99." In *Logistics of Warfare in the Age of the Crusades*, edited by John H. Pryor, 229–249. Aldershot, UK, 2006.

Muthesius, Anna. "Silken Diplomacy." In *Byzantine Diplomacy*, edited by Jonathan Shephard and Simon Franklin, 237–248. Aldershot, UK, 1992.

Naus, James. "The French Royal Court and the Memory of the First Crusade." *Nottingham Medieval Studies* 55 (2011): 49–78.

Neuss, Wilhelm. *Das Buch Ezechiel in Theologie und Kunst bis zum Ende des 12. Jahrhunderts.* Münster, 1912.

Nickel, Helmut. "A Crusader's Sword: Concerning the Effigy of Jean d'Alluye." *Metropolitan Museum Journal* 26 (1991): 123–128.

Nicolas, Nicholas Harris. *Testamenta vetusta: Being Illustrations from Wills of Manners, Customs, etc. as Well as the Descents and Possessions of Many Distinguished Families, from the Reign of Henry II to the Accession of Queen Elizabeth.* 2 vols. London, 1826.

Nicolau d'Olwer, L. "L'escola poetica de Ripoll en els segles X–XIII." *Anuari del Institut d'Estudis Catalans* 6 (1915–20): 3–84.

Niles, John D. *Homo Narrans: The Poetics and Anthropology of Oral Literature.* Philadelphia, 1999.

Norgate, Kate. *England under the Angevin Kings.* 2 vols. London, 1887.

O'Callaghan, Joseph. *Reconquest and Crusade in Medieval Spain.* Philadelphia, 2004.

Oexle, Otto Gerhard. "Welfische und staufische Hausüberlieferung in der Handschrift Fulda D 11 aus Weingarten." In *Von der Klosterbibliothek zur Landesbibliothek: Beiträge zum zweihundertjährigen Bestehen der Hessischen Landesbibliothek Fulda,* edited by Artur Brall, 203–231. Stuttgart, 1978.

O'Neill, John Phillip, ed. *Enamels of Limoges: 1100–1350.* New York, 1996.

Pacaut, Marcel. *Louis VII et son royaume.* Paris, 1964.

Pagès, Amédée. "Recherches sur la chronique Catalane attribuée à Pierre IV d'Aragón." *Romania* 18 (1889): 233–280.

Painter, Sidney. *William Marshal: Knight-Errant, Baron, and Regent of England.* Baltimore, 1933.

Paterson, Linda. "Syria, Poitou, and the *Reconquista* (or: Tales of the Undead): Who Was the Count in Marcabru's *Vers del lavador?*" In *The Second Crusade: Scope and Consequences,* edited by Jonathan Phillips and Martin Hock, 133–149. Manchester, UK, 2001.

Paul, Nicholas L. "Crusade, Memory, and Regional Politics in Twelfth-Century Amboise." *Journal of Medieval History* 31 (2005): 127–141.

——. "The Chronicle of Fulk le Réchin: A Reassessment." *Haskins Society Journal* 18 (2007): 19–35.

——. "A Warlord's Wisdom: Literacy and Propaganda at the Time of the First Crusade." *Speculum* 85 (2010): 534–566.

——. "The Fruits of Penitence and the Laurel of the Cross: Poetics of Crusade and Conquest in the Memorials of Santa Maria de Ripoll." In *A Storm against the Infidel,* edited by Iben Fonnesberg Schmidt and Torben K. Nielsen. Leiden, forthcoming.

Paviot, Jacques. *Projets de Croisade (v. 1290–v. 1330).* Paris, 2008.

Perry, David. "Paul the Martyr and Venetian Memories of the Fourth Crusade." In *Remembering the Crusades: Myth, Image, and Identity,* edited by Nicholas Paul and Suzanne Yeager, 215–232. Baltimore, 2012.

Petrakopoulos, Anja. "Sanctity and Motherhood: Elizabeth of Thuringia." In *Sanctity and Motherhood: Essays on Holy Mothers in the Middle Ages,* edited by Anneke B. Mulder-Bakker, 259–296. New York, 1995.

Phillips, Jonathan. *Defenders of the Holy Land: Relations between the Latin East and the West, 1119–1187.* Oxford, 1996.

——. "The Murder of Charles the Good and the Second Crusade: Household, Nobility, and Traditions of Crusading in Medieval Flanders." *Medieval Prosopography* 19 (1998): 55–75.

——. *The Second Crusade: Extending the Frontiers of Christendom.* New Haven, CT, 2007.

Pieper, Lori. *Saint Elisabeth of Hungary: The Voice of a Medieval Woman and Franciscan Penitent.* N.p., 2007.

Porta, Dolores. "El poema de Roda en honor de Ramón Berenguer IV." *Argensola* 11:44 (1960): 297–310.

Pössel, Christina. "The Magic of Early Medieval Ritual." *Early Medieval Europe* 17:2 (2009): 111–125.

Powell, James. *Anatomy of a Crusade, 1213–1221.* Philadelphia, 1986.

——. "Myth, Legend, Propaganda, History: The First Crusade, 1140–c.1300." In *Autour de la première croisade: Actes du Colloque de la Society for the Study of the Cruasdes and the Latin East (Clermont-Ferrand, 22–25 juin 1995),* edited by Michel Balard, 127–141. Paris, 1996.

Power, Daniel. "The Stripping of a Queen: Eleanor in 13th-Century Norman Tradition." In *The World of Eleanor of Aquitaine: Literature and Society in Medieval France,* edited by Marcus Bull and Catherine Léglu, 115–135. Woodbridge, UK, 2005.

Pratt, Karen. *Meister Otte's "Eraclius" as an Adaptation of "Eracle" by Gautier d'Arras.* Göppingen, 1987.

Pryor, John H. "The Eracles and William of Tyre: An Interim Report." In *The Horns of Hattin: Proceedings of the Second Conference of the Society for the Study of the Crusades and the Latin East,* edited by Benjamin Z. Kedar, 270–293. Jerusalem, 1992.

Puigvert i Planagumà, Gemma. *Astronomia i astrologia al Monestir de Ripoll: Edició i estudi dels manuscrits científics astronomicoastrològics del Monestir de Santa Maria de Ripoll.* Bellaterra, 2000.

Pujol y Tubau, Pere. "Mudança en la elecció de sepultura per la rey Alfons I." *Boletín de la Real Academia de Buenas Letras de Barcelona* 7 (1913): 86–89.

Purcell, Maureen. *Papal Crusading Policy.* Leiden, 1975.

Purkis, William. *Crusading Spirituality in the Holy Land and Iberia, c. 1095–c. 1187.* Woodbridge, UK, and Rochester, NY, 2008.

Queller, Donald, and Thomas Madden. *The Fourth Crusade.* 2nd ed. Philadelphia, 1997.

Reiffenberg, Frédérick-Auguste de. *Le chevalier au cygne et Godefroid de Bouillon.* 4 vols. Brussels, 1846–59.

Reilly, Bernard F. *The Contest of Christian and Muslim Spain, 1031–1157.* Oxford, 1992.

Rémy, Christian. *Lastours et les Lastours du X au XVI siècle.* Mémoire de maîtrise: Université des Sciences Humaines–Strasbourg 2. 2 vols. Strasbourg, 1990.

Reuter, Timothy. "Past, Present, and No Future in the *Regnum Teutonicum.*" In *The Perception of the Past in Twelfth-Century Europe,* edited by Paul Magdalino, 15–36. London, 1992.

Riant, Paul. *Exuviae sacrae Constantinopolitanae.* 2 vols. Geneva, 1877–88. Reprint, Paris, 2004.

Riley-Smith, Jonathan. "Peace Never Established: The Case of the Latin Kingdom of Jerusalem." *Transactions of the Royal Historical Society,* 5th series, 28 (1978): 87–102.

——. *The First Crusade and the Idea of Crusading.* London, 1986.

——. "Family Traditions and Participation in the Second Crusade." In *The Second Crusade and the Cistercians,* edited by Michael Gervers, 101–108. New York, 1992.

332 **BIBLIOGRAPHY**

——. *The First Crusaders, 1095–1131*. Cambridge, 1997.

——. "King Fulk of Jerusalem and the 'Sultan of Babylon'." In *Montjoie: Studies in Crusade Hisory in Honour of Hans Eberhard Mayer,* edited by Benjamin Kedar and Jonathan Riley-Smith, 55–66. Aldershot, UK, 1997. Reprinted in Jonathan Riley-Smith, *Crusaders and Settlers in the Latin East* (Aldershot, 2008), chap. 11.

——. "Islam and the Crusades in History and Imagination, 1 November 1898–11 September 2001." *Crusades* 2 (2003): 151–167.

——. "The Crusades, 1095–1198." In *The New Cambridge Medieval History,* vol. 4, *c. 1024–c. 1198,* pt. 1, edited by David Luscombe and Jonathan Riley-Smith, 534–563. Cambridge, 2004.

——. *The Crusades: A History.* 2nd ed. New York, 2005.

——. *The Crusades, Christianity, and Islam.* New York, 2008.

Riquer, Martí de. "El trovador Giraut del Luc y sus poesías contra Alfonso II de Aragón." *Boletín de la Real Academia de Buenas Letras de Barcelona* 23 (1950): 209–248.

Roland, C.-G. "Un croisé ardennais: Manassès de Hierges." *Revue historique ardennaise* 14 (1907): 197–212.

Rubenstein, Jay. "Putting History to Use: Three Crusade Chronicles in Context." *Viator* 35 (2004): 131–168.

——. "What Is the *Gesta Francorum* and Who Was Peter Tudebode?" *Revue Mabillon* 16 (2005): 179–204.

Ryan, Vincent. "Richard I and the Early Evolution of the Fourth Crusade." In *The Fourth Crusade: Event, Aftermath, and Perceptions: Papers from the Sixth Conference of the Society for the Study of the Crusades and the Latin East (Istanbul, Turkey, 25–29 August 2004),* edited by Thomas F. Madden, 3–13. Aldershot, UK, 2008.

Sauerland, H. V. "Aus Handschriften der Trierer Seminarbibliothek." *Neues Archiv der Gesellschaft für altere deutsche Geschichtskunde* 17 (1895): 601–611.

Schein, Sylvia. *Gateway to the Heavenly City: Crusader Jerusalem and the Catholic West (1099–1187).* Aldershot, UK, 2005.

Schenk, Jochen. "Forms of Lay Association with the Order of the Temple." *Journal of Medieval History* 34 (2008): 79–103.

Schubert, Ernst. "Drei Grabmäler des Thüringer Landgrafenhauses aus dem Kloster Reinhardsbrunn." In *Skulptur des Mittelalters: Funktion und Gestalt,* edited by Friedrich Möbius and Ernst Schubert, 211–242. Weimar, 1987.

Senseby, Chantal. "Entre *gesta,* chronique, et nécrologe: Une *notitia memorialis* de Saint-Julien de Tours (début xii siècle)." *Journal des savants* (2006): 250–251.

Shepard, Jonathan. "The Uses of the Franks in Eleventh-Century Byzantium." *Anglo-Norman Studies* 15 (1992): 275–305.

Shideler, John C. *A Medieval Catalan Noble Family: The Montcadas, 1000–1230.* Berkeley, 1983.

Shils, Edward. *Tradition.* Chicago, 1981.

Shopkow, Leah. *History and Community: Norman Historical Writing in the Eleventh and Twelfth Centuries.* Washington, DC, 1997.

Siberry, Elizabeth. "The Crusading Counts of Nevers." *Nottingham Medieval Studies* 34 (1990): 64–70.

——. *The New Crusaders: Images of the Crusades in the Nineteenth and Early Twentieth Centuries.* Aldershot, UK, 2000.

Simmonet, Jules. *Essai sur l'histoire et la généalogie des sires de Joinville (1008–1386).* Langres, 1876.

Smith, Caroline. *Crusading in the Age of Joinville.* Aldershot, UK, 2006.

——. "Saints and Sinners at Sea on the First Crusade of Saint Louis." In *Crusades: Medieval Worlds in Conflict,* edited by Thomas F. Madden, Vincent Ryan, and James Naus, 161–172. Farnham, UK, 2010.

Smith, Damian. *Innocent III and the Crown of Aragón: The Limits of Papal Authority.* Aldershot, UK, 2004.

Sommerlechner, Andrea. "Kaiser Herakleios und die Rückkehr des Heiligen Kreuzes nach Jerusalem: Überlegungen zu Stoff- und Motifgeschichte." *Römische Historische Mitteilungen* 45 (2003): 319–360.

Southern, Richard. *History and Historians: Selected Papers of R. W. Southern,* edited by R. J. Bartlett. Oxford and Malden, MA, 2004.

Spiegel, Gabrielle. *The Chronicle Tradition of Saint Denis: A Survey.* Brookline, MA, 1978.

——. *Romancing the Past: The Rise of Vernacular Prose Historiography in Thirteenth-Century France.* Berkeley, 1993.

——. *The Past as Text: The Theory and Practice of Medieval Historiography.* Baltimore, 1997.

Stablein, Patricia Harris. "Menace and Delight: The Catalan Image in the Poetry of Bertran de Born." In *Studia in honorem Profesor M. de Riquer,* 3: 453–464. Barcelona, 1988.

Stalls, William Clay. "Queenship and Royal Patrimony in Twelfth-Century Iberia: The Example of Petronilla of Aragón." In *Queens, Regents, and Potentates,* edited by Theresa M. Vann, 49–61. Denton, TX, 1993.

Staunton, Michael. *Thomas Becket and His Biographers.* Woodbridge, UK, 2006.

Stein, Henri. *Bibliographie générale des cartulaires français ou relatifs à l'histoire de France.* Paris, 1907.

Stewart, Susan. *On Longing: Narratives of the Miniature, the Gigantic, the Souvenir, the Collection.* Durham, NC, 1993.

Stoclet, Alain, J. "À la recherche duban perdu: Le trésor et les dépouilles de Waïfre, duc d'Aquitaine (d. 768), d'après Adémar de Chabannes, Rigord et quelques autres." *Cahiers de civilisations médiévales* 42 (1999): 343–377.

Strickland, Matthew. *War and Chivalry: The Conduct and Perception of War in England and Normandy, 1066–1217.* Cambridge, 1996.

——. "Senlis, Simon (I) de, Earl of Northampton and Earl of Huntingdon (d. 1111x13)." In *Oxford Dictionary of National Biography.* Oxford, 2004. doi:10.1093/ref:odnb/25091.

Stringer, Keith. "Senlis, Simon (II) de, Earl of Northampton and Earl of Huntingdon (d. 1153)." In *Oxford Dictionary of National Biography.* Oxford, 2004. doi:10.1093/ref:odnb/25092.

Stroll, Mary. *Calixtus II, 1119–1124: A Pope Born to Rule.* Leiden, 2004.

Sturm-Maddox, Sara, and Donald Maddox, eds. *Transtextualities: Of Cycles and Cyclicity in Medieval French Literature.* Binghamton, NY, 1996.

——. "Cyclicity and Medieval Literary Cycles." In *Transtextualities: Of Cycles and Cyclicity in Medieval French Literature,* edited by Sara Sturm-Maddox and Donald Maddox, 1–14. Binghamton, NY, 1996.

Sunderland, Luke. *Old French Narrative Cycles: Heroism between Ethics and Morality.* Cambridge, 2010.

Sweeney, James Ross. "Hungary in the Crusades, 1169–1218." *International History Review* 3 (1981): 467–481.

———. "*Summa potestas post Deum:* Papal *Dilectio* and Hungarian *Devotio* in the Region of Innocent III." In *The Man of Many Devices Who Wandered Full Many Ways: Festschrift in Honor of János M. Bak,* edited by Balázs Nagy and Marcell Sebök, 492–498. Budapest, 1999.

Talbot, Alice-Mary. "Byzantine Pilgrimage to the Holy Land from the Eighth to the Fifteenth Century." In *The Sabaite Heritage in the Orthodox Church from the Fifth Century to the Present,* edited by Joseph Patrich, 97–110. Leuven, 2001.

Tanner, Heather J. *Family, Friends, and Allies: Boulogne and Politics in Northern France and England, c. 879–1160.* Leiden, 2004.

Tarracó, Emilia. "La pintura mural romànica en el monestir de Ripoll." In *Miscellània in homenatge a Joan Ainaud de Lasarte,* 1: 161–169. Barcelona, 1998.

Taylor, Andrew. *Textual Situations: Three Medieval Manuscripts and Their Readers.* Philadelphia, 2002.

———. "The Challenge of Editing Sung Objects: Editing Digby 23." In *The Book Unbound: Editing and Reading Medieval Manuscripts and Texts,* edited by Siân Echard and Stephen Partridge, 78–104. Toronto, 2004.

Taylor, Nathaniel L. "The Will and Society in Medieval Catalonia and Languedoc, 800–1200." PhD diss., Harvard University, 1995.

———. "Testaments, publication de testaments, et ordre public en Catalogne et en Languedoc (IX–XII siècle)." *Annales du Midi* 118 (2006): 447–451.

Tebruck, Stefan. *Die Reinhardsbrunner Geschichtsschreibung im Hochmittelalter: Klösterliche Traditionsbildung zwischen Fürstenhof Kirche und Reich.* Frankfurt, 2001.

Tenant de La Tour, Geoffroi. *L'homme et la terre de Charlemagne à Saint Louis: Essai sur les origines et les caractères d'une féodalité.* Paris, 1943.

Teunis, Henk. *The Appeal to the Original Status: Social Justice in Anjou in the Eleventh Century.* Hilversum, 2006.

Thompson, Kathleen. "Family Tradition and the Crusading Impulse: The Rotrou Counts of the Perche." *Medieval Prosopography: History and Collective Biography* 19 (1998): 1–33.

Thompson, Michael W. *The Medieval Hall: The Basis of Secular Domestic Life, 600–1600 AD.* Aldershot, UK, 1995.

Thompson, Rodney M. *William of Malmesbury.* Woodbridge, UK, 1987.

Thompson, Stith. *Motif-Index of Folk-Literature: A Classification of Narrative Elements in Folktales, Ballads, Myths, Fables, Mediaeval Romances, Exempla, Fabliaux, Jest-Books, and Local Legends.* Rev. and enl. edition. 5 vols. Copenhagen, 1955–58.

Throop, Susanna. *Crusading as an Act of Vengeance, 1095–1216.* Farnham, UK, 2011.

Tonnerre, Noël-Yves. "Henri II et l'Anjou." In *Plantagenêts et Capétiens: Confrontations et héritages,* edited by Martin Aurell and Noël-Yves Tonnerre, 211–225. Histoires de famille: La parenté au Moyen Âge 4. Turnhout, 2006.

Trotter, D. A. *Medieval French Literature and the Crusades (1100–1300).* Geneva, 1988.

Tummers, H. A. *Early Secular Effigies in England: The Thirteenth Century.* Leiden, 1980.

Turner, Ralph V., and Richard Heiser. *The Reign of Richard Lionheart: Ruler of the Angevin Empire, 1189–1199.* Harlow, 2000.

Tyerman, Christopher. *England and the Crusades, 1095–1588.* Chicago, 1988.

———. "Were There Any Crusades in the Twelfth Century?" *English Historical Review* 110:437 (1995): 553–577.

Tyssens, Madeleine. *La geste de Guillaume d'Orange dans les manuscrits cycliques.* Paris, 1967.

Ubieto-Arteta, Antonio. "La peregrinación de Alfonso II de Aragón a Santiago de Compstela." *Estudios de la edad media de la corona de Aragón* 5 (1952): 438–452.

———. *Historia de Aragón: Creación y desarrollo de la Corona de Aragón.* Zaragoza, 1987.

Ubieto-Arteta, Antonio, and Federico Balguer Sánchez. "L'aparición del falso Alfonso el Batallador" and "Alusiones de los trovadores al Pseudo-Alfonso." *Argensola* 9 (1958): 29–47.

Udina Martorell, Federico. *El Archivo condal de Barcelona en los siglos ix-x: Estudio crítico de sus fondos.* Consejo superior de investigaciones científicas: Escuel de estudios medievales textos 18. Barcelona, 1951.

Valdez del Alamo, Elizabeth. "Lament for a Lost Queen: The Sarcophagus of Doña Blanca of Nájera." *Art Bulletin* 78 (1996): 311–333.

Van Houts, Elisabeth. *Gesta Normannorum ducum: Een studie over de handschriften, de tekst, het geschiedwerk en het genre.* Groningen, 1982.

———. "Normandy and Byzantium in the Eleventh Century." *Byzantion* 55 (1985): 544–559.

———. "Le roi et son historien: Henri II Plantagenêt et Robert de Torigni, abbé de Mont-Saint-Michel." *Cahiers de civilisation médiévale* 37 (1994): 115–118.

———. *Memory and Gender in Medieval Europe: 900–1200.* Basingstoke, UK, 1999.

———. "Wace as Historian." In *Family Trees and the Roots of Politics: The Prosopography of Britain and France from the Tenth to the Twelfth Century,* edited by K. S. B. Keats-Rohan, 104–132. Woodbridge, UK, 1997.

Venarde, Bruce L. *Robert of Arbrissel: A Medieval Religious Life.* Washington, DC, 2003.

Ventura, Jordi. *Alfonso el Cast: El primer comte-rei.* Barcelona, 1961.

Verbruggen, J. F. *The Art of Warfare in Western Europe during the Middle Ages.* Translated by Sumner Willard and R. W. Southern. 2nd ed. Woodbridge, UK, 1997.

Vercauteren, Ferdinand. "Note sur Gislebert de Mons, rédacteur de chartes." *Mitteilungen des Instituts für Österreichiche Geschichtsforschung* 62 (1954): 238–253.

———. "Gislebert de Mons, auteur des épitaphes des comtes de Hainaut Baudouin IV et Baudouin V." *Bulletin de la Commission Royale d'Histoire* 125 (1959): 379–403.

Vespremy, Laszlo. "*Dux et Praeceptor Hierosolymitanorum,* König Ladislaus (Lasxlo) von Ungarn als Imaginarer Kreuzritter." In *The Man of Many Devices Who Wandered Full Many Ways: Festschrift in Honor of János M. Bak,* edited by Balázs Nagy and Marcell Sebök, 470–477. Budapest, 1999.

Villanueva, Jaime. *Viage literario a las iglesias de España.* 22 vols. Madrid, 1803–52.

———. *Memorias cronológicas de los condes de Urgel.* Transcription and notes by Cristian Cortés, prologue and revisions by Eduardo Corredera Gutiérrez. Balaguer, 1976.

Villegas-Aristizábal, Lucas. "The Anglo-Norman Intervention in the Conquest and Settlement of Tortosa, 1148–1180." *Crusades* 8 (2009): 63–129.

Vincent, Nicholas. "The Pilgrimages of the Angevin Kings of England, 1154–1272." In *Pilgrimage: The English Experience from Becket to Bunyan,* edited by Colin Morris and Peter Roberts, 12–45. Cambridge, 2002.

Ward, John O. "Memorializing Dispute Resolution in the Twelfth Century: Annal, History, and Chronicle at Vézelay." In *The Medieval Chronicle,* edited by Erik Kooper, 1: 269–284. Utrecht, 1991.

Warner, David A. "Ritual and Memory in the Ottonian Reich: The Ceremony of Adventus." *Speculum* 76 (2001): 255–283.

Warren, Wilfred L. *Henry II.* New Haven, CT, 2000.

Wattenbach, Wilhelm. "Die Apologie des Guido von Bazoches." *Sitzungsberichte der Königlich preussischen Akademie der Wissenschaften zu Berlin* (1893): 395–420.

Weiler, Björn. "The *Rex Renitens* and the Medieval Idea of Kingship, ca. 900–ca. 1250." *Viator* 31 (2000): 1–42.

Weiner, Annette B. "Inalienable Wealth." *American Ethnologist* 12 (1985): 210–227.

——. *Inalienable Possessions: The Paradox of Keeping-While-Giving.* Berkeley, 1992.

Weltecke, Dorothea. "Die Konjunktion der Planeten im September 1186. Zum Ursprung einer globalen Katastrophenangst." *Saeculum* 54 (2003): 179–212.

Westerhof, Danielle. *Death and the Noble Body in Medieval England.* Woodbridge, UK, 2008.

Westfall-Thompson, James. *The Literacy of the Laity in the Middle Ages.* Berkeley, 1939.

Whalen, Logan E. *Marie de France and the Poetics of Memory.* Washington, DC, 2008.

White, Graeme J. *Restoration and Reform, 1153–1165: Recovery from Civil War in England.* Cambridge, 2000.

White, Stephen. *Custom, Kinship, and Gifts to Saints: The* laudatio parentum *in Western France, 1050–1150.* Chapel Hill, NC, 1988.

Willard, Charity Cannon. "Gilles de Chin in History, Literature, and Folklore." In *The Medieval Opus: Imitation, Rewriting, and Transmission in the French Tradition,* edited by Douglas Kelly, 357–366. Amsterdam, 1996.

Williams, John Bryan. "The Making of a Crusade: The Genoese Anti-Muslim Attacks in Spain, 1146–1148." *Journal of Medieval History* 23 (1997): 29–53.

Wolff, R. L. "Baldwin of Flanders and Hainaut, First Latin Emperor of Constantinople: His Life, Death, and Resurrection, 1172–1225." *Speculum* 27 (1952): 281–322.

Wright, Neil. "Epic and Romance in the Chronicles of Anjou." *Anglo-Norman Studies* 26 (2003): 177–189.

Wyard, Robert. *Histoire de l'abbaye de Saint Vincent de Laon.* Saint-Quentin, 1858.

Zimmermann, Michel. *Écrire et lire en Catalogne: ix-xii siècle.* 2 vols. Madrid, 2003.

✒ INDEX

Page numbers followed by letters *c, f, m,* and *t* refer to charts, figures, maps, and tables, respectively.

www.ingramcontent.com/pod-product-compliance
Lightning Source LLC
Chambersburg PA
CBHW021807270326
41932CB00007B/92